BOOK SALE

IMMIGRATION RESEARCH FOR A NEW CENTURY

IMMIGRATION RESEARCH FOR A NEW CENTURY

MULTIDISCIPLINARY PERSPECTIVES

NANCY FONER
RUBÉN G. RUMBAUT
STEVEN J. GOLD

EDITORS

RUSSELL SAGE FOUNDATION | NEW YORK

The Russell Sage Foundation

The Russell Sage Foundation, one of the oldest of America's general purpose foundations, was established in 1907 by Mrs. Margaret Olivia Sage for "the improvement of social and living conditions in the United States." The Foundation seeks to fulfill this mandate by fostering the development and dissemination of knowledge about the country's political, social, and economic problems. While the Foundation endeavors to assure the accuracy and objectivity of each book it publishes, the conclusions and interpretations in Russell Sage Foundation publications are those of the authors and not of the Foundation, its Trustees, or its staff. Publication by Russell Sage, therefore, does not imply Foundation endorsement.

Library of Congress Cataloging-in-Publication Data

Immigration research for a new century: multidisciplinary perspectives / Nancy Foner, Rubén G. Rumbaut, and Steven J. Gold, editors.
    p.   cm.
Includes bibliographical references and index.
ISBN 0-87154-260-9
    1. Emigration and immigration—Research.   I. Foner, Nancy, 1945—
II. Rumbaut, Ruben G.   III. Gold, Steven J. (Steven James)

JV6013.5 .I55 2000
304.8'2—dc21   00-036619

The paper used in this publication meets the minimum requirements of American National Standard for Information Sciences—Permanence of Paper for Printed Library Materials. ANSI Z39.48-1992.

RUSSELL SAGE FOUNDATION
112 East 64th Street, New York, New York 10021
10 9 8 7 6 5 4 3 2 1

Contents

Contributors

NANCY FONER is professor of anthropology at the State University of New York, Purchase.

RUBÉN G. RUMBAUT is professor of sociology at Michigan State University.

STEVEN J. GOLD is professor and associate chair in the Department of Sociology at Michigan State University.

RAFAEL ALARCÓN is professor and researcher in the Department of Social Studies at El Colegio de la Frontera Norte in Mexico.

NANCY C. CARNEVALE recently received her doctorate in American history from Rutgers University.

CATHERINE CENIZA CHOY is assistant professor of American studies and history at the University of Minnesota.

JOSH DEWIND is professor of anthropology at Hunter College, City University of New York. He is also director of the International Migration Program of the Social Science Research Council.

INGRID GOULD ELLEN is assistant professor of policy and planning at the Robert F. Wagner Graduate School of Public Service at New York University.

HERBERT J. GANS is Robert S. Lynd Professor of Sociology at Columbia University.

GRETA GILBERTSON is associate professor in the Department of Sociology and Anthropology at Fordham University.

JENNIFER S. HIRSCH is assistant professor in the Department of International Health at Emory's Rollins School of Public Health.

JON D. HOLTZMAN is visiting assistant professor in the Department of Sociology and Anthropology at Kalamazoo College.

JANE JUNN is associate professor of political science at Rutgers University.

KATHY A. KAUFMAN is assistant professor of sociology at Vassar College.

FRED KRISSMAN is lecturer of anthropology at the California State University, Northridge.

GALLYA LAHAV is assistant professor of political science at the State University of New York at Stony Brook.

JENNIFER LEE is assistant professor of sociology at the University of California, Irvine.

PEGGY LEVITT is assistant professor of sociology at Wellesley College and associate at the Weatherhead Center for International Affairs at Harvard University.

HOWARD MARKEL is George E. Wantz Professor of the History of Medicine and director of the Historic Center for the Health Sciences at the University of Michigan.

GASPAR RIVERA-SALGADO is assistant professor in the Department of Sociology and the program in American Studies and Ethnicity at the University of Southern California.

GEORGE J. SÁNCHEZ is associate professor of history and director of the Program in American Studies and Ethnicity at the University of Southern California.

AUDREY SINGER is associate in the International Migration Policy Program at the Carnegie Endowment for International Peace.

ALEXANDRA MINNA STERN is assistant professor of history at the University of California, Santa Cruz.

AYUMI TAKENAKA recently received her doctorate in sociology from Columbia University.

MARY C. WATERS is professor of sociology and Harvard College Professor at Harvard University.

STEVEN S. ZAHNISER is agricultural economist at the Economic Research Service, U.S. Department of Agriculture.

ARISTIDE R. ZOLBERG is University in Exile Professor of Political Science at the Graduate Faculty, New School University, and director of the International Center for Migration, Ethnicity, and Citizenship.

Acknowledgments

This volume has its origins in a June 1998 conference sponsored by the Committee on International Migration of the Social Science Research Council (SSRC). Entitled "Transformations: Immigration and Immigration Research in the United States" and held at Columbia University, the conference brought together for the first time a highly select group of scholars who had been awarded postdoctoral and predoctoral research fellowships under the SSRC's International Migration Program. These scholars, whose work spans the full range of the social sciences and who in many ways represent the cutting edge of a new generation of immigration research, presented the results of their work in a series of cross-disciplinary panels, alongside critical commentaries and reflections by established scholars in the field who had constituted the SSRC's International Migration Committee since its founding in 1994. Stimulated by the conference's wide-ranging critical discussions, the authors subsequently prepared formal papers, which went through several phases of refereed review and revision. Earlier versions of some of the papers were published in a special issue of the *American Behavioral Scientist* (June–July 1999); most appear here for the first time, and all have been revised for this volume.

We wish to thank a number of people who have helped in the preparation of this book. At the Social Science Research Council, Christian Fuersich, Walter Miller, and Veda Truesdale provided invaluable assistance at various stages along the way. We are grateful as well to the members of the SSRC's International Migration Committee and to the committee's staff director, Josh DeWind, for their participation and help in organizing the conference; and to the Andrew W. Mellon Foundation, whose support throughout has made possible the work of the committee, including the various fellowship programs and conferences organized under its auspices.

At the Russell Sage Foundation, David Haproff and Suzanne Nichols were consistently helpful in the production and publication of this volume. Rebecca Hanson and Kerry Woodward, who were at the Russell Sage Foundation in 1997 and 1998, were instrumental in coding and processing the data collected by the National Survey of Immigration Scholars, results of which were presented at the conference. The NASIS project itself, the first such survey conducted in the United States, was carried out under the auspices of both the Social Science Research Council and the Russell Sage Foundation. Indeed, this volume is the second produced as a result of the work of the SSRC's International Migration Committee, and both have been published by the Russell Sage Foundation; the first, *The Handbook of International Migration: The American Experience*, appeared in November 1999.

Finally, we are especially indebted to Herbert J. Gans, whose keynote address at the Columbia conference provided the basis for his chapter in this volume, and to all of the authors whose work is reflected in these pages for the quality of their contributions and the focused commitment they have brought to the enterprise.

Nancy Foner
Rubén G. Rumbaut
Steven J. Gold

Introduction

IMMIGRATION AND IMMIGRATION RESEARCH IN THE UNITED STATES

Nancy Foner, Rubén G. Rumbaut, and Steven J. Gold

Four decades into a new era of mass immigration, it has become commonplace to observe that the United States is undergoing its most profound demographic transformation in a century. Much less evident is the extent to which the social scientific study of immigration is itself being transformed in the process. This volume seeks to provide a glimpse of these dual transformations—indeed, it is itself a multidisciplinary product of the changes now under way. It reflects the work both of established scholars who have directed the Committee on International Migration of the Social Science Research Council (SSRC) since its formation in 1994 and, especially, of younger scholars from a wide range of disciplines who were awarded postdoctoral and predoctoral research fellowships under the SSRC's International Migration Program. The latter were chosen from a highly competitive national field of 263 applicants in 1996 and 1997. The fellows whose papers are included in this book were among the two dozen who presented their research at a SSRC conference held at Columbia University in June 1998.

Surely, the sheer magnitude of the phenomenon of immigration, whether measured in terms of its size, composition, or spatial concentration, is impressive. The immigrant stock population of the United States today numbers 55 million people—27 million immigrants and 28 million U.S.-born children of immigrants. That figure is already one-fifth of the total national population. If today's immigrant stock were to form a country, it would rank in the top 10 percent in the world in the size of its population—about twice the size of Canada and roughly the size of the United Kingdom, France, or Italy (see Rumbaut 1998).

This newest immigration is not only, by definition, of recent vintage, but it is also overwhelmingly non-European in national origin. Of the 27 million foreign born in the United States today, fully 60 percent arrived between 1980 and 1998, and an overwhelming 90 percent since 1960. Of those post-1960 immigrants, the majority (52 percent) have come from Latin America and the Caribbean, with Mexico alone accounting for 28 percent of the total. Another 29 percent have come from Asia and the Middle East. The Filipinos, Chinese, and Indochinese alone account for 15 percent of the total, or as much as all those born in Europe and Canada combined.

As in the past, today's newcomers are heavily concentrated in particular areas of settlement. Fully one-third of the immigrant stock population of the United States resides in California, and another third resides in Florida, Texas, and the New York–New Jersey region, with the concentrations denser still within metropolitan areas in these states. In Los Angeles County, for instance, a preponderant 62 percent of the area's 9.5 million people are of immigrant stock, as are 54 percent of New York City's and Orange County's, 43 percent of San Diego's, and 72 percent of Miami's population (Rumbaut 1998).

Unlike the last great wave of European immigration at the turn of the twentieth century, which was halted by the passage of restrictive legislation in the 1920s and by the back-to-back global cataclysms of the Great Depression and World War II, the current flows show no signs of abating. No draconian legislation that would drastically limit immigration is in sight. Moreover, inasmuch as immigration is a network-driven phenomenon and the United States remains the premier destination for a world on the move, the likelihood is that United States–bound immigration will continue for many years to come.

The rapid growth of this emerging population has led to a burgeoning research literature and an intensified public debate about the new immigration and its manifold impacts on American society. Virtually unnoticed by comparison has been the impact on American social science as it tries to grasp and grapple with the complexity of the subject. The papers in this volume, which address that interconnection, are organized into two parts. The focus of part I, "Studying Immigration," is not on the immigrants themselves but on research about them; these papers deal with various disciplinary perspectives that define the field, the social origins and intellectual orientations of immigration scholars themselves, and some critical reflections on future research needs. Part II, "Studies of Immigration," presents seventeen selected papers from a new generation of immigration researchers, the research fellows of the SSRC's International Migration Program.

Studying Immigration

Part I begins with a paper by Rubén Rumbaut that explores the social bases of the field of immigration studies itself. Rumbaut argues that the field will be advanced by making immigration research the object of systematic scrutiny and by analyzing it from the vantage of the sociology of knowledge. Studying immigration in the United States has been, in essence, a century-long affair, beginning in the first decades of the twentieth century, during a time of heavy European immigration in which nativist and racialist controversies were prevalent among commentators on "the immigration problem." In this early period, the emphasis was on the causes of immigration and on the full spectrum of the consequences of incorporating a mass migration of diverse strangers. The middle of the century saw a four-decade-long hiatus in mass immigration, during which the focus of immigration studies shifted to the processes of assimilation of a second and third generation and, after World War II, increasingly to issues of race and ethnic relations.

A third generation of scholarship can be said to span the newest era of mass immigration: paralleling the growth of immigration itself, this new era of research started out tentatively in the 1970s, expanded in the 1980s, and exploded in the 1990s into the growth industry it has become today. Because the study of immigration is socially and historically grounded, it is not surprising that today, as in earlier periods, the direction and emphasis of research are partly a reaction to, and have developed in conversation with, the dominant issues of the day. Thus, for example, the pressures of hegemonic Americanization at home and (for a time) isolationism abroad that stamped the early decades of the twentieth century contrast sharply with the era of hegemonic Americanization abroad and a domestic context of civil rights and ethnic reaffirmation in which today's researchers came of age intellectually.

Unlike the nascent scholarship on immigration at the turn of the past century, the present era has seen many immigrants themselves become leading scholars of immigration in certain disciplines, and the children and especially grandchildren of immigrants are prominent immigration scholars in others. In his opening contribution to this volume, Rumbaut reports some revealing empirical findings from the first National Survey of Immigration Scholars (NASIS), which provide valuable clues about their social origins and research orientations. The survey is based on a large sample of scholars, at various stages in their careers, who are immigration specialists in a wide variety of disciplines, principally sociology, history, anthropology, political science, and economics. The sample also includes substantial numbers of other immigration researchers whose doctoral training was in psychology, education, public health, urban planning, public policy, area studies, ethnic studies, religious studies, languages, literature, and other disciplines. In effect, the NASIS study paints a comparative cross-disciplinary portrait of those scholars who are most responsible for producing our scholarly knowledge base. It analyzes the extent to which that knowledge is produced by ethnic insiders or outsiders, and—by examining changes by gender, generation, ethnicity, and research focus over time—the extent of the transformation of the field in the present era.

The special commentaries that then follow, in chapter 2—on sociology, anthropology, history, and political science—offer a view of the perspectives of the different disciplines. They are supplemented by Josh DeWind's overview of the Social Science Research Council's activities in the immigration area. This is not the first time a SSRC committee has looked at immigration—an earlier committee, in the 1920s, was created to study immigration in the aftermath of the enormous turn-of-the-century influx. The earlier committee was also multidisciplinary in makeup; it drew its members from the fields of anthropology, psychology, economics, political science, and statistics. Yet there are important differences from the past. The Social Science Research Council itself had only just been created in 1923, and the committee on immigration—called the Committee on Scientific Aspects of Human Migration—was, as Josh DeWind and his colleagues have observed elsewhere, part of the effort by these disciplines to establish their scientific credentials, independent of efforts at social reform. The fledgling SSRC must have seen in the study of immigration and the integration of immigrants into American society a promising opportunity to demonstrate the importance of social science research as something more than fields of knowledge derived from the natural sciences (Hirschman, DeWind, and Kasinitz 1999, 5). Today, of course, the social sciences are firmly established as legitimate fields of study, and within each discipline there is a body of research and theory addressing immigration. In this context, one of the major goals of the present-day SSRC migration committee, as DeWind notes, has been to integrate this diverse body of scholarship and to promote the "theoretical coherence of immigration studies as an interdisciplinary subfield within the social sciences."

As a step in this direction, four members of the SSRC International Migration Committee offer their reflections on immigration research in their particular disciplines: sociology, anthropology, history, and political science. Each of the social science disciplines, of course, has distinct methods, emphases, and orientations that influence the interpretation, analysis, and conduct of immigration research. Sociologists studying immigration maintain a continuing interest in assimilation, residential segregation, occupational specialization, marginality, and ethnic and racial relations. Anthropologists, drawing on their research in cultures outside the United States, have emphasized migrants' links with their home societies. Political scientists have been concerned with explaining immigration policy, the political incorporation of migrants, citizenship, and the meaning of the nation-state, and historians, looking back to

America's past, have explored assimilation processes, the transplantation of immigrant cultures to America, and, increasingly, the role of race in newcomers' adaptation. Whereas once immigration history focused almost exclusively on the study of European immigrants, a growing number of historians are now studying Latin American and Asian immigrants.

There are differences, too, in the degree to which immigration to the United States is central to the concerns of the various social science disciplines. Immigration, as Mary Waters observes, is at the very core of American sociology—a legacy from the days of the Chicago School of sociology, with its studies of early-twentieth-century immigrants and their effects on American cities. It is not surprising that immigration has been a major topic in American history for many years, given its critical role in the making of the United States. It is noteworthy, however, that the first paper by a leading historian to propose a research agenda for establishing "the significance of immigration in American history," written by Arthur Schlesinger Sr., was published in 1921 in the *American Journal of Sociology*, the official organ of the Chicago School of sociology (Schlesinger 1921). Immigration actually became a field of specialization in American history in the period from 1926 to 1940, according to Philip Gleason's (1998) account; the field, in his words, "erupted" in the late 1960s to such an extent that by the 1970s, 1,813 doctoral dissertations in history focused on immigration or ethnicity. In anthropology, immigration to the United States is only beginning to develop as a legitimate topic of study, now that, as Nancy Foner notes, the people studied on their home turf end up living next door. In political science, according to Aristide Zolberg, immigration has, until recently, evoked little or no interest.

There is also variation in the degree to which scholars in the different disciplines are self-consciously reflecting on the role that their fields can, and will, play in understanding and studying the recent immigration. Whereas sociologists accept, as a matter of course, that immigration will be a central topic—indeed, as Waters notes, sometimes they even wonder why other disciplines are stepping on sociological turf—many anthropologists are concerned with carving out a distinctive anthropological approach to the new immigration now that a growing number are turning their attention to populations in the United States. In history, several contributors to a recent forum on immigration history, published in the *Journal of American Ethnic History*, speak of a field in crisis, torn between historians who have analyzed nineteenth- and early-twentieth-century European immigration and those studying immigration from Asia, Latin America, and the Caribbean in the past and present, and also between historians who define themselves as immigration historians and others who count themselves as ethnic studies scholars (see Gjerde 1999a; Sánchez 1999).

Although immigration researchers are, inevitably, influenced by their particular disciplines, they are increasingly crossing disciplinary boundaries and drawing on theoretical insights—and empirical data— from fields other than their own as they tackle particular problems, from the causes of international migration to what happens to the children of immigrants in the schools and the economy. At the same time, an interdisciplinary field of immigration studies is very much in the making. Sociological approaches to assimilation, for example, including the more nuanced concept of segmented assimilation, are influencing scholars studying immigrant incorporation, whatever their discipline. The same can be said of work on ethnic entrepreneurship; researchers in a variety of disciplines who study immigrant businesses cite and use models elaborated by sociologists to understand why particular groups go into business and why some are more successful than others. Transnationalism, a concept first elaborated by anthropologists to understand how—and why—present-day immigrants maintain ties with their homelands, has been taken up by sociologists, historians, and political scientists and is being examined and further developed from their own disciplinary perspectives. Historical studies of "whiteness" that bring out the contingent nature of race and analyze the "whitening" process among earlier European immigrants are helping to shape work on race and ethnicity among today's newcomers. Finally, researchers exploring immigration policy and the role of the state are gaining insights from the emerging political science literature on immigration, membership, and citizenship. Indeed, a recent call for the historiography of immigration law draws heavily on work by legal scholars and political scientists (Lee 1999).

The mix of disciplines in immigration studies, as Mary Waters notes, is creative and empowering, leading scholars to ask new questions and see old problems in new ways and to go beyond what are sometimes the limited concerns of their own fields. The anthropologist's emphasis on sending communities, the historian's on the contingencies of historical development, and the political scientist's on the way states shape the choices available to individuals are all, she says, correctives to the sometimes narrow focus of sociological thinking on immigration. In history, to give another example, George Sánchez has recently written that the future of immigration history depends on the field's ability to incorporate insights on race, nation, and culture that have primarily developed outside its own disciplinary boundaries (Sánchez 1999, 68). If, as Alejandro Portes notes, theoretical advances arise out of the ability to reconstitute a perceptual field and to identify connections not previously seen, then the interdisciplinary thrust of so much immigration research may be particularly productive as it brings new perspectives to bear on familiar issues, incorporates insights from different fields, and promotes the kind of "distance from reality" that Portes argues is important "in order to identify patterns lost at close range" (1997, 802, 803).

At the same time, efforts to create and sustain an interdisciplinary field of immigration studies raise some difficult questions and issues. On an intellectual level, there is the risk that scholars trained to study present-day immigration from a multidisciplinary perspective will lose the benefits that come from being steeped in the traditions and founding works of a particular discipline. This is something that worries some historians of immigration. The turn among recent graduate students to theory developed outside of history has led to concerns, among some historians, that classic works in immigration history are being neglected to the detriment of the field (Gjerde 1999b). There are also the hard realities of the hierarchy of disciplines and career concerns. As Waters points out, some methods and disciplines are privileged over others; and managing a career in a discipline—publishing and getting tenure, most importantly—when a scholar's work strays outside of disciplinary boundaries is a professional challenge in its own right.

Waters also alerts us to the importance of creating more linkages between immigration and the study of race, a theme that emerges in Sánchez's paper as well. Moreover, as Sánchez reminds us, immigration studies, past and present, need to consider the full range of groups arriving in every period. Just as historians need to remember that Asian and Latin American and Caribbean migration was occurring in the late nineteenth and early twentieth centuries, so, too, social scientists studying the present need to concern themselves with European immigration to the United States in the late twentieth and early twenty-first centuries. Finally, the establishment of new academic fields and departments—ethnic studies, women's studies, urban studies, American studies, city and regional planning, and the like (with which several of this volume's authors are affiliated)—have already begun to integrate existing approaches to create new disciplinary identities.

Although the huge influx of immigrants to the United States in the last four decades has stimulated an outpouring of research in all the social science disciplines, much remains to be done. Chapter 3, by Herbert Gans, concludes this first section by identifying six main "holes" or areas of needed immigration research. Three of these concern processes of immigrant incorporation: the persistent question of selectivity in emigration and immigration, which should be addressed much more systematically; intergenerational differences in adaptation, particularly between the first, 1.5, and second generations; and macro-level economic, political, and societal factors shaping those patterns of adaptation. Three other areas involve the field of immigration scholarship itself: insider versus outsider roles among immigration researchers, the need for more empirical research on the choices (and omissions) of topics and groups that draw the attention of immigration scholars, and the role of funding agencies in shaping the field of study—including the SSRC's International Migration Program itself.

As Gans admits, his research holes are mainly sociological holes. Clearly, there are additional anthropological, historical, economic, and political science holes that will need to be filled by future immigration researchers. A host of policy questions await further study in political science, as does the increasingly important role that immigrants are playing—and will continue to play—in U.S. politics: as immigrants become citizens (and voters) with the potential to determine the outcome of local, state, and even national elections; as foreign-born elected officials and political activists grow in number; and as immigrants become members of important political blocs and interest groups. Among the areas that await further careful study in anthropology are the dynamics of culture creation and invention among immigrants, cultural conflicts between immigrant and mainstream values, and the consequences of transnational connections for sending, as well as receiving, communities. In history, there are gaps to be filled in our understanding of the histories of Asian and Latin American immigrants in the United States; moreover, models and theories developed by social scientists to study America's latest arrivals may shed new light on the experiences of European immigrants in the past. Within disciplines—and across them—immigration research will also benefit from a range of comparisons that can offer new insights into the immigrant experience, among them comparisons of immigrants in the United States past and present and of immigration to the United States and other major receiving countries.

Finally, as to Gans' call for studies of immigration scholarship itself, this is largely unexplored territory. The massive immigration of the past few decades is, as we have emphasized, not only transforming American society and the immigrants themselves but is also transforming the way immigration is studied—that is, how researchers are trying to make sense of the very transformations immigration has created. To do this full justice, we need studies of the way knowledge is developed about immigration's causes and consequences, within and across disciplines, in concrete sociohistorical and intellectual contexts.

The Shifting Contexts
of Migration Research

In examining the ways immigration research has been recently transformed, it is worthwhile to reflect upon some of the shifting contexts that have brought about these changes. The unprecedented immigration that the United States has witnessed since the 1960s—in both numbers and diversity of origin—is obviously a major factor. The Cold War was associated with the arrival in the United States of more than two million refugees from Cuba, Southeast Asia, Central America, Eastern Europe, the former Soviet Union, and other countries as well as the expansion of military and political links with several source countries of migration. A related event, the collapse of the Soviet bloc, reduced the prominence of Marxist thought among both activists and academics while expanding the reach of global capitalism into regions in which its influence had previously been restricted (Antonio 1990).

Within the United States, the civil rights and feminist movements reframed American notions of social membership, economic opportunity, equality, and assimilation. Today's migrants thus enter a society transformed by the expansion of opportunities for minority group members and women and also by patterns of industrial restructuring that have drastically altered the economic environment. The huge influx of Third World immigrants itself has begun to change, in very basic ways, our notions about race and the structure of America's racial hierarchies. Migration scholarship has also been influenced by social movements that have championed a wide array of policy agendas from multiculturalism and affirmative action, through selective inclusion, to exclusionary nativism and restrictive welfare reform.

If these developments in the larger society have shaped migration scholars' perspectives on immigration and ethnic relations, so too have changes in their home turf—the academy, which has been perhaps the focal venue for debates about the meaning of immigration and ethnicity in American society. Many of society's most articulate and vehement spokespersons on topics of ethnic change and immigrant incorporation have been academics, and much campus activism has been directed at increasing resources for and representation of migrant and ethnic minority constituencies. Recent immigrants from Latin America, the Caribbean, and Asia, as well as Africa, the Middle East and Europe, are now among our nation's leading scholars (as well as athletes, artists, physicians, scientists, and entrepreneurs). Women of all ethnic groups are increasingly visible as authors of migration research in the social sciences and as part of higher education generally. A number of the most controversial policy efforts directed toward ethnic and gender inequalities have occurred on campuses—ranging from culturally sensitive speech codes to the outright banning of affirmative action programs in some of the nation's largest and most ethnically diverse state university systems. Immigrant and ethnic faculty and students have been major actors in these debates.

Finally, the writings of scholars have contributed significantly to deliberations about the meaning of immigration in a nation of immigrants. In addition to the myriad reports that have attempted to assess the impact of immigrants upon American culture and economy, scholars have begun to alter our basic understandings of the relations between immigrant communities and both the larger receiving society and their sending countries.

For example, before new understandings of ethnic community emerged, fostered by the ethnic revivals of the 1970s, both scholars and the wider public generally accepted as an article of faith that "American" culture was superior to that of migrant groups. Hence, the faster migrants abandoned their traditional customs and behavioral patterns in favor of those of the Anglo-American middle class, the better. Since that time, a wide range of studies has shown that immigrant and ethnic communities have the ability to provide their members with a variety of social, psychological, and economic benefits—ranging from business ownership and increased earnings to success in schools, protection from discrimination, moral support, and even superior physical and mental health.

These many changes in the field of migration studies have generally redirected its outlook and orientation, but certain contemporary conditions have also fostered the resuscitation of several approaches closely associated with the Chicago School's studies in the thirty years preceding World War II. These include the growing emphasis on community-based, qualitative studies in sociology and history, a revival of concern with the concept of assimilation in several fields, and an increased awareness of the importance of enduring ties to the country of origin (often in discussions of transnationalism). Fields such as sociology and history reveal a renewed interest in culture and identity, often explored through qualitative methods at the community level. Assimilation, a taboo word as recently as the late 1980s, is now a major topic in sociology, political science, education, and other fields. The concern with assimilation is visible in the work of senior scholars like Gans and Waters as well as that of the younger generation of social scientists represented here, including Jane Junn, Greta Gilbertson, and Audrey Singer. Just as sociologists and political scientists have devoted additional attention to issues of culture, community, and identity, anthropologists, who have always regarded these topics as central to their discipline, have become increasingly attuned to international and national political and economic contexts that frame their research settings. They are now as likely to discuss global capitalism or the world system as scholars in fields with a longer tradition of research on political economy.

Accordingly, a degree of convergence has occurred as topics and methods once associated with a single field are now shared by several disciplines. Chapters in this volume by Jennifer Lee, Jennifer Hirsch, Peggy Levitt, and Gaspar Rivera-Salgado each offer multidimensional analyses that emphasize contextual factors as well as immigrants' cultural patterns in trying to explain new social arrangements and organizations that arise within and beyond the United States.

New understandings of context and solidarity are being developed in a large body of work on the viability of ethnic self-help, the importance of ethnic niches, and an awareness of migrants' ties with the country of origin. Informed by theoretical understandings of ethnicity, race, and nationality as socially constructed rather than primordially determined, contemporary scholars are much more aware of the subtle, complex, and shifting array of social identities and sources of solidarity and conflict within ethnic and migrant populations than were earlier generations. For example, in their chapters in this book, Rafael Alarcón, Gaspar Rivera-Salgado, and Fred Krissman all report on Mexican migrants in the United States. Yet because of the distinct occupational, class, and ethnic characteristics of the three groups studied—Silicon Valley scientists, indigenous migrants, and migrant farmworkers—their subjects have little else in common. Nationality per se recedes into the background as a focal topic, and a more subtle analysis of class, ethnicity, and economic context takes its place. In general, as a consequence of the immense diversity found in contemporary immigrant experiences, scholars tend to specialize in certain types of immigration or locations of origin and settlement.

The younger generation of scholars, who are themselves often of immigrant origin, have brought a new level of concern with issues of belonging, identity, and social access. Having grown up after the modern civil rights and feminist movements, they are especially sensitive to issues of discrimination and marginalization among the immigrants they study, whatever their social class or educational level. For example, Jane Junn, Rafael Alarcón, and Catherine Ceniza Choy all ask to what extent skilled newcomers are stereotyped, blocked by "glass ceilings," or incorporated into forms of political participation that may be biased against them.

New perspectives on discrimination are reflected in recent studies of "whiteness," noted by Sánchez to be an issue of special interest to historians. By demonstrating that "white" ethnics were at one time considered to be "nonwhite," scholars such as Nancy Carnevale, Howard Markel, and Alexandra Minna Stern apply today's more critical models of racial and ethnic exclusion to an earlier period, demonstrating the extent to which racial discrimination once affected groups that are now accepted as members of the majority. At the same time, by exploring the selective incorporation of formerly racialized groups, these scholars reveal that racial classification continues to be a powerful basis of inequality in American society, even as our society increasingly accepts the social and ultimately political, rather than purely biological, basis of racial classification.

In sum, biographical, sociohistorical, and academic factors contribute to the evolution of immigration studies. Although some disciplinary differences and concerns have been retained, movement toward disciplinary convergence can be seen. Perhaps the most immediate evidence of this is the fact that a far greater number of disciplines than ever before—including several new fields—now regard the study of international migration among their integral concerns.

The topics and issues identified in this book will surely continue to take new forms because migrant populations, academic affairs, social history, political economy, legal developments—and the social and cultural origins of the scholars who track them—are not static phenomena. Yet it is our hope that this volume will contribute to our understanding of important transformations in migration research and help to identify important directions in its future development.

Studies of Immigration

The second part of this volume seeks to exemplify the diversity of a field in process of transformation by turning to a selection of quite distinct papers written by SSRC postdoctoral and dissertation research fellows. The papers illustrate a number of important new developments taking place in immigration research. The young researchers have been intensely influenced by recent changes in society, international migration, and intellectual life. They tend to be less immersed than senior scholars in the academic approaches of earlier periods, and, as Rubén Rumbaut's contribution makes clear, compared with the recent past, they include an unprecedented number of foreign-born and women scholars.

New Groups

Many of the populations, both large and small, that concern the new generation of immigration scholars were barely present in the United

States before the 1970s. These include groups that are the focus of papers in this book, from large populations like Dominicans, South Asians, Koreans, and Filipinos to small ones about whom little is known, like Nuer refugees and Japanese Peruvians. Others, such as Mixtec Mexicans, may have been in the United States in the past but were invisible to the classification schemes of an earlier era.

In addition, the social characteristics and legal status of contemporary migrants are unlike those prevalent earlier in the century. In recent decades, large numbers of highly skilled and educated migrants have entered the country, including the Indian and Mexican computer specialists, Korean entrepreneurs, and Filipino nurses described in the papers by Rafael Alarcón, Jennifer Lee, and Catherine Ceniza Choy, respectively. Furthermore, two of the largest and most controversial categories of recent entrants—refugees and the undocumented—were of far less prominence and interest before 1970.

Research Themes

The concern that animates the largest number of chapters in part II is social membership. As Gans and Waters both remark in their papers, despite its enduring relevance in some fields, the theory of straight-line assimilation has been deservedly challenged. As a consequence, contemporary migration scholars have generated a new and more complex awareness of the nature of group identity, national membership, racial divisions, and multiculturalism.

Several papers address these topics by examining the web of links that immigrants maintain between countries of origin and settlement. Conventionally, social scientists have assumed that authorized presence in a country, especially when legitimated through naturalization, resolves major questions about national membership. More recent scholarship challenges this conclusion, suggesting that identity, citizenship, and presence within a nation-state can and often do vary independently. In fact, whereas scholars once assumed that becoming naturalized proved a migrant's loyalty to the United States, today's researchers understand that naturalization may be motivated precisely by the desire to facilitate easy travel to another country.

Addressing the question of national membership and the role of the nation-state, Peggy Levitt, Gaspar Rivera-Salgado, and Fred Krissman variously illustrate the permeability of national borders and the benefits that individuals, corporations, social movements, and organizations often receive by accessing extranational resources. Elaborating on this process, Ayumi Takenaka, Greta Gilbertson and Audrey Singer, Steven Zahniser, and Gallya Lahav conclude that social, legal, and economic factors continue to make transnational existence a convoluted and difficult one. Furthermore, although ties to multiple nations offer new options, they also serve to further complicate matters of national membership for migrants and nation-states alike.

Another dimension of group membership around which recent studies of migration converge involves racial classification and the social construction of whiteness. For an earlier generation of scholars, full assimilation into the white, middle-class, English-speaking majority was seen as inevitable for the descendants of immigrants, although not for the immigrants themselves. Today's immigration scholars are questioning the inevitability of this process, seeing inclusion as selective, relational, and competitive and dependent on a wide range of factors, including the social, political, and economic concerns of the time and place. Focusing on the fit between the social characteristics of migrant groups and their contexts of reception—including race, health, language, location of entry and residence, gender, culture, social class, government policies, patterns of nativism, and discrimination—they show that migrants are first classified and then selectively offered or denied access to opportunities and membership in the larger society according to prevailing classification schemes.

For some groups, classification is the outcome of direct investigation by American authorities. Describing the medical practices used by immigration officials at several ports of entry early this century, Howard Markel and Alexandra Minna Stern argue in their chapter that the way immigrants were treated was a consequence of regional labor needs and eugenics-based beliefs about immigrants' origins. These factors, in turn, contributed to the medical treatments immigrants received and the rates of rejection they encountered. Similarly, Nancy Carnevale delineates the role literacy and English competence played in the racial classification of Italian and other European immigrants during the late nineteenth and early twentieth centuries.

Other chapters deal with more subtle processes of classification and incorporation. These center on migrants' ability to merge with existing American social institutions. Jane Junn explores the extent to which various minority groups have been incorporated into the American majority-rule political system. Ingrid Gould Ellen examines the ways immigrants of Asian and Latin American origins fit into racially segregated neighborhoods.

One of the burgeoning areas of social science research since the 1970s has concerned women, gender, and families. Before that time, social scientists focused on male wage earners and neglected immigrant women. If discussed at all, immigrant women were generally depicted as limited to the domestic sphere. Similarly, little attention was devoted to immigrant families and gender relations. Recent scholars, however, have devoted considerable attention to gender and family issues among migrants. As Rubén Rumbaut notes, the concern with women, gender, and families mirrors the increasing representation of women among migration scholars. Although women made up only 8 percent of migration researchers who received doctorates before 1965, they account for more than 60 percent of migration scholars who have received their doctorates since 1995.

Among the chapters concerned with gender issues, those by Catherine Ceniza Choy and Kathy Kaufman explore the experience and societal impact of migrant women in view of the demand for gendered workers like nurses and domestics. Taking a different approach, Jon Holtzman and Jennifer Hirsch describe the way in which the social, economic, and legal influence of American gender norms transforms the interactions of immigrant men and women in the country of settlement and, as Hirsch notes, extends to the country of origin as well.

A final topic that animates many of these projects is interest in economic incorporation. Before the 1970s, much of the research on immigrants' economic lives was rooted either in the individualistic assumptions of neoclassical economics or in cultural determinism. Since that time, scholars have developed more complex and contextualized understandings of economic incorporation, noting the importance of collective resources, labor markets shaped by class, ethnicity, gender, and legal status, and the influence of the United States on countries of emigration.

The chapters by Catherine Ceniza Choy, Fred Krissman, Peggy Levitt, Rafael Alarcón, and Steven Zahniser all describe the ways that U.S. political and economic interests contribute to the arrival of migrant workers, and several chapters show the dynamic processes involved in the establishment of niches for foreign-born engineers and scientists (Alarcón), nurses (Choy), private-household workers (Kaufman), farmworkers (Krissman), and small shopkeepers (Lee). Jennifer Lee considers the ways that immigrant and ethnic groups compete over the market for goods and services in urban ghettoes, and Kathy Kaufman seeks to explain why immigrants become heavily enmeshed in private household work in some cities but not others.

New Research

A closer look at the particular themes developed in the papers by the SSRC postdoctoral and dissertation research fellows that comprise part II of this volume brings out the sorts of problems, processes, and concerns that are the focus of a new generation of immigration scholars. Their papers have been organized in the following thematic triptych.

The first set of chapters examines issues of political economy, membership, and the state. In chapter 4, historians Stern and Markel (the latter is also a physician) draw upon historical data about the health screening and treatment of immigrants in four points of entry into the United States: the Atlantic and the Pacific coasts and the Mexican and Canadian borders. Their study reveals the ways in which labor needs and racial stereotypes intersected with medical knowledge to shape the nature of migrants' incorporation into the United States. Historian Choy (chapter 5) studies a skilled migrant group, Filipino nurses, tracing the presence of this gendered labor force to colonial education policies developed early this century and the U.S. Exchange Visitor program of the 1950s and 1960s. Focusing, in chapter 6, on the impressive level of political mobilization and cooperation displayed by Oaxacan Mixtec farmworkers in Mexico and California, sociologist Rivera-Salgado works to refine models of transnational community to incorporate the importance of networks and identities that existed before migration. Sociologists Gilbertson and Singer examine the complex patterns of connection that an extended, multigenerational family of Dominicans maintain between the United States and their country of origin as they explore decisions about naturalization, in chapter 7. In so doing, they reveal the various factors that frame migrants' views of citizenship and the reasons that dual citizenship, when available, appeals to many. Political scientist Junn utilizes several Texas voting surveys to assess the entrenched models of political participation across ethnic and nationality lines in chapter 8. Given the growing diversity of the American population, she asks if alternative means of political involvement will enhance newcomers' engagement in the democratic process. Comparing the United States and Europe, political scientist Lahav, in chapter 9, examines the current role of the nation-state, as well as that of nonstate actors, in regulating migration. In contrast to recent scholarship that sees a decline in the power of the nation-state, her research indicates that states continue to exert significant influence, sometimes through nonstate actors.

The second series of chapters concerns migration, economic incorporation, and the market. Economist Zahniser (chapter 10) applies a logit model to quantitative survey data to test a range of hypotheses about patterns of migration between Mexico and the United States. In explaining migration behavior and its determinants, he finds several intriguing differences for subgroups defined in terms of gender, legal status, and family composition. Anthropologist Krissman, in chapter 11, uses data culled during ethnographic fieldwork in California and Washington state to demonstrate the process by which U.S. employers access ethnic networks to recruit Mexican villagers to labor in agribusiness.

Unlike most scholars of migration who focus on unskilled laborers, urban planner Alarcón's research concerns highly skilled Indian and Mexican migrants working in Silicon Valley. His comparative case study, in chapter 12, presents the life histories and job trajectories of workers in one of the world's most technologically advanced and globally integrated industries. In so doing, he contributes to our understanding of an economically vital but understudied facet of human migration. Drawing on a growing body of research and theory on ethnic economies, sociologist Lee compares the small businesses owned by three ethnic groups—Jews, Koreans, and African Americans—in inner-city New York and Philadelphia (chapter 13). Her interviews and fieldwork reveal that the three groups specialize in distinct economic activities and, hence, limit competition. However, because their groups have higher rates of entrepreneurship, Jews and Koreans have access to greater levels of coethnic economic cooperation than is available to African Americans. Comparing two cities with small and large foreign-born populations but similar demand for domestic help, sociologist Kathy Kaufman determines that the presence of many immigrant women depresses wages for workers in this sector and permits employers to select household help according to their own ethnic stereotypes (chapter 14).

The third, and final, set of chapters examines issues of ethnicity, race, gender, and community. Anthropologist Hirsch did fieldwork with Mexican immigrant women in Atlanta and then traveled to their villages of origin, where she interviewed their mothers, sisters, and sisters-in-law. In this way, she was able to contemplate the ways in which generation and location shape women's opportunities and their relations with men. Based on her research, she argues in chapter 15 that social scientists should stop trying to determine only the effects of migration on women and instead consider how migration, generation, and other factors fashion what couples seek from their relationships. Anthropologist Holtzman conducted fieldwork among Sudanese refugees in Minnesota. In chapter 16, he analyzes the ways that American gender norms and views of marriage, and the U.S. criminal justice system, reorder power relations among Nuer men and women. Historian Carnevale discusses the importance of literacy and competence in the English language in views about the social acceptability of Italian and other European immigrants to the United States in the early twentieth century (chapter 17). Ellen, whose doctorate is in public policy, compares patterns of residential segregation between native whites and blacks and between Asian and Latino immigrants, in chapter 18. She finds that whites are leaving locations of migrant settlement faster than they are neighborhoods with a black presence and concludes that although issues of racial avoidance may play a part in this process, demographic and economic patterns also have an important impact. Sociologist Takenaka reports in chapter 19 on fieldwork she conducted on three continents (in North America, South America, and Asia) to examine the experience of Peruvians of Japanese ancestry. Upon returning to Japan from Latin America, they find themselves regarded as foreigners rather than countrymen. Accordingly, whether in Japan, Peru, or the United States, they learn to emphasize and deploy a hybrid identity reflecting their unique communal and cultural heritage. Finally, in chapter 20, sociologist Peggy Levitt investigates three Boston migrant populations—Dominicans, Brazilians, and Asian Indians—who maintain links with their countries of origin. She examines their distinct array of home-country links and United States–based resources to consider the effect of home-country affiliation on migrants' relationship to the host society.

Conclusion

These chapters, with their widely different disciplinary styles, theoretical concerns, and research methods, stand in marked contrast to what an earlier era of immigration studies produced. The work collected in this book serves at once the functions of describing and analyzing substantive social, cultural, economic, and political aspects of the complex transformations wrought by today's immigration while offering an augur of what a new generation of immigration researchers, now coming of intellectual age, is helping to create.

References

Antonio, Robert J. 1990. "The Decline of the Grand Narrative of Emancipatory Modernity: Crisis or Renewal in Neo-Marxian Theory?" In *Frontiers of Social Theory: The New Synthesis*, edited by George Ritzer. New York: Columbia University Press.

Gjerde, Jon. 1999a. "New Growth on Old Vines—the State of the Field: The Social History of Immigration to and Ethnicity in the United States." *Journal of American Ethnic History* 18(4): 40–65.

———. 1999b. "Response." *Journal of American Ethnic History* 18(4): 151–57.

Gleason, Philip. 1998. "Crevecoeur's Question: Historical Writing on Immigration, Ethnicity, and National Identity." In *Imagined Histories*, edited by Anthony Molho and Gordon S. Wood. Princeton: Princeton University Press.

Hirschman, Charles, Philip Kasinitz, and Josh DeWind. 1999. Introduction to *Handbook of International Migration*, edited by Charles Hirschman, Philip Kasinitz, and Josh DeWind. New York: Russell Sage Foundation.

Lee, Erika. 1999. "Immigrants and Immigration Law: A State of the Field Assessment." *Journal of American Ethnic History* 18(4): 85–114.

Portes, Alejandro. 1997. "Immigration Theory for a New Century: Some Problems and Opportunities." *International Migration Review* 31(4): 799–825.

Rumbaut, Rubén G. 1998. "Coming of Age in Immigrant America." *Research Perspectives on Migration* 1(6): 1–14.

Sánchez, George. 1999. "Race, Nation, and Culture in Recent Immigration Studies." *Journal of American Ethnic History* 18(4): 66–84.

Schlesinger, Arthur M. 1921. "The Significance of Immigration in American History." *American Journal of Sociology* 27(1): 71–85

Part I

STUDYING IMMIGRATION:
DISCIPLINARY PERSPECTIVES AND
FUTURE RESEARCH NEEDS

IMMIGRATION RESEARCH IN THE UNITED STATES: SOCIAL ORIGINS AND FUTURE ORIENTATIONS

Rubén G. Rumbaut

THIS collection of multidisciplinary essays is concerned not only with the fact that this giant sponge of a society is once again being transformed in the process of absorbing a mass immigration, but the field of immigration studies is itself in flux. Indeed, as must be increasingly plain to those actively involved in it, especially in disciplines like sociology, many immigration scholars in the United States today are immigrants, or the children or grandchildren of immigrants. In the absence of hard data to document the phenomenon, that perception, when it has been noticed at all, has rested entirely on serendipitous observations and educated guesses. Nevertheless, what bits of evidence occasionally surface raise intriguing questions—and implications. For example, an article several years ago in *Footnotes*, the monthly newsletter of the American Sociological Association (ASA), discussing the formation of the Section on International Migration within the ASA, pointed to a remarkable datum: of the 449 doctoral degrees in sociology produced from 1989 to 1990 in the United States, almost one-third (31 percent) were granted to students who had done their undergraduate work in non-U.S. universities (see Rumbaut 1994, 1995; Stevenson 1993).[1] In 1998, for the first time in its century-old history, the ASA elected as its president a prominent Latin American (Cuban-born) scholar, Alejandro Portes—who is also, incidentally, a member of the Committee on International Migration of the Social Science Research Council (SSRC).

As a first step to fill the lacuna of information, the National Survey of Immigration Scholars (NASIS) was designed specifically to inquire into the social origins and research orientations of those scholars who specialize in immigration studies and who are most responsible for producing our scholarly knowledge base. Drawing the NASIS sample was itself facilitated by the rapid expansion of formal organizations of immigration scholars, typically under the auspices of the professional associations of their respective disciplines, which provided us with their full membership lists. The oldest of these was the Immigration History Society (IHS), whose organized activities, meetings, awards, newsletter, and official quarterly, the *Journal of American Ethnic History*, have served the interests of historians of immigration over the past three decades.[2] The American Anthropological Association's Committee on Refugee Issues (CORI) was organized in the late 1980s, founded by a mix of academics and practitioners concerned about refugees and other displaced persons overseas and about refugee resettlement in the United States. In 1996, as Nancy Foner notes in chapter 2, CORI formally expanded its mandate to include immigrants and accordingly changed its name to the Committee on Refugees and Immigrants.[3] The above-mentioned Section on International Migration of the ASA was established in 1994, and with more than three hundred members (smaller than the IHS, more than twice as large as CORI) actively organizes formal paper sessions and roundtables on immigration issues at the annual ASA meetings and gives the Thomas and Znaniecki Award each year to the outstanding new book published in the field.[4] More recently, in 1996, political scientists and kindred scholars established the Ethnicity, Nationalism, and Migration Section of the International Studies Association (ENMISA), connecting a diverse group of researchers on these issues through a regular newsletter, syllabi collection projects, and organized panels at the International Studies Association annual meeting.[5] Finally, a complete list was obtained of all applicants for postdoctoral and predoctoral research fellowships from the SSRC's International Migration Program in 1996 and 1997—a total of more than 250 researchers in the early stages of their careers representing different social science disciplines, including economics and others not covered by the above organizations of immigration scholars.[6] The NASIS survey was mailed early in 1998 to those on the resulting master list of 1,189 immigration scholars, and a total of 753 completed surveys were returned—a return rate of 63.3 percent.[7]

Immigration Scholars: A Portrait

The NASIS sample, then, consists of immigration scholars in a wide range of disciplines and at all stages in their careers. Table 1.1 provides a detailed profile of their characteristics. The sample is nearly evenly divided among men (53 percent) and women (47 percent). Notably, by generation in the United States, almost half (48 percent) of the total are of immigrant stock themselves: that is, 30 percent are foreign born (first-generation immigrants), and 18 percent are U.S.-born children of immigrants (second-generation).[8] Another 29 percent are third-generation scholars who reported having one or more foreign-born grandparents, whereas less than a fourth (23 percent) reported no foreign-born grandparents (fourth generation or more). More than 150 different responses were tallied for the open-ended question on ethnic self-identity; table 1.1 reports only the main ones. More than one-tenth (12 percent) reported an Asian ethnicity or national origin, mostly Chinese, Korean, Japanese, Filipino, and Indian. Ten percent are of Latin American or Caribbean origin, mainly Mexicans, Cubans, Puerto Ricans, and Jamaicans, although 3 percent claimed a "Hispanic" or "Latino" panethnic identity. Much more numerous (almost 45 percent) are scholars of European origin, mainly Irish, German, Italian, and Polish; one hundred (13 percent) reported they are Jewish (of varying origins). A fifth of the sample (21 percent) claimed a plain "American" or "white" ethnic identity; the remaining 10 percent indicated various kinds of mixed ethnicity or gave other responses.[9]

As can be seen from table 1.1, the overwhelming majority of the NASIS scholars (87 percent) earned a Ph.D. in his or her particular discipline, with another small percentage reporting other doctoral or professional degrees. A tenth indicated that their highest degree is a master's. Only 6 percent received advanced degrees in universities outside of the United States.[10] The relative youthfulness of the sample is reflected by the fact that a third (34 percent) earned or expected to earn their highest degrees in 1995 or later, and another 27 percent got their degrees between 1985 and 1994. In fact, more than half got their doctorates in the 1990s. Seven percent earned their degrees before 1965, 17 percent between 1964 and 1975, and 16 percent during the period from 1975 to 1984. More of the scholars earned their highest degree in sociology (33 percent) than in any other discipline, followed by history (28 percent), anthropology (12 percent), and political science and economics (9 percent). The rest of the sample (19 percent) includes other researchers whose doctoral training was in psychology, education, public health, urban planning, public policy, area studies, ethnic studies, religious studies, languages, literature, and other disciplines. With respect to their professional status at the time, 21 percent of respondents were full professors, 11 percent associate professors, and 13 percent assistant professors; substantial numbers were advanced graduate students or scholars employed in research, administration, or other academic positions; 5 percent were retired.

Three out of four (77 percent) indicated that they specialized in particular immigrant ethnic groups (see table 1.1). By cross-tabulating their

TABLE 1.1   *National Survey of Immigration Scholars: Sample Characteristics*

Characteristic	N	Percent
Total sample	753	100
Gender		
Female	355	47.1
Male	398	52.9
Generation		
First (foreign born)	224	29.7
Second (U.S. born)	136	18.1
Third	217	28.8
Fourth+	176	23.4
Ethnic self-identity or national origin of researcher		
Chinese	29	3.9
Korean	15	2.0
Japanese	10	1.3
Filipino	9	1.2
Indian, other South Asian	15	2.0
Vietnamese, Cambodian	5	0.7
Iranian	5	0.7
Mexican	18	2.4
Cuban	8	1.1
Puerto Rican, other Latin American	10	1.3
"Hispanic," "Latino"	24	3.2
Jamaican, Haitian, other West Indies	15	2.0
African	11	1.5
African American, black	10	1.3
Jewish	100	13.3
Irish	65	8.6
German	44	5.8
Italian	26	3.5
Polish	16	2.1
Scandinavian	21	2.8
Other European	63	8.4
"American," white	156	20.7
Mixed, other	78	10.4
Highest degree		
Ph.D.	654	86.9
Other doctoral or professional degree	17	2.3
Master's	82	10.9
Year received highest degree		
Before 1965	52	6.9
1965 to 1974	127	16.9
1975 to 1984	119	15.8

TABLE 1.1   *Continued*

Characteristic	N	Percent
1985 to 1994	200	26.6
After 1994	255	33.9
Discipline of highest degree		
Sociology	246	32.7
Political Science, Economics	66	8.8
Anthropology	93	12.4
History	207	27.5
All other disciplines	141	18.7
Current position		
Professor	158	21.0
Associate professor	84	11.2
Assistant professor	95	12.6
Instructor	54	7.2
Researcher	85	11.3
Student, other	166	22.0
Administrative, other	74	9.8
Retired	37	4.9
SSRC research fellowship applicant?		
Yes	139	18.5
No	614	81.5
Specialized in particular immigrant groups?		
Yes	581	77.2
No	172	22.8
Ethnicity or national origin of groups of current research		
Asian	158	21.0
Latin American, Caribbean	168	22.3
African	43	5.7
Jewish	46	6.1
Irish	34	4.5
Other European	128	17.0
Other, or n.a.	176	23.4
Insider or outsider ethnicity of researcher		
Insider	280	37.2
Outsider	297	39.4
N.a. or n.d.	176	23.4
Principal topic of current or planned immigration research		
Politics, conflict, citizenship	96	12.7
Forced migration, refugees	62	8.2
Race or ethnicity, intergroup relations	62	8.2
Social mobility, inequality, discrimination	53	7.0
Communities, networks, enclaves	52	6.9
Economics, labor markets, business	44	5.8

(Table continues on p. 28.)

27

TABLE 1.1   *Continued*

Characteristic	N	Percent
Gender, immigrant women	38	5.0
Generation, children of immigrants	34	4.5
Identity	33	4.4
Health, mental health	31	4.1
Religion	30	4.0
Media, popular culture	29	3.9
Transnationalism, diaspora	25	3.3
Family, household, marriage	18	2.4
Education, language	18	2.4
Other topics (specified)	18	2.4
Ethnonational groups (specified)	39	5.2
Migration, adaptation (general)	47	6.3
History (general)	24	3.2

Source: Author's compilation.

own reported ethnicity with that of the groups that are the focus of their research, it is possible to classify the scholars, at least preliminarily, as ethnic "insiders" or "outsiders" in the researcher-researched relationship—that is, as either members or nonmembers of the ethnic groups they study (Merton 1972; Gans 1997). By this measure, more than a third of the sample (37 percent) are classified as insiders and 39 percent as outsiders; the remaining 23 percent of the cases do not focus on particular ethnonational groups (hence are also noninsiders). The data reported in table 1.1 shows the extraordinarily wide range of the principal substantive topics of the immigration scholars' current or planned research. Issues of political incorporation, conflict, and citizenship were focal concerns of 13 percent of the overall sample, followed by a multiplicity of other topics listed in order of frequency—and clustered here into main general areas, for ease of presentation.

Changes in the Characteristics of Immigration Scholars over Time

Table 1.2 provides some insights into the nature of the transformation of the field over the past few decades. It presents a cross-tabulation of basic social and professional characteristics of the immigration scholars by the time period in which they earned their highest degree. An immediately notable finding is the reversal in the proportion of male and female researchers over time. Among scholars who had earned their degrees before 1965, 92 percent are men and only 8 percent women; but

TABLE 1.2   *Characteristics of Immigration Scholars, by Year They Received Their Ph.D. or Highest Degree (Percentage)*

Characteristics	Before 1965	1965 to 1974	1975 to 1984	1985 to 1994	After 1994	Total
N	52	127	119	220	255	753
Gender						
Female	7.7	26.0	37.8	57.0	62.4	47.1
Male	92.3	74.0	62.2	43.0	37.6	52.9
Generation						
First (foreign born)	17.3	18.9	25.2	36.0	34.9	29.7
Second (U.S. born)	36.5	16.5	16.0	13.5	19.6	18.1
Third	30.8	37.8	37.0	29.5	19.6	28.8
Fourth +	15.4	26.8	21.8	21.0	25.9	23.4
Ethnicity or national origin of researcher						
Asian	0	4.7	7.6	14.5	17.3	11.7
Latin American, Caribbean	0	3.9	7.6	14.0	12.9	10.0
African	0	0.8	2.5	4.5	3.1	2.8
Jewish	25.0	15.0	15.1	11.0	11.0	13.3
Irish	9.6	11.8	8.4	4.5	10.2	8.6
Other European	21.2	33.9	26.9	22.5	15.3	22.6
"American," white	26.9	22.0	21.0	19.0	20.0	20.7
Mixed, other	17.3	7.9	10.9	10.0	10.2	10.4
Current position						
Professor	44.2	60.6	37.0	7.0	0	21.0
Associate professor	0	8.7	21.8	23.0	0.4	11.2
Assistant professor	0	—	1.7	26.5	15.7	12.6
Instructor	15.4	1.6	5.0	5.0	11.0	7.2
Research	0	12.6	12.6	11.5	12.2	11.3
Student, other	0	1.6	3.4	11.5	53.7	22.0
Administrative, other	1.9	7.1	15.1	14.0	7.1	9.8
Retired	38.5	7.9	3.4	1.5	0	4.9
Immigration-related dissertation						
Yes	28.1	25.7	43.7	58.2	77.2	55.4
No	71.9	74.3	56.3	41.8	22.8	44.6
Ethnicity of groups of current research						
Asian	13.5	10.2	18.5	24.0	26.7	21.0
Latin American, Caribbean	7.7	13.4	19.3	24.5	29.4	22.3
African	1.9	3.1	4.2	10.5	4.7	5.7
Jewish	15.4	6.3	5.9	5.0	5.1	6.1
Irish	5.8	7.1	5.9	1.5	4.7	4.5

TABLE 1.2   *Continued*

Characteristics	Before 1965	1965 to 1974	1975 to 1984	1985 to 1994	After 1994	Total
Other European	32.7	22.0	24.4	15.5	9.0	17.0
Other, or n.a.	23.1	37.8	21.8	19.0	20.4	23.4
Insider or outsider ethnicity of researcher						
Insider	25.0	29.1	36.1	43.0	39.6	37.2
Outsider	51.9	33.1	42.0	38.0	40.0	39.4
N.a. or n.d.	23.1	37.8	21.8	19.0	20.4	23.4

Source: Author's compilation.

the proportion of women has grown consistently and dramatically over time, such that among the youngest cohort of scholars, 62 percent are women and 38 percent men. Also notable are the generational changes that have been taking place, which roughly parallel the larger national patterns of immigration to the United States in this century. There has been a sharp increase in the proportion of first-generation immigrants, basically doubling from the 18 percent or so who earned their degrees before 1975 to the 35 percent who have gotten their degrees since 1985; and, as can be seen in the table, there has been an almost identical reversal in the proportions of each of the second and third generations since the period before 1965. These generational patterns, in turn, are reflected in the changing ethnic composition of immigration researchers. Until the early 1980s, the percentage of these scholars who were of Asian, African, Latin American, or Caribbean origin was minuscule, from virtually none among those who earned their doctorates before 1965 to merely single-digit percentages among degree recipients in the decade from 1975 to 1984. Those proportions have climbed along with immigration, especially among Asian-origin scholars, who collectively make up 17 percent of the most recent cohort of degree recipients, and scholars of Latin or Caribbean origin, who constitute another 13 percent of the most recent cohort. By contrast, the proportion of Jewish scholars has dropped over time, from 25 percent to 11 percent, as has that of scholars of other European ethnicity.

These changes by gender, generation, and ethnicity, in turn, have been accompanied by a notable shift in the focus of research. Particularly remarkable is the change in the proportion of scholars whose dissertation research was related to immigration. Among scholars who earned their highest degrees before 1975—during an era in which immigration had not reemerged as a significant public issue—only about a fourth wrote immigration-related dissertations, and most of these were in history; but among younger scholars who have earned their degrees since 1994, that proportion has tripled, to 77 percent. The patterns point to a heightened degree of specialization in the immigration field that now begins in graduate school, for most, in contrast to older scholars, who appear to have switched to immigration research after having first focused on other topics. Also clear is the concomitant change in the ethnicity or national origin of the groups that are now the focus of research attention. Among scholars who earned their degrees before 1975, only about a fifth focus on immigrants from Asia or Latin America and the Caribbean, compared with 38 percent of those who got their doctorates between 1974 and 1985, 48 percent of the next decade cohort, and 57 percent of the most recent cohort of degree recipients. At the same time, the proportion focusing research attention on European-origin groups has declined over time. Not surprisingly, perhaps, these changes have combined to increase the proportion of ethnic insiders among immigration scholars from 25 percent among the older cohort with pre–1965 doctorates to about 41 percent among younger cohorts with post–1984 degrees.

Characteristics of Immigration Scholars by Discipline

Thus far we have been discussing the characteristics of the NASIS sample of immigration researchers as a whole and by cohorts of older versus younger scholars. As the following chapters of this book make clear, however, there are also fundamental differences of focus and orientation by discipline in the study of immigration. Adding to those discussions of disciplinary distinctiveness, table 1.3 provides a breakdown of key social and professional characteristics by the major disciplines: sociology, political science and economics (combined because of both their smaller sample size[11] and commonality of patterns), anthropology, history, and all other social sciences. First, there are significant disciplinary contrasts by gender. Males constitute almost two-thirds of the historians (65 percent) and the majority of the political scientists and economists (55 percent), whereas females are in the majority among the anthropologists (57 percent). Among sociologists, the breakdown by gender is exactly even.

Generational differences by discipline are even more pronounced. There are more foreign-born (first-generation) scholars of immigration in sociology (42 percent) than in any other discipline; sociologists are followed by the political scientists and economists, with 33 percent, anthropologists, with 24 percent, and historians, among whose ranks only 14 percent are immigrants themselves. By contrast, far more historians

TABLE 1.3   Characteristics of Immigration Scholars, by Discipline of Ph.D. or Highest Degree (Percentage)

Characteristic	Sociology	Political Science, Economics	Anthropology	History	All Other Disciplines	Total
N	246	66	93	207	141	753
Gender						
Female	50.0	45.5	57.0	35.3	53.9	47.1
Male	50.0	54.5	43.0	64.7	46.1	52.9
Generation						
First (foreign born)	41.9	33.3	23.7	14.0	34.0	29.7
Second (U.S. born)	15.0	24.2	14.0	22.2	17.0	18.1
Third	18.3	22.7	34.4	45.4	22.0	28.8
Fourth+	24.8	19.7	28.0	18.4	27.0	23.4
Ethnicity or national origin of researcher						
Asian	17.1	12.1	7.5	6.8	12.1	11.7
Latin American, Caribbean	16.7	13.6	4.3	3.9	9.2	10.0
African	2.0	4.5	5.4	2.4	2.1	2.8
Jewish	8.5	13.6	12.9	19.3	12.8	13.3
Irish	5.7	4.5	5.4	14.0	9.9	8.6
Other European	16.3	9.1	19.4	33.3	26.2	22.6
"American," white	20.3	28.8	30.1	13.0	22.7	20.7
Mixed, other	13.4	13.6	15.1	7.2	5.0	10.4

Current position						
Professor	20.3	10.6	18.3	29.5	16.3	21.0
Associate professor	13.8	7.6	10.8	10.6	9.2	11.2
Assistant professor	16.3	22.7	3.2	9.2	12.8	12.6
Instructor	3.3	9.1	6.5	9.2	10.6	7.2
Researcher	13.4	12.1	16.1	9.2	7.1	11.3
Student, other	25.2	31.8	22.6	15.5	21.3	22.0
Administrative, other	5.7	6.1	19.4	8.2	14.9	9.8
Retired	2.0	0	3.2	8.7	7.8	4.9
Immigration-related dissertation						
Yes	56.9	53.8	50.0	58.2	52.8	55.4
No	43.1	46.2	50.0	41.8	47.2	44.6
Ethnicity of groups of current research						
Asian	26.0	9.1	37.6	7.7	26.2	21.0
Latin American, Caribbean	33.7	25.8	28.0	6.8	19.9	22.3
African	3.3	6.1	17.2	3.9	5.0	5.7
Jewish	2.4	3.0	3.2	12.6	6.4	6.1
Irish	0.8	0	1.1	12.6	3.5	4.5
Other European	6.5	3.0	4.3	36.7	21.3	17.0
Other, or n.a.	27.2	53.0	8.6	19.8	17.7	23.4
Insider or outsider ethnicity of researcher						
Insider	33.3	21.2	19.4	54.6	37.6	37.2
Outsider	39.4	25.8	72.0	25.6	44.7	39.4
N.a. or n.d.	27.3	53.0	8.6	19.8	17.7	23.4

Source: Author's compilation.

are third-generation scholars (45 percent) than is the case among any of the other disciplines, while sociologists have the fewest members of the third generation (18 percent). Curiously, and ironically, this pattern among historians recalls the "principle of third-generation interest" formulated long ago by Marcus Lee Hansen, the great immigration historian. "History," he wrote, "is usually written by the third generation following an event. The grandsons of immigrants are those who want to know all about the beginning of the American branch of the family" (Hansen 1990, 209). (The contrasting pattern among sociologists might merit my coining a "principle of first-generation interest"—and even adding, only partly tongue in cheek, a prediction that their grandchildren may well grow up to become historians!)

As would be expected, there are significant differences between disciplines in ethnic composition as well. Among sociologists of immigration, 34 percent are of Asian, Latin American, or Caribbean ethnic backgrounds, compared with only about a tenth of the historians and anthropologists and a fourth of the political scientists and economists. Jewish scholars and other European ethnics predominate among historians; scholars who identify as plain "American" whites prevail proportionately among the anthropologists, political scientists, and economists. Among the small number of African scholars in the sample, the greater proportion is found among the anthropologists. These patterns, in turn, are only partially reflected in the ethnicity of the groups of focal concern in these scholars' current research. Thus, among the sociologists, 63 percent report that they focus on Asian, Latin American, and Caribbean groups in their research, as do 66 percent of the anthropologists—17 percent of whom focus additionally on African groups—whereas relatively few historians focus on any of these populations. Instead, historians of immigration look back to the earlier waves of mass immigration from Europe, with more than 60 percent among them focusing on European-origin groups in their scholarship. That is a far greater proportion than is found among sociologists, political scientists, economists, and anthropologists, who pay little attention to Europeans in the contemporary U.S. immigration context. Indeed, and perhaps unexpectedly, one consequence of the foregoing is that by far the highest proportion of ethnic insiders is found among the historians, at 55 percent, compared with 33 percent among the sociologists and about 20 percent among the anthropologists, political scientists, and economists.

Table 1.4 goes a step further in the depiction of disciplinary differences by presenting a breakdown of the principal substantive areas of current or planned research reported by the NASIS scholars within each discipline. Here the thematic differences in disciplinary research come sharply into focus. Two-thirds of the political scientists and economists

TABLE 1.4   Principal Areas of Immigration Research, by Discipline of Ph.D. or Highest Degree (Percentage)

Principal Area of Immigration Research	Sociology	Political Science, Economics	Anthropology	History	All Other Disciplines	Total
N	246	66	93	207	141	753
Politics, conflict, citizenship	13.0	40.9	5.4	10.6	7.1	12.7
Economics, markets, business	9.3	22.7	0	1.0	2.8	5.8
Race or ethnicity, intergroup relations	6.1	7.6	3.2	13.5	7.8	8.2
Social mobility, stratification, netwcrks	19.1	3.0	12.9	14.5	9.9	13.9
Generation, gender, family, identity	20.7	4.5	15.1	16.4	14.9	16.3
Religion, language, culture, health	8.5	0	18.3	13.5	29.8	14.3
Forced migration, refugees	6.9	1.5	30.1	3.4	6.4	8.2
Transnationalism, diaspora	3.7	3.0	8.6	0.5	3.5	3.3
Migration, adaptation, history (general)	8.1	7.6	4.3	15.0	7.8	9.4
Specific ethnonational groups	2.0	1.5	2.2	11.1	5.7	5.2
All other topics, specified	2.4	7.6	0	0.5	4.3	2.4

Source: Author's compilation.

focus on issues of political and economic incorporation, compared with only about 22 percent of the sociologists, 12 percent of the historians, and 5 percent of the anthropologists. As is illustrated in the table, the research areas of comparatively greater sociological interest involve social mobility and stratification, networks, gender, generation, family, and identity. The anthropologists, most of whom are members of CORI, are overwhelmingly among the scholars who focus on issues of forced migration and refugees. They are also more likely to deal with issues of transnationalism and diasporas as well as religion, language, culture, health, and mental health (though here are also found high proportions of scholars from the other disciplines, including psychology). Historians appear to be more evenly balanced across those topical areas. These thematic differences are, of course, definitive of disciplinary identities. Chi-square statistics measuring the association of the variables given in table 1.4 are far more significant than the chi-squares for cross-tabulations of those same principal research areas by any other variables in NASIS, including gender and status as insiders or outsiders (for which the associations are statistically significant but weak) or ethnicity and generation (which scarcely reach statistical significance).

Characteristics of Insiders and Outsiders in Immigration Research

The finding reported earlier that nearly half of the total NASIS sample is of immigrant stock raises a set of empirical questions about the extent to which our knowledge of today's immigrants is a product of ethnic insiders or outsiders and a set of still other questions (epistemological, methodological, and theoretical) about the meaning and consequences of those patterns for immigration scholarship.

Table 1.5 presents a breakdown of ethnic insiders and outsiders among immigration researchers by generation, ethnicity, and the principal topics of their current or planned research.[12] The first panel of the table shows a clearly linear pattern of decreasing insiderness with increasing generation. That is, among foreign-born scholars, 50 percent are classified as coethnic insiders, as are 48 percent of the second generation, 31 percent of the third generation, and 19 percent of fourth or higher generations. In general, the greater the distance from the time of immigration, the greater the proportion of ethnic outsiders. The decisive break, however, appears to occur at the third (and higher) generations; the difference between first- and second-generation scholars in the proportion of insiders is small and not significant.

The second panel of table 1.5 shows the proportion of insiders and outsiders for all the main ethnonational groups in NASIS (ethnic identi-

TABLE 1.5   *Distribution of Ethnic Insiders and Outsiders Among Immigration Researchers, by Generation in the United States, Ethnic Self-Identity, and Principal Research Focus*

Characteristic	N	Insiders (Percentage)	Outsiders (Percentage)
Total sample	753	37.2	62.8
Generation			
First (foreign born)	224	50.4	49.6
Second (U.S. born)	136	48.5	51.5
Third	217	30.9	69.1
Fourth +	176	19.3	80.7
Ethnic self-identity or national origin of researcher			
Filipino	9	100.0	0
Korean	15	93.3	6.7
Chinese	29	75.9	24.1
Indian, other South Asian	15	73.3	26.7
Vietnamese, Cambodian	5	60.0	40.0
Iranian	5	60.0	40.0
Japanese	10	40.0	60.0
Mexican	18	83.3	16.7
Puerto Rican, other Latin American	10	80.0	20.0
Cuban	8	75.0	25.0
"Hispanic," "Latino"	24	54.2	45.8
African	11	90.9	9.1
Jamaican, Haitian, other Afro-Caribbean	15	86.7	13.3
African American, black	10	80.0	20.0
Italian	26	73.1	26.9
Scandinavian	21	66.7	33.3
Polish	16	50.0	50.0
German	44	40.9	59.1
Jewish	100	37.0	63.0
Irish	65	33.8	66.2
Other European	63	36.5	59.1
"American," white	156	0	100.0
Mixed, other	78	0	100.0
Principal topic of current or planned immigration research			
Politics, conflict, citizenship	96	20.8	79.2
Forced migration, refugees	62	27.4	72.6
Transnationalism, diaspora	25	32.0	68.0
Economics, labor markets, business	44	34.1	65.9

(Table continues on p. 38.)

TABLE 1.5   *Continued*

Characteristic	n	Insiders (Percentage)	Outsiders (Percentage)
Social mobility, inequality, discrimination	53	41.5	58.5
Race or ethnicity, intergroup relations	62	43.5	56.5
Communities, networks, enclaves	52	44.2	55.8
Family, household, marriage	18	38.9	61.1
Generation, children of immigrants	34	41.2	58.8
Identity	33	48.5	51.5
Gender, immigrant women	38	52.6	47.4
Education, language	18	22.2	77.8
Religion	30	26.7	73.3
Health, mental health	31	32.3	67.7
Media, popular culture	29	51.7	48.3
Other topics (specified)	18	16.7	83.3
Adaptation (general)	17	17.6	82.4
Ethnonational groups (specified)	39	48.7	51.3
Migration (general)	30	53.3	46.7
History (general)	24	54.2	45.8

Source: Author's compilation.

ties as self-reported by the scholars), ranked by decreasing degree of insiderness. (Note, however, that the small sample sizes of some groups make their estimates less stable.) The patterns here tend to combine immigrant-stock status with racial-minority (nonwhite) status to increase the likelihood of insiderness. Thus, among Asian-origin scholars, the Filipinos (100 percent) and Koreans (93 percent) have the highest proportions of coethnic insiders by far, followed by the Chinese (76 percent) and South and Southeast Asian groups; the Japanese (40 percent), interestingly, are the only Asian-origin group with a majority proportion of ethnic outsider scholars (and also the only Asian-origin group in the United States today who are primarily U.S.-born). African and Afro-Caribbean scholars exhibit very high insider rates (around 89 percent). Among Latin Americans, the Mexicans (83 percent), Puerto Ricans (80 percent), and Cubans (75 percent), in that order, show high proportions of ethnic insiderness, but the figure drops to 54 percent for those scholars who already self-identify panethnically as "Hispanic" or "Latino." Among European-origin groups, the highest proportion of ethnic insiders is registered among the Italians (73 percent), but for most others the rates falls below half, including Jewish (37 percent) and Irish American (34 percent) scholars, making the majority of them ethnic outsiders to the groups they study.

The final panel of table 1.5 breaks down the proportion of insiders and outsiders among the ranks of researchers by the main clusters of topics of current or planned immigration research. Here again there is substantial observable differentiation in the degree of insiderness or outsiderness and the chosen areas of research. Low insiderness is seen in the political and economic research theme areas, as well as in the mostly anthropological focus of interest in refugee issues, transnationalism and diasporas, and also education, religion, health, and mental health. The highest proportion of coethnic insiders is found among those scholars whose research focuses on gender and immigrant women, identity, media, and popular culture. Intermediate between these are the research topics of generations, children of immigrants, family, social mobility, and stratification, chosen mostly by sociologists and also by historians.

Given the multiple variables that show a significant correlation with our measure of insiderness versus outsiderness, logistic regression techniques were used to identify their independent effects on the likelihood of a scholar being a coethnic insider (coded as a dummy variable). For the model here reported, the classification table correctly predicted 78 percent of the cases as insiders or outsiders. Controlling for other variables, the strongest positive effects on insiderness were observed for scholars' ethnicity (Asian, African, and Latin American and Caribbean), with Italian and, to a lesser extent, Jewish ethnic identities also being significantly, though more weakly, associated with coethnic insiderness. Type of discipline followed ethnicity in predictive strength, with historians being significantly more likely to be associated with insiderness; political scientists and economists were significantly less likely to be associated with insiderness, and to a lesser extent sociologists and anthropologists were negatively associated with insiderness, controlling for all other factors. A strongly significant association was seen between having written an immigration-related dissertation and ethnic insiderness. Finally, although it had a weaker association than the others, generation mattered: being a member of the third or higher generation was significantly and negatively associated with being an ethnic insider. In other models tested, being foreign born (first generation) washed out of the regression equation, as did gender.

Conclusion

Herbert Gans' contribution to this volume (chapter 3) identifies six main "holes" or areas of needed immigration research. Two of the areas examined by Gans involve aspects of the field of immigration scholarship itself: insider versus outsider roles among immigration researchers and the need for more empirical research on the choices (and omissions) of topics and groups that draw the attention of immigration scholars. Data from the National Survey of Immigration Scholars presented here, analyzing the social origins and research orientations of a significant sample of the researchers who constitute the field today, may help to fill some of those gaps, if only in a preliminary way. It will be up to the next generation of immigration scholars, now coming of intellectual age, to tackle the more taxing tasks ahead and to venture creatively beyond them.

As noted in the introduction to this volume, the field of immigration studies will be advanced through our knowledge of its social bases. That is, there is value in making immigration research itself the object of systematic and reflexive scrutiny and analyzing it from the vantage of the sociology of knowledge. Unlike the nascent scholarship on immigration at the turn of the past century, the present era has seen many immigrants themselves become leading scholars of immigration in certain disciplines, and children, and especially grandchildren, of immigrants are prominent immigration scholars in others. The finding that almost half of today's immigration scholars are themselves of immigrant stock—including the majority of the sociologists and more than a third of the anthropologists and historians—underscores the profound impact of immigration on the field itself. Simply put, immigration is producing many of the scholars who study it and who will tell its story.

In the access to the new and old immigrant populations that their unique position may afford them—and in their particular mix of insiderness and outsiderness, nearness and distance, attachment and detachment—this new generation of scholars in a transformed context of scholarship may bring both unique advantages and disadvantages to the social scientific study of immigration. Perhaps they will manage to achieve a creative synthesis. Time alone will tell what turns out to be the balance of the mix.

A previous version of this chapter appeared in *American Behavioral Scientist* 1999, vol. 42, no. 9.

Notes

1. The American Sociological Association conducts a periodic census of its more than 13,500 dues-paying members. The census form collects demographic information on gender and race or ethnicity, but no question was asked about birthplace, making it impossible to determine the proportion of foreign-born sociologists in the

ASA. To obtain that information the ASA added an item on nativity in its 2000 census.

2. As George Sánchez notes in his paper in this volume (chapter 2), the IHS was renamed the Immigration and Ethnic History Society in 1998 by a vote of its members, in part to reverse the declining membership in its ranks—this, ironically, despite levels of immigration to the United States not seen since the pre–World War I era.

3. Each year CORI publishes a volume of selected papers on refugees and immigrants and gives a prize to the lead article; it also cosponsors the annual meetings of the Society for Applied Anthropology (SAA) and organizes academic panels both at the SAA and at the American Anthropological Association's annual convention. CORI maintains a web site at http://www.mason.gmu.edu/~cori.

4. The ASA's Section on International Migration maintains a web site at http://www.ssc.msu.edu/~intermig/, with current information on its full range of activities as well as listings of recent publications, a complete set of back issues of its biannual newsletter, *World on the Move*, and links to more than fifty immigration-related web sites worldwide.

5. ENMISA maintains a web page at http://www. csf.colorado.edu/isa/enm/. Just a few years ago most scholars working in the immigration field would not have imagined the level of information, organization, and disciplinary cross-linkages reflected in and facilitated by the web sites of these newly established groups.

6. A scholar may have been a member of more than one of these organizations or applied for an SSRC research fellowship (or both). All such duplicate cases were removed from the final master mailing list of scholars to whom the NASIS survey was sent.

7. Specifically, 282 surveys were returned out of 411 sent to members of the Immigration History Society (a 69 percent return rate); 235 (61 percent) of the 385 members of the ASA's Section on International Migration, 77 (64 percent) of the 120 members of CORI, 139 (55 percent) of the 253 SSRC applicants (not otherwise included in the other professional organizations), and another 20 ENMISA members, who were contacted via e-mail, brought the total received to 753. The resulting NASIS sample is probably quite representative of the sociologists and historians in the field but less so of the other disciplines. In particular, it should be noted that many anthropologists involved in immigration research are not members of CORI (whose members have focused more on refugee issues). Also, the NASIS subsamples of political scientists and especially economists are small and generally reflect a greater proportion of younger researchers (drawn from the pool of SSRC fellowship applicants) than established scholars from those disciplines.

8. Both figures are well above U.S. national norms, as spelled out in the introduction to this volume. By 1998, 10 percent of the U.S. population were foreign-born, and another 10 percent were second-generation native-born persons with at least one foreign-born parent.

9. It may be worth noting the responses of the NASIS scholars to the open-ended survey item on race, especially given its salience in the immigration research literature. Overall, 121 scholars (16 percent) answered "human" or "no such thing," left it blank, or otherwise debunked the question; these included more than 50 percent of those who reported a mixed ethnicity, 22 percent of those of Latin American or Caribbean origin, 15 percent of Jewish respondents, and 10 percent of Asian ethnics. Most in keeping with U.S. conventions were scholars who reported a plain "American" or Irish ethnicity, 94 percent of whom answered "white" to the item on race, as did more than 80 percent of the other Europeans; 95 percent of African respondents answered "black." Among all Asian nationalities, 80 percent identified themselves racially as "Asian." Most mixed were the Latin American and Caribbean respondents, a fifth of whom self-reported racially as "Latino," another fifth as "black," 30 percent as "white," and 10 percent as "multiracial."

10. One-third (34 percent) received their advanced degrees in universities in California, New York, and New Jersey; one-fourth in universities in Illinois, Michigan, Wisconsin, and Pennsylvania; 12 percent in Massachusetts, Connecticut, and Rhode Island; 3 percent in Texas; and 16 percent in the rest of the United States.

11. In this subsample of sixty-six, there are fifty-one political scientists and fifteen economists.

12. No other type of insiderness or outsiderness is covered by this measure, which is based solely on the ethnic homogamy (at least on the surface) of the researcher and the researched. It excludes gender (although the overwhelming majority of scholars whose research focused on gender were women), and it excludes a variety of other structural and cultural factors (from class to generation to political ideology) along which insiderness breaks down in the researcher-researched relation regardless of a putative common ethnicity or national origin. The study of insiders and outsiders in social science, like all else, ultimately must move from shallow correlation to full contextualization.

References

Gans, Herbert J. 1997. "Toward a Reconciliation of 'Assimilation' and 'Pluralism': The Interplay of Acculturation and Ethnic Retention." *International Migration Review* 31(4): 875–92.

Hansen, Marcus Lee. 1990. "Who Shall Inherit America?" In *American Immigrants and Their Generations: Studies and Commentaries on the Hansen Thesis After Fifty Years,* edited by Peter Kivisto and Dag Blanck. 1937. Urbana: University of Illinois Press.

Merton, Robert K. 1972. "Insiders and Outsiders: A Chapter in the Sociology of Knowledge." *American Journal of Sociology* 77(July): 9–47.

Rumbaut, Rubén G. 1994. "International Migration: New ASA Section to Form in Los Angeles." *Footnotes* (newsletter of the American Sociological Association) 22(5).

———. 1995. "Birth of a Section." *World on the Move* (newsletter of the Section on International Migration, American Sociological Association) 1(1): 2–4.

Stevenson, Robert J. 1993. "Where Do Sociologists Come From?" *Footnotes* 21(9).

2A

THE SOCIOLOGICAL ROOTS AND MULTIDISCIPLINARY FUTURE OF IMMIGRATION RESEARCH

Mary C. Waters

A<small>S A SOCIOLOGIST</small> I have always felt very much at home studying immigration. This is probably true for most sociologists, because immigration is at the very core of American sociology. The last great wave of immigration at the turn of the past century filled American cities with immigrants and their children. The social problems encountered by these immigrants, along with the problems arising out of urbanization and industrialization, gave rise to the body of sociological studies that came to be known as the Chicago School of sociology. Associated most often with one of its founders, Robert Park, the Chicago School gave rise to numerous studies of the first and the second generation of immigrants (Park 1922, 1928, 1950; Park and Burgess 1921; Park and Miller 1921; Thomas and Znaniecki 1984; Wirth 1956). Combining ethnographic methods and holistic inquiries with demographic data, these studies not only provide a wealth of data on particular groups, urban areas, and urban dynamics but also gave rise to many of the sociological concepts and theories we use today to try to understand the experiences of immigrants—assimilation, residential segregation, occupational specialization, marginality, and cycles in race relations. Hence, in many ways, it is natural for a sociologist to specialize in immigration, and as a group we have not been inclined toward self-reflection on, or justification of, the choice of the topic or the methods of the discipline.

Many sociologists, in fact, have reacted somewhat testily to the growing interest in immigration from other disciplines—wondering why these other disciplines are stepping on sociological turf and why they are using different concepts and methods to study phenomena we have been looking at for years. I have occasionally succumbed to this negativity myself as I encounter economists "discovering" generational

44

assimilation or anthropologists torturing their stories from the field so as to avoid ever using the term "assimilation." Yet my general reaction to seeing the study of immigration as part of a multidisciplinary emerging field is positive because it helps to undermine the tendency among sociologists to rely on tried and true methods and concepts to study the field.

The mix of disciplines and approaches that characterize the current Committee on International Migration of the Social Science Research Council (SSRC) and the work of SSRC fellows can challenge and embolden sociologists to develop new ways of seeing old problems. The anthropologist's insistence on understanding what is happening in sending communities, the challenge of the historian to avoid theories that completely abstract communities from the wider context of their existence, and the lessons of political scientists who look at the ways in which states shape the choices available to individuals all are correctives to the sometimes narrow focus of sociological thinking on the subject of immigration.

Yet as much as involvement in multidisciplinary working groups, conferences, and intellectual exchanges is creative and empowering for immigration scholars, we face some difficult questions and issues as we try to create and sustain a community of diverse scholars from many disciplines in the field of immigration studies. I review three issues here: the relationship between immigration and the study of race; the problem of being interdisciplinary within a context of a hierarchy of disciplines, some of which are valued more than others; and the problem of managing a career within a discipline when one's work strays outside of disciplinary boundaries.

Race and Immigration

Although the need for communication and collaboration across disciplinary boundaries in the study of immigration is apparent, there is also a great need for some linkages between the study of race in American society and the study of immigration. In my own discipline, sociology, there has been a large gap between those who study immigrants and those who study American race relations, the latter focusing mostly on the relations between blacks and whites. Yet most of those who have immigrated to the United States since 1965 have been people of color, and the question of how they react to American race relations and categories, and how America categorizes them, is paramount. Questions of the effect of immigration on native minorities—whether, for example, immigrants are leapfrogging over native American blacks in achievement—are difficult issues to study empirically for a variety of reasons, but there is also, perhaps, some political uneasiness among scholars about addressing the issues. Most liberal scholars in the academy want to be considered advocates of both immigrants and native minorities, and the question of whether these are contradictory goals is rarely asked.

The issue of tensions between new immigrants of color and black Americans is also a tough one for academics to take on. Where will the color line be drawn in the twenty-first century? Are some new groups "becoming white," as older groups of immigrants did? If so, what does that mean for black Americans and for immigration and poverty policy in the United States? These are issues that are often not addressed because of the ways in which scholars divide their attention and their energies and the ways in which funding agencies shape research agendas. To examine these issues, the SSRC has established committees to study poverty and the underclass and immigration, but despite the obvious commonality in subject matter, the structure of our disciplines and even of our interdisciplines has kept us from examining those linkages.

A related issue, equally sensitive, in this field is affirmative action and diversity in the academy. The discussions of insider-outsider issues in this volume raise interesting questions about ethnic and racial identities and how they affect research agendas and outcomes. University education is now witnessing an infusion of the children of the most recent great wave of immigration, who bring the diversity of this immigration stream into academia. Yet in my own university, most of the students of color are themselves immigrants, or the children or grandchildren of immigrants, rather than native-born Americans. It would be a sad irony indeed if the new immigrants and their descendants were to become insiders in academia and native minorities such as American blacks and Native Americans to remain underrepresented outsiders.

The Hierarchy of Disciplines

Although we are all in favor of interdisciplinary research, all disciplines are not created equal. All one need do is look at the average salaries by discipline to see that our society values some disciplines over others. Among those who study immigration, economists and political scientists are valued (at least as measured by salaries) over sociologists, historians, and anthropologists. Immigration is a hot political issue right now, and a great deal of public policy debate is currently being waged. Yet most of the research that is cited in these debates has been conducted by economists. Economists are now writing and doing research in immigration, but they tend to do so within their own disciplinary boundaries. There is little, or even negative, incentive for economists to become interdisciplinary; in fact, there is not a single economist on the SSRC International Migration Committee. Some years ago I served on a panel at the National Academy of Sciences on the demographic and economic impact of immigration on the United States (Smith and Edmonston 1997). The panel was made up mostly of economists, with a few sociologists included. It became clear to me then that, although we had a lot to contribute, the language of public policy debate is such that those of us working on immigration from outside the discipline of economics are often left out of the discussion. As we build our multidisciplinary community, we should also learn to communicate our work in a manner that allows us to join public policy debates on immigration, and we should be aware that only those disciplines with incentives to do so will join our multidisciplinary conversation.

The split between quantitative and qualitative research methods also challenges the emerging multidisciplinary field of immigration studies. A variety of methods and approaches exist in the social sciences and the humanities, and, of course, no single method is appropriate to all times and places; but as we shape the field we must be aware that some methods are privileged more than others in funding and respect in the policy world.

Careers

Finally, individuals doing interdisciplinary research face hard questions about their own careers and about how to judge the work of others. Young scholars feel pressure to make their mark, to gain the approval and respect of elder scholars in their discipline, and the prospect of interdisciplinarity poses a particular dilemma: the interdisciplinary scholar is seen, alternately, as creative, one who is capable of "thinking outside the box," and as somewhat unfocused and inadequately trained, one who asks the wrong questions. All too often, publishing and tenure decisions reward loyalty and convention rather than creativity and uniqueness. How can we encourage greater interdisciplinary research and still ensure that people are rewarded for their contributions within their disciplines? I do not have an answer to that question; but young scholars should be aware that interdisciplinary research will not translate into an effortless rise in their careers, that the packaging of their work may prove to be as important to their professional success as the work itself.

As we enter the twenty-first century sociologists once again are focusing in large numbers on immigration and its effects on American society. The legacy of the Chicago School shapes many of the methods and research questions sociologists ask about this new wave of immigration, and the infusion of scholars from many different disciplinary perspectives brings new tools and new research questions to bear on how immigration is transforming society. As Rubén Rumbaut points out in the preceding chapter, first-generation immigrants make up 30 percent of the total number of scholars, and 42 percent of the sociologists, in the National Survey of Immigration Scholars. Sociology has been quite welcoming of new immigrants into our ranks. This may be the legacy of the value-free, empirically based approach of the Chicago School. It is my hope that sociology as a discipline will be just as welcoming to the new methods and approaches in the study of immigration that emerge from our dialogues across disciplines. I also hope that other disciplines, particularly economics and political science, will recognize the value of the sociological approach. As we build a truly interdisciplinary community of immigration scholars we can look forward to new insights into the field and to the inevitable challenges that come from breaking new intellectual ground.

A previous version of this chapter appeared in *American Behavioral Scientist* 1999, vol. 42, no. 9.

References

Park, Robert. 1922. *The Immigrant Press and Its Control.* New York: Harper and Row.

——. 1928. "Human Migration and the Marginal Man." *American Journal of Sociology* 33(6): 881–93.

——. 1950. *Race and Culture.* Glencoe, Ill.: Free Press.

Park, Robert, and Ernest Burgess. 1921. Introduction to *The Science of Sociology.* Chicago: University of Chicago Press.

Park, Robert, and Herbert A. Miller. 1921. *Old World Traits Transplanted.* New York: Harper.

Smith, James P., and Barry Edmonston. 1997. *The New Americans: Economic, Demographic, and Fiscal Effects of Immigration.* Washington, D.C.: National Academy Press.

Thomas, William, and Florian Znaniecki. 1984. *The Polish Peasant in Europe and America.* Edited by Eli Zaretsky. 2 vols. 1918–1920. Urbana: University of Illinois Press.

Wirth, Louis. 1956. *The Ghetto.* 1928. Chicago: University of Chicago Press.

ANTHROPOLOGY AND THE STUDY OF IMMIGRATION

Nancy Foner

Anthropologists' interest in immigration to the United States is one of the changes taking place in the field as our nonindustrial societies around the world are being transformed in the face of dramatic globalizing forces. Villagers in the South Pacific island kingdom of Tonga, to give one example, regularly watch American television programs and videos—and more than one-quarter of the entire population of Tonga now lives in the United States (Small 1998, 52). Indeed, anthropological research on immigration is, to a large extent, about what happens when the people studied on their home turf turn up living next door.

Anthropologists' involvement in the study of recent immigration to the United States initially grew out of their research in sending countries. Fieldwork in another culture has long been a hallmark of anthropological training—a rite of passage along the way to becoming a full-fledged anthropologist. Until recently, the culture studied was meant to be in another region of the world, not in the United States, and there is still a strong bias in that direction. Anthropologists, of course, have long conducted research and commented on the American scene, as Micaela di Leonardo (1998, 28) points out, yet the traditional emphasis, especially in dissertation research, has been on cultures outside of the United States (other than the study of Native Americans).[1] When I was a graduate student at the University of Chicago in the late 1960s it was virtually unheard of to get the blessings of the department (not to mention a grant) to do fieldwork on a non-Native American group in the United States. As Sherry Ortner notes, the only such project to get department backing when she was a student at the University of Chicago was a study of American drag queens, and "one could argue that this was only because drag queens were seen as so exotic and 'other' that they might as well have been Australian aborigines" (1991, 163). My route to immigration research is typical of the path taken by many other anthropologists. I conducted my dissertation research in a Jamaican rural community; only several years later did I do research on Jamaican migrants, first in London and later in New York (see Foner 1973, 1978, 1987).

The fact that so many anthropologists who study migrants in this country have had field experience at both sides of the migration chain has shaped their research in many ways. They are particularly sensitive to the links that migrants maintain with their home societies; and they are concerned not only with migration's impact on those who move to a new setting but also with the consequences for those left behind. It is not surprising that the first major work on transnationalism among U.S. immigrants was written by anthropologists—all three of whom had field experience in both host and sending societies—and that anthropologists are often guided in their research by transnational perspectives (see Basch, Glick Schiller, and Szanton Blanc 1994).

Studying migrants in both sending and receiving societies has also made anthropologists sensitive to continuities as well as changes in immigrants' cultural and social patterns in the United States. Because of their familiarity with the culture migrants come from, they are attuned to subtle as well as dramatic changes that take place in this country. In addition, because many anthropologists use networks of people they have come to know in the home society to locate informants here—and conduct their studies through participant observation—their work often emphasizes the role of networks. In the tradition of participant observation and community studies, a number of projects on recent immigrants have explored relations between established residents and newcomers in neighborhoods and workplaces (see Lamphere 1992; Lamphere and Stepick 1994; Sanjek 1998).

This leads to the question of methods. As both the papers in this volume and a reading of the immigration literature show, anthropologists do not have a monopoly on ethnographic research. Yet what anthropologists mean by ethnographic research often differs from the way other disciplines define it. Anthropologists do not mean just in-depth interviews, nor do they mean a study that relies on in-depth interviews conducted by assistants. The anthropologist who is conducting ethnographic research does many, sometimes all, of the interviews and tries to incorporate participant observation into the project. This approach, of course, has its downside, in that it limits the number of people a particular anthropologist can study. Moreover, as a large literature in urban anthropology attests, participant observation in an urban setting is often difficult.

Anthropologists believe, however, that they are better able to understand what migrants' lives are like—and to understand their beliefs, values, and ideas as well as the complex ways they construct identities—by studying a small number of people, in depth and over a period of time. Through participant observation, it is possible to see, as one of cultural anthropology's founding fathers, Bronislaw Malinowski, observed long ago, that the way people behave is not always the way they say they behave.

Thus far the postmodern turn in much of anthropology has had little impact on immigration studies in the discipline, although this situation is likely to change. As more anthropologists branch into immigration research, we will be seeing studies of negotiated and contested cultural meanings and social practices—processes that stand out as immigrants construct new cultural forms and social arrangements in the context of change. A focus on cultural contestation, negotiation, and reinvention should enrich the field as long as agency is not overemphasized at the expense of structural circumstances and constraints and as long as shared cultural symbols, meanings, and values are not slighted in the quest to document multiple perspectives, resistance, and struggle. One can also expect interpretive analyses and "readings" of immigrant rituals, performances and texts, and cultural symbols as a way to elucidate the dynamics of change, conflict, and adaptation in immigrant communities. Issues of cultural relativism, long an anthropological concern, are bound to come to the fore as well. To date, the best-known and best-crafted account of the clash of immigrant and mainstream values is journalist Anne Fadiman's The Spirit Catches You and You Fall Down (1997), the story of a Hmong family's struggle to treat their ailing daughter by traditional means in the face of demands of the American medical system. As anthropologists become increasingly involved in understanding immigrant responses to American legal, medical, and governmental institutions, questions of the legitimacy and role of premigration cultural standards and practices in the American setting will undoubtedly be an important research topic (see chapter 16, this volume).

Although it hardly constitutes a groundswell, the growing number of anthropologists involved in immigration research in this country is beginning to have an impact on the field. As even the most remote cultures become incorporated into, and influenced by, global economies and cultures—and as "classic" subjects of anthropological study like the Nuer or Sherpa move to American cities—it is becoming more acceptable, and respectable, for anthropologists to study immigrants in the United States as their "first" research. Cultural anthropologists have tended to identify themselves in terms of the area of the world they study—Caribbeanists, Africanists, Latin Americanists—so it is noteworthy that a few years ago the Society for the Anthropology of North America (SANA) was founded as a section of the American Anthropological Association. No less a figure than Clifford Geertz has recently written that in the future, anthropology will no longer be defined by a concern with the distant or exotic: there will be an "increased extension of ethnographic approaches to the study of modern industrialized societies, including our own" (1997, 3).

A number of developments point to the growing interest in immigration in the discipline. A special unit of the American Anthropological Association is devoted to the study of immigrants. Founded in 1988 as the Committee on Refugee Issues (CORI), it extended its focus to immigrants in 1996 and changed its title (but not its acronym) to the Committee on Refugees and Immigrants. The Society for Urban, National, and Transnational Anthropology and SANA both have many members concerned with immigrant issues. Ethnographies that focus on immigrants in the United States are being used, as a matter of course, in introductory and other anthropology classes. Although at present only a few anthropology graduate students are writing dissertations on immigration—19 of the 258 cultural anthropologists who received a doctorates from 1996 to 1997 focused on immigrants, mostly in the United States—the number will no doubt grow. Already, there are signs of a self-conscious attempt to carve out distinctive anthropological approaches to immigration, particularly as a way to set off anthropological studies from those in sociology. Still, future anthropological work on immigration will, no doubt, continue to be influenced by research in other social science disciplines as well as in anthropology itself. Whatever direction anthropological research on immigration takes in the future, it seems safe to say that anthropologists will continue to emphasize their special ethnographic skills and strengths, and field experience in sending societies, as increasing numbers turn their attention to the expanding immigrant population in our midst.

A previous version of this chapter appeared in *American Behavioral Scientist* 1999, vol. 42, no. 9.

Notes

1. A count of all United States anthropology dissertations since 1930, according to di Leonardo (1998, 374), shows single-digit representation for United States non-Native American work until 1978, with proportions hovering around 15 percent thereafter.

References

Basch, Linda, Nina Glick Schiller, and Cristina Szanton Blanc. 1994. *Nations Unbound: Transnational Projects, Postcolonial Predicaments, and Deterritorialized Nation States.* Langhorne, Pa.: Gordon and Breach.

di Leonardo, Micaela. 1998. *Exotics at Home: Anthropologies, Others, American Modernity.* Chicago: University of Chicago Press.

Fadiman, Anne. 1997. *The Spirit Catches You and You Fall Down: A Hmong Child, Her American Doctors, and the Collision of Two Cultures.* New York: Farrar, Straus and Giroux.

Foner, Nancy. 1973. *Status and Power in Rural Jamaica: A Study of Educational and Political Change.* New York: Teachers College Press, Columbia University.

———. 1978. *Jamaica Farewell: Jamaican Migrants in London.* Berkeley: University of California Press.

———. 1987. "The Jamaicans: Race and Ethnicity Among Migrants in New York." In *New Immigrants in New York*, edited by Nancy Foner. New York: Columbia University Press.

Geertz, Clifford. 1997. "The Next Thirty-five Years of Anthropology." *The Sciences* 37(November/December): 3.

Lamphere, Louise, ed. 1992. *Structuring Diversity: Ethnographic Perspectives on the New Immigration.* Chicago: University of Chicago Press.

Lamphere, Louise, and Alex Stepick, eds. 1994. *Newcomers in the Workplace: Immigrants and the Restructuring of the U.S. Economy.* Philadelphia: Temple University Press.

Ortner, Sherry. 1991. "Reading America: Preliminary Notes on Class and Culture." In *Recapturing Anthropology: Working in the Present*, edited by Richard Fox. Santa Fe, N.M.: School of American Research Press.

Sanjek, Roger. 1998. *The Future of Us All: Race and Neighborhood Politics in New York City.* Ithaca: Cornell University Press.

Small, Cathy. 1998. *Voyages: From Tongan Villages to American Suburbs.* Ithaca: Cornell University Press.

RACE AND IMMIGRATION HISTORY

George J. Sánchez

In 1998, the Immigration History Society, the historical field's main organization for the study of immigration, officially changed its name to the Immigration and Ethnic History Society to better reflect the scope of interests among its members and to reverse the declining membership in its ranks. The *Journal of American Ethnic History* has been the official journal of the Immigration History Society since the late 1960s, but the relation between immigration and ethnicity has long served as a point of contention among historians (see Gabaccia 1999). Leading figures such as historian Oscar Handlin (1973) and sociologist Nathan Glazer (1971) describe immigrant groups to this country as representing varieties of intractability on a scale of eventual assimilation and incorporation into American life. Reinterpreting and extending earlier theories built by the immigration field as a whole, particularly the "race relations cycle," a concept attributed to Robert Park and the Chicago School of sociologists, even racial minorities were predicted to assimilate themselves eventually, like other newcomers to this country, once racial barriers toward integration were lifted in the 1960s.

Other historians, beginning with Rudolph Vecoli (1964), responded that ethnic persistence, rather than assimilation, more often characterized the response of immigrant newcomers to their American surroundings. The generation of immigration historians who first emerged in the 1960s were themselves following an older body of historical scholarship led by Marcus Lee Hansen and other students of Frederick Jackson Turner. Many of these scholars were of recent European heritage themselves and had engaged in transnational research as early as the 1930s and 1940s, tending to emphasize the transplanted nature of immigrant culture on the American frontier of the Midwest.[1] Immigration historians of the 1960s and 1970s built upon these earlier studies and, inspired by the ethnic revival movement of the period, produced study after study showing that European and other immigrants to the United States had selectively brought elements of their home culture to bear on their lives in their new adopted American nation.[2] This scholarly direction culminated in the publication of *The Transplanted*, by historian John Bodnar (1985), which drew upon a generation of historical literature to provide an alternative "botanical metaphor" to Handlin's *The Uprooted*, first published thirty-four years earlier.[3]

Both paradigms suffered from the same historical blind spot, however: cultural change among immigrants and their descendants was too often placed within a bipolar model of opposing cultures. Old World culture was depicted as static and unchanging, and any diversion in the New World was seen as evidence of assimilation. Whether scholars viewed assimilation as inevitable or consistently sought evidence for the persistence of Old World ways in the new surroundings in the United States, immigrant cultural patterns took on overwhelming significance for what they said about the openness of American society to absorb newcomers and the rigidity with which nations shaped unified and separate cultures.[4] In addition, change at the individual, or at most the familial, level drew the most sustained attention, because it served to verify or contradict the overriding "immigrant paradigm" of assimilation and incorporation, which continued to govern popular perceptions of the process of becoming American among immigrants of the past.

Race, if discussed at all by this generation of historians, tended to exist only as a characteristic that inhibited assimilation to a greater or lesser degree. As such, race came to be seen as one aspect of ethnicity rather than an independent feature of the American social structure. Indeed, as long as studies of European immigrants to the United States dominated immigration history, the dynamics of race in the United States remained a peripheral concern to the field. Two critical transformations have led to a major rethinking of the role of race in immigration to American society over the past thirty years. First, the Immigration Act of 1965 and other global events and processes have radically transformed the point of origin of most immigrants to the United States away from Europe and toward Latin America and Asia. Second, the emergence, growth, and maturity of scholarship focusing on African Americans, Latinos, and Asian Americans, particularly in various ethnic studies programs around the nation, has changed the treatment of race from a peripheral concern to one of central importance in understanding the place of insiders and outsiders in shaping American history and society.

Immigration historians, however, have begun to recognize that race has played and continues to play a critical role in facilitating the adaptation of certain European newcomers to American society.[5] Most of that recognition has developed because of the growing field of "whiteness" studies in the 1990s, particularly the work of David Roediger (1991). By discussing race as a relational concept rather than a biological or cultural one, Roediger and others have made it clear that part of the integration of European immigrants and their descendants into the American mainstream has been their positioning themselves as "white," as opposed to "black" (Barrett and Roediger 1997). Roediger has made the Irish the critical group in the nineteenth century for claiming their Americanness on the backs of blacks, and political scientist Michael Rogin (1996) and anthropologist Karen Brodkin (1994) have made similar claims for Jews in the twentieth century.[6]

New perspectives on race, however, have also informed studies that concentrate on immigrants of color in the late nineteenth and twentieth centuries. Recent work in Asian American studies, for example, examines the manner in which the perception of the "foreignness" of Asian Americans, despite their generations-long presence in the United States, has become a fundamental "racial" characteristic (Lowe 1996; Gotanda 1997). Indeed, historians of Asian America have been at the forefront of studies showing that European immigrants pushed for outright exclusion of Asian immigrants in the late nineteenth and early twentieth centuries as a way of claiming their "whiteness," a process that increasingly constructed white racial status as one of the attributes necessary for American citizenship.[7] More recently, historians have emphasized that these bars to immigration, particularly the Chinese Exclusion Act of 1882, served to prepare the United States for further limitations of immigration by national origins and expanded definitions of *race* (see Sayler 1995, especially 245; Hing 1993). Although John Higham admitted in 1963 that in writing his classic work on American nativism, *Strangers in the Land,* he "regarded opposition to certain non-European peoples, such as the Chinese and, to a lesser extent, the Japanese, as somewhat separate phenomena, historically tangential to the main currents of American nativism" (1963, iii), few writing today can afford to make that assumption. Asian exclusion provided a critical way to experiment with federal restrictions on immigration, which would later be used against Europeans, and it also supported the political culture that was accustomed to equating whiteness with full American citizenship.

Immigrants from Mexico have experienced a distinctive form of racialization based upon their presumed "foreignness." American-born newcomers to the American Southwest have had to "forget" the history of the imperial war with Mexico in 1846 and the subsequent movement of the United States–Mexico border as they assume the position of the "native" in the region by ascribing "alien" status to Mexican immigrants and Mexican Americans alike (Sánchez 1993, chapter 2). Indeed, the fact that Mexico and the rest of Latin America was not put under a quota system until after 1965 is a strong indication that the relation between race and immigration played different functions for Latin American and Asian immigrants. Race, for the most part, seemed to facilitate Mexican migration to America's railroad shops and agricultural fields, with employers arguing that unlike other groups, Mexicans returned to their native land like "homing pigeons," sparing American society the need to worry about their care and maintenance (Guerin-Gonzalez 1994). As historian David Gutiérrez (1995) has shown, the place of the Mexican immigrant in society has affected the perception of the Mexican American by Anglo-Americans throughout the twentieth century, with various racial advocacy groups taking different positions toward immigration policy in an effort to alter negative perceptions. As for other Latinos, their distinctive adaptation to the United States has depended upon the historical context in which they migrated, be it as colonials and citizens, as in the case of Puerto Ricans, or as political refugees, such as Cubans or Central Americans.[8]

The task for the next generation of historians is to weave together the insights of previous generations to begin to tell a whole story of immigration to the United States that excludes no one while taking into account the diversity of conditions that brought newcomers to the United States as well as the varieties of factors that influenced their adaptation to American society. It is as important for historians to remember that Asian and Latino migration to the United States was occurring in the late nineteenth and early twentieth centuries as it is for sociologists to concern themselves with European immigration to the United States in the late twentieth century.[9] The issue of race is likely to continue to emerge as a fundamental source of contention in analyzing immigrant adaptation to the United States, given the long history of racial discrimination in the country and the continued racialization of newcomers in contemporary American politics.

Notes

1. See Hansen (1940) for the best example of this generation's work.
2. This literature is simply too voluminous to list individually, but excellent review articles survey the most relevant literature. See Zunz (1985); Vecoli (1990); and Morawska (1990).
3. Jon Gjerde (1999) notes the widespread use of botanical metaphors in immigration studies in history.
4. See Sánchez (1993, 4–8), for a fuller description of this bipolar model and particularly its use among historians of Mexican immigrants.

5. For one of the latest reflections on the role of race in shaping American adaptation, see Gerstle (1997).

6. For recent examples of the growing field of "whiteness" studies in history, see Jacobson (1998); Lipsitz (1998).

7. One of the earliest examples is Saxton (1971).

8. For a fuller discussion of these groups, see Portes (1990).

9. For an early attempt at this sort of historical analysis, see Chan (1990).

References

Barrett, James R., and David Roediger. 1997. "In-between Peoples: Race, Nationality and the 'New Immigrant' Working Class." *Journal of American Ethnic History* 16 (3): 3–44.

Bodnar, John. 1985. *The Transplanted: A History of Immigrants in Urban America.* Bloomington: Indiana University Press.

Brodkin, Karen. 1994. "How Did Jews Become White Folks?" In *Race,* edited by Steven Gregory and Roger Sanjek. New Brunswick, N.J.: Rutgers University Press.

Chan, Sucheng. 1990. "European and Asian Immigration into the United States in Comparative Perspective, 1820s to 1920s." In *Immigration Reconsidered: History, Sociology, and Politics,* edited by Virginia Yans-McLaughlin. New York: Oxford University Press.

Gabaccia, Donna. 1999. "Ins and Outs: Who Is an Immigration Historian?" *Journal of American Ethnic History* 18(4): 126–35.

Gerstle, Gary. 1997. "Liberty, Coercion, and the Making of Americans." *Journal of American History* 84(2): 548–57.

Gjerde, Jon. 1999. "The State of the Field: The Social History of Immigration to and Ethnicity in the United States." *Journal of American Ethnic History* 18(4): 40–65.

Glazer, Nathan. 1971. "Blacks and Ethnic Groups: The Difference, and the Political Difference It Makes." *Social Problems* 18(4): 444–61.

Gotanda, Neil. 1997. "Race, Citizenship, and the Search for Political Community Among 'We the People.'" *Oregon Law Review* 76(2): 233–59.

Guerin-Gonzalez, Camille. 1994. *Mexican Workers and American Dreams: Immigration, Repatriation, and California Farm Labor, 1900–1939.* New Brunswick, N.J.: Rutgers University Press.

Gutiérrez, David G. 1995. *Walls and Mirrors: Mexican Americans, Mexican Immigrants, and the Politics of Identity.* Berkeley: University of California Press.

Handlin, Oscar. 1973. *The Uprooted: The Epic Story of the Great Migration That Made the American People.* 2d ed. Boston: Little, Brown and Company.

Hansen, Marcus Lee. 1940. *The Immigrant in American History.* Cambridge, Massachusetts: Harvard University Press.

Higham, John. 1963. *Strangers in the Land: Patterns of American Nativism, 1860–1925.* 2d ed. New York: Atheneum.

Hing, Bill Ong. 1993. *Making and Remaking Asian America Through Immigration Policy, 1850–1990.* Stanford: Stanford University Press.

Jacobson, Matthew Frye. 1998. *Whiteness of a Different Color: European Immigrants and the Alchemy of Race.* Cambridge, Massachusetts: Harvard University Press.

Lipsitz, George. 1998. *The Possessive Investment in Whiteness: How White People Profit from Identity Politics.* Philadelphia: Temple University Press.

Lowe, Lisa. 1996. *Immigrant Acts: On Asian American Cultural Politics.* Durham, N.C.: Duke University Press.

Morawska, Ewa. 1990. "The Sociology and Historiography of Immigration." In *Immigration Reconsidered: History, Sociology, and Politics,* edited by Virginia Yans-McLaughlin. New York: Oxford University Press.

Portes, Alejandro. 1990. "From South of the Border: Hispanic Minorities in the United States." In *Immigration Reconsidered: History, Sociology, and Politics,* edited by Virginia Yans-McLaughlin. New York: Oxford University Press.

Roediger, David R. 1991. *The Wages of Whiteness: Race and the Making of the American Working Class.* London: Verso.

Rogin, Michael. 1996. *Blackface, White Noise: Jewish Immigrants in the Hollywood Melting Pot.* Berkeley: University of California Press.

Sánchez, George J. 1993. *Becoming Mexican American: Ethnicity, Culture, and Identity in Chicano Los Angeles, 1900–1945.* New York: Oxford University Press.

Saxton, Alexander. 1971. *The Indispensable Enemy: Labor and the Anti-Chinese Movement in California.* Berkeley: University of California Press.

Sayler, Lucy E. 1995. *Laws Harsh as Tigers: Chinese Immigrants and the Shaping of Modern Immigration Law.* Chapel Hill: University of North Carolina Press.

Vecoli, Rudolph J. 1964. "*Contadini* in Chicago: A Critique of *The Uprooted.*" *Journal of American History* 51(3): 404–16.

———. 1990. "From *The Uprooted* to *The Transplanted*: The Writing of American Immigration History, 1951–1989." In *From "Melting Pot" to Multiculturalism: The Evolution of Ethnic Relations in the United States and Canada,* edited by Valeria Gennaro Lerda. Rome: Bulzoni Editore.

Zunz, Olivier. 1985. "American History and the Changing Meaning of Assimilation." *Journal of American Ethnic History* 4(1): 53–72.

THE POLITICS OF IMMIGRATION POLICY: AN EXTERNALIST PERSPECTIVE

Aristide R. Zolberg

INTERNATIONAL migration is an inherently political phenomenon, in that it entails not merely physical relocation but a change of jurisdiction from one state to another and eventually also a change of membership from one political community to another. Both aspects of the process, emigration and immigration, therefore, often elicit public concern and provoke political contention within and between countries. Yet until recently, the subject evoked little or no interest among political scientists, even within the subfield of American politics, notwithstanding the importance of immigration in the development of the society with which it is concerned.

The situation changed significantly from the late 1970s onward as a consequence of the reemergence of immigration issues on the political agendas of the United States and other advanced societies, as well as the concurrent escalation of refugee movements at the international level. The wide range of subjects covered reflects the fact that the discipline remains divided into distinct subfields that operate quite autonomously. Among political theorists oriented toward normative issues, interest has focused on matters of "membership" that involve questions related to conditions governing admission, naturalization, and voting rights for new citizens. Because democratic governance requires some minimal degree of community, liberal democracies must be "bounded" in some fashion, and hence it is legitimate for them to impose restrictions on access to membership; however, theorists disagree on what this implies for the formulation of actual immigration policies under present-day world circumstances (Walzer 1981; Barry and Goodin 1992; Carens 1987; Bauboeck 1994; Pickus 1998).

In the subfields of American politics and comparative politics (concerned with advanced industrial societies), most of the attention has focused on immigration policy as a dependent variable, seeking to account for variation within countries over time or between countries (Kubat 1993; Hollifield 1992; Cornelius, Martin, and Hollifield 1994; Brochmann 1996; Calavita 1992; Tichenor 1994; Castles and Miller 1993; Plotke 1999; Ireland 1994; Weil 1991; Zolberg 1989; Lahav 1997). Although much of this literature is grounded in the traditional analysis of policy making in terms of the dynamics of interest groups and political parties, as established in the few distinguished older works by political scientists dealing with American immigration policy (Divine 1957; Riggs 1950), some attempts have been made recently to develop more theoretical models derived from political economy and organizational theory (Freeman 1995; Fitzgerald 1996). Americanists have also been interested in the political incorporation of immigrants, including the political behavior of particular groups, notably Latinos (DeSipio and de la Garza 1992; DeSipio 1996; Jones-Correa 1997; Lin and Jamal 1999), and in the past as well as today (Mink 1986). On the European side, political scientists have been especially drawn to the analysis of political reactions to immigration, notably the emergence of extremist right-wing parties that exploit the issue in an opportunistic manner (Schain 1987, 1990; Layton-Henry and Rich 1986; Betz 1990; Kitschelt 1997).

At the international level, political scientists have contributed to the analysis of the escalation of refugee flows in the developing world from the late 1970s onward, and, more recently additional flows from the former Communist world, as well as the development of international institutions charged with managing these flows (Zolberg, Suhrke, and Aguayo 1989; Loescher and Monahan 1989; Loescher 1993; Skran 1995; Schmiedl, forthcoming). They have also explored the impact of both voluntary and forced international migration on the international system more generally, as well as the determinants and adequacy of international responses to these flows (Weiner 1995, 1996; Kennedy 1993; Money 1999; Zolberg and Benda, forthcoming).

Although, given the nature of the discipline, one should not expect the emergence of a unified, comprehensive framework that might integrate disparate literatures, it is nevertheless possible to construct a theoretically grounded field within which different elements can be located, and which would bring out links among them. Because immigration as a process is located precisely at the interface between the internal and the external, the framework deliberately seeks to overcome the conventional distinction between domestic and international spheres.

Viewed in a global perspective, immigration policies are shaped by the dynamics of world capitalism, on the one hand, and the international state system, on the other, within the context of epochal population dynamics and local circumstances (Davis 1974; Zolberg 1981, 1983,

1986). Although historically these policies have ranged widely, today they are strikingly similar: on a hypothetical continuum ranging from open to closed borders, they are clustered very narrowly around the "closed" pole. All affluent countries are determined to keep out most of the world's population and, despite musing about "loss of control" over their borders, effectively achieve this objective. However, in the post–World War II boom years most European states made provisions for temporary foreign workers as well as for a limited number of refugees seeking asylum; unexpectedly, this led to permanent settlement, followed by additional migration arising from family reunion. The traditional English-speaking "settlement" countries, including the United States, maintained a more immigrationist stance, providing for broader-based family reunion and also for the admission as permanent residents of persons who might contribute substantial capital or skills. The United States also recruited temporary foreign workers, by way of legal programs as well as by "informal" means; as in Europe, this eventually generated permanent settlement.

The restrictive immigration regime prevails worldwide because it constitutes a sine qua non for maintaining the Westphalian international state system as well as the privileged position of the "core" states and their populations amid highly unequal conditions (Wallerstein 1974; Nett 1971; Emmanuel 1972; Petras 1980; Hamilton and Whalley 1984). In addition, in the course of their formation, nation-states (as well as states that are genuinely multinational) tend to delineate their identities by distinguishing themselves from cultural "others" (Barth 1969). In some cases, this entails the elaboration of a conception of national citizenship that is explicitly ethnic (that in Germany, for example) (Brubaker 1992); however, even nations that adopt a more political conception of citizenship (notably, France and the United States) usually combine this with a more or less manifest ethnic identity as well. This ethnic dimension of nationhood is in effect "activated" if and when cultural "others" turn up as potential or actual immigrants and tends to generate efforts to exclude or at least restrict the flow.[1]

Accordingly, the process of decision making at the level of a given state is driven by two quite distinct types of considerations, each of which relates to a distinct sphere of social interactions. In the perspective of capitalist dynamics, immigrants of any kind—including refugees—are considered primarily as workers. Hence immigrants are characteristically welcomed by employers because they lower the average wage and also increase the elasticity of labor; conversely, they are characteristically resented by resident workers as unfair competitors willing to accept lower wages and below-standard conditions. At worst, they may not only lower wages but altogether displace natives. However, even the most profit-driven capitalists are unlikely to favor an increase in labor supply large enough to occasion a major social disruption; hence, in contemporary capitalist democracies, arguments on behalf of "open borders" appear perennially as the playful musings of free-market ideologues but almost never in policy debates. These considerations account for the tendency of advanced industrial societies to recruit guest workers from less developed countries (Castles and Kossack 1985). An alternative explanation is provided by the theory of labor segmentation (Piore 1979).

However, all types of immigrants—including even temporary workers—also constitute a political and cultural presence. This evokes a distinctive dimension of consideration pertaining to the putative impact of immigration on the host country's way of life, its cohesiveness, or, in current discourse, its identity. In almost any immigration situation, there are significant groups among the hosts who believe that newcomers in general, or particular groups among them, will jeopardize the established national ways. In the United States alone, just about every cultural attribute imaginable has been found objectionable at one time or another, notably "race"—as constructed in the nineteenth and early twentieth centuries, referring not only "Asiatics" and blacks but also "mixed-breed" Mexicans, different European nationalities, and Jews— religion (notably Roman Catholics, from the eighteenth century until quite recently), and language (German speakers in the late eighteenth century, Spanish speakers today). Similarly hostile responses have surfaced elsewhere, notably toward Jews from eastern Europe in most of western Europe a generation ago, Arabs and Muslims more generally throughout Europe today, and Sephardic and Ethiopian Jews in Ashkenazi-dominant Israel.

Although reactions like these are attributable in large part to persistent prejudice and xenophobia, it should be recognized that the settlement of any substantial group of people whose culture diverges markedly from the hosts' own is likely to call into question the established "cultural compromise" pertaining to religious, linguistic, and racial diversity and hence is a legitimate source of concern. The key questions are always "How different can we be?" and "How alike must we be?"— and, when they have been answered, how the answers are to be implemented organizationally and materially (Zolberg and Long 1999). Differing assessments along these lines precipitate confrontations not only between natives and foreigners but among the natives themselves, between those who perceive the newcomers as a threat in relation to what is deemed a fragile status quo and others who are more confident of the society's ability to weather change or welcome the diversity the newcomers would contribute as an enrichment. These alignments are probably related to a more comprehensive cultural cleavage that is emerging as the contemporary equivalent of the older rift between religious and secular camps.

The persistent coexistence of these two very different dimensions of consideration and, concomitantly, of interests, the one pertaining to the putative or actual effects of immigration on material conditions, the other its effects on cultural and political conditions, can be represented graphically by crosscutting axes, each axis having positive and negative poles, providing for a continuum of alignments from "for" to "against." Hence it is possible to adopt a positive position on immigration with respect to one dimension and a negative position in relation to the other. This accounts for the often noted tendency of immigration politics to straddle the ordinary liberal-conservative divide and the concomitant emergence of "strange bedfellow" coalitions for or against particular proposals. Successive attempts to resolve these disparate imperatives in the face of changing conditions shape immigration policy into complex and often inconsistent configurations, such as the segmentation of U.S. policy in the first half of the twentieth century into a "main gate" dealing with general immigration and a "back door" dealing with the procurement of temporary agricultural workers. In the post–World War II period, foreign policy imperatives led to the development of a third policy segment dealing with refugees.

Although the powerful social tendencies articulated in this framework underlie the elaboration of immigration and incorporation policies, they account for general dispositions rather than actual outcomes. This is so because in the advanced industrial societies in question, policy making is shaped in large part by the institutional apparatus of democratic politics, notably, the party system and representative institutions. Hence there is considerable variation in the translations of general dispositions into policies. This institutional mediation, which tends to be ignored by other social scientists, is precisely the area to which political scientists are drawn by the traditions of their discipline and in which they have made their most original contributions to our understanding of the dynamics of immigration policy, especially in the United States (Freeman 1994, 1995; Tichenor 1994; Fitzgerald 1996).[2] One noteworthy consequence is that despite perennial attempts to integrate the disparate segments of American immigration policy, they respond to different configurations of economic and political interests and hence continue to operate relatively autonomously, and to some extent at cross-purposes.

A previous version of this chapter appeared in *American Behavioral Scientist* 1999, vol. 42, no. 9.

Notes

1. This implies a critical revision of Brubaker's argument (1992), involving the transformation of the typology he developed to characterize nation-states into "dimensions of citizenship" shared to a varying extent by all states and subject to change over time.
2. For an elaboration of this point, see Zolberg (1999, 86–89).

References

Barry, Brian, and Robert E. Goodin, eds. 1992. *Free Movement*. University Park: Pennsylvania State University Press.

Barth, Fredrik, ed. 1969. *Ethnic Groups and Boundaries*. Boston: Little, Brown.

Bauboeck, Rainer. 1994. *Transnational Citizenship: Membership and Rights in International Migration*. Brookfield, U.K.: Edward Elgar.

Betz, Hans-Georg. 1990. *Radical Right-Wing Populism in Western Europe*. New York: St. Martin's Press.

Brochmann, Grete. 1996. *European Integration and Immigration from Third Countries*. Oslo: Scandinavian University Press.

Brubaker, Rogers. 1992. *Citizenship and Nationhood in France and Germany*. Cambridge, Mass.: Harvard University Press.

Calavita, Kitty. 1992. *Inside the State: The Bracero Program, Immigration, and the Immigration and Naturalization Service*. New York: Routledge.

Carens, Joseph H. 1987. "Aliens and Citizens: The Case for Open Borders." *Review of Politics* 49(2): 251–73.

Castles, Stephen, and Godula Kossack. 1985. *Immigrant Workers and Class Structure in Western Europe*. 2d ed. London: Oxford University Press.

Castles, Stephen, and Mark J. Miller. 1993. *The Age of Migration: International Population Movements in the Modern World*. New York: Guilford Press.

Cornelius, Wayne A., Philip L. Martin, and James F. Hollifield. 1994. *Controlling Immigration: A Global Perspective*. Stanford, Calif.: Stanford University Press.

Davis, Kingsley. 1974. "The Migrations of Human Populations." *Scientific American* 231(3): 91–97.

DeSipio, Louis. 1996. *Counting the Latino Vote: Latinos as a New Electorate*. Charlottesville: University Press of Virginia.

DeSipio, Louis, and Rodolfo O. de la Garza. 1992. "Making Them Us: The Political Incorporation of Culturally Distinct Immigrant and Nonimmigrant Minorities in the United States." In *Nations of Immigrants: Australia, the United States, and International Migration*, edited by Gary P. Freeman and James Jupp. Oxford, U.K.: Oxford University Press.

Divine, Robert A. 1957. *American Immigration Policy, 1924–1952.* New Haven, Conn.: Yale University Press.

Emmanuel, Arghiri. 1972. *Unequal Exchange: A Study of the Imperialism of Trade.* New York: Monthly Review Press.

Fitzgerald, Keith. 1996. *The Face of the Nation: Immigration, the State, and the National Identity.* Stanford, Calif.: Stanford University Press.

Freeman, Gary P. 1994. "Can Liberal States Control Unwanted Migration?" *Annals of the American Academy of Political and Social Science* 534 (July): 17–30.

———. 1995. "Modes of Immigration Politics in Liberal Democratic States." *International Migration Review* 19(4): 881–902.

Hamilton, Bob, and John Whalley. 1984. "Efficiency and Distributional Implications of Global Restrictions on Labour Mobility: Calculations and Policy Implications." *Journal of Development Economics* 14(1): 61–75.

Hollifield, James F. 1992. *Immigrants, Markets, and States: The Political Economy of Postwar Europe.* Cambridge: Harvard University Press.

Ireland, Patrick. 1994. *The Policy Challenge of Ethnic Diversity: Immigrant Politics in France and Switzerland.* Cambridge: Harvard University Press.

Jones-Correa, Michael. 1997. *Between Two Nations: The Political Predicament of Latinos in New York City.* Ithaca: Cornell University Press.

Kennedy, Paul. 1993. *Preparing for the Twenty-first Century.* New York: Vintage.

Kitschelt, Herbert. 1997. *The Radical Right in Western Europe: A Comparative Analysis.* Ann Arbor: University of Michigan Press.

Kubat, Daniel, ed. 1993. *The Politics of Migration Policies: Settlement and Integration: The First World into the 1990s.* New York: Center for Migration Studies.

Lahav, Gallya. 1997. "Ideological and Party Constraints on Family Reunification in Europe." *Journal of Common Market Studies* 35(3): 377–407.

Layton-Henry, Zig, and Paul B. Rich. 1986. *Race, Government, and Politics in Britain.* London: Macmillan.

Lin, Ann Chih, and Amaney Jamal. 1999. "Individual Inclusion and Group Exclusion: The Case of Arab Immigrants." Paper presented at the Eagleton Institute of Politics conference, Framing Equality: Inclusion, Exclusion, and American Political Institutions. Rutgers University, New Brunswick, N.J.(March 26, 1999).

Loescher, Gil. 1993. *Beyond Charity: International Cooperation and the Global Refugee Crisis.* New York: Oxford University Press.

Loescher, Gil, and Laila Monahan, eds. 1989. *Refugees and International Relations.* Oxford: Oxford University Press.

Mink, Gwendolyn. 1986. *Old Labor and New Immigrants in American Political Development.* Ithaca: Cornell University Press.

Money, Jeanette. 1999. *Fences and Neighbors: The Political Geography of Immigration Control.* Ithaca: Cornell University Press.

Nett, Roger. 1971. "The Civil Right We Are Not Ready For: The Right of Free Movement of People on the Face of the Earth." *Ethics* 81(3): 212–27.

Petras, Elizabeth. 1980. "The Role of National Boundaries in a Cross-National Labour Market." *International Journal of Urban and Regional Research* 4(2): 157–95.

Pickus, Noah M. J., ed. 1998. *Immigration and Citizenship in the Twenty-first Century.* Lanham, Md.: Rowman and Littlefield.

Piore, Michael. 1979. *Birds of Passage: Migrant Labor and Industrial Societies.* Cambridge, Mass.: Cambridge University Press.

Plotke, David. 1999. "Immigration and Political Incorporation in the Contemporary United States." In *The Handbook of International Migration: The American Experience,* edited by Charles Hirschman, Philip Kasinitz, and Josh DeWind. New York: Russell Sage Foundation.

Riggs, Fred W. 1950. *Pressures on Congress: A Study of the Repeal of Chinese Exclusion.* New York: King's Crown Press.

Schain, Martin. 1987. "The National Front in France and the Construction of Political Legitimacy." *West European Politics* 10(2): 229–52.

———. 1990. "Immigration and Politics." In *Developments in French Politics,* edited by Peter A. Hall, Jack Hayward, and Howard Machin. London: Macmillan.

Schmiedl, Susanne. Forthcoming. "Conflict and Forced Migration: A Quantitative Review." In *Global Migrants, Global Refugees: Problems and Solutions,* edited by Aristide R. Zolberg and Peter Benda. New York: Berghahn.

Skran, Claudena. 1995. *Refugees in Interwar Europe: The Emergence of a Regime.* Oxford, U.K.: Clarendon Press.

Tichenor, Daniel J. 1994. "The Politics of Immigration Reform in the United States, 1981–1992." *Polity* 26(3): 333–62.

Wallerstein, Immanuel. 1974. *The Modern World System: Capitalist Agriculture and the Origins of the European World-Economy in the Sixteenth Century.* New York: Academic Press.

Walzer, Michael. 1981. "The Distribution of Membership." In *Boundaries: National Autonomy and Its Limits,* edited by Peter G. Brown and Henry Shue. Totowa, N.J.: Rowman and Littlefield.

Weil, Patrick. 1991. *La France et ses étrangers: L'aventure d'une politique de l'immigration de 1938 à nos jours.* Paris: Calmann-Levy.

Weiner, Myron. 1995. *The Global Migration Crisis: Challenge to States and to Human Rights.* New York: HarperCollins.

———. 1996. "Bad Neighbors, Bad Neighborhoods: An Inquiry into the Causes of Refugee Flows." *International Security* 21(1): 5–43.

Zolberg, Aristide R. 1981. "The Origins of the Modern World-System: A Missing Link." *World Politics* 33(2): 253–81.

———. 1983. "'World' and 'System': A Misalliance." In *Contending Ap-*

proaches to World System Analysis, edited by William R. Thompson. Beverly Hills, Calif.: Sage Publications.

———. 1986. "Strategic Interactions and the Formation of Modern States: France and England." In *The State in Global Perspective,* edited by Ali Kazancigil. London: Gower/UNESCO.

———. 1989. "Reforming the Back Door: The Immigration Reform and Control Act of 1986 in Historical Perspective." In *Immigration Reconsidered,* edited by Virginia Yans-Johnson. New York: Oxford University Press.

———. 1999. "Matters of State: Theorizing Immigration Policy." In *The Handbook of International Migration: The American Experience,* edited by Charles Hirschman, Philip Kasinitz, and Josh DeWind. New York: Russell Sage Foundation.

Zolberg, Aristide, and Peter Benda, eds. Forthcoming. *Global Migrants, Global Refugees: Problems and Solutions.* New York: Berghahn.

Zolberg, Aristide R., and Litt Woon Long. 1999. "Why Islam Is Like Spanish: Cultural Incorporation in Europe and the United States." *Politics and Society* 27(1): 5–38.

Zolberg, Aristide R., Astri Suhrke, and Sergio Aguayo. 1989. *Escape from Violence: Conflict and the Refugee Crisis in the Developing World.* New York: Oxford University Press.

IMMIGRATION STUDIES AND THE SOCIAL SCIENCE RESEARCH COUNCIL

Josh DeWind

T HE SOCIAL Science Research Council has twice mobilized scholars to promote the study of immigration to the United States. Although they were conceived seventy years apart, the Committee on Scientific Aspects of Human Migration (1924 to 1927) and the Committee on International Migration (1994 to the present) were formed within similar demographic and political contexts. At the time each committee was created, large numbers of immigrants had been entering the nation for two or more decades, and, in the midst of extensive public debates, the Congress had passed comprehensive legislation to manage their entry and impact on American life. In both instances, public attention was beginning to turn from issues of immigration control to the integration and impact of immigrants on American life.

Although the earlier committee acknowledged being motivated by "questions of public policy involving issues of national prosperity and human rights," its members decided that "political exigencies ought not to determine our program." With prescience, they foresaw that "the immigration problem has been with us since the organization of our government and will undoubtedly remain with us for a long time to come. It was felt that research of a more fundamental character, even if painstakingly slow, might in the long run be more valuable" (Abbott 1927, 2–3). Similarly, the current committee seeks not to resolve policy disputes but rather to "clarify the nature of central issues, explain their origins and outcomes, and identify their wider social contexts and ramifications," with the intention of informing the public's ability to "assess the goals, consistency, and long-term implications of policy options being debated" (DeWind and Hirschman 1996, 41).

Despite the commonality of stepping back from public debates, the two committees defined the scope and focus of their work differently.

An examination of some of these differences illuminates the course immigration studies have taken in developing into a subfield within the social sciences during the twentieth century and suggests some future research goals. The earlier committee constituted the first interdisciplinary research program to be organized by the SSRC, which was created in 1923, and was organized to contribute to the council's goal of clarifying and legitimating the distinctive contributions that the social sciences—in this case, as distinct from the natural sciences—could make to public understandings of important public issues. Beginning with the legitimacy of the social sciences as a given, the current Committee on International Migration has focused on promoting the theoretical coherence of immigration studies as an interdisciplinary subfield within the social sciences. In so doing, this committee has built upon both prior scholarship, partly shaped by the earlier committee, and the council's by now considerable experience in training young scholars and orienting social science research.

The SSRC Committee on Scientific Aspects of Human Migration was created as an offshoot of an earlier group of scholars that had been convened in 1922 by the National Research Council (the research arm of the National Academy of Sciences) as the Committee on Scientific Problems of Human Migration "to consider, from the point of view of natural science, the complex migrational situation resulting from the World Wars and from the virtual elimination of space as a barrier to movements of man and to race intermixture" (Yerkes 1924, 189). The predominance of a natural science perspective within this committee and the alternative goal held by a minority of committee members of developing social scientific approaches and understandings of immigration led to the formation of the Committee on Scientific Aspects of Human Migration within the nascent SSRC. The two committees held some members in common, and their relationship was cited by the SSRC's president as an "excellent example of the possibilities, and also the difficulties, of bringing about successful cooperation between those interested in the social implications of natural science and those interested in social science" (Merriam 1926, 187).[1]

The SSRC committee brought together scholars from a number of social science disciplines including anthropology, psychology, economics, political science, and statistics. These scholars framed their study of U.S. immigration within the broader geographical and conceptual context of migration, which included both internal migration and global emigration and immigration flows. Employing such a broad definition of the field meant that, in addition to commissioning investigations of European and Mexican immigration to the United States, the committee also supported the collection of statistics on world migration and research on the internal migration of African Americans from the South to the North.[2] The studies supported were selected as representative of thematic divisions seen to comprise the migration field:

Statistical problems

Emigration conditions in Europe and other continents

Economic aspects of human migration

Legal and administrative policies in countries of immigration and emigration

Historical aspects of human migration

Social studies (Abbott 1927, 2)

To implement their research goals, the committee sought experienced scholars who could carry out sponsored research projects on approved topics without supervision. "In general," the committee reported at the end of its three-year life, "an attempt has been made to review the field as a whole, to select certain research problems that seemed to be significant either because they presented new problems of research or because the subject seemed of fundamental importance and promised a contribution upon which later research work might proceed" (Abbott 1927, 2–3). This thematic conception of the field notably brought together consideration of both international emigration and immigration with internal migrations under statistical, economic, and social thematic rubrics in order to develop fundamental social science understandings.

Though a critical assessment of the work and impacts of this committee will have to await further investigation, some hypotheses and lines of inquiry can be identified. The foremost contribution of the committee's commissioned studies and resulting publications would seem to be that they helped to establish the study of migration as a topic within the major social science disciplines. The committee's inclusive focus, however—its examination of international, national, and internal migration together—was lost. Perhaps because public concern about immigration waned as implementation of the Immigration Act of 1924 drastically cut the number of immigrants entering the United States, the committee was renamed, first as the Advisory Committee on Population and then the Joint Committee on Population (with the National Research Council) in order to refocus on international population issues in conjunction with the International Population Union. However, the committee soon became inactive, it was reported enigmatically, "through the failure of the plans for which it was created" (SSRC 1933, 61). The focus on internal migration was also dropped as other issues of African American life were taken up by a separate Advisory Committee on Interracial Relations. In 1931 the reorganized Committee on Population Review commissioned a survey of research in the field of population and was subsequently disbanded.

That immigration nonetheless continued to be considered a topic of importance within the social sciences was reaffirmed at the end of the decade. When the SSRC sought to clarify its role in promoting the scientific basis of research, it chose to do so through an evaluation of research publications held in highest regard by social scientists in different disciplines. The first study deemed meritorious enough for scrutiny of its scientific contributions was a study of immigration that had not been commissioned by the SSRC—William I. Thomas and Florian Znaniecki's five-volume *The Polish Peasant in Europe and America* (Thomas and Znaniecki 1918–1920).[3]

The current Committee on International Migration, established in 1994, is composed of senior scholars from the disciplines of sociology, anthropology, political science, economics, history, and law. In contrast to the earlier committee, this one has worked within a narrower conception of the field and focused on immigration to the United States. The committee's working groups have not addressed internal migration and have used international comparisons primarily to gain insight into the U.S. experience of immigrant incorporation. Within this smaller, national sphere, however, the committee has promoted research with a fuller view of the processes and impacts of immigration on American life—particularly as a transformative exchange between immigrants and native-born Americans—and has sought to enhance the field's interdisciplinary coherence by reinforcing intellectual and professional connections between researchers in the field.

The first field-building activity of the Committee on International Migration was organizing a conference to assess the theoretical state of immigration studies. Titled Becoming American/America Becoming: International Migration to the United States, the conference sought to link scholars from different disciplines to undertake critical syntheses of their theoretical perspectives regarding economic, political, and sociocultural aspects of immigrant incorporation (SSRC 1996).[4] The committee subsequently organized two comparative working groups that examined contemporary issues of immigrant incorporation within historical and international comparative perspectives. Working groups on transnational migration, on immigration, race, and ethnicity; and, in collaboration with another SSRC working group, on religion, immigration, and civic life are in the process of organization, with a primary focus still on immigration to the United States.

Although senior scholars have guided and participated in these research planning activities, the committee's research fellowship program has been designed to attract younger scholars into the field and has supported those whose research promises to contribute to "theoretical understandings of the origins of immigration and refugee flows to the United States, the processes of migration and settlement, and the outcomes for immigrants, refugees, and native-born Americans" (SSRC 1998). In addition, the committee has organized workshops to assist students of minority ethnic and racial backgrounds to prepare research and funding proposals. Unlike the earlier Committee on Scientific Aspects of Immigration, which sponsored senior scholars to research committee-designated topics, the contemporary committee has left applicants for fellowships to devise their own topics and research methods, with the purpose of encouraging the development of innovative theoretical perspectives within the field limited to U.S. immigration.

Although a focus on U.S. immigration has helped the SSRC to promote interdisciplinary coherence and attract new scholars to this subfield, it may soon be advantageous for social scientists to return to the broader conceptual and geographic boundaries of migration studies adopted by the SSRC's earlier committee. To this end, the Committee on International Migration is now sponsoring a collaborative research project on forced migration and human rights in Africa, and the Working Group on Religion, Immigration, and Civic Life is exploring how it might turn its attention to international issues. Study of local and global facets of migration would be responsive to both the dynamics of contemporary migration flows and to the SSRC's growing role in promoting international as well as national scholarship.

A previous version of this chapter appeared in *American Behavioral Scientist* 1999, vol. 42, no. 9.

Notes

1. The extent to which the natural science approach of the original National Research Council's Committee on Scientific Problems of Human Migration was influenced by the eugenics movement's concern that immigration was causing detrimental "race-mixing" and motivated the formation of an SSRC committee to develop a social science approach to the study of immigration is discussed by Casey Walsh (1997).

2. Specific immigration studies included Janson (1931), on Swedish migration; Taylor (1930, 1932), on Mexican labor; and Gamio (1930, 1931), on Mexican immigration. The results of a large international study were published as *International Migrations*, in two volumes. Volume 1 is a collection of statistics on migration within and be-

tween European, Asian, and North and South American countries, coordinated by Imre Ferenczi of the International Labour Office in Geneva and Walter F. Willcox of the Nation Bureau of Economic Research (Ferenczi and Wilcox 1929). Volume 2 is a compilation of analyses of country case studies of emigration and immigration, edited by Willcox (1931). Specific studies of the internal movements of African American migration include Kennedy (1930) and Kiser (1932), on migration from rural to urban regions, and Lewis (1932) and Ross and Truxel (1931), on migration more generally.

3. The appraisal and subsequent comments by the study's two authors were published by the SSRC in Blumer (1939).

4. Substantially revised and edited proceedings of this conference were published *as The Handbook of International Migration: The American Experience*, edited by Charles Hirschman, Philip Kasinitz, and Josh DeWind (1999).

References

Abbott, Edith. 1927. *Report of the Committee on Scientific Aspects of Human Migration, December 18, 1926.* Chicago: Social Science Research Council.

Blumer, Herbert. 1939. *Critiques of Research in the Social Sciences.* Part 1, *An Appraisal of Thomas and Znaniecki's "The Polish Peasant in Europe and America."* New York: Social Science Research Council.

DeWind, Josh, and Charles Hirschman. 1996. "Becoming American/ America Becoming: A Conference on International Migration to the United States." *Items* 50(2–3): 41–47.

Ferenczi, Imre, and Walter F. Willcox. 1929. *International Migrations,* vol. 1. New York: National Bureau of Economic Research.

Gamio, Manuel. 1930. *Mexican Immigration to the United States.* Chicago: University of Chicago Press.

———. 1931. *The Mexican Immigrant: His Life Story.* Chicago: University of Chicago Press.

Hirschman, Charles, Philip Kasinitz, and Josh DeWind, eds. 1999. *The Handbook of International Migration: The American Experience.* New York: Russell Sage Foundation.

Janson, Florence E. 1931. *The Background of Swedish Immigration, 1840–1930.* Chicago: University of Chicago Press.

Kennedy, Louise V. 1930. *The Negro Peasant Turns Cityward.* New York: Columbia University Press.

Kiser, Clyde V. 1932. *Sea Island to City.* New York: Columbia University Press.

Lewis, Edward E. 1932. "Economic Factors in Negro Migration." *Journal of the American Statistical Association* 27: 45–53.

Merriam, Charles. 1926. "Annual Report of the Social Science Research Council." *American Political Science Review* (February): 185–89.

Ross, Frank A., and A. A. Truxel. 1931. "Primary and Secondary Aspects of Interstate Migration." *American Journal of Sociology* 37: 435–44.

Social Science Research Council (SSRC). 1933. *Decennial Report, 1923–1933.* New York: SSRC.

———. 1996. "Becoming American/America Becoming: A Conference on International Migration to the United States." Unpublished conference outline, New York(January 18–21, 1996).

———. 1998. "Fellowships for the Study of International Migration to the United States, 1999–2000." New York. Unpublished promotional poster.

Taylor, Paul S. 1930, 1932. *Mexican Labor in the United States.* 2 vols. Berkeley: University of California Press.

Thomas, William I., and Florian Znaniecki. 1918–20. *The Polish Peasant in Europe and America.* Vols. 1 and 2, Chicago: University of Chicago Press. Vols. 3, 4, and 5, Boston: Richard Badger.

Walsh, Casey. 1997. "The Social Science Research Council and Migration Studies (1922–1930)." Unpublished paper. New School University.

Willcox, Walter F., ed. 1931. *International Migrations,* vol. 2. New York: National Bureau of Economic Research.

Yerkes, Robert M. 1924. 'The Work of Committee on Scientific Problems of Human Migration, National Research Council." *Journal of Personnel Research* 3(6): 189–96.

3

FILLING IN SOME HOLES: SIX AREAS OF NEEDED IMMIGRATION RESEARCH

Herbert J. Gans

FOR A social scientist, the only possible way to write about the future of immigration is to eschew predictions of what might be and instead propose what should be; but that is also the most personally satisfying assignment. Here, however, I fill it modestly, limiting myself to the presentation and discussion of six research "holes"—to borrow Rubén Rumbaut's metaphor—that deserve filling. As a sociologist, I see mainly sociological holes, and to keep the list from expanding into double digits, I stay within a favorite topic of sociological immigration research, the adaptation of immigrants and their descendants.

I use the word "adaptation" loosely, emphasizing both positives and negatives—including attempts to hold back acculturation, which some see as positive and others as negative. I also treat adaptation processes and all their conflicts as directly affected by macroeconomic and macrosociological factors that have an impact on immigrants; thus, these processes and conflicts are by their very nature different for different immigrants.

Emigration and Immigration

The first hole that should be filled is an old one that Charles Hirschman has called the selectivity question: who comes and who does not come to America? The traditional answer, which surely reflects the nationalism of some early American immigration researchers, is that the immigrants are the most ambitious and energetic people, and their lesser fellow nationals stay home.[1] I have never been convinced that this answer is accurate, but the question is worth raising again—this time, to determine whether and how immigrants are selected or self-selected, and by what criteria, including skills, and whether they actually use these skills after arrival.

Today, the selectivity question is also complicated by the fact that many, though by no means most, immigrants come as transnationals and that others come at least with the intention to be temporary, that is sojourners. Whatever their future plans at arrival, a significant number participate in what Peggy Levitt (1999) has called the remittance culture, which keeps them in America but also becomes a factor in encouraging and holding back some potential immigrants.

Sociologists must pay more attention as well to how people manage (and mismanage) their attempts to emigrate and immigrate, taking into account the political, bureaucratic, and financial obstacles in their old country, as well as in the United States, that now stand in their way. In addition, we need to learn more about what shapes success and failure in illegal immigration and the influence of illegal immigration on adaptation (Corcoran 1993). But then researchers interested in adaptation still need to ask whether and how the ability and willingness to take leave of an old culture, not to mention family and friends, affect emigration and immigration.

Sociological research has tended to ignore differences in the categories of immigration, especially the distinction between economic immigrants and political refugees. Another category needs to be added to these: politicoeconomic refugees, people fleeing from the failed or sabotaged attempts to correct the economic problems of their home countries. Sociologists have not done sufficient research on political refugees in the past, although these bear some resemblance to other kinds of involuntary immigrants. Moreover, some refugees remain here involuntarily all their lives, whereas others are so eager to become Americans that their refugee status plays only a minimal role in their adaptation. Today's research on political refugees must distinguish between poor ones (for example, the Hmong), those who have achieved a moderate or middle-income status (notably, Koreans), and especially former dictators and their friends from several countries, who are often adapting under luxurious conditions.

Yet perhaps in some way the most intriguing question in the adaptation of political refugees is how those who were well off in the old country dealt with sharp economic and social downward mobility when they first arrived here.[2] The findings might also be useful in helping native-born Americans who suffer from downward mobility owing to downsizing or other upheavals of postindustrial and global capitalism.

The First and Second Generations

The second hole in immigration research is, ironically enough, knowledge about the immigrants themselves. Although immigration research was a centerpiece of the "Chicago School," the University of Chicago sociologists and their colleagues elsewhere actually did not conduct as much research among the immigrants themselves as is now thought, and they seem frequently to have been more interested in the second generation.[3] For one thing, immigrants were hard to study because many did not speak English, and the researchers often spoke nothing else. In addition, by the time empirical research was fully under way, a large, English-speaking second generation was already available for study, and they were more accessible than immigrants to understaffed and under-funded researchers.

Many sociologists were actually more interested in how America affected the immigrants, which also attracted them to the second generation. This research preference may be repeating itself, for the second generation has already become a major research topic today, although there are still few second-generation adults in the post-1965 immigration.

A full-scale review of the old immigration research literature badly needs to be conducted, although, because the first generation of empirical researchers said little about their research methods, much less whom they interviewed (if anyone), such a review would not be an easy undertaking. For example, neither of Park's two books, *Old World Traits Transplanted* (1921) and *The Immigrant Press and Its Control* (1922), are fully empirical studies. The first consists mostly of quotes from other authors, few of whom were social scientists or researchers, and the second is drawn from newspaper stories and interviews with three or four immigrant press editors. In fact, the major Chicago study that actually obtained data from immigrants was W. I. Thomas and Florian Znaniecki's *The Polish Peasant in Europe and America* (1918–20), for even Louis Wirth's *The Ghetto* (1928) appears to have been based largely on data from the second generation.[4]

The principal later books, by Caroline Ware (1935) and W. Lloyd Warner and Leo Srole (1945) were multigenerational studies undertaken at a time when the second generation was already demographically dominant. Warner and Srole, who conducted their empirical work in the mid-1930s, say virtually nothing about where and how they obtained their data, but Ware, who researched her book in the 1920s, hired local residents to interview others. Although she never indicated the generational status of her interviewees, she reported that "younger residents were especially sought . . . (and) the sample was biased . . . partly by design in the direction of those who were . . . more Americanized" (Ware 1935, 192). Moreover, both Ware and Warner and Srole were more interested in acculturation and assimilation than in immigration.[5]

Judging from the scarcity of systematic empirical data on them, I now suspect that some of the original theorizing about the European immigrants used data from the second generation and then reasoned or imagined backward to a first generation coming to America with an old-country culture they were allegedly eager to preserve. From there, it was easy to proceed to what was later called "straight-line theory," in which unacculturated immigrants were succeeded by acculturating second generations and by socially assimilating third and fourth generations.[6]

Today's immigrants are being studied not only by sociologists but also by anthropologists, whose traditional preoccupation with preindustrial cultures makes immigrants especially attractive to them as populations of interest.[7] The major sociological contribution to immigrant research so far has been to study the post-1965 immigrants' economic adaptation, which also corrects the almost total failure of students of the European immigrants and their descendants to look at economic behavior.

Research conducted among the post-1965 immigrants has especially emphasized their entrepreneurial activities, many studies dealing with immigrant store owners and shopkeepers as well as owners of enclave enterprises, including garment sweatshops.[8] More research is needed on the workers, particularly the immigrants who have gone to work for big and small employers in the larger economy, often at the minimum wage rate and sometimes less. They may constitute the majority of immigrant workers. Although occasional journalistic and other studies report their exploitation, the details of their economic adaptation are still virtually unknown.

A large proportion of the other sociological studies of the immigrant generation are demographic or based on closed-ended survey questions, which are often too simple and too few in number to supply useful data either on behavior or attitudes. Also, too many studies are concerned with proving the inaccuracy of straight-line theory and immigrants' resistance, however it is conceptualized, to acculturation. Whatever the ideological and other impulses for these studies, they are premature from a research perspective, because straight-line theory can only be tested among the adults of the second and later generations. Instead, sociologists need to research the extent to which contemporary immigrants actually practice the cultures and maintain the social structures they bring with them from the country of origin. How much they themselves want, or must, Americanize in order to survive—and, if they are upwardly mobile, to succeed—must also be investigated.

In addition, the study of today's immigrant adaptation should include some analysis of what I call anticipatory acculturation. Because "globalism" and "transnationalism" have become popular buzzwords, many observers assume the immigrants' familiarity, while still prospective emigrants, with American life. Although these emigrants may be familiar with exported American mass media fare, our movies and television programs do not, and are not intended to, give an accurate picture of life in America. Still, the emigrants do learn from them, and in ways not anticipated by the creators of media fare. Evidently, foreigners often see the substructure of standard American culture patterns, one that is largely unconscious and taken for granted by all Americans and that holds up the superstructure of entertainment.[9]

Furthermore, an anticipatory acculturation study should look at the influence of fantasies about America from the mass media and other sources. Fantasies already played an anticipatory role in the European immigration: the notion of streets paved with gold, for example, and the resulting disappointment may explain why some European immigrants returned home, particularly before World War I. Whether such disappointments exist today and affect the rates of immigrant return deserves examination.

As long as second-generation research continues, by necessity, to deal with children and adolescents, additional work should be done on immigrant children as overachievers in school. This question is important not only for an understanding of the dynamics of successful school performance, perhaps for the benefit of Anglos as much as anyone else, but also for an understanding of why second- and third-generation immigrants often do not perform in school as well as immigrant students. Because many of the descendants of European immigrants experienced more success in school with each succeeding generation, we need to ask whether acculturation and "becoming American" now lead to educational decline—and, if so, why.

If the answer is positive, the data are relevant also for the selectivity question, for if immigration to America selects for the smarter and more ambitious, the underperforming children of immigrants may merely be behaving more normally. However, other factors could explain the decline in school performance, such as the low quality of schools that serve the poor and the limited occupational opportunities for poor children, particularly those with dark skin, in the economy.[10]

Once second-generation adults are present in large enough numbers, researchers can begin to test straight-line theory, if they are still so motivated. In addition, however, researchers should look more closely at differences in second generations among the various immigrant groups, gather empirical data on the comparative role of class opportunities and restraints, and see what difference, if any, race, ethnicity, and other factors make in the second generation. Other researchers should follow Roger Waldinger and Joel Perlmann's (1998) lead in comparing the second generations of the European and the current immigrations.

The racial diversity of the post–1965 immigration has already stimulated research on the role of race, particularly in immigrant economic adaptation. Other studies should be done on the ways in which Anglo constructions of race affect the adaptation of nonwhite immigrants at various socioeconomic levels, comparing, in particular, black immigrants with Asian and other nonblack newcomers. The differential fates of West Indians and Hispanics depending on their skin color must also be studied and compared with the extent to which a yet unknown number of Asian Americans appear to become "honorary whites," some as early as the second generation.

A related study should be undertaken on the ever increasing intermarriages of Asians and whites, focusing particularly on which whites are attracted to those who are officially still "nonwhite" as marriage partners. Such a study might also provide clues about the future possibilities of a dramatic shift in white constructions of, and reductions in, prejudicial attitudes toward at least some nonwhite races.

In addition, the study of the second generation should include an analysis of the adaptation of immigrants who came here as youngsters and are educated, or mainly educated, in American schools—whom Rubén Rumbaut has called the "1.5 generation," an analysis that was not undertaken during the European immigration. More important, a study of this cohort, as well as of the so-called 1.25 and 1.75 generations, should be used to determine what—if any—factors in childhood abroad and here play any roles in the adaptation processes and social or cultural conflicts of these generationally interstitial Americans. We know a little about how age of arrival affects the retention of foreign accents, but we know almost nothing about how it affects retention or rejection of old-country social structural, cultural, emotional, and other patterns.

Conversely, we need also to look at what is left from the sixth and later generations of the earlier nineteenth-century European immigrants, for example, among the Irish, Germans, and Scandinavians. Later in the twenty-first century, researchers can look at equivalent generations among the descendants of immigrant eastern and southern Europeans, as well as the Chinese and Japanese immigrants to California. Such research should indicate how the long-run adaptation process might be modeled and allow comparison of generational adaptations to the very different Americas experienced by the descendants of the various "old" (that is, European) and the current "new" immigrations.[11] Sometime in the twenty-first century, enough time may even have elapsed to begin to test classical straight-line theory systematically and determine the accuracy of its predicted outcome of total Americanization and the disappearance of ethnicity among whites and other races.

Macro-Level Factors in Immigration

A significant amount of immigration research, particularly that oriented toward adaptation, has emphasized microsocial factors, although the study of economic adaptation, and of the behavior of transnationals, has brought in macrosocial and macroeconomic issues. This is a constructive trend, for we need to understand how the nature of and changes in the American economy, polity, and society affect immigrant adaptation.

However, we need even more to know, and with as much specificity as possible, how economy, polity, and society affect the adaptation of, and opposition by, native-born white Americans to immigrants and their children. A related issue is the trends, among whites of various social classes, in the construction of ethnicity and race—as manifested, for example, in the determination of whether and which immigrants are treated as scapegoats or valued newcomers—and in the conditions that turn ethnic cultures from dangerous actions and threatening institutions into leisure-time experiences and tourist sites for people of all backgrounds.

Ultimately, sociologists should be able to understand all the macro-level factors that influence immigration and immigrants. This understanding might spur coordination with general macrosociology, which could in turn help reduce the marginality of immigration research in the discipline and aid its integration into the sociological mainstream.[12]

Insiders and Outsiders

The fourth area deserving of further work is the applicability of the insider-outsider dichotomy to immigration research. This dichotomy was first developed by Robert K. Merton (1973) to deal with the question of whether the black ghetto could be accurately studied only by blacks—that is, insiders—or whether it should also be studied by white outsiders. In an earlier paper (Gans 1997), I applied Merton's dichotomy to current immigration research, defining it in terms not only of a researchers' background but also attitudes toward sociocultural preservation of the immigrant group.

I borrowed Merton's dichotomy after noticing that much of the sociological research on today's immigrant groups was being conducted by researchers from these groups, who thereby constituted a new set of insiders (Gans 1997). I also noted that many of the writings of these researchers reflect their unhappiness with the concept of acculturation as well as their stated or unstated desire to preserve their ethnic and racial groups or traditions.

Much more conceptual and empirical work needs to be done in this area, although a giant empirical step has been taken by Rumbaut in his research reported in the opening chapter of this volume. My original hunch was tested on about 150 young immigration researchers who were applicants for SSRC dissertation and postdoctoral grants, but Rumbaut's work is based on about 750 respondents of all ages in five different researcher populations.

For the purpose of this paper, I need mention only that Rumbaut's analyses also support my initial suspicion that the insider-outsider dichotomy is particularly relevant to sociology. That discipline not only attracts more demographic insiders than the other social science disciplines but also allows them to pursue insider topics. Conversely, political scientists, being virtually limited to the study of politics and government, are thereby drawn to research on subjects relevant to all immigrant groups, for example, the politics of immigration policy. Perhaps for that reason, political science attracts fewer immigrants than sociology.[13]

The most interesting disciplinary cases are, at least judging from Rumbaut's data, anthropologists and historians, for they have the fewest first-generation and the most third-generation members.[14] Nevertheless, anthropologists appear to be studying the newest immigrants, especially those from Asia, Latin America, and Africa, although that should come as no surprise, given the discipline's traditional interest in people from these continents.

The historians surveyed are doing just as much immigration-related research, but they appear to be concentrating on immigrants from Europe—which has always been their most frequently studied foreign continent.[15] When combined, Rumbaut's data and mine suggest that in the end, disciplinary patterns may sometimes outweigh insider-outsider status in the selection of research topics.

Even so, Rumbaut's findings suggest again that information about the researcher, including the insider-outsider dimension, is an important area for future work by sociologists of immigration. To begin with, an analysis of insiders and outsiders must adapt Merton's original race-based dichotomy to the more complex situation of contemporary immigration research and the diverse origins of today's researchers. For example, although Anglo constructions of race classify all newcomers from Southeast Asia as Asian, one can debate whether a Korean American studying Japanese Americans is an insider or an outsider, not only because of ancestral national differences but also because of the long Japanese oppression of Korea and Koreans.

Furthermore, today's politics of the relation between the researcher and those researched is analytically more complex than the black-white issue facing researchers of the 1960s and 1970s that Merton discussed, for now class, gender, ethnicity, religion, identity politics, and other factors may come up as well. Thus, one must ask whether an affluent Dominican American studying poor Dominican newcomers is an insider or outsider, on class as well as generational grounds. A Lebanese American Christian woman conducting a study of Syrian Jewish immigrants may confront concurrent issues of gender, religion, nationality, and Arab-Israeli politics.

To be sure, not all these demographic differences between researcher and researched are new. DuBois and Frazier, two of the great African American researchers of the black community, both came from upper-middle-class families, and their pejoratively tinged observations about poor blacks reflect the class conflicts that stratified the black community of their times. Nonetheless, their class antagonism was little noticed when these men wrote—if only because their white readers shared their biases toward poor blacks. Meanwhile, the latter probably never had access to any social science research, whether by whites or blacks. Such class-related issues were not noted when Merton was writing, because in that moment in political time, the insider-outsider issue was defined solely as a racial one.

As for the normative aspect of the insider-outsider question, sociology's conventional wisdom holds that professional researchers should be able to detach themselves sufficiently to conduct objective studies. Professional researchers are generally trained to keep their explicit values out of their research, but other values and feelings sometimes sneak in nonetheless. Values also enter into the selection of topics, as well as the selection of hypotheses and concepts, whether the researchers are insiders or outsiders.

It would be wrong to assume, however, that all insiders seek to preserve their ethnic or racial communities. Many are sufficiently acculturated to have left them, and those departures may have influenced their decisions to become social scientists. Insiders are also sometimes hostile to their origins, using their research to attack or reject their own ethnic or racial group.[16] Furthermore, like all other people, immigrant researchers participate in disciplinary and other peer networks, some of which may expect fellow researchers to share the prevailing attitude toward ethnic and racial preservation. Other pressures come from funding sources when these are organizations dedicated to the preservation of the immigrant group.

The outsider concept carries its own complications. In Merton's original analysis, the white outsider was assumed not only to be a detached researcher but also to have no interests or values relevant to the black community. This was perhaps a justifiable assumption, given the

prevailing formulation of the issue in Merton's day, and it was surely a
rhetorically justifiable one in terms of the political arguments Merton
was confronting. Nonetheless, not all white researchers were detached:
many were integrationists. Though not overtly opposed to the preservation of the ghetto community, they did not always share the positive
feelings about it of its residents, or those of "Black Power" advocates.
More significantly, some researchers perceived themselves as detached
but appeared to the ghetto residents they studied as racially prejudiced
(although I suspect that the researchers' prejudice was often as much a
matter of class as of race).

Immigrant research raises some different issues. There have always
been detached nonimmigrant researchers of immigration, but others,
particularly in the early WASP-dominated cohorts of immigrant research, favored Americanization of newcomers, and some even supported the legislation that ended the European immigration in 1925. Yet
others were appalled by the behavior and values of poor immigrants,
particularly peasants and orthodox Jews, and expressed their class—and
religious—biases in their research.

Today's outsiders are not likely to repeat these normative errors, for
there are few advocates of rapid acculturation among sociologists of immigration. There are also few who openly express class antagonisms or
want to end immigration because of the imagined moral imperfections
of the immigrants. Actually, the more likely danger these days is the
opposite, among both insiders and outsiders: too much romanticization
of immigrant Gemeinschaften, tight-knit families, and integrated cultures.

In any case, a simple insider-outsider dichotomy is not applicable to
immigrant research. In the short run, it must become more qualified,
but in the long run, it may no longer be relevant. Meanwhile, it is worth
looking at the backgrounds, values, and conceptual and theoretical
schemes of all immigrant researchers—as well as the wording of questions in surveys and interview studies—to see whether, how, and in
what ways the researchers influence their findings. The researchers
themselves must, however, take the leading role in this process, engaging in more reflexivity and giving up the simple-minded positivism than
still too often prevails in empirical immigration research.

There remains a further insider-outsider question, one that is particularly important for empirical researchers: whether insiders have easier
and better access to the people being studied. In this case, the dichotomy is applied by the people being studied, but often immigrants are
more open to coethnics or coracials, and they will sometimes talk freely
only with them. Others talk freely only with an outsider, particularly a
depth interviewer who comes once and never returns. Conversely, some

immigrant groups do not seem to take their ethnicity very seriously and are more concerned that researchers are insiders with respect to gender, age, and other criteria.

Who will talk freely with whom, and about what subjects, are empirical topics. Researchers could even now informally share their experiences about these topics as a stopgap measure until systematic research on them can be undertaken.

The Sociology of Immigration Research

The fifth area requiring further research, the sociology of immigration, is closely connected to the previous one, for individual (and peer) reflexivity need to be supported by a sociology of immigration research that draws its theory and concepts in large part from the sociology of knowledge. A beginning research program for such an area will be easy to write, for it should aim to determine the reasons for the choices and omissions in immigration research topics and immigrants, past and present. For example, much of the research on the European newcomers in the early twentieth century was conducted among Jews and Italians but far less on equally numerous groups, such as the Polish and other Slavic groups.

Actually, a sociology of research is needed in all fields of the discipline and the rest of the social sciences. Although some postmodernist theoreticians have already moved in this direction, a revival of the older, Mannheimian tradition of the sociology of knowledge might help to ensure that the sociology of sociological research becomes more empirical and moves beyond the postmodern emphasis on textual analysis.

The Role of the Funding Agencies

A sociology of immigration research has to include an economic component: its funding and sources of funds and their effects on the shape of immigration research. At times, what funding agencies decide to approve and what to reject may have more effect on research than the researchers themselves, because without funds, most of the research cannot be done.

The funding agencies include not only federal agencies and foundations but also ethnic and racial organizations, including activist ones, that fund research only occasionally. Such research should include studies on where the agencies get their money, what topics and disciplines they fund and fail to fund and why, and whether they are more likely to support insiders than outsiders.

This area of study must, of course, include the SSRC and the funding agencies to which its immigration research is indebted, notably the Andrew W. Mellon and Russell Sage Foundations. The decisions of the SSRC's International Migration Program as to which applicants and projects to support have aided many of today's young immigration researchers but have thereby also left others unfunded. Understanding the logic of the program's choices will help future sociologists understand the direction American immigration research took at the turn of the millennium.

A previous version of this chapter appeared in *American Behavioral Scientist* 1999, vol. 42, no. 9.

Notes

1. Their answer to the selectivity question did not stop uncharitable Americans, including researchers, from complaining about the physical and moral faults of the immigrants once they had arrived.

2. The same question can be raised about immigrants, although many accept downward mobility for themselves as one cost of ensuring their children a better life.

3. Many of the Chicago researchers, Robert Park included, were actually more curious about relations between blacks and whites as well as the American black community. Martin Bulmer suggests in personal communication that this is evident from the scarcity of immigrant studies in his list of Chicago topics of study (Bulmer 1984, 3–4); and it is also implied by Stow Persons (1987).

4. Indeed, the Chicagoan with the most interest in immigrants may have been W. I. Thomas, who was also the real author of *Old World Traits Transplanted.* Park hired him to do the study because he was jobless, having been fired from the University of Chicago for sexual transgressions.

5. Ware's book was actually a community study of New York's Greenwich Village, but it was subtitled "A Comment on American Civilization in the Post-War Years."

6. In the Chicago School version of this theory, the second generation was beset with marginality. For a comprehensive account, see Persons (1987, chapter 6).

7. After World War II, historians also began to study the European immigrants, and by now there must be more historical than sociological studies about them.

8. Whether these immigrants are truly entrepreneurs deserves discussion, although I would also argue for more research attention to

entrepreneurs working with more capital or taking larger risks, including those who are turning the material culture of the new immigration into consumer goods for the larger American population.

9. A study of the role of overseas American mass media in anticipatory acculturation could also provide media researchers with another site for media effects research.

10. Yet other explanations include demographic and other differences between the old and new immigration and the peer pressures against high school performance, called "acting white" among poor black and Hispanic adolescents. It would be useful, for example, to look at the European immigration data again to see whether the poor children of the time pressed their peers to avoid the equivalent of "acting white," that is "acting WASP."

11. Needless to say, such a study would also provide a marvelous opportunity to see how race distorts long-term acculturation and assimilation, assuming that there is no basic change in white America's racial constructions in the meantime.

12. I make this observation with some hesitation because mainstream research, as in other institutions, can also be the most conventional, and the exciting ideas or creative activities too often come from elsewhere. Moreover, once immigrants are no longer perceived as a problem to mainstream society, funds for studying immigration may shrink considerably.

13. This will change if political scientists look for informal polities in immigrant groups, and it will surely change once the immigrants and their children vote in sufficiently large numbers in American elections.

14. These data are drawn from Rumbaut's table 1.3, in chapter 1 of this volume.

15. I should note a number of differences in our data sources that may affect the conclusions drawn here. My data came from SSRC's files of young immigration researchers applying for its dissertation and postdoctoral grants, Rumbaut's from the membership of the several disciplinary organizations, most of which is presumably older. Those who answered Rumbaut's survey may differ from the ones who did not, and organizational members may differ from the members of the larger discipline. Then again, SSRC applicants surely differ from their disciplinary colleagues as well.

    In addition, the SSRC had data on specific countries, both of research and researcher origin, and I also limited myself to first- and second-generation researchers, being unsure whether acculturation might have turned the third generation into outsiders. Rumbaut's survey was able to obtain data on later-generation researchers as well. He also used a demographic definition of insiders and outsiders. All this only proves once again that more research is needed, preferably using the same methods and definitions.

16. For example, Louis Wirth's (1928) study of the poor eastern European Jews of Chicago's West Side, *The Ghetto*, appears to have been hostile toward the people he studied, particularly those who were pursuing upward mobility in less than polite, or at least academic middle-class, ways. However, whether Wirth was an insider could be debated, for aside from the class differences between him and the people he studied, he was a German Jewish immigrant studying eastern European Jews, and the two populations had disagreed with and fought each other bitterly for generations.

References

Bulmer, Martin. 1984. *The Chicago School of Sociology: Institutionalization, Diversity, and the Rise of Sociological Research.* Chicago: University of Chicago Press.

Corcoran, Mary P. 1993. *Irish Illegals: Transients Between Two Societies.* Westport, Conn.: Greenwood Press.

Gans, Herbert J. 1997. "Toward a Reconciliation of 'Assimilation' and 'Pluralism': The Interplay of Acculturation and Ethnic Retention." *International Migration Review* 31(4): 875–92.

Levitt, Peggy J. 1999. "Social Remittances: A Local-Level, Migration-Driven Form of Cultural Diffusion." *International Migration Review* 32(124): 926–49.

Merton, Robert K. 1973. "The Perspective of Insiders and Outsiders." In *The Sociology of Science: Theoretical and Empirical Investigations,* edited by Norman W. Storer. Chicago: University of Chicago Press.

Park, Robert E. 1922. *The Immigrant Press and Its Controls.* New York: Harper.

Park, Robert E., and Herbert A. Miller. 1921. *Old World Traits Transplanted.* New York: Harper.

Persons, Stow. 1987. *Ethnic Studies at Chicago, 1905–1945.* Urbana: University of Illinois Press.

Thomas, William I., and Florian Znaniecki. 1918–20. *The Polish Peasant in Europe and America.* 5 vols. Boston: Badger.

Waldinger, Roger, and Joel Perlmann. 1998. "Second Generations: Past, Present, and Future." *Journal of Ethnic and Migration Studies* 24(1): 5–24.

Ware, Caroline F. 1935. *Greenwich Village, 1920–1930: A Comment on American Civilization in the Post-War Years.* Boston: Houghton Mifflin.

Warner, W. Lloyd, and Leo Srole. 1945. *The Social Systems of American Ethnic Groups.* New Haven: Yale University Press.

Wirth, Louis. 1928. *The Ghetto.* Chicago: University of Chicago Press.

Part II

STUDIES OF IMMIGRATION:
RESEARCH FROM A NEW GENERATION
OF SCHOLARS

4

WHICH FACE? WHOSE NATION? IMMIGRATION, PUBLIC HEALTH, AND THE CONSTRUCTION OF DISEASE AT AMERICA'S PORTS AND BORDERS, 1891 TO 1928

Howard Markel and Alexandra Minna Stern

SINCE the early days of the republic, anti-immigrant sentiment has played a part in the forging, expansion, and consolidation of America. Drawing from an extensive array of metaphors and explanations, nativist rhetoric has, at different times, been based on claims of religious incompatibility, cultural backwardness, and economic dependency. All these objections share a general belief that certain immigrants are inassimilable and potentially destructive to American society. One of the most insidious and powerful rationales for restricting immigration has been the need to safeguard the national public health against contagious or infectious diseases, deleterious genetic traits, and even chronic conditions or disabilities. Current concerns about immigrants introducing drug-resistant tuberculosis into American cities and the relatively recent quarantine of Haitians suspected of human immunodeficiency virus (HIV) seropositivity on Guantánamo Bay, Cuba, demonstrate that associations between outsiders and disease are very much with us today.

It was during the late nineteenth century, however, that the immigrant experience—of leaving one's homeland, traveling by land or sea, and being appraised on arrival to America—began to be increasingly mediated through the language and practice of public health. With the promulgation of the Immigration Act of 1891, which mandated the exclusion of persons suffering from a "loathsome or dangerous contagious disease" and, additionally, required steamship companies to disinfect passengers before transit and bear the costs of possible deportation, a new era of inspection began. This and subsequent laws—which re-arranged and expanded the criteria of exclusion—turned entry into the United States into a passage partially defined by a medical vocabulary of pathology and health. Moreover, as the U.S. Public Health Service (USPHS) began to play an important role at ports of entry throughout the country, the negotiation of immigration through a new set of medi-cal criteria became quite real for those migrating during this period. From Ellis Island to Angel Island, the hands, eyes, and instruments of public health officials assayed and scrutinized the physical condition of the nation's future citizens. After what was frequently a frightening ex-amination, the majority of newcomers were admitted; some, however, were deported or hospitalized for weeks or months as they underwent treatment for a number of illnesses ranging from ringworm to trachoma.

In this chapter, we explore the complicated nexus of American im-migration and public health during the Progressive Era. During these four decades, the first great wave of immigration brought more than twenty-five million individuals from Europe, Asia, and the Western Hemisphere to the ports and borders of America. At the same time that rapid urbanization, industrialization, and the settlement of diverse eth-nic groups in most major cities were reshaping the country, medical practice and knowledge were also being swiftly transformed. A water-shed period in modern medicine, the Progressive Era saw the elaboration of germ theory and bacteriology, which revolutionized the understand-ing of the etiologies of many infectious and contagious scourges and contributed to significantly improved means of sanitation and disease prevention. Within the clinic and hospital, as well, new technologies were being developed—such as the X ray and the electrocardiogram—that enabled physicians to extend their external gaze of the patient in-ward to assess the workings of the human body. This period was also characterized by the emergence of a series of novel theories about hered-ity and human capacity. The leitmotivs of the Progressive Era—science, efficiency, and order—cannot be understood without considering the popularity of a national eugenics movement that promoted, and helped to secure, laws to regulate the reproduction of the "unfit."

Although many facets of American immigration have been studied by historians, the dimensions of medicine and public health have only recently received close attention. In 1955, John Higham (1995) authored the first major study of the development of nativism, nationalism, and antiforeign sentiment that included health and disease within its rubric. The role of public health in the triumph of scientific racism in the 1920s, the passage of the Johnson-Reed Act of 1924, and the immigrant experience in general, however, has only begun to be more closely an-alyzed. In his excellent monograph, *Silent Travelers: Germs, Genes, and* the "Immigrant Menace," Alan Kraut (1994) explores the role of the USPHS and other agencies in the construction of foreigners as dangerous, diseased, and contagious. Along with several other scholarly papers (Birn 1997; Dwork 1981; Fairchild and Tynan 1994; Yew 1980), Kraut's book provides a picture of medical inspection at ports of entry— above all, Ellis Island—and describes the methods utilized by public health authorities to gauge the physical and mental constitution of the newly arrived. In spite of the ground broken by these works, there has been little attempt to analyze the intersections between immigration and public health from a synthetic perspective that considers regional differences. The preponderance of attention devoted to Ellis Island and the Atlantic seaboard, which received more than three-quarters of all immigrants during this period, obscures striking variations in the medical inspection process at the country's many immigration stations. From coast to coast and border to border, immigrants were subjected to divergent public health practices and were distinctly perceived according to skin color, nationality, citizenship status, and relationship to the labor market.[1] Taking these regional disparities into account is especially important given that it was during the Progressive Era that public health responsibilities were gradually transferred from local or state authorities to the domain of the federal government (see Marcus 1979). Highlighting and analyzing the nuances of these processes of nationalization and standardization also sheds light on the ways in which earlier patterns may be culturally embedded in the dynamics of contemporary immigrant health care.

Some readers are surprised to learn that contagious and infectious diseases actually played a relatively small role in the exclusion of immigrants; justifications were more frequently based on evidence—or suspicion—of the immigrant's extreme poverty, criminal or immoral behavior, work history as a contract laborer, or subversive political beliefs. At a time when epidemics were on the decline, many public health officials became less concerned with diseases such as cholera, typhoid, and plague and more interested in identifying more ambiguous conditions and syndromes, such as feeblemindedness, constitutional psychopathic inferiority, and poor physique. The three physicians who occupied the position of surgeon general during the Progressive Era reflected this trend and often voiced their anxieties and opinions about what "face" the nation should have and who should constitute the body politic. Between the ubiquitous racializing and "othering" discourses of the Progressive Era and the great ability of germs to level all differences of class, race, or gender, a fluid terminology of disease and pathology developed. Immigrants, public health officials, politicians, and social activists all fought over the definitions of such terms and, in so doing, helped change the landscape and limits of identity and ethnicity in early-twentieth-century America.

Although medical criteria were often used opportunistically to stigmatize specific immigrant groups in moments of perceived social crisis, the associations and metaphors generated by such incidents often created more durable stereotypes. Such associations of disease and disability affected not only the ways in which native-born Americans perceived immigrants during the Progressive Era but also had an impact on how various immigrant communities related to and worked with the American medical and public health establishment.

The View from New York

During the Progressive Era, when a premium was placed on efficiency and expertise, the immigration reception center at Ellis Island, in New York Harbor, was lauded by government officials, physicians, and journalists as a paragon of what Frederick Taylor (1911) characterized as "scientific management." As a result of the Immigration Act of 1891, which placed the administration of immigration issues under the control of the federal government, the Ellis Island immigration facility opened its doors in January 1892. A fire in 1897 destroyed the original wooden structure, and the beaux-arts, red-brick structure that now houses the U.S. Immigration Museum at Ellis Island began operating in 1901.

Built to process approximately five thousand immigrants a day as well as to inspect them for physical, economic, mental, and moral fitness, by 1907, the facility regularly received more than ten thousand immigrants on any given day and more than five hundred thousand annually. The overwhelming majority of these immigrants were from northern, eastern, and southern Europe, the Mediterranean, and, to a much lesser extent, Asia and Latin America. Despite the large number of immigrants requiring physical examinations, only a handful of physicians were on hand to conduct them. In 1892, only six USPHS physicians were assigned to staff the inspection line in the Great Hall of the Contagious Disease Hospital and to check first- and second-class passengers on board incoming ships. This number increased to eight physicians in 1902 and sixteen in 1905; and during the decade before World War I, when immigration reached its peak, twenty-five physicians were stationed at Ellis Island, processing four queues simultaneously. Referred to as "the Line," this form of medical inspection was stridently defended by its practitioners and, just as often, derided by a number of medical observers. The psychiatrist and superintendent of the Johns Hopkins Hospital, Henry M. Hurd, for example, viewed the mass inspection of thousands of immigrants in such a short period as superficial and clinically unsound. In 1892 he wondered aloud to a newspaper reporter, "How can a physician inspect two thousand persons as they should be in a couple of hours, when it sometimes takes a doctor twice as long to diagnose one patient?" ("Awake to Danger, Baltimore Requests the President to Stop Immigration," *Baltimore American*, September 2, 1892, 6).

The jurisdiction of state versus federal power over public health administration was a hotly contested issue in New York Harbor. To accommodate these concerns, incoming ships were first inspected by state health officers at the New York State Quarantine Station, off Staten Island, for evidence of the "quarantinable" diseases, including cholera, typhus, smallpox, bubonic and pneumonic plague, yellow fever, and leprosy. These diseases were believed to be extremely dangerous and easily spread to others by either direct or indirect contact. As a result of improved communication between seaports (via telegraph), sanitation on board the ships themselves, and rigorous medical inspections of immigrants before leaving for America, these epidemic diseases were a relative rarity and easily controllable during the early decades of the twentieth century, especially in comparison with their international spread during the eighteenth and nineteenth centuries.

Medical inspections in New York Harbor were structured by the hierarchies of class and socioeconomic standing. After the inspection at the quarantine station, USPHS physicians boarded transatlantic steamships for a brief and cursory examination of the first- and second-class passengers. Indeed, some immigrants were encouraged to spend the extra capital for a second-class ticket to avoid the more rigorous medical examinations carried out at Ellis Island and other ports. Cabin-class passengers suspected of having a dangerous or loathsome contagious disease or some physical condition that would interfere with their ability to earn a living were transferred by barge, along with those in steerage, for more complete physicals at Ellis Island. Despite repeated warnings from prominent bacteriologists that germs did not respect the boundaries of class, the focal point of these inspections was the most destitute—above all, impoverished Europeans—traveling in the dank, squalid quarters of the steerage.

Public health officials searched for a number of physical and mental conditions as immigrants passed through the labyrinthine, cordoned-off areas that contained the Line. At several checkpoints individuals were scrutinized for specific problems. As they climbed, baggage in tow, up the stairs to the Great Hall, for example, inspectors looked for shortness of breath and signs of cardiac weakness. Public health officers also checked for goiter by observing neck size and shape and attempted to identify rashes on the skin, nails, and scalp, which might indicate ring-worm, favus, or other fungal infections. Most vividly remembered by immigrants who passed through Ellis Island, however, was the dreaded eye examination for trachoma (for examples, see Brownstone, Franck, and Brownstone 1979; University Publications of America 1989). Known to be endemic in eastern Europe, the Mediterranean, and Asia, trachoma left anywhere from one to three out of four of its victims blind. Because its etiology was not yet well understood, physicians found trachoma ex-tremely difficult to diagnose; this situation of uncertainty made eye dis-eases a source of great anxiety for many public health officials and also helped to make the label "trachoma" especially fluid and nebulous. Stethoscopes were commonly employed as part of the inspection pro-cess, and, after 1910, X rays were used to detect pulmonary tuberculosis. The tools of the bacteriology laboratory, such as microscopes, slides, and stains, were also part of the public health officer's repertoire. These were especially important in the diagnosis of sexually transmitted diseases such as syphilis and gonorrhea, which although identifiable by genital examinations, by 1915 could be much more readily determined using culture methods. Other conditions that USPHS officials searched for in immigrants included feeblemindedness, chronic psychopathic inferi-ority, insanity, hernias, rheumatism, malignancies, senility, varicose veins, blindness, and poor eyesight.

In any given year between 1891 and 1928, fewer than 3 percent of those seeking entry to the United States were actually rejected for rea-sons of a contagious, infectious, or loathsome disease, mental disorder, or physical disability. In fact, only 1 percent of those turned away each year at Ellis Island during this period were rejected for medical reasons. What changed as the Progressive Era unfolded, however, as demon-strated by Elizabeth Yew (1980) and Alan Kraut (1994), was the per-centage of those debarred for medical reasons as a fraction of the total number of those debarred for any reason, including evidence of crimi-nal behavior, prostitution, being a contract laborer, untoward political beliefs, and insufficient financial resources. For example, in 1898, of the total number of immigrants excluded, only 2 percent were rejected based on medical criteria. This figure rose to 57 percent in 1913 and two years later to 69 percent (Kraut 1994, 66; Yew 1980, 492; data also drawn from U.S. Treasury 1891–1901, 1902–1911; and USPHS 1912–1930, for the years 1898 to 1924). More significant than the propor-tional increase, however, is the fact that these exclusions were the re-sult not of an increase in the incidence or detection of infectious or contagious diseases, such as trachoma or favus, but rather to expanded scrutiny for, and identification of, chronic disabilities that were deemed likely to inflict an immigrant, who might thereby become dependent on the state, or a "public charge," as codified in the Immigration Act of 1907.

Between 1897 and 1928, Ellis Island doctors moved further and further away from their original charge—to discern and prevent the entry of contagion that posed an immediate threat to the nation—toward the identification of more chronic syndrome-like conditions that seemingly placed the country's economic and productive strength in jeopardy. In the 1910s, for example, public health officers diagnosed higher numbers of cases of poor physique—a favorite "wastebasket" label of nativist groups such as the Immigration Restriction League, which argued that if allowed entry, such debilitated individuals would have an unhealthy impact on the body politic.[2] This was especially pronounced in the case of eastern European Jews fleeing pogroms in the Pale of Settlement; USPHS officials often observed their poor posture, rounded shoulders, and malnourished cast—beyond being effects of poverty these conditions were often traceable to occupations that required them to work "hunched over" at sewing machines in the needle or garment trades or at desks as religious scholars. Even with this trend, however, the number of immigrants excluded for medical reasons on Ellis Island remained low. There are several explanations for this. First, despite the greater role of medical terminology and inspections during this period, USPHS officers were never granted expanded powers by the Congress to actually reject any immigrant. More referees than judges, Ellis Island doctors were ultimately consultants and advisers to immigration officials rather than gendarmes with categorical powers to debar the newly arrived. Second, aid societies, such as the Hebrew Immigrant Aid Society, assisted immigrants in the appeal process and actively contested categories of exclusion such as poor physique and feeblemindedness. Once an immigrant was certified by a physician, his or her case was reviewed by a special board of inquiry, and the final determination depended upon the vagaries of the moment as well as the immigrant's negotiating skills and resources. Third, the citizenship status of Europeans arriving at Ellis Island was more secure than that of Asian immigrants. Usually considered white by law (Haney López 1996), although not according to popular stereotypes, Europeans—at least on paper—were eligible for naturalization and possessed certain political and legal rights. Freedom to migrate to America was not severely hampered until the enactment of strict quotas of 1921 and 1924. Based on a mixture of nativist thought, arguments about the potentially devastating economic effects of open immigration, and sensational eugenic "evidence" of the effects of immigrants on the national "germ plasm," these immigration restriction acts effectively slammed the gates shut to European and Asian immigrants for more than forty years.

At the Edge of the Pacific:
Angel Island, San Francisco Bay

Between 1910 and 1940, three thousand miles away from New York Harbor, a federal port of entry was maintained at Angel Island in the San Francisco Bay. Before 1910, Angel Island had served as a detention center for Chinese immigrants awaiting medical examination and processing by immigration authorities at the Embarcadero. Historian Roger Daniels (1997) contrasts, perhaps too starkly, Ellis Island—under the shadow, literally, of the Statue of Liberty—as an icon of "welcome and acceptance" to the smaller and more removed center at Angel Island, which was instead, he writes, a site of "suspicion and rejection." Indeed, the history of Asian immigration to the United States encompasses a very different story from the one that characterizes the eastern and southern European exodus from 1880 to 1924. As a result of several anti-Chinese congressional debates in the late 1870s and the passage of the Chinese Exclusion Act in 1882, which was extended for another ten years in 1892 and again in 1902, harsh numerical restrictions were placed on Chinese immigration. Within an economy of racial perception that revolved around fears of cultural and biological difference, Asians were viewed as distinct "others." Whereas they disparaged the "new" European immigrants as swarthy and sickly, many Americans viewed Asians as totally foreign and inassimilable, contending that "racial separateness between whites and Asians could never be blurred no matter how many coats of Americanization were painted on them" (Markel 1997, 85).

Although San Francisco authorities had long overseen an immigration reception center at the city's waterfront, they agreed to relinquish control in the early years of the twentieth century after a poorly managed epidemic of bubonic plague struck the Chinatown district and exposed the fissures between municipal, state, and federal powers with regard to public health.[3] The federally operated Angel Island facility, about a forty-five-minute boat ride from the San Francisco waterfront, opened in 1910. It was composed of a series of wooden structures that included a hospital, a small administration building, detention quarters, and a wharf; eventually, a laundry facility, extra barracks, and power-plant buildings were added. Like most immigration or quarantine stations in the United States at the turn of the century, the Angel Island facility was inadequate in terms of space, cleanliness, and staffing. Unlike these other stations, however, Angel Island was almost exclusively dedicated to the inspection, disinfection, and, at times, detention of Chinese, Japanese, and other Asian immigrants who sailed in steamships across the Pacific Ocean.

Exact numbers of immigrants processed at Angel Island are difficult to ascertain. Best estimates range between sixty thousand and one hundred thousand during the port's decades of operation, a mere fraction of the more than 10 million who passed through Ellis Island during this same period. The majority of those who came through Angel Island were Chinese merchants and their families, students, tourists, and those who could claim American citizenship. Chinese and Japanese diplomats and Europeans and Asians traveling first class were not required to stop at Angel Island. Sizable numbers of Japanese immigrants also passed through Angel Island. This group included roughly ten thousand "picture brides" and U.S.-born Japanese Americans who had been educated in Japan and were permitted to enter America as a result of the "gentlemen's agreement" signed by Theodore Roosevelt and the prime minister of Japan in 1907. There were also several thousand immigrants from India, Korea, and other Asian countries, a small number of Europeans, and fewer still from the Caribbean and West Indies (Daniels 1997).

Beyond the standard medical examination, Asian immigrants were inspected for several diseases that had been identified by surveillance studies of the most prevalent infectious and parasitic diseases in Asia at the time. These included trachoma, bubonic and pneumonic plague, hookworm (uncinariasis), threadworm (filiariasis), and liver fluke (chlonoriasis). The search for hookworm and other intestinal parasitic infections was especially embarrassing for Asian immigrants because it required them to submit a stool specimen, often on demand. Immigrants coming through Angel Island were also checked over for sexually transmitted diseases, tuberculosis, and chronic physical disorders such as cardiac abnormalities, hernias, varicose veins, and various mental disorders. As on Ellis Island, the severity of the medical examination was dictated by class distinctions. At Angel Island, however, these differences were compounded by contemporary racial prejudices. For example, when examining first-class passengers who came through San Francisco Bay—for the most part, white Europeans and other American citizens returning home after overseas travel—USPHS officers were far more conscientious about taking sanitary precautions, such as routine hand washing and the sterilization of clinical instruments, than when they handled the steerage class, made up principally of Chinese.[4] As on the eastern seaboard, those traveling first class were subjected only to a visual examination for trachoma and were spared the uncomfortable and startling eyelid aversion that was mandatory for Asian steerage passengers arriving at the San Francisco Bay. This conscious policy was communicated by a physician stationed at Yokohama, Japan, in a 1903 letter addressed to the surgeon general. This physician asserted that—on either side of the Pacific Ocean—manual inspections for trachoma be carried out only on "steerage aliens" because "the aversion of eyelids, essential for the diagnosis of trachoma, would, if practiced upon cabin passengers, be likely to embarrass the work of the Service here" (INS 1994b).

The racial dimension of these differences in treatment becomes more striking when the relatively high number of Chinese immigrants rejected is taken into account. For example, although trachoma was typically associated with eastern and southern European immigrants during the first decade of the twentieth century, at least one-third of all Chinese debarred from entry into the United States were also certified with this diagnosis. Even more telling, however, is the fact that of the approximately sixty thousand Chinese who passed through Angel Island during this period, close to ten thousand were deported. This rate, roughly 17 percent, is at least five times as great as the 1 to 3 percent noted at Ellis Island. Moreover, although the Chinese were never more than 1 percent of the nation's immigrant population during these years, they made up more than 4 percent of the number of immigrants deported each year (Daniels 1997, 6–7; Salyer 1995, 59–60; also see figures in U.S. Treasury 1891–1901, 1902–1911; and USPHS 1912–1930, for the years 1910 to 1930). A combination of factors—a general climate of Sinophobia supported by a wide spectrum of American society, associations of Asian immigrants with the debilitating diseases of trachoma and hookworm, and Asians' legal status as noncitizens—often translated into insensitive treatment on Angel Island. While detained in the barracks or hospital, many Chinese expressed their anger and sense of isolation by inscribing poems on the walls. In 1970, these traces of the past were discovered by a park ranger, and they have since been preserved. In one verse, an anonymous immigrant wrote,

> "I cannot bear to describe the harsh treatment by the doctors/Being stabbed for blood samples and examined for hookworms, was even more pitiful" (quoted in Lai, Lim, and Yung 1980, 100).

The Texas-Mexico Border: Laborers from a Nearby Land

Unlike Asians, who were subjected to the most exclusionary laws of any ethnic group from the late nineteenth to the mid-twentieth century, Mexicans—desired as laborers throughout the Southwest and in American cities and industries—were continually waived from the requirements of restrictive immigration laws. When the Immigration Act of 1917 was passed, for example, growers and industrialists were able to convince President Woodrow Wilson to exempt Mexicans from the literacy test, head tax, and contract labor clause (Reisler 1976). Nonetheless, a variety of intertwined factors—including high demands for Mexican labor until the Great Depression, the porosity of the two-thousand-mile boundary line that divides the two countries, and the outbreak of the Mexican Revolution in 1910—turned the border into a region marked by tension and complex migratory patterns.

Physicians from the USPHS were stationed at different points along the border as early as the 1890s; standardized procedures of medical inspection, however, were not put in force until the early twentieth century. During this period—before arrivals were grouped into nonstatistical locals and statistical immigrants with the intent of settling in the United States—between ten thousand and one hundred thousand immigrants were inspected annually at ports extending along the Rio Grande from Brownsville to El Paso. Carried out both in buildings next to the international bridges that spanned from Mexico to America and in bustling train stations, these examinations included checks for trachoma, favus, tuberculosis, syphilis, evidence of smallpox vaccination, and, on rare occasion, hookworm. The general clinical examinations on the Texas-Mexico border, unlike those in New York Harbor, were collapsed into a continuous and often assaulting process of entry.

Until the second decade of the twentieth century, the lack of epidemics and a fluid border economy of peoples, industries, and culture allowed for a relatively lax inspection procedure and easy passage through the El Paso and Laredo stations. During this early period, in fact, immigration and public health officials were primarily concerned not with Mexicans but with the Chinese, Syrians, and Greeks who were apparently avoiding Ellis Island and using the border as a back door into America.[5] Local oral histories of border residents and the records of the Immigration and Naturalization Service reveal that until the first decade of this century, Mexicans commonly came into the United States unquestioned; for this reason, Greeks and Syrians often sought to learn enough basic Spanish to enter America as mexicanos.[6]

As the twentieth century progressed, however, and Mexicans began to settle in the United States—often turning a temporary stay into permanent residence—the situation along the border began to shift. Partly for these demographic reasons, and also because the USPHS was in a general phase of expansion, a disinfection plant was built in 1910 alongside the El Paso immigration station in order to bathe "every arrival from Mexico" with "soap and warm water" ("All Immigrants Will Be Washed," El Paso Herald, July 21, 1910, 9). Nonetheless, contagious diseases were few and far between, and U.S.-Mexican relations were relatively harmonious during this period. In 1910, for example, fewer than 1 percent of all Mexican immigrants were debarred for medical reasons;

of 46,385 individuals inspected, only 328 were found to be suffering from a disease, mental defect, or condition that rendered them likely to become a "public charge" (U.S. Treasury 1902 to 1911, for fiscal year 1910, 163). The available annual reports from 1900 to 1930 reveal that, for Mexicans, these numbers remained consistently low; only rarely were Mexican immigrants diagnosed with diseases such as trachoma and favus, which were seen with much more regularity on the two coasts.

This situation changed drastically in 1917, however. After the Mexican Revolution erupted in 1911, USPHS and immigration officials became increasingly preoccupied with the openness of the border and the growing circulation of insurgents, refugees, and temporary laborers in the twin cities of El Paso–Juárez and Laredo–Nuevo Laredo. With news of a typhus epidemic in Mexico's interior beginning in 1915 and the discovery of several cases of the fever in El Paso in 1916, this concern became even more heightened, prompting the USPHS to send several high-ranking surgeons to the border to assess the threat of disease. In a climate of military tension, as General John J. Pershing futilely attempted to hunt down the revolutionary Pancho Villa in northern Mexico, and after a spate of several deaths, including that of El Paso's city physician, the USPHS decided in January 1917 that the moment for a full-scale quarantine had arrived. This unilateral decision on the part of U.S. officials did little to pacify or control augmenting tensions. On the morning the quarantine was put into effect, a group of two hundred Mexican women, most likely working as domestics in homes of the El Paso Anglo elite, stormed the immigration bridge and station. Led by what one local paper called the "auburn-haired amazon," these protesters attacked the public health and immigration officials, declaring they would not be subjected to degrading medical inspections ("Auburn-Haired Amazon at Sante Fe Bridge Leads Feminine Outbreak," *El Paso Times*, January 29, 1917, 1).

The purpose of the quarantine, according to the USPHS physician in charge at the time, was to disinfect and delouse "all persons coming to El Paso from Mexico, considered as likely to be vermin infested" (Pierce 1917, 427). Under the constant gaze of attendants, immigrants were stripped naked, showered with kerosene, examined for lice and nits, and vaccinated for smallpox if deemed necessary. At the end of this process, freshly sterilized clothing was returned to its owners, who also received a USPHS certificate verifying that the bearer had "been deloused, bathed, vaccinated, clothing and baggage disinfected" (Pierce 1917, 428). Several months after the quarantine had been in effect, officials reported that the threat of typhus had all but disappeared. Despite this fact, however, the border quarantine remained in effect until at least the 1930s; a public health response to an apparently impending epidemic had been transformed into an extended quarantine along the Texas-Mexico border (Stern 1999).

During the 1920s, disinfection plants were expanded and further outfitted at several Texas immigration stations. Delousing and fumigation were compulsory for daily laborers and immigrants; Mexican workers who lived in Juárez or Nuevo Laredo and commuted to El Paso or Laredo to work each day had to undergo sterilization on a weekly basis (INS 1994a). These requirements for entry into the United States were enforced both in the larger cities and in smaller towns with ports of entry such as Terlingua, Roma, and Rio Grande City. In 1926, John W. Tappan, a local physician affiliated with the USPHS, published an article in the *Journal of the American Medical Association* that placed the quarantine in a national perspective. Justifying the ongoing disinfections on the basis of typhus outbreaks in the middle of the preceding decade, Tappan wrote, "Conditions differ from those on the Canadian border. We have here to contend with an alien race: one with a different language, different customs, different moral standards, and different diseases" (1926, 1022). For their part, many Mexicans attempted to avoid passage through the border plants. In Laredo, the increasing number of Mexicans crossing into the United States at undesignated and illegal ports of entry to evade delousing, vaccination, and other immigration requirements caused sufficient alarm for the USPHS to create a mounted quarantine guard. This service, which should be seen as a precursor to the U.S. Border Patrol, began monitoring the Rio Grande for "aliens" in 1921, and their daily journals record activities ranging from apprehension to vaccination.[7]

On the Texas-Mexico border, the discrepancies between the constant demand of southwestern growers and industrialists for cheap labor and the mandate of the USPHS to protect the public health brought about a sui generis situation of protracted quarantine. Desired as laborers, Mexicans were allowed to enter the United States only after they had been cleansed and disinfected. This process, on the one hand, was pivotal to the construction of the border as a solid boundary line between the two nations and, on the other, worked to associate Mexicans, especially from the working classes, with filth and disease. During the late 1920s, when eugenicists and legislators sought to severely restrict Mexican immigration to a quota, stereotypes of the louse-ridden Mexican peon were common. Although Mexicans were not numerically restricted nor denied rights of naturalization based on "race," within the racist climate of the Progressive Era and the 1920s, the inclusion of Mexicans and Mexican Americans within the body politic came at a high cost of humiliating disinfections, economic disenfranchisement, and, frequently, the limits of de facto social segregation (see Gutiérrez 1995).

The Third Coast: Port Huron and Detroit, Michigan

The severity of the standardized quarantine along the Texas-Mexico border and the inspection procedures for immigrants coming through Ellis and Angel Islands is thrown into relief by an examination of the activities of the USPHS stationed along the Canadian border at Detroit and Port Huron, Michigan. Whereas more than a dozen officers rotated between Texas ports of entry, only a few physicians were stationed in Michigan. Overburdened with a demanding schedule of inspections at railway and ferry stations, until the 1920s, USPHS officers along the "third coast" lacked many medical instruments, hospital facilities, and central headquarters. Although these inspection stations were heavily trafficked, processing between two thousand and twenty thousand emigrants a year, the quiescence at Detroit and Port Huron is striking.

The absence of activity at Michigan immigration stations can be explained by several factors (Stern and Markel 1999). First, most immigrants entering through Detroit and Port Huron had already undergone quarantine inspections, when the transoceanic steamships they had boarded in Europe landed in cities along the eastern seaboard. Insulated by public health controls in cities such as New York, Boston, and Baltimore, Michigan was largely untouched by cholera, typhus, or plague epidemics. Second, an amicable relationship with Canadian immigration officials—which included an arrangement allowing USPHS officials to board trains and maintain stations in several provinces—obviated the kind of political strife that characterized U.S.-Mexican border relations. Finally, during an era of racial prejudices that deeply influenced medical inspections at Ellis Island, Angel Island, and Texas cities, the immigrants who passed through Michigan's gates were classified, in the words of the USPHS physician who worked at Port Huron for more than twenty years, as principally "the more desirable northern or western European" ("Annual Report: Medical Inspection: Aliens: Port Huron, Mich.," 1928, Domestic Stations, Port Huron, General Subject File, 1924–1935, NC 34 E10, Records of the USPHS).

Working conditions at Michigan's immigration stations, however, were less than optimal. Both the Port Huron and Detroit stations lacked instruments such as microscopes, stethoscopes, and other laboratory materials until the 1920s. Nor did the USPHS establish detention areas, hospitals, or even a room for basic medical consultations during the Progressive Era. For these reasons, public health officers were required to travel long distances from train depots to ferry stations—and, with the advent of the automobile, to the terminus of car tunnels—to examine immigrants. A 1914 report by a surgeon who had been directed to Port Huron to take stock of the immigration station wrote the surgeon general that "the physical facilities are poor, the officer being located in a small wooden building which has been condemned by the local health officer as unsanitary. It is poorly equipped. There is an unserviceable stethoscope and no microscope" (letter from Surgeon Louis L. Williams to the Surgeon General, August 12, 1914, file 460, Port Huron, Central File 1897–1923, Records of the USPHS).

Even at the largely neglected Michigan ports of entry, however, immigrants were excluded on the basis of medical criteria that drew directly from contemporary ethnic stereotypes. This was particularly true for the ambiguous diagnoses of feeblemindedness and poor physique. In the early 1920s, for example, after a young Jewish boy was certified as feebleminded, local public health authorities urged that he nevertheless be allowed to remain in the United States based on his ability "to take care of himself and manage money like others of his race" (letter from Dr. Frank J. Kilroy to Honorable Henry Behrendt, U.S. Marshal, September 14, 1921, file 3690, Detroit, Central File 1897–1923, Records of the USPHS). Despite such pleas on the boy's behalf, however, the surgeon general, Hugh S. Cumming, replied that the Immigration Act of 1917 mandated the deportation of the mentally defective, "not so much for the purpose of preventing the admission of alien paupers as it is for the protection of the race: the prevention of the propagation of feebleminded strains in our population" (letter from Surgeon General Cumming to Charles E. Townsend, November 22, 1921, file 3690, Detroit, Central File 1897–1923, Records of the USPHS). Beyond demonstrating the potential power of medical labels to deport immigrants, this incident also reflects the kinds of frictions between federal and local authorities that typified many immigration stations. Nonetheless, the inspection process at Port Huron and Detroit, Michigan—as with similar checkpoints along the Canadian border—was mainly one of an attentive guard on a quiet watch. Training and protocol dictated the same level of vigilance employed at other American ports and borders, but the fact remains, the enemy was nowhere near.

Conclusion

At the core of the many unsuccessful attempts to exclude immigrants for reasons of illness or disability are a series of interconnected questions: What were the categories of exclusion, and how were they employed? Who was eligible to become an American citizen? What face—

literally—should the nation have? Although broad patterns of exclusion characterized the country during the Progressive Era, it is important to recognize how local and regional social, physical, and cultural forces shaped immigrant inspections and the construction of disease at America's ports and borders. Medical examinations differed according to variations in geography, commercial activity, demography, relations between local, state, and federal governments, and institutional capacities. Dominant national perceptions about specific immigrant groups—in terms of skin color, facial features, and associations with a particular illness or condition (whether real, exaggerated, or perceived)—were also significant factors. Finally, the outcome of medical diagnoses was also structured by the immigrant's citizenship status, available social support mechanisms, level of education, and relationship to the labor market.

Perhaps the most compelling conclusion that can be drawn from this comparative sketch of medical inspections relates to the fluid nature of the exclusionary labels themselves. If one label failed to work in rejecting the most objectionable, a new one (albeit, typically, just as unsuccessful) was soon created, whether of contagion, mental disorder, chronic disability, or defective physique. Although some medical categories of exclusion were more popular in certain regions of the country, almost all were somehow tainted with the underlying idea that the immigrant group in question threatened the nation in a particular way.

The fluidity of medical labels is nowhere clearer than the way exclusionary language often worked in tandem with the demands of the labor market and capitalist enterprises. Eastern European Jews were seen on the Atlantic seaboard, for example, as a threat both to the economic and public health of America. As early as 1893, one immigration official equated the propensity of eastern European Jews to form labor unions and espouse socialistic beliefs with disease and ruination (Schulteis 1893, 25). Some sixteen years later, the secretary of the Immigration Restriction League, Prescott Hall, blamed the "poor physique of Hebrews" on their inability to find jobs in farming or other forms of "hard manual labor" and "to succeed in the struggle for economic independence" (1908, 50). This kind of logic, correlating disease with subversion and emasculation, bolstered arguments for the debarment of Jews from the American body politic. Conversely, along the Texas-Mexico border, where cheap labor was in constant demand, Mexicans—who for various reasons were less likely to be members of socialist or anarchist unions— might have been labeled as dirty and filthy, but physique was rarely a cause for debarment. In 1910, for example, before the outbreak of the Mexican Revolution, USPHS authorities at El Paso stated that "the majority of applicants for admission are healthy Mexican laborers from the interior, who, as a rule, are of fair physique" (U.S. Treasury 1902–1911, for the fiscal year 1910, 164). After the implementation of the quarantine, moreover, when Mexicans were increasingly associated with typhus and other ailments, their weakened bodily constitutions were seen as an asset to agricultural toil. In the 1920s, many farmers and industrialists in favor of continued waivers on immigration laws for Mexicans began to assert that the "physical attributes" of the Mexican "allowed him to be a perfect stoop laborer. Because the Mexican was small in size, agile, and wiry, growers explained, his ability in the fruit, vegetable, sugar beet, and cotton fields far exceeded that of the white man" (quoted in Reisler 1976, 138).

In an era in which differences in skin color and physical characteristics were becoming increasingly medicalized, it is not surprising that exclusionary labels of disease and disability became an essential aspect of repeated attempts to legislate immigration restriction. Though medical labels never became the predominant reason for debarring specific immigrant groups, their use helped to inspire more durable biological metaphors for describing the potential risks of open immigration to the physical, economic, and social health of the nation. Such metaphors only became more resilient as the language of eugenics gained ubiquity in medical and popular circles during the Progressive Era. Diseased newcomers, eugenicists effectively argued, not only jeopardized the present, with their propensity toward contagion, poverty, and alien beliefs; their admission also endangered the future of American society. Long after the arrival of the neurasthenic Jew, the criminally minded Italian, the dirty and lousy Mexican, and the trachomatous or parasite-infested Asian to American ports and borders, their defective genes would multiply and contaminate the national body. Fears of a country beset with chronic diseases and disabilities was central to the economic, social, and cultural arguments articulated by nativists during the 1920s and helped to ensure passage of the immigration restriction acts of 1921, 1924, and 1928 that reduced the flow of immigrants from Europe and Asia to a mere trickle.

A previous version of this chapter appeared in *American Behavioral Scientist* 1999, vol. 42, no. 9.

Notes

1. Gender and marital-familial status also played an important role in determining an immigrant's experience at both the hands of the

USPHS and the Immigration and Naturalization Service. For an excellent introduction to the history of immigrant women during the Progressive Era, see Gabaccia 1994. Also see Ewen 1985.

2. For a description of the conditions scrutinized by USPHS officers at immigration centers during this period, see USPHS 1917; for a description of the work of the Immigration Restriction League to have medical diagnoses applied to policies of immigration restriction, see Immigration Restriction League Papers; also see Solomon 1956.

3. The best social history of the San Francisco bubonic plague epidemic from 1900 to 1901 is McClain 1994; also see Risse 1992.

4. See INS 1994c, which details procedures and tensions over trachoma examinations of Chinese and Japanese immigrants on the Pacific Coast.

5. A. A. Seraphic, who was commissioned in 1906 to carry out undercover investigations of Syrian immigration from Mexico into the United States, consistently associated Syrians with trachoma and other contagious diseases; see INS 1994d.

6. For an incisive reconstruction of the voices of Mexican immigrants with respect to the solidification of the border, see Sánchez 1994, chapter 2.

7. The records of the USPHS from Laredo contain numerous such journals; see, for example, *Copy of Report of Mounted Guards Heston B. Martin and Alvis C. Taylor*, 1923, file 1169, Laredo and San Antonio, Texas, Central File 1897–1923, Records of USPHS.

References

Birn, Anne-Emanuelle. 1997. "Six Seconds per Eyelid: The Medical Inspection of Immigrants at Ellis Island, 1892–1914." *Dynamis* 17: 281–316.

Brownstone, David, Irene M. Franck, and Douglass L. Brownstone. 1979. *Island of Hope, Island of Tears.* New York: Rawson Wade Publishers.

Daniels, Roger. 1997. "No Lamps Were Lit for Them: Angel Island and the Historiography of Asian American Immigration." *Journal of American Ethnic History* 17(1): 2–18.

Dwork, Deborah. 1981. "Health Conditions of Immigrant Jews on the Lower East Side of New York, 1880–1914." *Medical History* 25(1): 1–40.

Ewen, Elizabeth. 1985. *Immigrant Women in the Land of Dollars: Life and Culture on the Lower East Side, 1890–1925.* New York: Monthly Review Press.

Fairchild, Amy, and Eileen A. Tynan. 1994. "Policies of Containment: Immigration in the Era of AIDS." *American Journal of Public Health* 84(12): 2011–17.

Gabaccia, Donna. 1994. *From the Other Side: Women, Gender, and Im-*

migrant Life in the United States, 1820–1990. Bloomington: Indiana University Press.

Gutiérrez, David G. 1995. *Walls and Mirrors: Mexican Americans, Mexican Immigrants, and the Politics of Ethnicity.* Berkeley: University of California Press.

Hall, Prescott F. 1908. *Immigration and Its Effects upon the United States.* 2d ed. New York: Henry Holt.

Haney López, Ian F. 1996. *White by Law: The Legal Construction of Race.* New York: New York University Press.

Higham, John. 1995. *Strangers in the Land: Patterns of American Nativism, 1860–1925.* 2d ed. New Brunswick: Rutgers University Press.

Immigration Restriction League Papers. Harvard University Rare Book and Manuscript Collection. Houghton Library.

Kraut, Alan. 1994. *Silent Travelers: Germs, Genes, and the "Immigrant Menace."* Baltimore: Johns Hopkins University Press.

Lai, Him Mark, Genny Lim, and Judy Yung. 1980. *Island: Poetry and History of Chinese Immigrants on Angel Island, 1910–1940.* Seattle: University of Washington Press.

Marcus, Alan I. 1979. "Disease Prevention in America: From a Local to a National Outlook, 1880–1910." *Bulletin of the History of Medicine* 53(2): 184–203.

Markel, Howard. 1997. *Quarantine! East European Jewish Immigrants and the New York City Epidemics of 1892.* Baltimore: Johns Hopkins University Press.

McClain, Charles. 1994. *In Search of Equality: The Chinese Struggle Against Discrimination in Nineteenth-Century America.* Berkeley: University of California Press.

Pierce, C. C. 1917. "Combating Typhus Fever on the Mexican Border." *United States Public Health Service Reports.* Washington: U.S. Government Printing Office.

Records of the U.S. Public Health Service (USPHS). Record group 90. College Park, Md.: National Archives.

Reisler, Mark. 1976. *By the Sweat of Their Brow: Mexican Immigrant Labor in the United States, 1900–1940.* Westport, Conn.: Greenwood Press.

Risse, Guenther B. 1992. "A Long Pull, a Strong Pull, and All Together: San Francisco and Bubonic Plague, 1907–1908." *Bulletin of the History of Medicine* 66(2): 260–86.

Salyer, Lucy E. 1995. *Laws as Harsh as Tigers: Chinese Immigrants and the Shaping of Modern Immigration Law.* Chapel Hill: University of North California Press.

Sánchez, George J. 1994. *Becoming Mexican American: Ethnicity, Culture, and Identity in Chicano Los Angeles, 1900–1945.* New York: Oxford University Press.

Schulteis, Herman J. 1893. *Report on European Immigration to the United States of America, and the Causes which Incite the Same; with Recommendations for the Further Restriction of Undesirable Immigration and the Establishment of a National Quarantine.* Washington: U.S. Government Printing Office.

Solomon, Barbara. 1956. *Ancestors and Immigrants: A Changing New England Tradition.* Cambridge, Mass.: Harvard University Press.

Stern, Alexandra Minna. 1999. "Buildings, Boundaries, and Blood: Medicalization and Nation-Building on the United States–Mexico Border, 1910–1930." *Hispanic American Historical Review* 79(1): 41–81.

Stern, Alexandra Minna, and Howard Markel. 1999. "All Quiet on the Third Coast: Medical Inspections of Immigrants in Michigan." *Public Health Reports* 114(2): 178–82.

Tappan, John W. 1926. "Protective Health Measures on the United States–Mexico Border." *Journal of the American Medical Association* 87(13): 1022–26.

Taylor, Frederick. 1911. *The Principles of Scientific Management.* New York: Harper and Brothers.

University Publications of America. 1989. *Voices from Ellis Island: An Oral History of American Immigration.* Frederick, Md.: University Publications of America.

U.S. Department of the Treasury. 1891–1901. *Annual Reports of the Surgeon General of the United States Marine Hospital Service.* Washington: U.S. Government Printing Office.

———. 1902–1911. *Annual Reports of the Surgeon General of the United States Marine Hospital Service.* Washington: U.S. Government Printing Office.

U.S. Immigration and Naturalization Service (INS). 1994a. Letter from Irving McNeil to John W. Tappan, Officer in Charge at El Paso, December 22, 1923. Reel 3. Casefile 52903/29, Record Group 85. Microfilm Records, Series A, Part 1, Asian Immigration and Exclusion, 1906–1913. Bethesda, Md.: American University Publications.

———. 1994b. Letter from Medical Officer in Command, Yokohama, Japan, to the U.S. Surgeon General, September 23, 1903. Reel 14. Casefile 52495/49, Record Group 85. Microfilm Records, Series A, Part 1, Asian Immigration and Exclusion, 1906–1913. Bethesda, Md.: American University Publications.

———. 1994c. Casefiles 52495/49, 52495/49A, 52495/49B, Record Group 85. Microfilm Records, Series A, Part 1, Asian Immigration and Exclusion, 1906–1913. Bethesda, Md.: American University Publications.

———. 1994d. *Seraphic Report Regarding Conditions on the Mexican Border, 1906–1907.* Casefile 51423/1, Reel 1, Record Group 85. Microfilm Records, Series A, Part 2, Mexican Immigration, 1906–1930. Bethesda, Md.: American University Publications.

U.S. Public Health Service (USPHS). 1912–1930. *Annual Reports of the Surgeon General of the United States Marine Hospital Service.* Washington: U.S. Government Printing Office.

———. 1917. *Book of Instructions for the Medical Inspection of Immigrants.* Washington: U.S. Government Printing Office.

Yew, Elizabeth. 1980. "Medical Inspection of the Immigrant at Ellis Island, 1891–1924." *Bulletin of the New York Academy of Medicine* 56(5): 488–510.

5

"EXPORTED TO CARE": A TRANSNATIONAL HISTORY OF FILIPINO NURSE MIGRATION TO THE UNITED STATES

Catherine Ceniza Choy

T HE INTERNATIONAL migration of Filipino nurses is often charac- terized as a post–1965 phenomenon. Between 1966 and 1985, an estimated twenty-five thousand Filipino nurses migrated to the United States (Ong and Azores 1994, 164); by the late 1960s, the Philip- pines had replaced Canada as the major country of origin of foreign- trained nurses in the United States; and in 1979, a World Health Organi- zation report observed that among nurse-sending countries, the largest outflow of nurses by far was from the Philippines (Mejía, Pizorkí, and Royston 1979, 43–45). The Philippines had became the world's largest exporter of nurses, with significant numbers of Filipino nurses working in the Middle East, Germany, and Canada as well as the United States.

To understand this phenomenon, sociologists, immigration histo- rians, and scholars of Asian American studies have generally turned to contemporary government policies. The U.S. Immigration Act of 1965, for example, encouraged the immigration of Filipino professionals through its occupational preference categories, which favored the entry of professionals with needed skills (Allen 1977). With the establishment of the Marcos dictatorship in 1972, the Philippine government focused on the development of an export-oriented economy, which included the export of labor as well as goods (Abella 1979; Hawes 1989).

Contemporary government policies help to explain the high levels of immigration among professionals—including doctors, accountants, nutritionists, and physical therapists, as well as nurses—from the Phil- ippines to the United States after 1965; however, they do not explain why so many Filipinas have become nurses, nor why Filipino nurses constitute such a significant portion of that migration. What enables and compels so many Filipino nurses to work abroad? This chapter addresses these questions historically by exploring connections between early-twentieth-century colonialist attitudes, mid-twentieth-century U.S. foreign policy, and post-1965 Filipino nurse migration.

Foundations: Americanized Credentials, Work Cultures, and Dreams

The contemporary international migration of Filipino nurses is inextricably linked to the history of American imperialism and the early-twentieth-century U.S. colonization of the Philippines. As a part of the establishment of an Americanized training hospital system in the Philippines during the colonial period, new standards were instituted to improve the professional skills and standing of the nursing labor force. These changes included an Americanized nursing-school curriculum, English language fluency, and professionalization of the nursing work culture. Studies by Paul Ong and Tania Azores (1994) and Tomoji Ishi (1987) have linked the Americanized nursing-school curriculum and the study of English in the Philippines to the later migration, but questions remain: What did this curriculum entail? How did it develop? Why did it take root so successfully in the Philippines? As American nursing leader and secretary of the International Council of Nurses, Lavinia Dock, noted in her early-twentieth-century history of nursing education, "nursing in the Philippines has a history on which we may look back with satisfaction, for, while carried on almost entirely by Americans in the early days of the occupation, its speedy adoption into the life and education of the Filipinos themselves and its wonderfully rapid development have probably not been surpassed elsewhere" (1912, 307–8).

The Americanized nursing curriculum was officially introduced into Philippine nurse training in 1907, with the establishment of St. Paul's Hospital, the Civil Hospital (which later merged with and became known as Philippine General Hospital), and University Hospital (later known as St. Luke's Hospital) in Manila. Dock reports that the course of study in these hospital programs included, "besides all the usual subjects, the nursing of tropical diseases, the sanitary work of the Bureau of Health, public instruction in dispensary and school work, English grammar and colloquial English, and industrial and living conditions in the islands" (1912, 316). The "usual subjects" included anatomy and physiology, practical nursing, materia-medica, massage, and bacteriology. The first Filipino nursing students also heard lectures on medicine, communicable diseases, and operating room techniques. Throughout American colonial rule, faculty and supervisors were predominantly American nurses and doctors. The study of English as an integral part of the curriculum was unique in colonial education in general and especially so in medical training. By contrast, for example, British colonial authorities originally trained Indian physicians in their native tongue and translated Western medical texts for their instruction.[1]

Although the improved standards and English language study theoretically enabled Filipino nurses to practice in the United States, their preparation in the Philippines was not a strictly academic affair. It also required an understanding of the social, cultural, and gendered dimensions of American nursing. The early training of Filipino nurses followed trends in nurse training in the United States, which was itself undergoing transformation in the early years of the twentieth century.

In the mid-nineteenth century United States, nursing was primarily the work of white, native-born, poor, and older women who entered nursing at the end of their working lives, often for lack of other options (Reverby 1987). Hospital nurses were often former patients, because the prevalence of cross-infection within hospitals made recruitment of nurses difficult. Responding to increasing concerns over the minimal requirements for career nursing, American professional nursing leaders in the early years of the twentieth century lobbied to raise the standards of nursing programs and professionalize the field in an effort to regulate the oversupply of ill-trained practitioners and increase nurses' prestige and autonomy (Reverby 1987). Professionalization involved measures such as the reduction of the number of nursing schools and more stringent entrance requirements.

Inspired by the work of Florence Nightingale, and in an effort to recruit younger women into their ranks, American nursing leaders also tried to recast the image of nursing as a profession that could provide "suitable employment" for young "gentlewomen," one that embodied the virtues and qualities of middle- and upper-class womanhood in Victorian America. Hoping to create the hospital training program as a "protected environment" managed by a "hospital family" (Reverby 1987, 48), leaders in the profession sought to institute sanitary measures as standard hospital procedure, and hospital nursing schools recruited young women from rural areas by promoting the "safe haven" the schools could provide in urban areas.

Like their American counterparts, the first Philippine nursing schools recruited young, healthy, "moral" women from "respectable" Filipino families. St. Paul's Hospital, Philippine General Hospital, and St. Luke's Hospital selected nursing students with the following qualifications: "good and sound physical and mental health, good moral character, good family and social standing, and recommendations from three different persons well known in the community" (Girón-Tupas 1952, 62). Students were recruited from areas as far away as Cebu in the Visayan islands (the middle region of the archipelago) to train in hospitals in Manila, on the island of Luzon (the northern region of the archipelago). The first Filipino nursing students traveled far from their families to live in American colonial government dormitories. In 1906, a dormitory opened for Filipino female students enrolled in the Philippine Normal School, whose program included training in "social graces" and methods of "home management" (Girón-Tupas 1952, 39). American and Filipino supporters acted as members of the hospital "family." Sofia de Veyra, a Filipina supporter for nursing schools in the Philippines, recalled, "We did a lot of mothering to the first girls and used a great deal of diplomacy and tact to keep them going and keeping up their interest in their work" (Girón-Tupas 1952, 34).

Philippine nursing schools followed the American example in educational standards as well as in recruitment practices. In 1907, the entrance requirements of the first government training school for Filipino nurses included completion of the seventh grade and satisfactory performance on a qualifying examination. In 1917, the largest hospital school of nursing, Philippine General, raised its entrance requirements, adding completion of the first year of secondary school, and in 1930, the completion of secondary school was made mandatory for entering students. By 1933, Philippine General Hospital School of Nursing gave preference for admission to applicants who had earned six units of credit in the University of Philippines College of Liberal Arts. Other schools of nursing in the colony followed Philippine General's example, raising their educational entrance requirements accordingly (Girón-Tupas 1952).

From the early twentieth century to the 1950s, the work culture of Filipino nursing students was similar to that of American students, combining academics, work, and daily living within and around the hospital school. Until the 1950s, in both the United States and the Philippines, virtually all nursing schools required that student nurses live in the hospital's nursing residence, under the close supervision of hospital superintendents and matrons. The strict discipline and hard physical work of nursing training (inspired by Nightingale's vision of models of order, duty, and discipline) bonded nursing students to one another. Purita Asperilla described her own training at the Philippine General Hospital in the late 1930s in this way: "You tend to become close to your friends, your classmates, because you live together. You sleep together. Our matron was very strict. . . . Nursing as [a] profession before the war, World War II, was militaristic. . . . They inspect[ed] you every morning before you [went] to the hall" (Asperilla, interview with author, November 11, 1994, New York).

Throughout the first half of the twentieth century, both American and Philippine hospital nursing schools depended on the labor of their nursing students. The "study" of nursing was in many ways "work." In the United States, hospital training schools used nursing students as an inexpensive source of labor, providing them with board and lodging and compensating their duties with small allowances, which in the first two decades of the twentieth century averaged about ten dollars a month. Nurses washed operating sheets and towels and scrubbed bathroom floors (Reverby 1987). The duties of Filipino nursing students were similar, and their compensation even more minimal. Purita Asperilla continued,

> You see at that time, our education was done in the morning, then we [were] on duty in the afternoon. We [were] depended upon for service. We were given a salary of eight pesos in the first year, ten pesos in the second year, and twelve pesos in the third year. We have free board and lodging. . . . But you know the first part of the curriculum is no hospital work. We were in the linen room. We were arranging linens, mending linens. (Asperilla interview)

Furthermore, the gendered construction of American nursing was deliberately reproduced in the Philippines. Although nursing changed, in the United States, from an option of last resort for women in the midnineteenth century into a respectable profession for women in the early twentieth century, it was still considered "women's" work. Dock's history of nursing education in the Philippines reveals the deliberate exclusion of men from the labor of nursing, accomplished by placing them instead in a training school for hospital attendants:

> When Miss McCalmont took charge of the nursing force in the Philippines, a peculiar state of affairs existed. All male patients, even the Americans, were cared for by male attendants only. . . . Baths, treatments, and nearly all surgical dressings were done by the attendants, who were generally ex–army corps men, with even less than ordinary training. . . . It seemed impossible to get the nurses back into the hospital habits of the United States, and an attempt was made to solve the problem by [establishing] a training school for men. (Dock 1912, 315)

As early as 1903, Major Edward Carter, surgeon of the U.S. Army and commissioner of health in the Philippines, had recommended the establishment of a training school specifically for Filipino nurses; but it was not until 1907, at the urging of the dean of women at the Philippine Normal School, Mary Coleman (who was responding, in turn, to the suggestion of Sofia de Veyra), that the U.S. colonial government established its first nursing school in the Philippines, at St. Paul's Hospital. In her history of Philippine nursing, Anastacia Girón-Tupas, chief nurse and superintendent of the Philippines, attributes the establishment of the school at St. Paul's Hospital to "the cooperation of American and Filipino ladies" (Girón-Tupas 1952, 34).

The first Filipino nurse graduates continued the collaboration. In 1922, Girón-Tupas joined 150 Filipino graduate nurses in organizing the Filipino Nurses Association (FNA). They elected Rosario M. Delgado, a graduate of the Philippine General Hospital nursing class of 1912, to be its first president. Alice Fitzgerald of the Rockefeller Foundation International Health Board, nursing adviser to the governor general of the Philippines, served as the organization's adviser.

The FNA took as its mission "to exalt the standard of the nursing profession and other allied purposes" (Girón-Tupas 1952, 299). Toward that end, the association created a special section, the League of Nursing Education. Although the league's membership was predominantly Filipino, American nurses, including Alice Fitzgerald and Lillian Weiser (chief nurse and superintendent of St. Luke's Hospital) participated as honorary members. In 1924, the league published its first "Standard Curriculum for Schools of Nursing." By 1946, the FNA drafted its first resolution, a petition for the creation of a College of Nursing at the University of the Philippines.

In addition to raising the standards of nursing education, the FNA shared other similarities with professional nursing organizations around the world. The FNA registered Filipino nurses, created a central directory for private-duty employment, advocated increased salaries for nurses and a government nurses' pension, provided financial assistance to elderly and sick nurses, and set up scholarship funds for nursing students. Based on its shared aims and activities with those of professional nursing organizations around the world, the Filipino Nurses Association became a member of the International Council of Nurses in 1929.

In the early twentieth century an elite group of Filipino nurse graduates was able to pursue postgraduate study in the United States, after which they returned to the Philippines to introduce the latest trends in American nursing practice. In the effort to "civilize" Filipinos and to "prepare" them for self-rule, the American colonial government in the Philippines sponsored a unique educational system involving universal primary and secondary education for the Filipino masses and higher education for young Filipinos of the elite class. Through the pensionado program, the American colonial government sponsored members of the

Filipino elite at universities and colleges in the United States to prepare them to assume top positions in American-established institutions in the Philippines. Philanthropic organizations and American individuals also contributed to this educational mission by financially sponsoring a few Filipinos to study in the United States. Although the vast majority of U.S.-sponsored Filipino scholars abroad were young men who studied politics, law, and medicine, this group also included a few Filipinas, who, it was proudly reported, "invaded the sacred and hitherto exclusively men's realm of business and politics" through their studies abroad (Ambrosio 1926, 1–2).[2] However, they remained a minority. For the most part American educational "opportunities" perpetuated gendered assumptions about women's work in the Philippines. While Filipino male students studied medicine and law, the majority of Filipina students who studied abroad took courses that would best prepare them for work in the home or in "female"-designated occupations. The most popular fields of study for Filipinas in the United States were home economics, social and religious work, and nursing.

In 1911, the first three graduates of St. Luke's School of Nursing, Quintana Beley, Veneranda Sulit, and Caridad Goco, completed their postgraduate coursework at Protestant Hospital in Philadelphia with the financial assistance of the wife of a former U.S. ambassador to England. They returned to the Philippines and assumed faculty positions at St. Luke's. In 1922, the Rockefeller Foundation sponsored another St. Luke's graduate, Escolastica Agatep, to study at Columbia University's Teacher's College. Agatep became the first Filipina nursing arts instructor at St. Luke's. In 1939, the Daughters of the American Revolution provided Imelda Tinawin with a scholarship that supported her studies for the bachelor of science degree in nursing education from Columbia University; from 1943 to 1945, Tinawin served as principal of St. Luke's School of Nursing. Study in the United States became a prerequisite for social and occupational mobility in the nursing profession in the Philippines. This historical link between study overseas (especially in the United States) and professional advancement in the Philippines laid the social and economic foundation for Filipino nurses' desire to go abroad.

The popularity of Americanized nursing in the Philippines needs to be understood within the context of limited educational opportunities for Filipinas under Spanish colonial rule. Before the American annexation of the Philippines in 1898, the colonial educational system under Spain offered separate and unequal opportunities for Filipinos based on gender as well as race and class. The Spanish university in the Philippines, the University of Santo Tomas, excluded women from programs of higher education. In the late nineteenth century, the Spanish colonial government also discouraged Filipinas from studying abroad at European universities, although it allowed elite Filipino men, known as "ilustrados," to do so; Filipinas were also excluded from the study and practice of medicine in the Philippines; during the Spanish colonial period, Spanish friars and priests cared for the sick.

By contrast, under U.S. colonial rule, all American-established institutions of learning, including the University of the Philippines, were coeducational from their inception. Through the pensionado program, the American colonial government enabled the first Filipinas to study abroad at colleges and universities in the United States, and the newly established Americanized training hospital system introduced young Filipinas to the study of nursing.

Given this particular historical context, some of the first Filipino nursing graduates interpreted the introduction of American nursing as an opportunity to enter a new and prestigious profession. As Apolonia Salvador Ladao, one of the first graduates of the Philippine General Hospital School of Nursing, recalled, "When we took up nursing, we did not know what it was all about; we were simply selected and recommended by our American teachers. We were thankful of this opportunity to enter a new profession and to serve our people" (Girón-Tupas 1952, 41).

The first Filipino nursing students were also able to interact with colonial government officials and to attend government functions. Filipino nursing students interpreted these opportunities as a form of prestige bestowed on them as a result of their study of nursing. Ramona Cabrera, another member of the first nursing class from Philippine General Hospital, explained that "the [American] people must have had a high regard for the work of nurses, as the high government officials were very kind and courteous to us. We were usually invited to accompany wives of the high government officials from Washington who were visiting the Islands. We were invited to the Governor-General's receptions and other important social functions" (Girón-Tupas, 42).

The opportunity to study abroad also inspired Filipino nurses and marked the beginnings of their idealization of the United States. In the second decade of this century, according to Filipino nurse Patrocinio Montellano, "to see America and have the opportunity to further my studies had been my dream." At first, "it seemed impossible . . . to have my dream come true." However, when one of her female friends was granted a government scholarship to study in the United States, Montellano recalls, "my obsession to go abroad was rekindled. I was determined to follow her by all means" (1962, 235).

During American colonial rule, the United States was a "land of promise" for Filipinos, like Patrocinio Montellano, who received American scholarships and professional opportunities unavailable to them during Spanish colonial rule. However, this promise was still reserved for an elite group of Filipinos. In the 1920s, male Filipino migrant workers constituted the overwhelming majority of Filipinos in the United States. They labored in the sugar plantations of Hawaii, the agricultural fields of California, and the canneries of Washington and Alaska, supplying an important source of labor to American industries, yet they faced considerable racism and prejudice in the form of segregation, poor working and living conditions, antimiscegenation laws, and racial violence.[3] This contradiction of American policies—privileging a few Filipinos, at times, at the expense of the general Filipino population—is a theme that would resonate in Philippine nursing, particularly in the mid-twentieth century.

To The Point of No Return: Filipino Exchange Nurses in the United States

The establishment of an Americanized training hospital system in the Philippines during the American colonial period created the professional and social foundations that enabled a Filipino nursing labor force to work and study in the United States. Furthermore, given the complex histories of Spanish and U.S. colonization of the Philippines, Filipinas, in general, and Filipino nurses, in particular, viewed work and study overseas in the United States as a "dream," a sure path to professional mobility upon their return to the Philippines. Transnational scholarship programs sponsored by the U.S. colonial government, U.S. philanthropic organizations, and American individuals allowed Filipino nurses to turn that dream into a reality.

These factors provide important historical linkages between early-twentieth-century colonization and the preponderance of Filipino nurses in the United States after mid-century, but how did opportunities for a few to study abroad develop into a mass migration of Filipino nurses in the post-1965 period? Furthermore, if study and work in the United States had become a path of professional mobility for Filipino nurses upon their return to the Philippines, why did so many emigrate to the United States through the occupational preference categories of the Immigration Act of 1965? Why did significant numbers of Filipino nurses in the late twentieth century remain in the United States as a permanent part of the American nursing labor force?

The socioeconomic and cultural significance of experience abroad for Filipino nurses changed dramatically in the mid-twentieth century. During this period, several exchange programs served as vehicles for the transformation of nursing into an internationally recognized profession.

While new international work programs in Germany and Holland recruited Filipino nurses to work outside of the Philippines, the U.S. Exchange Visitor Program (EVP) facilitated the first wave of mass migration of Filipino nurses abroad by providing several thousand Filipino nurses with the opportunity to work and study in the United States. Between 1956 and 1969, more than eleven thousand Filipino nurses participated in the EVP (Asperilla 1971, 52). Under the EVP, the experience of going abroad was transformed from an opportunity reserved for the few into one available to any Filipino registered nurse.

In 1948, the Exchange Visitor program was established by the American government, through the U.S. Information and Educational Act. The general objectives of the program were "to promote a better understanding of the United States in other countries and to increase mutual understanding between the people of the United States and the people of other countries." However, the motivations for establishing the program were rooted in Cold War politics. According to Senate reports, "hostile propaganda campaigns directed against democracy, human welfare, freedom, truth, and the United States, spearheaded by the Government of the Soviet Union and the Communist Parties throughout the world," called for "dynamic measures to disseminate truth" (U.S. Senate 1948, 4). One of the "dynamic measures" the Senate proposed was an educational exchange service involving the interchange of persons, knowledge, and skills.

Exchange Visitor Program participants from abroad engaged in both work and study in their sponsoring American institutions, for which they received a monthly stipend. Several thousand U.S. agencies and institutions, including the American Nurses Association and individual hospitals, served as sponsors. The American government issued EVP visas for a maximum stay of two years. Upon completion of the program, both the American and the sending-country governments expected the EVP participants to return to their countries of origin. In all, between 1956 and 1969, nurses made up more than 50 percent (11,136) of the total number (20,420) of exchange visitors from the Philippines (Asperilla 1971, 5).

Filipino nurses may initially have perceived the Exchange Visitor Program as "a dream come true," but exploitation in U.S. hospitals complicated romanticized Philippine narratives about work and study in America. Many sponsoring American hospitals actively recruited exchange nurses to alleviate growing nursing shortages in the post–World War II period. Some American hospital administrators took advantage of the exchange status of Filipino nurses by assigning them the work of registered nurses and compensating them with a minimal stipend. Other American hospital administrators abused the educational and professional component of the EVP by assigning Filipino exchange nurses the work of nurse's aides (Alinea and Senador 1973).

By the mid-1960s, the use of exchange nurses as employees appeared to be more the rule than the exception. A Philippine Department of Labor study committee characterized the EVP as "a handy recruitment device" and "a loophole for the circumvention of United States immigration laws" (cited by Asperilla 1971, 54). In 1966, the Philippine congressman Epifanio Castillejos, visiting the United States to survey the situation of Filipino exchange nurses, severely criticized the program: "Almost every Filipino nurse I met had problems which ran the gamut from discrimination in stipend, as well as in the nature and amount of work they are made to do, to the lack of in-service or specialized training in the hospitals they work in" (Castillejos 1966, 306–7). However, reports of discrimination and exploitation did not discourage further Filipino nurse migration to the United States through the EVP. Between 1967 and 1970, more than three thousand Filipino nurses participated in the program (Asperilla 1971, 52).

Why, despite reports of suboptimal living and working conditions, did several thousand Filipino nurses continue to come to the United States? The dissatisfaction of Filipino nurses with work schedules, opportunities, and salaries in the Philippines was a major factor. Several former exchange nurses I interviewed had used their exchange placements to leave unfavorable work conditions in the Philippines. Milagros Rabara, for example, applied for an exchange placement to avoid an evening work shift (Rabara, interview with author, March 21, 1995, New York). The limited number of days off at her hospital in the Philippines was a motivating factor for Lourdes Velasco to apply to the exchange program (Velasco, interview with author, February 6, 1995, New York).

Filipino nurses working in the Philippines also earned low wages and little professional respect. At some government agencies, nurses were paid lower wages than janitors, drivers, and messengers. In the mid-1960s, Filipino nurses earned between two hundred and three hundred pesos monthly for a six-day workweek, including holidays and overtime if required (Quijano 1968, 8). In the United States, in the mid-1960s, general-duty nurses earned twice as much, from four hundred to five hundred dollars a month.[4]

Filipino nurses were also attracted to the prestige attached to studying and working in the United States, a prestige originally created by the American colonial scholarship programs in the early twentieth century and revived in the mid-twentieth century. The Filipino Nurses Association contributed to the re-creation of this idealization through news stories in their official publication, the *Philippine Journal of Nursing* (*PJN*). Simply participating in the EVP was newsworthy. In 1960, the journal published the names and alma maters of the more than one hundred Filipino exchange nurses leaving for the United States every two to three months ("Local News: 104 Young Nurses Off to the United States" 1960; "Local News: 122 Young Nurses Departed to United States" 1960). The *PJN* also reported on the professional recognition that Filipino nurses had gained in the United States. When Chicago's American Hospital honored Juanita Jimenez as "Best Nurse of the Year," the *PJN* featured Jimenez as "a silver lining in our profession" (Bacala 1962, 192–93).

The ability of Filipino exchange nurses to improve their socioeconomic status through their earnings in American dollars, the acquisition of material goods unobtainable in the Philippines, and new forms of leisure also contributed to the prestige of work and study in the United States. Independent of wage differentials, which were considerable, the devaluation of the Philippine peso further increased the earning power of Filipino nurses working in America. The devaluation of the Philippine peso began in 1946 with the Tydings Rehabilitation Act, and by 1971, one American dollar was equivalent to six and a quarter pesos. As exchange nurse Ofelia Boado observed, "the pay [in the United States] was good compared to what I was getting in the Philippines. . . . It became so clear to me that many nurses come here not for advancement but for pay, for really good pay" (Boado, interview with author, February 6, 1995, New York).

Some Filipino exchange nurses manipulated the exchange visitor program to serve their own agendas, for example, by working sixteen-hour shifts to earn more money. With their stipends in American dollars, American credit cards, and layaway plans, the exchange nurses purchased stereos, kitchen appliances, and cosmetics unobtainable for all except the affluent elite in the Philippines. They enjoyed forms of leisure completely unavailable in the Philippines: Broadway shows, performances at Lincoln Center, travel within the United States and to Europe. They lived in their own apartments and stayed out late at night. According to Ofelia Boado, "You're very independent. You have your own apartment. In the Philippines, you live in the dorm where everything closes at 9:00 P.M. Or even if you stay at home, you don't go home late in the night or anything like that" (Boado interview).

Given these opportunities abroad, Filipino exchange nurses created a folklore of an America filled with social and economic promise. In their letters to Filipino nursing friends back in the Philippines, boasting of high salaries and "good living" in the United States, Filipino exchange nurses encouraged other Filipino nurses to follow their example (Asperilla 1971, 15–17, 72).

Going abroad became a trend among Filipino nurses. One study reveals that between 1952 and 1965 an average of slightly more than 50 percent of the 377 graduates from the University of the Philippines College of Nursing went abroad (Ignacio, Masaganda, and Sta. Maria 1967). Filipino exchange nurses, directly or by example, encouraged not only thousands of other Filipino nurses to go to the United States but also other young Filipinas to enter nursing school. In 1962 there were more student applicants for nursing studies than Philippine colleges and schools of nursing were able to accommodate (de la Vaca 1962); and going abroad after the study of nursing figured prominently in the plans of most of them. In 1963, FNA president Luisa Alvarez asked prospective nursing students why they chose that field of study. She reported, "This may surprise you but about 80 percent of those asked have answered me that it is because they want to go to the United States and other countries" (Alvarez 1963, 169).

By the early 1960s, many Filipino nurses hoped to remain indefinitely in the United States, as well. In 1960, Alvarez reported that many Filipino exchange nurses in Chicago complained about the length of their visits, claiming that a two-year period was insufficient time to "avail [themselves of] the benefits of the program" (1960, 133). They asked if it were possible to extend their visit to a period of three to five years. When extensions of the exchange visit did not materialize, some Filipino exchange nurses returned to the Philippines after their two-year stay. Others, however, attempted to bypass the two-year exchange limit and their mandatory return to the Philippines altogether and to change their "exchange" visa status while they were still in the United States.

According to the U.S. Mutual Educational and Cultural Exchange Act of 1961, exchange visitors were unable to apply for permanent residence until they had returned to their countries of origin and lived there for a period of at least two years after their departure from the United States. Yet Filipino exchange nurses employed multiple strategies to avoid returning to their homeland. Some married American citizens. Others immigrated to Canada. Filipino exchange nurses also exited the United States through Canada, Mexico, or St. Thomas and reentered on student visas. Some utilized a combination of requests by American universities, the Philippine Consul General, and American hospital employers to petition the Exchange Visitor Waiver Board of the Department of Health, Education, and Welfare for a waiver of the foreign residence requirement. When even these strategies failed and the Immigration and Naturalization Service (INS) set their dates for departure, some Filipino exchange nurses brought their cases to the U.S. Court of Appeals in an attempt to overturn INS rulings.

The widespread desire of Filipino exchange nurses to remain in the United States became a cause for alarm for Philippine government officials and nursing leaders. They interpreted nurses' duties as an integral part of Philippine nation-building. Songs, such as "The Filipino Nurses' Hymn," promoted this relationship between nursing and Philippine nationalism: "We pledge . . . to build a better nation that is healthy and great" ("The Filipino Nurses' Hymn" 1962, 34). The hymn conjures images of Filipino nurses "traveling on" to all regions of the Philippines: "In towns and upland terraces/In plains, in hills and mountains."

Philippine government officials and nursing leaders took pride in the professional achievements of Filipino nurses abroad and empathized with their desire to go to the United States and to remain there, given the potential social and economic opportunities. They also continued to endorse participation in the EVP and to believe that Filipino nurses' training abroad was necessary for the national development of the Philippines.

However, government health officials and nursing leaders also harshly criticized the new lifestyles of Filipino exchange nurses abroad, employing a rhetoric of spirituality and morality in their efforts to persuade Filipino nurses to return to or to remain in the Philippines. They characterized the economic ambitions of some Filipino exchange nurses to accumulate American dollars and to purchase American goods as a dangerous obsession. Critics charged that some Filipino exchange nurses had become financially as well as morally bankrupt—that they miscalculated their expenditures and, using credit and layaway plans, overspent their earnings. Others associated the nurses' new lifestyles in America with licentiousness. They claimed that the women smoked, drank, and talked behind each other's backs. The harshest criticism was leveled against Filipino exchange nurses who used marriage to American citizens to remain in the United States. The editor of the *Philippine Journal of Nursing* likened those nurses who "marr[ied] any American they could entice, if only to stay in the country of their husbands," to prostitutes: "This is 'selling' themselves" (Bacala 1963, 136).

The national problem that Filipino exchange nurses had become only worsened when it became clear that the vast majority of returning Filipino exchange nurses planned to go back eventually to the United States.[5] If they contributed at all to Philippines nation-building, it was not for very long. They compared their salaries, nursing facilities, equipment, and research opportunities in the United States with those of the Philippines and found the latter sorely lacking.

By the early 1960s, the international migration of nurses, particularly Filipino nurses, seemed unstoppable. Hospitals in Holland, Germany, the Netherlands, Brunei, Laos, Turkey, and Iran recruited Filipino nurses to alleviate their nursing shortages. Although Filipino nurses had to adjust to the different languages and foods as well as some new nursing procedures, nursing practices in Europe, such as the emphasis on bedside nursing, were generally similar to those in the Philippines. When officers of the Filipino Nurses Association visited hospitals in the Netherlands that had recruited Filipino nurses, they concluded that Filipino nurses in those hospitals were safe and well taken care of, and these reports—which also publicized favorable work conditions and bonuses—inspired further migration abroad.

Producing Nurses,
Exporting Women

In 1965, the U.S. Congress passed the Immigration and Nationality Act, which expedited a process that was already under way among Filipino nurses. The new law created a more equitable system of immigration involving worldwide ceilings and per country quotas. One major impact of the new legislation was the increased migration of highly educated and skilled persons into the United States through occupational preference categories. These categories dramatically affected Filipino professional immigration. Between 1966 and 1970, 17,134 Filipino professionals emigrated to the United States, constituting almost one-third of all Filipino immigrants (Cariño 1987, 309).

In the 1960s and 1970s, engineers, scientists, and physicians as well as nurses made up the bulk of professional immigrants from the Philippines. However, the demands for foreign-trained nurses to fill critical U.S. nursing shortages (exacerbated by the creation of Medicare and Medicaid programs in the mid-1960s), in combination with Filipino nurses' professional skills and historically shaped desires to work abroad, made the Philippines a dominant force in the international migration of nurses. By 1967, the Philippines became the world's top sending country of nurses to the United States, ending decades of numerical domination by European and North American countries. In 1967, Filipino nurses received the highest number of U.S. nursing licenses among foreign-trained nurses—1,521 licenses out of a total of 5,361 (Quraeshi, Quraeshi, and Mangla 1992, 61).

New American legislation also facilitated the adjustment of exchange visitor's status to that of permanent resident. A new law, passed in 1970, enabled exchange visitors to waive their two-year foreign residency requirement. Between 1966 and 1978, 7,495 Filipino exchange visitors adjusted their status to become U.S. permanent residents (Tullao 1982, 132–33). The growing exodus of Filipino nurses abroad through new avenues of immigration created new problems for nursing in the Philippines. As the demand for nursing education exceeded the enrollment spaces available in Philippine colleges and schools of nursing, Filipino businessmen and health educators opened new schools of nursing in the provinces as well as urban areas. Between 1950 and 1970 the number of nursing schools in the Philippines rose from 17 to 140 (Joyce and Hunt 1982).

As the number of nursing schools increased, so too did the demand for nursing school faculty. At the same time, the socioeconomic rewards of working abroad depleted the supply of Filipino nursing instructors. Although the Philippine Board of Examiners for Nurses required a ratio of one faculty member to ten to twelve students during clinical supervision, according to one nursing dean, Rosario S. Diamante, the ratio was "not possible due to the rapid turnover of faculty. This was mainly due to an exodus abroad either as immigrant or as participant of the Exchange Visitors Program or under a working visa" (Diamante 1972, 39). A 1974 summary of problems encountered by the Council of Deans and Principals of Philippine Colleges and Schools of Nursing included the "sprouting of many schools of nursing posing problems of lack of qualified faculty members." (Diamante 1975, 80). The council reported, "We conduct seminars for them only to find out that they have left the country" (Diamante 1975, 80).

As new avenues of entry to the United States exacerbated the trend of migration abroad, as the aggressive international recruitment of Filipino nurses continued unabated, and as nurses' wages in the Philippines lagged behind those of nurses abroad, Filipino nursing leaders, in collaboration with the Philippine government, employed new strategies to retain Filipino nurse graduates, if only temporarily. In the early 1970s, mandatory health service requirements for new nurse graduates replaced emotional appeals to nurses' selflessness and humanitarianism. However, these service requirements were only temporary.[6] Decrees by Philippine president Ferdinand Marcos mandating several months of health service in rural areas were token gestures to alleviate the maldistribution of Filipino health personnel in the country. At the same time, Marcos also committed the Philippines to an export-oriented economy, which included the export of people and skills as well as goods. Government officials thus promoted the export of laborers, including Filipino nurses, when the shortage of Filipino nurses serving the general population was most acute.

By the early 1970s the Marcos government was promoting "employment contracts" of Filipino laborers and a "dollar repatriation program" as a way both to alleviate unemployment and to revitalize a failing Philippine economy. Marcos's address to the Philippine Nurses Association at their 1973 convention in Manila revealed the government's new commitment to exporting womanpower: "And so, in short, what is the policy of nursing? . . . It is our policy to promote the migration of nurses. . . . We encourage this migration, I repeat, we will now encourage the training of all nurses because, as I repeat, this is a market that we should take advantage of. Instead of stopping the nurses from going abroad, why don't we produce more nurses? If they want one thousand nurses we produce a thousand more?" (Marcos 1974, 21–22). Like the revenues earned from agricultural exports, the earnings of Filipino nurses working abroad, deposited in Philippine banks, would help to build the Philippine national economy. Marcos encouraged Filipino nurses abroad to "earn for the country" as well as for themselves.

Given the shift to an export-oriented economy, Filipino nurses abroad were no longer seen as having abandoned their role in Philippine nation-building; rather, they were now considered integral to the process. Once criticized in the 1960s by the Philippine secretary of health for "turning their backs on their own people when the almighty dollar beckons," Filipino nurses abroad now became the new national heroes. Their work as nurses abroad continued to be associated with prestige. However, this time the prestige derived from indefinite working sojourns abroad, during which they would return a portion of their "precious dollars" to their country of origin. In his 1973 address to visiting Filipino nurses from abroad, a new Philippine health secretary, Clemente S. Gatmaitan, proclaimed, "We in the Health Department are happy that you have elected to stay and work abroad. . . . While in other countries, you give prestige to the Philippines because you are all virtually ambassadors of good will. . . . Another benefit that accrues from your work is the precious dollar you earn and send back to your folks at home. In this manner, you help indirectly in the improvement of our economic condition" (Gatmaitan 1973, 90).

These changes in the attitude of Philippine government officials' toward the mass migration of Filipino workers abroad led to the implementation of an official overseas labor policy. In 1974, the government created the Overseas Employment Development Board and the National Seamen Board. These agencies publicized the availability of Filipino labor in overseas labor markets, evaluated overseas employment contracts, and recruited Filipino laborers for work abroad.

Conclusion

At the close of the century, the Philippines continued to export its people as contract workers overseas through government agencies such as the Philippine Overseas Employment Administration. Filipinas have played a significant role in this phenomenon. In 1991, they constituted a larger proportion of the Philippine's overseas workforce (41 percent) than its domestic workforce (36 percent). Significant numbers of overseas Filipino workers in domestic services (housecleaning), entertainment, and the sex industry, in addition to the overseas working force, form a worldwide diaspora of Filipinas working in Japan, Canada, the Middle East, and several European countries, as well as the United States (Chang 1997, 135–37). This diaspora is a late-twentieth-century phenomenon, but a transnational history of Filipino nurse migration to the United States reveals that the migration of Filipino nurses has its roots in practices established earlier in the century. Although contemporary U.S. and Philippine government policies have facilitated migration in the tens of thousands since 1965, American educational policies during the U.S. colonial period in the Philippines and the U.S. Exchange Visitor Program of the 1950s and 1960s laid the social, economic, and political foundations for the Philippine export of nurses in the late twentieth century.

Notes

1. In British colonial India, a provincial medical board proposed the creation of a Native Medical Institution in 1822 to train Indian doctors in Western medicine. Regarding the language of instruction, the strategy described here was changed in the 1830s; see Arnold (1993, 54–55).

2. The original group of "pensionados" in 1903 consisted of 103 Filipino men and no women. In 1904, of thirty-nine pensionados, only five were women. In 1905, the gender imbalance continued, with three Filipinas and thirty-four Filipino men studying abroad under the auspices of the program. For a description of the original pensionado movement, see Sutherland (1953). For a comprehensive description of the pensionado program from 1903 to 1943, see Munden (1943).

3. By the 1930s, more than forty thousand Filipinos had migrated to the United States. Government-sponsored scholars constituted only several hundred of this total. The vast majority of historical literature on Filipino Americans focuses on this early-twentieth-century group of Filipino male workers. The classic account of these Filipino male migrant workers' experiences is Carlos Bulosan's *America Is in the Heart* (1943). For a history of Asian American laborers in the Northwest canneries, see Friday (1994). For a history of Asian American laborers, including Filipino laborers, in Hawaiian plantations, see Takaki (1983).

4. According to the Bureau of Labor Statistics in 1966, general-duty nurses in the United States earned a weekly average of $100.50. In 1969, an study by the American Nurses Association found that staff

nurses in the United States earned a weekly average of $133; see ANA Nursing Information Bureau (1969, 124).

5. In Purita Asperilla's study of 411 Filipino nurse returnees, 97 percent said that they would like to go back if possible, and 86 percent said that they had already made plans to go back (1971, 151).

6. In 1972, the Philippine Exchange Visitor Program Committee required medical and nursing graduates to serve in the Philippines for one year after the results of their board examinations before applying to the exchange program; see Luzon (1972, 65). In 1973, President Ferdinand Marcos issued a presidential decree requiring Filipino nurse graduates to serve for four months in a rural area as a condition for obtaining licensure; see "Rural Health Experience for New Graduates: A Must" 1973, 244, 246).

References

Abella, Manolo J. 1979. *Export of Filipino Manpower.* Manila: Institute of Labor and Manpower Studies.

Allen, James P. 1977. "Recent Immigration from the Philippines and Filipino Communities in the United States." *Geographical Review* 67(2): 195–208.

Alinea, Patria G., and Gloria B. Senador. 1973. "Leaving for Abroad? . . . Here's a Word of Caution." *Philippine Journal of Nursing* 42(1): 92–94.

Alvarez, Luisa A. 1960. "By the President." *Philippine Journal of Nursing* 29(3): 132–38.

———. 1963. "The President's Page: Words to Student Nurses." *Philippine Journal of Nursing* 32(4): 168–69.

Ambrosio, D. B. 1926. "Filipino Women in the United States Excel in Their Courses; Invade Business, Politics." *Filipino Student Bulletin* (special Filipino women students' issue) 5(8): 1–2.

American Nurses Association (ANA) Nursing Information Bureau. 1969. *Facts About Nursing.* New York: ANA.

Arnold, David. 1993. *Colonizing the Body: State Medicine and Epidemic Disease in Nineteenth-Century India.* Berkeley: University of California Press.

Asperilla, Purita Falgui. 1971. "The Mobility of Filipino Nurses." Ph.D. diss., Columbia University.

Bacala, J. C. 1962. "This Issue's Personality: Juanita J. Jimenez, A Silver Lining in Our Profession." *Philippine Journal of Nursing* 31(3): 192–93.

———. 1963. "The Trouble with Our Exchange Visitor Nurses." *Philippine Journal of Nursing* 32(3): 134–37, 142.

Bulosan, Carlos. 1943. *America Is in the Heart.* New York: Harcourt, Brace.

Cariño, Benjamin V. 1987. "The Philippines and Southeast Asia: Historical Roots and Contemporary Linkages." In *Pacific Bridges: The New*

Immigration from Asia and the Pacific Islands, edited by James T. Fawcett and Benjamin V. Cariño. Staten Island, N.Y.: Center for Migration Studies.

Castillejos, Epifanio B. 1966. "The Exchange Visitors Program: Report and Recommendation." *Philippine Journal of Nursing* 35(5): 306–7.

Chang, Grace. 1997. "The Global Trade in Filipina Workers." In *Dragon Ladies: Asian American Feminists Breathe Fire*, edited by Sonia Shah. Boston: South End Press.

de la Vaca, Tomas Antonio. 1962. "Should Filipino Students Take Their Basic Nursing Studies Abroad?" *Santo Tomas Nursing Journal* 1(3): 183–84.

Diamante, Rosario S. 1972. "Nursing Education in the Philippine[s] Today." *Philippine Journal of Nursing* 44(2): 35–42.

———. 1975. "Council of Deans and Principals of Philippine Colleges and Schools of Nursing, Inc." *Philippine Journal of Nursing* 44(2): 77–81.

Dock, Lavinia L. 1912. *A History of Nursing: From the Earliest Times to the Present Day, with Special Reference to the Work of the Past Thirty Years.* Vol. 4. New York: G. P. Putnam's Sons.

"The Filipino Nurses' Hymn." 1962. *Philippine Journal of Nursing* 31(1): 34.

Friday, Chris. 1994. *Organizing Asian American Labor: The Pacific Coast Canned-Salmon Industry, 1870–1942*. Philadelphia: Temple University Press.

Gatmaitan, Clemente S. 1973. "Closing Address for Visiting Filipino Nurses." *Philippine Journal of Nursing* 42(2): 90–91.

Girón-Tupas, Anastacia. 1952. *History of Nursing in the Philippines.* Manila: University Book Supply.

Hawes, Gary. 1989. *The Philippine State and the Marcos Regime.* Bloomington: Indiana University Press.

Ignacio, Teodora, Marlena Masaganda, and Leticia Sta. Maria. 1967. "A Study of the Graduates of the Basic Degree Program of the University of the Philippines College of Nursing Who Have Gone Abroad." *Academy of Nursing of the Philippines Papers* 11(4): 50–68.

Ishi, Tomoji. 1987. "Class Conflict, the State, and Linkage: The International Migration of Nurses from the Philippines." *Berkeley Journal of Sociology* 32: 281–95.

Joyce, Richard E., and Chester L. Hunt. 1982. "Philippine Nurses and the Brain Drain." *Social Science Medicine* 16:1223–33.

"Local News: 104 Young Nurses Off to United States." 1960. *Philippine Journal of Nursing* 29(3): 195–96.

"Local News: 122 Young Nurses Departed to United States." 1960. *Philippine Journal of Nursing* 29(4): 267–68.

Luzon, Col. Winnie W. 1972. "President's Report." *Philippine Journal of Nursing* 41(2): 59–66.

Marcos, Ferdinand E. 1974. "Address of His Excellency, President Ferdinand E. Marcos." *Philippine Journal of Nursing* 43(1): 13–23.

Mejía, Alfonso, Helena Pizorkí, and Erica Royston. 1979. *Physician and Nurse Migration: Analysis and Policy Implications*. Geneva: World Health Organization.

Montellano, Patrocinio J. 1962. "Years That Count." *Philippine Journal of Nursing* 31(4): 235–36, 255–57.

Munden, Kenneth. 1943. "Los Pensionados: The Story of the Education of Philippine Government Students in the United States, 1903–1943." Record group 350. National Archives, Washington D.C.

Ong, Paul, and Tania Azores. 1994. "The Migration and Incorporation of Filipino Nurses." In *The New Asian Immigration in Los Angeles and Global Restructuring*, edited by Paul Ong, Edna Bonacich, and Lucie Cheng. Philadelphia: Temple University Press.

Quijano, Alfredo S. 1968. "No Brain Drain, but There Is No Job Opportunity Here for Nurses." *Manila Examiner*, November 9.

Quraeshi, Nalini M., Zahir A. Quraeshi, and Inayat U. Mangla. 1992. *Foreign Nursing Professionals in the United States: Focus on Asian Immigration*. New Delhi: International Labour Organisation.

Reverby, Susan M. 1987. *Ordered to Care: The Dilemma of American Nursing, 1850–1945*. Cambridge: Cambridge University Press.

"Rural Health Experience for New Graduates: A Must." 1973. *Philippine Journal of Nursing* 42(4): 244, 246.

Sutherland, William Alexander. 1953. *Not by Might: The Epic of the Philippines*. Las Cruces, N.M.: Southwest Publishing.

Takaki, Ronald. 1983. *Pau Hana: Plantation Life and Labor in Hawaii*. Honolulu: University of Hawaii Press.

Tullao, Tereso Simbulan, Jr. 1982. "Private Demand for Education and the International Flow of Human Resources: A Case of Nursing Education in the Philippines." Ph.D. diss., Fletcher School of Law and Diplomacy.

U.S. Senate. 1948. "Promoting the Better Understanding of the United States Among the Peoples of the World and to Strengthen Cooperative International Relations." S. Rept. 811, 80th Cong., 2d sess., *Senate Miscellaneous Reports 1*. Washington: Government Printing Office.

6

TRANSNATIONAL POLITICAL STRATEGIES: THE CASE OF MEXICAN INDIGENOUS MIGRANTS

Gaspar Rivera-Salgado

O N FEBRUARY 10, 1997, the local media in Fresno, California, reported on a rally in front of the Mexican Consulate offices in that city, organized by a group of migrant farmworkers. What caught the attention of the media was that the group, composed of indigenous Mixtec farmworkers, had simultaneously organized a press conference in the northern Mexican border city of Tijuana and a caravan traveling from the Mixtec town of Juxtlahuaca to the city of Oaxaca.[1] Along the way the protesters had managed the symbolic takeover of the ancient city of Monte Alban. The main demand of this binational political mobilization, which had been coordinated across the two thousand miles that separate Oaxaca and California, was that the Mexican federal government recognize the agreement on culture and indigenous autonomy they had signed with the Zapatista Army of National Liberation (EZLN) in February 1996. The organizers of this mobilization also called for the governor of Oaxaca to address the specific demands of the twenty-two communities belonging to the Frente Indígena Oaxaqueño Binacional (Binational Indigenous Oaxacan Front).

This binational mobilization carried out by Mixtec migrants raises an interesting question: Where does Oaxaca begin or end for Mixtec migrants? On the streets of Los Angeles, California, where for the last seven years Zapotecs and Mixtecs have organized an annual cultural performance of traditional Oaxacan dance and music, called the Guelaguetza, for a massive audience that, in the summer of 1999, included almost two thousand people? In the agricultural fields of the San Joaquin Valley in central California, where more than forty thousand Mixtecs work and where they cheer for their favorite team of the pre-Hispanic handball game known as pelota mixteca every Sunday in the city of Madera? In the everyday practice of these indigenous Mexican migrants, their community of reference transcends the limits of the U.S. and Mexican borders and has become a "deterritorialized" space (sometimes called Oaxacalifornia, see Kearney 1995a), giving rise to novel forms of organization and political expression.[2]

The incorporation of large numbers of indigenous peoples in the U.S.-bound Mexican migratory flow illustrates just how dramatically migration patterns are changing. Not only are an increased number of Mexican migrants attempting to cross the border, but also new groups have joined the migratory stream (COLEF 1994a; Rivera-Salgado 1999). Mixtecs, Zapotecs, and Triques from Oaxaca, Nahuas from Guerrero, and Purepechas from Michoacan form the largest share of this new indigenous immigration wave (see Zabin et al. 1993; Anderson 1997).[3] Mixtec farmworkers now make up 7 percent of California's agricultural labor force. Many of these new indigenous migrants came to the United States for the first time during the mid-1980s, and they tend to concentrate at the bottom of the agricultural labor market in California, performing the most physically demanding and the lowest-paid jobs (Zabin et al. 1993). However, far from being passive victims of exploitative conditions, indigenous migrants have responded creatively to the multiple challenges they face in both countries. They have formed binational political organizations that allow them to undertake collective action both in their communities of origin and in the multiple satellite communities they have established along their migratory circuit. These indigenous organizations form part of a new wave of Mexican immigrants organized around a wide variety of cross-border civic organizations.[4]

Why have indigenous Mexican migrants been so effective in developing binational grassroots organizations to defend their political and economic rights and mobilizing politically on both sides of the border? How does the political activism of indigenous Mexican transnational communities affect politics on both sides of the border, at local, regional, and state levels? As the analysis in this chapter makes clear, the political involvement of indigenous peoples in Mexico—the desire for autonomy, long-term independence in local governance, and particular political structures—has had a crucial impact on indigenous Mexican migrant communities and transnational political activism. Just as indigenous people in Mexico distance themselves from the Mexican state and Mexican identity, so, too, Mixtec migrants in California create new forms of transnational organization that both reflect and strengthen their ethnic identity.

In analyzing the experience of Mexican indigenous migrants, I draw on my fieldwork and direct participation with one binational indigenous organization—the Frente Indígena Oaxaqueño Binacional. Between June

1996 and August 1998, I also conducted forty in-depth interviews on both sides of the border with a socially diverse sample of Mixtec, Zapotec, and Purepecha migrants. In addition, I carried out participant observation research in three municipalities in the Mixteca region in Oaxaca (Juxtlahuaca, Tecomaxtlahuaca, and Tlacotepec), one Zapotec municipality (Macuiltianguis), and one Purepecha municipality (Cheran) as well as in various communities of destination in California (Fresno, Madera, Watsonville, Santa Cruz, Los Angeles, and Oceanside). As part of the research, I attended various religious and community events and political rallies, and I was able to observe everyday activities both at work and at home.

Transnational Approaches to Migration

Recent literature on international migration has focused on the emergence of transnational communities. These studies have furthered our understanding of transnational action, community building, and the formation of transnational political communities in the United States, Mexico, and the Caribbean (for example, Basch, Glick Schiller, and Szanton Blanc 1994; Georges 1990; Glick Schiller, Basch, and Blanc-Szanton 1992; Glick Schiller, Basch, and Szanton-Blanc 1995; Goldring 1992; Kearney 1995b; Kearney and Nagengast 1989; Smith 1995). In this literature, transnationalism is defined as "the process by which immigrants forge and sustain multi-stranded social relations that link together their societies of origin and settlement" (Basch, Glick Schiller, and Szanton Blanc 1994, 7). At the heart of the transnational approach to international migration is the argument that the current restructuring of global capital produces a new set of political, economic, and social relations between sending communities and governments and citizens abroad. In this view, migration represents a "multi-level process (demographic, political, economic, cultural, familial) that involves various links between two or more settings rather than a discrete event constituted by a permanent move from one nation to another" (Gold 1997, 410).

In a transnational perspective, migration is conceptualized "as an on-going process through which ideas, resources, and people change locations and develop meaning in multiple locations, suggesting that by retaining social, cultural, and economic links with various locations and contexts, people can surmount the impediments traditionally associated with long-distance and international borders" (Gold 1997, 410). The emphasis in the transnational perspective is on the fact that migrants remain heavily involved in the life of their country of origin even though they no longer permanently live there. Transnational social relations thus allow migrants to develop and maintain multiple relations in more that one nation-state.

A key assumption of transnationalism is that race, ethnicity, and nationality are constructed categories that are reconfigured and strategically deployed both by nation-states and by individual transmigrants. It has been argued, for example, that Caribbean leaders have created "deterritorialized nation-states" that define state boundaries in social rather than geographical terms to include citizens abroad. Political leaders "who claim to lead deterritorialized states have taken steps both practically and symbolically to serve as representatives, protectors, and spokespeople for their dispersed populations" (Basch, Glick Schiller, and Szanton Blanc 1994, 18). Thus, in the wake of the 2000 presidential elections in Mexico, the opposition candidate Cuáuhtemoc Cárdenas appealed to thousands of Mexican migrants during a multicity tour through California, seeking to consolidate support for his party among Mexican migrants and possibly win votes (Mexican citizens can vote in elections if they return home, and migrants may also influence the voting behavior of relatives who have stayed behind). Cárdenas emphasized the importance of Mexican citizens abroad in constructing the "new Mexican nation," and his visit to California was an attempt to cement the loyalties of Mexicans in the United States by strengthening their identification with the Mexican nation and, by extension, the political contests of the Mexican state.

Whereas politicians and government officials are engaged in nation-building projects, transmigrants themselves construct transnational identities. Within a global context of economic uncertainty, transmigrants find full incorporation into the host country either difficult or undesirable. Nina Glick Schiller, Linda Basch, and Cristina Szanton-Blanc argue that transmigrants "settle in countries that are the centers of global capitalism but live transnational lives" for three reasons: global restructuring of capital leads to unstable social and economic conditions in both host and sending nations; racism in the United States and Europe further exacerbates transmigrants' economic and social vulnerability; and nation-building projects, attempting to ensure immigrants' loyalties, reinforce ties with their home communities (1995, 50). Consequently, transmigrants fashion multiple identities within a global landscape of the "delocalized transnation" (Appadurai 1996, 33). Such identities, transnationalist theorists argue, are reconfigured and deployed to "accommodate and resist their subordination within a global capitalist system" (Glick Schiller, Basch, and Blanc-Szanton 1992, 12).

The case of indigenous Mexican migrants points to the need to view the way transmigrant identity reflects shifting power relations in communities of origin and destination. In the literature on transnationalism, ethnic identity is frequently ignored or treated as a consequence of migration flows—a problem "here" but not "there." Much has been written about how various Caribbean groups, for example, have developed new racial and ethnic identities in the context of the American racial order (for example, Grasmuck and Pessar 1991; Glick Schiller, Basch, and Szanton-Blanc 1995). The few scholars of Mexican migration who have seriously considered ethnicity as an important point of departure to understand movement and migration of the Mexican population follow this approach (Kearney and Nagengast 1989; Zabin et al. 1993). For instance, Michael Kearney and Carol Nagengast argue that indigenous migrants, such as the Mixtecs, struggle to define cultural and ethnic identities in the United States and resist incorporation into the racial hegemony of a bipolar (black-white) system.

Important as it is to understand how U.S. racial and ethnic hierarchies, relations, and ideologies affect migrants, reconfigurations of racial and ethnic identities in the United States must be linked with the racial and ethnic experiences of immigrants in their countries of origin. Moreover, in the case of Mexican indigenous migrants it is necessary to appreciate the historical context and the specific politics and economics of their migratory experience to understand the ways they construct meaningful lives in situations not of their own choosing. Indigenous migrants become agents of social change by organizing and implementing creative strategies for collective action to fight for their survival—and this involvement in political organization builds on and reinforces ethnic identities that they bring from home.

Mexican Immigration to California

Indigenous migrants are relative newcomers in the flow of Mexican migration to California. In the last few decades the expansion of agriculture in the state has created a great demand for labor, deepening labor market links with Mexico and diversifying patterns of Mexican migration and settlement in rural and urban California. Until the early 1970s, the typical Mexican migrant was a lone male in his twenties who worked seasonally in U.S. agriculture and spent the rest of the year in his home community in west-central Mexico (Cornelius 1988; Massey et al. 1987). During the 1970s, the social networks of many migrant-sending villages "matured," and significant numbers of workers from them settled with their families in California, thereby increasing the proportion of women and children in the state's Mexican-born population (Massey et al. 1987; Cornelius 1988). Improvements in wages and working conditions of farmworkers in California between the mid-1960s and the early 1980s also bolstered this trend (Zabin et al. 1993).

In the 1990s, Mexican migration into the United States intensified dramatically with the incorporation of new groups of migrants—including indigenous peoples from Oaxaca, Michoacan, Guerrero, and other states—into the U.S.-bound migratory stream (COLEF 1994b).[5] Although indigenous migrant workers such as Mixtecs have a long history of migration outside the Mixteca region to other Mexican states such as Veracruz, Mexico City, and Sinaloa, they are only recently crossing the United States–Mexico border in large numbers (Kearney and Nagengast 1989; Zabin et al. 1993). The Mixteca region of western Oaxaca, in southern Mexico, is one of the poorest and ecologically most devastated areas in Mexico. This region is the homeland of some 635,000 Mixtec people, who constitute one of the largest ethnic groups in Mexico. In recent decades, as a result of deforestation and ensuing soil erosion, tens of thousands of Mixtecs have been forced to leave the Mixteca as circular and permanent migrants in search of wage labor. Since the 1960s and 1970s, large and increasing numbers of Mixtecs have been migrating into northwestern Mexico and into California, where they have now established sizable and growing communities.

The development of transnational communities among Mexican migrants, including indigenous peoples, has been hastened by, among other factors, the presence of ethnic enclaves, the proximity of Mexico, the constant renewal of the migrant flow, and the economic insecurity experienced by migrants on both sides of the border (Kearney and Nagengast 1989). For indigenous migrant workers, and for Mixtecs, in particular, the development of transnational communities is paralleled by the transnationalization of labor-intensive fruit and vegetable production. In terms of commercial agriculture, the Pacific Coast (northwestern Mexico and California) effectively constitutes a single production zone. Many of the same commodities are produced on both sides of the border, with the same basic technology and financing; both areas of this transnational agricultural production zone rely on the same kind of migrant labor force. Just as commercial agriculture in the Pacific Coast zone is dependent on indigenous regions of Oaxaca for migrant labor, so indigenous communities of southern Mexico are dependent on income earned in this production zone. Consistent with such a structural relationship, the subsistence agricultural communities of indigenous regions in southern Mexico and commercial agriculture in California and northern Mexico can be seen as interdependent (Zabin et al. 1993).

Indigenous migrants participate in a rich cultural exchange between the United States and Mexico by bringing back to their communities of origin commodities, styles, and attitudes acquired in the North. Para-doxically, migrants' insertion into the U.S. labor market also reinforces customs that appear to be quite "traditional" at home. For example, traditional fiestas, which are central to indigenous communities, have been not only perpetuated but actually made more elaborate with funds from migrant earnings. It is not uncommon for migrant workers who have done relatively well in el Norte to volunteer to serve as mayor-domos (sponsors) of festivities celebrating their community's patron saint. The expense for these festivities can run into thousands of dollars, all paid by the relatives and extended families of the main mayordomo. Many migrants living permanently or working temporarily in the United States return to Oaxaca during these celebrations, adding even more excitement to the events.

The Political Context of Transnational Political Activism

The consolidation of Mexican indigenous migrant organizations occurs within the context of U.S.-Mexican economic integration via NAFTA (the North American Free Trade Agreement) as well as the neoliberal restructuring of the Mexican economy in the current economic crisis, which has been especially harsh for rural and indigenous people. The sustained deterioration of the Mexican economy resulted in the 1994 Chiapas uprising, which demanded profound political and economic re-forms in the country and greater autonomy for indigenous communities. The increasing economic deterioration of living standards in rural Mex-ico, especially in southern Mexico, which is overwhelmingly indige-nous, has radicalized many indigenous and peasant organizations in the region. As indigenous organizations in Guerrero, Oaxaca, and Chiapas (these three states form the region known as the "Mexican poverty cor-ridor") increase their political activism, the response by state and federal governments has been the further militarization of the region, making even more tense the already volatile situation that existed there.

At the same time, post-melting-pot California has witnessed strong anti-immigrant backlash—indeed, initiatives like Propositions 187 and 209 and the "English for Our Kids Initiative" were conceived in Califor-nia. Although there was some activism against these propositions, spearheaded by well-established service-providing organizations, it did not spread to take the shape of a grassroots movement. Some efforts were made to try to build coalitions among different immigrant organi-zations in the state, but these efforts fell short of providing the bases for a long-term interethnic alliance.[6]

These events on both sides of the border provide the political context for the current activism of indigenous migrants. In examining the organizations forged by indigenous migrants in California, it becomes apparent that they are shaped by responses to the adverse working and living conditions they confront as migrant workers in the United States. Toward the end of improving these conditions, indigenous migrant organizations, such as the Mixtec-Zapotec coalition Frente Indígena Oaxaqueño Binacional (the Frente), have forged coalitions with unions (United Farm Workers), nongovernmental organizations (California Legal Rural Assistance), churches, student organizations (Movimiento Estudiantil Chicano de Aztlan), and Native American organizations to address the frequent violations of labor and human rights in this country. Meanwhile, in Mexico the activism of indigenous migrant organizations go beyond their own communities. In early 1996, the Zapatista Army of National Liberation invited several indigenous migrant organizations to participate in the first Indigenous National Congress in San Cristobal de las Casas, Chiapas. During that meeting the Frente, with offices in both California and Oaxaca, was appointed by the group's general assembly as the official conduit between the Indigenous National Congress and the indigenous migrant population in the United States.

The grassroots organizations that indigenous migrants formed in the 1990s are part of a long history of political activism among Mexican and other immigrants in the United States. Immigrant organizations based on home community ties are common to many immigrant groups who have settled in this country, and they have played a fundamental role in the economic empowerment and social incorporation of immigrants into U.S. society. Eastern European Jews who came to the United States during the Great Migration period between 1880 and 1923 provide perhaps some of the earliest forms of associations of immigrants from the same hometown with the development of "Landsmanschaftn" (Weisser 1985; Soyer 1997).[7] According to Michael Weisser, the importance of Landsmanschaften organizations was that they offered immigrants the possibility of "continuing the cultural and social traditions of the Old World in such undiluted form that there was little ambiguity about [their] cultural identity" (1985, 6). The problem of cultural identity continues to be an important issue for current debates about present-day immigrant groups such as Mexicans.

The Landsmanschaften principle was in no way peculiar to Jewish migrants. In fact, it is one of the most common forms of immigrant organization throughout the world, and groups as diverse as the Chinese in Singapore and the Ibo in Calabar, Nigeria, have formed associations based on village or region of origin.[8] Hometown associations have been crucial in allowing Mexican immigrants to participate in efforts and movements to change conditions in their homelands since the turn of the century. Mexican immigrants' concern about and loyalty to their communities of origin are an indication that these immigrants maintain ongoing connections and hold a meaningful stake in the affairs of their home communities, to which they hope someday to return.

The organization that serves as the case in this study, the Frente Indígena Oaxaqueño Binacional (hereafter the Frente), can be described as a coalition of organizations and communities of indigenous peoples— Mixtec, Zapotec, and Trique—from Oaxaca, most of whom have had to migrate temporarily or permanently from their state of origin to other northern Mexican states and the United States for their own economic survival. The members of the organization are concentrated in the Mexican states of Oaxaca and Baja California Norte as well as in the U.S. states of California, Oregon, and Washington.

The Frente was first formed in 1991, when five Oaxacan hometown associations met in California to form the Mixteco-Zapoteco Binational Front. Until that time, the main function of these Oaxacan hometown associations had been almost exclusively limited to financing public works projects in their communities of origin, following the same hometown-based political orientation established by previous mestizo migrants. For example, Mixtec hometown associations, like the Comité Cívico Popular Tlacotepense, were explicitly organized out of concerns with the internal problems facing San Miguel Tlacotepec. Arturo Pimentel, one of the founding leaders of this hometown association, explains in detail the chronology of this organization and its transformation from a hometown association to an ethnic regional organization:

> There were about twenty people among the group of people who founded the Comité Cívico Popular Mixteco; all of us were from Tlacotepec. We met at different times in different places. We had formed a sports club among Tlacotepenses who were going back and forth between Tlacotepec and Sinaloa and Mexico City. In the mid-1970s we started to organize a committee in response to some problems in our hometown. The PRIistas wanted to impose their own candidate for the municipal presidency. This committee was strengthened in California, but actually it emerged between people in our hometown and paisanos [countrymen] living and working in Mexico City, who had gone there to work in the construction of the subway system and other construction sites. . . .
>
> Originally we called ourselves Comité Cívico Popular Tlacotepense (Tlacotepense Popular Civic Committee) . . . but later when we would run into the same people in the agricultural fields in northern Mexico . . . we started to share our labor grievances in the labor camps in Sinaloa, Sonora, and San Quintín [Baja California Norte]. . . . That is why we later changed the name of our organization to Comité Cívico Popular Mixteco (Mixtec Popular Civic Committee). . . .

Later, in the mid-1980s I went to the United States. That was when the reform to the immigration laws took place with the Simpson-Rodino law. During that time the migrants from my hometown were concentrated mainly in the north of San Diego County, and they organized to send money and support to the municipal presidency in Tlacotepec.

We, in the Comité Cívico Popular Mixteco, were able to expand that project by incorporating people from other communities, and we also sought out other organizations such as the Asociación Cívica Benito Juárez (for people from San Juan Mixtepec) and the Organización del Pueblo Explotado y Oprimido (for people from San Miguel Cuevas). Mixtec migrant workers were the embryo of the Frente, the larger organization. Members of the Comité Cívico Popular Mixteco promoted between 1985 and 1987 some encounters with some Zapotec organizations in Los Angeles. . . . It was in this way that in 1991 we formed the Frente Mixteco-Zapoteco Binacional. (Arturo Pimentel Salas, interview with author, August 2, 1997, Juxtlahuaca, Oaxaca)[9]

The transformation of these indigenous migrant organizations from hometown associations to ethnic organizations was crucial for the formation of the Frente. In 1991, when the Frente was formed, six organizations of indigenous migrants—the Comité Cívico Popular Mixteco, the Organización de Pueblo Explotado y Oprimido, the Comité Tlacolulense en Los Angeles, the Organización Pro-Ayuda a Macuiltianguis, the Asociación Cívica Benito Juárez, and the Organización Regional de Oaxaca—met in Los Angeles explicitly to "join their efforts as indigenous peoples to fight for their rights."[10] The Organización Regional de Oaxaca was the only organization of the six that already worked as a coalition, coordinating the activities of eight other Zapotec hometown associations to produce and stage the Los Angeles–based cultural festival called the Guelaguetza.

By 1994 this initial group had enlarged its membership and became the Frente Indígena Oaxaqueño Binacional, whose current membership numbers about two thousand. The aim of the organization has changed dramatically from exclusively financing local public works projects in migrants' communities of origin to larger goals such as promoting and defending the human rights of all indigenous migrants and improving living and working conditions for indigenous migrants on both sides of the border. Additionally, the Frente has a strong rights orientation and carries out extensive education and advocacy on human, civil, and labor rights. At the same time, it organizes projects that address the economic development needs of its members both in Mexico and in the United States. The Frente is a member of the Congreso Nacional Indígena (Indigenous National Congress in Mexico) and has played a key role at the national level in the articulation of indigenous rights based on a grassroots perspective.

One of the Frente's most successful projects is the program for indigenous-language interpreters. Through this program fifteen Oaxacan indigenous interpreters were trained to provide relay interpretation (for example, between Spanish and Mixtec) in work, health, educational, social service, and legal settings in California. The languages represented were various dialects of Mixtec (including mixteco alto and mixteco bajo) and Zapotec (zapoteco del valle and zapoteco de la sierra). This program has been so successful that members of the government in Mexico City have contacted the leaders of the Frente to ask for advice in developing a similar program targeted at indigenous migrants who live in that city. In addition to the indigenous interpreter projects, the Frente also carries out projects in collaboration with other U.S. and Mexican partners and allied organizations. These include the Binational Indigenous Women's Project (with Lideres Campesinas), which focuses on issues of domestic violence and leadership development for indigenous women; the Defense of Human and Labor Rights Project (with California Rural Legal Assistance in the United States and Asesoria Legal Indígena in Baja California), which provides training and outreach services to educate indigenous migrants on their rights and, if need to, to defend those rights; and community development projects (with the Chicano Federation in San Diego County and Unidad de Capacitación e Investigación Educativa para la Participación in Oaxaca), which establish community gardens and other projects, especially focused on food security issues, in San Diego and in the Mixteca region of Oaxaca.

The Frente currently operates two regional offices from its headquarters in Fresno, California. The regional office in Juxtlahuaca coordinates the work of three municipal offices that serve more than twenty-two communities in five municipalities. The Maneadero office serves the Maneadero Valley and the San Quintín Valley region in Baja California Norte.

Transborder Political Activism of Mixtec Migrants

Since its inception, the Frente has promoted a new modality of membership that departs from the village-based and regional organizations that originally joined the coalition. First, the Frente recognizes in its bylaws both corporate and individual membership by declaring that "all organizations, communities, or individuals of Oaxacan indigenous origin, or non-Oaxaca indigenous origin, will be members of FIOB [the Frente Indígena Oaxaqueño Binacional] providing that they agree with our organization's principles, program of action, and political line."[11] This form of noncorporatist membership departs from the strictly corporate form of membership prevalent in village-based migrant associations, in which membership is restricted to persons born within the community or to migrants with direct kin ties to members of the village. In this respect the Frente has features of both a political party and a nongovernmental organization. It also has characteristics of a union—in part owing to the previous experience of leaders like Arturo Pimentel, who has been active in several union movements since the early 1970s.

The Frente sees itself not as a service-providing organization but rather as a grassroots social movement. It has developed a binational approach to political action, at times coordinating collective actions in both the United States and Mexico to defend and protect the human rights of its members and other Oaxacan migrants as they move from their home state northward to Baja California Norte and into the United States. Much of the Frente's work at the binational level has been framed within a rights perspective; the group also addresses labor issues and other issues that arise in migrants' communities of origin and carry forward into the United States.

A striking feature of Mixtec migrant workers' transnational activism is their active participation in the local political life of their communities even when they are not physically present. This political participation by migrants both strengthens and transforms their community's cultural and social resources (such as traditional forms of self-government, including the cargo system, leadership accountability to popular assemblies, and strong corporate community political identity). Peggy Levitt (1998) argues that the social remittances (ideas, behaviors, identities, and social capital) migrants send back home play an important role in transforming the social and political life of their communities of origin. The ideas and practices Mixtec migrants bring back are, in fact, remolded in the context of the home community, and traditional community practices are thereby adapted to the transnational context. During my fieldwork in California I met many Mixtec migrants who have been summoned back to their communities to perform tasks they had been elected to carry out by the local community assembly (a practice known as the "cargo"). Often, these migrants have been absent from their communities for many years, working and living as far away as Oregon, California, or New Jersey.

Pablo (a pseudonym) discussed mixed feelings that a lot of Mixtec migrants—including himself—have about returning to serve in elected positions in the local government of their communities of origin. Pablo had migrated from San Miguel Cuevas to Madera, California, when he was sixteen years old. After a brief stay in California he moved to Canby, Oregon, where he lived for eight consecutive years before returning to Cuevas. By that time, he spoke fluent Mixtec, English, and Spanish and had earned his general equivalency diploma and a bachelor's degree in social work from Oregon State University on a state scholarship. After graduating from college, he was recalled to his community to serve as secretary of the Committee of Communal Properties (Comité de Bienes Comunales). It is important, Pablo explained, to be a good citizen to his home community, despite the many hardships Mixtec migrants face in carrying out the community's mandate:

> I returned because I felt I did not have any other choice. It was either returning or losing my family's land. At first I did not want to do it [return]. Life is very hard here in Cuevas. You come and serve your community for no pay, and they do not care about how you are going to survive. At least the older people serving the community have their sons and daughters in el otro lado [the other side] who support them while they have their cargo [elected position]. I decided to return and serve, because I know that is what my father, if he was alive, would have wanted me to do, to be a good citizen. He was killed in a dispute for land with the neighboring community. I guess my job now is to try to keep the limits of our community intact. . . . I will ask for permission to go to work for a few months to el otro lado to make ends meet this year. The good thing is that this is my second and last year. (Pablo, interview with author, October 9, 1997, San Miguel Cuevas, Oaxaca)

The Mixtec community of Cuevas has taken a dramatic step in asserting its regulating mechanisms for membership in the community. Migrants have to fulfill some very strict requirements, which include the physical return of the migrant to perform a cargo, to maintain their good standing within the community. Failure to do so carries severe penalties, such as the confiscation of land and property, as Pablo mentioned in his interview.[12] After Pablo's period in his cargo had ended he did go back to the United States, where he struggled to find a new job and get back on his feet economically, after having exhausted his savings of three years. In reflecting back on this experience he felt that he did the right thing, because now his paisanos consider him a "good citizen" of his patria chica (literally, small country).

A similar desire to maintain good standing in the eyes of the community is found among Zapotec migrants in Los Angeles. The case of Angel (not his real name), a young single Zapotec migrant who has been migrating from San Pablo Macuiltianguis to Burbank for the last five years, illustrates this point. Angel usually works as a dishwasher at various restaurants in the area. He stays with an older brother, who resides permanently in Burbank and who, unlike Angel, is a permanent resident. Angel, who had just recently arrived after crossing the border illegally, described how he had been elected to a cargo in his community during a brief vacation from the United States.

> When I went to Macuiltianguis to visit my parents and enjoy the fiesta of my hometown I knew that I could be elected to a cargo. My father had already told me to prepare myself—and that is exactly what happened! I was elected to the school's Parents Committee. My father helped me to settle this matter by persuading an uncle to do the work for me so I could go back to my job in Los Angeles. That is the reason why I returned to California sooner than I had planned, since now I have to make enough money to pay one hundred dollars a month to my uncle who is doing the work required by my cargo in Macuiltianguis. That is the way all the migrants who do not reside in Macuiltianguis perform their cargos. If a migrant wants to be a "citizen in good standing" [ciudadano de bien], he could ask to be elected and then pay somebody to perform his duties in the community, and he can go back to his jobs in Mexico City or here in Los Angeles. . . . I want to be a citizen in good standing with my community so I give all my monetary contributions [cooperaciones] and my communal work [tequio]. I am a citizen in good standing [ciudadano al corriente], with all my rights. In this way whenever I return to Macuiltianguis no one would frown at me. (Angel [a pseudonym], interview with author, February 19, 1998, Burbank, California)

Notice that Macuiltianguenses have a very different notion of citizenship—more flexible—than Mixtecs from Cuevas, in the sense of its membership and requirements. Migrants from Macuiltianguis do not have to return physically to serve their cargo; instead, they can pay someone in the village to carry out their responsibilities for them. Another major difference is that sanctions are more symbolic than in the case of Cuevas—after all, being frowned upon by neighbors for not performing a cargo is a less drastic punishment than the confiscation of the family's farm by local authorities. Additionally, being a ciudadano al corriente (literally, up-to-date citizen) in Macuiltianguis does not carry big rewards for migrants like Angel. On the contrary, it involves investing a substantial amount of money in the form of unpaid labor or hard currency in the form of dues. Another incentive for Angel to maintain the status of ciudadano al corriente is that in Macuiltianguis membership in the community forestry cooperative depends on that status. Only citizens in good standing, those who are "up to date" on their cooperaciones and tequios, are considered "comuneros con voz y voto" (members of the community with a voice and a vote). This title carries more symbolic status, in terms of respect and standing in the community, than financial reward. Many indigenous communities, like San Miguel Cuevas and San Pablo Macuiltianguis, have decided to incorporate paisanos who have migrated into the local political process by redefining, through their community assemblies, their conceptualization of citizenship and community. According to their own redefinition of citizenship, a migrant who relocates abroad does not sever his or her ties with the community and can continue to enjoy the same rights and obligations as members of the community who stay, as long as the migrant continues to serve the cargos the community assembly decides to confer on him or her. In this way, the definition of community has been expanded to include the many members who reside abroad. People in indigenous villages in Oaxaca conceive of their community as made up of the local population as well as the population dispersed along the migratory network that extends to northern Mexico and into the United States. Thus, through the constant movement of migrants back and forth and the concurrent flow of information, money, and goods and services, the communities of origin and their various "satellite communities" in northern Mexico and the United States have become so closely linked that in a sense they form a single community, a transnational community. The transnational concept, the way I would like to use it here, has two relevant dimensions. The first is its geographic sense, referring to such phenomena as migration, commerce, and communication, which cross national borders. The second refers to the notion of transforming and transcending the nation-state as a modern social and cultural form (Kearney 1995b).

The political activism of migrant populations such as the Mixtecs and Zapotecs in California and their ability to participate in the political processes of their communities of origin directly challenges the hegemony of the Mexican state to define the boundaries of the "national political community" and the rights that its members can enjoy. One can hardly imagine an effective way that the state and federal governments in Mexico could regulate the process by which hundreds of indigenous municipalities and small villages elect their representatives every four years. The Mixtec municipality of Juxtlahuaca, where I carried out my fieldwork, is composed of sixty-two agencias municipales (villages), the smallest political organizational units in Mexico. Each of these agencias elects its own council of representatives according to its own usos y costumbres (customs and traditions). In other words, it is not the Mexican state that determines the boundaries of a Mixtec migrant "political" community, through judicial mechanisms (laws and regulations), but the indigenous community itself, which redefines and expands its contours through its political practice of incorporating the thousands of migrants who work and live two thousand miles away in a different country.[13]

The ability of Mixtec indigenous communities to adapt their political and cultural capital to the transnational process of migration is closely related to the high degree of autonomy they have traditionally exercised in regulating their internal affairs. In this sense, autonomy, understood as "the right to exercise collectively the free determination" of indigenous peoples, is not a concept or an idea that was born just yesterday (Regino 1996, 2). These indigenous communities have governed their communities and exercised authority through their own traditional mechanisms for a long time. This ability of the indigenous communities to regulate their community affairs turns out to be of great importance, especially for those communities with a high rate of out-migration.

In other words, Mixtec indigenous communities have completely reversed something that has traditionally been seen as a catastrophe for their long-term survival—extremely high rates of out-migration—and have transformed it into a source of synergy that assures their cultural, social, and economic reproduction. Indigenous autonomy, understood as the mechanism by which they govern themselves and exercise their authority, has been fundamental to their response to the migratory experience. Within this context, Mixtec indigenous communities have reconceptualized and expanded the concept of political community, redefining it in a way that allows for the incorporation of the immense indigenous population dispersed across many geographical borders.

The active participation of Mixtec migrants in the affairs of their communities of origin has strengthened their ethnic identity, which has allowed them, at the same time, to build binational political organizations that further strengthen close ties with communities in Oaxaca (see Kearney and Nagengast 1989). Many Mixtec migrants not only continue to be consulted about political decisions in their communities while they live in the United States but also still maintain rights and obligations as members of their specific political communities. In practice, Mixtec migrants have the right to participate in the internal governing process of their home community. Indeed, as I have indicated, they are eligible to be considered for public office within the local governing structures.

In this context, the transnational organizations of Mixtec migrants such as the Frente Indígena Oaxaqueño Binacional perform two basic tasks: first, they institutionalize political practices that allow for collective action in the different locations of the Mixtec migratory network (that is, the transnationalized space sometimes denominated Oaxacalifornia); second, they institutionalize cultural exchange practices and the circulation of information that give meaning to a political community that transcends many geographical borders, at the community, state, and international levels.

In the case of Mixtec migrants organized in the Frente Indígena Oaxaqueño Binacional and other Zapotec village-based migrant associations in Los Angeles, it is apparent that the cultural base of these organizations is a recently emerged sense of panethnic identity—namely, Mixtec and Zapotec ethnicity—that was formerly nonexistent in Oaxaca. There is a strong relation between this emergent identity and the formation of migrant political organizations among indigenous migrant communities, whose political participation and activism in California reinforce their ethnic identity, holding the community together as it becomes ever more extended throughout both Mexico and the United States.

Indigenous migrants have been able to mobilize and to transform cultural and social resources within their "traditional" society and culture to resist full incorporation into highly exploitative wage labor systems and to resist the forces of acculturation. Thus, whereas most conventional migration theory predicts that long-term extensive migration reduces ethnicity and promotes assimilation, this research points to an apparently contrary case.

As pointed out earlier, a key assumption of transnationalism is that racial, ethnic, and national identities are constructed categories that are reconfigured and strategically deployed by immigrants. Organizations such as the Frente are engaged not only in nation-building projects but also in the construction of transnational identities. Consequently, migrants fashion multiple identities within a complex geographical landscape that includes their communities of origin and multiple sites along their migratory network. Arturo Pimentel, one of the main leaders of the Frente, illustrates this point:

> Oaxacan migrant organizations are definitely village based. Our paisanos usually say that they are from Cuevas, Tunuchi, or Tlacotepec, as in my own case. But in a different context we are Mixtecs. Then, later, we are Oaxaqueños. However, village-based identification serves as the basis of our identity. For example, together with my paisanos we formed an organization that focused exclusively on our municipality. But later we realized that we were not alone, that we shared many things with our paisanos from other towns from the same region, then we had to say we were Mixtecos so that others would join the organization. Therefore, these are different levels of the organizational process. Also, we could compare this to the question of identity. When you come by yourself to the United States, you feel like you miss your homeland, your family, the music, the parties, the community celebrations, the ways of socializing. Well, everything there is in our communities. But in the moment your community or social circle grows, these customs regain force again, and this is a way to recuperate our community, what we are and our roots. (Arturo Pimentel, interview with author, October 21, 1997, Juxtlahuaca, Oaxaca)

As a result of migration, as the testimony of Arturo illustrates, ethnic and regional identities are foregrounded and become particularly prominent, as in the case of indigenous migrants. Such identities are reconfigured and deployed both to accommodate and to resist subordination within a transnational capitalist system.

The political practices of the transnational indigenous migrant organizations go far beyond the recent attempts by the Mexican state to recognize the particular situation of millions of Mexicans who have been incorporated in the U.S.-bound migratory process. It is not surprising that organizations such as the Frente Indígena Oaxaqueño Binacional consider the recent changes in the Mexican Constitution, which now allows Mexican immigrants who acquire U.S. citizenship to maintain their Mexican nationality, as too little too late. The main problem with this constitutional amendment, according to the Frente, is that it does not recognize the political rights of dual nationals, because they are unable to vote or be eligible for public office in Mexico. In other words, this recent change in the Mexican Constitution allows migrants to maintain their Mexican nationality and enjoy the protection of their civil rights by the Mexican state (such as the right to buy property along the coasts and borderlines), but they have to renounce such political rights as voting during presidential and local elections, and they are not allowed to hold elected office in Mexico. For indigenous migrants who are active participants in the affairs of their communities of origin, this represents a step back, rather than an improvement, for their political rights. Another recent development is a 1996 law granting Mexican citizens the right to vote in Mexican presidential elections while living abroad.[14] Some indigenous migrant leaders see this as a step forward in the recognition of the political rights of Mexican migrants in general. However, they claim that while electing the next Mexican president in the year 2000 is very important, it is more pressing to be able to shape policy at the state and local level, because the political institutions there affect indigenous communities the most. Indigenous migrant leaders want to be able to participate fully in political decisions at the local and community level in both the United States and Mexico—something that requires the recognition of dual citizenship: full membership in two nations, including all the rights and obligations they enjoy in their communities of origin in the Mixteca region in Oaxaca.

Conclusion

Recent patterns of migration that have developed in Mexican indigenous regions, along with the emergence of new transnational forms of organization, are having a profound impact on indigenous migrants' ethnic identities. On the one hand, long-term transnational migration strengthens and intensifies indigenous migrants' ethnic identity. On the other, indigenous migrants' political activism is dramatically transforming their communities of origin, allowing for the emergence of new forms of transnational political communities and identities and a new sense of who they are. These migrants and their transnational organizations will undoubtedly play an important role in national political discussions on both sides of the border, from immigration issues and labor to human rights in the United States and from the indigenous autonomy debate to the presidential elections in the year 2000 in Mexico.

A previous version of this chapter appeared in *American Behavioral Scientist* 1999, vol. 42, no. 9.

Notes

1. Mixtec migrants come from the southern Mexican state of Oaxaca, located 350 miles south of Mexico City. Oaxaca is the most culturally diverse and ethnically fragmented state in Mexico. This state's inhabitants are indigenous, with around 53 percent speaking one of sixteen indigenous languages. The two largest indigenous groups are the Zapotecs (861,200) and the Mixtecs (635,100). Indigenous peoples (pueblos indígenas) in Mexico are defined as those persons that have their origins and who maintain community attachment to any of the pre-Conquest inhabitants of the cultural region known as Mesoamerica.

2. For a more general discussion about the concept of "deterritorialized spaces," see Basch, Glick Schiller, and Szanton Blanc 1994.

3. A 1991 survey by the California Institute for Rural Studies found that among Oaxacan indigenous migrants in California, 203 Oaxacan communities were represented (among them Zapotec, Chinatec, Trique, and Mixtec communities), belonging to eighty-one different municipalities. These data suggest that indigenous Oaxacan migration has multiple sources in that state but tends to be concentrated in specific subregions. The best-represented communities were located in three districts in the Mixtec region: Juxtlahuaca, Silacayoapan, and Huajuapan de León (Runsten and Kearney 1994).

4. These binational civic organizations take many forms, ranging from immigrant hometown associations and related community development initiatives to cross-border indigenous rights movements and new advocacy networks for Mexican absentee voting rights (Smith and Guarzino 1998; Goldring 1998; Smith 1998; and Rivera-Salgado 1999).

5. Mixtecs, Zapotecs, and Purepechas form the largest share of these new migrants, but they also include other ethnic groups from Oaxaca, mestizo and indigenous groups from Guerrero and Puebla, and migrants from the most isolated villages in the traditional sending regions.

6. The San Francisco–based Immigration Network was the most developed effort on the part of a diverse group of immigrant service provider organizations to come together and provide some resistance to the anti-immigrant propositions. The efforts of the Immigration Network were concentrated in the San Francisco Bay area and some cities of the Central Valley. However, it did not develop a strong presence in southern California.

7. Daniel Soyer explains the meaning of "Landsmanschaften" as follows: "The Yiddish word *landsman* denotes a person (a man or woman, but usually a man) from the same town, region, or country as the speaker. The plural form is *landslayt*. A *Landsmanschaft* is thus a formal organization of *landslayt*, or, more loosely, the informal community of *landslayt*" (1997, 1). *Landsman* would be the equivalent of paisano in Spanish, among Mexican immigrants.

8. For a great description of Chinese, Ibo, and other immigrant organizations in a different context, see Fallers (1967).

9. Arturo Pimentel Salas is general coordinator of the Frente Indígena Oaxaqueño Binacional. The interview was conducted in Spanish, and this is my translation.

10. Editorial, *El Tequio*, no. 2 (July 1992): 2. *El Tequio* is the quarterly newsletter of the Frente.

11. "Será miembro del FIOB toda organización, comunidad o persona de origen indígena Oaxaqueño o sin ser indígena Oaxaqueño, que esté de acuerdo con su Declaración de Principios, Programa de Acción, Estatutos y Linea política"; see Frente Indígena Oaxaqueño Binacional (1998).

12. While doing fieldwork I was able to confirm only one case in which the land and house of a migrant who refused to go back to his community was seized by the authorities, in Santa Catarina Noltepec (a neighboring community of San Miguel Cuevas). Sometimes migrants can negotiate with the local authorities the duration of their cargo (as in the case of Pablo) or other alternatives, such as performing community service for short periods or paying a fine, if return to Oaxaca is not possible.

13. "Political community" is defined here in its broadest sense as the individuals who claim membership in an indigenous community and enjoy rights and responsibilities by participating actively in the internal decision-making process and the election of local authorities.

14. On June 30, 1999, the Institutional Revolutionary Party boycotted a session in the Senate that was crucial to implement the changes in the electoral code needed to enact the 1996 law on time for Mexican immigrants to vote in the presidential election in July 2000. Mexican immigrants now have to wait until the presidential elections of 2006 to be able to vote. (See, *La Jornada*,"Mexico: PRI Boicotea Debate de Reforma Electoral en el Senado," July 1, 1999, México, D.F.)

References

Anderson, Warren. 1997. "Familias Purépechas en el sur de Illinois: La (re)construcción de la identidad étnica." Paper presented to the Nineteenth Anthropology and Regional History Colloquium, Colegio de Michoacán. Ciudad de Zamora, Mexico (October 22, 1997).

Appadurai, Arjun. 1996. *Modernity at Large: Cultural Dimensions of Globalization.* Minneapolis: University of Minnesota Press.

Basch, Linda, Nina Glick Schiller, and Cristina Szanton Blanc. 1994. *Nations Unbound: Transnational Projects and the Deterritorialized Nation-State.* New York: Gordon and Breach.

Colegio de la Frontera Norte (COLEF). 1994a. *Encuesta sobre migración en la Frontera Norte.* Tijuana, Mexico: COLEF.

———. 1994b. *Estado actual de la migración interna e internacional de los Oriundos del Estado de Oaxaca.* Tijuana, Mexico: COLEF.

Cornelius, A. Wayne. 1988. *The Changing Profile of Mexican Labor Migration to California in the 1980s.* La Jolla: Center for U.S.-Mexican Studies, University of California.

Fallers, L.A., ed. 1967. *Immigrants and Associations.* The Hague: Mouton.

Frente Indígena Oaxaqueño Binacional. 1998. "Documentos Básicos del Frente Indígena Oaxaqueño Binacional," Downloaded from the world wide web in May 1998 at: http://www.laneta.apc.org/fiob/.

Georges, Eugenia. 1990. *The Making of a Transnational Community: Migration Development and Cultural Change in the Dominican Republic.* New York: Columbia University Press.

Glick Schiller, Nina, Linda Basch, and Cristina Blanc-Szanton, eds. 1992. *Towards a Transnational Perspective on Migration: Race, Class, Ethnicity, and Nationalism Reconsidered.* New York: New York Academy of Sciences.

Glick Schiller, Nina, Linda Basch, and Cristina Szanton-Blanc. 1995. "From Immigrant to Transmigrant: Theorizing Transnational Migration." *Anthropological Quarterly* 68(1): 48–54.

Gold, Steven. 1997. "Transnationalism and Vocabularies of Motive and International Migration: The Case of Israelis in the United States." *Sociological Perspectives* 40(3): 409–26.

Goldring, Luin. 1992. "Diversity and Community in Transnational Migration: A Comparative Study of Two Mexico–United States Migrant Communities." Ph.D. diss., Cornell University.

———. 1998. "The Power of Status in Transnational Social Fields." In *Transnationalism from Below*, edited by Michael P. Smith and Luis Guarnizo. New Brunswick, N.J.: Transaction Publishers.

Grasmuck, Sherri, and Patricia Pessar. 1991. *Between Two Islands: Dominican International Migration.* Berkeley: University of California Press.

Kearney, Michael. 1995a. "The Effects of Transnational Culture, Economy, and Migration on Mixtec Identity in Oaxacalifornia." In *The Bubble Cauldron: Race, Ethnicity, and the Urban Crisis*, edited by Michael Peter Smith and Joe R. Feagin. Minneapolis: University of Minnesota Press.

———. 1995b. "The Local and the Global: The Anthropology of Globalization and Transnationalism." *Annual Review of Anthropology* 24: 547–66.

Kearney, Michael, and Carol Nagengast. 1989. *Anthropological Perspectives on Transnational Communities in Rural California.* Davis: California Institute for Rural Studies.

Levitt, Peggy. 1998. "Social Remittances: Migration-Driven Local-Level Forms of Cultural Diffusion." *International Migration Review* 32(4): 926–48.

Massey, Douglas, Rafael Alarcón, Jorge Durand, and Hector Gonzalez. 1987. *Return to Aztlan: The Social Process of International Migration from Western Mexico.* Berkeley: University of California Press.

Regino, Adelfo. 1996. "La Autonomía una Forma Concreta del Derecho a la Libre Determinación y sus Alcances." Paper presented to the Indigenous National Congress. San Cristobal de las Casas, Chiapas, Mexico (January 10, 1996).

Rivera-Salgado, Gaspar. 1999. "Migration and Political Activism: Mexican Transnational Indigenous Communities in Comparative Perspective." Ph.D. diss., University of California, Santa Cruz.

Runsten, David, and Michael Kearney. 1994. *A Survey of Oaxacan Village Networks in California Agriculture.* Davis: California Institute for Rural Studies.

Smith, Michael P., and Luis Guarnizo, eds. 1998. *Transnationalism from Below.* Vol. 6 of *Comparative Urban and Community Research.* New Brunswick, N.J.: Transaction Publishers.

Smith, Robert. 1995. "Los Ausentes Siempre Presentes: The Imagining, Making, and Politics of a Transnational Migrant Community Between Ticuani, Puebla, Mexico, and New York City." Ph.D. diss., Columbia University.

———. 1998. "Transnational Localities: Community, Technology, and the Politics of Membership Within the Context of Mexico and U.S. Migration." In *Transnationalism from Below*, edited by Michael P. Smith and Luis Guarnizo. New Brunswick, N.J.: Transaction Publishers.

Soyer, Daniel. 1997. *Jewish Immigrant Associations and American Identity in New York, 1880–1939.* Cambridge: Harvard University Press.

Weisser, Michael R. 1985. *A Brotherhood of Memory: Jewish Landsmanschaften in the New World.* New York: Basic Books.

Zabin, Carol, Michael Kearney, Ana Garcia, David Runsten, and Carol Nagengast. 1993. *Mixtec Migrants in California Agriculture: A New Cycle of Poverty.* Davis: California Institute for Rural Studies.

7

NATURALIZATION UNDER CHANGING CONDITIONS OF MEMBERSHIP: DOMINICAN IMMIGRANTS IN NEW YORK CITY

Greta Gilbertson and Audrey Singer

R ESEARCH on naturalization and citizenship reflects increasing interest in the acquisition of citizenship as a process influenced by a multiplicity of forces. Scholars have begun to recognize the importance of destination conditions—including community structure, labor market, and federal policies—and their influence on citizenship acquisition (Yang 1994; Bloemraad 1999; Jones-Correa 1998). However, researchers have not adequately explored the ways in which contextual factors influence immigrants' propensity to naturalize by shaping their perceptions of citizenship. A critical feature of the current political and social context in the United States is the anti-immigrant legislation that was passed in 1996.[1]

Most sociological research on naturalization has focused on the individual characteristics of immigrants as predictors of naturalization.[2] According to Phillip Yang (1994), there are two complementary research traditions. One focuses on socioeconomic and demographic variables and finds that immigrants with higher levels of education, occupational status, and family income are more likely to naturalize (Portes and Curtis 1987; DeSipio 1987; Liang 1994a, 1994b). The other looks at the influence of various dimensions of assimilation, such as the cultural, economic, and structural, into the host society. These studies have found that immigrants who are more assimilated are more likely to naturalize (Liang 1994b). One interpretation of this finding is that cultural assimilation fosters in immigrants a sense of belonging to the receiving society by promoting familiarity with its language, values, government, and social system and nurtures positive associations with being an

American. Such experiences also enhance the ability of immigrants to meet the language and literacy requirements of the naturalization process (Yang 1994).

Although this research tells us which immigrant characteristics are associated with naturalization and demonstrates that naturalization rates vary by national origin, these studies neglect the role of immigrants' perceptions of the costs, benefits, and meaning of naturalization. This is an important oversight in the literature, especially in light of the fact that immigrant views of naturalization are likely to be the most direct determinants of naturalization behavior (Alvarez 1987; Yang 1994). One recent case study of naturalization by Michael Jones-Correa (1998) explores the context of naturalization decision making among Latin American immigrants in Queens. Jones-Correa argues that immigrants are reluctant to naturalize because they retain strong ties to their countries of origin. They see naturalization as a U.S. citizen as a betrayal of their country and of their plan to return. For many immigrants, becoming a U.S. citizen also means the loss of benefits in their home countries.

Jones-Correa's study provides insight into the process of naturalization; however, it does not explore the current context of citizenship acquisition in the United States in the late 1990s. The three laws passed in 1996 (the Welfare Act, the Immigration Act, and the Anti-Terrorism Act) and the accompanying anti-immigrant rhetoric appear to have created new incentives for legal permanent residents to naturalize by increasing the benefits of becoming a U.S. citizen and the costs of remaining a legal resident. The origins of the welfare law are found in Proposition 187, the 1994 California ballot initiative designed to deny all social and medical services to undocumented immigrants. The federal government took a step further with the Welfare Act in denying access to federally funded means-tested programs (Supplemental Security Income, food stamps, Medicaid, and Temporary Assistance for Needy Families) to all noncitizens, not just undocumented immigrants. The welfare law sent a strong message to noncitizen immigrants and appears to have been a catalyst for some legal permanent residents to become citizens.

In light of these concerns, this chapter employs a qualitative case study of an extended family group of Dominican immigrants residing in New York City to understand naturalization and the factors that influence immigrants' propensities to become citizens of the United States. As far as we are aware, this work is the first attempt to use a longitudinal case study to examine naturalization outcomes. The strength of this method is that it allows us to uncover the detailed reasons for immigrants' decisions to naturalize, which cannot be ascertained through other forms of data collection. It also permits us to document change in immigrants' perceptions of the costs, benefits, and meaning of naturalization and to assess the role of context—both family and community—on immigrants' views of naturalization and the decision-making process.

Dominicans in Washington Heights: Settlement and Naturalization in the Contemporary Context

The Dominican Republic is currently the fourth-largest source of immigrants to the United States (INS 1997). Dominicans form the largest immigrant group and the second-largest group, after Puerto Ricans, of Hispanics in New York City. In 1990, more than 80 percent of Dominicans in the continental United States lived in the New York–New Jersey region, with the overwhelming majority residing in New York City (Pessar 1995). Dominicans live in all five of the boroughs that constitute New York City, with the largest concentrations in Manhattan and the Bronx. The principal settlement area in Manhattan is Washington Heights, a multiethnic, predominantly working-class and Latino neighborhood.

Until recently, Dominicans have had relatively low rates of naturalization.[3] Low rates of naturalization among Dominicans are associated with several factors, including the clustering of Dominicans in a few high-density Latino areas in the city. An ethnically enclosed settlement pattern insulates immigrant groups from "mainstream" U.S. culture, increases their exposure to institutions and practices from the sending country, and limits cross-cultural contacts (see Jones-Correa 1998; Portes and Rumbaut 1996). Although residential concentration does not always lead to low levels of naturalization, it does appear to play such a role among Dominicans. Other factors that contribute to low naturalization rates among Dominicans are low levels of education and English language acquisition (Torres-Saillant and Hernandez 1998). Moreover, the proximity of the Dominican Republic to the United States and the relative ease and low cost of transportation facilitate high rates of movement back and forth between the two countries.[4]

Nevertheless, the number of applications for naturalization soared during the period of our study. Large numbers of Dominican immigrants—along with other groups of immigrants—made the decision to become U.S. citizens in the late 1990s. In 1997 alone, 1.6 million applications for naturalization were filed with the Immigration and Naturalization Service (INS), nearly five times the number of applications filed in 1994. Moreover, this surge in naturalization represents a major departure from the stable rates of approximately 250,000 applications a year during the 1980s and early 1990s. However, naturalization applications were already on the rise by the mid-1990s. Several factors contributed to the increase: the large cohort of legalization recipients who became eligible for naturalization under the Immigration Reform and Control Act at this time; the 1992 Green Card Replacement Program; the 1995 Citizenship USA initiative; and the INS's efforts to reduce the naturalization application backlog.

The change in policy mobilized local actors in immigrant communities to help immigrants to naturalize. In Washington Heights alone, a large number of private institutions and voluntary organizations provide services to the immigrant population. In response to the legislative changes and the anti-immigrant climate, some groups reoriented themselves toward providing naturalization services; other organizations expanded or initiated programs to assist immigrants with naturalization (Singer and Gilbertson 1996). Service providers reported in 1995 and 1996 that they were seeing a significant increase in the number of immigrants requesting assistance for naturalization.[5] In a politically savvy move, the City of New York, like several other local governments around the country, responded to the federal cuts in benefits for legal immigrants by funding a network of citizenship assistance centers (the Citizenship NYC program) to assist immigrants in naturalizing. The city government's explicit motive was to reduce costs associated with providing local funding to legal permanent immigrants who were no longer eligible for federally funded programs.

In tandem with the efforts of community organizations to provide immigrants with information concerning the benefits, procedures, and experiences of naturalization, the media was another source of information regarding U.S. citizenship. Channel 41, the most popular Spanish-language television channel, regularly broadcast news programs and public service announcements concerning changing laws and naturalization, including the names of community organizations that assist immigrants in the naturalization process. Spanish-language newspapers (such as El Diario de la Prensa) also provided similar information. However, the tone of the press coverage in the Spanish-language media was often alarmist, heightening the anxiety within the immigrant community regarding naturalization (see Cordero-Guzman and Navarro 2000).

Once an insular community that discouraged immigrants from naturalizing, Washington Heights was transformed into an environment in which information and resources concerning naturalization were readily available. Through a variety of sources, the public was showered with information on naturalization, and community organizations contributed by sponsoring citizenship drives, helping immigrants fill out paperwork, offering citizenship classes, and providing legal assistance. Various community actors, including city officials, took a proactive position by "packaging" U.S. citizenship as a way to preserve access to benefits and U.S. membership rights. This was arguably the most effective way to reach immigrants in a poor community with high participation in social welfare programs.

Other events in the Dominican community in New York City and in the Dominican Republic itself also appear to have encouraged more Dominican immigrants to naturalize. One such factor was the increased visibility of Dominicans in New York City political activities, including the election of several Dominicans to city and state offices in the mid-1990s (see Graham 1997). The election of Dominicans to public office reflects the growth of the Dominican electorate through naturalization, which, in turn, may have encouraged more Dominican noncitizens to naturalize in order to vote. The constitutional reform in the Dominican Republic, which allows Dominicans who become citizens of other countries to retain their rights as Dominican nationals, may also have increased incentives to naturalize. Many Dominicans became aware of dual nationality when Leonel Fernandez, the president of the Dominican Republic, in a televised speech, encouraged Dominicans in the United States to naturalize and assured them that they would not lose their rights as Dominican citizens: "If you, young mother, or you, elderly gentleman, or you, young student, feel the need to adopt the nationality of the United States in order to confront the vicissitudes of that society stemming from the end of the welfare era, do not feel tormented by this. Do it with a peaceful conscience, for you will continue being Dominicans, and we will welcome you as such when you set foot on the soil of our republic" (quoted in Graham 1997). With the advent of dual nationality, becoming a U.S. citizen no longer required Dominicans to relinquish their formal membership in the Dominican Republic.

Methodology

The aim of our study is to learn more about how people think and act about naturalization and the meanings they attach to U.S. citizenship within a context of changing sentiment and legislation regarding immigrants. We use a qualitative case study of an extended family group, the Castillo family, including intensive interviews and participant observation during a period of three years (1995 to 1998). Interviews and observations of the Castillo family were supplemented by interviews with community actors, including immigrant service providers and local leaders in Washington Heights and other New York City communities.

In the course of this research, we also spoke with about fifty other immigrants in the Washington Heights community and observed naturalization patterns among several other families. This information corroborated and complemented much of what we found in our more intensive study of the Castillos.

Selection of the Castillo family was, among other things, a matter of convenience. One of our authors resides in Washington Heights and, as a result of ongoing participation in the community as a researcher and resident, had extensive contact with several members of the Castillos and another family group originating from the same town in the Dominican Republic. We chose to focus on the Castillo family because of its large size and complexity, both in terms of generations and numbers of family members, its concentration in the New York City area, and its cohesiveness, which facilitated the gathering of information from all family members. Most of the adult members residing in the United States were legal permanent residents and, because they had been living in the United States at least five years, were eligible to become U.S. citizens.

There is no way to assess whether the Castillo family is representative of the Dominican community in the United States or in New York City. Although the extended family may be considered a single case, it is composed of a number of distinct nuclear and extended families. Individuals in these subfamilies have a broad range of characteristics, including legal status, age, time since arrival in the United States, life course stage, and settlement patterns. The characteristics of the subfamilies, including patterns of organization, residence, and social networks, also vary.

To what extent are the characteristics of the Castillo family members similar or different from Dominican immigrants resident in New York City? We cannot provide a definitive answer to this question, but comparing the Castillos to Dominican immigrants in New York City on several socioeconomic characteristics shows that in terms of education and occupation, the Castillos are similar to other Dominicans in New York City, according to 1990 census data (see Grasmuck and Pessar 1996). Levels of education of the first cohort are low (ranging from three to ten years of schooling), and as we would expect, those of their offspring are higher. However, among the second cohort, the earlier-arriving group has higher levels of education than the recent arrivals. The higher levels of education of the second cohort are partly a function of their younger age at arrival and education experience in the United States. Overall, 39 percent of all Dominicans aged twenty-five and over in New York City have a high school diploma or education beyond high school compared with 53 percent of the Castillos in the same age range.

In terms of occupation, the Castillo family members approximate the Dominican population residing in New York City. While about half (49 percent) of the Dominicans in New York were employed as operatives, laborers, and personal service workers according to the 1990 census, 55 percent of the Castillos were in these occupational categories.

Our findings on the naturalization patterns of the Castillos (elaborated later in the chapter) support research that shows a positive correlation between education, age at entry, time in the United States, and language skills. Those with higher levels of education entered the United States at younger ages and have spent more time in the United States. They have acquired higher levels of English language proficiency when compared with recent arrivals who arrive at later ages and have lower levels of English skills. Among the Castillos, more members of the second cohort—all of whom have higher levels of education and greater English language skills than the first cohort—naturalized and were more likely to have done so prior to the 1996 changes in the welfare laws. Those with higher levels of education in the second cohort were more likely to have naturalized than members of this cohort with lower levels of education.

The Castillo Family: Migration, Residence, and Citizenship

The Castillo family (excluding spouses) spans five generations and includes sixty-five members, fifty-three of whom reside in the United States. We interviewed two generations of the family during 1997 and 1998: the first sibling cohort, comprising six sisters and two brothers between the ages of thirty-nine and sixty-four, and their offspring, the second cohort, fourteen men and thirteen women ranging in age from eighteen to forty-five (see figure 7.1). The majority of both cohorts have resided in the United States for some time as legal permanent residents or U.S. citizens. The second cohort has a total of twenty-nine children whose ages in the fall of 1997 ranged from infancy to nineteen years. Twenty-one members of the third cohort reside in the United States, and more than two-thirds are U.S.-born citizens. One daughter of this cohort has a child, the first member of the next cohort.

The Castillos are members of an extended family group originating from the city of Mao, located in the largely agricultural province of Valverde in the Dominican Republic. Mao is the largest urban area (population sixty-eight thousand in 1993) in the northwestern region of the Dominican Republic, which historically has been a major source of mi-

FIGURE 7.1   *The Castillo Family*

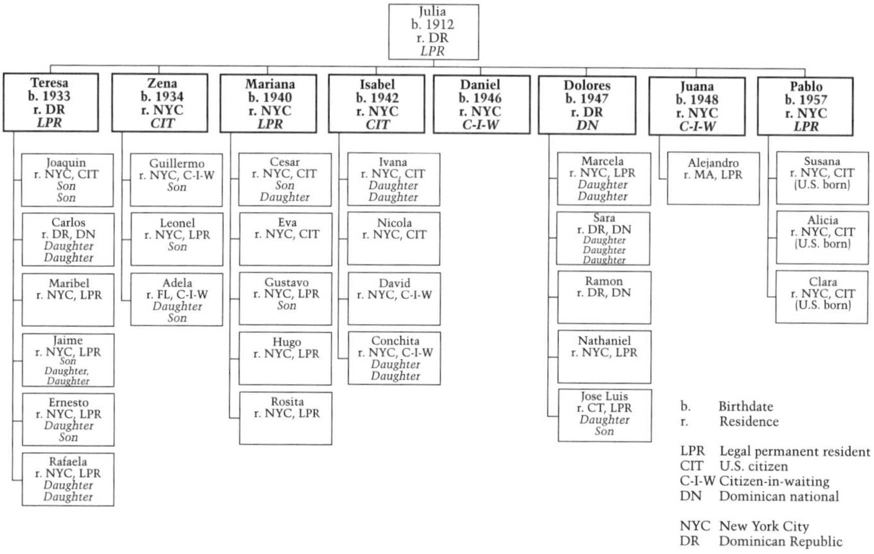

Julia b. 1912, r. DR, LPR

Teresa b. 1933, r. DR, LPR
- Joaquin r. NYC, CIT — Son, Son
- Carlos r. DR, DN — Daughter, Daughter
- Maribel r. NYC, LPR
- Jaime r. NYC, LPR — Son, Daughter, Daughter
- Ernesto r. NYC, LPR — Daughter, Son
- Rafaela r. NYC, LPR — Daughter, Daughter

Zena b. 1934, r. NYC, CIT
- Guillermo r. NYC, C-I-W — Son
- Leonel r. NYC, LPR — Son
- Adela r. FL, C-I-W — Daughter, Son

Mariana b. 1940, r. NYC, LPR
- Cesar r. NYC, CIT — Son, Daughter
- Eva r. NYC, CIT
- Gustavo r. NYC, LPR — Son
- Hugo r. NYC, LPR
- Rosita r. NYC, LPR

Isabel b. 1942, r. NYC, CIT
- Ivana r. NYC, CIT — Daughter, Daughter
- Nicola r. NYC, CIT
- David r. NYC, C-I-W
- Conchita r. NYC, C-I-W — Daughter, Daughter

Daniel b. 1946, r. NYC, C-I-W

Dolores b. 1947, r. DR, DN
- Marcela r. NYC, LPR — Daughter, Daughter
- Sara r. DR, DN — Daughter, Daughter, Daughter
- Ramon r. DR, DN
- Nathaniel r. NYC, LPR
- Jose Luis r. CT, LPR — Daughter, Son

Juana b. 1948, r. NYC, C-I-W
- Alejandro r. MA, LPR

Pablo b. 1957, r. NYC, LPR
- Susana r. NYC, CIT (U.S. born)
- Alicia r. NYC, CIT (U.S. born)
- Clara r. NYC, CIT (U.S. born)

b.   Birthdate
r.   Residence

LPR   Legal permanent resident
CIT   U.S. citizen
C-I-W Citizen-in-waiting
DN   Dominican national

NYC   New York City
DR   Dominican Republic

Source: Authors' compilation.

gration to the United States. In New York City, the majority (thirty-one) of the Castillos live in Manhattan; others live in the Bronx and Brooklyn. Three family members live in Connecticut, Massachusetts, and Florida.

The legal status of the Castillo family members over a twenty-seven-year period is summarized in table 7.1, which shows both the growth of the family over the period and their migration to the United States. The migration history of the Castillo family is characterized by the chain migration of legal immigrants sponsored by family members. The beginning of this chain is Zena, now sixty-four years old, who migrated in 1969 at the age of twenty-eight years, the first in her family to do so. After ending her marriage, she entered the United States via Puerto Rico, using a tourist visa; several years later she obtained legal permanent residency through an arranged marriage. By 1975, two members of the first cohort (Zena and Daniel), Zena's three children, and her mother Julia had acquired legal permanent residency and were living in the United States. Julia received her green card through her son Daniel's sponsorship and subsequently petitioned for five of her adult children, all but one of whom were granted legal permanent residency.

TABLE 7.1   *Legal Status of the Castillo Family, 1975 to 1997*

Legal Status	1975	1985	1997
Dominican national	27	24	12
U.S. legal permanent resident	6	15	20
"Citizen-in-waiting" or a naturalized citizen	0	1	13
U.S.-born citizen	0	4	20
Not yet born	32	21	—
Total	65	65	65

Source: Authors' compilation.

By 1985 the number of Castillo family members in the United States had increased from six to twenty members and included five of the eight members of the first cohort, eight members of the second cohort, and four U.S.-born members of the third cohort. By 1997 the bulk of the family had migrated to the United States, including seven of the eight members of the first cohort and the great majority of the second cohort. The members of the second cohort who live in the United States have a mixture of U.S.-born citizen children and Dominican-born children whose green cards they have sponsored. As of late 1997, thirteen members of the Castillo family had either naturalized or applied to naturalize (these are identified as "citizens-in-waiting" in figure 7.1 and tables 7.1 and 7.2).

Table 7.2 shows the current legal status of the Castillo family members by cohort, as of 1997. In the first cohort, two members have naturalized and two have applied for U.S. citizenship, all during or since 1996. Among the twenty-seven members of the second cohort, twenty-four reside in the United States (three of whom are U.S.-born citizens) and three are Dominican nationals. Of the twenty-one who are eligible to naturalize, five did so before 1996 and four have applied or natu-

TABLE 7.2   *Current Legal Status of Castillo Family Members, by Cohort, 1997*

Legal Status	First Cohort	Second Cohort	Third Cohort
Dominican national	1	3	8
U.S. legal permanent resident	3	12	4
U.S. "citizen-in-waiting"	2	4	0
U.S. citizen (naturalized)	2	5	0
U.S. citizen (U.S. born)	0	3	17
Total*	8	27	29

Source: Authors' compilation.
*Excludes Julia, mother of the first cohort members. She is a U.S. legal permanent resident.

ralized since 1996. Twelve of these are legal permanent residents. All legal permanent residents of the second cohort have lived in the United States long enough to be eligible to naturalize as of the date of their interviews. The third cohort consists of the offspring of the second cohort, and the majority are U.S.-born citizens.

To Become or Not to Become a Citizen: The Castillo Family

The requirements of naturalization have remained fairly consistent over the past two hundred years.[6] The law stipulates that immigrants must establish five years of permanent residence in the United States, demonstrate good moral character, prove knowledge of American history and civics, and be able to "read, write, and speak words in ordinary usage in the English language." The language requirement can be waived for certain elderly persons who have resided in the United States for at least fifteen years. Naturalizing citizens must also take an oath that affirms allegiance to the U.S. Constitution, promises a commitment to contribute to the national defense, and renounces allegiance to any foreign power (Aleinikoff 1998).

Beyond eligibility, the decision to naturalize must take into account an individual's ability to naturalize, the desirability of U.S. citizenship (Bloemraad 1998), and an assessment of the costs and benefits of naturalization. Ability refers to the factors that would facilitate or hinder an individual's progress through the naturalization process and includes literacy, language skills, and the relative ease of fulfilling bureaucratic requirements. The ability to naturalize also is influenced by an individual's ties to institutions or other individuals that can help him or her through the process. Ability and desire to naturalize are interrelated. Those who are most able to naturalize are more likely to choose to naturalize. Yet the ability to naturalize is not necessarily an incentive to naturalize.

Desire and ability to naturalize change over time as an immigrant's circumstances and perceptions of naturalization shift. The Castillos' perceptions of U.S. citizenship were influenced by the contemporary context of anti-immigrant legislation and rhetoric. The anti-immigrant context and community reaction to it heightened the incentives to naturalize and prompted many of the Castillos to change their assessments of their ability to naturalize, their views of the desirability of naturalization, and the meanings they attach to citizenship.

Yet despite new incentives to naturalize and changing views of U.S. citizenship, many of the Castillos did not apply for citizenship during the period during which we observed them. To illustrate how the Castillos understand naturalization, we classify family members into a typology that includes four groups: active sojourners, eventual return migrants, settled migrants, and recent arrivals. These categories are organized around the patterns of return migration and settlement because these plans and practices are important determinants of the decision to naturalize. All members of the first cohort, who are at or near retirement age, are either active sojourners or eventual return migrants. They have been abroad for a long period of time; return is often associated with retirement or the cessation of activity in the paid labor force in the United States, but it may occur earlier in the life course. Their goal is to be able to maintain a middle-class standard of living during their return visits to the Dominican Republic, which often depends on income generated abroad.

The second cohort consists of settled migrants and recent arrivals as well as the three U.S.-born children of Pablo. These individuals are younger, arrived in the United States at younger ages than their parents, and with a few exceptions, are economically active. Most have formed their own families in the United States, including U.S.-born children. They return to the Dominican Republic less frequently than their parents, they are less likely to own a home or property there, and they have fewer immediate family members residing there.

Although these categories are useful for describing the factors that influence individuals' perceptions and naturalization-related behaviors, they are not mutually exclusive, and they are subject to change. For example, some individuals do not fit well into a single category or have shifted from one to another over time. Several of the older members of the second group share some of the characteristics of the sojourners and eventual return migrants but are classified as settled migrants because they have lived in the United States for many years and entered at relatively young ages.

Active Sojourners
of the First Cohort

The active sojourners comprise four women of the first cohort who entered the United States as adults, have raised families in the United States, are no longer working, and currently spend at least several months a year in the Dominican Republic. Two of these four women have naturalized, and one has applied for citizenship.

To explain how the active sojourners view U.S. citizenship, we need first to discuss their adaptation to life in New York City. Their incorporation follows a model of coresidence with children, interaction in an extended family system, and the practice of recurrent return migration. Most of the first sibling cohort, including the active sojourners, have spent their working lives in the United States in low-paying jobs and have little in the way of savings that will last through their old age. In fact, some have used savings to travel to the Dominican Republic, and all have invested in housing there in anticipation of retirement. Many of the active sojourners have developed a patchwork of survival strategies in the United States involving coresidence and income pooling with other family members (see Kibria 1993). However, as immigrants age and their children form their own families, cooperative, coresidential strategies often become less feasible or desirable. Two other factors are critical in convincing these immigrants that they cannot continue to remain in New York City on a full-time basis: the cessation of paid labor and the increasing prevalence of health problems. As these women retire from their jobs, they find their lives in New York City increasingly unaffordable. They are also more likely to have chronic health problems that are aggravated by living conditions in New York.

Indeed, unlike other research that finds that immigrant women are more likely than men to want to remain in the United States (Grasmuck and Pessar 1991; Hagan 1994), we find that older immigrant women prefer living in the Dominican Republic because it allows them to better negotiate familial tensions and economic uncertainties. Especially for the older women of the first cohort, return migration or sojourning is perceived as a better option than remaining in New York on a permanent basis. All of the sojourner women worked in lower-paying, less secure jobs than their male counterparts and are more likely to face the prospect of negotiating retirement on a low income. Several do not have a partner or spouse. The option of living part time in their own homes in the Dominican Republic, therefore, is more desirable than living permanently in New York because it allows the sojourners to live more economically and have greater independence and control of their living arrangements.

Zena, who recently naturalized, does not feel comfortable living on a full-time basis in the household of her adult children, even though she stays in her son's household for several months at a time when she is in New York. She is single and cannot afford to live in New York on her own. Her monthly social security check and Supplemental Security Income (SSI) stipend total about five hundred dollars. Becoming a U.S. citizen has allowed Zena to continue to live in both the Dominican Republic and New York by securing her SSI benefit and allowing her to remain in the Dominican Republic for as long as she desires without fear that she may not be allowed back into the United States. Consequently, Zena lives in her own home in the Dominican Republic, which is located next door to her mother's house, for at least four months a year. Her home there is paid off, so she does not worry about paying rent. In addition, Zena finds the Caribbean climate and lifestyle more conducive to her physical and mental health.

Juana, who has also applied to become a U.S. citizen, is in a similar situation. She also is single, cannot afford to live in New York City on her SSI check, and does not consider permanent coresidence with her son feasible because he lives in Boston, far away from other family and friends. Like Zena, Juana also owns a home in Mao and finds living in the Dominican Republic easier because of a serious knee injury that impairs her mobility.

Isabel, who became a U.S. citizen in 1997, is married and shares a home in New York with her husband, two of her adult children, and two grandchildren. However, she finds coresidence with her children difficult on a full-time, year-round basis because she is responsible for most of the housework and the care of her youngest daughter's two children. U.S. citizenship allows Isabel to escape a difficult family situation while securing her membership rights in the United States.

Taken within this context, U.S. citizenship resolves several important tensions of a transnational residential strategy. First, it reduces the threat that individuals might lose benefits they are currently receiving or might need in the future. Zena was pushed to naturalize by recent legislation that threatened her only source of income:

> Well, I always said to my daughter-in-law, "I'm going to become a citizen," but I never made the effort. . . . But now with the problem of the checks. . . . I know with social security I won't have a problem, but because they're giving me a supplemental disability check [SSI], I got scared. If they take that check away, I'm not going to have anything to live on. How am I going to maintain myself in my old age? So, I came back from the Dominican Republic with the objective of getting citizenship, not only because of the problem of the checks, but there are problems with everything, now you've got to become a citizen if you want to live in this country. (Zena, April 4, 1997)

Second, naturalization reduces the risk that individuals could lose their legal permanent residency as a result of being outside the country for too long. Prolonged absences from the United States by legal permanent residents can sometimes result in problems upon reentry because the INS may question whether returning migrants have abandoned their permanent resident status. Since the passage of laws that have restricted the reentry to the United States of immigrants with a criminal history, and in the general context of anti-immigrant legislation, the question of how long legal permanent residents are permitted to be outside the country without risking the loss of their residency status was a great concern and source of anxiety among the sojourners. Even among immigrants who have not had any legal problems, there is a generalized perception that it is riskier now to spend even a few months outside of the United States than it was in the past.

The desire to retain the right to return to the United States also reflects immigrants' integration into their U.S.-based family group. Membership in the family is a critical facet of the Castillos' identity and forms the basis of their social integration both in New York City and in the Dominican Republic. Immigrant members said that their need to be with family was the most crucial reason for maintaining their right to reenter the United States. Thus, when asked why she was planning to naturalize, Mariana emphasized that it would allow her and her husband to spend time in the Dominican Republic without fear of losing their right to return:

> Well, because now you go and you have problems when you spend six or seven months in the Dominican Republic. And another is that the health of my husband is not very good now. . . . We think that we're going back to our country, and if you're not a citizen, you can't be coming and going every minute, because when you have family here, you're going to have to be coming back, but you can't be coming back every three months, every four months. This is one of the reasons. (Mariana, May 17, 1997)

Return to the United States is also seen as necessary because permanent reincorporation in the Dominican Republic is difficult for returnees. Because they have lived outside the Dominican Republic for many years, most of the first cohort have been involved in few Dominican institutions on a regular basis (church, politics, schools, for example), and their social networks are limited. Although living in a small town in the Dominican Republic is restful, many find it limiting, especially after years of New York City life. This, combined with some of the difficulties of life in the Dominican Republic—including irregular if not absent social services, water and electricity shortages, and limited availability of consumer goods—propels immigrants to return to the United States (see Guarnizo 1997).

For the active sojourners, resettlement in the Dominican Republic is feasible only if an opportunity structure can be negotiated that allows them to maintain their legal membership in the United States along with their Dominican settlement. In the Dominican Republic, this involves home ownership and maintenance of social ties with family members, and resources sufficient to cover basic living expenses and travel back and forth between the United States and the Dominican Republic. In the United States, this structure involves maintaining ties with children and grandchildren and securing the membership rights of U.S. citizenship.

Eventual Return Migrants of the First Cohort

For the eventual return migrants of the first cohort, return to the Dominican Republic may not be propelled by problematic adaptation in the United States but may, rather, reflect their desire to return to the Dominican Republic to retire. Of the three eventual return migrants of the first cohort, one has applied to naturalize and two have not.

Pablo and Daniel, two members of the first cohort, are both married and maintain stable residences and employment in New York. Each owns property or a home in Mao and envisions retiring in the Dominican Republic. Like the active sojourners, these individuals emphasized that acquiring citizenship was important because of changes in laws in the United States and the advantages of U.S. citizenship in light of their eventual return migration.

Daniel has worked in a plastics factory for the past twenty-six years and lives with his second wife and child. He owns land in the Dominican Republic and anticipates building a home and retiring there. For Daniel, the anti-immigrant climate and changing laws appear to have influenced the timing of his naturalization more than the decision to naturalize. Although he always intended to naturalize, Daniel said that he had planned to wait until he reached retirement age, having seen no immediate need to naturalize; however, given the change in laws, he now felt it important to begin the process.

> One thing is the change in laws, another is that the majority of countries are accepting double nationality. . . . That influences a lot, but really, the majority of people are doing it for the changes in laws. . . . For me it's really not relevant, because I've been working for twenty-six years and, God willing, I will have my pension, because I've always reported my income. But also, being an immigrant, you have to be practical. . . . You reach a certain age and you stop working and you want to go back to your country. (Daniel, April 20, 1997)

This example illustrates that naturalization is linked less to the immigrants' immediate situations in the United States than to their anticipation of return. Mariana and Pablo also anticipate eventual retirement in the Dominican Republic, but they have yet to naturalize. A detailed discussion of their situations reveals some of the complexities and contingencies of the naturalization decision-making process, as well as some of the difficulties of predicting why some immigrants decide to naturalize and others do not.

Pablo works in the same plastics factory as his brother, and, like his brother, he wants to naturalize and anticipates retiring to the Dominican Republic. He also views U.S. citizenship as facilitating his eventual return to the United States.

> When I reach retirement age, sixty or sixty-two years old . . . if I want to go to the Dominican Republic to live, it would be easy for me to say, "I'm not going back to the United States for the time being." I'm going to stay five, three, four years. I have a friend who worked with me, he spent ten years without coming here, but then he got sick, and the treatment there was very expensive. Here he had Medicaid because he had worked here for many years. It was easier to receive treatment here because over there it was very expensive. He was a citizen. I think it's an advantage. (Pablo, May 21, 1997)

Pablo stressed the importance of citizenship, citing the increasingly unfavorable laws and the importance of citizenship for Hispanics as a means to political power. An hour into the interview, however, Pablo revealed that citizenship would also help him resolve a problem he has had with the city welfare bureaucracy. His concern stems from the fact that several years ago it was discovered that he and his wife had been fraudulently receiving public assistance. Although he is now making payments to the state, his contributions, which are deducted from his paycheck by his employer, are often submitted late. Because of the advent of the antiterrorist law and the stricter screening of immigrants arriving into the country, Pablo stated, he feared that he may not be able to reenter the country if he travels to the Dominican Republic.

> If I travel now, for example, the way the laws are now, I could have problems when I return from there. They could check in the computer, and I could have problems. It's not that I'm afraid, because I have all the receipts, but it would be a hassle, I'd have to go to court, and so on. I was going to go back, but now I'm not because of this, not until I resolve this problem. This is one of the reasons for me becoming a citizen, and for many immigrants who are here. If I were a citizen, I could go back to the Dominican Republic without fear, and even if there was a problem, they couldn't deport me, because I'm a citizen. This is one of the main reasons for wanting to become a citizen. (Pablo, May 21, 1997)

However, as of February 1998, Pablo had not submitted his application to naturalize. In fact, Pablo returned to the Dominican Republic in December 1997 and successfully reentered the United States in January 1998. Pablo's reluctance to naturalize may be linked to a fear of being turned down for citizenship as a result of his legal problems. On the other hand, because he was able to leave and reenter the United States without any problems in the recent past, perhaps he feels less immediate pressure to naturalize. Yet another reason Pablo may not have applied is that he does not think he is prepared to pass the exam. During his interview he said that he would probably need to take a citizenship class in order to get ready for the examination.

As is clearly seen from Pablo's situation, the decision to naturalize is perceived as risk laden. The most benign dimension of this risk is the possibility of failing the citizenship examination. A more serious problem is detection by the immigration bureaucracy. Among the larger group of immigrants we spoke to in the study, we heard from immigrants who were afraid that any past wrongdoing (arranged marriages, illegal or off-the-books employment, tax fraud, immigration fraud, and the like) might disqualify them from citizenship. Heightening this uncertainty is the fact that the guidelines concerning eligibility in this regard are unclear. This confusion is not only a symptom of a lack of information among immigrants. Even among individuals working in community agencies, there was no agreement on which prior behaviors may make an immigrant ineligible for citizenship.

Social networks also influence immigrants' understanding of naturalization. Over the course of our study, a number of ominous naturalization stories were circulating, including tales of immigrants who had been turned down for citizenship, whose citizenship status had been revoked because of oversights by INS officials, and who had been deported. These stories discouraged some immigrants from pursuing naturalization and made others approach naturalization more cautiously. They also had the effect of shaping the naturalization process as a series of obstacles to be overcome and gave the process an adverserial tone.

Mariana's situation illustrates another factor that influences the timing of the decision to naturalize—the role of marital ties. Mariana and her husband, Armando, maintain an apartment in Washington Heights, where several of her adult children reside. Her husband owns a car repair shop in Brooklyn, where two of their three sons work. Mariana and her husband make annual trips to the Dominican Republic, staying several months at a time, and plan to retire there eventually. For Mariana, the decision to retire to the Dominican Republic revolves around her husband's failing health; over the years, Armando has suffered a heart attack and several bouts of serious depression. Mariana appeared ambivalent about return but felt that it was important for her husband's well-being.

At the time of our first interview in May 1997, Mariana said that both she and her husband were planning to naturalize. Mariana sees citizenship as important, as do her siblings, because of changing laws and advantageous because it will facilitate resettlement in the Dominican Republic and return migration. Yet as of January 1998, neither Mariana nor Armando had submitted their naturalization applications. Several factors could account for Mariana's hesitation, but it appears that the most important is that she is waiting until her husband qualifies to take the examination in Spanish so that they can apply together.[7] We found that many, though not all, married couples make the decision to naturalize together, around the same time. Alternatively, one partner naturalizes first and shortly thereafter convinces the other to naturalize. Of course, other reasons could account for the timing of Mariana and Armando's decision to naturalize, including the fact that Armando is still active in his business in the United States; thus, permanent resettlement does not lie in the immediate future. Indeed, Mariana and her husband have been traveling back and forth between the United States and the Dominican Republic as legal permanent residents without encountering any problems. Also, neither receive any form of benefits, and so they were not immediately threatened by loss of benefits. Finally, they may have been influenced by factors that have slowed the rush to naturalize, such as naturalization backlogs and the restoration of some benefits.

The experiences of the active sojourners and the eventual return migrants shows immigrants' understanding of naturalization is complex and their decision to naturalize is often a result of several factors. Indeed, our research underscores the importance of economic and familial circumstances of immigrants in shaping their view of naturalization. As immigrants age, they face economic, familial, and individual constraints to permanent settlement in the United States. These difficulties, combined with an opportunity structure that allows them to return to their home countries—including the maintenance of ties to both home country and the United States—makes a transnational lifestyle more feasible and desirable, for some, than permanent residence in the United States.

Settled Migrants of the Second Cohort

The settled migrants arrived in the United States at a young age and are better adapted to life in the United States than their parents or their recently arrived cousins. This group consists of twelve children of the second cohort who arrived in the United States at an average age of sixteen. Most work in semiskilled employment in either the manufacturing or service sectors and live in the Dominican enclave or a neighborhood of heavy Hispanic settlement in New York City. These immigrants are younger, are active in the labor force, and have families that include U.S.-born children.

Among the second cohort, we see differences in the propensity to have naturalized and to have begun the process by submitting the application. Several members of this group naturalized before the restrictive laws passed in 1996, whereas others appear to have been prompted by changing laws. For example, of the three children of Zena who immigrated in the early 1970s, two have recently applied to naturalize. Two of Isabel's four children naturalized in the early 1990s, and two have recently applied to naturalize. Two of Mariana's five children—who arrived in the mid-1980s—naturalized in the early 1990s. This contrasts with the experiences of the seven individuals who migrated during the 1990s—the children of Teresa and Dolores who have not yet chosen to naturalize.

There are several important differences both within the group and between this group and their parents. Unlike the first cohort, the settled migrant women of the second cohort were less likely to value U.S. citizenship for the rights it confers on individuals who plan to reside outside the country for long periods of time. Instead, they were more likely to see the benefits of naturalization from the vantage point of long-term residence in the United States. One of Isabel's daughters, Ivana, naturalized in the early 1990s to secure the rights of U.S. citizenship, including the right to vote. In addition, becoming a U.S. citizen made sense to her because she does not anticipate returning to the Dominican Republic. The decisions of two other women of the second cohort were also related to the fact that they anticipate remaining in the United States and feel comfortable here, but their decisions were complicated by the fact that both were romantically involved with Venezuelans and were traveling back and forth between the United States and Venezuela. They stated that they were motivated to naturalize to ease travel between the two countries and to facilitate possible residence there. Adela, a daughter of Zena, also said that she was naturalizing because she has three U.S.-born "American" children and she anticipates remaining in the United States. Adela recently applied for citizenship and was prompted by both the changing laws and the Green Card Replacement Program, which encouraged immigrants who were replacing their green cards to naturalize.

Members of this group, because of their longer residence in the United States, were generally able to meet the language and literacy requirements of naturalization. Most members of this group have some degree of English proficiency and have had some schooling in the United States. Thus, the application and examination components of the naturalization process were less daunting for them than for their parents. As a result, relatively few members of the second cohort relied on the services of a community agency, although many relied on other family members for help in the application process or said they were motivated to pursue citizenship after seeing another family member successfully complete the process.

The men of the second cohort who had arrived at younger ages were more likely than their female counterparts to say that they plan on returning to the Dominican Republic at some point in time, and their decisions to naturalize were not seen as a means to consolidate settlement in the United States. As a result, naturalization was approached with greater ambivalence. With several exceptions, the men of the second cohort were more likely to have naturalized since the advent of anti-immigration laws, and they appear to have been pushed to naturalize by developments linked to these laws. As a result, their views of naturalization were shaped by their desire to maintain active ties to the Dominican Republic—that is, to retain the right to travel, reside, and conduct business in the Dominican Republic.

The naturalization outcomes of this group vary. One settled immigrant, Leonel, indicated his desire to naturalize in order to return to the Dominican Republic, but as a result of a prior drug conviction, he has not submitted his application. He has consulted with two lawyers over the past several years; both advised him not to pursue U.S. citizenship at this time nor to leave the country. Guillermo and David both indicated that they were naturalizing to facilitate eventual retirement and business activities in both the United States and the Dominican Republic. Mariana's son Cesar was one of the earlier naturalizers among this group; his decision was linked to the fact that he feels settled in the United States, although he holds on to the idea of eventually moving back to the Dominican Republic or establishing a business there. Finally, Gustavo, another son of Mariana, refuses to naturalize on both political and practical grounds. One reason is that he anticipates returning to the Dominican Republic to establish a business with his father. He rejected citizenship for political reasons, as well, saying that he did not believe in becoming a U.S. citizen because it does not protect Hispanics from discrimination.

Another member of the second cohort, Joaquin, was the first Castillo family member to naturalize, in 1986. When asked why he naturalized, Joaquin said that when he first arrived in the United States, he wanted to buy a home and become a citizen. However, over the several decades that he has resided in the United States, Joaquin has decided that he would prefer to live in the Dominican Republic. Like the active sojourners, he and his wife have built a house in their hometown of Mao, and they stay there for periods as long as six or nine months. However, Joaquin's resettlement project is complicated by several factors: he cannot find employment in Mao, and his children and wife do not want to live there on a permanent basis. Joaquin's situation illustrates the dilemma of many would-be returnees. It also shows that U.S. citizenship is not always seen as a means to facilitate sojourning or return; however, it may help immigrants achieve this goal as it takes shape over time.

Recent Arrivals of the Second Cohort

The recently arrived immigrants of the second cohort arrived on average at the age of thirty, in the early 1990s. Among this group, no one has naturalized yet. These more recent arrivals are less well adapted to the United States than their cousins who arrived earlier. Their working lives tend toward informal jobs and intermittent work; some are currently not working. Those who are employed work in places where a majority of their co-workers are Latinos. Most speak little English, and several lack a stable residence. Despite some of the difficulties of this early stage of adaptation to the United States and a less than firm commitment to permanent residence in the United States, most of this group stated that they do not actively plan to return to the Dominican Republic.

Why have the members of this group neither naturalized nor applied? One reason may be lack of exposure to the concepts of naturalization and U.S. citizenship. Most of this group said that they had never seriously considered citizenship until the advent of anti-immigration laws. Another reason the recent arrivals have not become U.S. citizens is that most do not think it would bring them any immediate benefits. No member of this group envisions returning to the Dominican Republic in the near future (except for vacations), and none anticipates receipt of public benefits at the current time. In fact, although several members of this group lost their public assistance benefits during the period of study, they did not view U.S. citizenship as a means to retain or reestablish access to benefits.

More importantly, many of the recently arrived members of the second cohort believe that they are unprepared to naturalize. Many said that they do not have the money for the application fee, the time to begin the process, the willingness to study for the exam, and most important, the requisite English language skills. The language component of the naturalization examination appears to be the single most important barrier for this group. Their limited language skills largely owe to the group's migration at adult ages and the nature of their incorporation into jobs and residences in predominantly Latino neighborhoods in New York.

In addition to the anticipated difficulties of the naturalization process, a belief that the anti-immigrant legislation had been reversed helped to convince immigrants that they did not need to naturalize immediately. In the three years that we observed the Castillos, we witnessed a period of intense concern and interest in becoming U.S. citizens, which was followed by a significant decline in interest in naturalization. Immigrant service providers in Washington Heights confirmed the declining interest in naturalization, reporting a drop as of early 1998 in the number of immigrants seeking assistance with applications; nationally, naturalization applications have decreased, to approximately seven hundred thousand in 1999. The waning interest of some Castillo family members mirrors this trend.

The "naturalization fever" has died down for several reasons. Clearly, the heightened concern about naturalization was short-lived and was partly a result of intensive press coverage and community response to this issue. However, the restoration of some of the benefits that were taken away from legal permanent residents also eased the panic. The restoration of benefits appears to have discouraged some immigrants from naturalizing.[8] Teresa's husband Miguel said, somewhat cynically, that people were naturalizing "because the government is taking away benefits. But it's not true, people say a lot of things, there are a lot of rumors. For example, people were saying that you could only spend three months in the Dominican Republic. But that wasn't true either. The government makes a law and then they don't follow through on it. There are a lot of laws, but they're not enforced." (Miguel, July 15, 1997)

The long period of time required to naturalize discourages some immigrants from naturalizing. Media reports of backlogs and stories of friends and family members who have been waiting up to two years to hear back from the INS on the status of their applications appear to have convinced some immigrants not to naturalize. As a result of the large number of immigrants naturalizing in 1996 and 1997, the backlogs grew in many cities, including New York, where, during the period under study, the process averaged more than two years from application to the examination and interview.

The Social Process of Naturalization

Among those who naturalized after 1996, the laws and anti-immigrant climate seem to have pushed those who had considered naturalization or were favorably predisposed toward the idea of naturalization to hasten the process. Especially among the sojourners and immigrants anticipating return, the climate apparently influenced the timing of naturalization by pushing them to reassess their assumption that citizenship would be beneficial only for facilitating return migration. Daniel decided to naturalize earlier than he would have otherwise as a means of securing benefits associated with his retirement, such as his social security entitlements.

> I think what made me rush my decision to become a citizen was the changing laws that we're seeing now . . . because in any case I was going to become a citizen, but I thought I'd do it when I was sixty, if I were alive . . . when I was ready to receive my pension. . . . It's one way to return to my country, and you know when you're a citizen, you don't have to come back every year like you do when you're a resident. (Daniel, April 20, 1997)

Most of those who decided to naturalize have resided in the United States for many years, were exposed to information about naturalization, and had come into contact with individuals who had naturalized. This finding is consistent with quantitative studies that find length of U.S. residence to be a strong predictor of naturalization.

Those who decided to naturalize earlier than they had previously planned had to reassesses their ability to naturalize. Individuals who were discouraged from naturalizing because they lacked English skills were motivated to disregard these barriers in the face of changing conditions. Zena said, "My kids said, 'Mom, become a citizen,' . . . and an aunt of mine called me from Queens and said, 'You know that you can become a citizen?' And I said, 'And my English?' Because since I've been here I've been working, I never went to a school to learn English because I never thought I'd need to know it" (Zena, April 4, 1997). Isabel, also concerned about her English ability, took a course to prepare for the interview. Both Zena and Isabel naturalized in 1997.

Others who reassessed their options for U.S. citizenship changed their understanding of the meaning of U.S. citizenship, thus reconciling the idea of U.S. citizenship with their identity as Dominican immigrants and their allegiance to their home country. Many immigrants had been unwilling to "change flags" or renounce their Dominican nationality by applying for citizenship because they saw it as an act of betrayal of their country and their national identity or because they did not want to give up membership rights in their home country (see Jones-Correa 1998). It is also true, however, that many immigrants did not see the need to become U.S. citizens, because they already had, in effect, the status of "quasi citizen." As legal permanent residents, they had the right to live and work in the United States and to leave and enter at will (Aleinikoff 1998). They had had, until recently, access to most public benefits. Other factors that account for the changing social meaning of U.S. citizenship are the large increase in the number of immigrants becoming citizens and the passage of dual citizenship laws.

In addition, for most immigrants, being a resident was the normative status of their contemporaries. Their conceptions of citizenship had been shaped by racialized images of U.S. citizens as "white" and "native born." This is illustrated by the responses of Zena and Isabel when they were asked whether they thought of themselves as Americans, now that they had become citizens. When we asked Zena, who naturalized in 1997, about her identity, she replied, "I would say that one has to adapt and say, 'I am an American.' I say that I am an American citizen . . . but to say that I'm an American—no. Because American, American, that is someone who was born here, who is from this country. I would say to anyone that I am an American citizen" (Zena, April 4, 1997). Isabel, responding to this same question, said, "Well I would have to be sincere and say that I am an American citizen. But my origins, I cannot deny them, because I have a physical appearance, I have an accent that I can't erase, so really I am a 'Dominicana,' but an American citizen" (Isabel, April 5, 1997).

Among the Castillo family, issues of entitlement were an important component of the negotiation of citizenship, especially for the older migrants. Some immigrants made it clear that they felt entitled to the benefits of U.S. citizenship, whereas others emphasized that they were not naturalizing for the benefits. Daniel said that he had been employed continuously for the last twenty-six years and that he was not naturalizing to secure state assistance nor to receive it in the future.

Zena was adamant that she deserves her old age benefits (SSI) because she was employed for nineteen years and paid taxes, and during this time, while she was raising three children alone, she did not receive any government assistance. She believes that she has earned her right to be a U.S. citizen. However, Zena does not believe that everyone is entitled to the benefits of U.S. citizenship.

And another thing is that they make it too easy for people to enter this country. Do you know why? Look, I brought three kids here, but when I came welfare isn't what it is today. Back then, you had to wait five years before you could qualify for any aid, but now, you don't have to wait five years, only a year, a little over a year and you can get welfare. You hear, look at so-and-so [who] came a year and a half ago, and she's on welfare. What's the deal? This is the cause of some of the harsh changes that have occurred in New York. Someone who comes into the country with several kids isn't supposed to be able to get on public assistance like that! They should have to wait the five years, like the law says. Go to work, mother! Do you know the women who are getting welfare, who don't do anything except sit on their butts . . . because their husband is working? (Zena, April 4, 1997)

Many Castillos see citizenship as a set of rights that should be made available to deserving immigrants, but others resented government actions to take benefits away from immigrants and see citizenship as a form of coercion or an obligation. These individuals had more ambivalent attitudes toward naturalization, perhaps as the result of the mixed messages they were receiving. On the one hand, they were encouraged to naturalize: if they did not become U.S. citizens, they might risk losing their foothold in the United States, and perhaps there would be further negative consequences. On the other hand, they were told that they were abusing their rights to social welfare benefits. The resulting message, which many immigrants found disconcerting, was that immigrants were not deserving of U.S. citizenship because they were naturalizing for the benefits. Among those who naturalized, some felt that they were being coerced. Thus, when asked if she thought Hispanics should become citizens, Mariana answered, "In one sense I think so, but in another I think that it's a way of discriminating against us, like they're obligating us, that's how I see it, as if we're being obligated, that's how I understand it. . . . In the case that I might need help, I would ask for it, but I wouldn't like it. I came to this country not to look for a handout, or to ask for help, but to be with my family" (Mariana, May 17, 1997). One recently arrived immigrant of the second cohort said he would not naturalize at the current time because he did not want to appear as if he were doing it "for the benefits" (which he does not receive).

The Castillos' narrow interpretation of U.S. citizenship—as a change of legal status—reflects both the strength of the national identity of this group and the fact that many members retain ties to their country of origin and hold onto the idea of returning to the Dominican Republic at some point in time. It is also a function of their experiences as working-class immigrants and as members of a racialized Hispanic minority group. Achieving the status of naturalized citizen is not equivalent to becoming a "first-class" citizen and member of the United States, which many understand to be reserved for native-born whites. It also reflects the contemporary context of citizenship acquisition in which immigrants are encouraged to become citizens in order to retain rights, while at the same time they are told that they are abusing American generosity. One way of negotiating these changes is to minimize the significance of U.S. citizenship by viewing it narrowly as a set of legal rights and obligations rather than as a change in affective orientation or allegiance.

Conclusion

Clearly, our study relies on a small sample, and our results cannot be used to generalize about the experiences of all immigrants. However, our research does shed light on the complexity of the naturalization process and some of the important dimensions of the process, including the significance of the family and economic opportunities—in both the Dominican Republic and the United States—in shaping immigrant views of naturalization.

Many immigrants changed their ideas about becoming a U.S. citizen in the wake of extraordinary changes in the U.S. social and political climate in the 1990s. Naturalization was presented to immigrants as an option allowing them to retain or safeguard full membership rights in the United States. As a result, many immigrants revised their understanding of U.S. citizenship to correspond with this narrow rights-oriented approach. As the environment changed, immigrants reevaluated their understanding of U.S. citizenship, as well as their perception of their ability to become a citizen.

The case of the Castillos illustrates that immigrants define U.S. citizenship in terms of their own interests rather than those of the state. Naturalized U.S. citizenship does not necessarily signify permanent settlement or incorporation in the United States, and members of the first cohort have not pursued U.S. citizenship because of feelings of membership or belonging. For most of the second cohort, however, U.S. citizenship appears to have consolidated their plan to reside permanently in the United States. Although the changing conditions of membership have shaped immigrants' understanding of naturalization, these unique conditions do not determine the practice or content of citizenship. Indeed, the significance of being a U.S. citizen and the practice of U.S. citizenship—including their perception of themselves as Americans—may change over time. However, it will be influenced by the conditions under which they became citizens—including the contexts that shape immigrants' sense of belonging to U.S. society.

No doubt, the nature and meaning of citizenship will probably be different for the children of the second cohort. Most are U.S.-born citizens. They have fewer family ties to the Dominican Republic and less experience as transnational migrants. It remains to be seen whether they will claim their place in U.S. society or if, rather, the advantages of full membership will escape them. Their citizenship may matter less than the opportunities and barriers they confront in their quest for full membership.

The authors gratefully acknowledge support from the Social Science Research Council and the Open Society Institute. We also appreciate comments and suggestions from Mehdi Bozorgmehr, Charles Keely, Douglas Klusmeyer, Emily Rosenbaum, William Seltzer, and Steven Zahniser. We are most indebted to the Castillo family for their candid and unwavering participation in our study.

Notes

1. The Personal Responsibility and Work Opportunity Reconciliation Act of 1996 (known as the Welfare Act) made sweeping changes to the structure and access of public benefits for all residents of the United States; however, changes affecting the immigrant population were at the outset the most dramatic and the most draconian. The law established restrictions on the eligibility of legal immigrants for means-tested public assistance and broadened restrictions on public benefits for undocumented immigrants. It also required the INS to verify an immigrant's status in order for him or her to receive benefits. The Illegal Immigration Reform and Immigrant Responsibility Act of 1996 includes provisions to bolster control of U.S. borders, establishes measures to remove criminal and other deportable aliens, and provides for increased protection for legal workers through work-site enforcement. It also places added restrictions on benefits for immigrants, including tightening the requirements for an affidavit of support for sponsored immigrants, by making the long-required affidavit of support legally binding. The Antiterrorism and Effective Death Penalty Act of 1996 provides for expedited procedures for the removal of "alien terrorists" and for changes in criminal alien procedures such as authorizing state and local law enforcement officials to arrest and detain certain illegal aliens, providing access to certain confidential immigration and naturalization files through court order (INS 1997).

2. Another theme in the naturalization literature examines the relation between naturalization and political participation (see, for example, Garcia 1987; Pachon and DeSipio 1994; DeSipio 1996).

3. Naturalization rates vary widely by country of origin, by age at arrival, and by class of admission. In general, immigrants from Western Hemisphere countries and Western Europe are much less likely to naturalize than immigrants from Eastern Europe, Asia, and Africa. In an analysis conducted by the INS, 46 percent of the 1977 entry cohort of immigrants from all countries had naturalized by

1995 (INS 1997). The same cohort of Dominicans had a naturalization rate of 28.6 percent.

4. Numerous studies document the transnational nature of contemporary migration among Dominicans and others (see Glick Schiller, Basch, and Szanton Blanc 1992; Goldring 1992, 1996; Grasmuck and Pessar 1991; Graham 1997; Guarnizo 1994, 1997; Levitt 1996; Smith 1995).

5. Some service providers explained that their reorientation toward naturalization was, in part, an effort to serve the large cohort of immigrants who had legalized under the Immigration Reform and Control Act of 1986 (IRCA) and who were now applying for U.S. citizenship.

6. A history of various exclusions based on race, however, were imposed through 1952.

7. Immigrants who are over fifty-five years of age and have resided in the United States at least fifteen years as legal permanent residents or those who are over fifty years of age and have resided in the United States for at least twenty years as legal permanent residents are exempt from the English language requirement of the naturalization examination.

8. The budget agreement of 1997 restored SSI payments to permanent residents residing in the United States as of the date of the Welfare Act who were already receiving benefits, and in 1998, eligibility for food stamps was reinstated to immigrant children and the elderly who resided in the United States before the date of the passage of the Welfare Act.

References

Aleinikoff, T. Alexander. 1998. *Between Principles and Politics: The Direction of U.S. Citizenship Policy.* Washington, D.C.: Carnegie Endowment for International Peace.

Alvarez, Robert R. 1987. "A Profile of the Citizenship Process Among Hispanics in the United States." *International Migration Review* 21(2): 327–51.

Bloemraad, Irene. 1999. "Political Culture, State Institutions, Ethnic Organizations, and Immigrant Naturalization: Lessons Drawn from a Canadian-U.S. Comparison." Paper presented at roundtable discussion, From Immigrant to Citizen? Naturalization Decisions in Canada and the United States, held at the Carnegie Endowment for International Peace, Washington, D.C.(May 14, 2000).

Cordero-Guzmán, Héctor R., and Jose G. Navarro. 2000. *Managing Cuts in the "Safety Net": What Do Immigrant Groups, Organizations, and Service Providers Say About the Impacts of Recent Changes in Immi-*

gration and Welfare Laws? Unpublished manuscript. Robert J. Milano Graduate School of Management and Urban Policy, New School University.

DeSipio, Louis. 1987. "Social Science Literature and the Naturalization Process." *International Migration Review* 21(2): 390–405.

———. 1996. *Counting on the Latino Vote: Latinos as a New Electorate.* Charlottesville: University Press of Virginia.

Garcia, John A. 1987. "The Political Integration of Mexican Immigrants: Examining Some Political Orientations." *International Migration Review* 21(2): 372–89.

Glick Schiller, Nina, Linda Basch, and Cristina Szanton Blanc. 1992. *Towards a Transnational Perspective on Migration: Race, Class, Ethnicity, and Nationalism Reconsidered.* New York: New York Academy of Sciences.

Goldring, Luin P. 1992. "Diversity and Community in Transnational Migration: A Comparative Study of Two Mexico–United States Migrant Communities." Ph.D. diss., Cornell University.

———. 1996. "Blurring Borders: Constructing Transnational Migration in the Process of Mexico–United States Migration." *Research in Community Sociology* 6: 69–104.

Graham, Pamela. 1997. "Political Incorporation and Reincorporation: Simultaneity in the Dominican Migration Experience." Paper prepared for conference, Transnational Communities and the Political Economy of New York City in the 1990s. New School for Social Research, New York.

Grasmuck, Sherri, and Patricia Pessar. 1991. *Between Two Islands: Dominican International Migration.* Berkeley: University of California Press.

———. 1996. "Dominicans in the United States: First- and Second-Generation Settlement." In *Origins and Destinees: Immigration, Race, and Ethnicity in America*, edited by Silvia Pedraza and Rubén Rumbaut. Belmont, Calif.: Wadsworth.

Guarnizo, Luis. 1994. "'Los Dominicanyorks': The Making of a Binational Society." *Annals of the American Academy of Political and Social Science* 533: 70–86.

———. 1997. "The Emergence of a Transnational Social Formation and the Mirage of Return Migration Among Dominican Transmigrants." *Identities* 4: 281–322.

Hagan, Jacqueline Maria. 1994. *Deciding to Be Legal: A Maya Community in Houston.* Philadelphia : Temple University Press.

Jones-Correa, Michael. 1998. *Between Two Nations: The Political Predicament of Latinos in New York City.* Ithaca: Cornell University Press.

Kibria, Nazli. 1993. *Family Tightrope: The Changing Lives of Vietnamese Americans.* Princeton, N.J.: Princeton University Press.

Levitt, Peggy. 1996. "Transnationalizing Civil and Political Change: The Case of Transnational Organizational Ties Between Boston and the

Dominican Republic." Ph.D. diss., Massachusetts Institute of Technology.

Liang, Zai. 1994a. "On the Measurement of Naturalization." *Demography* 31: 525–48.

———. 1994b. "Social Contact, Social Capital, and the Naturalization Process: Evidence from Six Immigrant Groups." *Social Science Research* 23: 407–37.

Pachon, Harry, and Louis DeSipio. 1994. *New Americans by Choice: Political Perspectives of Latino Immigrants.* Boulder, Colo.: Westview Press.

Pessar, Patricia. 1995. *Visa for a Dream: Dominicans in the United States.* Boston: Allyn and Bacon.

Portes, Alejandro, and John W. Curtis. 1987. "Changing Flags: Naturalization and Its Determinants Among Mexican Immigrants." *International Migration Review* 21: 352–71.

Portes, Alejandro, and Rubén G. Rumbaut. 1996. *Immigrant America: A Portrait.* 2d ed. Berkeley: University of California Press.

Singer, Audrey, and Greta Gilbertson. 1996. "Naturalization Among Latin American Immigrants in New York City." Paper presented at the annual meeting of the American Sociological Association. New York(August 1996).

Smith, Robert C. 1995. "Los Ausentes Siempre Presentes: The Imagining, Making, and Politics of Transnational Communities Between the United States and Mexico." Ph.D. diss., Columbia University.

Torres-Saillant, Silvio, and Ramona Hernandez. 1998. *The Dominican Americans.* Westport, Conn: Greenwood Press.

U.S. Immigration and Naturalization Service (INS). 1997. *Statistical Yearbook of the Immigration and Naturalization Service, 1996.* Washington: U.S. Government Printing Office.

Yang, Phillip Q. 1994. "Explaining Immigrant Naturalization." *International Migration Review* 28: 449–47.

8

PARTICIPATION IN LIBERAL DEMOCRACY: THE POLITICAL ASSIMILATION OF IMMIGRANTS AND ETHNIC MINORITIES IN THE UNITED STATES

Jane Junn

Wↀ ITHIN the next decade, nearly one-third of the United States population will be classified as a race other than white. That proportion is projected to rise to 47 percent by 2050. At present, immigrants and their second-generation offspring constitute almost one-fifth of the U.S. population, and of these, more than three-quarters are from Central America, South America, the Caribbean, and Asia. How do changes in the ethnic composition of the U.S. population influence citizen participation in liberal democracy? Recent ballot proposals in California—where in the next decade, no one ethnic or racial group will constitute a majority of the population—showcase a spectacular example of political action aimed at restricting the political rights of immigrants and other minorities. In a society increasingly colored by a diversity of immigrants, to what extent can the structure and culture of liberal democracy in America permit the expression of difference that such compositional change engenders?

The study of the political consequences of international migration to the United States usually does not begin with an assessment of the ways current democratic institutions and practices either accommodate or constrain new entrants to the polity. Instead, emphasis has more often been placed on determining which factors enhance the political incorporation and assimilation of immigrants and ethnic minorities into American politics as it is presently constituted. In political science, perhaps the most common form of this type of analysis is the identification of individual-level characteristics, such as level of formal education, economic resources, generation of immigration, and ethnicity or national origin, on the propensity to be politically active. The implicit acceptance of the democratic system in its current state, combined with the normative position, at least among those on the left, that participation by immigrants and ethnic minorities ought to be increased, is a familiar theme. It is reasoned that the entrance into the democratic polity of immigrants and ethnic minorities as citizen voters creates opportunities for the development of group-based political power and better representation for previously marginalized groups. At the same time, it is precisely this compositional change and the possibility of enhanced political power for immigrants and ethnic minorities that contribute to restrictionist movements.

A number of key questions, however, rarely get addressed: Is more participation—especially among immigrants and ethnic and racial minorities—always better? How well do standard socioeconomic status models explain variation in political behavior across race and ethnicity? To what extent is the familiar interpretation of the results from these standard models consistent with the position that more participation is better?

Is More Participation Better?

More political participation is usually considered to be a good thing, and during times in which liberal democracy has few ideological rivals, there is little disagreement that more citizen participation is desirable—provided that this activity constitutes the free expression of voice through democratic deliberation.[1] Many Western feminist theorists have adopted the normative goal of more political participation (for example, Phillips 1994; Eisenstein 1994; Fraser 1992). Similarly, the ideal of political discourse in a "public sphere" described by Jürgen Habermas (1989), when practiced in a more deliberative democracy, places primary importance on the political and civic engagement of individual citizens (see also Gutmann and Thompson 1996). There are several common justifications for advocating more political activity in democracy. The most widely held belief among scholars is consistent with Western liberal and Enlightenment political theory, which argues that the participation of more citizens means that more individual opinions and preferences are taken into account. Increased individual voice in democracy translates into better representation, which produces a collective outcome that more closely approximates the common good and promotes equality and justice. In this view, the democratic process is conceived as a neutral mechanism that aggregates revealed individual preferences. A second reason for wanting more citizen participation in democracy has its origin in another set of democratic theories suggesting that political activity benefits citizens not by virtue of the outcomes of more equitable or efficient preference aggregation but rather by aiding individuals themselves in their development as citizens and in their connection to the political community. As individuals follow politics, collect information, express preferences, and deliberate about politics, they develop into capable democratic citizens more fit for inclusion in the polity. Finally, more participation is thought to be good for system-level stability; better-attended elections provide popular support for policies and leaders, thereby signifying the legitimacy and stability of both government and nation. These three justifications are not mutually exclusive but are linked with one another as compelling reasons to advocate the more participation in politics.

Indeed, more political activity—that is, more liberal democracy in the form of expanded expression of voice and deliberation among citizens—has been advocated as a procedural and substantive solution for distributional inequities in social and political goods. Increasing political activity among those traditionally disadvantaged and politically underrepresented can help create public policies that take their interests into account as well as empower those previously disenfranchised to take political stands to develop and forward their interests. Following this logic, differences in rates of participation among citizens are considered problematic, because differences in participatory input imply both inequality in political output and variation in the development of qualities desirable to democratic citizenship. Because immigrants and ethnic and racial minorities in the United States participate in politics at comparatively low rates, people in these groups have become the target of calls for political activity through drives for naturalization and voter registration. Such well-intentioned campaigns seek greater equality in political outcomes by making the electorate—the mass of citizens with some means of power in representative democracy—more descriptively representative of the population at large. The inference is that policies beneficial to those previously disenfranchised are most likely to be adopted when the face of the electorate approximates the face of the polity. Conversely, undesirable political outcomes are reasoned to be the result of a lack of activity among those with interests at stake. Under circumstances of modest rates of political activity among immigrants and minorities, what falls under scrutiny for change is the people who influence the institutions and process of democratic government rather than the institutions themselves.

Under what circumstances might we reasonably challenge the claim that more participation is good? More can be desirable only under circumstances in which two critical assumptions are met. First, for democracy to be better because of more participation, the process itself—

whether representative, parliamentary, or direct—must not privilege one group or ideology over others. Quite simply, it cannot be assumed that the structure, institutions, and culture of representative government in America present the same costs and incentives to participate for recently naturalized citizens and native-born English-speaking citizens, for example. Rather, the extent to which democratic practice is either neutral or constructed from already existing standards that systematically advantage some and disadvantage others must be considered when evaluating whether more participation is desirable. Second, more participation can be justified only if a common understanding of agency and citizenship is fluid; the conception of democracy cannot uphold some a priori static definition of the model citizen. Competing visions of citizenship must be recognized, and the construction of the meaning of being political must reflect the composition of the political community, including those who differ from the already existing cultural norm. As such, democracy cannot require assimilation to the current model; rather, the conception of democratic citizenship must itself be colored by the diversity of the population.

More Participation and Social Science Models

The notion that more participation is better has found a safe home in empirical investigations of mass political behavior in the United States. Political scientists have, for the most part, adopted some portion of this logic and directed their attention to studying what makes people active in politics. Models identifying which individual factors contribute to participation are thus deemed useful in developing strategies for increasing participation in the mass public. Most popular among the set of explanations for why people are active in politics is the socioeconomic status, or "SES," model. People with more social and economic resources are also more likely both to bear the costs of taking part in politics and to value and recognize the incentives for participation. As models of political behavior go, the SES model has thus far been a consistent and safe bet. It has succeeded in identifying among the most important individual-level characteristics that differentiate those who are more likely to be engaged in politics from those who do not take part. The two factors that have consistently proved to be the most important predictors of participation are the level of formal education and the level of family income, with the former accounting for the larger share of the variation in citizen activity. Political scientists Raymond Wolfinger and Steven Rosenstone (1980) describe the importance of formal education to voting as "transcendent"; and almost fifty years of

American National Election Study and other polling data demonstrate repeatedly that the more highly educated and those with more substantial economic resources participate in politics at higher rates than those with less formal education and more modest incomes. In this way, the SES model has been a resounding success. With respect to explaining political participation among nonwhite minority Americans, the SES model has also proved useful; once higher levels of education and family wealth among whites have been controlled for, African American and Hispanic citizens have been found to participate at or near the same rates as their more economically and educationally advantaged white counterparts.[2]

Despite its perceived success, however, the SES model suffers from several significant problems. First, although the SES model identifies the individual-level factors related to political activity, it says little about what it is exactly about education and income that make them such powerful predictors of participation. With some exceptions, the SES model is grossly undertheorized.[3] Second, and more damaging to its logic, the model yields predictions about political behavior in the wrong direction over time. What has been famously described by Richard Brody as the "puzzle of participation" is the expectation generated from the simple additive assumption of the SES model that participation should grow over time at a commensurate level with its determinants, at the same time that we observe decline or stasis in electoral activity (Brody 1978). Inconsistent with the prediction of the SES model, political engagement has not followed the upward trajectory of the main causal variable in the model; voting, campaign work, and other forms of engagement in electoral politics have declined or remained constant while average levels of formal education have increased dramatically over time.[4]

Finally, some have questioned the extent to which the model applies to a diversity of groups of people. For instance, higher resources do not necessarily drive similar rates of participation among Asian Americans, who are more highly educated but less active politically than whites (see Tam 1995; Lien 1997; Lee 1998). Even for those groups, such as African Americans, for which the SES model has a better fit to the data, the interpretation as "positive" of the finding that differences from whites in levels of political activity either disappear or recede significantly once disparities in resources are accounted for is problematic.[5] One could argue that making whites and minorities look like one another in statistical analysis by "controlling for" what in reality amount to substantial differences in income and education is an odd way to find optimism. Furthermore, a scenario of no variation in the independent variables (that is, in which everyone is well educated and wealthy) would be impossible in the American democratic system as it currently exists. Even if we are near "the end of history" in terms of ideological diversity, the hierarchical configuration of democratic-capitalist values, structures, and the institutions that support them (including formal education) are in no imminent danger of extinction.

Notwithstanding these difficulties, the implications of the SES model have been interpreted by fans of liberal democracy as encouraging. Potential participants in the polity can be brought into the political system by increasing their reserve of social and economic resources. In other words, resource-poor individuals can and should be enriched and compelled to participate through their incorporation into the social, political, and economic hierarchy. In the analysis that follows, I reinterpret the findings of the SES model for minority and white Americans. Formal educational attainment and income are conceived as surrogates for economic and political assimilation to liberal democratic practices and norms in America, and they predominate as explanations of more traditional system-directed political activities such as voting and campaign work. Yet the measures of assimilation (education and income) are less important for other more direct forms of political activity that require less interaction with formal political institutions.

What the Data Say About Political Participation

Two unique features of both the Citizen Participation Study (CITPART) of 1990 and the Texas A&M Minority Survey (TAM) of 1993 to 1994 set them apart from other data collections of mass political behavior. Instead of restricting the measurement of participation to the electoral realm, both surveys asked respondents about their engagement in a wide variety of activities. In addition to the range of political and social activities, a second unique feature of the CITPART and TAM studies is the large number of African Americans, Hispanics, and Asians included in the samples. Typical national surveys draw a sample of people to interview of between one thousand and two thousand adults who are representative of the United States population. Because minority Americans are outnumbered by whites by a more than four-to-one margin, only small numbers of minority Americans are interviewed in most national surveys. For example, in a typical survey of 1,500 adult Americans, between 90 and 120 Hispanics will be interviewed, and an even smaller proportion of Asian Americans, who make up less than 2 percent of the U.S. population. The Citizen Participation Study gathered data from interviews with more than fifteen thousand Americans—ten times the usual size of the typical national sample—yielding a much larger sample of minority Americans' behavior for analysis. The TAM survey also employed a strategy of stratified sampling to obtain roughly five hundred respondents from each of the four race or ethnicity groups in the state of Texas (Anglo whites, African Americans, Mexican Americans, and Asian Americans).[6]

Taken together, these two data collections present a unique opportunity to view the differences in the types, levels, and sources of political activity among Americans according to race or ethnicity. At the same time, however, the two studies differ significantly, in terms of their timing (one conducted before the 1992 presidential election, the other a year after the election), samples (one national, the other statewide, in Texas), and the questions asked. In particular, the 1990 CIT-PART study surveyed a random sample of the U.S. population about a wide range of political activities, incorporating both system-directed and more direct forms of political activity, though generation of immigration was not measured. Alternatively, the 1993 TAM study surveyed residents of the state of Texas about their political activity in a somewhat more narrow range of activities but included several important questions on generation of immigration and language spoken at home. The 1990 data is therefore used to examine differences between Anglo whites, African Americans, Hispanics, and Asian Americans in terms of their participation in system-directed and more direct forms of participation. The analysis of the 1993 Texas data examines more closely the impact of generation of immigration and language assimilation on overall political activity among the four groups in the study (Anglo whites, African Americans, Mexican Americans, and Asian Americans).

Table 8.1 shows the proportion of people in each group in the U.S. national survey who are active in each of nine different types of political activities, including electoral activity, contacting a public official, local community activity, organizational activity, and protesting. The participatory activities are divided into two categories, system-directed political activity and direct political activity. System-directed activities are those that are aimed at influencing elected representatives and other agents of government, whereas the activities classified as direct political activity include those types of participation that involve working directly with others, activities in which the action is not necessarily aimed at elected or appointed officials. The biggest differences between whites and minority Americans are in the activities of voting (both at the presidential level and for local candidates) and contacting a government official. Not surprisingly, these activities require interaction with bureaucratic institutions of government. Whereas blacks are only somewhat less active than whites in all of the system-directed activities (but significantly less likely to contact a government official), there are large

TABLE 8.1   *Involvement in Selected System-Directed Versus Direct Political Activities, United States, by Race or Ethnicity (Percentage)*

Political Activity	Anglo White	African American	Hispanic	Asian American
System-directed activity				
Registered to vote	82	82	57	46
		(0)	(−25)	(−36)
Voted in 1988 presidential election	74	67	45	35
		(−7)	(−29)	(−39)
Voted in most or all local elections	57	52	33	22
		(−5)	(−24)	(−35)
Worked on a political campaign in past five years	11	12	9	9
		(+1)	(−2)	(−2)
Gave money to a political campaign in past year	19	17	12	13
		(−2)	(−7)	(−6)
Contacted government official in past five years	37	22	18	20
		(−15)	(−19)	(−17)
Direct activity				
Served on a local board or council in past five years	8	11	8	4
		(+3)	(0)	(−4)
Worked with others in local community in past year	30	34	21	26
		(+4)	(−9)	(−4)
Participated in protest (not strike related) in past five years	5	9	5	9
		(+4)	(0)	(+4)
Percentage of population (sample %)	83	10	6	1
N	12,149	1,400	894	157

Source: 1990 Citizen Participation Study.
Note: Differences from whites are given in parentheses.

disparities between Anglo whites and Hispanics, as well as Asian Americans, in all of the system-directed activities. For instance, only half as many Hispanics contacted a public official as did whites, whereas less than half as many Asian Americans as whites voted in presidential and local elections.

The differences between groups recede dramatically when we consider forms of direct political activity, in which fewer structural and institutional barriers exist. In the 1990 national data, African American citizens are more active in all three types of direct participation (serving on local boards, working with others in the community, and participating in a protest) than whites. Similarly, Hispanics are less active only in working with others in the local community and as active as whites on the other two forms of direct activity. Asian Americans are almost twice as likely as whites to engage in protest but half as likely to serve on a board or local council or to work with others in the local community.

Table 8.2 shows the proportion of Anglo whites, African Americans, Mexican Americans, and Asian Americans who report taking part in each of the seven political activities asked about in the Texas survey. The patterns of lower activity among ethnic and racial minorities seen in the U.S. data are mirrored here, with larger differences between whites and blacks in Texas. Mexican Americans and Asian Americans are also less active than Anglo whites in all of the activities except protesting. Although the other measure of direct political activity in the 1993 TAM study—working with others to solve a local problem—is similar to questions in the U.S. data, the same pattern does not apply. Unlike the 1990 national data, which find that African Americans were more active than whites, Hispanics equally as active, and Asian Americans less active, minority respondents in the Texas data were, across all three groups, less likely to work with others to solve local problems. Of all of the types of political activity in both surveys, protesting is the only form in which minority Americans consistently outpace whites. Protest is a form of political activity that does not necessarily require working with and within current institutions of existing democracy. In-

TABLE 8.2   *Involvement in Selected Political Activities, Texas, by Race or Ethnicity (Percentage)*

Political Activity	Anglo White	African American	Mexican American	Asian American
Voted in 1992 presidential election	80	65 (−15)	52 (−28)	37 (−43)
Contributed money or worked for candidate or party	24	20 (−4)	17 (−7)	15 (−9)
Signed a petition	37	21 (−16)	21 (−16)	20 (−17)
Contacted a public official by writing or phone	34	19 (−15)	17 (−17)	13 (−21)
Attended a public meeting	25	24 (−1)	17 (−8)	19 (−6)
Worked with others to solve a local problem	38	35 (−3)	30 (−8)	18 (−20)
Attended a demonstration or rally	5	12 (+7)	12 (+7)	6 (+1)
N	566	513	550	500

Source: 1993 to 1994 Texas A&M Minority Survey.
Note: Differences from whites are given in parentheses.

stead, marching in the streets—the most readily available weapon of the weak—is often the only avenue by which the marginalized and disenfranchised can make their voices heard. Resorting to protest is often explicitly a statement of disenfranchisement from and opposition to current institutions and practices. The extent to which this characterization applies to the various groups in question, however, is not uniform. For African Americans, the tradition of mass demonstrations in the civil rights movement may best exemplify the motivation behind protest activity. For more recent and voluntary immigrants, however, protest activity may not reflect such opposition. Instead, concerned with political matters in their home countries, immigrants may find it easier to march in a demonstration to express their sentiments than to write a letter in English to a U.S. government official.[7]

In addition to the differences by race or ethnicity, the Texas data also provide the opportunity to consider how generation of immigration is related to political participation. Table 8.3 presents the proportion of Mexican Americans and Asian Americans—separated into three categories of generation of immigration (immigrant, second generation, and third generation and above)—who take part in each of the seven activities.[8] For both Mexican Americans and Asian Americans, the more recent the immigration, the less active respondents are. For Mexican Americans, the largest jump in activity occurs between immigrants and the second generation across all types of activities. For Asian Americans, the largest jumps in activity between immigrants and the second generation occur in voting, contributing money, signing a petition, and protesting, and between the second and third generations, in the remaining activities (contacting, working with others to solve a local problem, and attending a public meeting).

It is important to note that the two groups differ dramatically from one another in terms of proportion in each generation of immigration. Two-thirds of the sample of Mexican Americans in Texas are third generation or above, with the remaining third split between immigrant and second generations. The pattern of political participation among the largest group of Mexican Americans is strikingly similar to that of African Americans, with the proportion taking part in each activity diverging by no more than several points. Eighty-six percent of the Asian Americans in Texas are foreign-born immigrants. Although immigrants of both of these groups are the least active, relative to those who are second generation and above, Asian American immigrants are more active than Mexican American immigrants in all of the activities and are equally likely to take part in a demonstration or rally. The pattern of participation among third-generation Asian Americans in Texas is quite similar to that for Anglo whites.

TABLE 8.3   *Involvement in Selected Political Activities, Mexican Americans and Asian Americans, Texas, by Generation of Immigration (Percentage)*

Political Activity	Immigrant	Second Generation	Third + Generation
Mexican Americans			
Voted in 1992 presidential election	19	43	63
Contributed money or worked for candidate or party	9	14	19
Signed a petition	6	19	24
Contacted a public official by writing or phone	8	20	18
Worked with others to solve local problem	14	25	34
Attended a public meeting	6	17	20
Attended a demonstration or rally	5	13	13
Proportion of the sample in each generation	16	18	66
Asian Americans			
Voted in 1992 presidential election	31	65	79
Contributed money or worked for candidate or party	13	23	29
Signed a petition	17	33	46
Contacted a public official by writing or phone	12	10	33
Worked with others to solve local problem	16	10	40
Attended a public meeting	17	28	38
Attended a demonstration or rally	5	14	14
Proportion of the sample in each generation	86	6	8

Source: 1993 to 1994 Texas A&M Minority Survey.

Interpreting the Differences:
More Participation and the Trouble with the SES Model

What are we to make of the differences in levels of political participation among groups of citizens in the United States? The most common interpretation of the differences between whites and African Americans, Hispanics, and Asian Americans is to explain away the variation by the fact that white Americans on average have greater social and economic resources. Invoking the SES model is perhaps the easiest solution to explaining the disparity. Tables 8.4 and 8.5 present profiles of social and

TABLE 8.4   *Profile of Assimilation, Resources, and Other Characteristics, United States, by Race or Ethnicity (Percentage)*

Characteristic	Anglo White	African American	Hispanic	Asian American
Assimilation				
Respondent was born in the United States	97	95	60	22
First language spoken at home is English[a]	—	—	27	—
Social and economic resources				
Less than high school education	13	22	35	9
College degree and beyond	28	17	12	43
Family income less than $15,000	16	25	27	16
Family income more than $50,000	26	18	15	30
Respondent works outside the home full time	56	56	54	54
Respondent owns home	71	46	51	45
Political mobilization				
Respondent is strong partisan	30	42	23	20
Family and community				
Respondent is married	61	42	59	57
Average years of residence in community	20	22	16	9
Average age	44	40	37	35

Source: 1990 Citizen Participation Study.
[a]This question was asked only of Hispanics.

economic characteristics relevant to political activity for the 1990 CIT-PART (national) and the 1993 TAM (Texas) data, respectively.

The first set of characteristics are measures of place of birth and English language ability. In both the U.S. national and Texas data, the vast majority of whites and African Americans are native born. A significantly higher proportion of Mexican Americans in the Texas data (84 percent) were born in the United States, whereas only 60 percent of Hispanics nationally are native born. The proportion of Asians who are born in the United States is a third that of Hispanics in the 1990 CIT-PART data (22 percent), and only 14 percent of Asian Americans in Texas are native born. Only 27 percent of Hispanics in the 1990 CIT-PART data reported speaking English as their first language at home. In the Texas data, a much higher proportion of Mexican Americans (58 percent) reported that English is the language spoken most frequently at

TABLE 8.5   *Profile of Assimilation, Resources, and Other Characteristics, Texas, by Race or Ethnicity (Percentage)*

Characteristic	Anglo White	African American	Mexican American	Asian American
Assimilation				
Respondent is immigrant	2	5	16	86
Respondent is second generation	2	1	18	6
Respondent is third generation or above	96	94	66	8
English spoken most frequently at home	100	99	58	35
Social and economic resources				
Less than high school education	12	18	32	6
College degree and beyond	30	17	11	60
Family income less than $10,000	9	17	19	7
Family income more than $60,000	21	8	10	26
Respondent owns home	74	52	64	60
Political mobilization				
Respondent is strong partisan	26	38	23	15
Family and community				
Respondent is married	62	41	59	67
Average years of residence in community	20	16	17	8
Average age	46	39	36	37

Source: 1993 to 1994 Texas A&M Minority Survey.

home, whereas only a third of Asian Americans (35 percent) speak mostly English at home.

The next set of characteristics on social and economic resources shows a different pattern. In terms of education, Asians are the most advantaged, with 43 percent in the 1990 CITPART data and 60 percent in the Texas data reporting having earned a college degree or a higher degree. Asians are the most highly educated group in both data collections, followed by whites, of whom between one-third and one-half as many report having the same level of educational attainment (28 percent in the national data, 30 percent in the Texas sample). The most educationally disadvantaged group are Hispanics and Mexican Americans, one-third of whom in both samples report having less than a high school education. African Americans are similarly disadvantaged: one-fifth, on average, did not complete high school. The data on income show similar patterns: Asian Americans and whites have the most financial resources, African Americans and Hispanics have the least. In addition, many more whites own their own homes (more than 70 percent in both samples) than do minority Americans. In terms of political mobilization through strong political party affiliation, African Americans in both the 1990 CITPART data and the Texas sample were the most strongly affiliated, and Asian Americans appear to be the least likely to claim a strong affiliation with either the Democratic or Republican Party.

To allow identification of the importance of assimilation characteristics, social and economic resources, and mobilization to political participation, several models were estimated using ordinary least squares regression (OLS). For the Texas data from 1993 and 1994, system-directed and direct political activity were not separated, and an overall measure of political activity was created. Table 8.6 presents the results of the estimation of the model for the four separate groups. Being an immigrant has a significant negative effect on political participation for Mexican Americans, whereas immigrant and second-generation status reduces the likelihood that Asian Americans will be active. Similarly, speaking English at home affects only Asian American participation in a positive direction. Although the effect of education is positive and significant overall, it has the weakest effect for Asian Americans as compared with the other three groups. Income is a significant and positive predictor of activity for all but Asian Americans; for this group, strong party affiliation and home ownership correspond with a higher degree of political activity.[9]

Two sets of models were estimated with the Citizen Participation Study data. The first set of models predicting the two different types of political activity—system directed and direct—were estimated with all cases in the two samples. What differences remained between individuals of different racial or ethnic backgrounds were captured by dummy variables included in the model. A second set of models with an identical specification (with the exception of the exclusion of the race or ethnicity dummy variables) was estimated separately for each racial or ethnic group. Included in the specification of both of these regression models were the measures of being born in the United States and speaking English at home (for Hispanics only), the indicators of social and economic resources, a measure of strength of party affiliation as political mobilization, two measures of family and community, and control variables for gender and position in the life cycle.

Table 8.7 presents the estimates from the first set of models, which predict system-directed political activity and direct political activity. For system-directed activities such as voting, contacting, and working

TABLE 8.6   OLS Model Predicting Overall Political Activity, Texas, by Race or Ethnicity

Variable	Anglo White	African American	Mexican American	Asian American
Assimilation				
Respondent is immigrant	−.16	−.17	−.46**	−1.16**
	(.41)	(.34)	(.17)	(.23)
Respondent is second	.15	.24	−.08	−1.12**
generation	(.46)	(.64)	(.15)	(.31)
English spoken most	1.48	.28	.12	.35**
frequently at home	(.91)	(.71)	(.13)	(.13)
Social and economic resources				
Education	.37**	.33**	.36**	.22**
	(.06)	(.06)	(.05)	(.05)
Family income	.19**	.19**	.17**	.06
	(.04)	(.04)	(.04)	(.03)
Respondent owns home	.26	.13	.13	.29*
	(.16)	(.14)	(.12)	(.13)
Respondent is male	−.00	−.19	.10	−.05
	(.12)	(.12)	(.11)	(.12)
Political mobilization				
Respondent is strong partisan	.32*	.27*	.25*	.84**
	(.14)	(.13)	(.13)	(.16)
Respondent is married	−.08	.28*	−.09	−.30
	(.15)	(.14)	(.12)	(.16)
Length of residence in	.01	.01*	.01	.02*
community	(.00)	(.01)	(.00)	(.01)
Adjusted R^2	.27	.25	.35	.30
N	467	440	484	437

Source: 1993 to 1994 Texas A&M Minority Survey.
Note: Figures are unstandardized regression coefficients. Standard errors in parentheses.
*significant at .05.
**significant at .01.

on a campaign, being African American or Hispanic had no independent effect, accounting for all other factors. Being Asian American, however, has a strong and negative impact on system-directed activity, despite controlling for assimilation and social and economic resources. Being black or Hispanic, however, actually increases the likelihood of direct political activity, such as protesting and working with others in a local community, whereas being Asian American has a negative though small and statistically nonsignificant effect. Being born in the United States has no effect on direct political participation but a strong and positive influence on system-directed activity. Of the remaining explanatory variables in the model, the measures of social and economic resources,

TABLE 8.7   OLS Model Predicting Involvement in Selected
             System-Directed and Direct Political Activities,
             United States

Variable	System-Directed Activity	Direct Activity
Race or ethnicity		
Respondent is African American	−.00	.16**
	(.04)	(.02)
Respondent is Hispanic	−.04	.06*
	(.05)	(.03)
Respondent is Asian American	−.49**	−.05
	(.12)	(.06)
Assimilation		
Respondent was born in the United States	.76**	.04
	(.05)	(.03)
Social and economic resources		
Education	.16**	.05**
	(.00)	(.00)
Family income	.13**	.04**
	(.01)	(.00)
Respondent works outside the home full time	.04	−.04**
	(.03)	(.01)
Respondent owns home	.20**	.00
	(.03)	(.01)
Respondent is male	.03	.01
	(.02)	(.01)
Political mobilization		
Respondent is strong partisan	.67**	.10**
	(.03)	(.01)
Family and community		
Respondent is married	.12**	.02
	(.03)	(.01)
Length of residence in community	.01**	−.00
	(.00)	(−.00)
Adjusted R^2	.32	.09
N	13,152	13,152

Source: 1990 Citizen Participation Study.
Note: Figures are unstandardized regression coefficients. Standard errors in parentheses.
*significant at .05.
**significant at .01.

mobilization, and family and community have positive effects on both types of participation, though the size of the effects is larger for system-directed activity.[10]

Several patterns across the analysis of the system-directed versus direct forms of political activity are worth noting. First, as noted by the higher degree of model fit (adjusted R^2), the SES model does a much better job explaining the variation in the data for system-directed participation than for activity less mediated by current representative institutions, such as protest and communal work. Second, the coefficients for the indicators of race or ethnicity change both in sign and magnitude across the two types of activity for African American and Hispanics. Whereas being a minority appears to render one less active in traditional forms of political activity, all else equal, being black or Hispanic actually predicts more participation in direct activities. The model is able to "explain away" most of the effect of race or ethnicity for system-directed activity but not for direct participation.

Though revealing, this first set of models tells us only whether race or ethnicity matters; it provides little information on what factors influence political participation within groups of Americans. Table 8.8 presents the coefficients from the regression model predicting system-directed political activity, estimated separately for whites, African Americans, Hispanics, and Asian Americans. In the 1990 Citizen Participation Study data, being born in the United States is significantly related to participation in system-directed activities, with the strongest effect for African Americans and Asians. Both social and economic resources of education and family income are important for all racial and ethnic groups, with the exception of Asian Americans, for whom education is of the most modest importance and income of the greatest importance, compared with the other groups.

Table 8.9 details the model estimates for each of the four groups predicting direct political activity. The effect of assimilation characteristics has a statistically significant bearing on participation in direct political activities for none of the groups. In addition, although the effects of both education and family income—the building blocks of the SES model—are positive for Anglo whites, African Americans, and Hispanics, they have no significant bearing for Asian Americans. Where social and economic resources matter to direct political participation, the magnitude of their effects is far less important than for system-directed activity.

The analysis of the second set of regression models estimated for each of the four groups separately shows that there are actually many similarities in the combination of factors that encourage participation. The one group that differs systematically is Asian Americans, for whom characteristics of assimilation were more important than social and economic resources. Perhaps most telling, however, is the comparison between the prediction of the importance of social and economic resources for system-directed activity versus direct political activity. In the case of the former, education and family income have a much stronger impact

TABLE 8.8   OLS Model Predicting Involvement in Selected
System-Directed Political Activities, United States,
by Race or Ethnicity

Variable	Anglo White	African American	Hispanic	Asian American
Assimilation				
Respondent was born in the	.75**	.96**	.68**	.93**
United States	(.07)	(.17)	(.11)	(.30)
First language spoken at home	—	—	−.02	—
is English[a]			(.12)	
Social and economic resources				
Education	.17**	.16**	.10**	.05
	(.00)	(.01)	(.01)	(.03)
Family income	.12**	.11**	.13**	.19*
	(.01)	(.03)	(.03)	(.07)
Respondent works outside the	.04	−.06	.23*	−.06
home full time	(.03)	(.08)	(.11)	(.27)
Respondent owns home	.21**	.16*	.13	.32
	(.03)	(.08)	(.11)	(.28)
Respondent is male	.04	.02	−.05	−.06
	(.02)	(.08)	(.10)	(.24)
Political mobilization				
Respondent is strong partisan	.68**	.57**	.78**	.50
	(.03)	(.08)	(.12)	(.29)
Family and community				
Respondent is married	.15**	−.00	.05	−.05
	(.03)	(.08)	(.11)	(.28)
Length of residence in	.01**	.01**	.02**	.03*
community	(.00)	(.01)	(.00)	(.02)
Adjusted R^2	.30	.30	.36	.27
N	11,003	1,232	767	145

Source: 1990 Citizen Participation Study.
Note: Figures are unstandardized regression coefficients. Standard errors in parentheses.
[a]This question was asked only of Hispanics.
*significant at .05.
**significant at .01.

than they do on participation in more direct forms of political activity.
Thus, although resources facilitate political activity—it is far easier to
make a campaign contribution when one has extra money—economic
resources are but a partial explanation of political activity and do a better job differentiating who within groups is active than explaining the
disparity between racial or ethnic groups. Indeed, the importance of social and economic resources such as education and income to conventional forms of system-directed participation by African Americans and
Hispanics is evidence of the extent to which assimilation is a necessary

TABLE 8.9   *OLS Model Predicting Involvement in Selected Direct Political Activities, United States, by Race or Ethnicity*

Variable	Anglo White	African American	Hispanic	Asian American
Assimilation				
Respondent was born in the United States	.06	−.02	−.02	.25
	(.03)	(.10)	(.05)	(.14)
First language spoken at home is English[a]	—	—	.05	—
			(.05)	
Social and economic resource				
Education	.05**	.05**	.03**	.03
	(.00)	(.01)	(.01)	(.02)
Family income	.04**	.06**	.04**	.02
	(.00)	(.02)	(.02)	(.03)
Respondent works outside the home full time	−.05**	−.02	.02	−.11
	(.01)	(.05)	(.05)	(.12)
Respondent owns home	.02	−.09*	.05	−.21
	(.01)	(.05)	(.05)	(.13)
Respondent is male	.01	.04	.02	.05
	(.01)	(.04)	(.05)	(.11)
Political mobilization				
Respondent is strong partisan	.09**	.15**	.20**	.08
	(.01)	(.04)	(.05)	(.13)
Family and community				
Respondent is married	.03*	−.01	−.02	.15
	(.01)	(.05)	(.05)	(.13)
Length of residence in community	−.00	.00	.00	.01
	(.00)	(.00)	(.00)	(.01)
Adjusted R^2	.08	.08	.09	.04
N	11,003	1,232	767	145

Source: 1990 Citizen Participation Study.
Note: Figures are unstandardized regression coefficients. Standard errors in parentheses.
[a]This question was asked only of Hispanics.
*significant at .05.
**significant at .01.

condition for these types of activities. More conventional forms of political activity are facilitated by those social and economic characteristics that are valued as resources in American society. In particular, political participation directed at elected representatives is facilitated by exerting economic power, articulating reasoned opinion in American Standard English, and looking like others at political gatherings. In short, conventional democratic participation is facilitated by assimilation. However, other forms of activity may not be influenced as strongly by characteristics that signal assimilation. Instead, less conventional forms of activity—in particular, those that encourage group-based activity, not necessarily directed at official structures of government, or those at a local or communal level—may be less constrained by current structure and institutions in democracy.

Thus, all is not lost inferentially with the SES model as an explanation of political participation, for in one fundamental way, it accurately portrays the requirements for political access and influence in a social and economic system built on inequality. In this regard, the two central components of the SES model—formal educational attainment and income—are good surrogate measures of economic and political assimilation to norms of liberal democratic practice and resources necessary for participation in U.S. politics. Conceived in this way, the SES model should be a better predictor of engagement in political activities that are system directed and a poorer predictor of more direct forms of participation. For traditional system-directed forms of participation, social and economic resources predominate as predictors, and the SES model can "explain away" the effect of ethnicity. However, indicators of social and economic resources are less useful in predicting direct political activity, and the effect of being a minority remains significant.

Conclusion

Race and ethnicity remain significant predictors of political participation in the American political system, and the fact that systematic differences remain creates a problem for democracy in the United States. Unequal voice implies unequal policy outcomes; uneven participation means that not all members of society have the same chance to express their preferences; differences in rates of political activity foresee uneven political development. To the extent that one considers unequal rates of participation to be a problem, encouraging more activity among those who do not take part is most often seen as the solution, and identifying the determinants of participation is relevant to getting more participation from members of inactive groups.

Although I do not disagree with either the analytic strategy of uncovering antecedents to political activity or the proposition that more activity may be better for democracy, I have argued that an assumption implicit in analyses of race and participation should be held up for scrutiny rather than taken for granted. Simply put, the structure of the system of democracy in the United States cannot be assumed as neutral. Ample evidence attests to the contrary, and opportunities to take part and the rewards of political activity are not evenly distributed across the population. A particularly relevant example is the present system of single-member winner-take-all legislative districts, which legal theorist Lani Guinier characterizes as a situation in which majority rule may quickly turn into majority tyranny.[11] Fifty-one percent of the voters in any given district take 100 percent of the representative power. Under circumstances in which majority candidates consistently overwhelm minority candidates, voters with minority preferences become disillusioned and inactive. Guinier writes, "When voters are drawn into participation by seemingly fair rules, only to discover that the rules systematically work against their interests, they are likely to feel seduced and abandoned" (Guinier 1994, 12). As an alternative to winner-take-all majoritarianism, she suggests multimember legislative representation that might include cumulative voting, which provides individuals with multiple votes to distribute in any combination they choose. Guinier also discusses the possibility of supermajority voting, whereby a higher threshold for winning in a winner-take-all contest is set to empower small but cohesive minorities.

Voting in single-member winner-take-all legislative districts for permanent minorities provides an example of the extent to which taking or deferring an opportunity to participate in politics is not entirely voluntary. Individual agency is constrained by social context and placement. Nevertheless, the analytic emphasis on the individual-level subject has trained the focus for change on the nonparticipant citizen at the expense of a critical examination of the structure and institutions of democracy in which agency is acted out. The extent to which structural barriers to participation exist systematically by race is a question open to empirical investigation and not a condition that can be assumed. If we relax the assumption that the political process is neutral, then the comparatively lower rates of participation among minority Americans can be interpreted in another way, as an indicator of the structural inequalities present. In approaching the issue of political participation in this way, we can ask to what extent the patterns of persistent and racially segregated differences in participatory activity indicate a deficiency within the participatory system itself, in addition to identifying ways for individuals to enhance their ability to take part. Only under these circumstances can we evaluate the question of the desirability of more participation.

As an ideal, more participation is desirable; it expands the voice of groups and interests traditionally excluded from American politics. However, advocating more participation—especially by immigrants and traditionally disadvantaged minorities who have been systematically excluded from democracy—is justifiable only under circumstances in which the process of decision making incorporates difference. When the institutions and practices are biased, advocating more participation does not necessarily empower or emancipate those who have been previously dominated. Under such circumstances, more participation can work in exactly the opposite direction from which it is intended. Instead of eradicating domination and encouraging justice and equality, more participation amid institutions of democracy that replicate domination present in the society and the economy will only reinforce and legitimate the inequality.

Moreover, more participation in a polity in which behavioral norms are constructed from a static conception of the political being (as democratic citizen) forces those who differ to choose between assimilating to the standards of the actually existing democracy and exiting the polity.[12] In reducing barriers and gaining access to politics, we cannot neglect to reconstruct the politics we seek to influence. What it would take to make more participation good is a serious grappling with the meaning and problems of incorporating difference into the structures, institutions, and practices of democratic government in the United States. The solution cannot be a simple strengthening of already existing liberal democracy by asking for more participation among citizens. Instead, the challenge for politics in America is to create a democratic practice that views racial and ethnic differences in nonhierarchical terms and provides electoral space for the representation of group interests beyond the two political parties. In short, the task is to institutionalize a democratic practice that redresses rather than reproduces structural inequalities.

Appendix

TABLE 8A.1   *Life-Cycle Controls for Model Predicting Overall Political Activity, Texas, by Race or Ethnicity*

Life-Cycle Control	Anglo White	African American	Mexican American	Asian American
Age twenty-five to thirty-four	−.02	.12	.20	−.18
	(.23)	(.19)	(.16)	(.20)
Age thirty-five to forty-four	.49*	.44*	.44**	.32
	(.23)	(.18)	(.17)	(.23)
Age forty-five to fifty-four	.24	.10	.48*	.56*
	(.25)	(.23)	(.22)	(.26)
Age fifty-five to sixty-four	.61*	.60*	.52*	.38
	(.26)	(.25)	(.28)	(.29)
Age sixty-five +	.13	.37	.80**	.44
	(.25)	(.28)	(.27)	(.42)

Source: 1993 to 1994 Texas A & M Minority Survey.
Note: Figures are unstandardized regression coefficients. Standard errors in parentheses.
*Significant at .05.
**Significant at .01.

TABLE 8A.2 *Life-Cycle Controls for Models Predicting System-Directed and Direct Political Activity in 1990, United States*

Life-Cycle Control	System Directed Activity	Direct Activity
Age twenty-five to thirty-four	.36** (.04)	−.03 (.02)
Age thirty-five to forty-four	.79** (.04	.07** (.02)
Age forty-five to fifty-four	.98** (.05)	.04 (.02)
Age fifty-five to sixty-four	1.15** (.05)	.01 (.03)
Age sixty-five +	1.27** (.05)	−.04 (.03)

Source: 1990 Citizen Participation Study.
Note: Figures are unstandardized OLS regression coefficients. Standard errors in parentheses.
*Significant at .05.
**Significant at .01.

TABLE 8A.3 *Life-Cycle Controls for Model Predicting System-Directed Political Activity in 1990, United States, by Race or Ethnicity*

Life-Cycle Control	Anglo White	African American	Hispanic	Asian American
Age twenty-five to thirty-four	.34** (.05)	.54** (.11)	.28* (.15)	.21 (.35)
Age thirty-five to forty-four	.77** (.05)	.91** (.12)	.76** (.16)	.26 (.39)
Age forty-five to fifty-four	.96** (.05)	1.09** (.15)	1.07** (.19)	.52 (.53)
Age fifty-five to sixty-four	1.15** (.06)	1.32** (.16)	.93** (.22)	−.47 (.65)
Age sixty-five +	1.27** (.06)	1.27** (.17)	1.40** (.27)	.74 (.76)

Source: 1990 Citizen Participation Study.
Note: Figures are unstandardized OLS regression coefficients. Standard errors in parentheses.
*Significant at .05.
**Significant at .01.

TABLE 8A.4   *Life-Cycle Controls for Model Predicting Direct Political Activity in 1990, United States, by Race or Ethnicity*

Life-Cycle Control	Anglo White	African American	Hispanic	Asian American
Age twenty-five to thirty-four	−.03	.00	−.09	.06
	(.02)	(.07)	(.07)	(.16)
Age thirty-five to forty-four	.08**	.04	.03	−.03
	(.02)	(.07)	(.07)	(.18)
Age forty-five to fifty-four	.03	.14	.00	.34
	(.03)	(.09)	(.09)	(.26)
Age fifty-five to sixty-four	.01	.03	−.14	−.12
	(.03)	(.09)	(.10)	(.30)
Age sixty-five +	−.05	−.00	−.00	−.04
	(.03)	(.10)	(.12)	(.35)

Source: 1990 Citizen Participation Study.
Note: Figures are unstandardized OLS regression coefficients. Standard errors in parentheses.
*Significant at .05.
**Significant at .01.

A previous version of this chapter appeared in *American Behavioral Scientist* 1999, vol. 42, no. 9.

Notes

1. This has not always been the case. Important traditions of thought, frequently characterized as "elitist" theories of democracy, take quite the opposite position regarding the desirability of greater popular sovereignty. Arguments against more citizen participation reflect concerns about the political, moral, and cognitive capability of the mass public, regime stability, and decision-making gridlock. See, for example, Schumpeter (1942); Berelson, Lazarsfeld, and McPhee (1954); Lipset (1960); Michels (1962); Huntington (1968); and Crozier, Huntington, and Watanuki (1975). Though silent about the desirability of more citizen participation, perspectives from rational choice suggest that we should simply not expect more activity from individuals; see, for example, Fiorina (1990).

2. Recent examples of research reporting this finding include Verba et al. (1993); Bobo and Gilliam (1990); Calvo and Rosenstone (1989); Danigelis (1978, 1982); de la Garza et al. (1992); Ellison and Gay (1989); Guterbock and London (1983); Lien (1994, 1997); Shingles (1981); Tate (1993); Uhlaner, Cain, and Kiewiet (1989); and Welch, Comer, and Steinman (1972). The SES model has been revised to

include the importance of "ethnic political culture" and "group consciousness" to the political behavior of African Americans and Hispanics; see Nelson (1979); Miller et al. (1981).

3. In their "civic voluntarism model," Sidney Verba, Kay Schlozman, and Henry Brady go beyond the SES model by defining the elements of resources as time, money, and civic skills; see Verba, Schlozman, and Brady (1995) and Brady, Verba, and Schlozman (1995). See also Nie, Junn, and Stehlik-Barry (1996) for an analysis of the divergent pathways formal educational attainment takes to political participation. In addition, Wolfinger and Rosenstone (1980, chapter 2) provide a good explanation of how and why formal education is so important to voting.

4. See Nie, Junn, and Stehlik-Barry (1996, chapter 6), for a critique of the simple additive logic of the SES model and an explanation of rising aggregate levels of education amid stagnant and declining political engagement.

5. Although the SES model explains a good deal of political behavior among African Americans, the results are not always consistent; see Harris (1994); Dawson, Brown, and Allen (1990). Moreover, Jan Leighley and Arnold Vedlitz (forthcoming) make a strong case for the applicability of models of participation that go beyond the SES model for explaining political activity among Hispanics and Asian Americans.

6. The 1990 CITPART study was a representative sample of residents of the United States, whereas the TAM study surveyed residents of the state of Texas in 1993 and 1994. In the latter, approximately five hundred people from each of four groups were sampled: Anglo whites, African Americans, Mexican Americans, and Asian Americans. Country of origin was not asked of Asian Americans in either sample, but U.S. Census data from Texas indicate that more than 50 percent of Asians in Texas are of Chinese or Vietnamese origin. In the CITPART sample, the Hispanic population was made up of people from a variety of places, including Mexico (57 percent), Puerto Rico (12 percent), and Cuba (6 percent). For a more detailed description of the 1990 Citizen Participation Study, see Verba, Schlozman, and Brady (1995) and Leighley and Vedlitz (forthcoming).

7. See, for instance, the essays in Ahrari (1987) on ethnic group involvement in U.S. foreign policy.

8. Data for Anglo whites and African Americans are not included here, because 97 percent of whites and 95 percent of blacks were born in the United States. In addition, no measures of participation by immigrants in their home countries were included in either the Texas or the national survey. Immigration scholars such as Alejandro Portes and Rubén Rumbaut (1996, chapter 4) have docu-

mented the importance of such bidirectional participation to political adaptation.

9. Coefficients and standard errors for the age variables are detailed in appendix table 8A.1.

10. Coefficients and standard errors for the age variables in the analyses detailed below are shown in appendix tables 8A.2, 8A.3, and 8A.4.

11. In her 1994 collection of essays, *The Tyranny of the Majority*, Guinier writes, "When majorities are fixed, the minority lacks any mechanism for holding the majority to account or even to listen. Nor does such majority rule promote deliberation or consensus. The permanent majority simply has its way, without reaching out to or convincing anyone else" (Guinier 1994, 9; see also Amy 1995).

12. In his study of Latin American immigrants in New York City, *Between Two Nations*, Michael Jones-Correa (1998) argues that among the most significant reasons for the reluctance to become an American citizen is the requirement to renounce formal membership in one's country of origin and declare exclusive allegiance to the United States.

References

Ahrari, Mohammed E., ed. 1987. *Ethnic Groups and U.S. Foreign Policy.* Westport, Conn.: Greenwood Press.

Amy, Douglas J. 1995. *Real Choices/New Voices: The Case for Proportional Representation Elections in the United States.* New York: Columbia University Press.

Berelson, Bernard F., Paul M. Lazarsfeld, and William McPhee. 1954. *Voting.* Chicago: University of Chicago Press.

Bobo, Lawrence, and Franklin D. Gilliam Jr. 1990. "Race, Sociopolitical Participation, and Black Empowerment." *American Political Science Review* 84(2): 377–93.

Brady, Henry E., Sidney Verba, and Kay Lehman Schlozman. 1995. "Beyond SES: A Resource Model of Political Participation." *American Political Science Review* 89(2): 271–94.

Brody, Richard. 1978. "The Puzzle of Participation." In *The New American Political System*, edited by Anthony King. Washington, D.C.: American Enterprise Institute.

Calvo, Maria A., and Steven J. Rosenstone. 1989. *Hispanic Political Participation.* San Antonio, Tex.: Southwest Voter Research Institute.

Crozier, Michel J., Samuel P. Huntington, and Joji Watanuki. 1975. *The Crisis of Democracy.* New York: New York University Press.

Danigelis, Nicholas L. 1978. "Black Political Participation in the United

States: Some Recent Evidence." *American Sociological Review* 43(5): 756–71.

———. 1982. "Race, Class, and Political Involvement in the United States." *Social Forces* 61(4): 532–50.

Dawson, Michael C., Ronald E. Brown, and Richard L. Allen. 1990. "Racial Belief Systems, Religious Guidance, and African American Political Participation." *National Political Science Review* 2: 22–44.

de la Garza, Rodolfo O., Louis DeSipio, F. Chris Garcia, John Garcia, and Angelo Falcon. 1992. *Latino Voices: Mexican, Puerto Rican, and Cuban Perspectives on American Politics.* Boulder: Westview Press.

Eisenstein, Zillah. 1994. *The Color of Gender: Reimaging Democracy.* Los Angeles: University of California Press.

Ellison, Christopher G., and David A. Gay. 1989. "Black Political Participation Revisited: A Test of Compensatory, Ethnic Community, and Public Arena Models." *Social Science Quarterly* 70:101–19.

Fiorina, Morris P. 1990. "Information and Rationality in Elections." In *Information and Democratic Processes,* edited by John A. Ferejohn and James H. Kuklinski. Chicago: University of Illinois Press.

Fraser, Nancy. 1992. "Rethinking the Public Sphere: A Contribution to the Critique of Actually Existing Democracy." In *Habermas and the Public Sphere,* edited by Craig Calhoun. Cambridge: MIT Press.

Guinier, Lani. 1994. *The Tyranny of the Majority: Fundamental Fairness in Representative Democracy.* New York: Free Press.

Guterbock, Thomas M., and Bruce London. 1983. "Race, Political Orientation, and Participation: An Empirical Test of Four Competing Theories." *American Sociological Review* 48(4): 439–53.

Gutmann, Amy, and Dennis F. Thompson, eds. 1996. *Democracy and Disagreement.* Cambridge: Harvard University Press.

Habermas, Jürgen. 1989. *The Structural Transformation of the Public Sphere: An Inquiry into a Category of Bourgeois Society,* translated by Thomas Burger, with Frederick Lawrence. Cambridge: MIT Press.

Harris, Fredrick C. 1994. "Something Within: Religion as a Mobilizer of African American Political Activism." *Journal of Politics* 56(1): 42–68.

Huntington, Samuel P. 1968. *Political Order in Changing Societies.* New Haven: Yale University Press.

Jones-Correa, Michael. 1998. *Between Two Nations: The Political Predicament of Latinos in New York City.* Ithaca: Cornell University Press.

Lee, Taeku. 1998. "The Backdoor and the Backlash: Campaign Finance and the Political Opinions of Chinese Americans." Paper presented at the annual meeting of the American Political Science Association. Boston(September 3–6, 1998).

Leighley, Jan E., and Arnold Vedlitz. Forthcoming. "Race, Ethnicity, and Political Participation: Competing Models and Contrasting Explanations." *Journal of Politics.*

Lien, Pei-te. 1994. "Ethnicity and Political Participation: A Comparison

Between Asian and Mexican Americans." *Political Behavior* 16(2): 237–64.

———. 1997. *The Political Participation of Asian Americans.* New York: Garland.

Lipset, Seymour Martin. 1960. *Political Man.* New York: Free Press.

Michels, Roberto. 1962. *Political Parties.* New York: Free Press.

Miller, Arthur H., Patricia Gurin, Gerald Gurin, and Oksana Malanchuk. 1981. "Group Consciousness and Political Participation." *American Journal of Political Science* 25(3): 494–511.

Nelson, Dale C. 1979. "Ethnicity and Socioeconomic Status as Sources of Participation: The Case for Ethnic Political Culture." *American Political Science Review* 73(4): 1024–38.

Nie, Norman H., Jane Junn, and Kenneth Stehlik-Barry. 1996. *Education and Democratic Citizenship in America.* Chicago: University of Chicago Press.

Phillips, Anne. 1994. *Democracy and Difference.* University Park: Pennsylvania State University Press.

Portes, Alejandro, and Rubén G. Rumbaut. 1996. *Immigrant America: A Portrait.* 2d ed. Berkeley: University of California Press.

Schumpeter, Joseph. 1942. *Capitalism, Socialism, and Democracy.* New York: Free Press.

Shingles, Richard D. 1981. "Black Consciousness and Political Participation: The Missing Link." *American Political Science Review* 75(1): 76–91.

Tam, Wendy. 1995. "Asians: A Monolithic Voting Bloc?" *Political Behavior* 17: 223–49.

Tate, Katherine. 1993. *From Protest to Politics: The New Black Voters in American Elections.* Cambridge: Harvard University Press.

Uhlaner, Carole J., Bruce E. Cain, and D. Roderick Kiewiet. 1989. "Political Participation of Ethnic Minorities in the 1980s." *Political Behavior* 11(1): 195–232.

Verba, Sidney, Kay Lehman Schlozman, and Henry E. Brady. 1995. *Voice and Equality: Civic Voluntarism in American Politics.* Cambridge: Harvard University Press.

Verba, Sidney, Kay Lehman Schlozman, Henry Brady, and Norman H. Nie. 1993. "Race, Ethnicity, and Political Resources: Participation in the United States." *British Journal of Political Science* 23(4): 453–97.

Welch, Susan, John Comer, and Michael Steinman. 1972. "Political Participation Among Mexican Americans: An Exploratory Analysis." *Social Science Quarterly* 53(4): 799–813.

Wolfinger, Raymond E., and Steven J. Rosenstone. 1980. *Who Votes?* New Haven: Yale University Press.

9

THE RISE OF NONSTATE ACTORS IN MIGRATION REGULATION IN THE UNITED STATES AND EUROPE: CHANGING THE GATEKEEPERS OR BRINGING BACK THE STATE?

Gallya Lahav

N AN era of growing anti-immigrant sentiment and heightened state efforts to curtail immigration to the developed world, Western democracies are increasingly caught between their liberal ethos and their ability to effectively control immigration. Questions are being raised concerning the form of control industrialized democracies can use to effectively manage global migration flows. How can liberal democracies reconcile efforts to control the movement of people with those that promote free borders, open markets, and liberal standards? Are national actors, as some political analysts predict, "losing control" over migration? (Sassen 1996; Cornelius, Martin, and Hollifield 1994)

This chapter addresses two main questions: How do liberal nation-states manage the administration, elaboration, and implementation of immigration policy? And, who are the gatekeepers, and to what extent do they open up new channels and opportunities for state regulation over migration? In seeking to answer these questions, I offer a comparative analysis of the policy instruments and strategies adopted by the advanced liberal democracies of Europe (particularly France) and the United States. A disaggregated institutional view of the state, I argue, helps to explain why cultural variations may lead to particular domestic and international outcomes.[1]

In line with scholars who are "bringing back the state" into their studies of migration, the analysis that follows reconceptualizes and extends theories about political aspects of migration through a focus on state regulatory modes.[2] Going beyond a monolithic view of the state, this paper highlights a devolution or transfer of functions away from the central government and the proliferation of nonstate and transnational actors in migration regulation. The term "nonstate actor" refers to a diverse group of collective actors who have the economic, social, or political resources to facilitate or curtail immigration and return.

The argument is that nonstate and third-party actors represent reinvented state forms of power and governance in a world of increasing interdependence and changing boundaries. Liberal states are resorting to older—neocorporatist—means to reconcile demands to control borders for the movement of people with demands to promote open borders for trade and goods. The strategies increasingly used to control migration make clear that states are neither losing control nor abdicating sovereignty; rather, states seek to reduce the costs of immigration and to control migration at the same time that they allow the free flow of trade and goods. European countries undertaking regional integration may have significant lessons to teach traditional immigration countries, such as the United States. They are increasingly delegating policy elaboration and implementation to third-party actors as a way to increase policy effectiveness and diminish political fallout at the national level. That the United States is also moving in this direction suggests the possible emergence of an international migration regime oriented to protectionism and exclusion in combination with free trade in capital, goods, and services.[3]

Theoretical and Research Frameworks

The debate on how liberal states are responding to their market and democratic-rights-based tenets, on the one hand, and political pressures and needs to limit migration, on the other, is unresolved. The school of globalization, or interdependence, posits that in an increasingly global world, in which the lines between nation-states are becoming blurred, states are seeking international solutions to domestic problems. In this view, global population movements are seen as problem areas for national welfare because they increasingly take place outside the ambit of state control (Papademetriou and Miller 1983). The traditional notion of state sovereignty has been further challenged as the state no longer has complete control over the definition of citizenship and the decision as to who will enter a country (Layton-Henry 1990; Soysal 1994; Schuck 1989). Economic interdependence, the globalization of the economy, and the emergence of global cities, it is argued, have essentially eliminated the state's role in regulating migration (Sassen 1991, 1996).

Theorists of international political economy and political sociology support such liberal outcomes stemming from national and international constraints (see Hollifield 1992; Heisler 1992; Soysal 1994; Freeman 1995; Sassen 1996). According to these theorists, domestic liberal norms are "embedded," or institutionalized, in the international state system by human rights instruments and international agreements. Theorists of embedded liberalism contend that rights expressed in the form of constitutional norms and principles act to constrain the power and autonomy of states both in their treatment of individual migrants and in their relations to other states (Hollifield 1992; Ruggie 1982; Walzer 1980; Rawls 1971). Such arguments lend support to the hypothesis that immigration policy is an area in which states may be expected to defer to international regimes (Ruggie 1982; Krasner 1982). Proponents of globalization—whether sociologists or economists—often point to a growing convergence of national legislation in industrialized countries as testament to the effects of market globalization in contracting the state. The implications are limited state control over its migration interests.

National and international structures and standards may certainly impede state efforts to regulate immigration. Indeed, despite persistent cross-national differences in immigrant rights, all advanced industrialized nations of the OECD (Organisation for Economic Co-operation and Development) have made advances in this policy area (UN 1998; OECD 1997). Yet those who herald the decline of the nation-state have not paid enough attention to actual administrative mechanisms and domestic political processes or to the limitations of rights-based norms in determining migration outcomes (see Guiraudon and Lahav 2000; Guiraudon 1997; Lahav 1997a; Chekel 1995).

Critics of interdependence and neoliberalism argue that the assumption that globalization and international instruments undermine the state's capacity to control migration fail to realize the basis from which they derive: the state itself. State-centric and realist (or neorealist) theories assume that states have the power to protect and defend territorial integrity and that they continue to regulate international migration in accordance with their "national interests" (Waltz 1979; Zolberg 1981; Weiner 1985, 1990).

The theoretical debates about the role of the state in migration have, however, tend to neglect the mechanisms that states use to effectively manage immigration policy. There has been much discussion of the challenge immigration poses to liberal democracies (Layton-Henry 1990; Lahav 1993) but little exploration of state responses to immigration. Not much has been written, for example, on the actual instruments and policy measures used to restrict and shape immigration flows. Few attempts have been made to disaggregate the state and to identify the agencies and actors involved in regulating migration. Assessments of state capacities tend to be full of generalizations and devoid of specific claims, particularly concerning the practices and modes of policy implementation in migration regulation.[4]

It is also necessary to move beyond a unitary view of the state and adopt a neo-institutional perspective in analyzing the regulation of migration. In a neo-institutional approach, both norms and institutions are intricately related to inform policy outcomes. This approach poses the question, how does the state control migration in a way that corresponds to its policy interests, with a focus on the incentives and constraints political actors face in different national contexts? (See Thelen and Steinmo 1992, 7.) Going beyond the view of the state as a unitary actor facing global and domestic constraints allows us to understand the range of responses available to national governments when they face policy constraints and the number of actors and strategies that can be incorporated and deployed. In the context of an interdependent world, in which immigration is seen as a threat emanating from the international environment, what is interesting, then, is not only that the patterns of regulation and enforcement are increasingly conforming to public policy models, which are converging in the world, but those patterns, in particular, that involve increasing enforcement, via the transfer of state functions to international, transnational, private, and local jurisdictions.

Legislative and institutional analyses reflect converging policy norms and structures in the United States and Europe. The nature of policy implementation and the changes in the character of the gatekeepers reveal a trend toward more state commitment and increasing capacities to control borders. Although it is true that liberal international and domestic norms and pluralist politics have influenced the emergence of legal modes of migration, it is becoming more difficult to support the proposition that immigration is encouraged by a rights-based embedded liberalism (Schain 1995, 11; Joppke 1997; Lahav 1997a, 1997b; Money 1999). Analysis of policy implementation reinforces what has recently been suggested of contemporary surveys of program structures: namely, that states have considerable capacities to select migrants (Freeman 1994).

The empirical findings presented in this chapter suggest that the United States and European states are responding to and using global developments to extend and rethink control over immigration politics in the 1990s. A comparative analysis of the American and French cases reveals that liberal states are adopting policy tools or lessons that may be transferable across borders. Do they represent a new era of weak states in a global economy, or instead, an extension of state control whereby "the state" has changed the gatekeepers but is still able to define and control migration norms and outcomes? What are the implications of these regulatory modes for theories of state sovereignty and for transnational migration flows?

Bringing Back the State and Changing the Gatekeepers: Some Empirical Data

In order to assess the extent of state control over migration and migrant groups, it is important to identify how states manage policy outcomes that respond to their policy interests and commitments in an interdependent era. We need to consider policy structures and norms—that is, the instruments and organizations that states set up to achieve their policy goals. At the state level, the main provisions governing migration are normally established by law. The legislature has the prerogative to promulgate regulations or rules through ordinances. The executive may issue circulars, and administrative officials may give instructions, which are not always made public and may be modified or revoked. Guidelines for government action are deferred to the administrative discretion of different ministries and departments, such as Justice, State, Labor, Health and Human Services, and Treasury, in addition to the president's or prime minister's staff.

Although immigration issues, political structures, and policy making vary substantially among the advanced liberal democracies, one unmistakeable feature common to all is the rapid development of immigration legislation. The rate of change of immigration and asylum policy is evident from the density or flurry of legislation. In Europe, after the termination of guest-worker recruitment in 1973 (a process that did not always require legislation because it did not proceed from legislation in the first place), many countries passed little legislation for a decade, except to facilitate return migration (UNECE 1997, 168). Throughout the 1980s and early 1990s, however, nearly all European Union (EU) countries introduced restrictive legislation. From different starting points, most advanced industrialized countries have been converging toward more restrictive policies, and most have rapidly accelerated the pace of new legislative and administrative reforms to control immigration in the 1990s.

Although national legislation and immigration reforms represent the most obvious policy responses to regulate immigration, administrative decisions and policy implementation are also important. Because administrative structures and agencies have a substantial impact on policy elaboration and implementation, they are critical in analyzing state means to secure immigration and immigrant policy interests. New administrative categories (such as "temporary protection" status), for example, have been devised to accommodate authorized flows. In general, a key function of states in regulating migration is the creation of admissions and classification formulations, and this accounts for the difficulties in national comparisons (Lahav 1997b, 27). The means available to administrative agencies to create and recreate migrant categories and implement policy are considerable.

A sure sign of state efforts to adapt to migration challenges—and of a continuing state role in regulation—are the introduction of structural and institutional reforms to deal with enforcement. Some countries have adopted new institutions and commissions to deal explicitly with migration matters. Italy, for example, established the office of Extraordinary Commissioner for Immigration, who reports directly to the president of the Council of Ministers (OECD 1995, 99). More striking, however, has been the strengthening of traditional institutions dealing with migration, such as the U.S. Immigration and Naturalization Service (INS). Traditionally an agency plagued by low morale and negligible resources, in the 1990s the INS underwent a spectacular overhaul and became one of the few agencies in the government to grow.[5] The Clinton administration increased the INS budget to $3.1 billion for the 1996 fiscal, from $1.5 billion four years earlier (U.S. Department of Justice 1996). A significant proportion of the expanded budget has gone to tightening national borders, as attested by the gradual growth in the Border Patrol, scheduled to nearly double by 2001, and the adoption of new technology and automation (newly purchased computers, night-vision scopes, encrypted radios, and ground sensors).

The commitment to institutional effectiveness is perhaps nowhere better reflected than in administrative and implementation structures and norms. They are distinguished by two developments: the proliferation and diversification of third-party agents and nonstate actors and the devolution of decision making, policy elaboration, and regulation functions away from the central state (see figure 9.1). These phenomena are evident in policy making that focuses on immigrant intake as well as policies concerning the conditions of immigrants resident in the territory (Hammar 1985).

Increasingly, third-party actors define the immigration regulatory playing field as they deal with external and internal control sites, including questions of entry, stay, and exit of migrants. In terms of immigrant intake, these third-party actors include foreign states and intergovernmental groups as well as private companies such as airline carriers, transport companies, and security services. As for the control of migrants inside territories, this has increasingly become the domain of

FIGURE 9.1   *The State and Nonstate Actors in Migration Regulation*

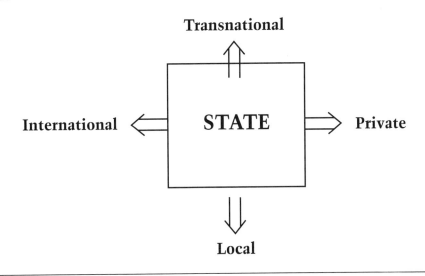

Source: Author's compilation.

employer groups and civic actors (at both the international and local levels) dependent on nongovernmental organizations, trade unions, and even the family for regulatory intervention. Three types of actors— private, local, and international—have a role in monitoring external and internal control sites in the United States and Europe. The focus of this chapter is on the United States and France, an EU country with a substantial foreign population and anti-immigrant popular agitation,[6] and I begin with private actors.

Private Actors

Private actors, or independent authorities who rely on market forces, have become crucial immigration agents in extending the area of what is referred to by Aristide Zolberg as "remote control" immigration policy (1999). Before World War I, the low level of movement and modest welfare entitlement facilitated international movement free of passports and an elaborate system of controls (Torpey 1998). Since the 1920s, an elaborate system of documentation has developed, including visas for entry, work permits, and residence permits.

The initial migrant appeal to the host country typically occurs in the country of origin at embassies or consulates, through visa bureaucrats. To a significant degree, visas are a means of extending the barriers of control into the sending country, where facts about applicants can be verified in ways impossible at receiving-country ports of entry.[7]

The external site of immigration regulation became increasingly developed, complex, and diversified in the 1990s. A major thrust of recent policy efforts in many countries is interdiction, defined broadly as activity directed toward preventing the movement of people at the source (UN 1997). Interdiction initiatives take various forms, including information campaigns to deter potential migrants, visa requirements, carrier sanctions, airline training, and liaison with foreign control authorities, as well as the actual interception of persons traveling on fraudulent documents. According to its proponents, interdiction is more cost effective, humane, and efficient than enforcement action taken after the migrant has arrived in a receiving country.

A core actor in the enlarged control system at the entry level is transport or carrier companies. This is not new. Carriers have long been obliged, at their own expense, to transport inadmissible passengers back to their countries of departure. Sanctions against ships have been in force since the Passenger Act of 1902. However, since the adoption of guidelines established by the 1944 Convention on International Civil Aviation (ICAO), transport companies have increasingly been forced to assume the role of international immigration officers imposed on them by states. The standards of the convention established the airline's responsibility to ensure that passengers have the necessary travel documents. Apart from ICAO guidelines, many countries have introduced laws that increase the responsibilities of carriers and levy fines against them for noncompliance. In 1994, all EU countries, with the exception of Spain, Ireland, and Luxembourg, passed laws increasing carriers' responsibilities.

The content, interpretation, and application of laws on carriers' liabilities vary among European member states (Cruz 1994). Nonetheless, they represent an effort by states to redirect the burden of implementation away from the central government and toward the sources of control, thereby increasing national efficacy and decreasing the costs to government in the process. It is noteworthy that in all the laws on carriers' liability, there is a striking absence of any provision to fine railways. A possible reason is that most railways are state owned, and the treatment of railways as airlines are treated (that is, charging them with fines unless they can provide convincing evidence discharging them of negligence) could cause embarrassing problems between European states (Cruz 1994, 25).

The abolition of internal borders, critical to European integration, is essentially mitigated by the flurry of legislation and implementation of the carriers' liability to check passengers. Indeed, more stringent security checks at airports—of identity cards, tickets, boarding passes, baggage, and so on—have virtually offset the absence of passport controls, owing to the increasing link between international crime, terrorism, drugs, and illegal immigration (Bigo 1996). International instruments have supported and enhanced the role of carriers in border control. European Union member states cite their obligations under Article 26 of the 1990 Supplementation Agreement of the Schengen Convention in relying on carriers to serve as immigration officers.

In the United States, devolution of interstate regulation to expert bodies can be traced back to the federal government's adoption of the Interstate Commerce Act of 1887, regulating railways, and with it the creation of a regulatory body, the Interstate Commerce Commission (ICC). In passing this legislation, the Congress delegated power to regulate an important part of interstate commerce—namely, railway traffic—to an agency designed especially for the purpose. This was an important institutional innovation at the federal level (Majone 1996, 16). Although the ICC is not a private agency per se, it was set up by statute as an independent commission, a compromise to those American political leaders who rejected nationalization and sought to establish an expert authority to operate outside the line of hierarchical control or oversight by the departments of central government (Fainsod 1940, 313; Majone 1996, 15).[8] It represented the transfer of activities of state interests to semiprivate actors and technical experts and away from legislators, courts, or bureaucratic generalists. In this way, market activities may be generally regulated in areas that are considered important and in need of protection as well as control. According to Giandomenico Majone, "this mode of regulation represents a new frontier of public policy and public management in Europe" in the 1990s (1996, 15).

Although there are differences between European cases and the U.S. experience, in which business interests have been more culturally and politically dominant and state intervention in the economy is more prohibitive, the cost-benefit logic of this exchange is similar. Airlines and shipping and travel services may provide unique resources of personnel, services, and access to migrants, whereas states, by virtue of owning airspace (according to the Paris Conference of 1919), subject all these industries to national restrictions. Thus, with little training investment, these private actors may be enlisted in an enlarged control system, providing the state with the technological and resourceful means to differentiate effectively between the legal passage of travelers or economic tourists and the illegal passage of would-be overstayers or migrants (Weber 1998).

Immigration control may be equally effective in the employment sector. Increasingly, approaches to stem illegal migration at the work site have been developed to extend and redistribute the liabilities of migration control outside of the central state and to make employer groups more significant actors. In the early to middle 1970s, most advanced European countries adopted and refined employer sanctions (see table 9.1).[9]

Strategies for enforcement of employer sanctions have evolved over time, involving a growing number of actors and leading to a complex web of laws. In the French case, for example, an employer who hires an illegal migrant is liable to an administrative fine from the Office of International Migrations and to judicial punishment following legal proceedings. Most citations for illegal alien employment are made by labor inspectors, but they also involve police gendarmes, judicial police, agricultural inspectors, and agents of customs, maritime affairs, and social security departments. In further removing immigration control from the central or federal government, a recent trend has been to contract out work-site enforcement to labor inspection agencies, security services, or police. In France, approximately four thousand police are qualified to enforce laws against illegal employment (Miller 1995, 23). In addition, French labor inspectors enjoy a great deal of discretion; they need not write up citations if they deem it not to be in the "public interest" to do so (Miller 1995, 23). Although the French practices and laws are controversial, there has been an unprecedented number of Special Contributions—2,498 in 1992 alone, compared with a total of 25,942 infractions for the entire previous fifteen-year period (Miller 1995, 18).

The French approach to stemming illegal migration at the work site

TABLE 9.1   *Third-Party Nonstate Actors in Immigration Regulation*

Country	Transport Companies (Sanctions)	Employers (Sanctions)	Immigrants (Punishment for Illegal Entry)	Civil Society (Sanctions for Harboring Illegal Immigrants)
Belgium	Yes	Yes	Yes	Yes
Canada	Yes	Yes	Yes	Yes
Denmark	Yes	Yes	Yes	Yes
Finland	Yes	Yes	Yes	No
Germany	Yes	Yes	Yes	Yes
Italy	Yes	Yes	Yes	No
Netherlands	Yes	Yes	No	Yes
Sweden	Yes	Yes	Yes	Yes
United Kingdom	Yes	Yes	Yes	Yes
United States	Yes	Yes	Yes	Yes

Source: Author's calculations.

has been considered a model for other Western countries, including the United States (see Miller 1995). The French model of department-level commissions, bringing together concerned enforcement services, elected officials, and representatives of employers and employees, is premised on the assumption that the battle for immigration control will be won or lost at the local level, in particular, in industries and places of employment (Miller 1995, 27). The 1995 agreement between the U.S. Department of Labor and the Immigration and Naturalization Service to allow labor inspectors to check I-9 compliance represents a step toward the French approach.

In the United States, elevated fines, random spot checks, raids, and removal of illegal immigrants from select industries known to rely heavily on illegal labor have actually threatened to close some small factories (for example, meatpackers in the Midwest, garment shops in Los Angeles and New York, and agriculture operations throughout the country). President Bill Clinton signed an executive order in February 1996 banning companies convicted of violating the employment provisions of the Immigration Reform and Control Act of 1986 (IRCA) from obtaining government contracts. Operation Jobs, begun in Dallas in 1995 and since expanded to eighteen states, and Operation SouthPAW (Protect American Workers), which operates in six southern states, have accounted for most of the eleven thousand illegal aliens the INS removed from work sites in 1995 (INS 1996). These figures are substantial and reflect a general increase in illegal deportations from roughly four thousand in 1993 to nearly seventy thousand in 1996 (*New York Times*, October 26, 1996; INS 1996).

There are substantial differences between European and American systems of labor control. In most European countries, the government's labor agency has responsibility for detecting and removing unauthorized workers from the workplace. France, for example, has a long history of protecting workers by controlling illegal migrants' access to the labor market; the French labor agency regards the removal of undocumented workers as a means of protecting and ensuring decent conditions for legal workers. In contrast, in the United States, the Immigration and Naturalization Service is interested in workers' legal status rather than their wages or working conditions, and the state labor inspectors are concerned about wages but not about workers' legal status. Recent controversies involving state labor inspectors who have failed to cooperate with the INS have led to a rethinking of the coordination policy.

Broadly speaking, these differences in European and American conceptual schemes have generated disparate outcomes, even when similar policies are adopted. In the United States, work-site sanctions come under the rubric of illegal migration rather than violations of employment standards. In contrast to France, where employer sanctions have been part of labor laws since the 1920s, in the United States, before the 1986 passage of the IRCA, illegal aliens were considered to be in violation of federal law by entering the country and working, but employers were not. Employer sanctions adopted in 1986 corrected this asymmetry and for the first time in U.S. history made the knowing hire of illegal aliens a violation of federal labor law. Employers are now also required to verify the status of new hires by examining a variety of documents and keeping records of their examinations. Nonetheless, owing to the European system's heavy social safety net, which sets employer payroll taxes and related overhead costs at higher levels than in the United States, the fine structure in Europe is typically far greater than in the United States (UN 1997). One scholar notes that differing policies give rise to different expectations in each case, and thus the measure of "effectiveness" also varies (Papademetriou 1993, 211).

There are also dramatic differences between the United States and France in the enforcement capacities of work control systems that stem from their different civic traditions and political cultures. Although France does not have a mandatory national identification document system, it is believed that more than 90 percent of French citizens carry a national identity card (Miller 1995, 26). Lacking such a tradition, American strategies to regulate the work site have been hampered in addressing the problem of fraudulent or counterfeit documents. Moreover, an American political culture averse to government intervention in business or corporate matters makes employers less vulnerable to liabilities than their European counterparts. Nonetheless, there are some changes. The INS revised the qualifications for issuance of the green card in 1989 and, in 1996, began replacing some of the older work authorization forms with a new "tamper-resistant" Employment Authorization Document (EAD), based on the worker's social security number and on improved documents to establish identity. The INS has also been developing and testing databases and access systems for businesses to use in verifying employment eligibility. The adoption of a worker authorization system has been viewed as a first step toward the introduction of a national identity card. Not surprisingly, it has come under substantial attack both from civil rights advocates and from conservatives and corporations who oppose expanding federal government involvement to hiring decisions.

The system of work-site control of immigration represents a coordinated effort to stem migration at the source. In both Europe (especially Germany) and the United States, there have also been a growing number of tripartite agreements between government, employers, and trade unions that emphasize the central role of employers in immigration control. These agreements have coincided with the reemergence of guest-worker programs, a feature of the thirty-year period following World War II. At their core is a system of quotas. Reminiscent of the bracero program in place from 1942 to 1964, a recent amendment to the 1995 Illegal Immigration Reform and Immigrant Responsibility Act granted temporary work visas to approximately 250,000 foreign farm-workers. The plan is designed to delimit permanent stays by withhold-ing 25 percent of foreign workers' wages until their return to their homelands (*New York Times*, March 6, 1996, 14). The rationale behind such programs, mostly involving seasonal workers, is to increase immi-gration control. Interestingly, most members of the House Agriculture Committee who supported the farmworker amendment had been the most vociferous in the fight for tighter restrictions on illegal immigra-tion (*New York Times*, March 6, 1996, 14). The company hiring the workers profits through lower wage rates and freedom from heavy fines imposed for hiring illegal migrants; and the United States reduces illegal immigration, the costs of border control, and resource-draining legal procedures for eventual deportation. In addition, the state can also bene-fit from taxes and social welfare contributions of the temporary or sea-sonal workers.

The devolution of immigrant control or issues of immigrant stays to private actors has emerged in many forms, both officially and un-officially. In the United States, the Immigration and Naturalization Service has increasingly focused on immigration enforcement, and its processing functions have increasingly been delegated to churches and trade unions who operate as go-betweens in legal services, educational programs, and information campaigns between immigrants and state bodies. Furthermore, the absence of INS offices or legal services in cer-tain areas of this vast country has contributed to the expansive role of municipal officers, jails, security services, and detention centers in regu-lating migrants (for enforcement functions) on behalf of federal inspec-tors (Conference on Immigration and the Changing Face of Rural Amer-ica, July 13, 1996).

Private actors have also been enlisted in deportation efforts in the United States.[10] A recent uprising at a detention center for illegal immi-grants exposed a trend in supervisory functions: the contracting out of detention centers and guards to private for-profit security services, com-panies, and space (*New York Times*, July 7, 1996, A1). In 1996, four of the thirteen national centers holding illegal immigrants or asylum seekers were run by private contractors. Moreover, the INS is said to rent thousands of beds in hundreds of state and local jails, with very little inspection. There has been speculation that the detention of immi-grants has become a lucrative business.[11]

States have also shifted the onus of regulation to private individuals and civil actors in other ways. Recent U.S. legislation imposes increased penalties for document fraud on illegal migrants, including civil fines and the barring of future entry (a serious penalty for someone with close or nuclear family members living in the United States). In France, a proposed government bill to prevent illegal immigration reflected, its critics argued, state efforts to "transform all citizens into police informers" (*New York Times,* February 20, 1997). The bill proposed that French hosts who had foreign guests on special visas had to inform the town hall when their guests left, allowing the French government to compile computer records on foreigners' movements. Although in response to heavy protests the bill was amended, the version that passed did extend the burden of regulation to foreigners, who are now required to submit their certificate of accommodation upon leaving the country. In the United States, the Illegal Immigration Reform and Immigration Responsibility Act of 1996 further shifted liabilities away from courts and toward individual migrants. By eliminating the federal courts' authority to review INS decisions in deportation and legalization cases, the act essentially strips noncitizens of the right to file complaints against the INS in court; it also reduces the courts' role in what had been the last line of defense against abuse of official power. The 1996 act practically places the INS beyond judicial scrutiny.

In privatizing regulations for immigrant stays, the family has an increasingly important role. In the United States, more restrictive sponsorship rules and enforceable practices place a burden on families. Until recently, individuals were required to assure that immigrants they sponsored would not become "public charges." Because these pledges had become unenforceable in court, several bills in the last few years have aimed to make this support binding. The sponsor's affidavit of support is now a legally enforceable document (for up to ten years or until the immigrant becomes a citizen). For the first time, the notion of "becoming a public charge" has been carefully defined, with the intention of making it a realistic ground for deportation. Moreover, the minimum income a person must have to sponsor relatives for admission has been increased.

In sum, the role and liabilities of nonstate actors in sharing the burden of regulation has been converging in the countries of Europe as well as in the United States and are manifest in the use of more stringent deterrent methods such as sanctions (see table 9.1). On one hand, these shifts in liabilities represent an incorporation of private actors in state regulatory functions; on the other, they constitute a general trend occurring in other policy areas, namely, a shift in the costs and liabilities of policy making outside of the central government. Privatization, loosely defined as the shift of a function from the public to the private sector, involves a dependence on market forces for the pursuit of social goods and may turn local actors or contractors into regulators (Feigenbaum and Henig 1994). Both the incorporation of private actors through sanctions and the privatization of migration regulation through the contracting out of implementation functions involve the extension of state control over migration outside and beyond its traditional boundaries.

Local Actors

States are increasingly relying on local actors, or decentralized bodies, for monitoring and implementation functions. Through decentralization, national governments have delegated substantial decision-making powers to local elected officials, often in a way considered to be exclusionary and detrimental to foreigners' rights. A major reason behind this kind of decentralization is that national elected officials concur and depend on local elected officials, who are under financial and political pressure to attract more funds and votes by adopting exceptionally harsh measures against immigrants.

What sort of decision-making powers have national governments delegated to local elected officials? In France, city halls now have the prerogative to inspect the veracity of marriages between nationals and foreigners. A 1993 law granted mayors the authority to refer a marriage involving an alien to the Procureur de la République (state prosecutor), who can delay the marriage for a month and then, if they see fit, prevent it. A 1996 survey revealed significant geographical diversity in the law's implementation; in some cases, it was used as a measure to arrest illegal aliens (Weil 1997).[12] Since 1982, when the Deferre laws on decentralization were passed in France, mayors have gained political powers. Mayors in urban areas and in the Southeast, where the National Front has made electoral headway, have used their new monitoring role in migration control policy to the fullest (Guiraudon and Lahav 2000, 21).

National governments have shifted other monitoring functions of immigrant stays and rights downward to local actors. Since 1993 legislation in France, foreigners living in the country illegally no longer qualify for social security (including child allowances, health insurance, old age pensions, and unemployment benefits) (UN 1997, 368), and local governments are bearing the direct costs. In the United States, Proposition 187 and the Gallegly Amendment, measures to bar the undocumented and their children from public schools and welfare programs, focused on the liabilities of local actors for implementation. These demands for more local power concur with national plans for restrictions of foreigners' rights. The 1996 Welfare Act marked the end of the sixty-one-year-old federal guarantee of cash assistance for the nation's poorest children; it revoked federal benefits like food stamps and Supplementary Security Income for noncitizen immigrants (*New York Times*, February 21, 1997, 18). This new law also gives states vast new authority to run their own welfare programs with lump sums of federal money. It thus represents renewed efforts to grant states (local actors) more control over traditionally unfunded mandates, creating a mechanism for uneven integration policies across states and regions.

Of course, as Gerald Neuman (1996) observes, in the United States, state and local governments have long regulated the movement of people across legal borders, through the use of criminal laws, vagrancy laws, quarantine laws, and registration requirements and, before 1865, through the law of slavery. In contrast to unitary states that have been decentralizing, such as France, the relation between state and federal governments in federal systems, such as the United States, has been laid out more clearly for a long time. Until the middle to late nineteenth century, states still carried a number of prerogatives in the area of migration, including the rights granted to aliens (Schuck 1998) and the bestowing of nationality (Neuman 1998). Part of the explanation stems from the fact that states with slave populations wanted control over nationality, and hence, it was not surprising that courts rescinded these state rights after the Civil War. Increasingly during the twentieth century, Supreme Court decisions emphasized the exclusive federal prerogatives in the area of immigration regulation, via the plenary power doctrine, and the dangers of state encroachment. Thus, although some argue that the devolution of immigration policy to states is a growing reality, and a legitimate one, given the handful of states that are major fiscal and political stakeholders of immigration (Spiro 1994), from a historical perspective, contemporary political demands for a state role in immigration policy is a call to turn back the clock.

In general, the delegation of immigrant policy to state and local governments is not new. However, by reinforcing the local authorities' responsibilities and autonomy in immigrant policy, federal governments have been able to effectively enlarge immigration control through burden-sharing exchanges. Still, as the legal scholar Peter Schuck (1998) has argued, it is ultimately up to the U.S. Congress to authorize states to play a role in immigration policy, as the latter did in 1996 with respect to welfare benefits. These trends have led to renewed conflicts between federal, state, and local mandates (see Neuman 1993; Olivas 1994). Thus, the 1996 Illegal Immigration Reform and Immigrant Responsibility Act, which permits the INS to train and deputize local police officers to enforce immigration laws, is likely to receive uneven political reception. The conflicts are likely to heighten contradictory goals of different arms of the state (the police, judiciary, public administration) and also to obscure the lines between national (and, in the EU case, supranational) and local mandates. The general implications of decentralization and incorporation of local actors for immigration flows are diverse local outcomes and uneven integration strategies, which often give the semblance of policy incoherence.

International, Third-State, and Transnational Actors

International and transnational actors have become important agents in the state's coordination of migration regulation. The collaboration between these actors and private and local ones has reinforced state interest in migration regulation. In policing and border control, for example, competition between different types of police at the national level makes participation in international forums an important source of domestic recognition and may be a means of expanding national jurisdiction.

In France, where the trend toward complete free movement of persons is critical for European integration, abolition of checks at internal borders have been offset by the proliferation of intergovernmental and supranational actors (the EU "third pillar," the Ad Hoc Immigration Group, TREVI, EUROPOL, the coordinating Rhodes Group, and the Schengen Group) who promote an effective migration control regime. Typically, they make decisions behind closed doors, with little or no formal debate in a public forum. Many intergovernmental cooperation groups do not have to answer to a representative body or international courts. The result is that it is difficult for certain national actors to oversee what international and regional organizations do, and they can be used to circumvent even the most liberal national constraints on migration control (Bunyan and Webber 1995; Guiraudon 1997). The proliferation and diversification of instruments used to restrict immigration in Europe fortify the state apparatus in immigration control, leading some even to speak about evolving images of police states (Pastore 1991; Bunyan 1991; Van Outrive 1990).

The strength of external controls is reinforced by international agreements and cooperation and the creation of transnational spaces. European integration, for example, has produced a "securitization" of internal and external controls through collaborative policy agency work and the extension of police and gendarmerie activities (Bigo 1998; Miller 1995). To a lesser degree, but in the same vein, the joint United States–Mexico border patrol task forces have attempted to coordinate strategies to deal effectively with illegal migration since the inauguration of

NAFTA (North American Free Trade Agreement). There has been a major shift in operational strategies from illegal apprehensions after crossing (Operation Hold the Line in El Paso, 1993, and Operation Gatekeeper in San Diego, 1994) to deterrence before entry. These changes in control sites essentially represent a border shift outward.

Similar border extensions exist in France as a result of Schengenland, which makes each member country the beneficiary of the police screening efforts of the others. International agreements have also generated substantial visa harmonization between France and other EU countries and expanded the role of third-party states in fortifying external controls. The joint visa list of the EU states established through the Dublin Convention in 1993 imposed visa requirements on travelers from 73 of the 183 non-EU states. In September 1995, a list of 110 countries whose nationals require visas to enter the EU region was established at a meeting of the EU Justice and Home Affairs Council.[13] In addition, some countries, such as Germany, station immigration officers at overseas airports to ensure that documentation is correctly checked (*Economist*, August 24, 1996, 40). Such measures not only can be seen as a border shift outward (for example, Schengenland, or the United States–Mexico border); they also mean that governments may rely on "remote control" immigration policy or the creation of international zones, such as airports, where intervention by lawyers and human rights associations is almost impossible. Foreigners' civil rights are, in fact, less likely to be respected in these juridical "no-man's-land" or transnational spaces (Guiraudon and Lahav 2000).

International cooperation and the incorporation of third-party actors have also created transnational spaces in the employment sector, where they can circumvent national protection of foreign workers' rights. One critical trend in the employment domain comes in the form of bilateral contracts or work agreements between EU or Eastern European firms, which are authorized to move their foreign workers in order to complete a project. Although the workers are physically present in France, for example, they cannot claim pension or social insurance benefits or be protected by labor law there (Faist 1994). In these ways, states have been able to delegate functions out to other states and third-party actors and thus shift levels of policy elaboration upward toward international and transnational political playing fields.

The potency of international actors and rules in sanctioning states to adopt all types of restrictive migration policies has been greatly underestimated by theorists of embedded liberalism. Coordination rather than competition, or, in political science terms, neocorporatist rather than pluralist, models of interest aggregation now dominate migration control in an interdependent world. The growing coincidence of state devolution has made the prospects of transnational cooperation and the establishment of an international migration regime more likely. It revises the image offered by globalists, international political economy theorists, constructivists, and sociologists who have overlooked the growing compatibility of international and national norms, especially the role of international agreements in bolstering national interests. Indeed, when the interests of several nations coalesce, favorable conditions may lead to migration coordination in order to upgrade common interests (Keohane and Hoffman 1990). European regional integration represents a supranational order consisting of strong states committed to pooling sovereignty based on restrictive migration policies and more effective control. Unlike international regimes for the movement of capital, goods, and services, which have sought to promote free trade, international cooperation on migration matters may serve to inhibit immigration rather than promote it. Indeed, thus far, cooperation predominantly exists in the prevention of migration (Ranier Munz, "The Migrants," *The Earth Times*, February 15, 1996, 14, Geneva). Although the shift in regulatory functions toward international or foreign state actors is in its infancy, it is becoming increasingly institutionalized (see Baldwin-Edwards 1997; Lahav 1998). In sum, the proliferation of transnational and international actors, agreements, and cooperation may be interpreted as national efforts to more effectively control migration.

Conclusion: Regulatory Norms and Outcomes

This chapter has argued that liberal states are oriented, not only in rhetoric but also in capacities, toward more restrictive immigration policy and that these states are shifting liabilities for migration control to nonstate actors. Implementation and enforcement functions have been delegated upward, to intergovernmental forums and cooperation (for example, the Schengen Group and the joint United States–Mexico border forces); downward, to local authorities (through decentralization); and outward, to nonstate actors (in particular, private companies, such as airline carriers, transport companies, security services, travel companies, employers, and churches). Does this represent a new era of weak states in a global economy, or does it reflect an extension of state control whereby the state is changing the gatekeepers and reinventing forms of state control?

In the search to build theoretical models that explain the role of the state in migration control, scholars need to consider the actors and modes of policy elaboration and implementation. In contrast to pluralist theories that yield liberal migration norms and outcomes (see Hollifield

1992; Freeman 1995), neocorporatist models focus on reconciliation by the state and its interlocutors. An analysis of institutions and process-tracking norms allows us to see a complex playing field that includes a plethora of nonstate actors who may act on behalf of the state. A neo-corporatist model considers that as the state expands, links between of-ficial bodies and social groupings of all kinds also proliferate. These models capture this type of increased "webbing" between various ele-ments of society more than liberal-pluralist ones, which reduce the rela-tionships to ones of power. The expansion of the state is not the enlarge-ment of a single entity but the increasing density of relationships that center on the official apparatus of the state.

The image of central governments as merely making and then im-plementing policy is much too simple. The regulatory relationships and interest exchanges between third-party actors and the state have become a significant part of national strategies. Fundamental to increased state commitment to control immigration is a tendency to pursue burden-sharing norms that rely on international and transnational private and local actors and spaces. This is developing not only in France and other EU countries, which have a rich history of neocorporatist arrangements, but also in the United States, which has now openly called for "burden sharing" in its latest Report of the Commission on Immigration Reform (U.S. Commission of Immigration Reform 1994). Immigration policy in the United States (also constrained by NAFTA considerations) is in-creasingly pursuing interagency coordination not only within and among its own national institutions but also with civil rights groups (concerned with racial profiling, human rights violations, and harass-ment of natives), outreach programs, and international police forces, of which the coordination of United States–Mexico border patrols has been most notably (albeit limitedly) successful.

Although these strategies are a revival of old approaches to immi-gration regulation, their adoption in the 1990s reflects something new: a formalization and institutionalization relying on third-party actors, such as industries, services, companies, local governments, and particularly other states. By bringing in private actors, for example, the state itself may be said to diffuse the costs of immigration and deflect a hostile anti-immigrant public opinion. The state may thus contain the political fallout of migration controls through a diffusing strategy that relies on a variety of third-party actors.

Actors at different levels have different incentives and constraints in participating in such neocorporatist arrangements with the state. For local authorities such as elected officials, the extension of their domain of jurisdiction coincides with a scapegoating of foreigners when bud-getary crises emerge. Economic incentives may be involved. With little investment in training, private security agencies and private carriers (for example, airline and shipping companies) reap rewards by participating in an enlarged migration control system as agents of the state. These private actors either find business opportunities or face economic constraints, such as the avoidance of fines, in this devolution. At the international level, civil servants and third-party state actors may enhance the degrees of freedom of national policy makers while gaining legitimacy and participation through expanded jurisdiction. For individual migrants, the cost may be high, at the price of liberal migration regimes. There have been many cases of stowaways thrown overboard ships to avert heavy carrier fines, reversals of due process of law, human right violations, and corruption and abuse. The risk to the state in these devolution processes is in the appearance of expropriated control or the retreat of the state, a risk that lends support to nationalist movements of the extreme right.

The incorporation of nonstate actors in migration regulation is consistent with a trend toward more selective and restrictive immigration policies. It is also consistent with trends in other policy areas, of shifting the externalities of policy making outside of the central government. The shifts in implementation to private, local, or cooperative arrangements reflect less an abdication of state sovereignty than an experiment in which national states make rational attempts to diminish the costs of migration. The impetus to immigration reform and stricter control, it should be remembered, have come from states themselves; private and local actors face ever more restrictions, either from central governments or from international agreements. In the face of global and international pressures in the post–Cold War system, state responses may serve to neutralize the contradictions between open borders for goods, capital, and services and limited borders for the movement of people.

It is important to emphasize that these developments are not changes in state functions but shifts in modes of regulation. The processes of devolution aim to enhance the political capacity of states to regulate migration, to make states more flexible and adaptable to all types of migration pressures, to shift the focus of responsiveness, and to generate more effective state legitimacy. In practice, liberal democracies can deploy a considerable battery of policy instruments to control migration. Effectiveness must be measured not only against demographic or migration outcomes but by the means used to contain and defuse political debates and to increase state efficacy and legitimacy. Critical distinctions between policy output and policy outcomes—between stated and hidden goals and consequences of migration control—must be considered. More research on motivations, attitudes, and training of nonstate gatekeepers as they relate to broader policy or political goals is clearly required to better understand the dynamic processes of regulation I have described.

Notes

1. See Thelen and Steinmo (1992) for a succinct overview of the neo-institutional literature in political science.

2. The notion of the "political" in migration analysis has not advanced much since the early 1980s, when the role of the state in migration was elaborated by Aristide Zolberg (1981). Reference here to the expression "bringing back the state" follows Max Weber's (1958) definition of the state as the legitimate owner of the means and apparatus of violence and force. It also reflects the work of Peter Evans, Dietrich Rueschemeyer, and Theda Skocpol (1985).

3. Following Stephen Krasner (1983), the term "international regime" includes principles, norms, rules, and decision-making procedures around which actor expectations converge on a given issue.

4. The United Nations Convention for the Rights of All Migrants, for example, has been commonly cited as testament to universal rights imposed on states by international human rights law. Nonetheless, considering how few states have signed or ratified the convention, its constraints become elusive. In order to make conventions or covenants relevant, states must go beyond signatory status to ratification, meaning the incorporation of legislation into national law. The approach of the United States to the Geneva Convention, one of the most widely revered international human rights instruments, underscores how ambiguous this process may be; the United States ratified the 1951 Convention and its 1967 Protocol in 1980 with the adoption of the Refugee Act, and only in the late 1980s did it actually devise regulations for implementation.

5. In addition, in 1993, the Crime Control Act appropriated funding (almost $50 million) to implement many proposed asylum reforms, the most notable of which was the doubling of the number of INS asylum officers (OECD 1995).

6. Note again that in these comparisons, differences may also arise because of structural differences that are specific to political systems: for example, the United States is a federal system, whereas France is a decentralized unitary state.

7. The United States, for example, calls its consulates in a place like the Dominican Republic, the largest source of immigration to New York City, "the front line in the struggle against illegal immigration." In the twelve-month period ending September 30, 1996, the

consulate in Santo Domingo processed 52,410 requests for immigrant visas (more than 40 percent of which were rejected) and 110,000 applications for nonimmigrant visas (*New York Times,* February 19, 1997).

8. In the United States, the tradition of regulation by independent bodies means combined legislative, judicial, and executive functions (rule making, adjudication, and enforcement, in the terminology of American administrative law). Such bodies allow public utilities and other industries deemed to affect the public interest to remain in private hands but subject to rules developed and enforced by specialized agencies or commissions (see Majone 1996, 15).

9. France decreed employer sanctions again in 1976; the United Kingdom adopted legislation prohibiting the harboring of illegal aliens, though not their employment (out of fear of fueling discrimination) in 1971; Switzerland has had antiharboring statutes since 1931 and adopted an employment statute in 1984; West Germany first prohibited the employment of clandestine aliens in 1975; the Netherlands did so in 1974, as did Austria in 1981, and Italy, Spain and Belgium have since followed suit (see Miller 1995).

10. In the United States, the number of illegal aliens deported in 1995 reached a record level of 51,600, up 15 percent from 1995 and up nearly 75 percent from 1990 (*New York Times,* December 28, 1995).

11. In Pennsylvania, a five-hundred-bed addition to York County local prison has been planned for the explicit rental to the immigration service. One county commissioner reported that the county would receive a reimbursement of fifty dollars a day per bed for what would cost only twenty-four dollars (*New York Times,* July 7, 1997).

12. The survey revealed that 41.6 percent of the marriages suspended by mayors involved an undocumented alien (Weil 1997).

13. In November, an additional requirement for airport transit visas was adopted for nationals of ten countries from which many asylum claims originated: Afghanistan, Ethiopia, Eritrea, Ghana, Iraq, Iran, Nigeria, Somalia, Sri Lanka, and Zaire.

References

Baldwin-Edwards, Martin. 1997. "The Emerging European Immigration Regime: Some Reflections on Implications for Southern Europe." *Journal of Common Market Studies* 35(4): 497–519.

Bigo, Didier. 1996. *Policies en Réseaux: Experiénce Européene.* (Police Networks: The European Experience.) Paris: Presses de la Fondation de Sciences Politiques.

———. 1998. "'Bond of Union.' Military Involvement in Internal Security." Paper presented at the annual meeting of the International Studies Association, Minneapolis, Minn.(1998).

Bunyan, Tony. 1991. "Towards an Authoritarian European State." *Race and Class* 32(3): 179–88.

Bunyan, Tony, and Frances Webber. 1995. *Intergovernmental Cooperation on Immigration and Asylum.* Brussels: Churches Commission for Migrants in Europe.

Chekel, Jeff. 1995. "International Norms and Domestic Institutions: Identity Politics in Post–Cold War Europe." Paper presented at the annual meeting of the American Political Science Association, Chicago (September 3, 1995).

Conference on Immigration and the Changing Face of America, Ames, Iowa (July 13–15, 1996).

Cornelius, Wayne, Philip Martin, and James Hollifield, eds. 1994. *Controlling Immigration.* Stanford, Calif.: Stanford University Press.

Cruz, Antonio. 1994. "Carrier Liability in the Member States of the European Union." Briefing Paper 17. Brussels: Churches Commission for Migrants in Europe.

Evans, Peter, Dietrich Rueschemeyer, and Theda Skocpol, eds. 1985. *Bringing the State Back In.* Cambridge, U.K.: Cambridge University Press.

Fainsod, Merle. 1940. "Some Reflections on the Nature of the Regulatory Process." In *Public Policy,* edited by Friedrich Mason. Cambridge, Mass.: Harvard University Press.

Faist, Thomas. 1994. "A Medieval City: Transnationalizing Labor Markets and Social Rights in Europe." ZeS-Arbeitpaper 9 (working paper 9.) Bremen, Germany: Universitat Bremen Zentrum fur Sozialpolitik.

Feigenbaum, Harvey, and Jeffrey Henig. 1994. "The Political Underpinnings of Privatization: A Typology." *World Politics* 46(2): 185–208.

Freeman, Gary. 1994. "Can Liberal States Control Unwanted Migration?" *Annals of the American Academy* 534(July): 17–30.

———. 1995. "Modes of Immigration Politics in Liberal Democratic States." *International Migration Review* 29(4): 881–902.

Guiraudon, Virginie. 1997. "Avoiding the Spotlight: Explaining the Evolution of Rights of Foreigners in Germany, France, and the Netherlands, 1974–1994." Ph.D. diss., Harvard University.

Guiraudon, Virginie, and Gallya Lahav. 2000. "A Reappraisal of the State Sovereignty Debate: The Case of Migration Control." *Comparative Political Studies* 33(2): 163–95.

Hammar, Thomas. 1985. *European Immigration Policy: A Comparative Study.* Cambridge, U.K.: Cambridge University Press.

Heisler, Martin. 1992. "Migration, International Relations, and the New Europe: Theoretical Perspectives from Institutional Political Sociology." *International Migration Review* 26(2): 596–622.

Hollifield, James F. 1992. *Immigrants, Markets, and States: The Politi-*

cal Economy of Postwar Europe. Cambridge, Mass.: Harvard University Press.

Joppke, Christian. 1997. "Asylum and State Sovereignty: A Comparison of the United States, Germany, and Britain." *Comparative Political Studies* 30(3): 259–98.

Keohane, Robert, and Stanley Hoffman. 1990. "Conclusions: Community Politics and Institutional Change." In *The Dynamics of European Integration,* edited by William Wallace. London: Pinter.

Krasner, Stephen. 1982. "Structural Causes and Regime Consequences: Regimes as Intervening Variables." *International Organization* 36 (Spring): 379–415.

———, ed. 1983. *International Regimes.* Ithaca: Cornell University Press.

Lahav, Gallya. 1993. "Immigration, Hypernationalism, and European Security." In *The Future of European Security,* edited by J. Philip Rogers. New York: St. Martin's Press.

———. 1997a. "The Evolution of Immigration Policy in Liberal Democracies Since 1965: Changing the Gatekeepers or 'Bringing Back the State'?" Paper presented at the German-American Academic Council (GAAC) Young Scholars' Institute on Immigration, Incorporation, and Citizenship in the Advanced Industrial Democracies, Berlin, Germany (July 14–25, 1997).

———. 1997b. "International Versus National Constraints in Family Reunification Migration Policy." *Global Governance* 3(3): 349–72.

———. 1998. "Immigration and the State: The Devolution and Privatisation of Immigration Control in the European Union." *Journal of Ethnic and Migration Studies* 24(4): 675–94.

Layton-Henry, Zig, ed. 1990. *The Political Rights of Migrant Workers in Western Europe.* London: Sage.

Majone, Giandomenico. 1996. "Regulation and Its Modes." In *Regulating Europe,* edited by G. Majone. London: Routledge.

Miller, Mark. 1995. "Employer Sanctions in France: From the Campaign Against Illegal Alien Employment to the Campaign Against Illegal Work." Research paper. Washington: U.S. Commission on Immigration Reform.

Money, Jeannette. 1999. "Human Rights Norms and Immigration Control." *Journal of International Law and Foreign Affairs* 3(2): 497–525.

Neuman, Gerald. 1993. "The Lost Century of American Immigration Law (1776–1875)," *Columbia Law Review* (93): 1833.

———. 1996. *Strangers to the Constitution: Immigrants, Borders, and Fundamental Law.* Princeton: Princeton University Press.

———. 1998. "The Effects of Immigration on Nationality Law." Paper presented to the European Forum seminar, European University Institute, Florence, Italy (June 4–6, 1998).

Olivas, Michael. 1994. "Preempting Preemption: Foreign Affairs, State Rights, and Alienage Classifications." *Virginia Journal of International Law* (35): 217–36.

Organisation for Economic Co-operation and Development (OECD). SOPEMI. 1995. *Continuous Reporting System on Migration: Trends in International Migration.* Paris: OECD.

———. 1997. *Continuous Reporting System on Migration: Trends in International Migration.* Paris: OECD.

Papademetriou, Demetrious. 1993. "Confronting the Challenge of Transnational Migration: Domestic and International Responses." In *The Changing Course of International Migration.* Paris: OECD.

Papademetriou, Demetrious, and Mark Miller. 1983. *The Unavoidable Issue: U.S. Immigration Policy in the 1980s.* Philadelphia: Institute for the Study of Human Issues.

Pastore, Massimo. 1991. "A Historical Critical Overview of European Intergovernmental Cooperation on Matters of Immigration, Asylum, and Internal Security." Paper presented to the Nineteenth Annual Conference of the European Group for the Study of Deviance and Social Control, Potsdam (September 4–8, 1991).

Rawls, John. 1971. *A Theory of Justice.* Cambridge: Cambridge University Press.

Ruggie, John. 1982. "International Regimes, Transactions, and Change: Embedded Liberalism in the Postwar Economic Order." *International Organizations* 36: 379–415.

Sassen, Saskia. 1991. *The Global City: New York, London, Tokyo.* Princeton, N.J.: Princeton University Press.

———. 1996. *Losing Control?* New York: Columbia University Press.

Schain, Martin. 1995. "Policy Effectiveness and the Regulation of Immigration in Europe." Paper presented at the annual meeting of the International Studies Association, (February 25, 1995).

Schuck, Peter. 1989. "Membership in the Liberal Polity: the Devaluation of American Citizenship." *Georgetown Immigration Law Journal* 3(1).

———. 1998. "The Reevaluation of American Citizenship." In *Challenge to the Nation State: Immigration in Western Europe and the United States,* edited by Christian Joppke. New York: Oxford University Press.

Soysal, Yasemin Nuhoglu. 1994. *Limits of Citizenship.* Chicago: University of Chicago press.

Spiro, Peter. 1994. "The States and Immigration in an Era of Demi-Sovereignties." *Virginia Journal of International Law* (35): 121–78.

Thelen, Kathleen, and Sven Steinmo. 1992. "Historical Institutionalism in Comparative Politics." In *Structuring Politics: Historical Institutionalism in Comparative Analysis,* edited by Sven Steinmo, Kathleen Thelen, and Frank Longstreth. Cambridge, U.K.: Cambridge University Press:

Torpey, John. 1998. "Coming and Going: Passport Control." Paper presented at the annual meeting of the International Studies Association, Minneapolis, Minn. (March 21–24, 1998).

United Nations. 1997. *World Population Monitoring, 1997: Issues of In-*

ternational Migration and Development. New York: Population Division of the Department for Social Information and Policy Analysis of the United Nations.

———. 1998. "Family Reunification Migration: Policies and Issues." In *International Migration Policies and Programmes: A World Survey.* New York: United Nations.

United Nations Economic Commission for Europe (UNECE). 1997. *International Migration and Integration Policies in the UNECE Region.* Geneva: Population Activities Unit.

U.S. Commission on Immigration Reform. 1994. *U.S. Immigration Policy: Restoring Credibility. 1994 Report to Congress.* Washington: Commission on Immigration Reform (September).

U.S. Department of Justice. 1996. Washington: U.S. Government Printing Office.

U.S. Immigration and Naturalization Service. 1994. *Statistical Yearbook of the Immigration and Naturalization Service: 1993.* Washington: U.S. Government Printing Office.

———. 1996. *Statistical Yearbook of the Immigration and Naturalization Service: 1994.* Washington: U.S. Government Printing Office.

Van Outrive, Lode. 1990. "Migration and Penal Reform: One European Policy?" Unpublished paper xviii, presented at the annual conference of the European Group for the Study of Deviance and Social Control, Haarlem, The Netherlands (1990).

Waltz, Kenneth. 1979. *Theory of International Politics.* Reading, Mass.: Addison-Wesley.

Walzer, Michael. 1980. *Radical Principles.* New York: Basic Books.

Weber, Frank Paul. 1998. "Participation of Carriers in the Control of Migration: The Case of Germany." Paper presented to the International Studies Association, Minneapolis, Minn. (March 21–24, 1998).

Weber, Max. 1958. *From Max Weber: Essays in Sociology,* edited and translated by H. H. Gerth and C. Wright Mills. New York: Oxford University Press.

Weil, Patrick. 1997. *Mission d'étude de la législation de la nationalité et de l'immigration: Rapports au premier ministre.* Paris: La Documentation Française.

Weiner, Myron. 1985. "International migration and International relations." In *Population and Development Review* 11(September): 441–55.

———. 1990. *Security, Stability, and International Migration.* Cambridge, Mass.: MIT Center for International Studies.

Zolberg, Aristide. 1981. "International Migration in Political Perspective." In *Global Trends in Migration: Theory and Research in International Population Movements,* ed. Mary M. Kritz, Charle Keely, and S. M. Tomasi. Staten Island, N.Y.: Center for Migration Studies.

———. 1999. "Matters of State: Theorizing Immigration Policy." In *The Handbook of International Migration: The American Experience,* edited by Charles Hirschman, Philip Kasinitz, and Josh DeWind. New York: Russell Sage Foundation.

10

ONE BORDER, TWO CROSSINGS: MEXICAN MIGRATION TO THE UNITED STATES AS A TWO-WAY PROCESS

Steven S. Zahniser

A NEW wave of research has reinvigorated the study of Mexican migration to the United States. Unlike previous, cross-sectional analyses of the migration decision (Taylor 1984; Massey and García España 1987; Sprouse 1991; García España 1992), these new works explicitly treat Mexican migration as a two-way phenomenon in which participants move in either direction across the United States–Mexico border. Most Mexicans in the migration stream eventually return to their native land, either to migrate again or to remain permanently in Mexico.[1] With this in mind, researchers are seeking answers to subtle questions about the transitional nature of Mexican migration, such as what determines the length of a migration spell (Kossoudji 1992; Lindstrom 1996; and Zahniser 1999) and under what conditions migrants elect to return to Mexico (Massey and Espinosa 1997). In contrast with earlier studies, these works generally deemphasize the importance of the expected wage differential between Mexico and the United States. Instead, they feature a heightened awareness of the myriad factors that influence Mexican migration, including U.S. immigration policies and conditions in migrants' communities of origin.

As part of these efforts, researchers are closely examining the retrospective life histories of Mexican heads of household. Like many previous studies, some of these works rely upon discrete-choice models, a class of econometric models that includes the logit and probit models. For instance, Douglas Massey and Kristin Espinosa (1997) evaluate the determinants of first, repeat, and return migration by estimating separate multinomial logit models for each of these three phenomena. However, one can also study the two-way nature of Mexican migration using a single econometric model. Two papers lay the foundation for this type of analysis. In a pioneering effort, James Heckman (1981) crafts a general probit model that includes previous decisions made by the individual, interactions among previous decisions, and a general lag operator. Heckman's work spurred Kazuo Yamaguchi (1991, 1990) to develop a similarly constructed logit model for the analysis of interdependent transitions observed in discrete time.

Corinne Deléchat (1996) effectively utilizes Heckman's model to gauge the sequential effects of previous migration decisions on the current one. This chapter, in turn, uses Yamaguchi's model to study two related questions. First, to what extent does the current migration decision depend on that made in the preceding period? The U.S. policy of apprehending and deporting persons who illegally enter the country clearly imposes a substantial cost on Mexican migrants who are not legally entitled to work in the United States. Because unauthorized entrants presently in the United States have already incurred this cost, they may be reluctant to return soon to Mexico, especially if they intend to work in the United States in the future. Second, how do the determinants of migration affect the transition from Mexico to the United States differently from the transition from the United States back to Mexico? For example, U.S. immigration status and migration networks are widely believed to reduce the costs of Mexican migration to the United States. Using the reasoning outlined above, these factors may foster the early return to Mexico of persons who plan to migrate again in the future. In addition, this chapter addresses the impact of changing macroeconomic conditions in Mexico and the United States on the migration decision.

To these ends, I apply Yamaguchi's model to a data set that describes the migration decisions of 5,689 heads of household from central and western Mexico during the period from 1971 to 1987.[2] This model has two special features: a dummy variable that indicates the individual's migration decision during the preceding year and a set of interaction terms between this variable and certain explanatory variables. This second feature enables one to distinguish the influences of explanatory variables on the two transitions.

The Mexican Migration Project

The data for this chapter are drawn primarily from the Mexican Migration Project, an ongoing study of the migration experiences of households throughout central and western Mexico (Mexican Migration Project 1997). The project, which is headed by Douglas Massey of the University of Pennsylvania and Jorge Durand of the University of Guadalajara, has its origins in a 1982 study of four communities in the states of Jalisco and Michoacán (Massey et al. 1987). Since 1987, the project has visited one or more new communities on an almost annual basis. Although the communities are not selected randomly, an effort is made to examine communities of varied sizes and economic bases in each state of the region. Within each community, the project typically studies two hundred randomly sampled households. In addition, a smaller number of interviews are conducted in the United States with persons originally from the survey community (usually twenty from each community). So far, the project has surveyed more than eight thousand households from forty-three different communities. The data collected in the first five survey communities are coded somewhat differently from the rest of the data, and one community's observations did not contain migrants during the period from 1971 to 1987. Therefore, these six communities are omitted from the data set. Sample information is provided in table 10.1.

Among the information collected by the project is a retrospective life history of each head of household, detailing his or her labor and migration experiences.[3] These histories include annual observations of the individual's place of work. Because some people work in more than one place during the course of a year, priority is given first to locations in the United States, second to locations in Mexico but outside the survey community, and third to the survey community itself. Using these histories, I construct the largest balanced data set possible for the period from 1971 to 1987. Thus, there are exactly seventeen annual observations for each individual in the data set.

The period from 1971 to 1987 is selected for two reasons. First, the Mexican Migration Project has assembled an assortment of variables describing the survey communities from 1970 to the present.[4] My econometric model includes some lagged variables, so the first year in the data set is 1971. Second, the series ends in 1987, the earliest survey year for the included communities. The resulting data set describes 5,689 individuals, all of whom were born no later than 1956. The youngest persons in the sample were thus age fifteen in 1971, which corresponds roughly to the age at which many Mexicans begin to make economic decisions for themselves.[5] Sample statistics are listed in table 10.2.

Economic Indicators

Econometric studies of Mexican migration to the United States often incorporate measures of changing economic conditions in the two countries. The most notable of these measures is the binational income differential. To some extent, this emphasis derives from the influential work of Michael Todaro (1969), whose theoretical model of rural-to-

TABLE 10.1   *Sample Information*

State and Political Category	Survey Year	1990 Population	Number of Respondents Mexico	United States	Total
Colima					
Municipal seat	1994	7,000	144	5	149
Guanajuato					
Municipal seat	1987	52,000	181	12	193
Municipal seat	1987	868,000	172	0	172
Municipal seat	1988	17,000	180	15	195
Tenencia	1988	2,000	134	5	139
Municipal seat	1990	21,000	154	14	168
Municipal seat	1991	363,000	159	9	168
Tenencia	1991	1,000	82	4	86
Municipal seat	1992	34,000	167	12	179
Municipal seat	1992	24,000	148	7	155
Guerrero					
Municipal seat	1993	101,000	64	0	64
Municipal seat	1995	7,000	116	0	116
Tenencia	1995	35,000[a]	80	0	80
Jalisco					
Municipal seat	1988	4,000	178	11	189
Municipal seat	1988	5,000	166	12	178
Tenencia	1988	3,000	173	5	178
Municipal seat	1991	31,000	152	15	167
Tenencia	1992	1,000	68	2	70
Municipal seat	1992	74,000	158	16	174
Michoacán					
Tenencia	1989	6,000	160	8	168
Municipal seat	1989	32,000	156	15	171
Tenencia	1989	2,000	126	13	139
Municipal seat	1990	7,000	160	7	167
State capital	1991	493,000	155	11	166
Municipal seat	1992	217,000	129	2	131
Nayarit					
Municipal seat	1990	20,000	156	16	172
Tenencia	1990	12,000	150	7	157
San Luís Potosí					
State capital	1993	526,000	170	0	170
Municipal seat	1994	42,000	147	0	147
Municipal seat	1995	13,000	143	0	143
Tenencia	1995	1,000	93	0	93
Tenencia	1995	1,000	80	0	80
Zacatecas					
Municipal seat	1991	8,000	288	19	307
Tenencia	1991	1,000	151	0	151
State capital	1994	109,000	170	4	174
Tenencia	1995	2,000	93	0	93

(Table continues on p. 246.)

TABLE 10.1   Continued

State and Political Category	Survey Year	1990 Population	Number of Respondents		
			Mexico	United States	Total
Municipal seat	1995	34,000	152	0	152
Tenencia	1995	1,000	88	0	88

Source: Mexican Migration Project 1998; for the population of the community in Colima, Zahniser 1999; and for the population of several communities surveyed in 1995, INEGI 1993.
Note: Population figures are rounded to the nearest nonzero thousand. A "tenencia" is a community that is not the seat of municipal government.
ªFigure reflects the population of the entire municipality (similar to a U.S. county) and not just the population of the town.

urban migration focuses on the expected difference between rural and urban real incomes. Various measures of this differential have been utilized. Real gross domestic product (GDP) per capita in Mexico and the United States (see Zahniser 1999), the ratio of the hourly wage in the U.S. nonagricultural sector to hourly earnings in the Mexican manufacturing sector (see White, Bean, and Espenshade 1990), and farm wages in the two countries (see Jenkins 1977; Frisbie 1975) are but a few examples. However, these variables may not closely reflect the wage expectations of prospective migrants, because they do not account for the specific occupational distributions of Mexican migrants in the United States and prospective migrants in Mexico.

Massey and Espinosa (1997) avoid this problem by utilizing data from the Mexican Migration Project to estimate an expected wage ratio for each observation in their study. However, one may also search for external measures that better reflect wage expectations. This chapter employs an original, alternative measure of the expected income differential that accounts for the occupational distribution of Mexican migrants.[6] In place of U.S. income, I estimate the average annual salary of a Mexican-born person in the U.S. state of California. The U.S. Department of Commerce's County Business Patterns (1971 to 1987) contains annual observations by economic sector of the number of employees and total payroll for the state. From this information, the average salary per employee in each sector can be calculated. Data for California are used because the state is the principal U.S. destination for approximately three-quarters of the data set's observations of individuals who spend some part of the year in the United States. The average salaries are then weighted by the number of Mexican-born individuals employed in each economic sector and averaged to form a single indicator of the expected salary in California for a person of Mexican birth. The sectoral distributions of Mexican-born persons in California are drawn from the 1970, 1980, and 1990 U.S. Censuses.

The Instituto Nacional de Estadística, Geografía, e Informática (IN-EGI), Mexico's centralized statistical agency, publishes similar wage and employment data for Mexico in its *Censos Económicos* (INEGI 1995). However, this information is not available for the period covered by my data set. Instead, I employ an estimate of annual consumption per worker in Mexico. This variable equals the household consumption component of Mexican GDP divided by the estimated number of economically active Mexicans aged twelve years or older. The sources used to calculate this variable are the International Monetary Fund's *International Financial Statistics Yearbook* (IMF 1993, 1998), the United Nations' *World Population Prospects* (UN 1993), and from INEGI, the *Anuario Estadístico de los Estados Unidos Mexicanos 1987* and the Banco de Información Económica (BDINEGI) web site (INEGI 1988, 1998).[7]

The econometric models in this chapter contain different combinations of macroeconomic indicators. The first combination consists of the alternative binational income ratio described above and the average consumption per worker in Mexico (in 1994 new pesos). Consumption per worker is included along with the ratio because some respondents in the Mexican Migration Project expressed the opinion that migration to the United States is primarily driven by unemployment and underemployment in Mexico and not by the binational wage gap (Zahniser 1999). If this hypothesis is correct, then individuals with adequate employment in Mexico are not likely to migrate, even if much higher-paying work is available in the United States. A second combination includes Mexico's real GDP per capita (also in 1994 new pesos) and the binational ratio of GDP per capita. The third and fourth combinations are identical to the first and second combinations, respectively, except that they include additional macroeconomic variables used in Massey and Espinosa (1997): the annual depreciation of the peso-to-dollar exchange rate, the Mexican inflation rate, and the real interest rate in Mexico.

Econometric and Theoretical Models

The logit model for analyzing interdependent, discrete-time transitions differs very little from a standard logit model.[8] Several innovations make the two-way analysis possible: the selection of one and minus one as the values of the dependent variable; the inclusion of a lagged dependent variable as an explanatory variable; and the inclusion of interaction terms between selected explanatory variables and the lagged dependent

TABLE 10.2   *Sample Means and Standard Deviations for Selected Variables*

Variable	All Observations		Migrant in Year t $[Y_t{}^* = 1]$	
	Mean	SD	Mean	SD
Migration decision				
Current year				
$[Y_t{}^*]$	−0.7551	0.6557	1	0
Previous year				
$[Y_{t-1}{}^*]$	−0.7594	0.6506	0.6296	0.7770
Individual characteristics				
Female	0.1547	0.3616	0.0471	0.2118
Age (in years)	41.0379	14.2077	37.1202	11.6916
Education (in years)	4.1155	4.1035	4.2792	3.4067
College educated	0.0548	0.2275	0.0222	0.1475
U.S. interview	0.0441	0.2054	0.2752	0.4466
Migration experience				
(in months)	20.5200	54.1670	105.6522	94.9361
Family responsibilities				
Married	0.7863	0.4099	0.8116	0.3910
Number of minor-age				
children	2.8883	2.6630	2.9623	2.5519
Single parent	0.0557	0.2293	0.0350	0.1838
Single mother	0.0368	0.1882	0.0116	0.1072
Migration networks and				
immigration status				
Networks and resi-				
dency	0.0474	0.2125	0.3122	0.4634
Residency but not				
networks	0.0122	0.1098	0.0659	0.2482
Networks but not				
residency	0.3740	0.4839	0.4442	0.4969
U.S. citizen	0.0025	0.0495	0.0190	0.1364
Additional income				
sources				
Number of adult				
offspring	1.5166	2.5595	1.1005	2.2530
Agricultural land				
(in hectares)	3.4776	51.5100	3.5263	22.9014
Business ownership	0.1686	0.3744	0.1333	0.3399

Source: Author's calculations.

Nonmigrant in Year t [$Y_t^* = -1$]		1971		1987	
Mean	SD	Mean	SD	Mean	SD
-1	0	-0.8220	0.5695	-0.7545	0.6563
-0.9533	0.3022	-0.8285	0.5601	-0.7506	0.6608
0.1697	0.3754	0.1547	0.3616	0.1547	0.3616
41.5846	14.4400	33.0379	11.3375	49.0379	13.3375
4.0927	4.1910	4.0215	3.8835	4.1376	4.1612
0.0593	0.2362	0.0416	0.1998	0.0571	0.2320
0.0119	0.1084	0.0441	0.2054	0.0441	0.2054
8.6386	30.5471	11.0723	36.8115	30.5412	70.3374
0.7828	0.4123	0.6431	0.4791	0.8408	0.3659
2.8780	2.6780	2.4877	2.7862	2.7305	2.3834
0.0586	0.2348	0.0402	0.1964	0.0639	0.2446
0.0403	0.1966	0.0233	0.1510	0.0459	0.2094
0.0104	0.1016	0.0305	0.1720	0.0766	0.2660
0.0047	0.0685	0.0077	0.0875	0.0210	0.1434
0.3642	0.4812	0.3205	0.4667	0.3980	0.4895
0.0002	0.0125	0.0016	0.0402	0.0036	0.0598
1.5747	2.5941	0.6783	1.6765	2.5964	3.1453
3.4708	54.3175	2.6520	31.2791	5.3594	122.9264
0.1735	0.3787	0.1066	0.3086	0.2446	0.4299

variable. Conveniently, these innovations do not affect the basic structure of the likelihood function, so the parameters may be estimated as if
the model were a standard logit model.

Let Y_t^* indicate an individual's migration decision for year t, where
Y_t^* equals one if the individual spends some part, if not all, of year t in
the United States and negative one if he or she does not. Some migrants
to the United States spend only a portion of the calendar year there.
Accordingly, the term "year of U.S. migration" refers in this instance to
a calendar year in which the individual spends at least part of the year in
the United States. Casual trips to the United States that do not involve
employment are not treated as episodes of migration; examples of casual
trips include a visit to family or friends, a business trip, and vacations
and sightseeing trips.

Let P_t measure the probability that Y_t^* equals one. Using the general
structure outlined by Yamaguchi, consider a logit model with the following log-odds ratio:[9]

$$\ln[P_t/(1 - P_t)] = b_0 + b_1 Y_{t-1}{}^* + b'_2 X_t$$
$$+ b'_3 Z_t + b'_4 Z_t Y_{t-1}{}^* + \varepsilon_t. \tag{10.1}$$

X_t consists of explanatory variables that are not hypothesized to interact
with the previous year's migration decision $(Y_{t-1}{}^*)$, and Z_t contains explanatory variables that are hypothesized to interact with $Y_{t-1}{}^*$. As
Yamaguchi illustrates, the interaction terms permit the estimation of
the separate effects of Z_t on the probability of migrating from Mexico to
the United States and the probability of returning from the United
States to Mexico. The difference, $b_3 - b_4$, measures the influence of Z_t
on the Mexico-to-United States transition, and $- (b_3 - b_4)$ gauges its
impact on the United States-to-Mexico move. In contrast, X_t has a symmetrical influence on the two transitions: b_2 on the Mexico-to-United
States transition and $-b_2$ on the United States-to-Mexico transition.

Despite its unusual configuration, the two-way logit model may
be linked to a conventional, dynamic model of the migration decision
under imperfect information. The only modification that is necessary
is to allow the possibility that the net benefit of spending year t in
the United States varies according to the country in which the individual spent the preceding year. The literature contains a number of models
suitable for this purpose, such as Deléchat (1996) and Olea (1988).
Because the focus of Deléchat's work is similar to that of this paper,
a modified version of her theoretical model is presented in appendix
10B.

Explanatory Variables

The explanatory variables may be divided into seven groups: (1) the previous year's migration decision $(Y_{t-1}{}^*)$, (2) individual characteristics, (3) family responsibilities, (4) additional income sources, (5) migration networks and immigration status, (6) fixed effects for time and national economic conditions, and (7) cross-sectional effects for the individuals' communities of origin.[10] The following section presents empirical results from several specifications of the model. Some specifications include fixed effects for time, and others include national economic conditions.

With a few exceptions, all the explanatory variables are included in Z_t so as to ascertain whether they differentially affect the two transitions. Age, total U.S. migration experience, and their squares may not be placed in Z_t because age and sometimes experience are one year greater than their one-period lags. Interacting these variables with $Y_{t-1}{}^*$ thus would result in perfect collinearity. The time and community dummies also are included in X_t, because their primary function is to serve as statistical corrections. Finally, the economic indicators are placed in X_t for want of a theoretical reason to include them in Z_t.

State Dependence

The indicator variable $Y_{t-1}{}^*$ measures the state dependence associated with the migration decision, and its parameter provides the most basic insight into how the previous period's migration decision influences the subsequent period's decision. Persons who wish to spend the coming year in a country different from their current location typically face a variety of migration costs. The most modest of migrants will incur minimal expenses for food and transportation; others may need to sell possessions or to make arrangements for property and family members left behind. If these costs discourage the average individual from moving from his or her current location, the parameter estimate for $Y_{t-1}{}^*$ should be positive, indicating positive state dependence.

Individual Characteristics

The individual characteristics describe the head of household's gender, age, educational level, and total U.S. migration experience (measured in months), as well as whether the interview was conducted in the United States or Mexico. Historically, Mexican women have been less likely than Mexican men to participate in international migration. Although this difference has narrowed in recent years, it should still be prevalent during the period under study. Indeed, Katherine Donato (1993) finds that this is true for the period from 1980 to 1989, using data from the Mexican Migration Project for ten survey communities. Gender differences in migration reflect a sexual division of labor that is still common in Mexico. Accordingly, social experiences that reproduce this pattern, such as gender-differentiated treatment in the educational system, are also likely to discourage female migration, although this particular division of labor is becoming less prominent in Mexican society.

Pierrette Hondagneu-Sotelo (1994) emphasizes that the social contacts that facilitate male migration are often less useful to Mexican women. In fact, she links increased female participation in Mexican migration to the development of separate support systems among female migrants. Gender differences may also exist in the value Mexicans place on leaving one's family for extended periods of time, making women less likely to migrate across the border and also more likely to return home once in the United States.

However, if the wage-earning ability of Mexican women is for some reason lower than that of Mexican men (for instance, if women experience a lower degree of human capital accumulation), being female may increase the probability of migrating. This may explain the migration of young Mexican women to areas of relatively high employment within Mexico and their increasing rate of U.S. migration. Moreover, the economic benefits of migration may be compounded by an improvement in the social status of female migrants. Hondagneu-Sotelo (1992, 1994) indicates that female migrants from Mexico tend to experience greater autonomy, exercise greater authority within the family, and perform less housework than they had in Mexico. Sherri Grasmuck and Patricia Pessar (1991) identify a similar phenomenon for female immigrants from the Dominican Republic. If this analysis is correct, then female migrants may stand to lose some of these gains by returning to Mexico.

Middle-aged Mexicans should be more likely to migrate than the very young and the very old (Sprouse 1991; Taylor 1984, 1987; García España 1992; Massey and García España 1987). Previous cross-sectional studies indicate that the probability of migration first climbs as a person initially gets older and then decreases as he or she becomes increasingly aged. Edward Taylor (1987) identifies the age of thirty-four as the point at which this probability begins to decline, and Taylor (1984) and Terry Wayne Sprouse (1991) the age of thirty-seven.[11] The parameter estimates for age and its square should therefore be positive and negative, respectively.

If the training and knowledge acquired in the Mexican educational system is not completely transferable to the United States, then the net return to migration and the probability of migration should decrease as educational level rises. College-educated Mexicans should be particularly less likely to migrate. Once in the United States, many highly educated migrants find themselves limited to low-wage manual labor jobs, of the same sorts less-educated migrants perform. With no additional incentive to remain in the United States, migrants with higher levels of education should be more likely to return to Mexico.

Researchers have long suspected that the accumulation of U.S. work experience coincides with positive changes in the migrant's human capital that increase the net return to migration (Chiswick 1978). The migrant is likely to receive on-the-job training, to become more familiar with the labor markets in specific U.S. locales, and to improve his or her English proficiency (Espinosa and Massey 1997). Accordingly, the probability of migration should rise with U.S. experience. In addition, if the marginal return to experience decreases as experience rises, then the parameter for the variable's square should be negative.

Whereas the respondents in Mexico were selected randomly, U.S. respondents were located using "snowball" sampling techniques. Both Mexican and U.S. respondents were asked at the end of the interview to volunteer the names and contact information of potential respondents in the United States. To account for any sample bias that may have resulted from this process, the econometric models include a dummy variable that identifies the country in which the interview was conducted. Respondents from the United States should be more likely to migrate from Mexico to the United States and less likely to return once in the United States.

Family Responsibilities

Family responsibilities generally influence the migration decision by altering the head of household's preferences for labor relative to leisure. Earlier studies have accounted for the number of dependents per adult member of the household (Massey and García España 1987), the proportion of dependents in the household (García España 1992), and household size (Sprouse 1991; Taylor 1984). However, variables measuring marital status and single parenthood have been largely absent from previous econometric models of the migration decision.

The migration decisions of married heads of household are likely to be influenced, at least in part, by their desire to spend time with their spouses. In addition, through his or her own labor power, a spouse increases the economic resources available to the household, making it less necessary for the head of household to migrate. For these two reasons, being married should reduce the probability of migration. Married migrants should also be more likely to return to Mexico for extended periods of time.

253

As the number of minor-age children increases, it is quite plausible that the head of household will seek to earn more income. One method of doing so is to work in the United States. On the other hand, minor-age children may deter migration if the household head forgoes migration opportunities in order to spend time with the children or if minors are put to work in the household. These competing rationales may cause the household head to be more likely to migrate from Mexico to the United States but also more likely to return home to Mexico after a period of migration.

The migratory behavior of single parents from Mexico has not been extensively studied. Two factors that are likely to influence this behavior are the country in which the individual's children reside and the availability of child care at both the origin and the intended destination of the prospective migrant. If adequate child care is not available at the children's current location, movements by single parents to the other side of the border seem unlikely unless the parent brings along the children. Unfortunately, the Mexican Migration Project collects limited information about the migration of children and no information about child care. Thus, the influence of single parenthood and single motherhood on the two transitions is uncertain.

Additional Income Sources

Additional income sources alleviate the need of the head of household to participate in international migration. Often, adult offspring are thought of as potential income sources for the household. Taylor (1984, 1987), for instance, routinely includes the number of adults in the household in his econometric models. Therefore, the probability of migration should decrease as the number of adult offspring rises. Individuals who operate businesses or own agricultural land in Mexico should also be less likely to migrate.

Presumably, migrants eventually want to return home to monitor the status of their household's economic activities. Thus, the probability of making the United States-to-Mexico transition should increase with business ownership and the amount of land owned. With respect to adult offspring, migrants may be motivated to return by the prospect of reuniting with their grown sons and daughters and their families.

Migration Networks
and Immigration Status

Three dummy variables indicate different combinations of immigration status and the presence or absence of migration networks:

1. "Networks and residency" denotes persons in year t who possess legal residency in the United States and have at least one member of the immediate family (a parent, sibling, or grandparent) with previous U.S. migration experience;

2. "Residency but not networks" denotes legal residents whose immediate family lacks such experience; and

3. "Networks but not residency" denotes nonresidents whose immediate relatives have U.S. experience.

The excluded group consists of persons who have neither legal residency nor immediate relatives with U.S. experience. For the purposes of this chapter, legal residents are defined as those persons who legally immigrated to the United States, including both noncitizens and naturalized citizens. Nonimmigrants who enter the United States on tourist visas are not considered to be legal residents.

Legal residents are able to cross the border relatively freely, thus incurring lower migration costs. They are legally entitled to participate in the U.S. labor market and thus are likely to secure a higher wage. In addition, the probability of being deported is much lower for the legal resident than for the undocumented migrant, although it is not zero. The U.S. government is empowered to deport legal resident aliens who are convicted of serious crimes and in recent years has done so. Finally, if businesses are reluctant to employ persons whom they suspect to be transient, the probability of finding work may be higher for the legal resident than for the undocumented migrant. For these reasons, legal residency should increase the probability of migrating to the United States.

What is the effect of legal residency on the United States-to-Mexico transition? Obviously, legal residents need not hire the services of a coyote[12] should they wish to return to Mexico and then reenter the United States, so legal residency may encourage returning to Mexico. While they are in Mexico, however, legal residents miss the prized opportunity of working in the formal U.S. labor market. Therefore, it is unclear whether legal residency increases or decreases the probability of returning to Mexico. In most instances, a person who has taken the additional step of obtaining U.S. citizenship has decided to settle in the United States. Thus, U.S. citizens should be more likely to make the Mexico-to-United States transition and less likely to make the reverse transition.

A migration network may be broadly defined as any socioeconomic link between the origin and destination of a prospective migrant that facilitates migration between the two points. As noted earlier, this chapter uses a network measure that indicates whether the head of household has a parent, sibling, or grandparent with U.S. migration experience in or before year t. Taylor (1984, 1987) and Sprouse (1991) measure networks with a dummy variable indicating the presence of close friends or family in the United States, and Douglas Massey and Juan Felipe García España (1987) and García España (1992) use the proportion of households in the community with U.S. migration experience. The previous literature points to networks as having a strongly positive and statistically significant influence on the probability of migrating to the United States.

Migration networks reduce the costs of migration and limit its associated risks. Audrey Singer and Massey (1998) underscore the importance of family and friends with U.S. experience who accompany first-time migrants to border-crossing staging areas. Expertise is transferred to the migrant, making him or her more astute in negotiating with coyotes and more aware of "the rules of the game" should the migrant be apprehended by the Immigration and Naturalization Service. Relatives who are living in the United States at the time that the individual migrates often provide an initial place to stay at little or no cost. Some networks yield valuable contacts in the search for work (Massey et al. 1987; Zahniser 1999). In some cases, the migrant is able to secure U.S. employment before arrival in the United States. Thus, migration networks should increase the probability of finding work in the United States and perhaps even the actual wage received.

Similar to legal residency, migration networks have an ambiguous net effect on the United States-to-Mexico transition. Although networks reduce the costs of reentering the United States, they also increase the value of job opportunities in the United States that the return migrant must forgo while in Mexico. In addition, the presence of family and friends in the United States can make life north of the border more agreeable (Massey et al. 1987). However, some migrants encounter "bad" migration networks, marked by abusive employers and relatives who shun their arriving kin (Zahniser 1999). Thus, it is not possible to predict the direction in which the three network and residency variables affect the United States-to-Mexico transition.

Macroeconomic Conditions

Of the five two-way logit models, models 2 through 5 feature several indicators of macroeconomic conditions in Mexico and the United States. Models 2 and 4 include real Mexican consumption per worker and the alternative binational income ratio. Models 3 and 5 use real per capita GDP in Mexico and the binational ratio of per capita GDP. As indicated earlier, the probability of migration should rise with the expected income differential and fall as expected real income in Mexico increases.

Models 4 and 5 include three additional economic indicators used in Massey and Espinosa (1997): the Mexican inflation rate, the annual depreciation rate of the Mexican peso versus the U.S. dollar, and the real interest rate in Mexico. The authors link inflation and a deteriorating exchange rate to the erosion of peso-denominated savings, which increases the cost of hiring coyotes, who usually must be paid in dollars. Thus, migration should be less likely when inflation is high and the rate of depreciation is sharp. These twin threats lead many Mexican households, including some of modest means, to hold savings in dollars. Massey and Espinosa find that the odds of first and repeat migration increase with the real interest rate, as migration and borrowing are substitute methods of financing household, farm, and business investments.

Empirical Results

Table 10.3 displays the parameter estimates from the standard logit model and five two-way logit models. A likelihood ratio test (LR = 7,773.36 with 16 degrees of freedom, $p < 0.0001$) confirms that the two-way specification of model 1 is superior to that of the restricted, standard logit model. One difference between the standard model and the two-way models warrants brief attention. With respect to age and its square, the standard logit results are consistent with previous cross-sectional studies in which the parameter estimate for age is positive (albeit insignificant in this case) and that for the squared term is negative. In the two-way models, the estimates for both variables are negative and significant.

Two-Way Results

Table 10.4 summarizes the hypotheses for the explanatory variables and the findings from the two-way models. Across the five two-way specifications, the results are quite similar. Outside of the macroeconomic variables, none of the parameter estimates change in sign from one model to the next, and the estimates are generally of similar magnitude and comparable significance across specifications.

Table 10.5 lists the estimated net effects of selected explanatory variables on the Mexico-to-United States and the United States-to-Mexico transitions. These estimates are calculated using the formulas presented in equation (10.1) and the parameter estimates in table 10.3. Because the net effects for the interacted explanatory variables Z_t are

TABLE 10.3   Parameter Estimates from Logit Models

Variable	Standard Logit[a]	Two-Way Logit Models				
		Model 1[a]	Model 2	Model 3	Model 4	Model 5
Intercept	-2.9182***	-1.2529***	-0.3208	-0.7810***	-0.9299	-1.9107***
Y_{t-1}*	—	1.6715***	1.6848***	1.6838***	1.6821***	1.6812***
Individual character-istics						
Female	-0.7890***	-0.3430***	-0.3497***	-0.3504***	-0.3511***	-0.3514***
Interaction term		0.7460***	0.7421***	0.7404***	0.7416***	0.7404***
Age (in years)	0.0027	-0.0333***	-0.0273***	-0.0288***	-0.0270**	-0.0285***
Age squared	-0.0012***	-0.0004***	-0.0004***	-0.0004***	-0.0004***	-0.0004***
Education (in years)	-0.0293***	-0.0152**	-0.0133*	-0.0141*	-0.0130*	-0.0137*
Interaction term		0.0347***	0.0345***	0.0344***	0.0344***	0.0343***
College educated	-0.5277***	-0.3828***	-0.3815***	-0.3783***	-0.3837***	-0.3807***
Interaction term		-0.0685	-0.0721	-0.0717	-0.0695	-0.0698
U.S. interview	2.0448***	1.7302***	1.7244***	1.7252***	1.7245***	1.7258***
Interaction term	—	0.2611***	0.2695***	0.2678***	0.2709***	0.2708***
Migration experience (in months)	0.0462***	0.0272***	0.0272***	0.0272***	0.0272***	0.0272***
Migration experience squared ($\times$ 0.1)	-0.0008***	-0.0005***	-0.0005***	-0.0005***	-0.0005***	-0.0005***
Family responsibilities						
Married	-0.1296**	-0.1371**	-0.1150*	-0.1214*	-0.1149*	-0.1213*
Interaction term	—	-0.1942***	-0.2050***	-0.2053***	-0.2024***	-0.2029***

TABLE 10.3   *Continued*

Variable	Standard Logit[a]	Two-Way Logit Models				
		Model 1[a]	Model 2	Model 3	Model 4	Model 5
Agricultural land (in hectares)	-0.0090***	-0.0077***	-0.0076***	-0.0076***	-0.0077***	-0.0077***
Interaction term	—	0.0024**	0.0023**	0.0023**	0.0023**	0.0023**
Business ownership	-0.8969***	-0.5256***	-0.5265***	-0.5266***	-0.5238***	-0.5232***
Interaction term	—	0.0956*	0.0973*	0.0976*	0.0990*	0.0987*
National economic conditions						
Real consumption per worker in Mexico (× 0.0001)	—	—	-0.2000	—	-0.0251	—
Expected income ratio	—	—	-0.0779***	—	-0.0181	—
Real per capita GDP in Mexico (× 0.001)	—	—	—	-0.0069	—	0.0460**
Ratio of real per capita GDP	—	—	—	-0.0320***	—	0.0617**
Mexican inflation rate	—	—	—	—	-0.0020	-0.0052**
Real interest rate in Mexico	—	—	—	—	-0.0052**	-0.0088***
Devaluation rate	—	—	—	—	0.0020	0.0043**
Log-likelihood (intercept and covariates)	-15,748.45	-11,861.77	-11,893.11	-11,894.65	-11,891.06	-11,888.78

Source: Author's calculations.

Note: Results for community dummy variables and time effects are not reported. Results of Wald chi-squared test on significance of parameter estimate: *** passes at 99 percent level; ** passes at 95 percent level; ** passes at 90 percent level; and * passes at 90 percent level.

[a] The standard logit model and mode. 1 also contain dummy variables measuring time effects.

Number of minor-age children	0.0588**	0.0575***	0.0545***	0.0551***	0.0544***	0.0549***
Interaction term	—	0.0234***	0.0224***	0.0225***	0.0225***	0.0227***
Single parent	-0.2674**	0.0602	0.0850	0.0800	0.0837	0.0746
Interaction term	—	0.4035**	0.3962**	0.3953**	0.3990**	0.3975**
Single mother	0.3597**	-0.1913	-0.1800	-0.1807	-0.1723	-0.1701
Interaction term	—	-0.9469***	-0.9403***	-0.9378***	-0.9370***	-0.9344***
Migration networks and immigration status						
Networks and residency	1.8482***	1.1709***	1.1725***	1.1715***	1.1723***	1.1712***
Interaction term	—	-0.1470*	-0.1569*	-0.1522*	-0.1608**	-0.1569*
Residency but no networks	2.6578***	1.8574***	1.8588***	1.8580***	1.8578***	1.8578***
Interaction term	—	-0.7230***	-0.7377***	-0.7331***	-0.7388***	-0.7332***
Networks but no residency	0.5372***	0.3352***	0.3404***	0.3387***	0.3403***	0.3385***
Interaction term	—	-0.3979***	-0.3985***	-0.3979***	-0.3991***	-0.3988***
U.S. citizen	0.6918*	-0.6834	-0.7044	-0.7006	-0.6920	-0.6834
Interaction term	—	0.5515	0.5751	0.5715	0.5758	0.5700
Additional income sources						
Number of adult offspring	0.0824***	0.0778***	0.0776***	0.0775***	0.0778***	0.0778***
Interaction term	—	0.1283***	0.1278***	0.1277***	0.1282***	0.1280***

(Table continues on p. 260.)

TABLE 10.4   *Summary of Hypotheses and Findings from Two-Way Models*

Variable	Hypothesized Influence on		Evidence for	
	Mexico-to-United States Transition	United States-to-Mexico Transition	Mexico-to-United States Transition	United States-to-Mexico Transition
Y_{t-1}*	Positive	Negative	Positive	Negative
Individual characteristics				
Female	Negative	Negative	Negative	Negative
Age (in years)	Positive	Negative	Negative	Positive
Age squared	Negative	Positive	Negative	Positive
Education (in years)	Negative	Positive	Negative	Negative
College educated	Negative	Positive	Insignificant	Positive
U.S. interview	Positive	Negative	Positive	Negative
Migration experience (in months)	Positive	Negative	Positive	Negative
Migration experience squared	Negative	Positive	Negative	Positive
Family responsibilities				
Married	Negative	Positive	Insignificant	Positive
Number of minor-age children	Positive	Positive	Positive	Negative
Single parent	Uncertain	Uncertain	Insignificant	Negative
Single mother	Uncertain	Uncertain	Positive	Positive
Migration networks and immigration status				
Networks and residency	Positive	Uncertain	Positive	Negative
Residency but not networks	Positive	Uncertain	Positive	Negative
Networks but not residency	Positive	Uncertain	Positive	Insignificant
U.S. citizen	Positive	Negative	Insignificant	Insignificant
Additional income sources				
Number of adult offspring	Negative	Positive	Negative	Negative
Agricultural land (in hectares)	Negative	Positive	Negative	Positive
Business ownership	Negative	Positive	Negative	Positive
National economic conditions				
Real consumption per worker in Mexico	Negative	Positive	Insignificant	Insignificant
Real per capita GDP in Mexico	Negative	Positive	Mixed results	Mixed results

TABLE 10.4   *Continued*

Variable	Hypothesized Influence on		Evidence for	
	Mexico-to-United States Transition	United States-to-Mexico Transition	Mexico-to-United States Transition	United States-to-Mexico Transition
Expected income ratio	Positive	Negative	Mixed results	Mixed results
Ratio of per capita GDP	Positive	Negative	Mixed results	Mixed results
Mexican inflation rate	Negative	Positive	Mixed results	Mixed results
Real interest rate in Mexico	Positive	Negative	Negative	Positive
Depreciation rate	Negative	Positive	Mixed results	Mixed results

Source: Author's calculations.

essentially the sum of parameters b_3 and b_4, one must account for both the variances of $\hat{b}_3$ and $\hat{b}_4$ and the covariance of the two estimates when evaluating the statistical significance of the estimated net effects. This is done using a series of t-tests in which the standard error equals $\sqrt{\text{var}(\hat{b}_3) + 2\text{cov}(\hat{b}_3, \hat{b}_4) + \text{var}(\hat{b}_4)}$. The results of these tests are noted in table 10.5.

The similarity of the two-way results allows us to concentrate on model 1. The parameter estimate for $Y_{t-1}{}^\star$ is positive and highly significant (see table 10.3), which indicates positive state dependence within the model. Heads of household who spend all of one calendar year in Mexico are less likely to migrate to the United States during the following year, and those who spend some part of the calendar year in the United States are more likely to do so. Given the characteristics of the average observation in the panel and using the parameter estimates from model 1, the probability of migrating equals 0.4146 when the individual has spent some part of the previous year in the United States and 0.0155 otherwise.

Females are less likely than males to make either the Mexico-to-United States or the United States-to-Mexico transition (see table 10.5). The negative relationship between gender and the Mexico-to-United States transition is consistent with the results of previous studies (Sprouse 1991; Taylor 1984, 1987). However, the negative relationship between gender and the United States-to-Mexico transition is a new quantitative finding. It meshes neatly with qualitative evidence that shows that female migrants are often reluctant to return to their country of origin.

The probability of migration decreases with age at an increasing rate, a result that sharply contrasts with previous cross-sectional

TABLE 10.5   *Estimated Net Effects of Selected Variables on Mexico-to-United States and United States-to-Mexico Transitions*

Variable	Model 1	Model 2	Model 3	Model 4	Model 5
Mexico-to-United States transition					
Female	−1.0890***	−1.0918***	−1.0908***	−1.0927***	−1.0918***
Age	−0.0333***	−0.0273***	−0.0288***	−0.0270***	−0.0285***
Age squared	−0.0004***	−0.0004***	−0.0004***	−0.0004***	−0.0004***
Education	−0.0499***	−0.0478***	−0.0485***	−0.0474***	−0.0480***
College educated	−0.3143	−0.3094	−0.3066	−0.3142	−0.3109
U.S. interview	1.4691***	1.4549***	1.4574***	1.4536***	1.4550***
Migration experience	0.0272***	0.0272***	0.0272***	0.0272***	0.0272***
Migration experience squared (× 0.1)	−0.0005***	−0.0005***	−0.0005***	−0.0005***	−0.0005***
Married	0.0571	0.0900	0.0839	0.0875	0.0816
Number of minor-age children	0.0341**	0.0321**	0.0326**	0.0319**	0.0322**
Single parent	−0.3433	−0.3112	−0.3153	−0.3153	−0.3229
Single mother	0.7556*	0.7603*	0.7571*	0.7647*	0.7643*
Networks and residency	1.3179***	1.3294***	1.3237***	1.3331***	1.3281***
Residency but not networks	2.5804***	2.5965***	2.5911***	2.5966***	2.5910***
Networks but not residency	0.7331***	0.7389***	0.7366***	0.7394***	0.7873***
Number of adult offspring	−0.0505***	−0.0502***	−0.0502***	−0.0504***	−0.0502***
Agricultural land (in hectares)	−0.0101***	−0.0100***	−0.0099***	−0.0100***	−0.0100***
Business ownership	−0.6212***	−0.6238***	−0.6242***	−0.6228***	−0.6219***
United States-to-Mexico transition					
Female	−0.4030**	−0.3924**	−0.3900**	−0.3905**	−0.3890**
Age	0.0333***	0.0273***	0.0288***	0.0270**	0.0285***
Age squared	0.0004***	0.0001***	0.0004***	0.0004***	0.0004***
Education	−0.0195*	−0.0212*	−0.0203*	−0.0214*	−0.0206*
College educated	0.4513*	0.4536**	0.4500*	0.4532*	0.4505*
U.S. interview	−1.9913***	−1.9939***	−1.9930***	−1.9954***	−1.9966***
Migration experience	−0.0272***	−0.0272***	−0.0272***	−0.0272***	−0.0272***
Migration experience squared (× 0.1)	0.0005***	0.0005***	0.0005***	0.0005***	0.0005***
Married	0.3313***	0.3200***	0.3267***	0.3173***	0.3242***

(Table continues on p. 264.)

TABLE 10.5   *Continued*

Variable	Model 1	Model 2	Model 3	Model 4	Model 5
Number of minor-age children	−0.0809***	−0.0769***	−0.0776***	−0.0769***	−0.0776***
Single parent	−0.4637*	−0.4812*	−0.4753*	−0.4827*	−0.4721*
Single mother	1.1382***	1.1203***	1.1185***	1.1093***	1.1045***
Networks and residency	−1.0239***	−1.0156***	−1.0193***	−1.0115***	−1.0143***
Residency but not networks	−1.1344***	−1.1211***	−1.1249***	−1.1190***	−1.1246***
Networks but not residency	0.0627	0.0581	0.0592	0.0588	0.0603
Number of adult offspring	−0.2061***	−0.2054***	−0.2052***	−0.2060***	−0.2058***
Agricultural land (in hectares)	0.0053***	0.0053***	0.0053***	0.0054***	0.0054***
Business ownership	0.4300***	0.4292***	0.4290***	0.4248***	0.4245***

Source: Author's calculations.
Note: Net effects are calculated using the parameter estimates in table 10.3. Results of two-tailed t test: ***$|t| \geq 2.576$; **$1.960 \leq |t| < 2.576$; *$1.645 \leq |t| < 1.960$

studies. However, the evidence regarding U.S. migration experience resembles that of Taylor (1987). The large parameter estimate for experience (0.0272) and the much smaller parameter estimate for the squared term (−0.00005) (table 10.3) mean that the probability of migration increases until twenty-four years of U.S. experience have been accumulated. A modest amount of migration experience offsets the negative influence of age on the probability of migration: thirty-two months of U.S. experience negate the effect of twenty years of age, and fifty-four months of experience counteract thirty years of age.

There is less unanimity in the cross-sectional literature regarding education's impact on migration. Taylor (1984) finds no significant relationship between these variables, but Sprouse (1991) discovers the contrary. Sprouse includes both years of education and its square and finds that the probability of migration first rises and then falls as education increases. Massey and García España (1987) use a trio of dummy variables that reflect different levels of education. Their results mirror those of Sprouse, as persons with one to three years of education are more likely to migrate than persons with no education, and persons with four or more years are less likely to migrate.

In the two-way models, education reduces the likelihood of both transitions. The finding regarding the Mexico-to-United States transition is consistent with the works of Sprouse and García España. However, the negative relationship between education and the United States-to-Mexico transition provides a fresh insight regarding schooling and migration. Better-educated migrants are less likely to return to Mexico, perhaps because their U.S. earnings are higher than those of less-educated migrants. These returns do not seem to extend to college-educated migrants, who are more likely to make the United States-to-Mexico transition.

Being married exerts a positive and significant effect on the United States-to-Mexico transition but an insignificant effect on the Mexico-to-United States transition. Thus, the additional labor power afforded to a household through marriage does not necessarily deter the household head from migrating, as was hypothesized. Nor is the spouse an appreciable burden that forces the head of household to migrate. Instead, married migrants alternate years of migration to the United States with substantial amounts of time spent in Mexico, apparently with their families.

The probability of making the Mexico-to-United States transition rises with the number of minor-age children. Taylor (1984, 1987) obtains a similar result, but the number of dependents in the household is insignificant in the works of García España (1992), Sprouse (1991) and Massey and García España (1987). In contrast, the probability of making the United States-to-Mexico transition falls with this variable. Thus, increasing numbers of dependent children lead Mexican heads of household not only to enter the migration stream but also to remain in it year after year.

Relative to the average observation, the variable indicating single parenthood has no significant impact on the Mexico-to-United States transition and a weakly significant, negative effect on the reverse transition. Because the estimated net effects for both the single-parenthood variable and the number of minor-age children are negative, single parenthood unambiguously discourages the United States-to-Mexico transition. If single parents on average have invested less in their human capital, then the returns to their employment in Mexico are likely to be smaller. Thus, it should not be surprising that once in the United States, single parents tend not to leave.

In contrast, the variable indicating single motherhood positively affects both the Mexico-to-United States and the United States-to-Mexico transitions. However, when one considers all the variables associated with single motherhood (minor-age children, single parenthood, and gender), single motherhood increases only the probability of the United States-to-Mexico transition, and only for those women with no more than three children. Still, this result is intriguing in that certain migrant single mothers prefer to return to Mexico for extended periods of time, perhaps because of more substantial family support there.

Legal U.S. residents, as well as nonresidents with migration networks, are more likely to make the Mexico-to-United States transition than nonresidents who lack a network. This difference is most profound for legal residents who have no network and next strongest for persons who possess both networks and U.S. residency. Regarding the United States-to-Mexico transition, legal residents are less likely to undertake this transition than nonresidents without networks. In the absence of legal residency, migration networks have no significant effect on the United States-to-Mexico transition. This latter result suggests that the influence of such networks is limited to the Mexico-to-United States transition.

Additional income sources have a significant effect on both transitions. Increasing amounts of agricultural land owned by the household discourage the Mexico-to-United States transition and encourage the reverse. The direction of business ownership's effects is identical. Other researchers have obtained similar results. García España (1992) and Massey and García España (1987) find a negative relationship between migration and the ownership of agricultural land or a business, and Taylor (1987) demonstrates a negative relationship between land ownership and migration. Sprouse (1991) and Taylor (1984), who use a variable measuring the value of total assets, discover no significant relationship.

The probability of the Mexico-to-United States transition falls with the number of adult offspring. Presumably, heads of household with more adult offspring have less need to migrate. However, the probability of the United States-to-Mexico transition decreases with the number of adult offspring, in contrast to the hypothesis that migrants opt not to migrate during the following year in order to spend time with their extended families. The presence of adult offspring at home in Mexico may assure the head of household that affairs at home are in good hands, thus encouraging him or her to work in the United States year after year.

In model 1, eighteen of the thirty-six community dummy variables (whose results are not reported) are significant at the 90 percent level or better. Fourteen of these are significant at the 99 percent level. Fifteen of the significant community dummies are positive in sign, and three are negative. In addition, all of the time effects in model 1 (whose results are also not reported) except 1972, 1981, 1983, 1986, and 1987 are statistically significant. Each significant time effect is positive.

National Economic Conditions

The primary measures of national economic conditions produce mixed results (see table 10.3). The alternative indicators of expected income in

Mexico (consumption per worker in models 2 and 4 and real GDP per capita in models 3 and 5) are insignificant, except in model 5, in which higher levels of Mexican consumption are shown to encourage migration. Moreover, models 2 and 3 suggest that migration becomes less likely (rather than more likely) when the United States-to-Mexico income ratio widens. Only model 5 obtains the conventional result that the probability of migration rises and falls with this ratio.[13]

The poor performance of expected income in Mexico and the binational income ratio in the various models is extremely surprising, especially given the wild fluctuations of the Mexican economy from 1971 to 1987. One possibility is that the aggregate variables utilized do not capture the changing economic prospects facing the typical Mexican head of household, despite my best efforts to incorporate new and more accurate measures. Another possibility is that migration is largely insensitive to marginal changes in Mexico's macroeconomic performance. If this is the case, improvements in this performance will not substantially decrease migration to the United States unless the changes are fairly dramatic.

The three economic variables added to models 4 and 5 perform somewhat better. Higher rates of inflation lessen the probability of migration. This finding supports the theory that inflation restricts migration by eroding the savings of prospective migrants. The depreciation rate, which is significant in model 5 but not in model 4, exercises the opposite effect. Lower real interest rates are found to encourage migration, as borrowing money to finance the costs of migration becomes easier. The results for currency depreciation and the interest rate run contrary to the findings of Massey and Espinosa (1997). However, the sensitivity of the results to different specifications raises doubts about the usefulness of these economic variables, as they are employed here and by Massey and Espinosa.

Conclusion

This chapter uses Yamaguchi's logit model for the analysis of interdependent, discrete-time transitions to study Mexican migration to the United States. Estimates of the separate effects of various explanatory variables on the Mexico-to-United States and the United States-to-Mexico transitions yield a number of important findings, some of which would not have been uncovered using a standard logit or probit model. First, once a Mexican head of household migrates to the United States, migration becomes a persistent behavior. These data indicate that individuals who spend some part of the year in the United States are 26.8

times more likely to do so again the following year than persons who spend the entire year in Mexico.

Second, migrants who become legal U.S. residents are more likely to work in the United States from one year to the next. However, the data yield no clear evidence regarding the United States-to-Mexico transition of nonresidents who form part of a migration network, as measured by the previous migration experience of parents, grandparents, or siblings. Therefore, the impact of such networks on the costs and benefits of migration may not extend beyond the Mexico-to-United States transition.

Third, females are more likely to follow one year of U.S. migration with another. However, Mexican men are still more likely to participate in U.S. migration, and they are more likely to undertake the Mexico-to-United States transition. According to Hondagneu-Sotelo (1992, 1994) and Grasmuck and Pessar (1991), the tendency of female migrants to remain in the United States is rooted in their perception that returning to their country of origin would endanger hard-earned economic gains and more profound changes in relations between the sexes. To ascertain whether this perception is accurate, closer attention should be paid to the changing face of gender relations within Mexico, as well as the interplay between migration and these relations. Quantitative analysis of this issue and others related to female migration from Mexico will require new data sets. In particular, there is a pressing need to develop data sets that are specifically designed to study both male and female migrants and to scrutinize existing data from the Mexican government about the country's labor market.

Fourth, married migrants typically follow a year of migration with one or more years spent entirely in Mexico. These individuals appear committed to both supporting their families through employment in the United States and spending significant amounts of time with their loved ones. This pattern seems most amenable to a proposed guest-worker program for Mexican migrants to the United States.

Fifth, heads of households with larger numbers of dependent children tend to be repeated participants in international migration. As the number of dependent children increases, the head of household is more likely to spend part of the year in the United States as a migrant, regardless of the previous year's migration decision. Mexico's successful efforts to reduce its rate of population growth should help to make international migration a less common feature of Mexican life.

Finally, two innovative variables were utilized to measure expected income in Mexico and the United States: Mexican consumption per worker and the average salary in California of the Mexican born. Lamentably, these variables performed little better than traditional measures based on GDP per capita, and they yielded few insights into the relationship between macroeconomic conditions and migration. Other explanatory variables may prove more useful. Candidates include measures of local economic conditions in migrants' communities of origin, such as access to credit, and indicators of local weather conditions severely detrimental to agriculture, such as droughts, floods, and hurricanes.

Appendix 10A: Description of Variables and Their Sources

Unless otherwise specified, the variables are drawn from the data set LIFEFILE of the Mexican Migration Project (1997).

Adult offspring: Number of adult offspring in year t

Age: Age of individual in year t, in years

Agricultural land: Amount of agricultural land owned by household in year t, in hectares

Average California salary of the Mexican born: Average salary in California of persons born in Mexico, weighted by the estimated number of Mexican-born employees in each economic sector (in current U.S. dollars). Variable is calculated using salary information from U.S. Department of Commerce, *County Business Patterns* (1971 to 1987), and sectoral distributions of employment in the 1970, 1980, and 1990 U.S. Censuses (U.S. Department of Commerce 1997a, 1997b, 1997c). Sectoral distributions for years between census years are linearly interpolated. Salary information for the transportation industry is used in place of missing data for the railroad sector and the U.S. Postal Service. Salary information for elementary and secondary school is used in place of missing data for certain government employees.

Business ownership: Dummy variable that equals one if the household owned a business in year t and zero otherwise

College educated: Dummy variable that equals one if the individual had more than twelve years of education in year t and zero otherwise

Community effects: Dummy variables that equal one if the individual is from the specified community and zero otherwise

Depreciation rate: Annual depreciation of the exchange rate between the Mexican peso and the U.S. dollar. Variable is calculated using the mid-period average of the exchange rate of the peso to the dollar in IMF (1998).

Education: Years of schooling

Expected income ratio: Mexican consumption per worker divided by the average salary in California of the Mexican born. Mexican consumption is converted to dollars using the period-average exchange rate found in IMF (1998).

Female: Dummy variable that equals one if the individual is female and zero otherwise

Married: Dummy variable that equals one if the individual was married in year t and zero otherwise

Mexican consumption per worker: Household consumption expenditure of Mexico, including nonprofit institutions serving households, divided by the estimated number of economically active Mexicans, aged twelve years or older (in current new pesos). The numerator is from IMF (1998). The denominator equals total Mexican population (IMF 1998) times the estimated percentage of the population aged twelve years or older (United Nations 1993) times the percentage of the population aged twelve years or older that is economically active (INEGI 1988, 1998). The estimated percentage of the population aged twelve years or older is calculated by adding the percentage aged fifteen years or older to the quantity of the percentage aged five to fourteen years times 0.3.

Mexican inflation rate: Annual rate of Mexican inflation. Variable is calculated using consumer price indexes in IMF (1993, 1998).

Mexican GDP per capita: Per capita income of Mexico in year t, in current new pesos. Variable is calculated using GDP and population figures in IMF (1998).

Migration experience: Total U.S. migration experience as of year t, in months

Minor-age children: Number of minor children of the head of household in year t

Networks and residency: Dummy variable that equals one if the individual is a legal resident of the United States and at least one person among his parents, siblings, and grandparents has previous U.S. migration experience in year t. Otherwise, the variable equals zero.

Networks but not residency: Dummy variable that equals one if the individual is not a legal resident of the United States and at least one person among his parents, siblings, and grandparents has previous U.S. migration experience in year t. Otherwise, the variable equals zero.

Ratio of per capita GDP: Ratio of U.S. per capita GDP to Mexican per capita GDP. The latter is converted to U.S. dollars using the period-average exchange rate (IMF 1998).

Real consumption per worker in Mexico: Mexican consumption per worker, in 1994 new pesos. Variable is calculated using consumer price indexes from IMF (1993, 1998).

Real per capita GDP in Mexico: Mexican GDP per capita, in 1994 new pesos. Variable is calculated using consumer price indexes from IMF (1993, 1998).

Real interest rate in Mexico: Average cost of funds in Mexico minus the Mexican inflation rate. The average cost of funds for the period from 1975 to 1987 is from IMF (1998). For the period from 1971 to 1974, estimates from Massey and Espinosa (1997) are used. These estimates (provided by Massey and Espinosa) are obtained by regressing observed values of the average cost of funds on the Mexican money supply and then using the resulting parameter estimates to predict the missing values.

Residency but not networks: Dummy variable that equals one if the individual is a legal resident of the United States and not one person among his parents, siblings, and grandparents has previous U.S. migration experience in year t. Otherwise, the variable equals zero.

Single mother: Dummy variable that equals one if the individual was a single mother in year t and zero otherwise

Single parent: Dummy variable that equals one if the individual was a single parent in year t and zero otherwise

Time effects: Dummy variables that equal one if year t is the specified year and zero otherwise

U.S. citizen: Dummy variable that equals one if the individual was a U.S. citizen in year t and zero otherwise

U.S. GDP per capita: Per capita income of United States in year t, in current U.S. dollars. Variable is calculated using GDP and population figures in IMF (1998).

U.S. interview: Dummy variable that equals one if the individual was interviewed in the United States and zero otherwise

Y^*_t: Equals one if the individual migrated to the United States in year t and -1 otherwise

Appendix 10B: Theoretical Model

Define R_t to equal the net return from working in the United States during year t. To facilitate the structuring of the optimization problem, let us also create a more standard variable for the migration decision: define Y_t to equal one if the individual spends at least some part of year t in the United States and zero otherwise. Just before year t, the individual selects the sequence of migration decisions that maximizes the net expected present discounted value of lifetime utility, given Ω_t, the information set that is available at that time. The individual thus faces the following optimization problem:

$$V_t = \max_{\{Yt\}^T_{s=t}} E_t[\sum_{j=t}^{T} \rho^{j-t} R_j | \Omega_t], \qquad (10B.1)$$

where ρ is the discount rate. Bellman's equation allows equation (10B.1) to be reduced to a one-period problem:

$$V_t = \max_{\{Yt\}}\{R_t + \rho E_t[V_{t+1}(\Omega_{t+1})] | Y_{t-1}\}. \qquad (10B.2)$$

R_t can be expressed as the difference between the increment to indirect utility that results from working in the United States in year t and the costs associated with participating in the U.S. labor market in year t:

$$R_t(Y_{t-1}) = Y_t[\gamma(X_t^{\gamma}, Z_t^{\gamma}, Y_{t-1}^{*})$$
$$- C(X_t^{C}, Z_t^{C}, Y_{t-1}^{*})], \qquad (10B.3)$$

where X_t^{γ} and Z_t^{γ} are those variables in X_t and Z_t respectively that influence incremental utility and X_t^C and Z_t^C are those variables in X_t and Z_t respectively that affect migration costs.

Variables in X_t and Z_t may affect both incremental utility and migration costs. By virtue of their interaction with Y_{t-1}^*, the variables in Z_t differentially influence the net return, depending on the migration decision of the previous year.

Finally, define M_t to be an indicator function of whether the individual spends year t in the United States:

$$M_t = Y_t[\gamma(X_t^{\gamma}, Z_t^{\gamma}, Y_{t-1}^{*}) - C(X_t^{C}, Z_t^{C}, Y_{t-1}^{*})] +$$
$$\rho\{E_t[V_t + 1(\Omega_{t+1}) | Y_t = 1] - E_t[V_t + (\Omega_t + 1) | Y_t = 0]\}. \qquad (10B.4)$$

The individual spends year t in the United States when M_t exceeds zero. Assuming that M_t is a linear function of X_t, Z_t, and Y_{t-1}, reexpressing equation (10.B4) as the log-odds ratio (equation 10.1) provides the final link between the theoretical and econometric models.

A previous version of this chapter appeared in *American Behavioral Scientist* 1999, vol. 42, no. 9.

Notes

1. Using the same general data source as this chapter, Belinda Reyes (1997) finds that about half the migrants in her sample return to Mexico after two years and almost 70 percent do so after ten years or less.

2. Appendix 10B presents a corresponding theoretical model in which determinants of migration differentially affect the net return to migration, depending on the previous year's migration decision.

3. These are found in the data set LIFEFILE of the Mexican Migration Project (1997).

4. Because these variables are not yet available for all the survey communities, they are not used here, though they may appear in future work.

5. Mexican employment data generally focus on persons aged twelve years or older; U.S. data examines those aged sixteen years or older.

6. Appendix 10A provides a more complete explanation of the calculation of this variable.

7. Mexican census data indicate that in 1970, 43.6 percent of Mexicans aged twelve years or older were economically active, as compared with 50.9 percent in 1980 (INEGI 1988). Out of concern that this increase is the product of a methodological change, the 1980 figure is used when calculating consumption per worker for 1971 to 1980, and interpolations between the 1980 figure and an average of 1987 quarterly data are used for 1981 to 1987.

8. Much of this section draws from Yamaguchi (1991), especially 49–50, which contain a clear exposition of his model. Whenever possible, this chapter follows Yamaguchi's notation.

9. In the discussion that follows, variables X_t and Z_t, parameters b_2, b_3, and b_4, and parameter estimates $\hat{b}_2$, $\hat{b}_3$, and $\hat{b}_4$, are all non-scalar vectors. Subscripts denoting individuals are dropped.

10. A detailed description of the variables and their sources is located in appendix 10A.

11. In the comparable models in Massey and García España (1987) and García España (1992), the parameter estimates for age and its square are not statistically significant.

12. Coyotes, also known as polleros, help undocumented migrants to enter the United States illegally in exchange for a fee.

13. Similar results are obtained when the economic variables are included in standard logit models that correspond to models 2 through 5. In a set of two-way models in which the alternative measures of expected income in Mexico and the binational income

273

ratio are included one at a time, the economic variables are statistically insignificant.

References

Chiswick, Barry R. 1978. "The Effect of Americanization on the Earnings of Foreign-born Men." *Journal of Political Economy* 86(5): 897–921.

Deléchat, Corinne. 1996. "The Dynamics of the Migration Process: The Case of Mexican Migration to the United States." Unpublished paper.

Donato, Katherine M. 1993. "Current Trends and Patterns of Female Migration: Evidence from Mexico." *International Migration Review* 27(4): 748–71.

Espinosa, Kristin E., and Douglas S. Massey. 1997. "Determinants of English Proficiency Among Mexican Migrants to the United States." *International Migration Review* 31(1): 28–50.

Frisbie, Parker. 1975. "Illegal Migration from Mexico to the United States: A Longitudinal Analysis." *International Migration Review* 9(1): 3–13.

García España, Juan Felipe. 1992. "Determinants of Internal and International Migration from Rural Areas of Mexico." Ph.D. diss., University of Pennsylvania.

Grasmuck, Sherri, and Patricia R. Pessar. 1991. *Between Two Islands: Dominican International Migration.* Berkeley: University of California Press.

Heckman, James J. 1981. "Statistical Models for Discrete Panel Data." In *Structural Analysis of Discrete Data with Econometric Applications,* edited by Charles F. Manski and Daniel McFadden. Cambridge: MIT Press.

Hondagneu-Sotelo, Pierrette. 1992. "Overcoming Patriarchal Constraints: The Reconstruction of Gender Relations Among Mexican Immigrant Women and Men." *Gender and Society* 6(3): 393–415.

———. 1994. *Gendered Transitions: Mexican Experiences of Immigration.* Berkeley: University of California Press.

Instituto Nacional de Estadística, Geografía e Informática (INEGI). 1988. *Anuario Estadístico de los Estados Unidos Mexicanos, 1987.* Aguascalientes, Mexico: INEGI.

———. 1993. Sistema Para la Consulta de Información Censal. "Resultados definitivos: Onceno Censo General de Población y Vivienda, 1990." CD-ROM. Aguascalientes, Mexico: INEGI.

———. 1995. *Censos Económicos 1994: Resultados Oportunos, Tabulados Básicos.* Aguascalientes, Mexico: INEGI.

———. 1998. Downloaded on December 24, 1998, from Banco de Información Económica website on the worldwide web at: http://dgcnesyp.inegi.gob.mx/cgi-win/bdi.exe.

International Monetary Fund (IMF). 1993. *International Financial Statistics Yearbook*. Washington: IMF.

———. 1998. *International Financial Statistics Yearbook*. Washington: IMF.

Jenkins, J. Craig. 1977. "Push/Pull in Recent Mexican Migration to the United States." *International Migration Review* 11(2): 178–89.

Kossoudji, Sherrie A. 1992. "Playing Cat and Mouse at the U.S.-Mexican Border." *Demography* 29(2): 159–80.

Lindstrom, David P. 1996. "Economic Opportunity in Mexico and Return Migration from the United States." *Demography* 33(3): 357–74.

Massey, Douglas S., Rafael Alarcón, Jorge Durand, and Humberto González. 1987. *Return to Aztlán: The Social Process of International Migration from Western Mexico*. Berkeley: University of California Press.

Massey, Douglas S., and Kristin Espinosa. 1997. "What's Driving Mexico-U. S. Migration? A Theoretical, Empirical, and Policy Analysis." *American Journal of Sociology* 102(4): 939–99.

Massey, Douglas S., and Juan Felipe García España. 1987. "The Social Process of International Migration." *Science* 237: 733–38.

Mexican Migration Project. 1997. LIFEFILE (machine-readable downloaded file). Philadelphia: Population Studies Center, University of Pennsylvania (February).

———. 1998. "Table 1: Sample Information." Downloaded on December 31, 1998, from the worldwide web at: http://lexis.pop.upenn.edu/mexmig/sampletable.html.

Olea, Héctor Alonso. 1988. "The Economics of Undocumented Immigration: Mexican Participation in the U.S. Labor Market." Ph.D. diss., Rice University.

Reyes, Belinda. 1997. *Dynamics of Immigration: Return Migration to Western Mexico*. San Francisco: Public Policy Institute of California.

Singer, Audrey, and Douglas S. Massey. 1998. "The Social Process of Undocumented Border Crossing Among Mexican Migrants." *International Migration Review* 32(3): 561–92.

Sprouse, Terry Wayne. 1991. "Household Labor Decisions and Migration in San Luís Potosí, Mexico." Master's thesis, University of Arizona.

Taylor, J. Edward. 1984. "Migration Networks and Risk in Household Labor Decisions: A Study of Migration from Two Mexican Villages." Ph.D. diss., University of California, Berkeley.

———. 1987. "Undocumented Mexico–U. S. Migration and the Returns to Households in Rural Mexico." *American Journal of Agricultural Economics* 69(3): 626–38.

Todaro, Michael P. 1969. "A Model of Labor Migration and Urban Unemployment in Less Developed Countries." *American Economic Review* 59(1): 138–48.

United Nations (UN). 1993. *World Population Prospects: The 1992 Revision*. New York: United Nations.

U.S. Department of Commerce. 1971–1987. *County Business Patterns.* Washington: U.S. Government Printing Office.

———. 1997a. *1990 Census of Population and Housing.* Public Use Microdata Sample, 5 Percent Sample, California. Machine-readable data file. Obtained from the University of Colorado at Boulder, Institute for Behavioral Science. Washington: U.S. Government Printing Office.

———. 1997b. *1980 Census of Population and Housing.* Public Use Microdata Sample, 5 Percent Sample, California. Machine-readable data file. Obtained from the University of Colorado at Boulder, Institute for Behavioral Science. Washington: U.S. Government Printing Office.

———. 1997c. *1970 Census of Population and Housing.* Public Use Microdata Sample, 5 Percent Sample, California. Machine-readable data file. Obtained from the University of Colorado at Boulder, Institute for Behavioral Science. Washington: U.S. Government Printing Office.

White, Michael J., Frank D. Bean, and Thomas J. Espenshade. 1990. "The U.S. 1986 Immigration Reform and Control Act and Undocumented Migration to the United States." *Population Research and Policy Review* 9(2): 93–116.

Yamaguchi, Kazuo. 1990. "Logit and Multinomial Logit Models for Discrete-Time Event-History Analysis: A Causal Analysis of Interdependent Discrete-Time Processes." *Quality and Quantity* 24(3): 323–41.

———. 1991. *Event History Analysis.* Applied Social Research Methods Series. Vol. 28. Newbury Park, Calif.: Sage Publications.

Zahniser, Steven S. 1999. *Mexican Migration to the United States: The Effects of Migration Networks and Human Capital Accumulation.* New York: Garland.

11

IMMIGRANT LABOR RECRUITMENT: U.S. AGRIBUSINESS AND UNDOCUMENTED MIGRATION FROM MEXICO

Fred Krissman

A CADEMIC discourse, media attention, and public policy initiatives in the United States have been riveted on "supply-side"
factors in the debate over undocumented migration from Mexico. The general consensus is that endemic poverty in Mexico is the
problem and the apprehension and deportation of "illegal aliens" in the
United States is the solution. However, poverty in the migrants' homeland is not an adequate explanation for large-scale undocumented immigration;[1] nor have such flows ever been terminated through policing
without the wholesale violation of basic human rights (Dunn 1996;
Hoffman 1974). Rather, the international migrant networks that provide
the social infrastructure to support sustained migratory activity develop
from long-term socioeconomic integration between specific labor-sending and labor-receiving countries, and the level of state repression that is
politically palatable merely makes new immigrant workers more desirable to many cost-conscious employers.[2]

My research examines the "demand-side" of the migration equation, shifting the onus from "them" to "us." I found that many labor-
intensive industries in the United States have crafted personnel practices to foster the proliferation of labor recruitment agents. Among
other dubious activities, these agents facilitate the flow of new workers
across the United States–Mexico border even as undocumented migration becomes an increasingly volatile political issue.

The Recruitment of Immigrant Workers

Sustained migratory flows around the world are generally tied to a demand for low-cost labor.[3] In North America, political leaders from Alex-

ander Hamilton to California governor Pete Wilson have helped make the United States a nation of immigrants in order to ensure an ample supply of workers for the country's burgeoning industries. The correlation between U.S. immigration policy and labor demand is demonstrated by the remarkable symmetry between the annual levels of legal admissions and contemporaneous economic growth, as measured by the overall unemployment rate and/or a growing gross national product (see, for example, Portes and Bach 1985, 33, 57). In sum, U.S. immigration policy and practice have, from the onset, been driven by the needs of the national economy. How has the supply of immigrant labor to the United States been so carefully calibrated to demand?

Both the public and private sectors have engaged in recruitment activities since the 1790s, beginning with the "[saturation of] Europe with promotional campaigns to stimulate emigration" (Calavita 1989, 153, 154). Over the next two centuries recruitment activities fostered inflows of contract workers from around the world.[4] Contracted labor has linked the workers recruited abroad to the demands in particular domestic labor markets. Indeed, labor recruiters have targeted workers from different labor-sending nations for specific job niches in the United States.[5]

Targeted labor recruitment helps to explain how certain ethnic groups become concentrated in specific industries while also accounting for the advent of ethnic communities in proximity to those firms.[6] As a significant number of new immigrants from one country are funneled to one or more industries in a region, they settle in association with one another, leading to the development of an ethnic community that may continue to attract co-nationals to that area (Portes and Rumbaut 1990, 86–88). As ever more workers from the same foreign country respond to the demand of U.S. industries for low-cost labor, international migrant networks between specific labor-sending and labor-receiving nations are created and strengthened.

Because supply rather than demand factors have been emphasized in the immigration literature the development of these networks typically has been analyzed from the point of view of the migrants.[7] From this perspective would-be migrants will seek out the assistance of family, friends, and co-nationals in deciding when to migrate, where to go, and how to get jobs, housing, and other assistance upon arrival. By relying upon fellow countrymen already living in the nation of destination new immigrants can minimize a variety of risks and maximize the opportunities for adjusting successfully to life and work in the new country. These are some of the benefits—or "positive" social capital—associated with the development of networks (Portes 1998, 9–13).

This upbeat assessment may be true for many individual immigrant families (especially for those children raised in the United States) when assessed over the course of the household life cycle. However, these international networks also provide the means for labor-intensive industries to access a continuous flow of immigrant workers from year to year, guaranteeing substandard conditions for these new workers in the short term as well as lower labor costs for employers over the long term. Therefore, the development of networks can also be examined from the perspective of the employers who prefer to hire new immigrant workers.

There are a number of benefits to employers of using networks to fill their labor needs. Aside from ensuring access to an ample low-cost workforce exactly when needed, many responsibilities that employers usually shoulder (such as worker recruitment, training, and supervision) can be foisted on employees who are members of the network. In addition, the social relations of production in firms using immigrant workers can be effectively controlled in spite of substandard workplace conditions through the manipulation of these networks.[8] Dissatisfied workers are loathe to cause a ruckus when their immediate supervisors are members of the same migrant network. Instead, these workers "vote with their feet," leaving such jobs as soon as they find better employment opportunities. As a result of the high turnover rates in these revolving-door labor markets, the growth of networks is constantly reinforced as more new immigrants are recruited to replace those who abandon substandard jobs.

These networks have their roots in the cooperative relations elaborated by families and communities within subsistence economies in their rural homeland. However, within the context of out-migration, employers use these networks to reduce the costs of production. Alejandro Portes (1998, 15–18) has referred to the potential for the abuse of networks by employers as constituting a type of "negative" social capital. Although the negative aspects of networks have been largely neglected in the literature, there have been some important case studies. Larissa Lomnitz (1982) has described both positive and negative social capital (which she labels as horizontal [symmetrical] and vertical [asymmetrical] network relations) in virtually every sector of the Mexican economy. Robert Alvarez and George Collier (1994) discuss both types of relations in the development of ethnic enterprises that span the United States–Mexico border. My research further contributes to this literature by correlating the abuses of networks with the substandard conditions maintained in many immigrant-dominated labor markets in the United States.

Although many U.S. industries have benefited from the use of international migrant networks, the agricultural sector is arguably the most salient case over a long historical period. Agribusiness in the southwestern United States has maintained access to an abundant supply of new immigrant workers for more than a century, exploiting successive waves of new immigrants from Mexico. In recent decades this model has been adopted by virtually every labor-intensive industry in the region (see, for example, Cornelius 1998). Now there is growing evidence (for example, *Migration News* 1998) that the personnel practices permitting the continued recruitment of new Mexican immigrants in the Southwest are spreading across the United States, especially within but not limited to the agricultural sector. Therefore, the agricultural sector provides the case study par excellence for the examination of immigrant labor recruitment.

Agribusiness is the largest economic sector in the United States, generating more than 150 billion dollars annually with the labor of about 2.8 million people. The agricultural sector has always required a large seasonal and migrant workforce that has few options but to accept the low wages, inadequate annual earnings, and arduous conditions characteristic of the nation's farm labor markets. Whereas the national and ethnic backgrounds of those filling these positions were once quite diverse from one regional labor market to another, today the majority of farmworkers across the United States are new immigrants from Mexico. The ability of growers to obtain Mexican immigrant workers has led to the creation of both the world's most profitable agricultural sector and the most disadvantaged class fraction of America's working poor.[9] How have an ever larger number of agribusiness firms across the United States been able to obtain Mexican labor during the past century?

The development of the Southwest depended upon the recruitment of immigrant workers from the outset. Between 1880 and 1910 the U.S. railroads recruited workers within north-central Mexico, and other labor-intensive industries such as mining and agriculture recruited both in Mexico and at the border into the 1920s. Incessant recruitment linked the men from a handful of Mexican states to specific workplaces in the United States, in the Southwest and beyond. Only the depression of the 1930s—during which at least four hundred thousand Mexicans and even Mexican American citizens of the United States were forcibly "repatriated" in violation of their basic human rights—stalled the growth of these international migrant networks.

When World War II stimulated an economic upturn, growers lobbied for the reactivation of the migrant networks from Mexico. In response, the U.S. government established official recruitment centers in Mexico to import hundreds of thousands of men annually, creating an army of contract workers for agribusiness in the Southwest in the midtwentieth century even though the importation of contract labor had been outlawed in 1885. The ready availability of foreign contract workers forced thousands of families of Mexican origin already settled in the

Southwest to migrate farther north in search of seasonal jobs. The dual migration system that resulted supplied much of the western United States with low-cost farm labor, resuscitating preexisting international networks and increasing socioeconomic integration between ever expanding portions of Mexico and the United States into the 1960s.

In the face of the conspicuous recruitment of millions of Mexican workers by U.S. industries and the government between the 1880s and the mid-1960s the immigration literature has dismissed the continued importance of recruitment in the contemporary era. Douglas Massey and his colleagues (1987, 40–44, 302) follow Alejandro Portes and Robert L. Bach (1985, 5–7) in stating that international migrant networks have become self-sustaining. However, this conventional wisdom neglects three modern realities. First, the formal activities of highly visible institutions have been transferred to individuals who continue to engage in labor recruitment activities. Second, the increasing costs and risks of unauthorized entry and employment make the services of intermediaries particularly important today, when the deteriorating Mexican economy leaves would-be migrants without sufficient resources to finance the journey north themselves. Third, the new sending regions of Mexico and receiving regions of the United States have only undergone socioeconomic integration in the past few decades, long after the formal recruitment program had been terminated. This chapter presents documentation of these three realities in a set of case studies of the contemporary agricultural sector in the United States.

I used ethnographic methods to answer the following question: How have a growing number of farm employers across wider portions of the United States obtained new immigrant workers since the demise of the contract labor program and a shift in federal policy against undocumented immigration? I found that labor recruitment is still critical for labor-intensive industries, such as agriculture, that demand an ample supply of new immigrant workers. Although new workers are recruited in a number of ways, there are two common alternative personnel practices. Many employers encourage supervisory personnel to recruit new workers as needed, and others pay fees to farm labor contracting firms (FLCs) to provide growers with their seasonal labor. My research includes data on both practices, so that the importance of labor recruitment can be assessed regardless of the strategy used by individual employers.

The Research Sample

I conducted intensive fieldwork within three labor-intensive crop industries in California and Washington state, collecting data from a representative sample of twenty-four firms. I also compiled regional and community data in both the United States and Mexico to examine the development of the international migrant networks that are used by labor recruiters to provide these industries with workers.[10]

I interviewed an owner, manager, or delegated representative from each firm in the sample. These meetings typically involved detailed discussions regarding the history and contemporary situation for each company, as well as a tour of the production facilities. The firm representatives also help me to identify and obtain subsequent interviews with one recruitment agent at each firm (or at an FLC firm used by the grower). I also met with between three and eight workers at each company employing seasonal workers. My principal aim in all of these interviews was to identify the personnel practices and labor recruitment activities within each firm. My data were compiled from these interviews, meetings with other family and community members, and participant-observation in various events encountered during an extended period of field research in both the labor-sending and labor-receiving nations.

The firm sample was not random; rather, it was shaped to provide proportional representation of the types of companies found in the three regional industries. Three types of firm diversity were considered to determine the total sample: the two alternative personnel practices (direct versus contract employees); firm ownership types (corporate, family-owned, and cooperative); and, the scale of operation (based on the size of the payrolls).

Despite my attention to diversity, all twenty-four firms that employ seasonal farm labor rely on hiring methods that differ dramatically from the classical economic model of free markets in the buying and selling of labor (see Krissman 1997). Individual workers are not hired based upon their previous experiences, schooling, or skills; indeed, there seems to be a preference for new immigrants without any on-the-job experience. Rather than advertising or using public or private employment agencies to find the most qualified workers, the representatives of these firms reported using "employee referrals," "word of mouth," and "walk-ins" to obtain most of their seasonal workers. These are usually euphemisms for the use of international migrant networks. Why do employers use networks?

Not only are new workers prescreened by current employees, but employers can expect that once hired, they also will be trained and supervised by the employees that refer them to the firm. Employers know that new hires are beholden to the referring employees and therefore under considerable pressure to justify the referral by working hard without complaint. In sum, all these firms make extensive use of the international networks of their current employees to obtain new workers as needed while maintaining a high degree of control over the social relations of production. Networks allow employers to lower their labor costs. In addition, networks are a highly efficient means of obtaining seasonal labor.

Each of the twenty-four firm representatives said that sufficient workers have been readily obtained in short order by their supervisors or FLCs year after year; however, most expressed concern for the future in the event that tougher immigration enforcement is implemented. Although all the employers acknowledged the critical importance of seasonal and migrant labor to the productive process, nineteen of the twenty-four firm representatives claimed not even to know the specifics of the personnel practices at their firms. These firm representatives referred me to supervisory employees or their FLC firms for details on the methods by which the bulk of the workforce is obtained. I refer to the field supervisors, labor contractors, and their assistants mentioned by the employers as labor recruitment agents.

The recruitment agents interviewed include eleven supervisors working directly for growers, three owners (or co-owners) of FLC firms, and ten FLC firm supervisors. The average age of the labor recruiter sample is forty-one years, with the youngest twenty-nine and the oldest fifty-seven. Twenty-three are men, and all but one were born and raised—at least until their teens—in Mexico. (The recruiter born in the United States is also of Mexican origin but was born and raised in south Texas.) None are native English speakers; twenty-two are native Spanish speakers, and two speak indigenous languages (one from Oaxaca and one from Michoacan). Nineteen cannot carry on a general conversation in English, although twelve know sufficient English to discuss work tasks with English-speaking superiors. The average level of schooling is 7.3 years. However, if the U.S.-born agent is excluded, the average educational level falls to less than 5 years. Every recruitment agent worked as a seasonal farm laborer in one or more of the crop industries under study before attaining a supervisory position. The average number of years spent as a farmworker is nine (with a range of two to thirteen years), and the average number of years as a recruitment agent is twelve (with a range of two to eighteen years).

Twenty of the twenty-four recruitment agents were reported to earn supplemental income for services provided to their workers.[11] Many of the services related to recruiting or supporting the basic needs of new workers are questionable, unethical, or even illegal for one or more reasons. Furthermore, such supplemental income, obtained in cash, is unlikely to be reported as earned income for tax purposes. Indeed, a principal reason for state regulatory activity of FLC firms concerns the violation of tax laws.[12]

The most commonly reported sources of nonwage income are as follows. Fourteen labor recruiters earned interest on cash advances or loans; twelve from fees for rides to work; eleven for rent of housing and/or bedding items; nine for sales of food and/or drink at work and seven from sales of food or drink where workers are housed; and, seven from fees to cash payroll checks. In addition, several services provided to workers by others may also provide recruitment agents with income. Agents commonly refer new immigrant workers to the people who sell false work papers; other entrepreneurs operate mobile gambling, drinking, or prostitution services, which typically appear on payday at the locations where single male workers are housed by recruiters or their employers.

Services are usually provided by labor recruiters at highly inflated prices. Obligatory rides to work cost from three to five dollars daily per worker. Food and drink are sold at profit margins of between 33 and 100 percent. Garage, shed, or trailer spaces are often rented out to groups of workers as sleeping spaces, at a minimum charge of fifteen dollars per person weekly. Bedding, space heaters, and other essentials come at additional cost. Checks are commonly cashed for a fee of between 3 and 10 percent of net value. When the services are provided on credit, interest rates of 20 to 30 percent monthly are typically charged. Many new immigrants are dependent upon these services. Nonetheless, the large deductions from their paychecks are a principal source of job dissatisfaction, which is reflected in employee turnover rates averaging 65 percent annually.

Owing to high turnover, labor recruiters rely on familial and community contacts to maintain the size of their workforce. All twenty-four agents have immediate family members on the payroll (most commonly spouses, siblings, children, and parents, in that order). The average number of immediate family workers is seven, with a range from two to seventeen. If in-laws and other, more distant, relatives are considered, these figures rise, on average, by a factor of four. Indeed, one agent claimed to have provided transportation to more than two hundred members of his kindred from a labor smuggler's "safe house" in Los Angeles to the Yakima Valley during the past decade.

Most of the workers not related to the labor recruiters are still from the same region in Mexico as their benefactors. Nineteen agents agreed that most of their subordinates were from their hometowns. Twenty-three agents said that they primarily hired workers based on personal acquaintance or the referral of current employees. Thirteen agents were reported to recruit new workers from within Mexico. Eleven admitted to transporting new immigrants to the border from the Mexican interior, and seven said they helped new workers that had crossed the border illegally to arrive at their ultimate destinations in the United States.

Finally, it is crucial to underscore the link between the subterranean activities of recruitment agents and the personnel practices of the agribusiness firms that use this labor. Twenty-two of twenty-four agents said that the most important services they provide their employers are recruitment, training, and supervision of the crews. (Most of the agricultural firm representatives, it will be recalled, claim not to know the actual process by which new workers are hired, yet they report that the supply provided is adequate to their highly seasonal needs.) Yet, despite the critical assistance the recruitment agents provide their employers, their wage earnings are substandard. Indeed, seventeen agents justified the supplemental income obtained from services to immigrants, at least in part, by mentioning the low wages or fees they earn on the job. Farm labor contractors are forced to engage in "cutthroat" competition to get contracts from growers, resulting in razor-thin profit margins. Meanwhile, year-round farm supervisors average about eight dollars an hour, a low wage in comparison with urban counterparts. The fees charged for services to the farmworkers provide the income necessary to support labor recruitment agents and their families in the United States.

The culpability of agricultural employers is further demonstrated by the unanimous testimony of twenty-four agents, all of whom began recruiting new workers in response to the requests of their employers. Indeed, seven of the thirteen FLC firms were actually founded at the behest of agribusiness firms that wished to divest themselves of direct responsibility for their workers. These firms usually sought out FLCs in response to pressure by union activists and government representatives, both of which attempt to improve some of the substandard conditions that have persisted in U.S. farm labor markets for more than a century.

The Case Studies

The pervasive and exploitative recruitment activities encouraged by the personnel practices of agribusiness firms in the western United States are revealed in the life and work histories of agribusiness representatives, labor recruitment agents, workers, and others impacted by the agricultural economy. The three agents described in this section are representative of the total sample of labor recruiters and include one from each of the crop industries studied. There is abundant evidence of the continued demand for new immigrant labor by U.S. farm employers, as well as the fundamental role labor recruitment agents play in supplying farm labor markets in the contemporary period. These accounts also document the substandard conditions endured by all new immigrant workers once they are incorporated in regional labor markets in the United States, regardless of their international migrant network affiliation.

Case One: Umberto Rodriguez

Umberto (a pseudonym), a forty-six-year-old mestizo man, came to the San Joaquin Valley in California with his family from Huanusco, Zacatecas, in northern Mexico, in the mid-1960s.[13] His father, a bracero-era worker, was among the tens of thousands of beneficiaries of a massive legalization effort that accompanied the end of the program. In 1968, at the age of sixteen, Umberto joined his parents and older siblings in the fields, harvesting a variety of crops, including table grapes. The family became members of the United Farm Workers union (the UFW) when their principal employer, a corporate subsidiary with seven hundred acres of vineyards, signed a collective bargaining agreement in 1970 after a five-year strike and product boycott. The new contract raised wages by more than 30 percent and provided previously unheard-of benefits.

Umberto became a company crew foreman in 1975 and a field supervisor in 1976. Although the company refused to renew the union contract in 1973, the UFW persisted in attempting to renegotiate an agreement. In response to the pressure of union activists, the corporate manager of the vineyard approached Umberto with a proposition—to start an FLC to provide the company with its harvest labor. As Umberto recalls, it was an offer he could not refuse. The manager helped Umberto obtain a loan to cover initial business expenses and arranged for an accountant to provide payroll and other business services.

Along with the assistance of the corporation, Umberto had his large family as an asset. The family's collective work experience enabled Umberto to fill supervisory positions for four crews. Each crew was headed by a sibling or an in-law and was supported in other key positions by spouses, parents, or other close relatives. The FLC's new workers were initially recruited from among the corporation's preexisting labor force, already made up mainly of Zacatecans. All benefits not mandated by the government were eliminated, giving the corporation total labor savings of more than 10 percent annually.

The decline of the union threat was followed by a slow but marked reduction in wages. Umberto says that increased FLC competition for contracts has forced wages down about 8 percent during the past decade. Although he claims that working conditions in his firm are better than those prevailing among his competitors, Umberto does admit to suffering turnover rates of more than 60 percent annually. He has replenished his workforce by recruiting among the residents of his native Zacatecas town (his paisanos).[14] Umberto's entire management hierarchy is from Huanusco, permitting easy and ubiquitous access to the community's migrant network. His efforts are facilitated by the fact that Zacatecan migration to the San Joaquin has become well entrenched. As Umberto's firm grew, and as management personnel left to start their own contracting firms, FLCs controlled by immigrants from Huanusco soon provided at least five thousand jobs in the valley. More paisanos are resettled in the San Joaquin than continue to reside in Huanusco, which suffered a negative 11 percent population growth rate between 1980 and 1990.

Although the already large immigrant population in the San Joaquin attracts many first-time migrants from Huanusco, Umberto's firm also influences migration decisions. Umberto has strengthened his position in the town through the elaboration of symmetrical ties within his kindred and hometown philanthropy. For hard work and complete loyalty while an FLC supervisor, Umberto eventually rewarded two of his brothers by helping them to set up their own contracting operations. Meanwhile, Umberto is a founding member of a social club that engages in a number of small projects in Huanusco, including providing a monthly stipend of twenty dollars to about a dozen destitute individuals. Umberto is also among the expatriate elite whose names are emblazoned on plaques commemorating donors to the community's revitalization fund. Umberto's parents sponsor both a public Christmas party (a posada) and part of a special Christmas mass in Mexico. Both sponsorships are bestowed by the priest in return for financial support to the parish.

While Umberto focuses upon symmetrical relations and philanthropy, his large family of FLC management agents strengthen asymmetrical relations with potential immigrants. Many serve as godparents (compadres), providing financial sponsorship for the material expenses that families incur in baptisms, quinciñeras, and marriages. Furthermore, Umberto's in-laws own a general store where would-be migrants apply for FLC jobs as well as arrange the cash loans needed to make the journey north for the summer grape harvest. The store's loans, provided at an interest rate of 30 percent monthly, ensure that migration is within the reach of virtually any able-bodied adult in Huanusco and also serve as a principal recruiting tool for Umberto's FLC.

During the 1990 summer harvest I canvassed two of Umberto's work crews in the vineyards. Each crew was a "family," and each foreman a paterfamilias, while the foremen, in turn, are closely related to Umberto. Paisanos filled every position in both forty-odd-member crews. When I questioned the dominance of the Zacatecans, Umberto replied that "his people" train paisano newcomers at no cost to him, "cause no trouble," and have a special talent for harvesting table grapes. Each vine row had a core picker and packer team (equipo), almost all of whom were young people between the ages of about eighteen and thirty.

Most of the teams were composed of close kin—a husband and wife, siblings, or first cousins (primo hermanos). In addition, in many rows elderly and preteen relatives augmented the labor of the core team.

Evidence for both symmetrical and asymmetrical relations were habitually displayed within the FLC. When Umberto came by to check on harvest progress, he was greeted as "don" or "patron" (sir) by the workers, whereas foremen hailed Umberto more familiarly as "hermano" (brother), "tio" (uncle), or "compadre." In a similar fashion, foremen were referred to by crew workers in familial terms or as compadres. Within each level of the hierarchy symmetrical relations were more pronounced. Evidence of symmetrical relations among workers and within the supervisory strata include low- or no-interest loans, mutual aid, and cooperative exchanges of labor and other resources throughout the year.

Case Two: Refugio Lopez

Refugio (a pseudonym), a forty-five-year-old indigenous Mixtec man, is a longtime worker in the San Joaquin Valley's citrus industry and a recruitment agent for an FLC. During the past twenty years he has moved up the farm job ladder from field harvester to foreman.

Refugio was raised in a remote hamlet near Tecomaxtlahuaca (known by its diminutive, *Teco*) in the southern Mexican state of Oaxaca.[15] Refugio worked from the age of seven to provide for himself (as well as to help support his mother and her two other children). He began earning his living by shepherding goats for a childless village couple, but at the age of twelve Refugio joined the hundreds of thousands migrating from the Mixteca, leaving Teco first to labor in a Mexico City tortilla-producing plant for four years before working in the American-controlled agribusiness sector, first on a northern Mexico tomato plantation, until he was recruited to work in California.

In 1981, at the age of twenty-nine, Refugio settled in the San Joaquin Valley with his common-law wife, two of her brothers, and a family of paisanos. Another paisano on a citrus harvest crew provided them with employment. The firm, one division of a conglomerate, controls more than ten thousand acres of navel oranges in the region. However, the firm divested itself of both its field labor and trucking operations as a result of labor-organizing activities in 1983. The company encouraged key supervisory personnel within these two divisions to become independent entrepreneurs, providing harvest labor and transport services under contract to the firm.

Refugio was recruited into a new harvesting FLC through his foreman. The FLC offered the same piece-rate wage of ten dollars per thousand-pound bin but annulled previously negotiated (non-government-mandated) benefits. Worker complaints about lost benefits were met with selective discharges. Meanwhile, the piece rate remained static in the intervening eleven years, thereby declining more than 20 percent in relation to the rising cost of living. The deterioration of workplace conditions has ensured high employee turnover and led to a recurrent need to replenish the crews. Refugio has obliged his foreman by recruiting paisanos from Teco.

By assisting the foreman Refugio benefited in three ways. He enhanced his status within the Oaxacan expatriate community as a labor broker. He was awarded a "raitero" franchise (transporting seven to ten workers in his van each day at three dollars per person), increasing his earnings by 60 percent. Finally, he was promoted to the less arduous task of forklift operator. With this change in status Refugio agreed to increase his recruitment activities for the foreman. He says that this was not a problem, because he had been reinforcing preexisting ties to his migrant network. He has provided a "safe house" to scores of paisanos passing through in search of work along the wide-ranging Pacific migration circuit. Furthermore, he has remained a member in good standing in his home community. In 1987 Refugio received residency documents, legalizing his status as a U.S. worker and allowing him to make periodic return visits to Oaxaca without fear of problems on reentering the United States.

In Teco, Refugio purchased a house, officially married, and distributed gifts from California. He also expanded his godparent relations, participating in many of the celebrations that visiting migrants indulge in during visits home. With his new van, well-fed and well-dressed family, and fat billfold, Refugio serves as yet another local example of the benefits of international migration relative to the endemic poverty of the Mixteca. Refugio also passes on information about living and working conditions in California to villagers who may be considering a trip to the United States and makes loans to those who cannot afford to self-finance their migration.

On trips back up north, Refugio often ferries new migrants in his van. At the border he knows a labor smuggler (a "coyote") who will assist the undocumented across and reunite them with Refugio in San Diego. In addition, he has driven from his San Joaquin Valley home to the border in response to collect calls from migrants needing rides north. Indebted migrants stay with Refugio until transportation, housing, and meal expenses have been paid off through payroll deductions at an interest rate of 20 to 30 percent a month. The size of Refugio's household during the winter-to-spring citrus harvest season averages about twenty-two adults and five children lodged in various rooms within the house as well as in several other shelters erected on the lot.

In 1991, Refugio was elevated to foreman status by his patron, who began his own FLC. Refugio asserts that as a foreman he is working harder and longer hours than ever before. He stresses the difficult responsibility a foreman has to satisfy the grower and the FLC owner, on the one hand, and his crew members, on the other. He says that workers can exert considerable influence on him to provide reasonable wages and decent working and living conditions. After all, these are his paisanos, even family members, not mere strangers.

Perhaps in part because of this tension, Refugio is often critical of the FLC owner, remarking that the patron earns too much money. Refugio has recited a litany of the material possessions that the FLC owner has accumulated, including a restaurant (and two catering trucks that sell the restaurant's food to farmworkers in the orchards), several houses, and ostentatiously equipped four-wheel-drive vehicles that the owner and other family members use to supervise the six harvest crews. However, Refugio has also displayed new wealth as a result of becoming an FLC agent. In 1990 he purchased an acre parcel with a ramshackle four-bedroom house and a number of outbuildings, where the constant flow of paisanos passing through can be more easily accommodated. He has also purchased a large van, which permits Refugio to carry fifteen crew members to the field each day at three dollars per head.

Case Three: Lorenzo Ramirez

Lorenzo (a pseudonym), a forty-four-year-old mestizo man, is an orchard manager who oversees two crews for an intermediate-sized apple operation in Yakima Valley, Washington. Reared in Pajacuaran, Michoacan, in central Mexico,[16] he migrated to the United States, at the age of seventeen, in 1970. Lorenzo joined his father in Salinas, California, where they harvested lettuce and other vegetables.

In 1975 the agribusiness firm was organized by the UFW, raising wages more than 40 percent and instituting benefits, including a seniority system that helped guarantee jobs for older farmworkers such as Lorenzo's father in spite of their reduced productivity. However, in 1979 the firm decertified the union and abolished the seniority system. The following year his father retired to Pajacuaran, and Lorenzo migrated north to the Yakima Valley. Lorenzo's new employer offered him free housing in an orchard and helped him regularize his residency status. Within a year, five other disgruntled Salinas workers followed Lorenzo north.

The grower is a farm equipment retailer who has purchased about 250 acres of apple orchards bit by bit, primarily from clients who either retired or went bankrupt. Lorenzo claims that the owner's interest in the orchards is limited to obtaining tax breaks that reduce his total liabilities. Lorenzo says that he rose to the position of field supervisor in five years, becoming "both a general and private." The owner provided Lorenzo with a salary, a larger cottage, a company truck, and a simple mandate—to keep production costs low.

Lorenzo was promoted in 1986, when the U.S. government was preparing to award residency papers to millions of "illegal aliens" under the Immigration Reform and Control Act (IRCA). His employer, fearful that the implementation of new border controls and paperwork provisions might lead to a labor shortage, paid Lorenzo to recruit new workers in Michoacan. During his hometown visit, Lorenzo provided at least thirty paisanos with papers certifying that they had already worked at least ninety days picking apples, allowing them to qualify for the residency program. However, Lorenzo admits that few had ever been as far north as Yakima, and some had never been to the United States before. Several paisanos claim that Lorenzo actually sold the certification papers for up to five hundred dollars each. If true, Lorenzo, and perhaps his employer, may have earned more than ten thousand dollars from the sale of these letters.

The paisanos came to Yakima in 1987 as instructed, only to find the apple harvest delayed owing to unseasonable weather. Without adequate funds to support themselves, these men wanted help to purchase necessities. Lorenzo says that the grower refused to advance wages because of uncertainty about the harvest. The paisanos began agitating for compensation for their long wait. The employer became edgy, making Lorenzo worry about retaining his own post. In the end Lorenzo did not hire eighteen of the paisanos, even when the harvest finally did begin. Although he claims that many owed him money for cash advances, Lorenzo says that he no longer had confidence ("confianza") in these workers.

The Washington State Apple Commission had also responded to growers' fears concerning the IRCA by unleashing an unprecedented advertising campaign in California during 1987 to lure farmworkers northward. When the harvest was delayed the result was an industry-made disaster for the stranded workforce. (In 1992, the Apple Commission finally settled a class-action lawsuit brought on behalf of destitute workers for more than six hundred thousand dollars). Nonetheless, the unemployment crisis proved a boon for Lorenzo's employer. One of his forklift operators, an indigenous worker from the Purepecha Plateau of central Michoacan, recruited replacement workers from among paisanos who had come to the San Joaquin Valley from California in response to the advertising campaign. The indigenous men bunked up six to a cabin until Lorenzo's paisanos moved on in search of work elsewhere. Lorenzo still employs ten workers from Pajacuaran, but seven are close kin. Lorenzo has since delegated responsibility for obtaining the bulk of his seasonal workforce to the machine operator, insulating himself from both his employer and his workers.

Lorenzo admits that the current situation for apple workers is poor. Wages have been stagnant for more than a decade, the cabins have deteriorated as a result of age and high occupancy rates, work crews have been expanded, and total work hours per season have declined. Lorenzo says that even he is not paid very well, estimating that his annual salary of eighteen thousand dollars breaks down to about seven dollars an hour. Although his family lives in an orchard cottage and he has a ranch pickup truck at his disposal, Lorenzo says that his standard of living has declined since coming to Washington. In addition, his wife does not like the isolation of their rural home, far from neighbors, stores, and other conveniences.

However, the isolation of living in the orchard has provided some economic advantages. Workers must rely on Lorenzo to ferry them to town to cash their checks and pick up basic supplies. Between trips the workers have to pay top dollar to buy necessities that Lorenzo has stockpiled. The convenience store owner deducts 5 percent of net pay from each worker's paycheck, but Lorenzo prefers to use this store because the owner gives him a six-pack of beer for each check cashed by a worker. Back at the orchard, Lorenzo puts the beer cans on ice and sells them back to the workers for a dollar a pop.

Conclusion

A labor system of not very benign neglect has been erected in the agricultural sector in the United States, permitting agribusiness firms to maintain access to a low-cost immigrant workforce despite popular opinion or public policy. A combination of the personnel practices of these firms and the activities of their recruitment agents have created and sustained an ever expanding number of new international migrant networks between Mexico and the United States.

In the first case study, the mestizo owner of a large-scale FLC firm is generally above the face-to-face provisioning of "services for indenture." Instead, Umberto, a member of a well-entrenched international migrant network linking a town in northern Mexico with grape growers in rural California, cultivates symmetrical relations (viewed as positive social capital) among the agents that recruit for his firm and engages in hometown philanthropy to maintain his status as a paisano. In turn, a score of his agents elaborate asymmetrical relations (considered negative social capital) with their workers as well as with would-be migrants in their hometown, who may enter this network to earn U.S. wages.

The asymmetrical relations elaborated between recruitment agents and new workers are underscored in the second and third case studies. Refugio is a new foreman from the Mixteca, a region in southern Mexico inhabited by indigenous peoples. He must engage in constant recruitment activities to maintain his crew in the face of high turnover rates. Periodic trips home, labor-smuggling activities, and the provision of loans and services are all necessary to secure sufficient low-cost labor. Although Mixtec adults have long migrated within Mexico to support their families, this region has only recently been linked to international labor markets as a result of the efforts of U.S. agribusiness recruiters. However, because the pay is so poor and the working and living conditions so harsh in California's citrus industry, new migrants must be constantly recruited from home to replace those that abandon the FLC after paying off their debts. One result of this process is that the bulk of Refugio's total income is derived not from his labor in the orchards but from the fees and interest he charges new immigrant workers for his services.

Lorenzo, a mestizo immigrant from central Mexico, is now a field supervisor in the Pacific Northwest. Although he works directly for his Anglo employer, Lorenzo is responsible for maintaining an adequate supply of apple harvesters. He must offer free grower-provided housing to lure workers to this distant and isolated area. Nonetheless, he has found ways of obtaining supplemental income. Although he does not write up the payroll, Lorenzo is able to tap his workers' wages when they cash their checks. Lorenzo sells basic necessities at highly inflated prices, and he may have profited inordinately from the hysteria whipped up by the IRCA, selling fraudulent letters certifying previous employment in the United States. Finally, he has passed on most recruitment responsibilities to a machine operator who taps his own network, based in the indigenous Purepecha Plateau of Michoacan.

By passing on recruitment responsibilities to a subordinate, Lorenzo has insulated himself from direct ties to, or complete responsibility for, the workforce. On one hand, the international network of indigenous workers is too new to provide better alternative employment options, forcing them to be more accommodating than Lorenzo's own mestizo paisanos. On the other hand, the orchard owner can be deflected from criticizing Lorenzo for any actions these workers might undertake. Meanwhile, the indigenous labor recruiter has cemented his relations with both Lorenzo and his employer by providing recruitment services, strengthening the links between his hometown in Mexico and jobs in the Pacific Northwest even as he becomes another cog in the system of labor recruitment.

These data underscore four points of particular relevance to U.S. immigration policy. First, my study demonstrates that the continued development of international migrant networks is inextricably linked to the demand for immigrant workers. My own research was informed by analyses of the regional demand for low-cost labor, as well as macro data demonstrating the increasing use of immigrant workers in a variety of labor-intensive industries across the United States.

I found that agribusiness employers have purposefully adopted new personnel practices during the past few decades to evade government regulation and inhibit unionization. The new agribusiness personnel strategies shift hiring decisions to their most trusted Mexican employees or to nominally independent contractor firms, fostering the creation and expansion of international migrant networks. These labor recruitment agents place large numbers of their family members and friends in jobs so that they can tap both the positive and negative social capital available within their networks. However, the actual mechanisms of job placement for family and paisanos have been given little attention in the literature on immigration, networks, or labor markets.

Until now, studies of immigrant-dominated labor markets have been replete with euphemisms such as "word-of-mouth," "worker referrals," and "walk-ins," and the network literature refers to immigration "pioneers," enclave "anchors," and employment "brokers." These catchphrases describe personnel practices and network development vaguely, implicitly acceding to the point of view of employers and recruiters, which is that they are bystanders in processes they neither cause nor have control over. The use of these euphemisms contributes little to an understanding of how and why an increasing number of labor-intensive industries are dominated by new immigrant workers, nor do they indicate how and why international migrant networks are spreading across both the United States and Mexico in the absence of formal recruitment activities. Indeed, this mystification of the actual social relations of production has led to the inaccurate conclusion in the immigration literature that recruitment is no longer an important factor in the continuing flow of undocumented migrants into the United States.

The second point of relevance involves methods. The ethnographic approach provided here highlights the micro-organizational processes that are largely absent from macro analyses of international migration. These processes include the shifting of responsibility for the workforce from the personnel departments to field supervisors or independent FLCs; the continued recruitment of new immigrant workers to maintain the size of work crews in the face of high employee turnover rates; and the services provided by labor recruiters to new immigrant workers for fees deducted from wages. Only in-depth research is likely to bring to light the importance of these subterranean practices to supplying immigrant-dominated labor markets, thereby demonstrating the importance of the continued recruitment of new immigrants in the contemporary era.

Third, this study reveals how agribusiness personnel practices help divide the workforce. Over the past century growers have constantly shifted among potential employees, pitting one group of farmworkers against the other. In the current period recruitment agents typically obtain most of their workers from within their own home region in Mexico. As more farmworkers (including indigenous Mexicans) advance to the supervisory roles that require active recruitment activities, a labor force often thought of as homogenous is actually becoming more diverse. Although all these workers are Mexican citizens, they vary by region of origin, ethnicity, and native speech. This diversity has created significant cleavages within regional farm labor markets, with important ramifications for both labor activists and institutions in rural towns across the United States. The personnel practices pursued by agribusiness firms have ensured that undocumented migration has spread over time from a handful of Mexican states to the dozen or more that are important today. These personnel practices have maintained longtime, and created new, international migrant networks over the decades. The lack of workplace regulatory activities by the federal government allows the continuation of the abuses systemic to immigrant-dominated labor markets, encouraging ever more employers to tap international migrant networks to obtain an ample supply of low-cost labor.

Finally, this study documents the strong and ever expanding linkages between rural Mexico and farm labor markets across the United States, underscoring the role of socioeconomic integration in shaping migrant flows. The historical development of international migration from each Mexican state occurred during a different period, under distinctive socioeconomic conditions within that state, as well as between that state and the regions in the United States to which out-migrants have increasingly directed their migratory efforts. In each case recruitment activities have clearly been critical in creating and maintaining such far-flung international migrant networks. A myopic and largely self-serving focus on supply-side factors will continue to waste public resources, increase the death toll along a highly militarized international border, and stimulate periodic efforts by political opportunists to blame the victims of this system of indentured servitude. Only when public policy comes to grips with the demand side of the immigration equation can legislation be fashioned and regulatory regimes be implemented that lead to effective and humane outcomes. To lead the media and policy makers in this direction, academic research must focus on the link between the informal labor recruitment activities promoted by the personnel practices of labor-intensive sectors of the nation's economy and the continued flow of new migrants into the United States.

Notes

1. Although poverty is one of a number of factors that may contribute to an individual would-be migrant's decision-making process, poverty is not the precipitating or perpetuating factor for large-scale immigrant flows. Our preoccupation with poverty is confounded by a number of facts. First, most nations are considerably more impoverished than Mexico (*UNICEF* 1989), yet the majority have much lower rates of emigration (*UNFPA* 1993). Second, most impoverished people—including rural Mexicans—live their entire lives and die within a few kilometers of their place of birth, never having migrated anywhere (Martin 1994, 48). Third, emigration from Mexico typically begins with the members of families in the middle stratum of the local economy (Massey, Goldring, and Durand 1994), primarily from a dozen states (Cornelius 1993), most of which are not among the nation's poorest. Fourth, many Mexicans migrate to the United States even though they were gainfully employed at home (see, for example, Chavez 1992, 24). Fifth, many immigrants come to the United States not because they were impoverished in their homelands but, rather, because their expectations for upward mobility appear difficult to achieve in their homelands (Portes and Rumbaut 1990). Sixth, the high cost of undocumented immigration to the United States, estimated at more than four thousand dollars in the late 1990s, is well beyond the reach of most rural Mexicans unless someone else—often a labor recruiter—loans them the money to make the trip.

2. Western Europe, southern Africa, Japan, and the United States provide examples of advanced industrial nations, within which many employers prefer new immigrant workers, especially the undocumented, who must overcome a greater number of structural barriers to fight substandard workplace and living conditions (Cornelius 1998; West and Moore 1989; Cockcroft 1986; Burawoy 1981; Castells 1977).

3. See Cornelius, Martin, and Hollifield (1994); Guerin-Gonzales and Strikwerda (1993), and Sassen (1988) for instances of labor recruitment in various historical, national, and international contexts.

4. See Hutchinson (1981, 438); Benton (1985, 51, 54); Cheng and Bonacich (1984); and Cardoso (1980) on the use of contract labor from three continents in the United States during the nineteenth century; for the twentieth century, see Galarza (1964).

5. For example, throughout the nineteenth century, U.S. industrialists recruited skilled labor from northern Europe and unskilled labor from southern and eastern Europe (Cummings 1980, 9).

6. See Waldinger (1996) for an elaborate description of both ethnic labor markets and communities in New York City. See Portes and Bach (1985, chapter 7) regarding Mexican incorporation into U.S. labor markets.

7. The literature on network development is voluminous and covers both internal (for example, Hirabayashi 1993) and international (for example, Massey et al. 1987) migration.

8. See Wells (1996, chapter 5) and Krissman (1997, 218, 219) for the limits on the control employers can exert over workers via international migrant networks.

9. See Griffith and Kissam (1995) and Heppel and Amendola (1992) regarding the shift toward the use of farmworkers from Mexico across the United States. See Fix and Passel (1994, 47–54) concerning the scope of immigrant labor use throughout the U.S. economy. I have discussed the deleterious effects of labor recruitment upon entire regions of rural Mexico elsewhere (Krissman 1996, chapters 5 and 6).

10. My fieldwork with California's farmworkers was conducted from 1988 to 1992; Washington's farmworkers were studied from 1995 to 1998. The research was supported at various stages by the Social Science Research Council, the Rockefeller Foundation, the Wenner-Gren Foundation for Anthropological Research, the Center for U.S.-Mexican Studies, at the University of California, San Diego, the North-South Center, at the University of Miami, the Agricultural Personnel Management Program, at the University of California, Berkeley, and the Center for Chicano Studies, at the University of California, Santa Barbara.

11. The data were observed or provided during interviews with agribusiness representatives, recruitment agents, and the farmworkers. The latter data are used here only if obtained during at least two different interviews and are qualified as "reported" recruitment activities. Only one FLC owner, two supervisors for apple firms, and one table-grape supervisor apparently did not earn supplementary income from their workers. However, some of the supervisors working for the one FLC owner did provide such services for their crews.

12. Seven of the thirteen agricultural firms using FLCs reported that contractors they had used have been targets of federal investigations concerning tax-related violations. These violations involved payroll deductions that were neither transferred to the federal government nor claimed as earned income. Only two FLCs confirmed these reports.

13. Zacatecas is one of the top four Mexican emigration states, having sent tens of thousands of wage laborers to the United States annually since before 1900. In the 1990s an estimated half a million Zacatecans resided in California alone. Remittances from the United States provide about 80 percent of total revenues in rural Zacatecas, more than 104 million dollars annually.

14. Rural Mexicans use the term paisano ubiquitously to refer to fellow countrymen, particularly non-family members from the same town, region, or state. In the 1980s the Mexican federal government created Programa Paisano, ostensibly to promote migrant rights.

15. The Mixteca, mainly within western Oaxaca, generates more than 80 percent of its total regional revenues from remittances. Although Oaxacans began to migrate to the United States in large numbers only during the 1970s, Oaxaca is now among Mexico's top ten labor-sending states, with at least 55 million dollars in remittances annually.

16. Michoacan is one of the top four Mexican emigration states, having sent tens of thousands of wage laborers to the United States annually since the 1940s. Mestizos in the western part of the state have a longer tradition of migrating than indigenous residents of the central plateau. All told, about 2 million currently reside in the United States, remitting at least 310 million dollars annually.

References

Alvarez, Robert, and George A. Collier. 1994. "The Long Haul in Mexican Trucking." *American Ethnologist* 21(3): 606–27.

Benton, Barbara. 1985. *Ellis Island*. New York: Facts on File Publications.

Burawoy, Michael. 1981. "The Functions and Reproduction of Migrant Labor." *American Journal of Sociology* 81(5): 1012–50.

Calavita, Kitty 1989. "The Immigration Policy Debate." In *Mexican Migration to the United States*, edited by Wayne A. Cornelius and Jorge Bustamante. La Jolla: Center for U.S.-Mexican Studies, University of California, San Diego.

Cardoso, Lawrence. 1980. *Mexican Emigration to the United States, 1897–1931*. Tucson: University of Arizona Press.

Castells, Manuel. 1977. "Immigrant Workers and Class Struggles in Advanced Capitalism." In *Peasants and Proletarians*, edited by Robin Cohen, Peter C. W. Gutkind, and Phyllis Brazier. London: Monthly Review Press.

Chavez, Leo. 1992. *Shadowed Lives*. Fort Worth, Tex.: Harcourt Brace College Publishers.

Cheng, Lucy, and Edna Bonacich. 1984. *Labor Immigration Under Capitalism.* Berkeley: University of California Press.

Cockcroft, James D. 1986. *Outlaws in the Promised Land.* New York: Grove Press.

Cornelius, Wayne A. 1993. "Mexican Immigrants in California Today." In *Immigration and Entrepreneurship,* edited by Ivan Light. New Brunswick: Transaction Publishers.

———. 1998. "The Role of Immigrant Labor in the U.S. and Japanese Economies." Unpublished report to the Irvine Foundation.

Cornelius, Wayne A., Philip L. Martin, and James F. Hollifield. 1994. *Controlling Immigration.* Stanford: Stanford University Press.

Cummings, Scott. 1980. *Self-help in Urban America.* New York: Kennikat Press.

Dunn, Timothy J. 1996. *The Militarization of the United States–Mexico Border, 1978–1992.* Austin, Tex.: Center for Mexican American Studies.

Fix, Michael, and Jeffrey Passel. 1994. *Immigration and Immigrants.* Washington, D.C.: Urban Institute.

Galarza, Ernesto. 1964. *Merchants of Labor.* Santa Barbara, Calif.: McNally and Loftin.

Griffith, David, and Ed Kissam. 1995. *Working Poor: Farmworkers in the United States.* Philadelphia: Temple University Press.

Guerin-Gonzales, Camille, and Carl Strikwerda. 1993. *The Politics of Immigrant Workers.* New York: Holmes and Meier.

Heppel, Monica L., and Sandra L. Amendola. 1992. *Immigration Reform and Perishable Crop Agriculture.* New York: University Press of America.

Hirabayashi, Lane. 1993. *Cultural Capital.* Tucson: University of Arizona Press.

Hoffman, Abraham. 1974. *Unwanted Mexican Americans in the Great Depression.* Tucson: University of Arizona Press.

Hutchinson, Edward P. 1981. *Legislative History of American Immigration Policy, 1798–1965.* Philadelphia: University of Pennsylvania Press.

Krissman, Fred. 1996. "Californian Agribusiness and Mexican Farm Workers (1942–1992)." Ph.D. diss., University of California, Santa Barbara.

———. 1997. "California's Agricultural Labor Markets." In *Free and Unfree Labour,* edited by Tom Brass and Marcel van der Linden. Berne: Peter Lang.

Lomnitz, Larissa. 1982. "Horizontal and Vertical Relations and the Social Structure of Urban Mexico." *Latin American Research Review* 17(2): 51–74.

Martin, Philip L. 1994. "Commentary." In *California Immigration.* Sacramento: California Research Bureau.

Massey, Douglas, Rafael Alarcón, Jorge Durand, and Humberto Gonzalez. 1987. *Return to Aztlan.* Berkeley: University of California Press.

Massey, Douglas, Luin Goldring, and Jorge Durand. 1994. "Continuities in Transnational Migration." *American Journal of Sociology* 99(6): 1492–1533.

Migration News. 1998. Downloaded from the world wide web at: http://www.migration.ucdavis.edu.

Portes, Alejandro 1998. "Social Capital." *Annual Review of Sociology* 24: 1–24.

Portes, Alejandro, and Robert Bach. 1985. *Latin Journey*. Berkeley: University of California Press.

Portes, Alejandro, and Rubén G. Rumbaut. 1990. *Immigrant America*. Berkeley: University of California Press.

Sassen, Saskia. 1988. *Mobility of Labor and Capital*. Cambridge: Cambridge University Press.

United Nations Population Fund (UNFPA). 1993. *The Individual and the World*. New York: United Nations.

United Nations Children's Fund (UNICEF). 1989. *The State of the World's Children*. New York: United Nations.

Waldinger, Roger. 1996. *Still the Promised City?* Cambridge: Harvard University Press.

Wells, Miriam J. 1996. *Strawberry Fields*. Ithaca: Cornell University Press.

West, Michael, and Erin Moore. 1989. "Undocumented Workers in the United States and South Africa." *Human Organization* 48(1): 1–10.

12

SKILLED IMMIGRANTS AND CEREBREROS: FOREIGN-BORN ENGINEERS AND SCIENTISTS IN THE HIGH-TECHNOLOGY INDUSTRY OF SILICON VALLEY

Rafael Alarcón

Hewlett-Packard Laboratories, located in the core of Silicon Valley, has been the prime research unit of Hewlett-Packard for three decades. Researchers at HP Labs have developed such innovative products as inkjet printers, cardiac ultrasound imaging, scientific calculators, and telecommunications software. HP Labs has stretched its global reach from its research and development headquarters in Silicon Valley to include locations in Bristol, England; Tokyo, Japan; and Haifa, Israel. However, globalization has also a local expression at the Palo Alto site. Most names posted on the doors of the researchers' cubicles would seem "foreign" to some people visiting the facility.

The arrival of a large number of skilled migrants during the early 1990s gave rise to a heated debate over their impact on the U.S. workforce. Because many of the highly skilled migrants are employed by high-technology firms, the debate focused on this industry. In the first months of 1996, former senator Alan Simpson attempted to reduce the number of skilled migrants allowed to enter the United States each year, arguing that these migrants take jobs away from U.S. citizens and lawful permanent residents.

In his attempt to curb the immigration of highly skilled migrants, Simpson proposed to reduce the number of employment-based visas and to impose a fee on companies that hire skilled workers from abroad. Simpson accused high-technology companies of bringing in highly skilled migrants on temporary visas, paying them one-third less than the going rate for U.S. workers, and offering the incentive for obtaining green cards (certification of legal permanent residency) in the future (*Wall Street Journal*, "Immigrant Engineers," March 4, 1996). In the same vein, former labor secretary Robert Reich alleged that some companies misuse temporary migration programs, such as the H-1B, by laying off workers to hire foreigners. According to the Immigration and Nationality Act of 1990, the H-1B nonimmigrant visa program is designed for temporary workers employed in "specialty occupations" that require highly specialized knowledge and at least a bachelor's degree or its equivalent. Reich cited the example of Syntel, a Michigan-based software consulting service that is run by natives of India and whose labor force is mainly composed of H-1B workers. According to Reich, the New York insurance company American International Group laid off 250 computer programmers and hired Syntel to provide programming services in September of 1994 (Schibsted 1995).

Against this perspective, high-tech entrepreneurs from Bill Gates, chairman of Microsoft, to owners of small start-up companies contend that immigrants are a key factor in the industry's impressive growth. A cadre of CEOs and managers maintain that because their companies are competing in a global economy they need to have access to the best and brightest workers of the world. For example, T. J. Rodgers, president and CEO of Cypress Semiconductor Corporation, a Silicon Valley company, notes that immigrants hold a disproportionate number of research-and-development (R&D) jobs at Cypress. He argues that each R&D job creates nine additional jobs and that eliminating the immigrants would result in a loss of 720 jobs at Cypress, most of which are held by native-born Americans. According to Rodgers, four out of ten of his senior vice presidents are foreign born, as are two of Cypress's four outside directors. He also mentions that José Arreola, a Mexican immigrant with a doctorate in transistor physics, is Cypress's top scientist (McLaughlin 1997).

I use the term "skilled immigrants" to refer to the engineers and scientists who are permanent residents or naturalized citizens and are employed by high-tech companies. "Cerebreros" are the same professionals who hold temporary visas like the H-1B. These workers are also known as "high-tech braceros." I prefer to call them "cerebreros" because, unlike Mexican braceros in the past, who worked with their arms (brazos) with temporary contracts, cerebreros work with their brains (cerebros) on a temporary basis.[1]

This chapter examines the integration of foreign-born engineers and scientists in the high-technology industry of Silicon Valley, located in the San Francisco Bay area. By studying the migration experiences of these workers and the recruitment practices implemented by high-tech companies, I seek to investigate the many legal vectors skilled migrants use to enter the United States. The study focuses on the experiences of immigrant groups from two developing countries: India and Mexico.

U.S. immigration policy and geographical location have created completely different migration processes originating in the two countries. India provides the United States with the largest number of highly educated immigrants, and Mexico is the source of the largest number of unskilled workers and of a small but growing number of engineers and scientists. Ironically, India has a very high illiteracy rate, higher than that of Mexico (see table 12.1). It also is a much poorer country than Mexico and still has a dominant agrarian economy, with a gross national product (GNP) per capita ten times lower than that of Mexico and seventy-nine times lower than that of the United States (World Bank 1997).

There are also important similarities between India and Mexico. After a long period of import substitution, the two countries began liberalizing their economies in the mid-1980s. In the 1990s, India became a global producer of software, and some Mexican cities have solidified their role as preferred locations for in-bond manufacturing in the electronics industry, a role that now, under the North American Free Trade Agreement (NAFTA), is expanding.

The data used in this analysis come mainly from twenty case studies of engineers and scientists from Mexico and India (ten from each country). Most of these engineers and scientists are employed by three major

TABLE 12.1   *Economic Development Indicators for Mexico, India, and the United States*

Indicator	Mexico	India	United States
Total population in 1996 (millions)	93	945	265
Average annual population growth from 1980 to 1996 (%)	2.1	2.0	1.0
Life expectancy at birth in 1995 (years)	72	62	77
Females in labor force in 1995 (%)	31	32	46
Labor force in agriculture in 1990 (%)	28	64	3
Labor force in industry in 1990 (%)	24	16	28
Average annual growth of GDP from 1990 to 1996 (%)	1.8	5.8	2.4
GNP per capita in 1995 (dollars)	3,320	340	26,980
Population living on less than $1 a day from 1981 to 1995 (%)	14.9	52.5	0
Female adult illiteracy in 1995 (%)	13	62	> 5
Male adult illiteracy in 1995 (%)	8	35	> 5

Source: World Bank 1997.

Silicon Valley corporations. The names used to refer to these professionals and to their current employers are fictitious, to keep the identity of respondents confidential. I use the Public Use Microdata Samples (PUMS) of the 1990 Census of Population and Housing to analyze the demographic and employment characteristics of these workers. The PUMS used in this chapter contain records representing 5 percent of the housing units and their occupants (U.S. Department of Commerce 1992).

Both the census data and the ethnographic materials refer to engineers and scientists who are employed in the high-technology industry. These professionals are employed in occupations that are defined by the Bureau of the Census as "professional specialty occupations," including fourteen types of engineers, five types of mathematical and computer scientists, and nine types of natural scientists (U.S. Department of Commerce 1993). "High technology" refers to the industry that encompasses the following manufacturing sectors: computing and office equipment, communications equipment, electronic components, guided missiles, and space vehicles and instruments. From the service industry, it also includes the software and data processing sector (Saxenian 1994, 209).

Skilled Migrants
in the Global Economy

Since the 1980s, immigration has been a key feature in the economic restructuring of the United States, as an unprecedented number of immigrants have entered the country. For instance, from 1982 to 1991, approximately 8.6 million immigrants were granted permanent residency, a figure approaching the highest levels of admissions that took place from 1905 to 1914, when 10.1 million immigrants were admitted into the United States (INS 1992). Most of the newcomers are low-skilled immigrants who have settled in the central cities of the most important metropolises of the United States. There is also, however, a smaller group of highly educated immigrants who have established homes in the wealthiest suburbs of many of the same metropolises.

Contemporary immigrants to the United States reflect a bifurcated pattern of educational attainment (Fix and Passel 1994; Portes and Rumbaut 1996). According to Michael Fix and Jeffrey Passel (1994), immigrants concentrate at the extremes of the educational spectrum in comparison with natives. They are much more likely than natives to have very low educational attainment, but at the same time they are more likely than natives to have advanced degrees. In 1990, 26 percent of the foreign born over the age of twenty-five had less than nine years of education, compared with only 9 percent of the native population.

Twenty percent of both natives and immigrants, on the other hand, have college degrees, and recent immigrants (24 percent) are more likely than natives to have college degrees. Most of the immigrants with less than nine years of education come from Latin America, and the most highly educated immigrants originate in Asia. In spite of this, most academic research and policy debate addresses only the low-skilled component of the process. As a result little is known about the social and economic integration of the highly skilled migrants into the United States.

The theoretical analysis of the role of skilled migrants in a global economy requires a combined examination of the mobility of capital and the mobility of labor. Although these two processes are directly related, they have been traditionally examined by different groups of analysts, who are divided by solid disciplinary borders. In general, economists, regional planners, geographers, and political scientists have focused on the aspect of the mobility of capital that has to do with industrial location. Sociologists and social anthropologists, on the other hand, have studied the movement of people searching for better job opportunities outside their regions of origin. Saskia Sassen (1988) notes that the literature on international trade and investment and on international labor migration is characterized by the absence of mutual references. This discussion seeks to redress the omission by combining labor immigration and regional development theories.

Apparently, there is a global labor market. Filipino women work as nurses in the United States. Ethnic Japanese Brazilians are employed by subcontractors of big corporations in Japan. India, with arguably the second-largest scientific community in the English-speaking world, has 140,000 scientists working abroad (Stremlau 1996). In spite of increased border enforcement, Mexican migrants, documented and undocumented, are the preferred labor force in key sectors of the food industry of the United States. It has been argued that the engineers and scientists employed in the high-technology industry are part of an international class of "symbolic analysts" who are not constrained by national borders (Reich 1992).

Manuel Castells denies the existence of a truly global labor market, on the ground that the global economy is segmented. "In other words, the global economy does not embrace all economic processes in the planet, it does not include all territories, and it does not include all people in its [workings, although] it does affect directly or indirectly the livelihood of the entire humankind" (Castells 1996, 102). In Castells' view the global economy is based on three major regions: North America, the European Union, and the Asian Pacific region. The rest of the world depends on these regions, and the different countries compete with one another to attract capital, human skills, and technology (Castells 1996). Castells concedes, however, that that there is a global labor market for the small but growing segment of professionals and scientists who are involved in innovative research and development, cutting-edge engineering, financial management, advanced business services, and entertainment.

The globalization of the high-technology industry began in the 1960s, when semiconductor manufacturers began shifting their assembly operations to Asia. In this context, the theory of the international division of labor originated to try to explain the global relocation of manufacturing. Friedrich Frobel, Jurgen Henricks, and Otto Kreye (1980) argue that because of changing market and production conditions in advanced industrial countries, multinational corporations began moving labor-intensive manufacturing to Third World countries that supplied cheap and unskilled labor. The new technologies available at the time allowed the multinational corporations to relocate production through the linking and coordinating of production by telecommunications and computers. Such relocations began to generate a world market for labor and industrial sites, as different regions in the Third World began to compete with one another to offer the best conditions for the reproduction of capital (Parthasarathy 1994).

World systems theory can be useful in understanding the migration of professionals that is caused by the relocation of manufacturing plants to developing countries. This theory builds on the work of Immanuel Wallerstein (1974) and considers international migration as a natural consequence of economic globalization and market penetration across national boundaries. In this sense, the international movement of labor generally follows the movement of goods and capital in the opposite direction (Massey et al. 1994). In this vein, Sassen (1990) contends that international migration to the United States often follows previous flows of U.S. investment, military actions, or the implementation of U.S. foreign policies. World systems theory suggests that direct investment by U.S. high-technology companies establishing manufacturing plants in developing countries inadvertently creates the conditions for the future migration to the United States of local engineers and scientists. These professionals, who obtain specific training and work under the discipline of the U.S. labor system, also learn about better employment opportunities in the parent company in the United States through daily contact with U.S. managers and co-workers.

According to the social capital approach to the study of labor migration, the migration of a few professionals in the beginning becomes a self-perpetuating institutionalized process over time. Douglas Massey and colleagues (1987) argue that once international migration begins, social networks develop that make foreign employment increasingly accessible to all classes of the sending society. Migrant social networks consist of social ties that link sending communities to specific points of destination in receiving societies. These ties bind migrants and non-migrants within a complex web of complementary social roles and interpersonal relationships that are maintained by an informal set of mutual expectations and prescribed behaviors.

Social networks increase the likelihood of international movement because they lower the costs and risks of movement and increase the expected net return to migration. International migration becomes institutionalized and over time becomes progressively independent of wage differentials and employment rates (Massey et al. 1994).

An emerging new research field, known as transnationalism, offers new perspectives for understanding the migration experiences of skilled migrants. Some analysts contend that some migrants retain multi-stranded social relations linking their lives in their societies of origin and settlement. (Basch, Glick Schiller, and Szanton Blanc 1994). Donald Nonini and Aihwa Ong (1997) argue that the globalization of the world economy has led to the appearance of transnational professionals and technocrats with expertise in managerial, financial, legal, technical, and commercial services. These professionals, like the Chinese, have developed "new lifestyles grounded in high mobility (both spatial and in terms of careers), new patterns of urban residence, and new kinds of social interaction defined by a consumerist ethic" (Nonini and Ong 1997, 11). This is also the case of former Indian engineers who have become high-tech entrepreneurs in Silicon Valley and maintain close relationships with India (Saxenian and Edulbehram 1998).

Silicon Valley: Regional Development and Human Capital

Since the 1970s, Silicon Valley and Route 128, located in Eastern Massachusetts, have attracted international attention as the world's leading centers of technological innovation. Both regions had common origins in university-based research (Stanford University and MIT, respectively) and postwar military spending. However, after years of economic turmoil, Silicon Valley has prevailed as the most successful high-technology region in the world. The region is home to one-third of the hundred largest high-technology companies created in the United States since 1965, and Silicon Valley firms also generated 150,000 new high-technology related jobs between 1975 and 1990 (Saxenian 1994).[2]

AnnaLee Saxenian (1994, 2) argues that the different experiences of Silicon Valley and Route 128 (growth in the former and decline in the latter) are based on the fact that the two regions have developed fundamentally distinct industrial systems. Silicon Valley entrepreneurs have created a regional-network-based industrial system that promotes collective learning about changing markets and technologies and flexible adjustments. At the same time, social networks and open labor markets encourage experimentation and entrepreneurship. On the other hand, Route 128 is dominated by a small number of relatively integrated and independent corporations organized under a centralized authority. In general, practices of secrecy and corporate loyalty govern relations between firms, customers, suppliers, and competitors in this region.

The analysis of the economic development of the two regions suggests that the dissimilar industrial systems that emerged in Silicon Valley and Route 128 explain a great deal of Silicon Valley's success. However, one factor has been largely ignored: the role of foreign-born engineers and scientists. There is a much larger concentration of foreign-born engineers and scientists in Silicon Valley than in the firms located along Route 128.[3] According to PUMS data, nearly one-third of the engineers, mathematical and computer scientists, and natural scientists employed in the high-technology industry of Silicon Valley were born outside the United States (32.3 percent). The corresponding figure for Route 128 (16.7 percent) is almost half that proportion.

This difference seems to be the result of two factors: the existence of a larger immigrant pool in Silicon Valley and the operation of an industrial system in this region that is more open to new migrants. Interviews with engineers from India and Mexico who have worked in the two regions reveal that there is a more favorable environment in Silicon Valley than in Route 128. This issue, however, deserves further research.

Engineers and scientists in Silicon Valley are mostly young, with a median age of thirty-seven for the native born and thirty-four for immigrants. The group is overwhelmingly male: native and foreign-born females constitute only 17.5 percent of the total. This situation is similar in Route 128.

Education is a crucial factor in high-technology because it is a knowledge-based industry, and R&D is, therefore, one of its major components. Table 12.2 compares educational attainment among native and foreign-born engineers and scientists in Silicon Valley and Route 128. In general, immigrant engineers and scientists in both regions have much higher levels of education than their native-born counterparts. The majority of the immigrants in Silicon Valley have postgraduate degrees, and they are twice as likely to have obtained doctoral degrees than native-born engineers and scientists. In the Route 128 region, the percentage of immigrants with postgraduate degrees is more than twice that of native-born professionals who have obtained these degrees. The large disparity between the native and foreign-born engineers and scientists is repeated among those who have obtained doctorates.[4]

TABLE 12.2 *Educational Attainment Among Native and Foreign-Born Engineers and Scientists Employed in High Technology, Silicon Valley, California, and Route 128, Massachusetts, 1990 (Percentage)*

	Silicon Valley		Route 128	
	Native	Foreign Born	Native	Foreign Born
No college degree	19.6	5.8	17.4	9.8
Graduate degree[a]	58.1	41.4	61.4	43.3
Master's or professional degree	18.4	45.0	19.9	39.4
Doctoral degree	3.9	7.9	1.3	7.5
Unweighted *N*	1,834	846	1,266	254

Source: U.S. Department of Commerce 1992.
[a]Includes individuals with bachelor's or associate degrees in college occupational and academic programs.

Although Taiwan, India, and China are the principal sources of professionals for the two regions, Silicon Valley and Route 128 tap into different sources of highly skilled immigrants, as table 12.3 shows. This suggests the existence of different recruitment processes and social networking. Although Asia is by far the largest contributor, geographical location (East Coast versus West Coast) seems also to play an important role. For this reason, European countries send more immigrants to Route 128 than to Silicon Valley. The table also shows that the immigration of professionals from African and Latin American countries is negligible. In particular, the immigration of Mexican professionals is comparatively very small (data not shown in the table). Mexican engineers and scientists contribute only 0.8 percent of the professionals in Silicon Valley and 0.4 percent along Route 128.

Census data reveal that immigrant engineers and scientists play a crucial role in the development of the information technology industry because of their large concentration and their contribution of human capital. Who are these immigrants, and how are they recruited by high-tech companies?

Indian and Mexican Engineers and Scientists in Silicon Valley

My interviews with Indian and Mexican engineers and scientists in Silicon Valley reveal four main avenues through which highly skilled migrants coming from developing countries find employment in Silicon

TABLE 12.3   *Country of Birth of Foreign-Born Engineers and Scientists Employed in the High-Technology Industry, Silicon Valley, California, and Route 128, Massachusetts, 1990 (Percentage)*

Silicon Valley		Route 128	
Taiwan	16.4	India	9.8
India	11.9	Taiwan	8.7
China	9.9	China	6.3
Vietnam	8.9	USSR	5.5
Hong Kong	6.1	Hong Kong	5.1
Philippines	5.1	Canada	5.1
Iran	5.0	England	4.7
Japan	3.0	West Germany	3.1
Korea	2.8	Greece	3.1
Germany	2.2	Vietnam	3.1
England	2.0	Germany	2.8
Canada	1.7	Ireland	2.8
Pakistan	1.4	Italy	2.4
Poland	1.2	United Kingdom	2.4
France	1.1	Lebanon	2.4
West Germany	1.1	Colombia	2.4
United Kingdom	1.1	Israel	2.0
Other countries	19.1	France	1.6
		Poland	1.6
		Iran	1.6
		Morocco	1.6
		Burma	1.2
		Japan	1.2
		Philippines	1.2
		Other countries	18.3
Unweighted *N*	846		254

Source: U.S. Department of Commerce 1992.

Valley. Some of them entered the United States as children of immigrant families. Others are former employees of subsidiaries of U.S. high-tech companies located abroad. Another group is composed of former foreign students at U.S. universities. Finally the cerebreros work in Silicon Valley companies under temporary visas.

Children of Immigrant Families

This group comprises immigrants who come to the United States as children accompanying their families. In most cases the mode of entry for these immigrants is through immigration policy provisions that favor family reunification. According to the Immigration and Nationality Act of 1990, 480,000 visas are issued every year for this purpose. The act allocates these visas, giving unlimited access to the immediate relatives of U.S. citizens and then granting 226,000 visas under a system of four preferences benefiting the adult children of U.S. citizens and the direct relatives of permanent residents.

Although the children of immigrant families enter the United States at different ages, carrying disparate educational experiences, they more or less resemble the native population because of their exposure to the U.S. educational system and their multiform integration into the economic, political, social, and cultural institutions of the United States. Rubén Rumbaut (1997) refers to some members of this group as the "1.5 generation" to distinguish them from the second generation that comprises persons who are born in the United States. Rumbaut states that the children of the "1.5 generation" are socialized and begin their primary education outside the United States and complete their education in the United States. The age of arrival of an immigrant is an important factor in his or her integration into the United States: for example, those who arrive before the age of six are considerably more likely to speak English without an accent. Shiv and Mario illustrate the experiences of two children of immigrant families.

Shiv clearly belongs to the 1.5 generation. Born in India, he came to the United States at the age of seven, when his father, who had completed a doctorate in bacteriology in India, obtained a research fellowship in a Boston hospital. The family moved to the San Francisco Bay area a year later, and Shiv eventually obtained a bachelor of science degree in chemical engineering from the University of California, San Diego. After graduating, he joined General Motors for a brief period and then transferred to Electronic Data Systems, where he received three years of rigorous internal training in programming. After working for a few years for IBM, he moved to another major Silicon Valley corporation, where he currently works as a project manager.

Mario was eighteen years old when he came to the United States. He was born in a rural municipality of Michoacan, Mexico. In 1985, one year into his studies in medical school, he moved to Sacramento, California, with his family. He began working in construction, the only available job, through the contacts of his relatives. After three years, he decided to go back to school and enrolled in a community college. He later obtained a bachelor of science degree in electrical engineering from the University of California, Berkeley. After his graduation, he was recruited to be an operations engineer by a high-tech company that is a leading provider of fixed-network wireless data communications services.

Former Employees of Subsidiaries
Located Outside the United States

Another group of foreign-born engineers and scientists is made up of former workers at subsidiaries of Silicon Valley companies located in India, Mexico, or other countries. These workers were able to enter the United States and find employment in Silicon Valley thanks to the personal contacts they established while working outside the United States.

The relocation of high-tech plants began in the 1960s, when semiconductor manufacturers began moving assembly operations outside the United States. Fairchild started its first foreign manufacturing facility in Hong Kong in 1962, and Intel opened its first plant in Malaysia in 1972, followed by others in the Philippines, Barbados, Puerto Rico, and Singapore (Florida and Kenney 1990). An international division of labor within the high-tech industry began to emerge when research and development was carried out in core areas such as Silicon Valley while assembly and testing were performed in the periphery. Offshore assembly plants were later relocated to Southeast Asia and to a lesser extent to Latin America and Western Europe (Scott and Angel 1986). The stories of Sujai, Laura, and Manuel illustrate how some engineers working for offshore plants end up in Silicon Valley.

Sujai was born in New Delhi, India, and was an excellent student at BMS College of Engineering in Bangalore. He obtained ample international professional experience before moving to Silicon Valley by working in India, Germany, and Singapore. In 1995, he attended an international telecommunications conference in Geneva, where he met the section manager of his company, who worked in the Silicon Valley headquarters. To the manager's delight, Sujai helped him find the solution to a technical problem they had not been able to solve in Santa Clara. Two years later, the company advertised a position for a network management software professional. The manager contacted Sujai and in a few weeks recruited him to work in Silicon Valley. The company decided to get him an L-1 visa, which is a temporary visa for intracompany transferees. Currently, Sujai manages a team of eleven engineers and an offshore development team located in India.

Laura, born in Mexico, was one of the few women in the electrical engineering program at the Instituto Tecnológico de Monterrey, where she was one of the best students in her class. In the early 1980s, she began working as an assembly engineer in an offshore plant of Raytheon Semiconductors, one of the oldest semiconductor companies of Silicon Valley, located in Tepic, Nayarit. After receiving some training in the parent plant in Silicon Valley, she was put in charge of transferring technology to the plant in Mexico. In her frequent trips to Silicon Valley, she met an Anglo engineer, who later became her husband. Laura is now a test engineer in another Silicon Valley semiconductors company and is in charge of a team of technical workers who test the "waffles" containing the computer chips that are manufactured in Singapore.

Manuel was born in Mexico and got his degree in chemical engineering at the Instituto Politécnico Nacional. After a short stay at Du Pont he was offered employment at Hewlett-Packard de México. At the end of the 1970s, the company offered him a job in its headquarters in Silicon Valley. The company arranged the immigration visas for Manuel and all the members of his family. He moved to San Jose with his family and continued working for Hewlett-Packard for some time. In the late 1980s he joined a Mexican company that has an office in Silicon Valley. This company sells telecommunications technology used in financial data communications networks, automated teller machines, and airline and hotel reservations systems in developing countries that lack reliable telephone systems.

Former Foreign Students at U.S. Universities

The third group includes adult foreign-born persons who initially come to the United States to pursue studies in science or engineering fields. High-tech companies recruit these immigrants immediately after they get their degrees and often obtain permanent residency for their workers, thanks to immigration law provisions that favor skilled persons. This process has been reinforced by the Immigration and Nationality Act of 1990, which expanded the proportion of employment-based immigrant visas, increasing their number from 54,000 under previous immigration law to 140,000 a year. Before 1990, fewer than 10 percent of all immigrants could enter the United States each year based on their job skills. Thanks to the 1990 law, approximately 21 percent of the new immigrants each year are now admitted on the basis of their occupational skills. The 140,000 employment-based visas granted to the principal immigrants and their families are allocated under a system of five preferences that encourage the immigration of artists, professors, athletes, religious workers, investors, and engineers and scientists, among others.

David North (1995) contends that the rapid growth in the number of foreign-born engineers and scientists derives in part from the fact that there are more foreign students than native-born U.S. citizens entering graduate programs in science and engineering. He argues that a very small percentage of college-educated native-born students seek graduate degrees in science and engineering because a large percentage instead opt for degrees in medicine, law, or business or go directly into the labor market. This is in part the result of changes in the labor markets during the past forty years whereby the financial rewards to physicians, lawyers, and business executives have increased exponentially whereas the relative compensation to engineers and scientists has decreased. North provides some evidence to illustrate the competition between foreign-born students and natives in science and engineering graduate programs. In 1991, for instance, of the 8,504 doctorates granted by U.S. universities in these fields, more than one-third went to students from China. Other recipients were, by order of importance, from South Korea, India, Canada, Iran, Greece, Mexico, the United Kingdom, Japan, and Germany (North 1995, 16). Atul and Martin originally entered the United States on student visas and later obtained permanent residency because of their employment in high-tech companies.

Atul is a citizen of the world. He was born in Madras, India, went to high school in Hong Kong, and obtained a bachelor's degree at Stanford University and a master's degree at the University of Pennsylvania. His wife is Puerto Rican, and he became a U.S. citizen in 1996. Atul came to the United States in 1982 to pursue undergraduate studies at Stanford. He got his first job in a Silicon Valley corporation that is the leading supplier of software for enterprise information management. A few years ago, Atul decided to transfer to a smaller software company founded by Indian immigrants.

Martin was born in Mexico City and holds a doctorate in computer science from the University of California, Berkeley. While a student at Berkeley, he married an American citizen and as a result became a permanent resident. They moved to Mexico City, where Martin obtained a teaching position at the Universidad Nacional Autónoma de México. After a few years, he played a key role in the founding of the computer science department at the university. Martin and his wife decided to return to the United States when she became ill. They settled in San Jose because Martin got a job at National Semiconductors, thanks to a friend from Berkeley. After working in many different companies, Martin was hired in 1994 by a major corporation, where he became a senior manager overseeing twelve engineers.

The Cerebreros

The "cerebreros," like the Mexican braceros in the past, work in the United States temporarily with visas such as the H-1B, which allows the temporary stay of workers employed in "specialty occupations." Until 1998 there was an annual cap on H-1B visa holders of 65,000 workers, who were allowed to stay in the United States for a maximum of six years. The American Competitiveness Act, which was approved in October 1998, increased the number of H-1B visas by 142,500 over the following three years, from 1999 to 2001. The annual ceiling on the number of H-1B visas issued is 115,000 in 1999 and 2000 and 107,500 in 2001. In the year 2002 the number of visas will return to the original quota of 65,000 a year (*Migration News* 1998).

Data from the INS for 1994 show India as the most important contributor of H–1B workers, closely followed by the United Kingdom. Other important sending countries are Japan, the Philippines, France, Germany, Canada, and Mexico (INS 1996). Some Indian computer companies that are involved in the practice of "body shopping" use this program intensively because they provide Indian engineers to foreign firms for a fee (Lakha 1992). The cases of Daniel and Charnjeet illustrate the experiences of H-1B workers.

Daniel is currently working in a Silicon Valley software company as a support technical engineer. Although he did part of his education in Madison, Wisconsin, while his father worked on his doctorate there, he obtained a degree in computer systems from the Universidad de las Americas in Mexico. His dedication to school helped him obtain full scholarships during his five years of study. In 1994, while working for a small software company in Mexico City, he was assigned to work on a major project with one of the most important Mexican banks. In this project, Daniel met some engineers from a Silicon Valley company that was providing the software for the project. Unfortunately, the project was canceled; but before the American engineers returned to Silicon Valley, they invited Daniel to join the company because he already had the specific programming skills they use in their business. Initially, Daniel declined the job offer, but at the end of the year, with the devaluation of the Mexican peso, he changed his mind. The company hired him immediately, and Daniel flew in to the San Jose airport with an H-1B visa.

Charnjeet is not yet a cerebrera but intends to become one in the near future. She is a young Indian engineer who recently got her master's degree in computer engineering from a university in South Carolina. As a graduate student with an F-1 visa, she is currently doing her practical training in a big Silicon Valley company. After graduating, foreign students are allowed to work for some time in the United States in their fields of study. The company is helping Charnjeet obtain a H-1B visa, but they have to wait for a while until the newly allocated H-1B visas become available. For now, the Immigration and Naturalization Service has stated that the visas for this year have been used up. Charnjeet landed her current job, as a technical support engineer, when she attended a job fair in Silicon Valley and was given an interview on the spot. Her employers are so pleased with her work that they want to get her a H-1B visa and later a green card.

Conclusion

This nonrandom sample of stories about the experiences of Indian and Mexican engineers and scientists offers valuable insights into the various avenues by which skilled migrants enter the United States. The research shows that Indian and Mexican engineers and scientists find employment in Silicon Valley thanks to social networks they establish with relatives, co-workers, managers of subsidiaries of U.S. high-tech companies located abroad, and people they meet at U.S. universities. Skilled migrants are less restricted than unskilled migrants in participation in U.S. labor markets: immigration policy, corporate power, and their own class resources allow them to cross borders with greater ease than low-skilled migrants. This should be considered an important factor in developing more-comprehensive theories and models of contemporary labor migration.

Transnational professionals enjoy a privileged position because they are vital to companies involved in global production processes and markets. The engineers and scientists I interviewed are among the best and the brightest workers of the world. Some of them were the top students at their universities or launched successful careers before coming to the United States. This finding coincides with census data that show educational attainment to be higher among immigrants than among native-born engineers and scientists.

This talent, produced elsewhere, represents a net gain for information technology companies that have the power and the luxury to select workers from within a global pool. It represents a "brain drain," however, from developing countries. Developing countries subsidize the industrialized countries to the extent that the rewards of their costly investment in human capital are reaped by high-tech companies in the developed world. The movement of highly skilled immigrants into the high-technology regions of developed countries supports the main contention of the international division of labor theory: these engineers and scientists are solidifying the location of research and development activities in the core regions of the industrialized world.

The research on which this chapter is based also suggests that Silicon Valley's small innovative firms more effectively incorporate migrant professionals than the large-scale corporate companies along Route 128. This process reflects a historical trend: until the 1960s, white ethnics and immigrants were excluded from major U.S. corporations and industrial companies, though they were regularly employed by smaller, less established companies—some of which they had started (Kanter 1993). It can also be argued that a flexible industrial system in a knowledge-based industry depends on a flexible immigration system that allows the continuous arrival of workers with the newest skills and ideas. In fact, "body-shopping" companies, with their intense use of H-1B workers, seemed to sustain a flexible industrial system because they provide Indian professionals with the specific training required by high-tech companies.

The new trends in the evolution of the information technology industry support this position. Since the late 1960s, information technology has shifted from a hardware-driven to a software-driven industry (Parthasarathy 2000). However, software is still a complex, labor-intensive, and expensive process that depends on talent. Castells (1989) notes that the software industry is the ultimate expression of a scientific labor-intensive activity because it sells pure knowledge, with fabrication being reduced to the minimum material expression.

In this context, Indian engineers and scientists have a comparative advantage over other professionals in the developing world. The apparent difference in the social and economic backgrounds of Mexican and Indian professionals—Indian professionals generally come from more affluent families—supports the notion that Indians, like other Asian immigrants, have already experienced a more severe selection process when trying to emigrate to the United States (Portes and Rumbaut 1996). In addition, owing to the particular characteristics of the history of emigration from India, professionals from this country have many more options in the global economy. The fact that Indians migrate to many different countries allows them a much richer international experience than Mexican professionals, who, like their less-skilled co-nationals, are more constrained to work in the United States.

Indian immigrants have been able to become "global software engineers" because of industrial policies implemented by the Indian government that have supported the development of the software industry (Parthasarathy 2000). Finally, it is also easier for Indian professionals to find employment in the United States because they are fluent English speakers upon arrival, English being the official language of higher education in India.

In this regard, Alejandro Portes (1996) observes that although both Mexico and India have highly unequal patterns of income distribution, migration is far more common for Indian than for Mexican professionals, in both absolute and relative numbers. Portes contends that neoclassical theory, which predicts migration on the basis of the cost-benefit analysis supposedly performed by potential migrants, is irrelevant. As he has noted, Douglas Massey and colleagues (1987) provide a more solid empirical explanation when they argue that migration displays a strong intrinsic tendency to become more extensive over time because social networks forged from the relationships of kinship, friendship, and "paisanaje" facilitate the movement of people and information.[5]

From the immigrants' perspective, a job in Silicon Valley leads to much higher wages, better research opportunities, and a middleclass status unattainable in their native countries. Among those I interviewed, neither the Indian nor the Mexican professionals complain about receiving lower wages than native-born professionals in similar positions. What they complain about is the existence of a "glass ceiling" that prevents them from obtaining significant management positions. In fact, the Federal Glass Ceiling Commission found that Indian males with at least a bachelor's degree were less likely than either the total Asian and Pacific Islander male population or white males to be in management positions (Fernandez 1998).

The concern for the discrimination against immigrant professionals is not new. In the late 1960s, Bradley Parlin (1976) conducted a case study of the employment practices of a large manufacturing plant. In comparing the experiences of citizen and immigrant professionals who were recent college graduates in engineering and science fields, he found that U.S. citizens in general were considerably more likely to find employment than immigrants and that noncitizens coming from non-Western countries were less likely to find employment than noncitizens from Western countries. According to Parlin, employers' decisions were based on factors other than merit or competence.

Issues of discrimination notwithstanding, the recent debate on immigration policy seeking to favor occupational skills over family reunification considerations is a clear invitation to new skilled immigrants and cerebreros who have access to the right social networks to look for employment in the United States.

The Social Science Research Council through its International Migration Program and the Center for U.S.-Mexican Studies at the University of California, San Diego, granted me doctoral fellowships, which allowed me to write this chapter. The chapter is based on my dissertation (Alarcón 1998) and a previous version, which appeared in *American Behavioral Scientist* 1999, vol. 42, no. 9. (Alarcón 1999). I am greatly indebted to Nancy Foner, Rubén Rumbaut, Steve Gold, and an anonymous reviewer for their valuable comments and ideas.

Notes

1. In 1942, because of the diversion of manpower for World War II, the governments of Mexico and the United States enacted the Bracero

Program, which granted temporary work contracts for Mexican farmworkers and which remained in effect until 1964. Drawing on the experience of braceros, two colleagues, Rubén Rumbaut and Michael Kearny, in two different conferences have suggested to me the use of the term "cerebreros" to describe the foreign-born engineers and scientists who hold temporary visas.

2. I include the case of Route 128 to compare and contrast trends taking place in Silicon Valley.

3. Silicon Valley includes the counties of Santa Clara, San Mateo, Santa Cruz, and a small portion of Alameda County, in California. Route 128 includes the counties of Essex, Middlesex, Suffolk, and Norfolk, in Massachusetts (see Saxenian 1994).

4. The difference in educational attainment between the foreign and the native born in Silicon Valley and Route 128 is consistent with the findings of a study that uses a national sample of engineers and scientists employed in all industries (Bouvier and Martin 1995).

5. "Paisanaje" describes the feeling of belonging to a common community of origin.

References

Alarcón, Rafael. 1998. "Migrants of the Information Age: Foreign Born Engineers and Scientists and Regional Development in Silicon Valley." Ph.D. diss., University of California, Berkeley.

———. 1999. "Recruitment Processes Among Foreign-Born Engineers and Scientists in Silicon Valley." *American Behavioral Scientist* 42(9): 1381–97.

Basch, Linda, Nina Glick Schiller, and Cristina Szanton Blanc. 1994. *Nations Unbound: Transnational Projects, Postcolonial Predicaments, and Deterritorialized Nation-States.* New York: Gordon and Breach.

Bouvier, Leon, and John Martin. 1995. *Foreign-Born Scientists, Engineers, and Mathematicians in the United States.* Washington, D.C.: Center for Immigration Studies.

Castells, Manuel. 1989. *The Informational City: Information Technology, Economic Restructuring, and the Urban Regional Process.* Oxford: Blackwell.

———. 1996. *The Rise of the Network Society.* Cambridge, Mass.: Blackwell.

Fernandez, Marilyn. 1998. "Asian Indian Americans in the Bay Area and the Glass Ceiling." *Social Perspectives* 41(1): 119–49.

Fix, Michael, and Jeffrey Passel. 1994. *Immigration and Immigrants: Setting the Record Straight.* Washington, D.C.: Urban Institute.

Florida, Richard, and Martin Kenney. 1990. *The Breakthrough Illusion: Corporate America's Failure to Move from Innovation to Mass Production.* New York: Basic Books.

Frobel, Friedrich, Jurgen Henricks, and Otto Kreye. 1980. *The New International Division of Labor.* Cambridge: Cambridge University Press.

Kanter, Rosabeth Moss. 1993. *Men and Women of the Corporation.* New York: Basic Books.

Lakha, Salim. 1992. "The Internationalization of Indian Computer Professionals." *South Asia* 15(2): 93–113.

Massey, Douglas, Rafael Alarcón, Jorge Durand, and Humberto González. 1987. *Return to Aztlan: The Social Process of International Migration from Western Mexico.* Berkeley: University of California Press.

Massey, Douglas, Joaquin Arango, Graeme Hugo, Ali Kouaouci, Adela Pellegrino, and Edward Taylor. 1994. "An Evaluation of International Migration Theory: The North American Case." *Population and Development Review* 20(4): 699–752.

McLaughlin, Ken. 1997. "Immigrants Called Vital to the Valley: New Point Man in Senate Criticized, Praised in San Jose Visit." *San Jose Mercury News,* January 15, 5.

Migration News. 1998. "INS: Congress: H-1Bs Approved; Farm Workers Rejected. Naturalization, Deportations." Download from the worldwide web at: http://www.migration.ucdavis.edu (December).

Nonini, Donald, and Aihwa Ong. 1997. "Chinese Transnationalism as an Alternative Modernity." In *Ungrounded Empires: The Cultural Politics of Modern Chinese Transnationalism,* edited by Aihwa Ong and Donald Nonini. New York: Routledge.

North, David. 1995. *Soothing the Establishment: The Impact of Foreign-Born Scientists and Engineers on America.* Lanham, Md.: University Press of America.

Parlin, Bradley. 1976. *Immigrant Professionals in the United States: Discrimination in the Scientific Labor Market.* New York: Praeger.

Parthasarathy, Balaji. 1994. "Marxist Theories of Development: The New International Division of Labor and the Third World." *Berkeley Planning Journal* 9: 109–24.

———. 2000. "Globalization and Agglomeration in Newly Industrializing Countries: The State and the Information Technology Industry in Bangalore, India." Ph.D. diss., University of California, Berkeley.

Portes, Alejandro. 1996. "Las Ciencias en Conflicto: Tipo y Funciones de la Transgresión Interdisciplinaria" (Contentious Science: The Forms and Functions of Trespassing). *Estudios Sociológicos* 14(42): 595–626.

Portes, Alejandro, and Rubén Rumbaut. 1996. *Immigrant America: A Portrait.* Berkeley: University of California Press.

Reich, Robert. 1992. *The Work of Nations: Preparing Ourselves for Twenty-first-Century Capitalism.* New York: Vintage Books.

Rumbaut, Rubén. 1997. "Assimilation and Its Discontents: Between Rhetoric and Reality." *International Migration Review* 31(4): 923–60.

Sassen, Saskia. 1988. *The Mobility of Labor and Capital: A Study in*

International Investment and Labor Flow. Cambridge: Cambridge University Press.

———. 1990. "U.S. Immigration Policy Toward Mexico in a Global Economy." *Journal of International Affairs* 43(2): 369–83.

Saxenian, AnnaLee. 1994. *Regional Advantage: Culture and Competition in Silicon Valley and Route 128.* Cambridge: Harvard University Press.

Saxenian, AnnaLee, and Jumbi Edulbehram. 1998. "Immigrant Entrepreneurs in Silicon Valley." *Berkeley Planning Journal* 12: 32–49.

Schibsted, Evantheia. 1995. "Border Gods." *Forbes ASAP,* December 4, 1995, p. 63.

Scott, Allen, and David Angel. 1986. *The U.S. Semiconductor Industry: A Locational Analysis.* Los Angeles: University of California, School of Architecture and Urban Planning.

Stremlau, John. 1996. "Dateline Bangalore: Third World Technopolis (India)." *Foreign Policy* 102: 152–68.

U.S. Department of Commerce, Bureau of the Census. 1992. *1990 Census of Population and Housing: Public Use Microdata Samples (5%).* U.S. Machine Readable Data Files. Washington: U.S. Government Printing Office.

———. 1993. *1990 Census of Population and Housing: Public Use Microdata Samples: Technical Documentation.* Washington: U.S. Government Printing Office.

U.S. Immigration and Naturalization Service (INS). 1992. *1991 Statistical Yearbook of the Immigration and Naturalization Service.* Washington: U.S. Government Printing Office.

———. 1996. *1994 Statistical Yearbook of the Immigration and Naturalization Service.* Washington: U.S. Government Printing Office.

Wallerstein, Immanuel. 1974. *The Modern World System, Capitalist Agriculture, and the Origins of the European World Economy in the Sixteenth Century.* New York: Academic Press.

World Bank 1997. *World Development Report, 1997: The State in a Changing World.* Oxford: Oxford University Press.

13

IMMIGRANT AND AFRICAN AMERICAN COMPETITION: JEWISH, KOREAN, AND AFRICAN AMERICAN ENTREPRENEURS

Jennifer Lee

O NE OF the chief sources of tension between immigrants and African Americans in the United States is the notion that immigrant entrepreneurs who open businesses in predominantly black neighborhoods take business opportunities away from native-born blacks. Given their prevalence—particularly in black communities—one might assume that immigrant businesses owned by Koreans, Jews, Chinese, and Asian Indians compete with African American entrepreneurs, thereby inhibiting the development of African American small business. Do immigrant entrepreneurs compete with African Americans in the retail industry? The question of who owns the stores in the community is laden with symbolism, translating into far beyond what these businesses generate in profit. Business ownership is a visible and powerful indicator of social mobility and opportunity, and for this reason the debate concerning competition between immigrants and African Americans is much deliberated in the fields of economics and sociology (Bean and Bell-Rose 1999; Borjas 1994; Hamermesh and Bean 1998; Light and Rosenstein 1995).

Immigrant entrepreneurs have made distinct inroads in many large U.S. cities. Approximately one-third to one-half of Korean families are engaged in small business (Light and Bonacich 1988; Min 1996), figures that parallel the self-employment rate of Jewish immigrants in the early twentieth century (Steinberg 1989; Marx 1967). Both immigrant groups have also prospered by serving the black community.[1] Judging from Jewish and Korean entrepreneurial success in these communities, it may seem that immigrant entrepreneurs undeniably compete with and thereby inhibit African American entrepreneurial development.

My research reveals a more complex and nuanced picture, however.

Because immigrant groups enter and dominate retail niches different from those of African Americans, there tends to be little interethnic competition; competition is far more likely to be intraethnic in nature.[2] Previous studies confirm that the presence of immigrant entrepreneurs does not, in fact, increase competition among black small businesses but instead fills economic niches that were previously unfilled (Light and Sanchez 1987; Wilson and Martin 1982). However, this is not the end of the story.

Although larger statistical studies have been unable to find evidence of competition strictly defined, qualitative studies are sometimes able to fill in the missing blanks. Large-scale, quantitative studies cannot always capture the subtle ways in which immigrant entrepreneurs may compete with or affect African American small business development (Fairlie and Meyer 1998). There are both intended and unintended consequences of retail niche domination—what Roger Waldinger (1995) aptly phrases, "the 'other' side of embeddedness," which can work to exclude other ethnics from entering these industries, resulting in blocked opportunities for outsiders who attempt to penetrate ethnically saturated niches. Retail niche domination gives the ethnic majority cumulative business advantages, what I refer to as "coethnic advantages." Entrepreneurship is embedded in ethnic networks that act as coethnic advantages for some and blocked opportunities and exclusion for others. Coethnic advantages include vertical integration, the extension of credit from coethnic suppliers to retailers, the ability to pool orders, and the formation of business associations. Yet for entrepreneurial groups, ethnic clustering also translates into coethnic disadvantages, such as market saturation, resulting in fierce intraethnic competition.

Research Design and Methods

The research methods include semistructured interviews with seventy-five merchants from five research sites and both participant and nonparticipant observation. I located five largely black neighborhoods in New York City and Philadelphia, three of which are low income and two middle income. The three low-income neighborhoods are East Harlem, West Harlem, in New York, and West Philadelphia; the two middle-income neighborhoods are Jamaica, Queens, and East Mount Airy, Philadelphia. Table 13.1 illustrates various characteristics of the research sites, including median household income, percentage living below the poverty line, racial composition, employment status, and level of education.

Each of these neighborhoods has bustling commercial strips lined with small businesses that offer a variety of merchandise, some of

TABLE 13.1   *Characteristics of Research Sites*

Characteristic	West Harlem	East Harlem	Jamaica, Queens	West Philadelpha	Mount Airy, Pennsylvania
Total population	55,142	28,448	53,127	48,672	27,675
Income					
Median household income (dollars)	16,767	11,348	35,224	18,394	35,152
Public assistance in household (%)	22	42	8	21	8
Below poverty line (%)	34	46	13	27	8
Race (%)					
Black	60	54	28	93	95
White	26	18	39	5	4
Other	14	27	33	2	1
Nativity (%)					
Native born	81	90	51	96	97
Foreign born	19	10	49	4	3
Gender (%)					
Male	44	46	49	44	45
Female	56	54	51	56	55
Employment (%)					
Employed	48	40	61	46	67
Unemployed	7	9	6	8	7
Not in labor force	45	51	33	46	26
Education (%)					
High school or more	64	42	72	58	79
College or more	27	4	26	8	17

Source: U.S. Department of Commerce 1992.

which is geared specifically toward a black clientele, including wigs, ethnic beauty supplies, inner-city sportswear, and beauty salons and barber shops serving black customers. There are also a variety of other businesses that sell furniture, better apparel, sneakers, jewelry, fruits and vegetables, fresh fish, electronics, and discount household supplies. However, the large, chain retail stores that are nearly ubiquitous in white, middle-class neighborhoods and suburban shopping malls are noticeably absent from these shopping strips, leaving a vacant niche for willing entrepreneurs. The merchants in these neighborhoods are a mixed lot and include Koreans, Jews, Asian Indians, Latinos, African Americans, and West Indians, although the customers are primarily black.

Between March 1996 and May 1997 I interviewed fifteen store owners from each site. Twenty-five of these merchants were Jewish, twenty-nine Korean, and twenty-one African American. My original goal was to interview an equal number of Jewish, Korean, and African American merchants from each site, but some neighborhoods had very few African American store owners along the major avenues; therefore, there is an underrepresentation of African American merchants in the sample. I interviewed merchants from many different industries and also tried, whenever possible, to interview Jewish, Korean, and African American merchants from the same lines of business in order to understand how their practices and outcomes differed, even when holding the industry constant. Table 13.2 illustrates the variety of industries in the sample of merchants.

The businesses were not randomly selected, nor are they representative; rather, they reflect the diversity of small businesses in these communities. The interviews with the store owners, lasting between one-and-a-half and two hours, were tape-recorded and were later transcribed verbatim. I asked the merchants many questions about their businesses: why and how they opened their business, why they chose to enter the particular retail niche, what were the credit terms with their suppliers, and what economic and ethnic resources they utilize in business. I also did a great deal of nonparticipant observation in these stores, visiting each store at least twice. In addition, I benefited from participant observation while I worked as a bag checker in a store on 125th Street in West Harlem and as a cashier in a store on 52d Street in West Philadelphia. These experiences allowed me to observe the daily lives of the merchants and have been invaluable to my research.

I chose to study both New York City and Philadelphia because both are large eastern cities, and they are similar on a number of key dimensions, such as the self-employment rate, the proportion of service sector employment, the rate of unemployment, and the percentage living below the poverty line (Carpenter 1992). My research design thus allows for a comparative analysis of retail niche domination among Jewish, Korean, and African American entrepreneurs in five largely black neighborhoods in two cities.

Identifying and Occupying Retail Niches: An Evolutionary Chain

Immigrant entrepreneurs choose self-employment as a means of relatively quick upward mobility in the face of blocked mobility in the primary labor market. Their relatively poor English language skills, and consequent inability to transfer their educational credentials, and their

TABLE 13.2   *Ownership of Businesses in the Sample, by Type of Business*

Type of Business	Jewish	Korean	Black	Total
African cultural products	0	0	1	1
Apparel				[17]
Army-navy, industrial	2	0	0	2
Inner-city sportswear	1	4	0	5
Ladies' dresses	0	3	1	4
Ladies' better casual	0	0	1	1
Men's and ladies' better casual	0	0	2	2
Men's dress apparel	2	0	0	2
Men's better casual	0	0	1	1
Auto repair	2	0	0	2
Baked goods, coffee shop	0	0	1	1
Barber shop	0	0	1	1
Beauty salon	0	0	3	3
Bookstore	0	0	1	1
Cards and gifts	1	0	1	2
Carry-out food	0	1	1	1
Dry cleaner	0	2	0	2
Electronics	1	0	0	1
Ethnic beauty supplies	1	4	0	5
Eyeglasses	1	0	0	1
Fish market	0	2	0	2
Furniture	7	1	2	10
General merchandise	0	1	0	1
Grocery	0	4	0	4
Hardware	0	0	1	1
Jewelry	1	1	0	2
Lingerie	1	0	1	2
Music	0	0	1	1
Pawnshop	1	0	0	1
Pharmacy	1	0	1	2
Shoe repair	0	1	0	1
Sneakers	1	2	0	3
Thrift store	0	0	1	1
Variety, household supplies	1	0	0	1
Wigs	1	3	0	4
Total	25	29	21	75

Source: Author's calculations.

unfamiliarity with the American corporate structure and customs lead the foreign born to enter self-employment to achieve socioeconomic mobility (Lee 2000). However, immigrant entrepreneurs set up shop specifically in low-income black neighborhoods for three primary reasons. First, because there is little competition from larger, chain corporations in these underserviced communities, immigrant-owned small businesses can thrive. Second, rent is relatively inexpensive compared with predominantly white and middle-class neighborhoods, making the operation of a small business financially more feasible. Finally, immigrants claim that running a business in a middle-class, white neighborhood is more difficult because they do not have the English language fluency and middle-class mannerisms required to deal with a more affluent and more educated clientele. For example, when asked why she opened a business in a low-income, black neighborhood as opposed to a middle-income, white neighborhood, the Korean owner of a take-out restaurant in West Harlem replied,

> Because easier. First of all, you don't have to have that much money to open up the store. And second of all, easier because you don't need to that much complicate. White people is very classy and choosy, and especially white people location is not like this, mostly they go to mall. Here they don't have many car, so easier, cheaper rent. When you go to white location, Second Avenue, Third Avenue, rent is already cost twenty thousand dollar [per month], you know, and they don't have any room for us. But black people area, other people hesitate to come in because they worry about crime and something like that, so they got a lot of room for Koreans.

When Jewish and Korean merchants have gathered enough experience and capital doing business in low-income neighborhoods, some opt to leave inner cities and open stores in safer, middle-income neighborhoods, where their businesses may be less profitable (because of increased competition) but there is less crime. Interestingly, Korean store owners in Mount Airy, the most affluent black neighborhood of my research sites, noted that their businesses are not as profitable as those in poorer neighborhoods because many middle-class customers own cars and can therefore drive outside of their communities for services and products. Immigrant-owned businesses flourish in inner cities because low-income consumers are often confined to shopping in the neighborhoods in which they live.

Immigrant entrepreneurs cluster in vacant niches in black neighborhoods, and the process of retail niche domination can be best described as "an evolutionary chain."[3] The newest immigrant store owners locate in the most physically exhausting, labor-intensive businesses, which require relatively little start-up capital and have low profit margins, such as grocery stores, take-out restaurants, and fish markets. The long hours and physically demanding labor often ensure that first-generation immigrants will be the ones to occupy these lines of business. Korean immigrants presently dominate these niches, but they are merely the successors in a line of immigrant ethnic groups who occupied these business niches before them.

Jewish store owners are the veterans in black neighborhoods; most are second- or third-generation shopkeepers whose businesses have been in these neighborhoods for more than four decades. Jewish merchants have moved up the retail chain and now occupy the most profitable and most desirable business niches. Their retail mobility, coupled with their mobility out of retail altogether, has left room for newer immigrants to penetrate the less desirable niches that Jews and other white ethnic groups have long since abandoned. Jewish retailers did not begin with high-ticket merchandise such as furniture, jewelry, and expensive apparel; they, like the Korean immigrants, began with businesses requiring low capital investments. For example, a Jewish merchant who sells industrial apparel explained how his father acquired his first business: "My father sold ice cream from a pushcart and sold second-hand dishes in front of Macy's to make a living, and when he accumulated enough money, he could afford to go into business."

The Jewish and Korean-owned businesses that line the major avenues are often not the immigrants' first businesses. Like the father of this Jewish merchant, most immigrants begin with labor-intensive businesses, and once they have amassed enough capital from their first business, they move toward larger, more capital-intensive businesses. For example, a Korean merchant in West Philadelphia owned three businesses before purchasing her fourth and most recent business, a profitable sneaker store. She began by opening a grocery store with her brother, where she worked seven days a week for three years. When she grew tired of the long hours every day, she decided to sell the grocery business and bought a discount variety store. After several years, she sold the variety store for a profit and bought a clothing store, which required greater capital but was significantly less labor-intensive than either the grocery or variety stores. Eventually, she bought the sneaker store she currently owns. In each successive move, the Korean business owner made a profit by selling her former business and moving toward a less physically demanding business that required more economic capital.

Retail niche domination is an evolutionary process: As immigrant entrepreneurs gather experience and capital, they penetrate more capital-intensive industries, leaving room for newer immigrants to occupy the abandoned retail niches. Korean immigrants have largely succeeded the Jewish immigrants, and as we enter the twenty-first century, newer immigrant entrepreneurs are already beginning to fill the niches and storefronts vacated by upwardly mobile Koreans. For example, Asian Indian and Middle Eastern immigrant groups have entered retail niches such as delicatessens and discount variety stores. As long as second- and third-generation immigrants find better opportunities in the mainstream labor market, retail self-employment (particularly businesses that cater to a low-income clientele) will remain a protected occupational niche among immigrant communities, who will continue to succeed one another.

Although immigrant groups replace one another, African Americans tend to dominate different retail niches altogether, such as barbering and hair styling salons, restaurants, and music stores—niches that require little start-up capital and are protected by the distinct tastes of their coethnic clientele. Timothy Bates (1997) refers to these businesses as "traditional lines of black enterprise." Given capital constraints, African American retailers in black neighborhoods are more likely to enter service-oriented industries, most notably the hair service industry.[4] African American salon owners purchase their businesses with very little capital, typically beginning with only one hair station and slowly expanding the number of stations and services they offer.

The hair service industry is a protected market for blacks because it relies heavily on coethnic tastes and preferences and also because other ethnic groups are unable or unwilling to enter this market. For instance, a former Jewish beauty salon owner in West Philadelphia candidly admits why he changed his line of business from hair styling to hair products (such as wigs and hair pieces) with the change of the neighborhood's racial composition: "In 1975, it was no longer a hair salon. By 1975, we were strictly selling hair products: wigs and hair accessories. I didn't feel like doing hair any more. I don't want to do black hair. I don't want to offend them, but I just don't want to do it." In addition, because beauticians and barbers need to acquire licenses in order to serve clients, immigrant ethnic groups who choose self-employment strictly as a means to upward mobility do not consider this labor-intensive industry as a cost-effective option.

Differences in economic and social capital among ethnic groups dictate which retail niches they are able to occupy. African Americans lack access to the economic and social capital in the form of loans from family and fellow ethnics that Jewish and Korean merchants enjoy. These coethnic resources play a crucial role in the formation and development of immigrant-owned businesses, giving immigrant entrepreneurs a distinct advantage over African Americans, who are generally unable to develop the economies of scale to effectively compete with more affluent immigrant groups. Because of capital constraints, few black-owned businesses overlap with Jewish- or Korean-owned businesses in these neighborhoods, and because these three groups occupy separate niches, business competition is more likely to be intraethnic in nature.

Mass Marketing a Once
Exclusive Product

Some immigrant entrepreneurs succeed in those industries in which they are able to "mass market" a once exclusive product. In other words, they take a luxury product or service and sell it at a lower cost, thereby making it more accessible for a wider population. This is the structural component in the study of immigrant entrepreneurship that has been missing in previous work. For instance, before Korean-owned manicure salons opened on virtually every block in New York City, manicures used to be available only in full-service beauty salons. In these salons, manicures cost about twenty dollars, making them accessible only to an elite group of people, namely upper-class and upper-middle-class white women. Koreans mass marketed the manicure by charging only seven dollars, taking this luxury service out of the beauty salon and making it more available to a wider clientele (Kang 1997). Koreans have used the same strategy in selling fresh flowers, which could once be had only at florist shops but now are readily available at corner delis. These business owners have successfully adapted to the changing demands of the service economy by bringing small, full-service retail shops close to both high- and low-income consumers (Sassen 1991). Korean-owned manicures and delis have become a ubiquitous symbol of New York City, as attested by the complaint of a woman who had moved out of the city that "there are no Koreans. . . . which explains why you can never find flowers and why manicures cost $15" (Zigman, *New York Times*, 1996, C6).

Korean immigrants have also used the same strategy with ethnic beauty supplies, including both hair care and skin care for an ethnic clientele. These products were once available only through beauty salons, but again immigrant entrepreneurs have mass marketed these goods by offering them to the general population on a retail level, thereby making them available at much cheaper prices. Interestingly, the retail sale of ethnic beauty supplies is a relatively new industry, dating back only ten years, and of the three hundred beauty supplies stores in New York City, 80 percent are Korean owned. Ethnic clustering like this leads to advantages, such as the ability to pool orders with several store owners, form business associations, and negotiate with manufacturers in order to receive cheaper wholesale prices.

This strategy of mass marketing transcends industries and also explains immigrants' success in lower-line apparel. According to the 1993 *Consumer Expenditure Survey* (U.S. Department of Labor 1995), blacks, compared with whites, spend a greater percentage of their income on apparel and services (Landry 1987; Rauch 1996). African Americans in inner cities also have distinctive tastes in apparel and accessories, creating a demand for what people in the business call "ethnic urban sportswear" or "inner-city sportswear." One large component of ethnic urban sportswear is imitation designer knock-offs of Ralph Lauren Polo, Tommy Hilfiger, and Moschino. Koreans have capitalized on this industry. An African American employee of a Korean-owned store illustrates the immense demand for this line of less expensive, designer-imitation clothing: he explained the difference between the Korean-owned store in which he works and the more expensive Jewish-owned clothing stores on 125th Street in West Harlem: "For example, you have this Ralph Lauren look-alike. JJ [a Jewish-owned clothing store] is too expensive, so people that are, quote drug dealers, hustlers, they can afford JJ and DJ. Welfare recipients, people who just receive money twice a month, or maybe once every month, they want that look. So what they do is they'll come in, and we'll cater to their needs."

Because low-income blacks cannot afford to purchase designer clothing, Korean-owned businesses that sell designer imitations prosper in poor neighborhoods. Although Korean merchants currently dominate this market, they were not the first to identify it. Jewish retailers once dominated the lower-line apparel industry, but they have left this niche and entered a more exclusive one in which they now carry higher-priced apparel, including dress wear and authentic designer sportswear.

Vertical Integration: Coethnic Advantage and Disadvantage

Aside from the regional monopoly in industries such as inner-city sportswear and higher-priced apparel at a retail level, there is also a Jewish and Korean monopoly in these industries on a wholesale level. One Korean merchant on 125th Street in West Harlem asserts that of the forty suppliers with whom he does business, only three are not Korean. This translates into ethnic advantage in terms of vertical integration, the importance of which in small business should be underscored, because coethnics are more likely to extend credit and offer better price points to one another than to outsiders. Korean merchants have stressed the importance of and the facility with which they are able to receive merchandise on credit from their coethnic suppliers. For instance, a Korean retailer in West Harlem remarked,

> Korean companies are really new, and they don't do credit checks or whatever. It's just through yes, no, handshake deals. But, like, all these American companies, they do a credit check. They look at a lot of different factors, a lot of hassles, but Korean companies, it's no hassle. When the

invoice is due, you pay them when it's due. Or when business is bad, you pay them on a weekly basis until your business is better. That's how they work. That's how a lot of these Korean wholesalers became big because if you think about it, the urban clothing business is predominantly—I would say, Koreans own a predominant market-share in that area.

A neighboring Korean merchant explained how he was able to get merchandise for his first business from coethnic suppliers without having any prior credit history: "My first business, I sold costume jewelry and general merchandise like stockings, and handbags, things that people can buy from all Korean stores. Most Korean people carry same kind of merchandise. The wholesalers on 32d Street, they give you credit. Wholesalers not organized in the credit. No application, no research the credit history. We just talk. They see your personality, your character, and that's it." Korean merchants are not the only group that profits from vertical integration; Jewish merchants also benefit from this structural advantage. For example, a Jewish merchant in West Harlem similarly explained the ease with which he was able to receive jewelry on credit from his coethnic wholesalers when he opened his first business, even though he had no prior credit or business history: "I started out in jewelry because I have some friends in the business. They helped me out. My friends helped me out to get credit, so the wholesalers gave me credit right away. I guess I got a lucky break." Steven Gold (1994a, 1994b) notes comparable patterns of coethnic economic cooperation among the Chinese-Vietnamese and Israeli business communities in California. Although coethnic vertical integration is not a prerequisite for setting up shop, it is undoubtedly a valuable resource that can pull a business through a rough period.

Credit is vital to the success and growth of small businesses, particularly at the start-up phase or when business is slow. Merchants who receive stock on credit have an economic advantage over those who must pay for their merchandise C.O.D. (cash on delivery), because stock purchased on credit gives retailers more flexibility by allowing them to keep money in the business for a longer period of time. Receiving credit from suppliers has historically been and continues to be a problem for black merchants. David Caplovitz's (1969) early study of Harlem merchants reveals that in comparison with white business owners, black merchants were more likely to have to pay C.O.D., even when type and size of business was held constant, indicating that suppliers consider them poor credit risks. Decades later, today's African Americans who pursue more skill- and capital-intensive businesses also find themselves in the difficult position of not being able to establish credit lines with their suppliers (Woodard 1997). Coethnic vertical integration increases the probability that merchants will receive credit from their suppliers.

Kenneth Wilson and Allen Martin (1982) note that vertical integration serves another important function: the creation of additional spending within the coethnic community. They argue that vertical integration characterizes the success of the Cuban enclave in Miami, which is composed of highly interdependent industries. In comparison, the black economy in Miami is composed of weakly interdependent industries, in which even the potential for vertical integration is absent. My findings support those of Wilson and Martin; African American–owned businesses are not vertically integrated and thus are denied even the potential for coethnic advantage in terms of supplying credit or generating additional capital among African American entrepreneurs. African American merchants realize their inability to do business with other African Americans, although some expressly commented that, given the choice, they would prefer dealing with coethnics. For example, an African American coffee shop owner commented, "I would love to have been able to do business with my own, but there really isn't anybody that sells what I need. That's unfortunate, that I can't do business with my own ethnic group." In addition, she explained that while working in a Jewish-owned business after graduating from high school, she learned the prevalence, and relevance, of vertical integration. "I would say that 95 percent of the business that they did, their supplies and so forth, were with other Jewish people. They supported their own [by buying from each other]. So I learned that . . . the black companies that they dealt with, the reason that they were dealing with them is because they had something that the Jewish companies needed [that Jewish suppliers did not have]."

Another African American merchant who sells Afrocentric women's apparel buys from Pakistani and Asian Indian suppliers who have entered the wholesale market for Afrocentric clothing. He remarked, "I have Pakistanis, Indians, who are *big* in African fabrics, and African designs making billions of dollars, on black culture. Pakistanis!" Because he operates strictly on a cash basis with his suppliers, he receives no credit from them, even in emergency situations, for instance, when his store was burglarized. He explained the problems that resulted from this misfortune: "They broke in and they cleaned out the whole store. Everything was stolen empty. . . . No way to really get credit because we were mostly on a cash basis with our suppliers, and we were in a very bad condition." In this case, if he had been dealing with coethnic suppliers who would have extended him credit, he would have received merchandise and been able to go back into business more quickly. In retail, where cash flow can be tight at times, and in low-income neighborhoods, where crises such as break-ins are not uncommon, the option of purchasing merchandise on credit from suppliers becomes an invaluable advantage.

Given the low rate of self-employment among African Americans at a retail level, the paucity of African American businesses on the wholesale end is not surprising. Entering wholesale or manufacturing requires even more capital than entering business on the retail end. Suppliers must plan and invest in merchandise well in advance and amass enough capital to carry them over for long periods of time. An African American retailer explained,

> You don't have black suppliers because you got to remember that being on the wholesale end of it means you have to plan for a season ahead or two seasons ahead in some places if you're dealing with major department stores. You have figures and money and layouts and things, if you don't have the bank credits or the bank backing or the bank whatever, you cannot do it. You cannot produce a year in advance. You don't have the wherewithal. You don't have the resources, so as a result, we're limited that way.

Even Afrocentric products such as apparel, books, greeting cards, and wedding invitations are often made by non–African American wholesalers. For instance, the African American merchant who sells women's apparel also offers Afrocentric wedding invitations and explained that although all of the merchandise from his supplier is Afrocentric, the company is white owned. He commented regretfully, "What happens is a lot of times everybody knows how to make money from our community but us. We don't make money off our community." Because many Asian Indians lived in Africa before immigrating to the United States, these "twice migrants" have excellent import connections in Africa (Bhachu 1985). Immigrant entrepreneurs such as Jews, Asian Indians, Koreans, Armenians, and Chinese often have access to capital and imported merchandise from their countries of origin that American-born blacks lack. These resources offer competitive business advantages in both the retail and wholesale markets.

Although not all African American business owners agree that coethnic vertical integration is either economically advantageous or symbolically significant, for Jewish and Korean retailers, it can be a critical resource in business, especially at the start-up phase and when business is slow. The option of purchasing stock on credit allows merchants to keep funds in their businesses for longer periods. Vertical integration also generates additional revenues in the ethnic business community at large. However, whether or not African American retailers prefer to do business with their own ethnic group, the potential for coethnic vertical integration is not available, thereby limiting structural advantages such as extended credit.

Ethnic solidarity, facilitating the trust needed to supply credit to coethnics in retail, is stronger among some groups than others. Dense coethnic ties based on shared immigrant experience, common language, lifestyle, and involvement in coethnic institutions provide a firm basis for intraethnic economic cooperation (Gold 1994b). Given that as many as one-half of the Koreans in New York City are self-employed, with a sizable proportion serving inner-city consumers, their coethnic networks intersect in many different spheres: business, church, family, and social activities. As the newest immigrant group in the sample, Korean entrepreneurs exhibit the densest coethnic ties. By contrast, Jews, and even more so African Americans, are large, diverse, and long-established ethnic groups in the United States. Both groups are marked by diversity in religion, migration experience, generation, and class. The greater the heterogeneity within an ethnic group, the less basis for cooperation. Coethnicity alone does not secure economic cooperation.

Advantages of Ethnic Clustering

Ethnic clustering in niches results in coethnic advantages and disadvantages alike. Coethnic advantages include the ability to pool orders and form associations with other business owners to receive better prices from manufacturers. Suppliers generally allocate better wholesale prices to retailers who order larger quantities of merchandise, so some Korean merchants whose businesses are located in close proximity to one another pool their orders. Korean and Jewish retailers have also formed various business associations to collectively bargain with manufacturers. For example, the Korean Beauty Supplies Association works with manufacturers in marketing products with redeemable coupons or advertisements to encourage customers to shop in Korean-owned businesses. Similarly, the Korean-American Grocers Association of New York uses tactics such as price bargaining, collective purchasing, and threatening to endorse a competitor's products in order to guarantee better prices on major grocery items from non-coethnic suppliers (Min 1996). Because Korean merchants cluster in select industries, they are able to mobilize and pool their resources to derive benefits, ensuring that ethnic clustering translates into coethnic advantages.

Ethnic and Economic Exclusion: The "Other" Side of Embeddedness

Coethnic advantages enjoyed by some groups have negative consequences for others, both intended and unintended—what Waldinger (1995) describes as "the 'other' side of embeddedness." Ethnic clustering facilitates the entry of fellow ethnics into similar social structures but may also disadvantage other groups who are excluded from business opportunities simply by virtue of their nonmembership in these networks. For instance, non-Korean grocers and ethnic beauty supplies business owners do not receive the same price discounts and redeemable coupons from their suppliers simply because they are not members of these ethnic business associations.

Retail niche domination can also have more detrimental and serious consequences for other ethnic groups that go far beyond the receipt of better prices from wholesalers. The case of one African American pharmacist in Philadelphia illustrates how coethnic advantage can translate into disadvantage for other groups. She explained the ways in which she is excluded from business networks and the difficulties of being one of very few black pharmacists in a predominantly white field. Because she has opened her own business, other pharmacists in the community will no longer communicate or work with her, even though they worked with her in the past when she served as a manager for a Jewish-owned pharmacy in the same neighborhood. She explained, "When I worked for the Jewish guy, I used to call Gary [another Jewish pharmacist in the neighborhood] and say, 'Gary, I need such and such [medication]. Can I buy it off you? Can I borrow it?' 'Sure.' He'd call and say, 'Do you have such and such?' He'd come and we'd swap [medications], and we'd send our drivers over there. As soon as I moved over here [and opened my own business], no more. Pharmacy is a closed network field."

Favors, such as swapping medications and transferring patients' drug histories—favors pharmacists normally do for one other as common, professional courtesies in the interest of the patient—ceased when the African American pharmacist decided to branch out on her own. Commenting on the pharmacist's unprofessional behavior, she remarked, "I just can't understand it. And I think if someone asked him why he don't speak to me, he's going to say because she's my competition. That's the only reason why I can think he's not speaking to me anymore." Yet competition cannot be the only reason for this type of exclusion, given his cooperation while she was working for another Jewish pharmacist in the same neighborhood, who also served as his competition. Now that she can no longer rely on neighboring pharmacists to exchange favors, she finds herself disadvantaged compared with those who work together. She responded in disbelief at their grave concern with her newly established business, "See, that's what I can't understand. Why ya'll worried about me? You're already established. You already put your kids through college. You already got your boat and your house down at the shore. Why you worrying about me?!"

Michael Woodard's study of African American business owners similarly finds that one of their greatest external barriers is their exclusion from markets and distributor networks. An African American entrepreneur who owns a commercial furniture business revealed,

> We are often excluded from opportunities. . . . It's not because minority businesses don't reach out, but they're not competitive because they've been excluded from the distributor network. And the companies who exclude offer a thousand reasons why minorities can't be a part of their network, such as financial strength and other factors they manage to get around with our white counterparts. The biggest obstacle is that we don't know how it's done and we've never seen it done, since we're not even in the loop. There are too many industries that exclude us that we don't even look at—food service, sports equipment. Consequently, we're not in those industries. (Quoted in Woodard 1997, 69)

Coethnic embeddedness can work to exclude other ethnic groups from deriving business advantages or even gaining entry. Regardless of the ways in which exclusion operates—whether subtle or blatant—it can have deleterious social and economic consequences for outsiders who fall beyond these networks. In the retail industry, it is often African Americans who pay a heavy price for their exclusion from business networks. Therefore, although it may initially appear that there is no interethnic retail competition because Jews, Koreans, and African Americans occupy separate niches, retail niche domination often precludes the possibility of interethnic competition. Like Waldinger's study of competition between blacks and immigrants in Los Angeles, my study finds "little evidence of competition strictly defined" (1997, 383). However, interethnic competition is far more nuanced and is better depicted as a combination of blocked opportunities, constraints, and exclusion from business networks—ultimately resulting in exclusion from certain retail niches altogether. Business communities embedded in ethnic networks have dual functions: helping coethnics and excluding outsiders. African Americans have never been able to compete with immigrant entrepreneurs on a level playing field; instead, they have found better opportunities for employment and mobility in the public sector (Waldinger 1996). Were African Americans equally able to penetrate all retail niches, interethnic competition would undoubtedly take a different form.

Coethnic Disadvantage and Intraethnic Competition

Although there are distinct advantages for coethnics who cluster in retail niches, from the merchants' perspective, coethnic disadvantages can outweigh the advantages when niches become saturated. The notion of niche saturation resulting in coethnic disadvantage departs theoretically from Waldinger's (1996) thesis that niche concentration benefits ethnic groups. Market concentration can lead to market saturation, creating fierce intraethnic competition, most notably among immigrant groups, like Koreans, who enter only a select number of industries. In fact, the majority of Korean retail business owners in Chicago and Los Angeles regard coethnics as their primary competitors (Yoon 1997). Immigrants' concentration in industries such as grocery stores, nail salons, ethnic urban sportswear, and sneakers has made competition severe in the inner-city market.

The saturated market in certain industries has further consequences: immigrant entrepreneurs are now wary of coethnic "training systems" in which employers hire and teach coethnic employees about the business (Bailey and Waldinger 1991). Although immigrant entrepreneurs may have once preferred to hire coethnics (Light and Bonacich 1988; Portes and Bach 1985; Wilson and Portes 1980), immigrant store owners, such as Koreans, are far more reluctant to do so today, because they are essentially "training today's co-ethnic employees to be tomorrow's competitors" (Gold 1994b, 122). In fact, some Korean merchants have explained that they now refuse to hire coethnic employees for fear they will learn the business and then open a store in the same neighborhood, creating even greater competition in the same line of business. Coethnic training systems and coethnic loyalty function only when they serve profitable economic ends. Because these coethnic systems are no longer advantageous for merchants, many have withdrawn from helping fellow ethnics who are all too eager to learn the business.

In lieu of coethnic labor, immigrant entrepreneurs in black neighborhoods are increasingly hiring black and Latino immigrant employees (Lee 1998). Hiring other ethnics thereby removes the threat of future competition in the inner-city market. However, there is another underlying economic reason that coethnic hiring is no longer as prevalent in recent years: coethnic wages have become too costly, nearly double the wages for non-coethnics. For example, black employees in Korean-owned businesses in Harlem are paid on average $250 to $300 for a six-day workweek, whereas Korean employees' weekly wages fall between $450 and $500. The large wage differential makes it difficult for small business owners who work on a low profit margin to hire coethnics who expect far higher salaries than non-coethnics (Gold 1994a; 1994b; Kim 1999). In addition, taking into account immigration trends, the 1990s saw a sharp decline in the number of Korean immigrants to the United States, a decline that translates into fewer available newcomers to fill the demand for bottom-level jobs in Korean-owned businesses. Consequently, Jewish and Korean merchants increasingly turn to a cheaper labor source to fill an occupational niche once exclusively reserved for fellow ethnics.

Thus, although ethnic clustering in niches has valuable advantages such as collective mobilization on the retail level, it also has negative consequences in the form of severe intraethnic competition, most notably, in low-income black neighborhoods. Before market saturation in these retail niches, immigrants relied heavily on training systems to acquire skills and experience from coethnics who had already established their businesses. Because the inner-city market is already saturated with immigrants who congregate in only a few select industries, intraethnic cooperation has given way to cutthroat competition. Immigrant entrepreneurs lament the days of booming business—the days when intraethnic competition was minor and relatively inconsequential. Today, immigrant shopkeepers increasingly complain of slimmer profit margins and failed business ventures. Retail self-employment once may have been the quickest pathway to success, but immigrant entrepreneurs are finding that this route—now fraught with intraethnic competition—is no guarantee to social and economic mobility. Niche concentration does not always bestow rewards.

Although Jewish- and black-owned businesses are also clustered in a few business niches, these store owners maintain that intraethnic competition is not as severe because their businesses do not rely exclusively on local customer patronage but instead draw in a wider clientele base. Beauty salons proliferate on nearly every corner of these commercial strips, but they distinguish themselves by offering a variety of hair-, skin-, and nail-care services. Salons also serve clients from many different neighborhoods because clients follow their hair stylists, even after the stylists have moved to different salons or neighborhoods; clients remain loyal to their stylists, not the salons.

Similarly, Jewish business owners who sell furniture in East Harlem specialize and target different clientele bases, with each store offering a different price range for furniture. Some Jewish furniture store owners target a more middle-income customer base; others rely more heavily on the poorer local patronage. Because these furniture stores supply credit for customers who do not have or cannot afford credit cards, many of the customers return to shop in East Harlem even though they have moved to different neighborhoods and cities.[5] The diversity in both the customer base and merchandise or service offered in Jewish- and black-owned businesses reduces intraethnic competition. In contrast, Korean-owned retail businesses suffer greatly from intraethnic competition because they are vertically integrated (leaving little room for diversity in the merchandise they offer), cluster in only a few retail niches, and rely exclusively on local consumers.

Conclusion

Media images often portray immigrants streaming into America's urban landscape, depicting the foreign-born as a group who takes away business opportunities from the native-born, particularly native-born African Americans. Nowhere is this portrait more contentious than in America's inner cities, where competition among immigrant and African American business owners is one of the principal sources of tension between the foreign- and native-born populations in low-income black neighborhoods. This issue quickly spilled over into the public and academic discourses alike, with economists and sociologists leading the charge.

Do immigrant entrepreneurs take opportunities away from the native-born, and do immigrant entrepreneurs compete with and inhibit self-employment opportunities for African Americans? Economists Robert Fairlie and Bruce Meyer (1998) find that although the levels of immigration have virtually no effect on African American self-employment, the industry distributions for African American and immigrant entrepreneurs in the retail trade and personal services are similar enough that direct competition must exist between these groups. I argue that although self-employed immigrants and African Americans may converge in similar industries, such as retail and personal services, this does not necessarily mean that these groups compete with one another.

In fact, a different and more complex portrait of immigrant and African American competition is taking place. Within the retail trade industry, there are many different retail niches. Immigrant entrepreneurs, in fact, do not directly compete with African American business owners because Jewish, Korean, and African American business owners occupy distinct retail niches. Jews, for example, occupy retail niches that deal with furniture, jewelry, and expensive apparel, while Koreans are enmeshed in fruit and vegetable markets and inner-city sportswear niche. These areas of retail concentration are different from those of African Americans who dominate the hair styling and music store niches. Furthermore, although both immigrants and African Americans converge in the personal services industry, there is a breadth of personal services that business owners can offer their clientele. Here too, immigrants and African Americans occupy distinct niches; African Americans retain a stronghold on barbering and hair styling, while Koreans dominate the nail service industry. Therefore, when unraveling the question of interethnic competition at the industry level, it is crucial to bear in mind that there is an enormous amount of heterogeneity within industries, and immigrants and African Americans largely occupy separate retail niches within the same industry. Consequently, there is little direct interethnic competition.

Although immigrant entrepreneurs may not directly compete with African American business owners, the retail niches in which these groups specialize should be understood as a result of ethnic succession, differential opportunities, constraints, and exclusion. The inequality of economic and social capital combined with their exclusion from business networks leave African Americans severely disadvantaged. They are unable to penetrate more costly retail markets and effectively compete with their immigrant counterparts. Exclusion comes with a heavy price—ranging from not receiving the best prices from wholesalers (which limits a business owner's ability to effectively compete with other retailers), to blatantly excluding African Americans from business networks, to facing barriers that limit penetration into ethnically saturated retail niches. These types of exclusion can have deleterious economic consequences for outsiders who fall beyond ethnic networks, stripping them of advantages that other groups utilize and rely on in business.

I would like to thank Nancy Foner, Herbert Gans, Steven Gold, Rubén Rumbaut, Roger Waldinger, and the anonymous reviewer for helpful comments on an earlier version of this paper. The International Migration Program of the Social Science Research Council, the Andrew W. Mellon Foundation, and the National Science Foundation, SBR–9633345, provided generous research support on which this paper is based. I am also grateful to the University of California President's Office for their support during the writing of this paper. A previous version of this chapter appeared in *American Behavioral Scientist* 1999, vol. 42, no. 9.

Notes

1. "Black," as used in this chapter, refers to a generic category that includes African Americans, West Indians, and Africans.

2. "Retail niche" refers to a line of business in the retail sector in which ethnic groups concentrate or specialize. For example, in the inner city, Koreans dominate the urban ethnic sportswear retail niche, Jews the furniture niche, and African Americans the hairstyling niche.

3. The concept "evolutionary retail chain" diverges theoretically from Waldinger's concept of "ethnic musical chairs" (1996,. 260). Whereas Waldinger refers to ethnic groups succeeding one another in the re-

tail trade altogether, the concept of "evolutionary retail chain" refers to the process by which ethnic groups succeed one another in particular retail niches or lines of business. As older, more experienced entrepreneurs penetrate more capital-intensive industries, they leave room for newer groups to occupy the abandoned retail niches.

4. Timothy Bates (1997) and Michael Woodard (1997) argue that although "traditional lines of black enterprise" may be common in inner-city neighborhoods, today's African American entrepreneurs are entering new "emerging lines of business" that are far more capital- and skill-intensive and serve a racially diverse clientele, including corporations and the government.

5. Often, the credit terms offered by furniture stores in low-income communities are exorbitantly high and are a form of exploitation for poor consumers, who pay more for interest than the price of the merchandise itself. Usually, the owners require one-third of the retail price in cash as a down payment (which covers the wholesale cost of the merchandise), and the rest is paid over a period of one, two, or more years. The longer it takes the consumer to pay off the balance, the higher the interest payments and the total cost for the furniture.

References

Bailey, Thomas, and Roger Waldinger. 1991. "Primary, Secondary, and Enclave Labor Markets: A Training Systems Approach." *American Sociological Review* 56(4): 432–45.

Bates, Timothy. 1997. *Race, Self-Employment, and Upward Mobility.* Baltimore: Johns Hopkins University Press.

Bean, Frank D., and Stephanie Bell-Rose, eds. 1999. *Immigration and Opportunity: Race, Ethnicity, and Employment in the United States.* New York: Russell Sage Foundation.

Bhachu, Parminder. 1985. *Twice Migrants: East African Sikh Settlers in Britain.* New York: Tavistock.

Borjas, George J. 1994. "The Economics of Immigration." *Journal of Economic Literature* 32(4): 1667–1717.

Caplovitz, David. 1969. *The Merchants of Harlem.* New York: Columbia University, Bureau of Social Science Research.

Carpenter, Allan. 1992. *Facts About Cities.* New York: H. W. Wilson.

Fairlie, Robert W., and Bruce D. Meyer. 1998. "Does Immigration Hurt African American Self-Employment?" In *Help or Hindrance? The Economic Implications of Immigration for African Americans,* edited by Daniel S. Hamermesh and Frank D. Bean. New York: Russell Sage Foundation.

Gold, Steven J. 1994a. "Chinese-Vietnamese Entrepreneurs in California." In *The New Asian Immigration in Los Angeles and Global Re-*

structuring, edited by Paul Ong, Edna Bonacich, and Lucie Cheng. Philadelphia: Temple University Press.

———. 1994b. "Patterns of Economic Cooperation Among Israeli Immigrants in Los Angeles." *International Migration Review* 28(1): 114–35.

Hamermesh, Daniel S., and Frank D. Bean, eds. 1998. *Help or Hindrance? The Economic Implications of Immigration for African Americans.* New York: Russell Sage Foundation.

Kang, Miliann. 1997. "Manicuring Race, Gender, and Class: Service Interactions in New York City Korean-Owned Nail Salons." *Race, Gender, and Class* 4(3): 143–64.

Kim, Dae Young. 1999. "Beyond Coethnic Solidarity: Mexican and Ecuadorian Employment in Korean-Owned Businesses in New York City." *Ethnic and Racial Studies* 22(3): 581–605.

Landry, Bart. 1987. *The New Black Middle Class.* Los Angeles: University of California Press.

Lee, Jennifer. 1998. "Cultural Brokers: Race-Based Hiring in Inner-City Neighborhoods." *American Behavioral Scientist* 41(7): 927–37.

———. 2000. "Striving for the American Dream: Struggle, Success, and Intergroup Conflict Among Korean Immigrant Entrepreneurs." In *Contemporary Asian America*, edited by Min Zhou and James V. Gatewood. New York: New York University Press.

Light, Ivan, and Edna Bonacich. 1988. *Immigrant Entrepreneurs.* Berkeley: University of California Press.

Light, Ivan, and Carolyn Rosenstein. 1995. *Race, Ethnicity, and Entrepreneurship in Urban America.* New York: Aldine De Gruyter.

Light, Ivan, and Angel A. Sanchez. 1987. "Immigrant Entrepreneurs in 272 SMSAs." *Sociological Perspectives* 30(4): 373–99.

Marx, Gary T. 1967. *Protest and Prejudice.* New York: Harper and Row.

Min, Pyong Gap. 1996. *Caught in the Middle.* Berkeley: University of California Press.

Portes, Alejandro, and Robert L. Bach. 1985. *Latin Journey.* Berkeley: University of California Press.

Rauch, James. 1996. "Trade and Networks: An Application to Minority Retail Entrepreneurship." Working paper 100. New York: Russell Sage Foundation.

Sassen, Saskia. 1991. "The Informal Economy." In *Dual City: Restructuring New York*, edited by John H. Mollenkopf and Manuel Castells. New York: Russell Sage Foundation.

Steinberg, Stephen. 1989. *The Ethnic Myth.* Boston: Beacon Press.

U.S. Department of Commerce. 1992. *1990 Census of Population and Housing.* Summary. Washington: U.S. Government Printing Office.

U.S. Department of Labor. 1995. *Consumer Expenditure Survey, 1993.* Washington: U.S. Government Printing Office.

Waldinger, Roger. 1995. "The 'Other Side' of Embeddedness: A Case Study of the Interplay of Economy and Ethnicity." *Ethnic and Racial Studies* 18(3): 555–80.

———. 1996. *Still the Promised City? African-Americans and New Im-*

migrants in Postindustrial New York. Cambridge, Mass.: Harvard University Press.

———. 1997. "Black/Immigrant Competition Re-Assessed: New Evidence from Los Angeles." *Sociological Perspectives* 40(3): 365–86.

Wilson, Kenneth L., and Allen W. Martin. 1982. "Ethnic Enclaves: A Comparison of the Cuban and Black Economies in Miami." *American Journal of Sociology* 88(1): 135–60.

Wilson, Kenneth L., and Alejandro Portes. 1980. "Immigrant Enclaves: An Analysis of the Labor Market Experiences of Cubans in Miami." *American Journal of Sociology* 86(2): 295–319.

Woodard, Michael D. 1997. *Black Entrepreneurs in America.* New Brunswick: Rutgers University Press.

Yoon, In-Jin. 1997. *On My Own.* Chicago: University of Chicago Press.

14

OUTSOURCING THE HEARTH: THE IMPACT OF IMMIGRATION ON LABOR ALLOCATION IN AMERICAN FAMILIES

Kathy A. Kaufman

IMMIGRANTS employed as domestic workers have literally reorganized social life in many American communities. One has only to walk the streets of New York City to see this phenomenon at work. Parks are crowded with Caribbean women tending to fair, blue-eyed charges; each morning finds immigrant women heading into the elevators of residential buildings equipped with vacuum cleaners and dust mops; just a few miles away, suburban lawns are abuzz with mowers and hedge trimmers wielded by men from Mexico, Nicaragua, and El Salvador. Maintaining servants is no longer the exclusive domain of the well-heeled: Immigrant domestic workers increasingly take over what were the traditional household chores of middle-class mothers, fathers, and adolescent children, who, in turn, are frequently away at work themselves.

Three decades into this immigration wave, there is an opportunity to examine some of its more enduring effects on American society. This chapter describes the ways in which shifts in social stratification brought about by immigrant inflows have fundamentally altered the consumption and labor allocation patterns of American households. Specifically, I argue that ethnic concentrations in particular occupational niches cause crowding, which has a depressive effect on immigrant wages and increases income inequality in the local labor markets in which immigrants are concentrated. It is precisely this income inequality that makes service sector hiring affordable for middle-class families.

A complete understanding of the dynamics of service sector hiring requires attention not just to labor supply characteristics but also to the complementary role of household demand. By locating the source of labor demand in affluent consumption and declining manufacturing sectors, polarization theorists have overlooked the dramatic impact of the surge in the female labor supply on utilization of services in the United States. For American families the decision to outsource household work and enter the labor force is a complex one, shaped by an array of factors that span the continuum from the micro- to macro-level. On the one hand, individuals and households weigh the financial impact of entering the labor market against a variety of nonmaterial interests, including individual tastes, cultural values, and social norms. On the other hand, the financial feasibility of household hiring is largely contingent upon the macroeconomic forces affecting the price of domestic service. Ultimately, although macro-level perspectives on labor migration emphasize the intersubstitutability of unskilled workers, a highly differentiated domestic-service labor supply presents itself to household employers, who pick and choose among immigrant groups in the process of matching human capital characteristics of workers to the requirements of jobs.[1]

The findings described here are derived from a comparative study of the domestic service labor market in New York, a city with high rates of immigration, and Philadelphia, a city with low immigration levels. In-depth ethnographic interviews were conducted with domestic workers and middle-class families to examine the conditions under which families choose to outsource household work and the impact of the characteristics of the local domestic service labor supply on that decision-making calculus.

Methodology

In the spring and summer of 1997 in-depth ethnographic interviews were conducted with a total of sixty domestic workers employed in New York City and Philadelphia. By sample design, of the thirty domestic workers interviewed in each city, twenty were baby-sitters and ten were housecleaners. However, because there is some crossover between the two lines of work, a number of New York baby-sitters also did some cleaning, sometimes for households that were not their primary employers.

In addition, interviews were conducted between September 1996 and May 1998 with forty American-born middle-class women, also divided evenly between New York and Philadelphia. These interviews focused on how the material circumstances, perceptions, and preferences of families interact with contextual factors to produce particular labor force participation and domestic service hiring decisions. In Philadelphia these respondents were recruited from refresher childbirth classes and a parent-child education program offered by Pennsylvania Hospital. In New York City respondents were recruited through mailings sent to patients who had given birth at Columbia-Presbyterian Hospital over a five-year period. To control for the degree of labor-intensity of household production, only families with at least one child between the ages of two and five were recruited, and families with children under three months of age were temporarily excluded. Parents who were not native born were also excluded, and those without private medical insurance were eliminated from mailing lists in an attempt to solicit only middle-class households.

Background

Dramatic differences in immigration rates to U.S. regions and cities have resulted in variation in the size, composition, and degree of informality of the domestic service employment sector from one location to the next. This heterogeneity offers a unique opportunity for comparative research on the impact of immigration on the local social structure. New York City and Philadelphia were chosen as research sites because, despite many similarities, they represent extreme cases among American metropolitan areas with regard to immigration. These cities resemble each other on a number of key dimensions apart from immigration level: female labor force participation rate, proportion of service sector employment, proportion of industrial employment, unemployment and self-employment rates, and percentage living below the poverty line (Carpenter and Provorse 1996). New York City, however, has one of the highest percentages of foreign-born residents in the country (28.4 percent in 1990), and in 1992 almost a quarter of its residents (24.4 percent) were Hispanic. By contrast, in 1990 Philadelphia ranked thirty-seventh in the United States for foreign-born residents (6.6 percent), only 5.6 percent of whom were Hispanic (U.S. Department of Commerce 1991).

The racial-ethnic composition of these cities has notable consequences for the character of the domestic service labor supply in each city. More than two-thirds of the domestic service labor force in New York City (69.3 percent) is foreign born, compared with a mere 15 percent of Philadelphia's domestic-service labor force. In addition, domestic workers in Philadelphia are twice as likely to be African American as those in New York City. As a consequence, Philadelphia's domestics are much more likely to be American citizens (90 percent, versus 47 percent in New York) and to speak English proficiently (25 percent in New York do not). Philadelphia's domestic workers are also better educated, with 30 percent more having high school diplomas than their New York counterparts. As indicated by table 14.1, of the fraction of Philadelphia's domestics who are immigrants, the majority are European (47 percent), whereas nearly three-quarters of those in New York City are Caribbean

TABLE 14.1   *Country of Birth of New York City and Philadelphia Domestic Workers, 1990 (Percentage)*

Country of Birth	New York	Philadelphia
United States	27.4	85.4
Caribbean	21.7	3.7
Central America	12.5	1.2
South America	16.1	1.6
Europe	10.1	6.9
U.S. territories	3.3	—
Other	2.3	0.1

Source: U.S. Bureau of the Census 1992.

and Latin American, with minor concentrations of Colombian (7.5 percent), Jamaican (5.4 percent), Dominican (4 percent), Salvadoran (3.5 percent), Trinidadian (3.2 percent), Haitian (2.9 percent), and Guatemalan (2.9 percent) natives.

Impact of Immigration on Labor Supply Characteristics and Working Conditions

As Alejandro Portes and others have recently emphasized, the socially embedded nature of immigration leads to highly uneven concentrations of immigrants across American cities. These authors point out that because information about immigration and its potential rewards is spread through contact with others who have emigrated in the past, flows instigated by relatively few individuals may soon take on their own momentum and grow exponentially. Moreover, this process causes immigrants to settle in relatively few destination cities, where social contacts from home communities facilitate their settlement in housing and employment and ease the transition into a new society (Portes and Rumbaut 1990; Portes 1995). Once immigrants are in the United States, the process of job acquisition is similarly circumscribed by social networks, resulting in ethnic concentrations in relatively few occupational sectors. As Roger Waldinger explains, "Migrants . . . enter the economy under the auspices of friends or kin, which means that they begin with connections. Networks funnel the newcomers into specialized economic activities; as newcomers flow into the workplaces where earlier settlers have already gotten established, ethnic concentrations, or niches, gradually develop" (1996, 3–4).

Although immigration scholars have emphasized the positive im-

FIGURE 14.1   *Domestic Workers per Household Relative to the National Average, New York City and Philadelphia, Various Years*

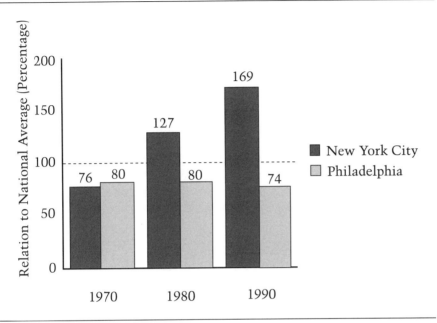

Source: U.S. Department of Commerce 1992.
Note: The middle line, at 100 percent, represents the national average. Thus, for example, in 1990, the density of domestic workers in New York City was 69 percent higher than that of cities nationwide.

pact of cohesive social networks on the economic adaptation of immigrants, labor economists note that the segregation of workers into a small number of industries may cause "crowding," leading to greater competition for jobs, reduced wages, and poor working conditions.[2] This certainly appears to be the case with New York City's domestic service labor market. Whereas Philadelphia had a slightly higher density of domestic workers per household than New York City in 1970, the foreign-born population of New York City has swelled to more than 25 percent since that time, and immigrants have come to dominate the domestic service labor supply. With the continued influx of newcomers into this labor market sector, the number of domestic workers per household in New York has come to greatly exceed the national average, whereas Philadelphia's relationship to the norm has been stable (see figure 14.1).

This has resulted in a density of domestic workers in New York City that is now more than double that found in Philadelphia.

New York City

Occupational crowding resulting from immigration has transformed New York's domestic service sector. The presence of many compatriots in an employment sector can offer an advantage to coethnics who gain access to valuable information about job opportunities. In New York, however, the domestic-service labor supply threatens to outstrip demand, generating cut-throat competition for jobs. This competition leads job seekers to lower their salary demands in order to find work, reducing wages to near subsistence levels. Moreover, once employed, the ease with which individual household workers can be replaced by their employers reduces their bargaining power, ultimately transforming domestic service in New York into an inferior occupation characterized by poor compensation and onerous working conditions.

Price

In New York City the price of domestic service is a function of labor supply rather than demand. Whereas Philadelphia's household employers must compete with other industries for a limited pool of workers, for a number of reasons, the size of the immigrant-dominated domestic service labor force in New York City is far less sensitive to price.[3] First, as a number of immigration scholars have noted, the threshold of what is considered a minimally acceptable salary is lower for first-generation immigrants, whose standard of living and earnings expectations are set in reference to conditions in their country of origin (Waldinger 1996; Foner 1986). Furthermore, an immigrant labor supply, constrained by a lack of social, financial, and cultural resources—and, in many cases, by language barriers as well—has fewer available venues for employment and is therefore less likely to respond to low wages by defecting to other sectors. The use of social networks for job acquisition confines workers' awareness of jobs to a limited number of niches already occupied by coethnics. Moreover, undocumented immigrants are legally restricted to a relatively few informal employment sectors. Even documented immigrants feel they must work "off the books" if a lack of skills would reduce their after-tax earnings in formal sectors to barely subsistence levels. Finally, although substandard wages and working conditions will cause some to retreat from domestic service, ongoing in-migration from abroad functions to replenish the domestic service labor supply, stabilizing wages at very low levels.

Competition

All the above factors combine to enlarge the domestic service labor supply in New York City, generating competition for jobs and reducing the average wage. Domestic workers interviewed for this study report answering advertisements and finding themselves competing with scores of other applicants for a single job. As one woman who has been baby-sitting and housekeeping in New York for twenty-three years observed, "Now it has become more and more difficult, because there are a lot of people searching for jobs. Everyone is after the ads in the paper and the ads in the parks. It is very difficult for most people." This competition is reflected in individual domestics' wage histories, which not only fail to show the consistently rising earnings that would indicate returns on increased experience but often demonstrate marked wage reductions upon changing jobs. A Guyanese baby-sitter who saw her wages drop by one-fifth when she changed jobs described her experience in the market this way: "You don't have a chance to set no price. I mean, when you need a job. . . . They just know when you need the job. You know? You just say, okay. They set the price. She raised me once and take it back and cut the hours. Hopefully I will get a raise."

Working Conditions

Ultimately, crowding not only undermines the wage of New York's domestic workers but also impairs their ability to assert control over their working conditions. Both baby-sitters and housekeepers described marriages disrupted for years by live-in work when no other jobs presented themselves. Baby-sitters, in particular, are likely to be responsible for housecleaning, laundry, and cooking, in addition to child care. According to a Honduran baby-sitter,

> They don't want to do anything, and leave all the work for the baby-sitter. . . . I had to do the cleaning, I had to take care of the children, I had to help them with their homework, I had to take them to the doctor, I had to bathe them, get them dressed, cook, and everything else. Absolutely everything. So when she finished telling all this that I had to do, and all what she demanded, I asked her if she didn't want me to sleep with her husband too!

In contrast to Philadelphia's domestics, who typically live with their own children if they have them, immigrant domestics in New York often leave their children behind in their home countries, enduring long and painful separations.[4] The reasons for this are multiple: Those without immigration documents sometimes migrate alone out of fear that they will be deported, potentially jeopardizing their custody of their children. Furthermore, domestics' low wages usually relegate them to housing in poor neighborhoods, where they fear their children would be affected by violent crime or an oppositional culture prevalent among other local adolescents. Finally, without dependent children, women are free to accept live-in jobs, which greatly increases the employment prospects of newcomers with few resources. The ties to employers' children, however, present new difficulties. Having endured the loss of their own children, these women find it even more painful to break with abusive employers once they have formed bonds with their young charges and have reared them as their own.

Ultimately, although in New York City domestics may enjoy some aspects of their jobs, the years of work in domestic service are clearly seen as a sacrifice by these women, who lack alternative employment possibilities. More recent arrivals to the United States often speak of plans to learn English, go to school, and move on to more lucrative or prestigious employment. Yet veterans in domestic service describe educational and career ambitions long-ago derailed by language barriers, financial difficulties, and legal obstacles. The story of Hilda, who came to the United States two decades ago from Ecuador, is typical in this regard. As she told it,

> I wanted to study to be a doctor. That was my greatest illusion. I did all the paperwork, and I went through all the requirements to go into college and study. I went to school to validate the credits I had taken in Ecuador, to take a high school equivalency exam, and to study English. Everything was going perfectly. Everything was beautiful. The director of the school was very nice. He told me he was going to help me get into school. I was very happy. But one day he came to me and said that everything was ready, but the only thing missing was my green card and my social security number. And that was exactly what I didn't have. He told me there was nothing to be done in such a situation. I was devastated. That was a terrible thing. Tough luck. What could I do? All the illusions crumbled down. In order to get my papers I had to get married or something like that, and I didn't really want to get married. I was too young. So I started to search for work. . . . For my condition as an alien here, for not being legal, I had to accept the jobs that are open for that condition. And that is housecleaning and baby-sitting. Maybe it's a lack of enthusiasm or momentum. I started to work and get involved in other things. What I needed the most at that time was money, and the studies were not so important anymore.

As Hilda's story implies, for immigrants with limited resources or without legal residency, the passage of time in domestic service is often accompanied by a lowering of expectations. Career ambitions give way to either realism or resignation, and a sense of merely biding time. "The important thing," as one woman put it, "is to work, even more when you have left your family in your country. Working in whatever doesn't really matter to me. I know that if I knew English well enough, and if I studied something here, obviously I would have better opportunities. But that is not the case." Another expressed the situation more starkly: "When one decides to come here, one is making a sacrifice to save some money, having always in mind to return. I do wish to return."

Philadelphia
Price

In contrast to New York City, the price of domestic service in Philadelphia reflects tight labor market conditions caused by the coincidence of growing demand and a relatively static labor supply. In 1993, the average hourly wage of private household employees in both cities was $7.68 (U.S. Department of Commerce 1995), but the cost of living is estimated to be 44 percent lower in Philadelphia than in New York (ACCRA 1998), resulting in much greater purchasing power for this city's domestic workers. Unlike their New York counterparts, Philadelphia's domestic workers are much more likely to report having set their own starting salary. In addition, their employers will sometimes spontaneously offer salary increases. The employer of one worker, for example, just said, "It's time for a raise," and gave her an increase from $6.50 to $8.00 an hour. Domestic workers in Philadelphia also report that they receive a wide assortment of benefits that are unusual in New York, including paid vacations, cash bonuses, and personal gifts. In extreme cases, women in Philadelphia report that their employers have loaned them money for down payments on houses, offered them apartments to live in rent free, or given them large gifts, such as expensive furniture or major appliances.

Competition

Philadelphia's domestic workers experience extremely high demand for their services and almost no involuntary unemployment. One baby-sitter's comment—"As soon as I get outa one job, I got a job right away—not even a week"—is typical in this sector. It is not uncommon for baby-sitters to be hired by pregnant employers, who begin to pay them immediately to ensure their availability after the baby is born. One woman pulled a wad of crumpled papers from her pocket and unfolded them to reveal the telephone numbers of mothers who had stopped her in the park to ask if she would keep them in mind if she became available. Ultimately, Philadelphia's domestics exercise a great deal of control over the circumstances of their employment. One housekeeper described the hiring process this way: "They interview me, I interview them. And I choose what I want to do—the people who I want to work for. I only work for people who are pleasant."

Working Conditions

In Philadelphia, baby-sitters' responsibilities are typically limited to child care and explicitly exclude other household chores. This results in a much more relaxed work schedule than that experienced by New York baby-sitters, who frequently juggle cooking, shopping, and housecleaning along with child care. In fact, in Philadelphia it is not uncommon for women who migrate from other occupations to comment about the more relaxed working conditions they encounter in domestic work. In contrast to their New York counterparts who are relegated to domestic service for lack of other opportunities, Philadelphia's domestics have chosen housekeeping and baby-sitting out of a strong preference for the activities that make up these jobs. Housecleaners express pride in their work and clearly derive a great deal of satisfaction from the quality of service they offer their employers. Baby-sitters describe being called to the profession by a lifelong fondness for children. During our interviews they spoke glowingly of their work and introduced each child to the interviewer as a proud parent might. As for future plans, the vast majority of domestic workers interviewed in Philadelphia intend to continue in their line of work. Significantly, those few who plan to leave private household employment prefer to remain in the same industry, hoping eventually to open their own day care centers or to start cleaning services. In contrast to New York City's domestics, who consider their years in the service sector a sacrifice, domestic service is an occupation of choice for Philadelphia's domestic workers.

The Structure of Demand: Household Hiring of Domestic Workers

According to the polarization thesis, demand for low-wage labor in recent years has been generated by affluent urban professionals whose taste for hand-crafted goods and labor-intensive services contrasts with the mass-produced fare favored by the middle class (Sassen 1991; Harrison and Bluestone 1982). Demand for services on the part of the wealthy, however, is relatively constant from a historical standpoint, in comparison with the massive substitution of services for women's unpaid labor occurring among the middle class. Although a large proportion of service sector utilization by the affluent represents a form of consumption, for those middle-class families who are allocating more labor to the market in order to maximize income in the face of stagnant wages and rising costs, such a trade-off represents not consumption but a necessary form of substitution in household production.

For the vast majority of households that fall into the middle income bracket, the decision to hire help hinges upon the disparity between the income of potential wage earners in the household and the local price of domestic service. Because wages of domestic workers are consistently at the bottom of national distributions, this disparity can be significant, offering a large cash advantage to families who outsource household work. In 1994, the average income for full-time working women, at $30,107, surpassed the salary of a full-time, year-round domestic employee by more than $17,000. Although that difference is reduced somewhat by taxes, even after taxes a married-couple family stood to gain more than $13,300 by trading off a wife's household labor for that of a paid, full-time household employee. These potential advantages are amplified in the case of college-educated women. Because the returns on higher education for women have made disproportionate advances in the last two decades, families who swap the services of a college-educated wife for those of a domestic employee realize an average annual boost in after-tax income of more than $20,000.[5]

These wage disparities reflect national averages, but because the crowding effect of immigration increases income inequality, the disparity between the median wage at the middle- and low-ends of the income distribution is greater in high-immigration cities than in low-immigration areas. Using gini coefficients as an indicator of income inequality, table 14.2 illustrates that in 1990 of the ten U.S. cities with the largest foreign-born populations only two—Washington, D.C., and San Diego–had below-average income inequality levels.[6] Eight cities had above-average levels of income inequality, and over one-half had income inequality levels at or above the 75th percentile. Even more striking is the relationship between income inequality and the number of domestic workers per household. Of these same cities, the density of domestic workers exceeds the national average in all cities except Chicago. Moreover, six of those cities have close to or greater than twice the average density of domestic workers, and Los Angeles has almost triple the national average.

The impact of immigration on the price of domestic service, and ultimately its consequences for domestic service hiring, is illustrated vividly in interviews with families in New York and Philadelphia. Many factors impact the labor supply decision of families, but the relatively

TABLE 14.2   *Income Inequality and Domestic Service Density in Cities with the Ten Largest Foreign Born Populations, 1990*

	Foreign-Born	Gini Coefficient	Gini Coefficient as Percent of National Average	Domestic Workers per 1,000 Households
Metropolitan area				
Los Angeles, CA	32	.430	+5.0	14.8
New York, NY	27	.447	+9.0	9.0
Washington, DC	12	.385	−6.2	10.3
Miami, FL	45	.461	+12.4	12.7
Houston, TX	13	.432	+5.5	9.9
San Diego, CA	17	.402	−1.9	8.6
San Francisco, CA	27	.418	+2.1	10.4
Chicago, IL	13	.423	+3.3	3.9
Dallas, TX	9	.412	+0.6	7.9
El Paso, TX	23	.425	+3.7	10.0
Top ten ranked cities, foreign-born population				
Mean	22	.424		9.8
Standard deviation	(10.9)	(.216)		(3.0)
One-hundred largest urban areas				
Mean	8	.410		5.1
Standard deviation	(7.5)	(.199)		(2.3)

Source: Adams (1992); gini coefficients courtesy of Sanjoy Chakravorty (see Chakravorty 1996 for methodology).
Note: For an explanation of gini coefficients, see note 6 in text. Jersey City, N.J., and Nassau-Suffolk counties (N.Y.) are excluded from this table due to unavailable gini coefficients.

minor disparity between female wages and the price of domestic service in Philadelphia makes hiring much more costly for Philadelphia families. As a result, middle-class families in Philadelphia who attempt to hire baby-sitters or housekeepers at a price they consider affordable are limited to workers whose lack of human, cultural, or social capital relegate them to the bottom of the local earnings distribution. Ultimately, potential employers find this poor and largely African American subset of the domestic service labor force deficient with regard to key skills or work habits. One Philadelphia mother who went through the hiring process but ultimately placed her infant son in day care described the experience this way: "I felt like they were very scarce, very scarce. I guess I should clarify that it's a scarcity in quality, in people that I felt I would definitely choose. I never felt like I had to choose among several people. I felt like I was getting sort of the best of people who maybe didn't have a terrific amount to offer."

These factors result in contrasting norms with regard to the utilization of services in Philadelphia and New York. Although the majority of families report having interviewed prospective employees, only 6 percent of families in this study's Philadelphia subsample actually used baby-sitters as their primary form of child care. Similarly, fewer than one in three families hired housecleaners, compared with almost double that rate in New York. Families in Philadelphia enlist relatives, juggle split shifts, or reduce mothers' work hours to provide familial child care for infants. Because more lax state regulations render day care costs slightly lower in Pennsylvania than in New York, Philadelphia's parents strongly favor day care for older children over much more expensive private baby-sitters.[7] In contrast to the vast majority of families in New York City who declined to use day care centers, calling them "cold" and "institutional," more than half of those interviewed in Philadelphia chose day care centers as their primary form of child care.

These differences in prevailing utilization patterns are salient for the labor force participation rates of mothers. The importance of trust in the intimate sphere of domestic service makes employee recommendations and referrals from friends and relatives particularly crucial to household hiring. Despite the fact that domestic service remains slightly more costly than group child care in New York City, group childcare seldom receives more than cursory consideration. Thus, the paradoxical result of less costly private domestic services in New York is that, relative to women's average wage, families face a more narrow array of child care choices and actually spend more for child care than do their Philadelphia counterparts. Whereas the average wage of middle-class women interviewed for this study was equal across the case study cities, women's wages *net child care expenditures* were significantly lower in New York than in Philadelphia, a point not lost on study respondents.

Ultimately, twice as many mothers in the New York City subsample chose to stay home with their children full time, and for a significant number, cost was key to the decision to remain out of the labor force. As one woman expressed it, "Combined, we have a lot of money, but for me to justify putting [my daughter] in day care, I'm not going to spend more for the day care than I'm earning. It's just kind of ridiculous. I should come out with something! I should have something in my bank account!" U.S. Census Bureau figures, in fact, reflect this divergence in work patterns between the two cities. In 1989, the disparity in labor force participation rates was striking, with two-thirds (66.1 percent) of mothers in Philadelphia in the labor force versus only 57.4 percent of those in New York City. This gap of almost 9 percentage points holds true both for mothers of infants and toddlers and for mothers of school-age children (U.S. Department of Commerce 1990). The fact that labor force participation rates among women without minor children were actually slightly higher in New York lends additional support to the hypothesis that the cost, quality, and availability of child care services play a critical role in mothers' propensity to work.

The Demand for Skills and Racial-Ethnic Correlates to Quality Among Immigrant Domestic Workers

Once families do decide to trade off their own labor for the services of a paid employee, another dynamic comes into play. With respect to the hiring of baby-sitters (who represent more than one-third of all private-household workers), a family's labor supply combines with the ages of children in the household to determine the types of characteristics required of domestic service employees. These requirements interact with racially tinged perceptions of domestic service quality to influence hiring decisions, ultimately creating differential levels of demand for immigrant and nonimmigrant workers.

In terms of market labor supply, families can be divided into two analytical categories. The first is made up of dual-earner families, which have two parents who work full time; the second category contains families with at least one parent who works less than full time, including both those with stay-at-home parents and those with at least one parent who is a part-time worker.[8] Furthermore, the characteristics sought in domestic service employees vary depending upon whether the family has an infant (under the age of one), a toddler (ages one through four years), or school-age children.

The Limits of Surrogacy

Despite the fact that substitutes for parental child care are now widely utilized, their appeal is still limited by a powerful preference for maternal care for young children. Occasionally this preference is attributed to the superiority of maternal care as indicated by statements such as, "There's no substitute for a mother's love," or "No one takes care of a baby like her own mother." However, the preference seems equally driven by the needs of mothers who repeatedly reiterated their deep desire to participate in the care of their own small children.

Although some mothers do prefer to work full time outside the home, those mothers who cannot realize their desire to provide some daytime parenting for small children seem to find the emotional costs almost unbearable. There are generally two causes for such an involuntary separation: a spouse with low-wage or unstable employment or labor-supply inflexibility associated with the mother's profession. One mother who worked full time while her husband completed his graduate education described her experience in this way:

> In the early days it was incredibly difficult. I mean, I was extremely resentful because I wanted to be with her. I hated going back to work. I had a huge breast pump that I took into the office. I would go to the nurse's office at lunchtime and pump, and I would sit in my office and cry and take naps because she never slept. I was a zombie, and I was resentful toward my husband because I didn't have the option of staying home. I actually asked him for a long time to leave the program and he wouldn't do it. Because he decided to do that, I had no choice.

The situation is equally painful for women whose work does not afford the flexibility of part-time hours. Some of these are highly ambitious women who have invested heavily in careers that pay off in terms of high salaries, social recognition, and job satisfaction but do not allow for daytime parenting. One such woman, who eventually decided to scale back her work hours, described the strain she experienced when repeated efforts to restructure her job in order to spend more time with her children failed:

> I was doing those hours even after I had my first child and I was really torn. And so when I came back after my second child, I tried to make this arrangement, but within a month, I was back into the same hours. . . . I did that for almost two and a half years and got to the point where I literally was on the verge of a nervous breakdown. I just couldn't handle home and work. I was working nights and five days a week and sometimes on weekends. And I found myself trying to run faster and faster on a treadmill just to keep up with that. It got to the point where I just couldn't handle it anymore. I had a month-long migraine that just debilitated me. I was missing stuff at the school and forgetting to respond to the kids' birthday invitations and missing their plays and their parent-teacher conferences. And collection notices would come in for bills that I had never even seen. It was just a mess. I was shaky all the time. I was really, really a wreck. I went to this great neurologist who just finally sat me down and said, well, what's going on in your life? I burst into tears and we talked and I decided I've just got to take a break. My kids are growing up, and, you know, all through this I still never really became fully reconciled. I felt guilty and remorseful that I had missed out on my son's early childhood and I finally

realized I was just going to live with this regret for the rest of my life if I didn't do something about it.

Maternity

Couples who place a high value on parental care resort to a number of strategies, including working split shifts, working at home, altering career paths to reduce work hours, and even moving to cities with lower living costs in order to increase time with their children. Where these strategies are not viable, however, families mitigate the strain by turning to paid child care providers who not only provide for their children's physical well-being but also can serve as emotional surrogates. This factor represents a critical distinction in the hiring patterns of full-time and less-than-full-time working households, and it is also a key element of the hiring requirements of parents with younger rather than older children. For parents who work full-time, as well as parents of infants and young toddlers, a primary requirement of child care arrangements is that children receive individual attention and that their emotional needs be met. Parents refer to "warmth," "kindness," and "motherliness" as the qualities they look for in potential hires. This desire for one-on-one attention and affection also results in a strong preference for baby-sitters over institutional arrangements for infants and children under the age of three. For interviewed mothers who work full-time, this affective quality in a sitter was key to satisfying the mother's concern that she was not neglecting her children through her own absence.

The preference for maternal qualities in baby-sitters coincides with ethnic stereotypes about immigrants, advantaging nonnative workers in this labor market. Perhaps because immigrant women are perceived as products of cultures in which women traditionally do not work outside the home,[9] American respondents repeatedly commented on their suitability for infant care. As one woman put it, "I think certain cultures just love babies. A lot of my other friends have women from the islands and they seem to be more happy and less frustrated with this line of work." Another mother said, "I think that Puerto Ricans are more experienced with kids and where babies are concerned they can be much more helpful." By contrast, American caretakers, it was frequently noted, lack this quality. The problem was put this way: "[American caretakers] don't have any desire to love a baby. They don't want to stay at home. They want to be out in the car, running around town, taking the kids shopping. Or sitting around, having play dates with their friends who are also nannies so that the kids would baby-sit themselves essentially, and they would be chatting away."

This maternal stereotype of immigrant women is paradoxical, first because baby-sitters are replacing the labor of biological mothers who in many cases would also prefer not to work full time outside the home, and second, because the immigrant sitters themselves frequently foster out their own children in order to enter the domestic service labor market. Thus, maternal child care remains a primary value despite the execution of a chain of surrogacy in which each biological mother in turn trades off maternal child care for wages.

Language and Education

Whereas immigrants are favored for the care of infants, once children become verbal, middle-class parents become preoccupied with providing them with developmental and educational advantages. At this point more educated, native baby-sitters with fluent English-language skills become preferred employees. For New York City's households, this transition often involves replacing the immigrant child care provider who has cared for the child since its early infancy. As one woman remarked, "I was happy with that person. Then as the kids get older their needs change. When they're very young you want nurturing, caring, safety. And then when they get older you need somebody who can drive, who has a clue. Who has a clue, and who can speak English so your kids don't start sounding like they're from some other country, and who can just teach them sort of how life works."

In the case of foreign language skills, part-time and full-time working parents tend to diverge. Whereas full-time working parents stress the need for English-speaking employees as their children approach school age, some parents who work part time see development of foreign-language skills as an adjunct to English-language training that they provide to their children themselves. As a respondent with a Cuban baby-sitter explained, "I felt that whoever takes care of the kids should be able in the event of an emergency to talk on the phone. Beyond that, though, my intent was to have her speak Spanish exclusively to the kids. They were getting plenty of English from us. I wanted them to hear a second language."

Reliability

Another highly sought-after quality in child care workers by households in which both parents work full time is reliability. Because time for these families is an extremely scarce commodity and lapses in child care coverage can be disastrous, a stable child care provider is a necessity. This produces a strong preference for baby-sitters who do not have their own custodial children and can therefore maintain consistent availability, ultimately advantaging immigrant baby-sitters who have fostered their children out. As this mother's testimony indicates, having dependent children clearly reduces the appeal of a potential hire in this labor market:

> I have a lot of friends who decided to go the baby-sitter route. . . . I didn't feel like dealing with it. I had a taste of dealing with a baby-sitter for five months and I don't feel like dealing with their personal problems, or having them call up at six in the morning [to cancel] and then I have to scramble. It's bad enough when I get up in the morning and [my daughter] is sick. But then, for somebody else not to show up, is a big pain in the neck.

Self-Assurance

For all parents who hire caretakers, trust in their competency is an absolute necessity. In particular, parents who work full time, and consequently have fewer opportunities to observe their baby-sitters, seem to look for signs of competency in the employee's demeanor. However, there is often a tension between the desire for competency and confidence and the desire for an employee who will take direction. This issue was discussed in particular in reference to West Indian immigrants, whom employers regarded either as extremely competent or as "bossy," depending upon their perspective. A mother who fired her West Indian baby-sitter because she found her manner abrasive said, "My problem with the Caribbean sitters was that there's this attitude that they know all about children, and of course, we're struggling to figure out about ours. This was kind of obnoxious and I didn't want to deal with it anymore. I didn't need somebody coming in and elbowing around." Moreover, this image of West Indians as self-assured occasionally spilled over into concerns that the discipline customarily applied to children on the islands would be too harsh for American children. Another mother who eventually fired her West Indian nanny explained that "she was overdisciplinarian. Her theory was, you have to bend a tree when it's young. Very strict. She had five boys and she grew up in Jamaica. You know, maybe they hit kids with sticks down in Jamaica."

Personality

Like most workers, domestic service employees have frequent contact with their employers, making interpersonal compatibility a factor in families' hiring decisions. Because in this case the domestic's workplace is also the employer's home, however, smooth, congenial relations are not only important, they are critical to the selection of an employee. Although respondents refer to personality conflicts in less explicit terms than those used to describe human capital deficits, their salience in both hiring decisions and turnover is unmistakable. One respondent decided not to hire a particular baby-sitter because "there was so obviously something wrong with this person. She was just really mousy, timid, not outgoing." Another woman hired a Caribbean caretaker but fired her soon afterward because "I thought she was a little strange. I didn't understand her at all. She would talk to herself and I just couldn't deal with it. I thought she was a little unbalanced, but in retrospect I don't think she was. I think it was a cultural thing. She really got on my nerves." Another found her baby-sitter insubordinate. She reported, "I hired this Polish woman and I was very sensitive because I wanted things done my way. And at one point I asked her to give me the baby and she said no. I said yes. She said no. And I sat her down and I said, 'Listen to me. These are my children. When I ask you for them, you give them to me.' She said she was worried about my back. I said, 'I will worry about my back.' I just couldn't get past that."

Conclusion

Although the presence of an ethnic niche in the domestic-service sector can aid immigrants by increasing their access to jobs, in this context, coethnic ties constitute a double-edged sword. The tendency of immigrant communities to grow through chain migration combines with a process of job acquisition, which relies on the cohesive social networks of coethnics to convey information about employment opportunities. As the size of the immigrant community grows, so does the proliferation of social network connections, which converge on a limited pool of jobs.

Thus, while the ethnic niche may ease the incorporation of individual immigrants into the local job market, it simultaneously functions to erode the quality of the occupational niche as a whole, reducing the collective prospects of immigrant workers. In the case of New York's domestic-service sector, workers encounter fierce competition, demanding employers, onerous working conditions, and earnings that border on the subsistence level. In contrast, the paucity of domestic workers in Philadelphia, which lacks a large immigrant labor supply, strengthens the bargaining position of domestic workers vis-à-vis their employers. This results not only in higher wages and, on average, a much richer array of non-cash benefits, but also in a fundamentally distinct definition of what constitutes a domestic-service job. The typical baby-sitting job in Philadelphia does not require housecleaning, and the typical housecleaning job does not require baby-sitting. By altering not only the working conditions of individual domestics, but also the collective perceptions of what is customary and permissible to demand from domestic workers in general, labor supply conditions in Philadelphia have elevated the circumstances of domestic service workers across the spectrum.

These findings not only suggest a less uniformly positive view of the impact of coethnic ties than is prevalent in the immigration literature, but they also contradict the notion, common among students of domestic service, that the "subservient" nature of these occupations renders them intrinsically unprestigious. By altering the structure of domestic-service work, labor market conditions in Philadelphia raised the social standing of domestic-service occupations and engendered the development of a professional role for domestic-service workers. In contrast to New York where domestic work is considered unskilled labor, domestic workers in Philadelphia view themselves, and are often viewed by their employers, as professionals who bring both experience and special expertise to their jobs.

Although I speculated that labor demand might be a key factor instigating or perpetuating labor migration to the United States, it appears that in this case, labor supply characteristics outweigh the role of demand in driving the process of domestic-service hiring. The decision by workers to emigrate was not directly related to their perceptions of labor demand in receiving communities. Rather, workers migrated because of preexisting social ties to prior migrants in accordance with the classic chain migration model.

In interaction with local labor supply characteristics, however, demand still plays a crucial role in shaping domestic-service consumption patterns in the high immigration context. While the movement of immigrant workers into New York's domestic-service labor force is not directly spurred by local labor demand, immigration has altered social norms governing the consumption of domestic services in ways that are self-perpetuating. Crowding in the domestic-service sector has driven down domestics' wages, widening the income gap between domestics and their potential employers and ultimately rendering services affordable to middle-class families. Moreover, immigration has altered the actual and perceived compatibility of workers' characteristics to jobs by changing the racial and ethnic make-up of the domestic-service labor force. As a result of both of these trends, domestic-service hiring has become normative in New York. Therefore, New York families are many times more likely to hire private household workers than their counterparts in Philadelphia, *even* in cases where household hiring is significantly more costly than alternatives, such as day care centers or commercial housecleaning services.

This study points to a number of issues that deserve additional research. The consistency with which scholars find that social processes, rather than purely economic factors, play a primary role in immigration and job acquisition makes the possibility of crowding in immigrant-dominated employment sectors a subject of both interest and concern. Although the finding of crowding by this study may stem from the idiosyncrasies of domestic-service work, such as its low skill requirements or informality, other ethnic niches are likely to share these characteristics, thereby rendering crowding a relatively pervasive phenomenon.

Furthermore, income inequality emerges here as a crucial, albeit unpredictable, factor influencing the economic adaptation of immigrants. For example, a polarized opportunity structure may benefit newcomers and unskilled immigrants in the short-term by increasing the availability of low-wage jobs; however, these same conditions may stifle socioeconomic mobility and be a disadvantage to more settled and skilled immigrants. Due to the complexity of this variable, a more nuanced understanding of the impact of income inequality on immigrants' prospects will require additional empirical research.

Finally, the observation that employers perceive fine distinctions in the attributes of workers of different national origins is also important. Household employers not only demand a variety of skills from "unskilled" workers, but the personalities of workers—which often emerge in interaction with cultural traits specific to national-origins groups—can be crucial to the success of employer-employee relationships. Although this effect is probably accentuated in the case of domestic–service employment because of its intimate nature, it is likely that personality and culture also impact outcomes in other occupational sectors as well. These conclusions suggest that employers' perceptions of cultural as well as human capital differences among immigrant workers deserve further attention.

This research was supported by the Social Science Research Council and the National Science Foundation (award number 9701367).

Notes

1. The presence of immigrant domestic workers in the United States is hardly a new phenomenon. Immigrant domestics have intermittently played a crucial role in American household production since the mid-nineteenth century. However, unlike earlier in this century, when service sector demand was generated by growing affluence, recent demand has been created by growth in labor supply to the market, caused partially by wage stagnation. Useful sources for historical descriptions of the domestic service labor market are Katzman (1981) and Rollins (1985).

2. Crowding hypotheses were first proposed by Millicent G. Fawcett (1918) and F. Y. Edgeworth (1922) in relation to female employment.

3. A number of authors have documented the experiences of domestic workers. Immigrant domestics in particular are the subject of works by Shellee Colen (1989) and Evelyn N. Glenn (1986). David M. Katzman (1981) offers a useful historical perspective.

4. Julia Wrigley (1995) has also documented this phenomenon.

5. Estimates of tax liability are calculated based upon contributions to Social Security (6.2 percent) and Medicare (1.45 percent), and average tax rates by adjusted gross income for married couples filing separately in 1994 (IRS 1997, table 1.2). In 1996, mean income was $30,107 for all females and $41,339 for female college graduates. Average after-tax income was $26,107 for all females and $33,464 for female college graduates, compared with the mean salary of $12,720 for full-time year-round domestic service employees (U.S. Department of Commerce 1999). Tax liability was not added to the cost of domestic service salaries because of estimates that income tax compliance rates for household employees are below 14 percent (Johnston 1998). Nonwage compensation in the form of benefits is also not considered, but because domestic workers receive a much smaller than average proportion of compensation in the form of benefits, these figures probably understate the potential net gain from substituting women's unpaid household labor with that of a paid employee.

6. Gini coefficients express how close a distribution is to perfect equality or inequality. In the case of perfect equality the coefficient equals zero, and as the distribution approaches absolute inequality, the coefficient approaches one. As a summary measure, the gini coefficient does not specifically describe income differences between various points in the distribution.

7. In Pennsylvania, the caregiver-to-child ratio permitted in state-licensed day care centers is higher than that permitted in New York State for children in three age groups. The law permits six twenty-seven-month-old children for each caregiver, versus five per caregiver in New York, ten three-year-olds, versus seven in New York, and ten four-year-olds, versus eight in New York.

8. Even households with stay-at-home parents now frequently use some form of paid child care (Hofferth 1989).

9. This is merely an impression. Studies show that immigrant domestic workers often have high levels of labor force participation in their home countries before emigrating (see Foner 1987; and Grasmuck and Grosfoguel 1997).

References

Adams, Terry K. 1992. *Census of Population and Housing, 1990: Extract Data* (computer file). Ann Arbor, Mich.: Economic Behavior Program, Survey Research Center. American Chamber of Commerce Research Association (ACCRA). 1998. *Cost of Living Index* 31(1).

Carpenter, Allan, and Carl Provorse. 1996. *Facts About the Cities.* New York: H.W. Wilson.

Chakravorty, Sanjoy.1996. "Urban Inequality Revisited: The Determinants of Income Distribution in U.S. Metropolitan Areas." *Urban Affairs Review* 31(6): 759–77.

Colen, Shellee. "'Just a Little Respect': West Indian Domestic Workers in New York City." In *Muchachas No More: Household Workers in Latin America and the Caribbean,* edited by Elsa M. Chaney and Mary Garcia Castro. Philadelphia: Temple University Press.

Edgeworth, F. Y. 1922. "Equal Pay to Men and Women for Equal Work." *Economic Journal* 32(128): 431–57.

Fawcett, Millicent G. 1918. "Equal Pay for Equal Work." *Economic Journal* 28(109): 1–6.

Foner, Nancy. 1986. "Sex Roles and Sensibilities: Jamaican Women in New York and London." In *International Migration: The Female Experience,* edited by Rita J. Simon and Caroline Brettell. Totowa, N.J.: Rowman and Allanheld.

———. 1987. *New Immigrants in New York.* New York: Columbia University Press.

Glenn, Evelyn Nakano. 1986. *Issei, Nisei, Warbride: Three Generations of Japanese Women Domestics.* Philadelphia: Temple University Press.

Grasmuck, Sherri, and Ramon Grosfoguel. 1997. "Geopolitics, Economic Niches, and Gendered Social Capital Among Recent Caribbean Immigrants in New York City." *Sociological Perspectives* 40: 339–63.

Harrison, Bennett, and Barry Bluestone. 1982. *The Deindustrialization of America: Plant Closings, Community Abandonment, and the Dismantling of Basic Industry.* New York: Basic Books.

Hofferth, Sandra. 1989. "What Is the Demand for and Supply of Child Care in the United States?" *Young Children* (July): 28–33.

Internal Revenue Service (IRS). 1997. *Individual Income Tax Returns: Statistics of Income, 1994.* Publication 1304. Washington: Statistics Division.

Johnston, David Cay. 1998. "Despite an Easing of Rules, Millions Evade 'Nanny Tax.'" *New York Times,* April 5, 1996, p. A6.

Katzman, David M. 1981. *Seven Days a Week: Women and Domestic Service in Industrializing America.* Urbana, Ill.: Illinois University Press.

Portes, Alejandro. 1995. *The Economic Sociology of Immigration: Essays on Networks, Ethnicity, and Entrepreneurship,* edited by Alejandro Portes. New York: Russell Sage Foundation.

Portes, Alejandro, and Rubén G. Rumbaut. 1990. *Immigrant America: A Portrait.* Berkeley, Calif.: University of California Press.

Rollins, Judith. 1985. *Between Women: Domestics and Their Employers.* Philadelphia: Temple University Press.

Sassen, Saskia. 1991. *The Global City: New York, London, Tokyo.* Princeton, N.J.: Princeton University Press.

U.S. Department of Commerce, Bureau of the Census. 1990. *Census of Population and Housing.* Summary Tape File 3C. Table P073. Washington: U.S. Government Printing Office.

———. 1991. *County and City Data Book.* Washington: U.S. Government Printing Office.

———. 1992. *Census of Population and Housing, 1990: Public Use Microdata Samples, 5 percent File.* Washington: U.S. Government Printing Office.

———. 1995. *Current Population Survey, March 1994.* Washington: U.S. Government Printing Office

———. 1999. Table P-27, "Educational Attainment: Full-Time, Year-Round Workers Eighteen Years Old and Over by Mean Earnings, Age, and Gender: 1991 to 1997." Downloaded on February 3, 1999, from the worldwide web at: http://www.census.gov/hhes/income/histinc/p27.html.

———. 1999. Table P-30, "Full-Time, Year-Round Workers (All Races) by Mean Income and Gender: 1970 to 1997." Downloaded on February 3, 1999, from the worldwide web at: http://www.census.gov/hhes/income/histinc/p30.html.

———. 1999. Table P-37, "Occupation of Longest Job: Full-Time, Year-Round Workers (Both Sexes Combined) by Median and Mean Earnings: 1982 to 1997." Downloaded on February 3, 1999, from the worldwide web at: http://www.census.gov/hhes/income/histinc/p37.html.

Waldinger, Roger. 1996. *Still the Promised City? African Americans and New Immigrants in Postindustrial New York.* Cambridge, Mass.: Harvard University Press.

Wrigley, Julia. 1995. *Other People's Children.* New York: Basic Books.

15

EN EL NORTE LA MUJER MANDA: GENDER, GENERATION, AND GEOGRAPHY IN A MEXICAN TRANSNATIONAL COMMUNITY

Jennifer S. Hirsch

WOMEN and men in rural western Mexico and their relatives in Atlanta discuss differences between life in the United States and Mexico in terms of gender: "En el norte," they say, "la mujer manda"—in the North, that is, women give the orders. Young Mexican women on both sides of the border, however, call our attention to the role of history rather than migration in the transformation of gender: they say they are not as easily pushed around as their mothers. Although older women in this community have hardly been powerless, in the space of a generation men and women have begun to express a different, companionate ideal of marriage—an ideal with significant implications for the politics and emotional terrain of marriage. Younger women (and some of their husbands) on both sides of the border articulate a vision of intimate partnership influenced both by the true love of soap opera and by the increasing economic and social possibility of leaving a violent or even merely unsatisfying marriage. "En el norte, la mujer manda" has specific meaning, as well, however: young Mexican women have greater opportunities for realizing these companionate ideals in the United States. This chapter discusses two trajectories—generational and geographic—of change in gender. Each story would be incomplete alone, but interwoven they relate the complex recent history of gender in this transnational community.

Theorists of transnationalism have presented a valuable critique of simplistic ideas about assimilation by pointing to the ways that strong social ties, frequent travel, and constant communication facilitate the construction and maintenance of cross-border social identities (for example, Glick Schiller, Basch, and Blanc-Szanton 1992). In so doing, however, they tend to underemphasize the real contrasts in social context between sending and receiving communities. In addition, transnational communities are located in time as well as in space, and so to understand the "gender regime" (Connell 1987, 119) of a transnational community we need to talk not just about migration-related change but also about history—in particular, the history of the sending community. Important cultural changes accompany migration, but these changes can only be understood in the broader historical context of how the sending communities themselves are changing.

Although migration scholars have made great strides over the past two decades in including women in migration research (for example, Goodson-Lawes 1993; Grasmuck and Pessar 1991; Cornelius 1991) and even some significant progress in exploring the ways in which gender shapes and is, in turn, shaped by migration (for example, Foner 1997, 1998; Pessar 1998; Hondagneu-Sotelo 1994; Pedraza 1991), it is time to reorient the question of whether or not migration empowers women, to move away from the relentless search for one or two universal causes for this empowerment. The emphasis on the relative increase in women's empowerment with migration has become a set of theoretical blinders, focusing our attention excessively on the question of women's resources and bargaining power, rendering male gender invisible, and obscuring the fact that what changes with migration may be not only the resources and style with which women and men bargain, but also what couples bargain for—that is, their marital goals.

Research Design and Methods

This chapter presents results from an ethnographic study of two generations of Mexican women. The sample comprises twenty-six women between the ages of fifteen and fifty-one years, all from the same sending community in western Mexico. At the time the study was conducted, half of the women lived in Atlanta; the others (their sisters or sisters-in-law) had remained in or returned to the sending community. Most of these women's mothers were interviewed as well. (Throughout the chapter, "younger women" refers to the younger of the life-history informants—generally speaking, those under the age of thirty-five; "older women" refers to the older informants, between thirty-five and fifty-one years of age, and to the mothers of the life-history informants.) The primary method of data collection was the life-history interview: six interviews were conducted on childhood and family life; social networks and stories of migration from Mexico to the United States; gender and household division of labor; menstruation, reproduction, and fertility management; health, reproductive health, sexually transmitted diseases and infidelity; and courtship and sexuality. Interviews were also conducted with nine of the informants' husbands.

The interviews were conducted during fifteen months of participant observation in Atlanta and in the sending community in western Mexico. The substantive focus on gender and sexuality dictated working with a relatively small sample of women in order to develop the necessary rapport. At the same time, the goal was to produce results that could be generalized to the experiences of other Mexican women in transnational communities. A method of systematic ethnographic sampling that builds on existing social networks was employed. (I discuss the methodology in greater detail elsewhere; see Hirsch 1998; Hirsch and Nathanson 1997.) In brief, this method entailed several months of preliminary research in the migrant receiving community (Atlanta), both to select the sending community and the research participants in Atlanta and to understand how their specific experiences might compare with those of the larger Mexican migrant population. The sending communities were Degollado, a town of approximately fifteen thousand in the state of Jalisco, and El Fuerte, a small agricultural community outside Degollado. In Atlanta, some informants lived in Chamblee, an urban neighborhood of small apartment complexes with good public transportation and a heavy concentration of Mexican and Vietnamese immigrants, and others lived in trailer parks on the outskirts of the city.

Once the first group of life-history informants had been interviewed in Atlanta, I traveled to Degollado. As with others who move between locations of this transnational community, my arrival was no secret; those I was hoping to interview were expecting me, looking forward not just to meeting "la gringa" who had been visiting their sisters in Atlanta but also to receiving the letters, photos, and small gifts that their sisters had given me to carry. These "encargos" put my introduction to the families in Mexico in a familiar context—that of any member of their transnational community who, as a routine part of the frequent back-and-forth travel, aids in the construction and preservation of social ties across borders. In the course of the six trips I made between Atlanta and Degollado, I carried "huaraches," wedding videos, yarn, baby clothes, jewelry, cash, herbal remedies, birth control pills, letters, and photographs for the families of the women I was interviewing. As a U.S. citizen, my border crossings were quite different from those of my informants, many of whom were more likely to cross with a "coyote" than in an air-conditioned jet. Nevertheless, my deliberate insertion into these migrant social networks and the use of these networks to build a research sample helped identify informants and build rapport.

Flexibility was another key aspect of the research design. My interest in generational changes in marriage grew in response to repeatedly hearing, "Ya no somos tan dejadas como las de antes" (We are no longer as easily pushed around as the women of the past). As the months passed I saw that in spite of my neat construction of two similar groups of women to be studied, the women themselves would not sit still long enough to be compared: during the course of the fieldwork, several of those interviewed in Atlanta either moved permanently back to Mexico or spent months at a stretch living there, and some of the women interviewed in the Mexican field sites have since journeyed northward. Women's physical mobility makes it hard to compare those who go with those who stay—perhaps one of the reasons that studies of transnational communities have focused more on cultural continuity than on change. The analysis of differences between the communities focused of necessity much more on differences in social and economic context (and thus in women's opportunities) than on a strict comparison of women in Atlanta and Degollado.

From "Respeto" to "Confianza"

A generational change is evident in the shift from the older women's focus on "respeto" (respect) to the younger women's discussion of "confianza" (trust). The change goes beyond ideals: young couples were more likely to make decisions jointly, to regard a spouse as a companion, to share the tasks of social reproduction, and to value sexual intimacy as a source of emotional closeness. Doña Elena, now sixty-two years of age and a widow, still remembers vividly, more than forty years later, her grandmother's instructions to her on the art of the successful marriage: " 'Just be quiet—don't answer back, and don't talk to him this way or that way. . . . You need to serve them with love.' " To have a good marriage, Doña Elena said, she tried to "have his food ready for him, his clothes all nicely ironed, and all mended like we used to do, and . . . take care of him as best I could." He, in turn, should "provide all that one needs, food and clothes, and not run around misbehaving." At the core of this marital bargain is the idea of separate spheres (with women in the house and men in the street) and respect for one's spouse. Women of this generation evaluate their marriages against a gendered standard of respect rather than in terms of intimacy or sentiment. (Some were also quite fond of their spouses—Doña Elena started to cry while telling me how much she missed her husband, Miguel.) Doña Elena credits her marital success to her husband's gentle character—she notes that he never hit her—and to her own ability to get what she wanted "por las buenas" (by being nice). This meant keeping conflict underground, carefully managing her speech to stay within the bounds of respect. Doña

Elena married a kind man, but other women were less fortunate. Any inability to get along (saberse llevar) cast shame on the woman's natal family; women knew their parents would not take them back once they had married: "Mi'ija," they would say, "es tu cruz" (My daughter, it's your cross to bear).

The interviews with the older women ended with a question I hoped would tell me what their marriages were really like, rather than the way they were supposed to be. "Señora," I would say, "some people tell me that in Mexico the man has to be the boss at home, but it seems to me that you all are not so 'dejadas' (easily pushed around)—you let the man think that he is in charge but you know how to get your way. Is this true?" Those women whose husbands had a history of being violent or otherwise abusive said to me that no, this was not true—that really one does have to obey. Other women, though, would smile conspiratorially in response. As long as you are respectful, they would tell me, you can do what you want.

In contrast to their mothers' emphasis on respect, younger women talk more about "confianza." Confianza implies trust, particularly trust that one's secrets will be kept. Confianza denotes a relationship between social equals, in contrast to respect, which implies a hierarchy appropriately acknowledged. Confianza also suggests the ability to admit to sexual knowledge: women say they did not ask their mothers about menstruation because they had a lot of respect for them and not enough confianza, and it is a mark of that same confianza to tell a sexual joke among married women. Young women say that they waited until they had confianza with their boyfriends before giving in to their requests for a kiss, and they talk a lot about the role of confianza in building a strong marriage. These women have imbued the word with new meaning, combining previously separate concepts of privacy, sexual behavior, and the freedom to be oneself into an idea of a special, shared, sexual intimacy. The younger women did not disregard the importance of respeto—many of them, for example, talked about courtship as a time of testing how respectful a young man might be as a husband—but they have also redefined respect, using it to claim new areas of power in marriage, such as the basic expression of respect of being allowed to voice their opinions; for their mothers, in contrast, direct disagreement with one's husband was hardly an indication of respect on anyone's part. Space does not permit a discussion of heterogeneity among the marriages of younger women; it should be noted, however, that not all the younger women achieved this new ideal of confianza combined with respeto, but they all surely took it as the ideal.

In these marriages of confianza among the younger generation, both men and women were more likely than their parents to say that they make decisions together. In response to the question, "Quién manda en su casa?" (Who gives the orders in your house?), they each (separately) told me that they both give orders, or that neither one does. The meaning of women's speech has been redefined: whereas for their mothers, to voice disagreement with their husbands would have been considered "resongona" (sassy), some of the young couples took pride in the fact that they did not always automatically do what the man said. Unlike their fathers, these younger men do not automatically interpret a woman's disagreement as an attack on their authority and thus their manhood. As one young woman in Atlanta said, "Tengo opiniones" (I have opinions). Her mother, doubtless, also had her own opinions, but she had to be much more careful about how she shared them with her husband.

A second feature of marriages of confianza is heterosociality, expressed as the erosion of the gendered boundaries of space between the house and the street (Rouse 1991; Gutmann 1996). In the context of explaining what it meant to share "el mando" (the power), younger women and their husbands frequently mentioned spending time together. Whether staying at home together or going to the plaza or the mall as a family, this heterosociality stands in strong contrast to the idea that men belong in the street and women in the house and that choosing to be in the house somehow lessens a man's masculinity just as too much time in the street imperils a woman's moral virtue. The notion that men and women can be companions lessens the social distance implied by respeto.

A third feature of the younger generation's marriages is the loosening of the boundaries of gendered tasks. Their mothers helped their fathers in myriad ways, but generating income was considered to be the exclusive responsibility of the men. Women worked in the past, but the labors of social reproduction were defined into invisibility, falling under the rubric "quehacer" (that which must be done). "El hombre tiene que mantener la casa," they said: the man has to support his house. Both in Degollado and Atlanta, men are still publicly evaluated by their ability to provide and women still judged by the tidiness of their daughters' braids and the spotlessness of their floors, but there has been a generational movement toward helping (ayudando) each other with their gendered tasks. Although helping out does not change the gendered primary responsibility for certain tasks, offering to help—or accepting an offer of help—no longer casts feminine virtue and masculine power in doubt. Behind closed doors some men sweep, cook meals, clear the table, and wash dishes. Women's "helping" is even more widespread: almost half of the women interviewed in Mexico and most of those in Atlanta were involved in some kind of income-generating activity.

In other ways, too, the younger men and women were striving to create families different from the ones in which they had been raised. They continued to say, as did their mothers, that "los hijos son la felicidad de la casa" (children are the happiness of a home), but none of the younger women aspired to having quite as much of that happiness as did their mothers: the average parity of the life-history informants' mothers was just above nine, whereas the life-history informants (admittedly much earlier in their reproductive careers) had an average of three children each, and many wanted no more. This striking decline in fertility reflects, among other things, the transformation of sexuality's role in the work of making a family.[1] Young couples want smaller families so that they have the time and energy to focus on each other; the affective relationship at the core of the family has shifted from that between the mother and her children to that between the husband and wife. For their mothers, children—the sooner after marriage the better—were the bond that built a family ("tener familia"—literally, to have a family—means to have a child), but for the younger women and men sexual intimacy has become in and of itself constitutive of family ties. Sexual closeness has taken on a new, productive (as opposed to reproductive) aspect (see Hirsch, forthcoming).

For older women, sexual intimacy within marriage held a husband's attention (and his resources) and served to generate children; a woman's sexual pleasure was certainly a bonus but hardly a requirement. For younger women, the mutual pleasure and emotional sharing are in and of themselves a goal. For example, many of the older women—even those who seem to have shared a pleasurable intimacy with their partners—employ the word "usar" (to use) to describe vaginal intercourse (they might say, for example, "cuando él me usa"—"when he uses me"—to describe sexual relations). "Usar" connotes the utilization of an inanimate object; it is the word one might employ to talk about an iron, or a plow. Younger women, in contrast, talk about making love (hacer el amor) or being together (estar juntos) or having relations (tener relaciones).

Together, these qualities (an emphasis on a new kind of confianza in addition to respect, more room for explicit disagreement, a growing heterosociality, increased helping, new meanings for marital sexuality) combine to form a new marital ideal. Both women and men deliberately frame this ideal as modern: women (whether in Mexico or the United States) told me repeatedly that they were not as easily pushed around as their mothers, and many men strove to convince me that they were not macho like their fathers. A thorough discussion of how these ideological changes are the product of deliberate choices men and women make in response to changing social conditions—an explanation, in other words, that integrates both structure and agency—is beyond the scope of this paper, so here I will just note some of the macro-level changes and strategic advantages that have facilitated this trend. In addition to the influence of migration (both on the migrants themselves and, via return migration, on the sending communities), factors worthy of mention include increasing neolocal residence, access to mass media through satellite dishes, rising rates of female education, three decades of government-sponsored family planning programs and sex education, and even the Catholic Church's efforts to co-opt this new discourse of sexuality (see Hirsch 1998).[2]

The question arises, of course, of what benefit women and men think they will derive from being modern. Some men say that living as bachelors in the United States has taken away the shame of grabbing a broom or heating a tortilla—but it did not do so for their fathers, and some of the men who "help" their wives have spent little or no time in el norte. Men's helping women can only be understood together with the ground that men have ceded in decision making and the fracturing of the sharply gendered distinction between the house and the street as part of a larger redefinition of masculinity. These men are not just helping with the housework: they are helping with the work of making a family. What men stand to gain is "cariño" (tenderness). The benefits to men of a marriage of confianza are emotional; they gain access to an intimacy that their fathers sacrificed as part of the cost of being "respetados" (respected). Some men in the sending community see this new masculinity as a strategy for social mobility; the way that Mexican "telenovelas" and advertisements portray modern, successful men speaking softly to their wives over cell phones, rather than as machos with mustaches and guns shouting at their women, does not escape notice among both men and women in Degollado.

For male migrants there are additional advantages to this alternative masculinity. The aggressive postures of the stereotypical macho are just the behaviors most likely to catch the attention of "la migra" (the Immigration and Naturalization Service) or the local police. Furthermore, many Mexicans in Atlanta work for gringo bosses who care more about whether they show up on time and work hard than whether they are suspect as "maricones" (a deprecatory term for homosexuals) because they refuse to go drinking with their buddies. More subtly, Mexican men in Atlanta see the pervasive image of the leisure time togetherness of the gringo nuclear family at the mall, in television commercials, in public parks, and in church. Ultimately, men's embrace of this alternative masculinity seems to be the result of a combination of influences: their family history, their age, and situational factors that make the new attitude advantageous. It is a strategy for social mobility and self-protection, but it also feels good.

The companionate marriage has many benefits for women, and women press their husbands as far as they can toward this model. One benefit women see is pleasure in the possibility of closeness. Another is a path to power and a means to ensure marital security. Women who felt that they had significant input in matters pertaining to their family (whether economic or social) proudly told me, "I have opinions" (that is, opinions that count). Companionate marriage gives women a moral language with which to define the limits of acceptable behavior. Women believe these strong emotional ties guarantee not just a better marriage but one that is more likely to endure, so that maintaining affective bonds is part of the work women do to strengthen their marriages. Finally, some women use this new marital ideal as a justification for migration and for working outside the home. For example, young women make marital togetherness an explicit negotiation point during courtship: they tell their boyfriends that if they are planning to go north they should save or borrow to pay the coyote for both of them, because "no me voy a casar para estar sola" (I am not getting married to be alone). The companionate ideology lends weight to women's desire to participate in the previously largely male adventure of migration.

Though women may see a promise of power in these new ideas about confianza, companionate marriage as an ideology has more to say about the emotional intimacy couples can achieve through talking than it does about who gets the last word. Furthermore, these ideas about marriage emphasize the extent to which it is a bond of desire rather than of obligation—which may put women in a difficult position when, as is so often the case, desire falters. Several women mentioned that the message that they could support themselves, if for some reason they had to, was not lost on their husbands: seeing their wives' work and earn money sometimes diminished men's feeling of obligation to take care of them. In the United States, the transformation of marriage into a relationship that ideologically (though not actually) is purely affectionate (as opposed to both affectionate and economic) has lessened women's claim on men's resources after a marriage breaks up (see Giddens 1992, on the "pure relationship"). It is easy to see that the continued incorporation of an ideology that privileges the emotional work of a relationship over the man's economic role could lessen his feeling of obligation to his family. Furthermore, these companionate marriages can be very isolating for women, especially for migrants, as the ideal encourages women to invest time and energy primarily in the marital relationship rather than in a wider social network of female friends and relatives.

En el Norte la Mujer Manda:
Migration-Related Differences
in Gender

In addition to discussions of historical changes in the nature of gender, another constant refrain in both Atlanta and Mexico was that "en el norte la mujer manda"—in the North, women are in charge. When Doña Elena criticized Maria and her other daughters in Atlanta for answering back to their husbands, she said that Maria responded, "No, mom, here the woman is the boss, it's not like back in Mexico where the men are the boss. . . . No, here they don't hit you. . . . Here, the men are the ones who stand to lose" ("No, 'ama, aquí uno manda, no es como allá en Mexico que los hombres mandan. . . . No, aquí no me friegan. . . . Aquí los hombres la llevan de perder"). Comments such as this direct our attention to differences between various locations of the same transnational community. In terms of shared culture, the intensity of physical movement, and social and economic links, Degollado and El Fuerte are typical of the kinds of transnational communities others have discussed (for example, Glick Schiller, Basch, and Blanc-Szanton 1992). When people in Mexico asked me, for example, how long I had been "here" (in Mexico) doing my research, they expected an answer dated from my first entry into the community in Atlanta and including all the time I had been talking with their relatives in either place: "here with us" encompasses the expanded social space of their transnational community. There are, however, important differences between geographic locations of a transnational community, many of which are cast in terms of the social organization of gender. I identified key differences between the sending and receiving communities in three areas: privacy and the social organization of public space, domestic violence, and economic opportunities for women. Combined, these factors make women less socially and economically dependent on men.

Gender does not mark the division between house and street in the United States quite as strongly as it does in Mexico. As noted above, in the United States the danger of being picked up by "la migra" while in the street raises the costs of a certain type of flamboyant behavior. As anthropologist Roger Rouse (1991) has pointed out, Mexican men do not "own" the street in Atlanta; they are well aware they are just visiting. Women's widespread participation in the formal labor market in Atlanta further neutralizes the street's gendered aspects; going to and from work gives women as much justification as men to be outside. Women use the ideology of family progress ("salir adelante como familia"—to "make it" as a family) to justify their embrace of other previously masculine privileges, such as driving and owning a car. In Degollado and El

Fuerte, only women from the wealthiest families drive at all, and very few women own cars. For migrant women, mobility is power. The Mexican women I know in Atlanta who do drive never tire of the thrill of the freedom to go wherever they want without having to ask, of their new mastery of the street.

Furthermore, the audience in the U.S. street is not the same as in small-town Mexico. The sense of shared vigilance of all public behavior (characteristic, perhaps, of any small town) is lost in the urban United States. A feeling of freedom accompanies the realization that "aquí nadie te conoce"—that here no one knows you. In the field sites in Mexico, women put on stockings and hair spray to walk two blocks to the market to buy tortillas. In Atlanta they relax this resolute appearance management, dressing more for comfort than to express social status. Older women whose husbands never would have let them wear slacks, let alone jeans, in Mexico go out in Atlanta in sweatpants without asking permission. Upon her return to Mexico after living with her older sister, one unmarried woman left behind all the Bermuda shorts she had bought in Atlanta; she knew without asking that her father would never let her wear them in the rancho.

Women in Atlanta still dress up to go out at night with their husbands, but on a day-to-day basis they feel almost invisible and thus freed from some of the performative demands of gender and class. Although they delight in the relatively low prices and wide selection in U.S. stores, they stockpile their treasures to wear for the first time on visits back to Mexico. This invisibility is expressed in other ways, as well. In Mexico women sweep outside their front doors first thing in the morning and sometimes again in the afternoon, but never in all my visits in Atlanta (some quite early in the morning) did I see anyone sweeping outside her door. Women hint that privacy expands the range of the possible, joking about how easy it would be to take a lover—all you would need to do would be to hop on the bus, or in your car, and go meet him. In Degollado, a woman seen riding in a car with an unknown man would have some serious explaining to do, but in all likelihood her transgression would pass completely unnoticed amid Atlanta's urban anonymity. Staff at family planning clinics—or even abortion providers—are not inevitably the "comadre" of one's mother's cousin or some other relative. More than likely they do not even speak Spanish, which complicates delivery of services but certainly increases the feeling of privacy. The lack of an audience monitoring gendered behavior as an indicator of prestige greatly increases the possibilities for experimentation (and transgression).

One example of the greater privacy in Atlanta is the way the Catholic Church in the United States loosens its hold on women's reproductive behavior. Couples who marry in Degollado and El Fuerte are routinely (though not always) asked if they will accept "todos los hijos que Dios les manda," all the children God sends them. Women and their husbands are scolded in confession (the priests ask them directly) for using anything but periodic abstinence as a method of contraception. The women and men who do use a method either forgo communion altogether (which also means forgoing any "compadrazgo" [godparent relationship] that would be formalized at a Mass) or else confess their sin once a year, do penance, take communion, and then resume using contraception. The authority of the confessional is absolute; lying in confession is a mortal sin, perhaps even worse than the initial sin of nonprocreative sex. In Atlanta, in contrast, some priests ask about contraception and some do not, and women can cannily choose their confessors. Furthermore, some women—especially those who do not drive and live far from public transportation—sidestep the question altogether by no longer attending Mass. Others drift toward other Christian sects, such as Southern Baptist or Jehovah's Witnesses.

Men say that one reason Mexican women have more power in the North is that a man cannot hit his wife without expecting the government to interfere. In contrast to Mexico, where police are reluctant to intervene in cases of men's violence toward their wives or parents' toward their children, Mexicans—whether or not they live in the United States—know that in the United States help is literally a phone call away. Consider the difference between Maria in Atlanta and Josefina in Degollado, both of whom had been slapped by their husbands. Josefina admitted it to me, saying that the reason that Pedro could always get the last word ("la mujer con el hombre nunca va a poder") is that he could always beat her up ("me puede chingar"). Maria, meanwhile, told her mother, with great bravado, that men could not hit women in the United States, that they were the ones who stood to lose if they resorted to violence. It is, of course, a myth that men's violence toward women does not exist in the United States, just as it is untrue that there are no social controls against men's violence in Mexico. Domestic violence does take on new meanings in the United States, however, and the U.S. legal system—combined with the legal vulnerability of many Mexicans who live in fear of deportation—gives women important leverage. Eva and Pancho, for example, were fighting constantly during the time I was getting to know her, but she said she could usually get him to calm down by threatening to call her lawyer. Whether she really had a lawyer (or, more likely, a domestic violence counselor), the function of having a lawyer was clear; they both knew that if things got bad enough she could get a restraining order and he would have to leave the house.

Some women do call the police, but the reasons not to involve the authorities are as significant as the possibility that they might. Juan, who has been working in the United States since before his twentieth birthday, is now in his early thirties and is a U.S. citizen. He and Mercedes have one son, who was born in Atlanta. Juan spoke of Mercedes' right to have her own opinions, even to correct him, and of wanting to create a family bonded by warmth and physical affection rather than the respectful reserve his parents showed each other. The most important way a man respects his wife, he said, was in not forcing her to have sex against her will; intimacy should always be mutual and voluntary. Yet Juan reserves the right to slap his wife "to get her to calm down" and to remind her that he is ultimately the boss. He suggests that "getting along well" and having a "happy and harmonious home" depends on her understanding that there are only one pair of pants in their home, and that they belong to him. Their interactions around violence—his slapping her, her refraining from calling the police—are messages not just about gender hierarchy per se but also about the gendered nature of Mexican identity for immigrants to the United States. He is not just showing her her place—he is making sure that it is the same place she occupied in Mexico. By not dialing 911, she allows him to continue to believe that he really has the last word, that although they are in the United States now she has not forgotten what she learned as a girl about how to get along "por las buenas," by being nice. Under these conditions direct resistance resonates with meaning; just because a woman lives in a country in which the police will respond to her call does not make it easy to pick up the phone. This may explain at least in part why a woman like Maria, who has been in the United States for ten years, drives her own car, speaks English, and earns more than her husband does not call the police when he hits her. By enduring the violence, she allows him to reassert his power; she pays for her mobility and economic success with bruises.

The other reason Mexican women have more power in the United States than in Mexico, men say, is that they work for wages. "El mando," the power to give the orders, is an economically earned right: men have traditionally had the last word because they have the ultimate responsibility for supporting their families. Women's labor force participation in the United States is perceived as an encroachment on men's sole right to el mando, but this is hardly just a case of female employment translating directly into domestic power. Leaving aside the point that social reproduction is work as well, albeit unpaid and undervalued, women also work in Mexico. Three of the thirteen life-history informants in Mexico had their own businesses, and another five occasionally sold cheese, needlework, goats, or chickens or did housework. Older women were economically active as well. One of the older women was available to be interviewed only on Wednesday afternoons because in addition to running a small grocery store she manages her son's restaurant (he lives in the United States), which is open every night of the week except on Wednesdays. Another ran a workshop out of her home, sewing piecework for a factory in a large town nearby. Though it was hardly the norm, I met a number of older women who had accompanied their husbands north at least once, to try their hands at factory work or fieldwork.

The difference, then, is not that women work for wages in the United States and do not in Mexico; rather, it is that women's labor in the United States brings them much closer to economic independence than do their sisters' efforts south of the border. In Atlanta it is eminently possible for a woman to support her children earning just above the minimum wage—especially if she has only a few children, or if they are U.S. citizens (and hence qualify for access to Medicaid), or if she has her own family nearby to help. In Degollado and El Fuerte, few full-time jobs available to women of limited education pay even half the weekly minimum wage (about three hundred pesos—not quite forty dollars—at the time of my fieldwork). A housekeeper who works from eight in the morning until three in the afternoon, for example, earns seventy pesos a week; by taking in washing and ironing it might be possible to earn another seventy. One hundred and forty pesos a week would not feed a family of four (which would be a small family) even the barest meals of beans, tortillas, and chiles, much less provide for housing, clothes, shoes, schoolbooks, and the occasional medical emergency.

The net effect of all these differences (violence, women's work, increased privacy) is that Mexican women do not need men in the same way in Atlanta as they do in the sending communities. They are economically able to provide for themselves. Socially, a single mother can be respetada (respected) in a way that would be difficult in Mexico without a man. This is not just an abstract set of differences in the social construction of gender. Several years ago, Maria's husband began staying out all night drinking. In the morning, he would refuse to drive her to work. He stopped giving her any of his paycheck, and she suspected he was spending time with other women. She threatened to buy her own car and learn to drive, but he just laughed—so she took her savings, called a friend, and bought a car. Once she could drive, she asked him to leave. She told him she did not need his nonsense—"mejor sola que mal acompañada" (better to be alone than in bad company)—and that he should not come home until he could be a more responsible husband and a better father to his two children. Several weeks later he was back, asking for forgiveness. They still have occasional difficulties, but for the most part they live well together.

Maria had certain advantages that not all migrants have: there is not one story to be told about women's migration from Mexico to the United States but, rather, many stories. As I discuss elsewhere (Hirsch n.d.), whether these stories have happy or sad endings depends in part on a number of factors—such as legal status, kin networks, the moment in the family cycle at which migration takes places, and individual personalities—that make women more or less able to take advantage of the social and economic opportunities offered by life in the United States.

Implications for Future Research

On a methodological note, the life-history method—combined with patient participant observation, hours spent knitting and watching telenovelas, and repeated visits—proved to be extremely useful for sexuality research with Mexican women. Once I was able to establish confianza with these Mexican women they were quite willing to talk about sex in a variety of ways, ranging from sharing the ribald jokes told among married women to answering questions (in the final life-history interview) about the nature of desire, sexual positions, pleasure, and communication. The repeated visits and the gradual growth of my relationships with them were crucial in promoting this confianza. The findings here also underline the importance of flexibility in research strategy (and, by implication, in regard to the research questions themselves). I turned my attention to generational change only after being told repeatedly and by many women that their lives and marriages were different from those of their mothers—"Ya no somos como las de antes." Those embarking on migration studies should remember that migrants can offer much more than grist for an academic's mill: if we listen carefully, we can find in their words important messages about the theoretical and methodological approaches that best suit the problem at hand.

Rather than looking at the sending community only as the cultural and social control group in order to foreground the changes that accompany migration, we should also explore how the sending communities themselves are changing. Without acknowledging historical processes in the sending communities, we imply that we are comparing life in the traditional developing world and the modern developed world—an error that many of us have sought to avoid, in the first place, by adopting the transnational perspective, with its emphasis on the intensity of connection between sending and receiving communities. After all, the sending communities are a moving target, subject to historical change just as the receiving communities are. In addition, as anthropologist Nancy Foner

(1997) has noted, "traditional" migrant culture is not a fixed body of norms but rather a category manipulated deliberately by migrants as they forge new cultures, drawing on both the old and the new. The main point here—and this is both a theoretical and a methodological recommendation—is that studies of gender that neglect historical transformations in the sending communities miss key cultural developments without which migration-related changes cannot be fully understood. Even if our research designs are cross-sectional, our theoretical and methodological approaches can be longitudinal.

I have also addressed here theoretical concerns about migration and cultural change. At first glance the emphasis on intimacy, choice, and cooperation in younger women's and men's descriptions of their marriages might seem to be directly influenced by North American ideals of companionate marriage (see Simmons 1979 and Giddens 1992). The comparative perspective employed here, however, highlights the way in which the cultural changes in this community are a result both of transnational linkages and of social processes within Mexico. Women in the U.S. and Mexican field sites shared similar ideals for marriages of confianza; the key difference was that women in the United States seemed to have more leverage in negotiating toward that ideal—or, perhaps, that men are more willing to adopt this new paradigm away from the watchful eyes of their fathers and uncles in Mexico. The generational paradigm shift from marriages of respeto to marriages of confianza, the trend toward companionate marriage, has interesting parallels in Africa, Europe, and North America (see, for example, Inhorn 1996; Smith n.d.; Gillis, Tilly, and Levine 1992; Simmons 1979)—parallels that suggest the value of exploring links between widespread processes such as industrialization and technological change and ideologies of the nuclear family. My point is not that Mexicans are adopting some universally homogeneous ideal of family relations but rather that they are actively transforming a globally available ideology into a specifically Mexican companionate marriage.

This study suggests a route to disaggregating the ideological and material components of cultural change that would also hold true for areas of interest other than gender. Comparative historically grounded research in migrant sending communities could lay a solid foundation for sorting out which aspects of cultural change in migrants are actually a product of migration and which are the result of changes in the sending community. Of course, changes in the sending community cannot be separated from migration-related changes: one of the key historical processes in these sending communities is their increasing integration into international migrant circuits. A comparison of the gender culture of towns and ranchos such as Degollado and El Fuerte with that of other towns and ranchos less intensely tied to migration might disentangle the influences of migration and returning migrants from those of more specifically Mexican historical forces—if it were possible to find any such towns.

More important, the time has come to move away from bargaining as the metaphor guiding our approach to gender and migration. Although the ideas of bargaining and negotiation have been useful for the way they highlight the constrained agency of migrants (see Pessar 1998), the ethnographic evidence presented here suggests that our focus on the causes of women's empowerment has limited our understanding of gender and migration in a number of ways. First, the debate about the relative importance of wage labor versus the broader cultural and legal differences of life in the United States (see Hondagneu-Sotelo 1994; Gibson 1988) in giving women more power misses the interrelatedness of these factors—Maria would not have thrown her husband out if she could not have supported herself on her own, but in Mexico she never would have been working as a waitress, because the contact with unknown men that such a job entails would have risked her honor and that of her family. Second, whether women can take advantage of these economic, cultural, and legal opportunities depends on a number of other factors, such as legal status, kin networks, and experience in the labor force. There is not, and never will be, one answer to the question of how migration affects gender. A simplistic focus on the effects of migration on gender-related issues takes us back two decades in gender theory, to the idea of "woman" as a unified category. As Patricia Pessar (1998), a leading theorist in the area of gender and transnationalism, has argued, gender may not even be the defining axis of women's lives; we need to look at race and class as well.[3] In addition, we should not assume that migration to the United States is always beneficial to women; in fact, this may not be the case. Migration can limit some women's power in important ways; rather than being able to walk next door to her mother's house, a Mexican woman seeking social support may have to struggle with language difficulties and public transportation if, in fact, she is lucky enough to have her own kin nearby. Again and again, women who do not work told me, "Me siento como en la cárcel"—"I feel as if I were in jail"; others have found similar experiences (for example, Pessar 1995, 45).

Conclusion

The question of why migration empowers women, or even which women are empowered, makes other aspects of changes in gender construction invisible. As Micaela di Leonardo (1991) has argued, gender is relational—that is, it is not possible to understand gender without interviewing both women and men. As described above, men's preferences are perhaps the most important constraint on the kinds of marriage that Mexican women in this community can negotiate. Without attention to how masculinity is changing, it is impossible to make sense of these new marriages of confianza. Looking at the issue of gender and migration by focusing on women's changing resources posits male gender as the invisible, immutable reference category; it assumes that Mexican men in the United States continue to want what they wanted in Mexico—and that what men in Mexico want has not changed. Although some, such as Rouse (1991) and Pessar (1995), have looked at the ways male migrants' resources (especially their social power as men) change, not enough attention has been paid to the way the goals themselves may be changing. Foner has noted that the Jamaican women she interviewed were influenced by "American values extolling the ideal of marital fidelity and 'family togetherness'"(1997, 967). The Mexican couples in this study are influenced both by those "American values" and by new, Mexican ideas about marital intimacy and togetherness. Some Mexican men, although they may not long to pack their children's lunches or clean the toilets, do yearn for a different kind of family life, and they are remaking their families with that goal in mind. As Juan said, of his parents' marriage, "I've never seen them kiss, or even hug." He said he wants to do both, to act "closer so that the children really know you love each other, that you feel both tenderness and respect" (mas unido para que conozcan que uno se quiere y que tiene uno cariño y que hay respeto). Ethnography can remind us to listen to the voices of our research subjects; in this case, those voices remind us that they, too, though they are poor and struggling and sometimes undocumented, deserve the basic humanity of being understood to make decisions not merely with an eye to strategy and advantage but, as we all do, from love and longing as well.

A previous version of this chapter appeared in *American Behavioral Scientist* 1999, vol. 42, no. 9.

Notes

1. A number of other factors have contributed to this sharp decline in fertility. Though the subject can hardly be discussed adequately here, factors worthy of mention include social changes such as rising rates of education among both men and women and a concur-

rently rising age at first marriage; economic transformations such as women's increased labor force participation and the increased availability of nonagricultural jobs for which a secondary education is desirable, if not necessary; and political factors such as the Mexican government's concerted effort, since the 1970s, to slow population growth through national family planning campaigns.

2. Neolocal refers to married couples immediately setting up their own households as opposed to patrilocal, living with the man's family, or uxorilocal, living with the woman's family.

3. Although this chapter focuses on ideals and practices within marriage, there are certainly other relationships that are relevant to broader issues of how migration affects the social construction of gender. As Katherine Donato (1993) and Pierrette Hondagneu-Sotelo (1994) point out, not all women who migrate do so with their husbands; some move north under the moral protection of other male relatives such as fathers or brothers, and still others (in particular, those who become pregnant outside of marriage) migrate to distance themselves deliberately from their male kin. Further research should go beyond both a narrow emphasis on women's resources within marriage and the tendency to look at gender as if it structures only marital relationships.

References

Connell, Robert W. 1987. *Gender and Power.* Stanford: Stanford University Press.

Cornelius, Wayne. 1991. "Los Migrantes de la Crisis: The Changing Profile of Mexican Migration to the United States." In *Social Responses to Mexico's Economic Crisis,* edited by Mercedes González de la Rocha and Agustín Escobar Latapí. San Diego: Center for U.S.-Mexican Studies, University of California, San Diego.

di Leonardo, Micaela. 1991. Introduction to *Gender at the Crossroads of Knowledge.* Berkeley: University of California Press.

Donato, Katherine M. 1993. "Current Trends and Patterns of Female Migration: Evidence from Mexico." *International Migration Review* 27(4): 748–71.

Foner, Nancy. 1997. "The Immigrant Family: Cultural Legacies and Cultural Changes." *International Migration Review* 31(4): 961–74.

———. 1998. "Benefits and Burdens: Immigrant Women and Work in New York City." *Gender Issues* 16(4): 5–24.

Gibson, Margaret A. 1988. "Punjabi Orchard Farmers: An Immigrant Enclave in Rural California." *International Migration Review* 22(1): 28–50.

Giddens, Anthony. 1992. *The Transformation of Intimacy.* Stanford: Stanford University Press.

Gillis, John R., Louise A. Tilly, and David Levine. 1992. *The European Experience of Declining Fertility, 1850–1970.* Cambridge: Blackwell.

Glick Schiller, Nina, Linda Basch, and Cristina Blanc-Szanton. 1992. "Towards a Transnational Perspective on Migration: Race, Class, Ethnicity, and Nationalism Reconsidered." *Annals of the New York Academy of Sciences* 645.

Goodson-Lawes, Julie. 1993. "Feminine Authority and Migration: The Case of One Family from Mexico." *Urban Anthropology* 22(3–4): 277–97.

Grasmuck, Sherri, and Patricia R. Pessar. 1991. *Between Two Islands: Dominican International Migration.* Berkeley: University of California Press.

Gutmann, Mathew C. 1996. *The Meanings of Macho: Being a Man in Mexico City.* Berkeley: University of California Press.

Hirsch, Jennifer S. 1998. "Migration, Modernity, and Mexican Marriage: A Comparative Study of Gender, Sexuality, and Reproductive Health in a Transnational Community." Ph.D. diss., Johns Hopkins University.

———. n.d. "'Que, pues, con el pinche NAFTA?' Gender, Power, and Migration Between Western Mexico and Atlanta." *Urban Anthropology,* in review (submitted in 1998).

———. Forthcoming. "'Un Noviasgo Despues de Ser Casados': Companionate Marriage, Sexual Intimacy and the Modern Mexican Family." In *Qualitative Demography: Categories and Contexts in Population Studies,* edited by Simon Szreter, Arunchalam Dharmalingam, and Hania Sholkamy. New York: Oxford University Press.

Hirsch, Jennifer S., and Constance A. Nathanson. 1997. "Demografía informal: Cómo utilizar las redes sociales para construir una muestra etnográfica sistemática de mujeres mexicanas en ambos lados de la frontera." *Estudios Demográficos y de Desarollo Urbano* (El Colegio de Mexico) 12(1–2): 177–99.

Hondagneu-Sotelo, Pierrette. 1994. *Gendered Transitions: Mexican Experiences of Immigration.* Berkeley: University of California Press.

Inhorn, Marcia. 1996. *Infertility and Patriarchy: The Cultural Politics of Gender and Family Life in Egypt.* Philadelphia: University of Pennsylvania Press.

Pedraza, Silvia. 1991. "Women and Migration: The Social Consequences of Gender." *Annual Review of Sociology* 17:303–25.

Pessar, Patricia. 1995. "On the Homefront and in the Workplace: Integrating Immigrant Women into Feminist Discourse." *Anthropological Quarterly* 68(1): 37–47.

———. 1998. "The Role of Gender, Households, and Social Networks in the Migration Process: A Review and Appraisal." In *Becoming American/America Becoming,* edited by Josh DeWind, Charles Hirschman, and Philip Kasnitz. New York: Russell Sage Foundation.

Rouse, Roger. 1991. "Mexican Migration and the Social Space of Postmodernism." *Diaspora* 1(1): 8–23.

Simmons, Christina. 1979. "Companionate Marriage and the Lesbian Threat." *Frontiers* 4(3): 54–59.

Smith, Daniel J. n.d. "Sexual Relationships and Social Change: Linking Fertility Preferences and Contraceptive Use to the Social (Re)Construction of Gender and the Individual." Emory University. Unpublished paper.

16

DIALING 911 IN NUER: GENDER TRANSFORMATIONS AND DOMESTIC VIOLENCE IN A MIDWESTERN SUDANESE REFUGEE COMMUNITY

Jon D. Holtzman

A YOUNG wife went into the forest to collect firewood with the other village women, or so the story goes. Chatting as they went, their conversation quickly turned to the beatings their husbands had given them, with each describing in turn the violent treatment they had received. Everyone had a story to tell of this beating or that, this fight or that; yet when it came to the young wife's turn all were aghast: Married for more than a year, she revealed that she had never been beaten! The women wondered out loud what her life must be like, and what kind of man her husband must be, and the women quickly came together to remedy this situation. She must, they instructed, take her husband's ceremonial leopard skin and soil it. When he knew it had been soiled she should throw it in the cooking fire. She went home and did this, and as the other village women had promised, her husband had no choice but to beat her.

This folk story, in various forms, was related to me—often quite spontaneously—by Nuer men in Minnesota during the course of my research there from 1995 to 1998. When Nuer began to resettle in Minnesota in the mid–1990s as refugees from the civil war in southern Sudan, domestic violence quickly emerged as a significant issue within the Nuer community and served, as well, to construct certain attitudes toward the Nuer within social service agencies and the host community at large. The fact of this violence may be attributed to a variety of sources stemming from both long-standing patterns of gender relations within Nuer marriages and their transformations in the context of re-settlement. In this sense a consideration of domestic violence is significant as a "flash point" that crystallizes a host of tensions derived both from the recasting of gender roles within the household and the interaction of the household with broader institutions within the host community.

In regard to the latter point, state intervention has had wide-ranging effects in the process of recasting Nuer marital relations, in ways that are sometimes unintended and not always entirely positive. The sources of bias in the Nuer folk story about domestic violence—and the emphasis on women's need to be beaten—are, of course, patently obvious. As a Nuer woman chuckled when I asked her about this tale, "That is a man's history," informed by male Nuer attitudes concerning gender relations, female motivations, violence, and the like. Yet it is also important to consider the biases intrinsic in American approaches to understanding family dynamics—and domestic violence—which, if less obvious and less self-serving than the example given above, nonetheless are salient in shaping the ways American communities respond to issues of violence within immigrant populations. In fact, significant differences between Nuer and American conceptions of family life and decision-making processes can lead to a misreading of conflict within the home. The result is, in some cases, policy decisions that are incongruous with the goals of Nuer women and men alike.

Acknowledging the incongruity between policy and its consequences in the case of domestic violence puts one on slippery ground. There is a thin line, which should not be crossed, between explaining domestic violence—which is a necessary step in addressing it—and justifying it, which neither I nor anyone else would wish to do. That it is necessary to understand the family dynamics that feed domestic violence in particular cultural contexts certainly does not mean that cultural differences justify domestic violence among immigrants in the United States (see Koptiuch 1996 for a discussion of the legal notion of "cultural defense"). Nor does it mean that domestic violence should not be addressed as a serious issue within immigrant communities. Rather, I suggest, the serious disjunctures between American and immigrant (in this case Nuer) models of the family, and related attitudes toward domestic violence within it, require that close attention be paid to these differences, lest the consequences of domestic violence become magnified in ways that may bring unintended and negative effects for the very victims the U.S. law is intended to protect.

Immigration and Family Change

Family relations have long been recognized as one of the most significant areas of social change among immigrants. The families in which immigrants live have typically been shaped by cultural and historical factors very different from those they face in the United States, so that domestic relationships necessarily are reworked in the context of immigration. Economic organization, educational opportunities, broad societal norms, ideologies of the family, and their embodiment in policy and law all play a role in transforming relationships between men and women, and between old and young, within the family.

Gender relations are a particularly salient area for family change. Broad-ranging changes in daily life resulting from immigration have been found in a variety of contexts to have significant effects on the status of women and the relationships between women and men (Foner 1998; Pessar 1995; Grasmuck and Pessar 1991; Donelly 1994; Pedraza 1991; Tienda and Booth 1991). Among Korean immigrants, for instance, economic life in the United States has drawn many married women into the outside labor force, in contrast to the situation in Korea, where married women were more likely to be at home playing a domestic role. When Korean women assume a more important economic role—and their husbands' status as providers thereby declines—significant marital tension and conflict often results (Min 1998). Similarly, Southeast Asian women who have gone to work in meat-packing plants in Kansas have found that access to an independent income has given them greater autonomy and, along with it, greater assertiveness, but it has resulted in higher rates of divorce, as well (Benson 1994).

Tensions arising from changing gender relations in immigrant families frequently have implications for family violence, as well. The frequent absence of close kin sometimes results in the removal of social curbs on family violence (Hagan 1994), and other factors may remove protections afforded to women in their home countries (Ong 1995). Even if rates of domestic violence are unchanged, or even diminished, in the United States, the causes of domestic violence may differ in this country. The fact that it is also, here, illegal has significant implications for immigrant family life (Kibria 1993; Donelly 1994).

Ethnographic Background

The Nuer are among the most recent immigrants to the United States, having begun to arrive in significant numbers only in the mid-1990s. In the African context, however, they are well known within anthropology, representing one of the discipline's most important case studies. Agropastoralists from southern Sudan, the Nuer are best known through the classic ethnographies of E. E. Evans-Pritchard (1940, 1951, 1956), which have been central to the twentieth-century theoretical development of anthropology—both from Evans-Pritchard's own work and from count-less reexaminations of his material (for example, Sahlins 1961; Kelly 1985; Gough 1971; Southall 1986; Beidelman 1966, 1971; Newcomer 1972). More recently, excellent historical (Johnson 1994) and eth-nographic restudies (Hutchinson 1996) have provided important updates to scholarly understandings of the Nuer.

The fate of the Nuer has, unfortunately, in recent decades been en-twined with the civil war in southern Sudan. The war, which is rooted in deep north-south divisions based on cultural, political, economic, his-torical, and religious differences, has raged off and on in Sudan since independence in the 1950s. Nuer life has been severely disrupted by the conflict, as their fields and pastures have become a war zone and their livestock the larder for rebel and government forces alike. Tens of thou-sands of southern Sudanese have been killed in the civil war, and by 1988 more than a quarter million had fled war and famine to the relative safety of refugee camps across the border in Ethiopia (Hutchinson 1996). With the Ethiopian revolution of the early 1990s, however, insecurity became a significant issue there, as well, and many Nuer now fled to neighboring Kenya in search of permanent third country resettlement. Resettlement programs were at this time being orchestrated in Kenya, at camps run by the United Nations High Commissioner for Refugees. Nuer, along with other southern Sudanese, applied for permission to resettle in a number of countries—Canada, Australia, and the United States.

By the mid-1990s, significant numbers of Nuer had gained permis-sion to resettle in the United States. Largely church-based resettlement agencies placed the refugees in selected communities around the United States. Sites were selected based on the availability of willing sponsors in the community or on other criteria that seemed to make the commu-nity suitable for refugee resettlement—for instance, a low level of preex-isting diversity, which they hoped would limit preexisting biases toward refugees. A community of approximately four hundred Nuer was estab-lished in the Twin Cities metropolitan area, primarily in the northern outer-ring suburbs, though this number was reduced substantially in early 1997 through out-migration to Nebraska in search of subsidized housing. Approximately half of the Twin Cities Nuer population moved directly to Minnesota from Africa; the other half came as secondary mi-grants from other U.S. cities that had been sites of Nuer resettlement, such as Dallas, San Diego, Rochester (New York), and Sioux Falls (South Dakota). The resettling population mainly consisted of young families, with some unmarried young men. There are few older individuals, and most families live independently, with few close relatives in the com-munity.

Nuer Marriage and Gender
Relations in the Sudanese Context

Nuer marriage in Sudan is a process that occurs not simply between two individuals but between the families and extended kinship networks of both bride and groom. Although there is some marital choice—a man usually takes an active role in finding his own bride, and a woman's approval, at the least, of the man she is marrying is required—the families play a central role in arranging the marriage. A fundamental component of marriage is the payment of "bridewealth" from the family of the groom to the family of the bride, typically on the order of twenty-five cows (Evans-Pritchard 1951). These are collected from a range of the groom's kin and subsequently distributed among the kin of the bride. The bridewealth payment brings about the social transfer of the bride from her natal family and descent group to those of the groom. Perhaps more important, "progeny rights" are transferred—any children born will be members of the groom's family, even should the couple separate.

The "gol" (family) represents an important unit in Nuer society Evans-Pritchard 1951. A family includes a man, his wife, and any children of the union. Because Nuer men are frequently polygynous, a man may have more than one wife, each with her own house in the homestead. Family units typically live in their own homestead within loosely defined villages, and both agricultural and pastoral production are organized at the family level. Resource distribution typically occurs within the gol, although in polygynous families it takes place independently within the house of each wife.

Although the family formed in marriage is a significant independent unit, kin nevertheless continue to play a central role in the conjugal relationship, even after all marriage ceremonies are completed. Through marriage, new kinship relationships and new networks of property exchange are created. Indeed, because the continued maintenance of these relationships and networks is largely contingent on the well-being of the conjugal bond, kin have material interests in the stability of the marriage. Should the marriage end in divorce—particularly before the birth of several children—bridewealth cattle must be returned. This is an odious prospect for the bride's family in particular, not only because of the economic importance of cattle but because of their social importance, as well. A family that received cattle when a daughter married may have already used the cattle to pay bridewealth for a son. Being forced to return these cattle may, thus, result in the weakening or even dissolution of the son's marriage—what Sharon Hutchinson (1996) calls "chain divorce." Not surprisingly, kin seek to ensure the stability of any marriage.

Significant gender divisions exist among the Nuer, both within the family and in the society at large. This is most visibly demonstrated by the divisions of male and female space. Within the homestead each woman has her own house, which constitutes her rightful space. Men do not typically spend significant time in these houses. They generally congregate together and sleep in a separate structure constructed for men. There is a fairly well-defined division of labor, with men focused on the herding of livestock and the cultivation of fields and women engaged in milking, food preparation, and care of the home. Men are jurally defined as dominant within the home, are expected to be decision makers, and may legitimately resort to violence if they deem it necessary. Women, however, also have influence in the home, which they may exercise through cessation of their domestic tasks, most notably by refusing to cook (Hutchinson 1996; Holtzman n.d.). As couples age, the authority of women in Nuer families typically increases, and they may more freely contradict, swear at, and insult their husbands without fear of reprisal (Hutchinson 1996)

Although affection certainly exists between many Nuer couples, the marriage relationship is not centrally defined along those lines. Whatever affection exists between couples generally develops over time, as the result of familiarity and shared experiences (Duany 1992). The Nuer characterize a Nuer couple as "two people who can't agree about anything" (Hutchinson 1996, 229), and Evans-Pritchard's (1951) discussion of latent hostility between husbands and wives is now famous in anthropology.

> Nuer have told me . . . that there is what we would call a latent antagonism between husband and wife and indeed between man and woman. They say that when a man has begotten several children by his wife he wants her to die, and may even pray for this to happen, for he does not want to die before her and another man to cohabit with her, rule in his home, use his cattle, and perhaps illtreat his children and rob them of their birthright. Men also say that in their hearts women wish for their husbands' deaths. (Evans-Pritchard 1951, 133)

Given such underlying attitudes it is not surprising that Nuer marriages in Sudan are not without conflict. A number of aspects of Nuer marriage in Sudan are important to consider before examining their transformation in the United States. The basis of marriage is wholly different from that in Western marriage. Nancy Folbre (1988) has examined in depth the Western assumptions of affect and altruism that may bias interpretations of married life in other cultural contexts. Nuer marriage is seen not so much as a relationship between two people based on mutual affection and common purpose as a relationship between groups. The emphasis is on creating a social network, through the conjugal bond, for the purpose of distributing rights, privileges, and responsibilities concerning people and livestock. Contrary to Western ideals of family life, there is no assumption of accord between husband and wife—indeed, quite the opposite. The interests of husbands and wives are not the same, and conflict is expected. Although men may attempt to dictate their will, women may disagree, arguing with their husbands, refusing to cook, goading and insulting them—situations all parties understand can result in violence.

It is important also to emphasize that severe conflict, even physical violence—generally by men against women, though occasionally the inverse (Hutchinson 1996)—is not considered pathological but is, rather, expected as a normal, if undesirable, part of marriage (see also Micaela di Leonardo's (1979, 1991) discussion of evidence of female-male violence in the work of E. E. Evans-Pritchard (1951, 103). Both men and women are socialized to understand marriage in this way, and the behavior of husbands and wives is structured toward pushing each other to the breaking point. In fact, violence serves as a signal for other parties to intervene to defuse tension. Marriage partners are not expected to be able to resolve serious conflicts themselves; rather, they do so through a kinship network. If conflict reaches a point of violence, a woman normally leaves, seeking assistance from her own, or her husband's, kin. These outside parties are expected to resolve the problem not so much by assessing the competing claims but by simply imploring the husband and wife to come back and treat each other in a proper way—for the husband to refrain from violence and for the wife to refrain from the behavior that makes her husband angry. The outside parties emphasize the importance of returning to the marital relationship, both for the couple's sake and for the sake of kin who also have strong extrinsic interests in the success of the marriage.

Transformations in Gender Relations in Minnesota

What happens to marriage and gender relations among the Nuer in the United States? It goes without saying that migration represents a radical change for Nuer refugees resettling in Minnesota. Although all immigrants experience pronounced changes, the Nuer represent the far end of the continuum with respect to the differences between the life to which they were accustomed and life in urban America. Virtually all Nuer refugees grew up in rural African communities, oriented toward subsistence agropastoralism, and left their homes because of war and famine.

Time spent outside of their home communities was generally in refugee camps in rural areas, surrounded by other Nuer. Few had spent much time in an urban setting, and many men and virtually all women were monolingual in Nuer when they arrived in the United States. Most men, and all the women, had little in the way of formal education.

Given this background, changes in Nuer life in Minnesota are pervasive, affecting virtually all areas of their lives. Nowhere is this more apparent than in gender relations and marriage. As Pierrette Hondagneu-Sotelo (1999, 366) notes, the majority of immigration studies are still conducted as though gender relations are largely irrelevant to the way the lives of immigrants are organized. Although attention has been paid to the experiences of women (Pedraza 1991; Tienda and Booth 1991), it does not extend fully to current conceptions of gender per se, which are now dominant within anthropology and other social sciences (compare Benson 1994). Current approaches view gender as encompassing the full range of sociocultural processes that construct the identities and positions of both men and women, as well the relations between them (for example, Collier and Yanagisako 1987; Collier 1988). Gender is seen as having an important influence in structuring a broad range of domains including economics, religion, and political organization. The emphasis is also on the ways that the lives of men and women, as well as ideal categories of masculinity and femininity, are socially constructed in relation to one another.

In the Nuer case, adaptation to a new environment has not only led to a reworking of patterns of individual behavior, social relationships, and social identities; fundamental aspects of gender relations within which Nuer have been socialized have also begun to shift. So far, there is little evidence that outside employment has increased the status of women in either a general sense or vis-à-vis their husbands as is found in a plethora of immigrant groups (Foner 1998; Min 1998; Benson 1994; Pessar 1987; Grasmuck and Pessar 1991; Zhou and Nordquist 1994). Among the Nuer, both men and women have had difficulty finding jobs, with women particularly lacking language and job skills necessary for employment.

More prominent is a general, quite conscious perception that it is impossible to continue to follow long-standing Nuer ways of organizing family life given conditions in the United States. One example concerns the physical separation of men's and women's spaces that is characteristic of Nuer life in Sudan. Such separation is simply not possible in a one- or two-bedroom American apartment. This new closeness is not merely physical but entails far greater levels of mutual dependency as well. In Sudan, the division of labor is relatively clear-cut, and both women and men can accomplish their tasks, and function as successful adults, without widespread marital cooperation in daily activities. In contrast, the Nuer have found that life in the United States requires substantial coordination between husbands and wives.

The Nuer understand that their old family patterns are, of necessity, being modified, yet no new normative patterns have clearly developed. A lack of general agreement about how daily life should now be organized can lead to jostling between men and women who are consciously trying to negotiate family roles. In some cases, the reorganization of daily life has pushed men to assume responsibilities that are highly problematic within ritually constituted cultural constructions of Nuer manhood. The most obvious example is cooking. A Nuer youth, after he has been initiated into manhood, is strictly forbidden to cook food. However, because Nuer women may be out of the house at odd hours in the United States—particularly among the few women who are engaged in some type of employment—men sometimes are required to prepare meals, lest they or their children go hungry until late at night.

Gender Conflict in the United States

It is not surprising that sources of gender conflict differ significantly between Nuer in Sudan and those in the United States. Interviews with Nuer informants in the United States and Hutchinson's (1996) work in Sudan suggest that quarrels in Sudan frequently revolve around men's perceptions of women's failure to cook or perform other household duties. Female adultery—real or imagined—may also be a source of tension. These concerns may continue to be present in the United States, though broader changes in daily life inflect them in different ways. Failure to perform household duties may still be an issue, but it is now sometimes constructed through values drawn from life in the United States. One man remarked that his friend "is working and his wife is not working, and he [came home from work and] didn't get any food, and he tells his wife, 'Why didn't you cook and you are here and you are not working.' And the wife says, 'How can I cook and see my video?' Can you comment on that? Leave your hunger in your car, yunno."

In this instance, the tensions stem from issues concerning the organization of work in the United States: a man is entitled to find his dinner waiting for him when he returns from work, and the provision of that meal is considered the responsibility of his wife. The single greatest source of gender conflict is, however, money. Once subsistence agropastoralists, the Nuer have had to adjust to the need for cash for rent and day-to-day needs. This can be highly stressful on an individual level and is a general source of tension between husbands and wives. On top of this, the Nuer bring expectations to the United States—which are rein-forced by the American consumer culture—that fuel desires for a wide range of material goods. Women question whether their husbands are hiding money for their own purposes. Men, in turn, complain that women's material desires and expectations far outstrip their budgets—and that their (almost uniformly uneducated) wives cannot understand basic mathematical realities.

The significance of money in gender conflict frequently goes beyond conflicts over household budgets and reaches to the very legitimacy of a union. Many relationships were formed in the exigencies of displace-ment rather than in a village context. Kin frequently had little role in arranging the marriage, and an official marriage ceremony—whether Christian or Nuer—was often not completed. Most important, bride-wealth was either absent or only partially paid. It may have been diffi-cult or impossible in the context of refugee flight to acquire the neces-sary livestock to make marriage payments, and the appropriate kin may not have been available to discuss the details of the marriage. Both Nuer in Minnesota and kin remaining in Africa understand and accept that circumstances have forced a couple to join together without a proper and complete marriage ceremony, but they do expect, nevertheless, that steps will be taken to legitimate the marriage.

The most obvious way to do this is to remit money to kin remain-ing in Africa, either as a substitute for marriage cattle or for the hus-band's kin to purchase cattle, which will be transferred to the bride's family. To fail to do this may call into question a women's identity as a married woman: rather than being properly married, she has run off with a man, and her family has received nothing in return. At the same time that women press to send money home to pay off bridewealth debts, men may also wish to remit money to their own families because of the hardships they continue to face. Both men and women are eager to remit money to kin remaining in Africa, but the recipients, amounts, and purpose of remittances may be bitterly contested. Given the meager household budgets of most Nuer refugees, there is rarely enough money to satisfy all desires to remit money.

The Changing Context of Conflict and Conflict Resolution in the United States

The new tensions arising in Nuer marriages in the United States com-monly result in open conflict and sometimes in violence. Scholars of domestic violence have long suggested that increased domestic violence is an almost inevitable consequence of social change, when social relationships and cultural values are disrupted (Gelles and Cornell 1983). Recent studies, however, have found the relationship of social change to domestic violence to be much more complex (Morley 1994). In some instances, social change increases family violence (Savishinky 1966); in others, the opposite effect has been observed (Erlich1966). David Levinson (1989) argues that there is no simple relationship between social change and increases in family violence and stresses the need to specify the types of relationships that can mitigate or reduce family violence in situations of social change.

In the case of the Nuer, there is, in fact, no clear indication of any change in the rates or severity of domestic violence in Minnesota. Some amount of domestic violence has occurred in most homes, on at least one occasion, with an estimated 25 percent experiencing police intervention at some time. Some informants claim that this is indicative of increased domestic violence in the United States owing to greater marital strains, but there is no question that domestic violence is also common in Sudan. What is clear is that the causes of domestic violence and its implications differ substantially from those found in the Sudanese context.

A key factor underlying domestic violence in the United States is the significant transformation of gender-based authority in Nuer families. These changes are one immediate consequence of Nuer resettlement and appear to have been set in motion before families set foot on American soil. In contrast to Nuer gender relations in Sudan, a message of gender equality has been actively promoted among the Nuer, beginning with cultural orientation programs in refugee camps. Before resettlement, Nuer men and women were instructed by the United Nations High Commissioner for Refugees that in the United States, domestic violence is a criminal offense.

Once in the United States, Nuer women are responsive to the message of gender equality and the relative freedom of American women. Nuer men recognize the equality and freedom that American women enjoy, and they claim to recognize its legitimacy, as well. They argue, however, that their own wives present a very different case. Noting the lower educational experience and English facility of Nuer women compared with Nuer men, men argue that women lack the social and linguistic skills to exercise the type of freedom that American women exhibit. In the words of one Nuer man, "Our women are very primitive." Such views add another potential dimension to conflicts within a relationship in which the struggle for power is already an intrinsic feature. As Nuer women have recognized their equality within American life, they have become emboldened in asserting their own agendas within the home. Like many immigrant men from other patriarchal societies (see Pessar 1995; Margolis 1994; Min 1998; Lessinger 1996; Donelly 1994), Nuer men are not enthusiastic about relinquishing their culturally constructed domestic dominance. Within this context, domestic violence is a frequent outcome.

Dialing 911

When it comes to the structure and rhetoric of institutionalized conflict between Nuer husbands and wives, not much has shifted in the short period since Nuer began to settle in Minnesota. The context of conflict and its implications for both men and women, however, have changed radically. Thus, a Nuer husband in his late twenties noted that in Minnesota, as in Sudan, "when a man and woman argue, the first thing she says is that she is going." In Sudan "going" means returning to her family or going to her husband's brother, who will seek to fruitfully resolve the conflict—both for the benefit of the couple and also because of the extrinsic stake the kin themselves have in the marriage. In the United States, however, this kinship network is absent or greatly diminished. It is not unusual to have a sibling or two within the community, but large kinship networks are absent. Furthermore, the influence of any kin who are present is greatly diminished, because in the United States there are no bridewealth cattle to be returned in the event of divorce. Hutchinson notes the effects of British-initiated policies in decreasing the influence of the kinship network on Nuer marriage—in the words of one Nuer, "the fate of marriage was increasingly put into the hands of two people who couldn't agree about anything —[1996, 229]—and in Minnesota, this condition has been pushed to the extreme. There, the "two people who couldn't agree on anything" are placed in the position of resolving disputes without the presence of significant kin who might calm the parties and clarify the issues involved.

Consequently, in the United States, when a woman says, "I am going," it implies recourse to a legal system whose goals are very different from those held by kin. Nuer women have developed a readiness to seek resolution of disputes outside of the Nuer community, through the involvement of police and women's shelters. The concept of "dialing 911" has itself taken on a life of its own, with the propensity of women to seek police assistance becoming an additional source of gender-based tension. Nuer men acknowledge that it is sometimes appropriate for women to seek police intervention, but they also maintain that women sometimes make calls simply to further their own cause. Men feel that the threat of dialing 911 has become part of the rhetoric of conflict—a weapon to be used against men regardless of the threat of physical violence. A Nuer husband in his early thirties claimed, for instance, that "if you just look at a woman like you are serious she dials 911."

An added complication is that the police and other government agencies are perceived as inherently biased toward women, a perception the Nuer share with other immigrants (Kibria 1993). Not surprisingly, this sentiment is felt most strongly by men, but women, as well, sometimes recognize that police and court actions and decisions are sometimes incongruous with Nuer cultural assessments. As one Nuer man complained, "The police only care if you hit your wife, but they don't care about all the things she might have done." The point of his line of argument was not that the violence is justified but rather that a husband's acts of violence occur within a context of conflict. A wife might have done something to cause the conflict, or engaged in behaviors during the course of the conflict that both Nuer men and women consider to be far worse than physical assault—insulting her husband, demeaning his manhood, being intentionally neglectful of the home, or repeatedly committing adultery. The police, however, are interested only if violence results. This is not to say that violence is justified—not necessarily even to Nuer men. The Nuer, both men and women, have traditionally perceived violence as something arising out of patterns of mutual contestation and conflict within the home: violence is sometimes a natural (if undesirable) outgrowth of these circumstances, not the only bad thing, or even the worst thing, that men and women do to one another. Nuer immigrants feel that by privileging violence over other negative behaviors, the government provides advocacy for women in the context of disputes within the home rather than seeking a fair resolution to family problems.

As the threat of police intervention has made some men reticent to hit their wives, the inability of men to resort to violence has entered the rhetoric of goading within domestic conflict. Given the Nuer view that conflict in marriage is normal, men's inability to resort to violence may be taken by women to be a weakness rather than a virtue. One woman, for instance, teased her husband, "Why are you so good to me now when you weren't before?"—ostensibly throwing in his face the idea that he is now weak and no longer able to exert control over her. In response to the threat, he refused to eat any food she prepared (a statement tantamount to refusal of sexual relations) and then sought legal separation; she eventually apologized for her statements.

Disjunctures in Models of the Family and Domestic Violence

In focusing on Asian immigrants, Kristin Koptiuch (1996) highlights some of the ways the American legal system has dealt with various forms of domestic violence in immigrant populations. She notes in particular the recent legal turn to the "cultural defense," in which cultural differences have been used as a legal defense in cases of domestic violence, rape, and murder among Asian immigrants. Koptiuch focuses primarily on the level of discourse and the ways in which both proponents and opponents of the cultural defense revisit and reinforce stereotypes that she sees as products of colonial discourses—exoticness, primitiveness, and (for opponents of the cultural defense argument) the necessity for whites to protect brown women from brown men (Spivak 1988). She thus raises significant issues that are applicable to the Nuer case, as well, regarding the way that domestic violence has served to structure attitudes toward the Nuer among social service workers and the general population. One American woman, for instance, questioned whether Nuer men should be allowed to be included at an international crafts show she was helping to organize because she had "heard that they beat their wives."

Koptiuch does not, however, examine in detail the crux of this issue of "cultural defense"—the extent to which cultural differences might reasonably be seen to construct certain types of criminal action in ways that render them very different from the ways they are understood within the American legal system. With respect to domestic violence, the goal is not the acceptance—much less decriminalization—of criminal behavior but simply the recognition that different cultural understandings and goals can result in unanticipated, unintended, and sometimes harmful consequences. Effective policy must be cognizant of these issues, lest existing problems become amplified or new ones created.

The values, understandings, and agendas of the Nuer set them at odds with American practice with regard to marital conflict and domestic violence. Violence in the United States is stigmatized as a pathological and criminal act, and policy is rightly geared toward the protection of the victims of this crime. The Nuer, in contrast, see violence as an expected outgrowth (albeit an undesirable one) of conflict within marriages, conflict that may have been initiated by either or both parties. Whereas Americans perceive violence as a signal that a marriage should, perhaps, be dissolved, Nuer perceive it more as an indication that a couple requires assistance in resolving their difficulties.

This cultural disjuncture may have negative implications for women as well as for men. Indeed, even when Nuer women involve the state in their marital conflict, their own goals do not necessarily mirror those of the state. In only a minority of domestic violence cases do Nuer women want to dissolve their marriages. As husbands and wives, through rhetoric and actions, push conflict to a point at which violence may occur, the involvement of outside authorities pushes the conflict to yet a higher level (see Kibria 1993 on Vietnamese immigrants). The arrest of men frequently creates further animosity, leading many to refuse (at least for a time) to return to wives who may actually want them back. In essence, then, although violence within the traditional context represents a point at which intervention will occur for resolution of the conflict, in the United States it represents a point at which the conflict is escalated to potentially permanent separation.

It is also important to consider the ways in which the influence of government agencies has served, in some ways, to further the destabilization of Nuer marriages in the United States. Theoretical models of "cooperative conflict," which have gained prominence in household analysis within recent years, are useful for thinking about this issue (Sen 1984; Wilson 1991; Kabeer 1991). These models analyze household behaviors in a way compatible with Nuer cultural models of the family. Rather than positing an ideal Western model of the family in which altruism and shared interest are paramount in shaping household cooperation, cooperative conflict models recognize the poles of interest that exist within the family—based most significantly on gender—and seek to explain the ways in which particular cooperative forms emerge out of the bargaining position of opposing parties.

A central component of understanding individuals' bargaining positions is to consider the strength of their breakdown positions, that is, the consequences they will face if cooperation breaks down—divorce or separation, for example. Clearly, the social and legal context of the United States has significantly recast this "breakdown position" for Nuer actors and for Nuer women in particular. In Sudan, divorce or separation are difficult to pursue—a woman's husband has legal rights in her, the cessation of which may usually occur only with the cooperation of her male natal kin—but in the United States separation is actively promoted, particularly in the context of domestic violence. Women are encouraged to leave abusive husbands, and indeed, for women on public assistance, there are economic incentives for them to do so. Nuer women in the United States are typically awarded custody of the children—in contrast to normative patterns in Sudan, where the fact that children stay with the husband is perceived by Nuer to make marriages much more resilient. When Hutchinson described American custody patterns to an older female informant in Sudan, the woman laughed: "Oh, we Nuer thought of that [possibility] long ago but rejected the idea because, if the children were to remain with the mother, all wives would leave their husbands—and so, with us, it's always the father who keeps them" (1996, 183–84). The awarding of custody to Nuer women in the United States has economic implications, as well. In receiving custody, women also receive full control of the welfare check and may also be eligible for additional funds aimed specifically at recently separated women. Given the prominence of money as the focal point of Nuer domestic conflict, legal institutions thus also play an unintended role in fueling conflict by presenting women with opportunities to gain access to resources through divorce that are not available in marriage.

Such policies are, of course, quite reasonable within American models of family processes. Based in the assumption that (ideally) American couples strive for accord in their relationships, violence is seen as an indication that the relationship itself has broken down. Official policies—of law enforcement and social services—are aimed at picking up the pieces of failed relationships and assisting women and children, in particular, in putting their lives back together. In contrast, Nuer couples are not expected to see eye to eye, and even domestic violence may be seen as a normal outgrowth of the mutual conflict between them—conflict that is not pathological but is fundamental to the constitution of a relationship between two people with opposing interests. To this extent these policies do not serve, as they are intended, to deal with the consequences of conflict but rather become themselves an integral part of the conflict equation.

It is interesting, in this regard, that Nuer couples sometimes meet secretly after restraining orders have been put into place. Although they understand that a judge has ordered them to be separate, they may wish to resolve their differences and be together, although economic incentives may work against this. (A women may receive additional public assistance for a period of time following separation; should she again live with her husband in the same home, this money will be lost. If the two live together and fail to report it, they may be forced to pay the money back if they are caught.) As Nancy Donelly (1994) notes for the Hmong, there is a general perception by Nuer men, as well as many women, that the state tries to keep people apart rather than letting them resolve their differences.

Conclusion

Events of domestic violence represent a crystallization of wide-ranging changes in gender relations among Nuer refugees. As new tensions have arisen in Nuer marriage within the context of refugee resettlement, Nuer marriage—normally characterized by institutionalized conflict—has been further destabilized by its extrication from the kinship network that traditionally forms the medium for conflict resolution.

Disjunctures between Nuer and American approaches to family and domestic violence have at times resulted in actually feeding domestic conflict and magnifying the consequences of violence in unfortunate ways. Although American approaches emphasize the protection of victims in pathological—indeed, criminal—circumstances of violence, Nuer see violence as a more natural, if unfortunate, outcome of the behavior of men and women within marital relationships, which are inherently conflictual. Consequently, Nuer approaches to marital conflict emphasize the resolution of disputes in ways that are in the best interests of both parties and the broader social group. This model of domestic life continues to inform the behavior of both Nuer women and men; yet it is sometimes at odds with the emphasis on the protection of women and the punishment of wrongdoers within American social and legal models of domestic conflict. Although efforts to prevent domestic violence are positive, indeed essential, steps, some of the consequences in the Nuer community suggest a need to develop more nuanced, culturally appropriate strategies that take into account the full range of gender relationships and family processes within the target population.

References

Beidelman, Thomas O. 1966. "The Ox and Nuer Sacrifice." *Man* 1: 453–67.

———. 1971. "Nuer Priests and Prophets: Charisma, Authority, and Power Among the Nuer." In *The Translation of Culture*, edited by T. O. Beidelman. London: Tavistock.

Benson, Janet. 1994. "Reinterpreting Gender: Southeast Asian Refugees and American Society." In *Reconstructing Lives, Recapturing Meanings: Refugee Identity, Gender, and Culture Change*, edited by Linda Camino and Ruth Krulfeld. Basel: Gordon and Breach.

Collier, Jane. 1988. *Marriage and Inequality in Classless Societies*. Palo Alto: Stanford University Press.

Collier, Jane, and Sylvia Yanagisako. 1987. *Gender and Kinship: Essays Towards an Unified Analysis*. Palo Alto: Stanford University Press.

di Leonardo, Micaela. 1979. "Methodology and Misinterpretation of Women's Status: A Case Study of Goodenough and the Definition of Marriage." *American Ethnolgist* 6(4): 627–37.

———. 1991. "Gender, Culture, and Political Economy: Feminist Anthropology in Historical Perspective." Introduction to *Gender at the Crossroads of Knowledge: Feminist Anthropology in the Postmodern Era*, edited by Micaela di Leonardo. Berkeley: University of California Press.

Donelly, Nancy. 1994. *Changing Lives of Refugee Hmong Women*. Seattle: University of Washington Press.

Duany, Wall. 1992. "Neither Palaces nor Prisons: The Constitution of Order Among the Nuer." Ph.D. diss., Indiana University.

Erlich, Vera. 1966. *Family in Transition: A Study of Three Hundred Yugoslav Villages*. Princeton: Princeton University Press.

Evans-Pritchard, E. E. 1940. *The Nuer.* Oxford: Oxford University Press.
———. 1951. *Kinship and Marriage Among the Nuer.* Oxford: Oxford University Press.
———. 1956. *Nuer Religion.* Oxford: Clarendon Press.
Folbre, Nancy. 1988. "'The Black Four of Hearts': Towards a New Paradigm of Household Economics." In *A Home Divided: Women and Income in the Third World,* edited by Daisy Dwyer and Judith Bruce. Palo Alto: Stanford University Press.
Foner, Nancy. 1998. "Benefits and Burdens: Immigrant Women and Work in New York." *Gender Issues* 16(4): 5–24.
Gelles, Richard, and Claire Cornell. 1983. *International Perspectives on Family Violence.* Lexington, Mass.: D. C. Heath.
Gough, Kathleen. 1971. "Nuer Kinship: A Reexamination." In *The Translation of Culture,* edited by T. O. Beidelman. London: Tavistock.
Grasmuck, Sherri, and Patricia Pessar. 1991. *Between Two Islands.* Berkeley: University of California Press.
Hagan, Jacqueline. 1994. *Deciding to Be Legal: A Maya Community in Houston.* Philadelphia: Temple University Press.
Holtzman, Jon D. n.d. *Politics and Gastropolitics: Gender and the Power of Food in Two African Pastoralist Societies.* Unpublished manuscript.
Hondagneu-Sotelo, Pierrette. 1999. "Introduction: Gender and Contemporary U.S. Immigration." *American Behavioral Scientist* 42(4): 565–76.
Hutchinson, Sharon. 1996. *Nuer Dilemmas: Coping with War, Money, and the State.* Berkeley: University of California Press.
Johnson, Douglas. 1994. *Nuer Prophets.* Oxford: Oxford University Press.
Kabeer, Naila. 1991. "Gender, Production, and Well-Being: Rethinking the Household Economy." Discussion paper 288. Sussex, U.K.: Institute of Development Studies.
Kelly, Raymond. 1985. *The Nuer Conquest.* Ann Arbor: University of Michigan Press.
Kibria, Nazli. 1993. *Family Tightrope: The Changing Lives of Vietnamese Americans.* Princeton: Princeton University Press.
Koptiuch, Kristin. 1996. "'Cultural Defense' and Criminological Displacements: Gender, Race, and (Trans)Nation in the Legal Surveillance of U.S. Diaspora Asians." In *Displacement, Diaspora, and Geographies of Identity,* edited by Smadar Lavie and Ted Swedenburg. Durham: Duke University Press.
Lessinger, Johanna. 1996. *From the Ganges to the Hudson: Asian Indians in New York City.* Boston: Allyn and Bacon.
Levinson, David. 1989. *Family Violence in Cross-Cultural Perspective.* Newbury Park, Calif.: Sage Publications.
Margolis, Maxine. 1994. *Little Brazil: An Ethnography of Brazilian Immigrants in New York.* Princeton: Princeton University Press.
Min, Pyong Gap. 1998. *Changes and Conflict: Korean Immigrant Families in New York.* Needham Heights, Mass.: Allyn and Bacon.

Morley, Rebecca. 1994. "Wife Beating and Modernization: The Case of Papua New Guinea." *Journal of Comparative Family Studies* 25(1): 25–52.

Newcomer, Peter J. 1972. "The Nuer Are Dinka: An Essay on Origins and Environmental Determinism." *Man* 7(1): 5–11.

Ong, Aihwa. 1995 "Women Out of China: Traveling Tales and Traveling Theories in Postcolonial Feminism." In *Women Writing Culture,* edited by Ruth Behar and Deborah Gordon. Berkeley: University of California Press.

Pedraza, Silvia. 1991. "Women and Migration: The Social Consequences of Gender." *Annual Review of Sociology* 17: 303–25.

Pessar, Patricia. 1987. "The Dominicans: Women in the Household and the Garment Industry." In *New Immigrants in New York,* edited by Nancy Foner. New York: Columbia University Press.

———. 1995. "On the Homefront and in the Workplace: Integrating Immigrant Women into Feminist Discourse." *Anthropological Quarterly* 68(1): 37–47.

Sahlins, Marshall. 1961. "The Segmentary Lineage: An Organization of Predatory Expansion." *American Anthropologist* 63(2): 322–45.

Savishinsky, Joel. 1966. *Stress and Mobility in an Arctic Community: The Hare Indians of Colville Lake, Northwest Territories.* Ann Arbor, Mich.: University Microfilms.

Sen, Amartya. 1984. *Resources, Values, and Development.* Oxford: Basil Blackwell.

Southall, Ian. 1986. "The Illusion of Nath Agnation." *Ethnology* 25(1): 1–20.

Spivak, Gayatri. 1988. "Can the Subaltern Speak?" In *Marxism and the Interpretation of Culture,* edited by Cary Nelson and Lawrence Grossberg. Urbana: University of Illinois Press.

Tienda, Marta, and Karen Booth. 1991. "Gender, Migration, and Social Change." *International Sociology* 6: 51–72.

Wilson, Gail. 1991. "Thoughts on the Cooperative Conflict Model of the Household in Relation to Economic Method." *Institute of Development Studies Bulletin* 22(1): 31–36.

Zhou, Min, and Regina Nordquist. 1994. "Work and Its Place in the Lives of Immigrant Women: Garment Workers in New York City's Chinatown." *Applied Behavioral Science Review* 2: 187–211.

17

LANGUAGE, RACE, AND THE NEW IMMIGRANTS: THE EXAMPLE OF SOUTHERN ITALIANS

Nancy C. Carnevale

THE ONGOING debate on whether to make English the official language of the United States is only one reminder that language remains a social, political, and cultural issue of direct significance to this nation of immigrants. To date, immigration scholars, including historians, have taken a limited approach to language, focusing largely on English language acquisition as an index of assimilation.[1] A historical approach to language within an interdisciplinary framework, however, allows for a broader range of possibilities for the study of language and immigration. This chapter examines the role of language in the social construction of race at the turn of the century. During this period of mass migration, language was one of the criteria used to categorize immigrants racially. Language also facilitated the change in the perception of the racial status of southern and eastern European immigrants, from an "in-between" position (Orsi 1997, 335; Higham 1992, 169; Barrett and Roediger 1997) to one in which they were accepted as unambiguously "white."[2]

Americans in the early years of this century were both obsessed with and confused by race. This preoccupation was fueled by the arrival of the so-called new immigrants, vast numbers of southern and eastern Europeans who did not appear to fit easily into existing racial categories. As Americans of northern European extraction struggled with the question of how to define the newcomers, the term "race" itself took on varied and often inconsistent definitions. Thus, although it may seem contradictory to readers today, in early-twentieth-century America it was possible to grant someone legal status as a white person while still impugning his or her "whiteness." This was the situation faced by southern and eastern Europeans, including southern Italians, my focus here; in Matthew Jacobson's words, they were at that time among those considered "probationary white[s]" at best (1998, 8).

The racial definitions imposed on the newcomers had a direct bearing on their place within American political as well as social life. The struggle to define southern and eastern European immigrants racially occurred within the context of intense Americanization efforts aimed at the large number of new arrivals. Within this setting, nationality and race became easily conflated, so much so that "the processes of 'becoming white' and 'becoming American' were intertwined at every turn" (Barrett and Roediger 1997, 6). That is, Americanization implied a change in racial status as much as a transfer of national allegiance for some immigrant groups. Language—a knowledge of English or the perceived ability to learn the national language—became one indication of the capacity of the new immigrants to begin this race-dependent process of Americanization.

A consideration of issues of language in this period offers an unusual opportunity to examine the fluidity of racial boundaries and affords insight into the complex relationship between race and nation in the history of U.S. immigration. Such a focus follows those who have suggested that immigration studies would benefit from moving away from an emphasis on assimilation toward greater attention to questions of racial identity (Orsi 1992; Barrett and Roediger 1997; Jacobson 1998).

The example of southern Italian immigrants illustrates the connections between language, race, and immigration in early-twentieth-century America. The overwhelmingly working-class southern Italian immigrants who arrived in the United States formed one of the largest new immigrant populations and were among those groups considered racially inferior. The racial views that prompted the social scientist Edward Ross to write in 1914 of the potential for the "Italian dusk" to "quench . . . the Celto-Teutonic flush . . . in the cheek of the native American" (quoted in Solomon 1956, 167) were not limited to academics but reflected the popular view.[3] Because of their high rates of illiteracy, their poor command of the English language, and American perceptions of them as dark-skinned, a study of Italian immigrants and language provides an excellent opportunity to examine how race and language operated in the Americanization process.

Two significant areas of American public policy reveal the ways in which language, race, and entry into American life were linked. The congressional debates surrounding the literacy test for immigrants, mandated in 1917, suggest that language was used both to categorize racially and to exclude immigrants considered incapable of assimilating. Yet the need for national unity during World War I led to a muting of the emphasis on racial difference as Americanization efforts were intensified by the Bureau of Naturalization, the forerunner of the Immigration and Naturalization Service. Instruction in the English language was a major component of the bureau's efforts to assimilate completely those immigrants allowed into the country.[4]

Two distinct views of how language and race operated in the assimilation of immigrants undergirded these policies—conflicting yet coexisting views, even before World War I. This incongruity suggests the degree to which racial ideologies were undergoing a profound reorganization at this time. The contradictions and inconsistencies evident in these views of the relationship between immigrants, language, and race were resolved over time as the racial categories of black and white became fixed.

Language, Literacy, and Race

The extent to which the new immigrants could be considered white was a subject of great and ongoing debate among academics and within society at large. Numerous physical and cultural characteristics considered to be evidence of racial status were put forward to help make this determination, including language. Race theorists and social scientists of various stripes believed that there was an inherent association between language and race, although the exact nature of the relationship between the two was unclear (Gossett 1963, chapter 6; Dyer 1980, 59–60).

A Dictionary of Races or Peoples, produced as part of the 1911 Immigration Commission's well-known forty-two-volume report on the new immigrants, reflected this uncertain understanding of how language and race were related. The *Dictionary* legitimated the practice of distinguishing national groups by language and referring to them as "races." It recognized five "great races"—Caucasian, Ethiopian, Mongolian, Malay, and American, also known as "the white, black, yellow, brown, and red races"—and drew distinctions within these categories "largely upon a linguistic basis" (Immigration Commission 1911, 3). The rationale given for this classificatory system was twofold: it reflected the thinking of anthropological authorities of the day such as A. H. Keane and Daniel G. Brinton, and it was in keeping with the practices of immigration officials and census statisticians, who tracked different groups according to their languages. The *Dictionary,* however, also acknowledged the uncertainty surrounding the relationship between language and race. In a reference to this relationship, the authors noted, "The sciences of anthropology and ethnology are not far enough advanced to be in agreement upon many questions that arise in such a study" (Immigration Commission 1911, 3).

Generally speaking, two competing understandings of the relationship between language and race existed within academic circles and the larger society. One held that language was a racial characteristic, which might or might not be mutable, according to the unique logic of the time. The other position was that language was a learned cultural feature. Both views were used to support public policy including restrictionist and Americanization efforts. The first view was exemplified by many early anthropologists who considered language a hereditary racial trait rather than the result of learning or historical development. The anthropologist Albert Galloway Keller, for example, used language as a criteria for determining race in the chart he designed for this purpose (cited in Fairchild 1947, 30). Other anthropologists and social scientists believed that even acquired traits like language could be transmitted genetically and that the environment had the potential to transform the social and even physical features of a given group (Stocking 1968). As Theodore Dyer notes regarding social scientific thought in this period, "distinctions between race and culture were hazy" (1980, 38).

A related strain of thought regarding language and race emphasized the role of language in assuring racial unity and extending racial influence (Dyer 1980, 59–60). Popular notions of Anglo-Saxon moral, intellectual, and political superiority were linked with use of the English language, which itself was considered by some to be the highest form of speech. Henry Cabot Lodge Sr., the Massachusetts legislator and a founding member of the Immigration Restriction League, was one of the most forceful proponents of this idea (Solomon 1956; Lodge 1909).

In an 1896 speech to the Congress in support of a test of literacy, Lodge asked rhetorically, "How, then has the English-speaking race, which to-day controls so large a part of the earth's surface, been formed?" (Lodge 1909, 253). Lodge explained that a fusion of Germanic peoples, Saxons and Normans, over the course of centuries had resulted in "a new speech and a new race, with strong and well-defined qualities, both mental and moral" (254). This new intellectually and morally superior people was closely associated with democratic government. By the time of the Reformation, claimed Lodge, the "English-speaking people were ready to come forward and begin to play their part in a world where the despotism of the church had been broken, and where political despotism was about to enter on its great struggle against the forces of freedom" (255). It was members of this "stock" who migrated to the colonies and formed the democratic republic of the United States.

In a bit of complicated logic, Lodge managed to include all of the older migration groups, such as the Dutch and the French Huguenots, under the rubric of the superior English-speaking peoples. Even the much maligned Irish, "although of a different race stock originally," were by Lodge's time considered more acceptable because of their ability to speak English and their close association with English-speaking people who had presumably civilized them (259).[5]

Nevertheless, for Lodge and other restrictionists, knowledge of the English language did not transform the essential character of the individual. Language, like physical traits and culture, was "in the last analysis only the expression or the evidence of race" (261). The core of racial difference lay in the moral and intellectual character of a people, which constituted "the soul of a race, and which represent the product of all its past, the inheritance of all its ancestors, and the motives of all its conduct" (262). Lodge and his ilk saw restriction as the only solution to the degradation of the English-speaking people in America and a test of literacy as the natural instrument of exclusion.

Americanizers represented a second view, an alternative to that of Lodge and the race-based social scientific thought of the period. They saw language, in the form of American English, as the best way to incorporate the foreign born into American society. Their position was buttressed by the work of Franz Boas, who challenged the prevailing understanding of language. Boas, known as the father of cultural anthropology, argued that it was a fallacy to single out certain languages—and peoples—as superior. He specifically challenged the connections between "the blond type," or Aryan people, and the so-called "Aryan languages" (1915, 4) made by racialist thinkers who argued that just as the blond northern European or Aryan was superior to other races, so too were the Aryan languages. Boas, however, was well ahead of his contemporaries in his rejection of any notion of linguistic or racial hierarchies (Hyatt 1990).

Although they rejected the notion of language as race based, the mainstream of the Americanization movement nevertheless believed their language—like their political institutions—to be superior. They glorified the English language and attributed transformative powers to it that suggest the linguistic and racial divide many Americans perceived between themselves and the new European "others." As George Gordon, a proponent of Americanization through the use of the English language, wrote, "Let no American citizen hug his foreign tongue . . . and shut out the light of the great English language which carries all our ideals as Americans! The very vessel of the Lord it is. . . . This tongue consecrates the immigrant who would be a citizen; he can never be a citizen of the United States without that, never" (quoted in Talbot 1920, 86–87). Gordon, himself an immigrant, could be speaking here of his own "conversion" from immigrant to truly American.

In addition to the issue of whether or not immigrants were capable of learning English, literacy and illiteracy were subjects of some concern in the period of mass migration, when a great number of immigrants arriving in the United States were illiterate in their own languages. Indeed, the stereotype of the poorly educated, illiterate immigrant likely has its roots in this period (Leibowitz 1984). As with its assessment of immigrant languages, the Immigration Commission's report on literacy ultimately deemed literacy in any language a racial trait. Although the report discussed the effects of environment and class, the high rate of illiteracy among the new immigrants was attributed to "inherent racial tendencies" (Handlin 1957, 121).

The importance attached to literacy most likely reflects, in part, the understanding that a democracy requires the literacy of its citizens in order for them to make informed decisions in the voting booths and fulfill other civic duties. Literacy in any language was also important, however, because it was considered prerequisite to learning English. The literacy test, which required that immigrants, in order to enter the country, read and demonstrate comprehension of a selected piece of text translated into their own language or dialect, was based in part on this logic. Restrictionists believed that the general illiteracy of southern and eastern Europeans in their own native languages indicated that they were inherently less capable of learning English. Americanizers, however, believed that the new immigrants could learn English and thus foster their transformation from immigrants into Americans.

The English language, then, became one vehicle for the new immigrant's entry into American society. This was literally the case by 1906 when, for the first time in the history of the nation, prospective citizens were required to pass an English test, albeit a nominal one, to become naturalized citizens. The implementation of this requirement for citizenship—along with the initial calls for a literacy test in the 1890s—signaled the formal beginning of the association of linguistic ability with entry into American life. For certain European groups like Italians, language and literacy were used initially to hinder and ultimately to facilitate their acceptance into society. Adoption of the national language allowed immigrants to begin to redefine their national status, a status based on a particular racial identity.

Restriction Through Language and Literacy

The literacy test, passed by Congress over President Woodrow Wilson's 1917 veto after three previous attempts to override presidential vetoes in twenty years, was a thinly veiled attempt to stem the massive influx of immigrants from southern and eastern Europe.[6] Although laws restricting Chinese immigration were already in effect, the literacy test represented the first effort to limit immigration for a broader base of immigrants, an effort that culminated in the restrictive immigration legislation of the 1920s.

Many different and sometimes overlapping groups, including Progressives, Americanizers, nativists, organized labor, and eugenicists, were represented in the congressional hearings on the literacy test. Their discourse on literacy and immigrants encompassed diverse and contradictory elements. The congressional records of the hearings provide a window through which to view how racial ideologies of the time informed this early restrictionist legislation. A test of literacy may have suited the refined sensibilities of patrician politicians (Higham 1992, 101), but it also reflected a belief in the racial basis of language and literacy, which was formed in part in response to the new mass immigration.

Although Italians were not explicitly named in the literacy test legislation, most references to specific groups in hearings and reports on the issue were to southern Italians. Southern Italians (the distinction between northern and southern Italians was a racial one commonly drawn both in Italy and in the United States) constituted perhaps the largest group of temporary sojourners in America and had one of the highest illiteracy rates (Caroli 1976). Indeed, southern Italians were consistently among what some congressional representatives referred to as "the illiterate races" (U.S. Congress 1916, 38). In testimony presented in the hearings, these Italians were also often accused of working for less than native workers. Americans considered them particularly foreign in their resistance to shedding their native ways and especially in their refusal—eugenicists, and those who agreed with them, would say their inability—to learn English.

In congressional discussions of the literacy test in 1916, the illiteracy of the new immigrants was discussed within the larger context of their ambiguous racial position. Records of the hearings include a number of allusions to the difficulty of assimilating southern Italians, in particular, and suggestions of their nonwhite status. The chairman of the Committee on Immigration, John Burnett of Alabama, reported that the Italian minister of education explained to him that northern Italians had much higher rates of literacy than southern Italians because "the north Italian is white; the south Italian is not white" (U.S. Congress 1916, 38). In interpreting these remarks to a bewildered Italian community leader who testified before Burnett's committee against the imposition of the literacy test, Burnett stated, "I suppose the meaning of it is that the people in the south of Italy have mixed their blood with the people across the Mediterranean and they are not entirely white" (U.S. Congress 1916, 38).[7]

While Congress debated the whiteness of southern and eastern Europeans, the whiteness of northern Europeans was plain. Similarly, the literacy of northern Europeans was also beyond dispute. In the same hearings, Senator Knute Nelson of Minnesota rhapsodized over the northern European immigrant who, unlike his southern European counterpart, had no problem learning English and fitting easily into American society:

> The literacy test . . . does not affect any of the immigrants from northern Europe. They can all read and write. . . . Many of them come from countries in which the principles of free government prevail to as great an extent as they do in this country. So it is no difficulty for them when they come here to assimilate themselves with our institutions. . . . I have noticed they readily acquired the language of this country; and under the operation of our naturalization law recently, which requires that they must be able to speak the English language before they can become naturalized, it is wonderful to see how readily they adapt themselves to that situation (*Congressional Record* 1916, 225–26).

This example suggests that, in keeping with contemporary notions of Anglo-Saxon supremacy, the linguistic superiority of northern Europeans reflected their superior political evolution, just as it did their racial predominance.

The literacy test was aimed at limiting the immigration of the "illiterate races" in large part because restrictionists believed that they were incapable of assimilating. Americans and their legislators offered many reasons for restricting the new immigration, but the means by which they chose to do so reflects a significant assumption of the time; namely, that literacy in any language is a sign of inborn character, if not intelligence. These assumptions underlying the legislation may help explain why many congressmen advocated the literacy test as a means of restricting immigration when other options were available and when the test—as predicted by some at the time—proved ineffectual. The same 1917 bill that authorized the use of the literacy test also restricted the entry of specific groups by using geographical boundaries to demarcate areas from which no immigration would be allowed—a blatant attempt to restrict the immigration of Asian peoples, who were perceived as unambiguously nonwhite. Only four years after the imposition of the literacy test, what were in effect racial quotas, discussed as numerical quotas limiting immigration to a percentage of a group's prior immigration, were imposed upon southern and eastern Europeans. The initial use of a test of literacy to restrict this immigration suggests both the special resonance literacy and English held in this period and the uncertainty with which restrictionists regarded the possibility of assimilating these immigrants.

Assimilation Through Language

While restrictionists were trying to keep immigrants of objectionable racial status from entering the country, Americanizers came to view the English language as a primary means of their assimilation. The efforts to Americanize immigrants gained urgency with the entry of the United States into World War I and the related hysteria over national loyalties. Questions regarding the racial status of the new immigrants were temporarily muted as the practical need for national unity in the face of war led to an all-out effort to incorporate them.

Although Americanization efforts can be seen as ways to foster national loyalty and patriotism, national identity and racial identity were closely linked. One of the favored means to develop a patriotic citizenry, the acquisition of English language skills, was also one important way of fostering the change in racial status necessary to become an American.

The records of the Immigration and Naturalization Service reveal the extent of the connection between language and entry into American society and the lengths to which numerous organizations were willing to go to make sure that as many immigrants as possible learned English. The Bureau of Naturalization was authorized to supply the names of aliens applying for citizenship to local school boards, who would in turn contact immigrants to encourage them to enroll in evening English and civics classes. The bureau widely promoted the evening classes. It encouraged and helped organize mass meetings on behalf of churches, schools, employers, and other organizations with the aim of spurring foreigners to enroll in evening classes and generally raising awareness regarding citizenship.

The public schools also received material support from the bureau to prepare aliens for naturalization. The bureau was so involved in this effort that in at least one instance, when it was not satisfied with the pace at which New York City public schools were being supplied the names of aliens applying for citizenship, it insisted that the district superintendent accept additional staff whom the bureau had provided for this purpose (letter from Richard Campbell to H.K. Jenkins, February 9, 1916, Records of the Bureau of Naturalization, entry 152, box 1).

What did it mean to become American? Learning the English language was a key component of the Americanization process; Americanization, it was thought, would naturally proceed from a knowledge of the national language. As one author of a civics text wrote, "Unity of speech will bring unity of thought, unity of feeling, unity of patriotism" (Downer 1924, 100). The centrality of the English language is evident in a 1918 speech submitted by the commissioner of naturalization to the famous Four-Minute Men—whose task it was to rouse patriotic fervor during World War I through street-corner addresses—asking that they direct their efforts toward the Americanization of foreigners. After noting the vast numbers of immigrants who can neither speak, nor read, nor write English and who are ignorant of American government and institutions, the speech states that in the evening classes for citizenship preparation, "the first thing they teach them is how to speak, read, and write in our tongue. Every foreigner wants to learn to do that. He is ambitious to be told he speaks United States like an American" ("Proposed Four-Minute Speech," Records of the Bureau of Naturalization, entry 152, box 4). (Indeed, the notion that English was distinct from "American" was gaining currency at this time [Mencken 1967]). The idea was simply captured in the slogan suggested by the bureau, "One language, one country, one flag" ("An Appeal to Every Citizen" [1919], Records of the Bureau of Naturalization, entry 152, box 4).

The same document suggests that one can learn the true meaning of what it means to be an American only by someone fluent in the English language: "Often the only source thru which they can gain impressions of our customs and habits and standards of living, is the self-appointed member of their nationality or race, who has learned to speak some English, and induces them to believe that he is a competent instructor in Americanization. A high standard of true Americanism can be taught only by American people whose blood tingles with patriotism, loyalty, love, and honor for America alone." The image of "blood" here hints at a racial basis for nationality as well as the capacity of the English language to transform immigrants.

The belief that a knowledge of the English language led to Americanization was coupled with the conviction that English fluency bestowed intelligence, a racial characteristic considered necessary for American citizenship, which the new immigrants were thought to lack but might be capable of acquiring. Anyone unwilling to "become thoroughly American in thought and deed" by clinging to foreign customs, including language, threatens to "lower the standard of intelligence." ("Proposed Four-Minute Speech"). Fortunately, "the public school [sic] have worked wonders in teaching English and Citizenship—in the making of intelligent and loyal Americans" ("Proposed Four-Minute Speech"). The bureau encouraged the evening schools to offer prizes to those who were most proficient in English, so that "their transformation from uninformed foreigners, not comprehending our language, customs, or governmental institutions, to intelligent, loyal, and productive members of society" could be celebrated (letter from Richard Campbell to Chief Examiner, New York, January 29, 1916, Records of the Bureau of Naturalization, entry 152, box 1).

Women were as much the target of the Americanization program as men. Although Americanization efforts aimed at immigrant women placed strong emphasis on reinforcing American gender hierarchy and inculcating immigrant women with American standards of child rearing and homemaking (McClymer 1991), English language instruction was also emphasized in the Americanization of women, even though women could not become naturalized citizens independently of their husbands. Mothers provided an American home not merely by serving American foods but by speaking the American language. Indeed, one approach the bureau took to promoting its campaign was to suggest that if immigrant parents learned English, the real beneficiaries would be the immigrant sons who were currently abroad fighting the war: "Every American soldier has the right to demand and be given the opportunity to come home to an American home with American speaking and thinking parents upon his return from the great adventure across the waters. He should not be compelled to return to an alien home when he is himself in all of his speech and nature American" (letter from Raymond Crist to Raymond Moley, October 4, 1918, Records of the Bureau of Naturalization, entry 152, box 3).The bureau's efforts to Americanize immigrants through the English language echo the words of Theodore Roosevelt. A longtime student of racial thought, Roosevelt stated that the English language was "the crucible [that] turns our people out as Americans" (quoted in Dyer 1980, 134). Although, like other Americanizers, Roosevelt also questioned the racial status of the new immigrants, he, too, believed that they could pass through the "crucible" of language to become Americans, whereas blacks, and others such as Asians, and Latin Americans could not.

Conclusion

Whereas the immigrant language was a signifier of racial difference, the English language provided a means through which those immigrants considered capable of assimilating—or at least their children—could begin to gain full entry into American society. As James Barrett and David Roediger write in their study of the racial positioning of the new immigrants, "Americanization . . . was never just about nation but always about race and nation" (1997, 14). Becoming American required a clarification of the newcomer's uncertain racial status. Although from a contemporary perspective, they would unquestionably have been considered white, the racial identity of southern Italians and other new immigrants was not a given. Their racial status, and thus their position within American society, was the outcome of lengthy and complex negotiations that ultimately drew clearer racial distinctions between European groups and African Americans, along with other darker-skinned immigrants seeking legal and civic rights at the time.

The foregoing suggests the need for immigration studies scholars to conceptualize language issues more broadly. A shift in focus from assimilation models toward frameworks that examine the social construction of race creates greater possibilities for the study of language and immigrants. The use of a historical method in this study does not merely provide historical context; it also suggests theoretical innovations of potential interest to immigration scholars in other fields.

Notes

1. The work of immigration historians since the 1960s has largely taken the form of community studies in which language issues are most often treated peripherally. In sociological studies, English language acquisition has been used as evidence of assimilation; see, for example, Alba (1990). Sociolinguistic studies of immigrants have focused primarily on language maintenance. Fishman (1966) remains a standard work in this area.

2. Though this chapter examines language from the perspective of the dominant society, it is only a prelude to a larger project, which emphasizes the immigrant side of the equation; see Carnevale (2000).

3. In a recent study, David A. J. Richards situates the nonwhite status of southern Italians in the United Sates within the context of American and Italian constitutional history.

4. Although these areas have been examined by immigration scholars, they have not been explored within the context of the racial and civic construction of the immigrant through language.

5. Irish immigrants were by this time much less problematic for Lodge and his kind. Like the Germans and the Scandinavians also designated "old immigrants," the Irish had gained a certain level of acceptance, in part owing to a measure of political clout (Carlson 1975). Although, like the Italians, they were the object of anti-Catholic nativist sentiment, the association of illiteracy and immigrant languages with nonwhite status occurred well after the major wave of Irish immigration. The racism directed against the Irish developed in the antebellum era, under very different circumstances (Roediger 1991).

6. Primary sources used throughout this section include the Congressional Record 1916; U.S. Congress 1916; and Records of the Immigration and Naturalization Service. Specific sources for quotes are cited in the text.

7. Burnett and like-minded legislators drew on the racialist thinking of northern Italians, who themselves had long insisted on the racial inferiority of southerners (Verdicchio 1997), to justify their racial impressions of immigrants in the U.S. context.

References

Alba, Richard. 1990. *Ethnic Identity: The Transformation of White America.* New Haven: Yale University Press.

Barrett, James R., and David R. Roediger. 1997. "In-between Peoples: Race, Nationality, and the 'New Immigrant' Working Class." *Journal of American Ethnic History* 16(3): 3–44.

Boas, Franz. 1915. "Race and Nationality." *International Conciliation Special Bulletin,* 3–15. In *Leonard Covello Papers,* Box 53, folder 6. Philadelphia: Balch Institute for Ethnic Studies.

Carlson, Robert F. 1975. *The Quest for Conformity: Americanization through Education.* New York: John Wiley and Sons.

Carnevale, Nancy. 2000. "Living in Transition: Language and Italian Immigrants in the United States, 1890–1945." PhD. diss., Rutgers University.

Caroli, Betty Boyd. 1976. "The United States, Italy, and the Literacy Act." *Studi Emigrazione/Etudes Migrations* 13(41–44): 3–22.

Congressional Record. 1916. 64th Cong., 2d sess., vol. LIV, pt. I. Washington: U.S. Government Printing Office.

Downer, H. 1924. *Chats with Possible Americans.* Davenport, Iowa: Friendly House Drookery. Located in the Records of the Bureau of Naturalization. INS Record Group 85. National Archives, Washington, D.C.

Dyer, Theodore G. 1980. *Theodore Roosevelt and the Idea of Race.* Baton Rouge: Louisiana State University Press.

Fairchild, Harry P. 1947. *Race and Nationality as Factors in American Life.* New York: Ronald Press.

Fishman, Joshua. 1966. *Language Loyalty in the United States.* London: Mouton.

Gossett, Thomas. 1963. *Race: The History of an Idea in America.* Dallas, Tex.: Southern Methodist University Press.

Handlin, Oscar. 1957. *Race and Nationality in American Life.* Boston: Little, Brown.

Higham, John. 1992. *Strangers in the Land: Patterns of American Nativism, 1860–1925.* 2d ed. New Brunswick: Rutgers University Press.

Hyatt, Marshall. 1990. *Franz Boas, Social Activist: The Dynamics of Ethnicity.* Westport, Conn.: Greenwood Press.

Immigration Commission. 1911. *A Dictionary of Races or Peoples.* Washington: U.S. Government Printing Office.

Jacobson, Matthew F. 1998. *Whiteness of a Different Color: European*

Immigrants and the Alchemy of Race. Cambridge, Mass.: Harvard University Press.

Leibowitz, Arnold H. 1984. "The Official Character of Language in the United States: Literacy Requirements for Immigration, Citizenship, and Entrance into American Life." *Aztlan* 15(1): 25–70.

Lodge, Henry Cabot. 1909. *Speeches and Addresses, 1884–1909.* Boston: Houghton Mifflin.

McClymer, John F. 1991. "Gender and the 'American Way of Life': Women in the Americanization Movement." *Journal of American Ethnic History* 10(3): 3–20.

Mencken, H. L. 1967. *The American Language.* 4th ed. New York: Alfred A. Knopf.

Orsi, Robert. 1992. "The Religious Boundaries of an In-between People: Street Feste and the Problem of the Dark-Skinned Other in Italian Harlem, 1920–1990." *American Quarterly* 44(3): 313–47.

Records of the Bureau of Naturalization. INS Record group 85. National Archives, Washington, D.C.

Richards, David A.J. 1999. *Italian American: The Racializing of an Ethnic Identity.* New York: New York University Press.

Roediger, David R. 1991. *The Wages of Whiteness: Race and the Making of the American Working Class.* London: Verso.

Solomon, Barbara. 1956. *Ancestors and Immigrants.* Cambridge, Mass.: Harvard University Press.

Stocking, George, Jr. 1968. *Race, Culture, and Evolution: Essays in the History of Anthropology.* New York: Free Press.

Talbot, W. 1920. *Americanization.* New York: H. W. Wilson.

U.S. Congress. 1916. Committee on Immigration and Naturalization. *Restriction of Immigration: Hearing on H.R. 558.* 64th Cong. 2d sess. Washington: U.S. Government Printing Office.

Verdicchio, Pasquale. 1997. *Bound by Distance: Rethinking Nationalism Through the Italian Diaspora.* Madison, N.J.: Fairleigh Dickinson University Press.

18

A NEW WHITE FLIGHT? THE DYNAMICS OF NEIGHBORHOOD CHANGE IN THE 1980s

Ingrid Gould Ellen

BOTH academic and popular writings today display a growing concern that Latinos and Asians are becoming more and more residentially segregated from non-Hispanic whites (Bean and Tienda 1987; Frey 1995; President's Commission for a National Agenda for the Eighties 1980). In addition, some warn of a "new white flight" from communities populated by immigrants, particularly those of Asian and Latino descent, that is driving residential separation (Filer 1992; Frey 1994, 1995; Holmes 1997; Rich 1995). Such trends also raise concerns about the changing prospects for immigrant assimilation more generally in the United States.

On the one hand, these observers are correct that segregation levels of Latinos and Asians are growing—albeit slowly. In the 153 metropolitan areas with nonnegligible Hispanic populations, the mean dissimilarity index for Hispanics rose from 42.2 in 1980 to 42.7 in 1990.[1] Asian segregation rose somewhat more on average—from 40.7 in 1980 to 43.0 in 1990. By contrast, average black segregation levels fell from 68.8 to 64.3 over the same time period (Farley and Frey 1994). As will be shown later in the chapter, during the 1980s, the proportion of non-Hispanic whites in an integrated neighborhood was more likely to decline when the dominant minority group was Latino or Asian than when the dominant group was African American.

The notion that a "new white flight" is responsible for these trends may not be accurate, however. The evidence here (examining changes over time in ethnically mixed neighborhoods) suggests that white avoidance generally plays a lesser role in the growing residential isolation of Latinos and Asians than it does in the segregation of African Americans, and more benign factors appear to play a more prominent role. One such factor is a desire for ethnic clustering. Another seems to be the rapid influx of Asian and Latino immigrants into many metropolitan areas. In this regard, the growing levels of segregation observed may not necessarily be a cause for concern.

A second problem with much commentary and analysis of Asian and Latino segregation is that it tends to treat Asians as a single ethnic group and Latinos as another. Grouping all Latinos into a single ethnic category, however, is misleading. This chapter looks separately at Puerto Rican, Mexican, and Cuban households and demonstrates that the shifting residential patterns of these groups are quite different. It is no doubt true that treating Asian Americans as a single ethnic group is also misleading, but unfortunately the data were not available to disaggregate this population.[2]

The Causes of Neighborhood Racial and Ethnic Change

This chapter focuses on changes over time in neighborhoods shared by non-Hispanic whites and ethnic minority groups. Certainly, the process of change in these communities does not tell the full story of ethnic and racial segregation. (The question of why minorities fail to move into predominantly non-Hispanic white communities in larger numbers, for instance, cannot be addressed by this analysis.) Exploring these mixed communities, however, is an important (and often overlooked) window into understanding segregation: if every time minorities gain a foothold in non-Hispanic white communities, the whites quickly disappear, then the prospects for lasting integration are dim. Furthermore, by exploring the contextual factors that appear to make mixed neighborhoods more or less stable, we are likely to gain insight into the underlying causes of racial and ethnic segregation.

The theoretical tool that has been used most widely to characterize the process of neighborhood ethnic change is the ecological succession model. The model, originally developed to describe the process by which new plants come to inhabit an environment, stresses that new plants taking hold in an area tend to create conditions that make the habitat more attractive for their own kind and less attractive for others. A classic example is the pine tree. Pine trees help to make their environment more inviting to other pine trees by shedding their needles and making the soil more acidic, thus fostering evergreen development. This acidity, however, together with the heavy shade created by their branches, makes it difficult for most other plants to thrive (Taub, Taylor, and Dunham 1984).

In the 1920s, Ernest Burgess, Robert Park, and other Chicago School sociologists borrowed this basic framework and applied it to urban development. They created an ecological succession model to describe the process through which one land use or population group replaces another in a given community (Park, Burgess, and McKenzie 1925; Park 1936). The model was commonly used to study neighborhood racial change during the 1950s and 1960s after the great migration of blacks from the rural South to the urban North (Duncan and Duncan 1957; Taeuber and Taeuber 1965). The studies generally concluded that racial change within neighborhoods is inevitable and irreversible—once black households enter a neighborhood, that is, the black population increases until the area becomes predominantly black.

Although the ecological model provides an analogy that, at least in the past, has proved generally congruous with the reality of neighborhoods shared by blacks and whites, it does not really address the question of what it is about black entry that makes neighborhoods uninviting to whites or particularly attractive to blacks. What is it about black entry into a neighborhood that has generally made its habitat (neighborhood) a favorable environment for blacks, inducing other blacks to move there, and an inhospitable one for whites? To truly understand racial and ethnic change (and variation in this change), we need to clarify these underlying motivations and dynamics and understand how they vary across different ethnic groups.

There are generally four hypotheses offered—at least implicitly—for why mixed neighborhoods typically lose non-Hispanic whites and become largely minority areas. The first is that the transition is driven principally by differences in income and education: racial and ethnic separation, that is, may be more a matter of class than of race or ethnicity (Leven et al. 1976). The argument is that households—regardless of their race—generally settle in communities with other people of similar means and status. This may result from class prejudice or from the simple fact that wealthier people can afford more extensive amenities. To the degree that non-Hispanic whites have higher incomes and more advanced education than minorities, they will tend to avoid areas populated by minorities.

The second hypothesis is that neighborhood change is mainly the result of minorities' desires to live among others of similar backgrounds and culture (Clark 1991). Even if whites are entirely indifferent to racial composition, minority preferences for cultural affinity may lead integrated communities to become areas dominated by a particular minority. This argument seems particularly compelling in the case of recent immigrants, for as these new immigrants arrive in this country, it seems natural that they would choose to settle—at least initially—in communities with people who share their language and customs.

A third and related hypothesis is that neighborhood change is fueled largely by rapidly growing minority populations (Taeuber and Taeuber 1965). If the minority population in a given metropolitan area is growing rapidly relative to the white population, all neighborhoods will become increasingly minority, even assuming neutral preferences. Consider the case of Los Angeles during the 1980s, for instance. Owing in large part to immigration, the Hispanic population in the metropolitan area grew by 60 percent between 1980 and 1990, while the non-Hispanic population grew by just over 2 percent. Even assuming that these population shifts were evenly spread across all neighborhoods, we would expect to see fairly substantial changes in mixed neighborhoods. On average, neighborhoods that were 20 percent Hispanic in 1980, for instance, would be expected to become 28 percent Hispanic in 1990; those that were 40 percent Hispanic in 1980 would shift to 50.9 percent in 1990. These are certainly not the kinds of dramatic and sudden changes experienced by some racially integrated neighborhoods in the 1950s and 1960s, but they do represent significant shifts.[3]

Each of these three hypotheses suggests a fairly benign and natural process; the fourth—namely, white avoidance—suggests a more invidious one. According to this view, non-Hispanic whites are assumed to dislike sharing communities with minority groups. Thus, they either systematically leave mixed communities at accelerated rates or move into them at slower rates.

In summary, there are four dominant explanations for the causes of ethnic (or racial) change: class differences, ethnic clustering, minority population growth (in particular immigration), and white avoidance. In the case of neighborhoods shared by non-Hispanic whites and African Americans, ample evidence suggests that the widespread transition that has occurred in neighborhoods shared by non-Hispanic whites and African Americans has been caused in great part by white avoidance and accelerated by discriminatory tactics on the part of realtors (Ellen 2000; Farley et al. 1978; Galster 1990; Massey and Denton 1993; Yinger 1978).[4]

Far less research has been conducted to explore the dynamics of change in neighborhoods shared by non-Hispanic whites and Asians and those shared by non-Hispanic whites and Latinos—despite the fact that Asians and Latinos together made up more than 12 percent of the national population in 1990, as large a share of the population as blacks. Douglas Massey and Brendan Mullan (1984) examine the extent of non-Hispanic white loss occurring in black and Latino mixed neighborhoods during the 1960s and find that non-Hispanic white loss was much more likely to occur in the communities of blacks and whites; and when such losses occurred, they were typically more dramatic. What is more, whereas class was irrelevant in the black-white communities, the rate of change appeared to be closely related to class in Hispanic-white areas. When the Hispanic population had lower levels of education and income, the loss in non-Hispanic white population tended to be more rapid.

It is not at all clear, however, that these conclusions will hold today. First, neighborhoods shared by blacks and non-Hispanic whites are becoming more stable (Ellen 1997). Second, owing to immigration, the Asian and Latino populations have grown substantially since 1970, and with this growth has come what appears to be an increasingly anti-immigrant "nativism" (Perea 1997). Considerable evidence suggests a disturbing and growing tendency to view the new nonwhite immigrants arriving in this country as culturally and intellectually inferior and therefore unlikely to fully assimilate into the dominant culture. Moreover, many Americans believe that immigrants are taking jobs away from the native-born and disproportionately utilizing our government services, such as welfare and education (Feagin 1997).

Such fears are increasingly visible in the political arena. In the 1996 presidential campaign, two candidates for the Republican nomination (Pat Buchanan and Pete Wilson) made immigration a central theme. Consider, too, the many recent federal and state laws that take aim at immigration: Proposition 187 in California, which denied public services to undocumented aliens; the Temporary Assistance to Needy Families legislation, which offered restricted benefits to immigrants; and the nineteen new state laws that were passed in the 1980s to establish English as the official language (Tatalovich 1997).

Thus, it seems likely that some of this rising tide of nativist sentiment would manifest itself in the residential arena as well. Native-born whites, that is, might exhibit a growing resistance to sharing neighborhoods with immigrants, and in particular, with Asians and Latinos. As a result, native-born whites might flee more rapidly from (or more assiduously avoid) neighborhoods with growing Latino and Asian populations. Thus, a fresh look at the pace of non-Hispanic white loss in ethnically mixed neighborhoods seems warranted.

This chapter explores the dynamics of change in different types of ethnically integrated communities. It should be stressed that the analysis here relies solely on aggregate data. As such, the evidence is ultimately only suggestive. Analysis of individual household decisions would be required to prove any hypotheses concerning the dynamics and motives underlying neighborhood ethnic change.

Data and Methodology

This analysis relies on social, demographic, and economic data from areas known as census tracts. Determined with an eye to reproduce the

427

real neighborhoods in metropolitan areas, census tracts typically include between twenty-five hundred and eight thousand people. When the discussion below mentions "neighborhoods," the term refers to census tracts.

The census tract data used here are taken from the Urban Institute's Underclass Database (UDB), which includes social, demographic, economic, and housing variables for census tracts in the United States from the 1970, 1980, and 1990 censuses. The chief advantage of the UDB is that the Urban Institute has linked 1970 and 1990 tracts and their associated data forward and backward to their 1980 geographic dimensions.[5] Thus, by using this data set, it is possible to examine changes in neighborhoods over time, from 1970 through 1980 to 1990. Without such a data set, boundary changes between decennial census years make comparisons in certain neighborhoods impossible.

The primary analysis examines the change (and, in particular, the loss in the non-Hispanic white population) that occurs in ethnically mixed communities. The change occurring in integrated neighborhoods composed of non-Hispanic whites and blacks is compared with that occurring in neighborhoods made up of Hispanics and non-Hispanic whites and in those made up of Asians and non-Hispanic whites. To be considered integrated, between 10 and 50 percent of a tract's population must belong to the minority group in question. So as not to confound different processes of change, the other two minority groups must constitute less than 10 percent of the tract's population. Any cut-off used to define integrated communities is arbitrary, of course, but this definition tries to reflect the fact that non-Hispanic whites greatly outnumber all three of these minority groups as well as the fact that integration is usually taken to be about sharing on relatively equal grounds. For ease of presentation, the neighborhoods are referred to as "black-white," "Hispanic-white," and "Asian-white."

The study also separately considers three types of Hispanic-white neighborhoods: those in which the Hispanic portion of the neighborhood is predominantly Mexican, Puerto Rican, or Cuban. These neighborhoods are considered integrated if the particular Hispanic group in question makes up between 10 and 50 percent of the tract population and if the other two Hispanic groups (as well as blacks and Asians) each represent less than 10 percent of the population.

Although the UDB covers the entire United States, these neighborhoods are naturally clustered in certain parts of the country. The Cuban-white census tracts, for instance, are concentrated in Florida and New Jersey, and the Puerto Rican–white census tracts are primarily located in New York, New Jersey, and Massachusetts. The Mexican-white neighborhoods are more geographically dispersed, located in some twenty-five

TABLE 18.1   *Measures of Non-Hispanic White Loss in Ethnically Integrated Tracts, 1980 to 1990*

Measure	Black-White	Hispanic-White	Asian-White
Mean percentage point loss in percentage non-Hispanic white	7.3	12.8	9.1
Proportion of tracts in which the percentage non-Hispanic white declined by at least 10 percentage points	34.4%	56.5%	43.0%
N	4,776	3,383	279

Source: Author's calculations.
Note: Tracts are defined here as integrated if the minority group in question constitutes between 10 and 50 percent of the tract population and each of the other two minority groups constitutes less than 10 percent.

different states. A full 93 percent of these neighborhoods, however, are located in the southern and western regions of the country. The Asian-white census tracts are spread across nineteen different states, but 77 percent are located the western region.

The Pace of Non-Hispanic White Loss During the 1980s

The first question to address in exploring the stability of neighborhood integration is simply the extent and pace of non-Hispanic white loss occurring in different types of integrated communities. Table 18.1 describes the loss in non-Hispanic white population that occurred during the 1980s in three types of integrated neighborhoods: black-white, Hispanic-white, and Asian-white. Again, integrated tracts are those in which between 10 and 50 percent of the population belong to the minority group in question and the other two minority groups make up less than 10 percent of the neighborhood population. The table reports on two measures of non-Hispanic white loss. The first row shows the mean difference between the proportion non-Hispanic white in 1990 and the proportion non-Hispanic white in 1980. The second row displays the share of tracts in which the proportion non-Hispanic white declined by at least 10 percentage points over the decade.

By both measures, the pace of non-Hispanic white loss appears to be most rapid in the Hispanic-white tracts and slowest in the black-white tracts. To show that these results do not reflect a different underlying distribution of tracts (for instance, the black-white tracts might be typically closer to 50 percent black), figure 18.1 shows the mean loss in the

FIGURE 18.1   *Mean Loss in Percentage Non-Hispanic White, by Initial Minority Proportion, 1980 to 1990*

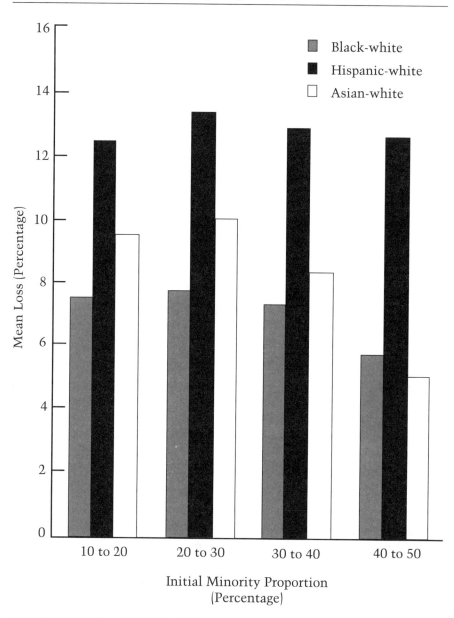

Source: Author's calculations.

TABLE 18.2   *Measures of Non-Hispanic White Loss in Hispanic Integrated Tracts, 1980 to 1990*

Measure	Mexican-White	Cuban-White	Puerto Rican–White
Mean percentage point loss in percentage non-Hispanic white	12.3	18.7	15.5
Proportion of tracts in which the percentage non-Hispanic white declined by at least 10 percentage points	56.5%	82.4%	63.3%
N	2,094	91	319

Source: Author's calculations.
Note: Tracts are defined here as integrated if the minority group in question constitutes between 10 and 50 percent of the tract population and blacks, Asians, and the other two Hispanic groups each constitutes less than 10 percent.

proportion non-Hispanic white by decile of minority representation. It compares, that is, the mean non-Hispanic white loss for tracts that are 10 to 20 percent black, Hispanic, and Asian, 20 to 30 percent black, Hispanic, and Asian, and so on. As shown, the same pattern holds up for all of these deciles. The relative loss in the non-Hispanic white population is greatest in Hispanic-white tracts and generally smallest in black-white tracts.

Notably, this first result runs contrary to the findings of Massey and Mullan (1984), who report that, at least during the 1960s, the pace of non-Hispanic white loss in Hispanic-white neighborhoods was smaller than that occurring in neighborhoods shared by blacks and whites. Thus, there clearly seems to have been a shift in the past few decades, and the prospects for residential integration of Hispanic households appear at first glance to be increasingly dim.

As for differences across Hispanic subpopulations, table 18.2 looks separately at the non-Hispanic white loss in tracts shared by non-Hispanic whites and Mexicans, Cubans, and Puerto Ricans. The magnitude of non-Hispanic white loss appears greatest in the Cuban-white tracts and smallest in the tracts shared by Mexicans and whites. Indeed, the proportion of non-Hispanic whites present declined by at least 10 percentage points in more than 80 percent of all Cuban-white tracts, compared with 57 percent of Mexican-white tracts. Despite this large difference, the extent and magnitude of non-Hispanic white loss was greater in all three of these types of Hispanic integrated tracts than it was in the black-white tracts.

The fact that the pace of non-Hispanic white loss is more rapid in certain types of mixed communities, however, does not mean that the non-Hispanic whites are more resistant to these communities or that the change in these neighborhoods should raise greater concerns. The underlying dynamics of change may be quite distinct across different types of integrated communities.

Decomposition of Neighborhood Ethnic Change

The changes reported above represent net losses in white representation, losses that could have occurred in several different ways. First, both the white and minority populations might in fact have grown, but the minority population may simply have grown more quickly. Alternatively, both populations might have shrunk, but the white population may have shrunk more rapidly. Finally, the minority population might have grown while the white population has shrunk.

To distinguish these different phenomena, three measures of the population changes in the integrated tracts that lost a substantial share of non-Hispanic whites are used. The first is overall population growth. High growth would suggest that the non-Hispanic white loss occurred not because whites were abandoning the community but because the minority population was simply growing more rapidly than the white population. The second measure is the percentage of growth in the non-Hispanic white population; and the third is the rate of growth in the foreign-born population, which yields a sense of the degree to which immigration may be fueling the pace of ethnic change.

Table 18.3 presents these comparisons. The total population growth between 1980 and 1990 was an average of just 8 percent in the black-white tracts, compared with 26 percent and 20 percent, respectively, in the Hispanic-white and Asian-white tracts.[6] The nonblack minority tracts, that is, gained significantly more residents in the process of losing non-Hispanic white population share than did the black-white tracts. Again, this difference would seem to suggest that the change in the non-black minority tracts is driven more by minority demand (crowding out) and less by white avoidance than the change that occurs in the black-white tracts. Similarly, the number of non-Hispanic whites declined by a significantly larger percentage in the black-white tracts. Specifically, the number of non-Hispanic white residents fell on average by 27 percent between 1980 and 1990 in the black-white tracts, compared with 12.5 and 9 percent, respectively, in the Hispanic-white and Asian-white tracts. Finally, as the third row in the table shows, much of this minority population growth appears to derive from immigration. The number of foreign-born residents increased by more than 140 percent in the Hispanic-white tracts and by nearly 80 percent in the Asian-white tracts.

TABLE 18.3   *Population Shifts in Integrated Tracts in Which the Percentage Non-Hispanic White Declines by at Least Ten Percentage Points, 1980 to 1990*

Measure	Black-White	Hispanic-White	Asian-White	Mexican-White	Cuban-White	Puerto Rican–White
Percentage Growth in population	8.3	25.9	20.0	30.0	36.9	13.3
Percentage Growth in non-Hispanic white population	−26.7	−12.5	−9.3	−10.5	−19.0	−35.4
Percentage Growth in foreign-born population	45.9	141.7	78.2	162.3	102.8	52.6
N	1,645	1,910	120	1,184	75	202

Source: Author's calculations.

Again, the picture is not identical across different Hispanic subgroups. Most notably, the neighborhoods with significant numbers of Puerto Ricans followed a very different pattern from that of the other Hispanic-white communities. Population gains were modest, and the number of non-Hispanic whites fell by more than one-third. Furthermore, the average increase in the foreign-born population was roughly 50 percent, a relatively modest increase when compared with the 162 and 103 percent immigrant growth experienced by the Mexican and Cuban neighborhoods. In other words, the change occurring in the Puerto Rican neighborhoods appeared quite similar to that taking place in black communities. This is consistent with Massey and Bitterman (1985) and others who have found that the residential patterns of Puerto Ricans more closely resemble those of African Americans than other Hispanic groups.

Correlates of Non-Hispanic White Loss

Another way to gain some insight into the dynamics of ethnic change is to explore whether integrated tracts with certain characteristics are more likely to lose non-Hispanic white population and whether these characteristics, in turn, vary with the ethnic group present. The focus here is on three key questions. First, to what extent does the size of the initial minority population determine the subsequent pace of white

TABLE 18.4 *Selected Coefficients from Regression of Loss in Percentage Non-Hispanic White, 1980 to 1990*

Variable	Black-White Tracts		Hispanic-White Tracts		Asian-White Tracts	
	Coefficient	Std. Error	Coefficient	Std. Error	Coefficient	Std. Error
Intercept	5.290	3.100	13.700*	2.740	.975	6.570
Percentage black	.133	.110				
Percentage black squared	−.006*	.002				
Percentage Hispanic			0.150	0.101		
Percentage Hispanic squared			0.004*	0.002		
Percentage Asian					0.277	0.304
Percentage Asian squared					−0.007	0.006
Change in percentage black, 1970 to 1980	.314*	.020				
Change in percentage immigrant, 1970 to 1980			0.323*	0.038	0.064	0.100
Percentage black families earning more than $25,000	.070*	0.14				
Percentage Hispanic families earning more than $25,000			0.010	0.014		
Poverty rate (percent)					0.161*	0.078
Selected metropolitan area variables						
Black-white growth difference	.061	.036				
Immigrant-white growth difference			0.101*	0.019	0.110	0.065
R^2	0.20		0.11		0.16	
N	2,505		3,065		259	

Source: Author's calculations.
*$p < .05$.

434

loss? (Both white avoidance and ethnic clustering would predict initial size to be important.) Second, does socioeconomic class appear to play a role in determining the pace of white loss in any of these types of integrated tracts? Third, does the pace of immigration or the relative rate of minority population growth in the metropolitan area appear related to non-Hispanic white loss?

To explore these questions, the change in percentage non-Hispanic white in a particular tract between 1980 and 1990 is regressed on a number of 1980 neighborhood characteristics, including racial and ethnic composition, socioeconomic status, levels and changes in the minority population of the metropolitan area, and control variables for region, the demographic makeup of the non-Hispanic white population, and local housing market conditions (see table 18.4). The regression controls, for instance, for the proportion of whites who are older than sixty-five, because these whites may leave neighborhoods more rapidly. The age and density of the housing stock are also taken into account, because the white population may be more apt to decline in older, dense urban neighborhoods (Wilson 1987). Once again, black-white, Hispanic-white, and Asian-white integrated neighborhoods are analyzed separately.

The three categories of variables of interest here are racial and ethnic composition, socioeconomic status, and the changing ethnic composition of the metropolitan area. Let us turn first to the variables representing racial and ethnic composition. Although it is commonly assumed that neighborhoods with larger minority populations lose whites more rapidly, the share of minorities present in 1980 is not significantly related to the subsequent decline in non-Hispanic white population in any of these types of neighborhoods.[7] This would seem to undermine the idea that non-Hispanic white loss is a function of simple racial or ethnic prejudice on the part of non-Hispanic whites or that it is explained by a desire for ethnic clustering. Yet in both the black-white and Hispanic-white cases, the magnitude of the decline is strongly related to growth in the black and immigrant population over the previous decade.[8] Black-white and Hispanic white tracts that experienced greater black or immigrant gain during the 1970s, that is, are likely to experience greater non-Hispanic white loss during the 1980s. It may be that these earlier changes critically shape expectations about a neighborhood's future and that many non-Hispanic white households fear living in a community that they believe is likely to become majority black or Hispanic. Similarly, high levels of recent growth in minority and immigrant populations may also serve as an inviting signal to minority groups or simply indicate that this is a neighborhood in which minority immigrants are settling.

Prior growth in the immigrant population is not significant in the case of the Asian-white tracts. This may reflect the fact that non-Hispanic whites are less fearful of living in a community that they believe is likely to become majority Asian, or it may reflect the reality that fewer communities actually become majority Asian. Because this is aggregate data, it is impossible to pinpoint precisely the underlying motivations.

Some interesting differences emerge with the socioeconomic variables. In particular, socioeconomic class appears to be relevant in the case of Asian-white communities, with poorer neighborhoods more likely to lose whites. Class, by contrast, appears irrelevant in the case of Latinos and blacks. Indeed, in the case of blacks, non-Hispanic white loss is predicted to be greater when the black population is *more* affluent (that is, when the share of black families earning at least twenty-five thousand dollars a year is greater).[9] This rather surprising finding might reflect the fact that whites are in fact more threatened by blacks when they are of similar social status.[10] (In a different specification, the coefficient on the poverty rate was statistically insignificant for both black-white and Hispanic-white tracts.) Note that the lack of significance of class in the case of Hispanic-white communities is once again contrary to the finding of Massey and Mullan (1984) that during the 1960s, more affluent Hispanic-white communities were less likely to lose non-Hispanic white residents.

As for the metropolitan area characteristics, the key question here is whether ethnic change should be more rapid in metropolitan areas in which the minority population is growing more rapidly (Taeuber and Taeuber, 1965). As shown, the differential between the growth rate of the black population and the non-Hispanic white population appears irrelevant to the magnitude of non-Hispanic white loss in the black-white tracts. In the Hispanic-white communities, by contrast, the coefficient on the growth rate differential between non-Hispanic whites and immigrants is positive and statistically significant. (Notably, the coefficient on the differential between the growth in the non-Hispanic white population and the growth in the immigrant population in the sample of Asian-white census tracts is only significant at the 10 percent level, perhaps because a smaller share of immigrants are Asian than are Hispanic.) This once again lends support to the idea that, in comparison with black-white areas, ethnic change in Hispanic-white areas is driven more by demographic realities and less by white avoidance behavior.

Conclusion

Although the results here are tentative, they seem to support five conclusions. First, in contrast to earlier decades, neighborhoods shared by

Latinos and non-Hispanic whites and Asians and non-Hispanic whites generally lost non-Hispanic white representation more rapidly than black-white communities during the 1980s. With this said, the second conclusion is that in comparison with the change that occurs in black-white communities, the ethnic change that occurs in Hispanic-white and Asian-white communities appears to be less the result of white avoidance. The non-Hispanic white loss that occurs in these neighborhoods appears to result more from growing minority demand.

Third, the growing minority demand may be rooted in the immigrant status of many Asians and Latinos. Like earlier European immigrants, they may find it helpful to settle in communities populated by other immigrants who share their language and customs and can offer them guidance in how to maneuver in this new society. The simple fact of rapid population growth generated by high levels of immigration has most likely contributed to the pace of non-Hispanic white loss in integrated communities and may have contributed, in turn, to the growing segregation of Latinos and Asians. Latino and Asian populations grew from 10 percent of the U.S. metropolitan population in 1980 to 14.1 percent in 1990. (The black population in the United States, by contrast, increased by only 0.3 percentage points over the same time period.)

Fourth, socioeconomic class appears to make a difference in integrated neighborhoods in which the dominant minority group is Asian but not in mixed tracts occupied by Hispanics and blacks. In particular, the non-Hispanic white population is more apt to remain steady in Asian-white neighborhoods when the neighborhood is of higher economic status. Yet there is no evidence that class can moderate the pace of white loss observed in black-white and Hispanic-white communities.

Finally, it must be noted that to consider Hispanics as a single, monolithic ethnic group is an oversimplification. The nature of change occurring in Puerto Rican–white tracts is shown here to be quite distinct from that occurring in Mexican-white and Cuban-white tracts. The change that takes place in the Puerto Rican areas appears much more similar to that occurring in black-white communities. Non-Hispanic white loss, that is, is not engendered by growing levels of immigration and occurs, instead, in the face of a relatively stable total population. Once again, this same conclusion is no doubt true for Asian subpopulations as well; but unfortunately, I did not have access to data that could explore such differences.

In short, the trends in the segregation of Latinos and Asians compare unfavorably with that of blacks. Whereas Latino and Asian neighborhoods are growing more segregated, black neighborhoods are becoming less so. Similarly, neighborhoods shared by Latinos and whites and Asians and whites are losing relative non-Hispanic white population more rapidly than black-white communities. Still, the data here suggest that the causes of this growing segregation may be quite different, and perhaps less permanent and troubling, than the forces that have historically driven black-white segregation.

Notes

1. The included metropolitan areas had to have at least twenty thousand Hispanic residents in 1990 or a Hispanic population share of at least 3 percent. Similar rules applied for measuring Asian and African American segregation. Derived from the Lorenz curve, the dissimilarity index may be understood as an indicator of how far the population distribution is from a world in which every neighborhood (or census tract) contains the same proportion of the minority group at hand—African Americans, for example. In particular, the index may be interpreted as the ratio between the number of households who must move for the area to be completely desegregated and the maximum number that would ever have to move, assuming that the population of every tract remains constant.

2. Michael White, Ann Biddlecom, and Shenyang Guo (1993) find that in 1980, Chinese, Japanese, and Filipinos were generally more segregated from non-Hispanic whites than other Asian groups that have arrived more recently in this country, such as Koreans, Asian Indians, and Vietnamese.

3. Of course, the decline in non-Hispanic population at the metropolitan area level may not be exogenous. William Frey provides documentation that during the 1980s, the non-Hispanic white population declined more rapidly in the states and metropolitan areas in which the immigrant population grew more rapidly; and he at least suggests a causal link (Frey 1994, 1995).

4. In the case of blacks, the evidence suggests that the pace of change was accelerated by the tactics used by speculative realtors (dubbed "blockbusters") to scare whites into selling their houses quickly and at much reduced prices. More generally, the evidence also suggests that widespread housing discrimination contributed to the pace of racial change by confining black housing options to a handful of neighborhoods and thereby building pressure for expansion (Yinger 1978).

5. If a tract was split between 1980 and 1990, the populations in the two 1990 tracts are summed to match the original 1980 tract. If two tracts merged (which is less common) over the decade, the matching is less precise, because the 1990 population must be divided into two tracts. In general, it is assumed that the relative

proportions between the two tracts in 1980 persist in 1990, and the 1990 population is allocated accordingly.

6. This difference does not simply reflect differences in fertility rates. The variation in the rate of growth of the adult population was almost identical.

7. The coefficients on percentage black squared and percentage Hispanic squared are significant and negative, indicating that marginal declines in the white population tend to become less likely as the overall white population declines.

8. It was not possible to get reliable information about the size of the Hispanic and Asian populations in 1970. The growth in the immigrant population, however, should serve as a good proxy.

9. Data on the incomes of Asian residents in tracts were not available.

10. Census tracts, of course, are not perfect representations of neighborhoods. Thus, when blacks have substantially lower incomes than their white neighbors, it might be a good indication that they are living in a subcommunity within the tract that is quite socially—and even physically—isolated from the more affluent white area.

References

Bean, Frank D., and Marta Tienda. 1987. *The Hispanic Population of the United States.* New York: Russell Sage Foundation.

Clark, William A. V. 1991. "Residential Preferences and Neighborhood Racial Segregation: A Test of the Schelling Segregation Model." *Demography* 28(1): 1–19.

Duncan, Otis D., and Beverly B. Duncan. 1957. *The Negro Population of Chicago: A Study of Residential Succession.* Chicago: University of Chicago Press.

Ellen, Ingrid Gould. 1997. "Stable Racial Integration in the Contemporary United States: An Empirical Overview." *Journal of Urban Affairs* 20(1): 27–42.

———. 2000. *Sharing America's Neighborhoods: The Prospects for Stable Racial Integration.* Cambridge, Mass.: Harvard University Press.

Farley, Reynolds, and William Frey. 1994. "Changes in the Segregation of Whites from Blacks During the 1980s: Small Steps Toward a More Integrated Society." *American Sociological Review* 59(February): 23–45.

Farley, Reynolds, Howard Schuman, Suzanne Bianchi, Diane Colasanto, and Shirley Hatchett. 1978. "Chocolate City, Vanilla Suburbs: Will the Trend Toward Racially Separate Communities Continue?" *Social Science Research* 7(December): 319–44.

Feagin, Joe R. 1997. "Old Poison in New Bottles: The Deep Roots of Modern Nativism." In *Immigrants Out! The New Nativism and the Anti-Immigrant Impulse in the United States,* edited by Juan F. Perea. New York: New York University Press.

Filer, Randall. 1992. "The Impact of Immigrant Arrivals on Migratory Patterns of Native Workers." In *Immigration and the Workforce,* edited by George Borjas and Richard Freeman. Chicago: University of Chicago Press.

Frey, William H. 1994. "The New White Flight." *American Demographics* (April): 40–48.

———. 1995. "Immigration and Internal Migration 'Flight' from U.S. Metropolitan Areas: Toward a New Demographic Balkanisation." *Urban Studies* 32(4–5): 733–57.

Galster, George C. 1990. "Neighborhood Racial Change, Segregationist Sentiments, and Affirmative Marketing Policies." *Journal of Urban Economics* 27: 334–61.

Holmes, Stephen A. 1997. "Leaving the Suburbs for Rural Areas: A Hint of Racial Undercurrent Behind Broad Exodus of Whites." *New York Times,* October 19, p. 34.

Leven, Charles L., James T. Little, Hugh O. Nourse, and R. B. Read. 1976. *Neighborhood Change: Lessons in the Dynamics of Urban Decay.* New York: Praeger.

Massey, Douglas S., and Brooks Bitterman. 1985. "Explaining the Paradox of Puerto Rican Segregation." *Social Forces* 64(2): 306–31.

Massey, Douglas S., and Nancy Denton. 1993. *American Apartheid: Segregation and the Making of the Underclass.* Cambridge: Harvard University Press.

Massey, Douglas S., and Brendan P. Mullan. 1984. "Processes of Hispanic and Black Spatial Assimilation." *American Journal of Sociology* 89(4): 836–73.

Park, Robert E. 1936. "Succession, An Ecological Concept." *American Sociological Review.* 1(April): 171–79.

Park, Robert E., Ernest W. Burgess, and Roderick D. McKenzie. 1925. *The City.* Chicago: University of Chicago Press.

Perea, Juan F., ed. 1997. *Immigrants Out! The New Nativism and the Anti-Immigrant Impulse in the United States.* New York: New York University Press.

President's Commission for a National Agenda for the Eighties. 1980. *Urban America in the Eighties: Perspectives and Prospects.* Washington: U.S. Government Printing Office.

Rich, Spencer. 1995. "U.S. Immigrant Population at Postwar High." *Washington Post,* August 29, A1.

Taeuber, Karl, and Alma Taeuber. 1965. *Negroes in Cities: Residential Segregation and Neighborhood Change.* Chicago: Aldine.

Tatalovich, Raymond. 1997. "Official English as Nativist Backlash." In *Immigrants Out! The New Nativism and the Anti-Immigrant Im-*

pulse in the United States, edited by Juan F. Perea. New York: New York University Press.

Taub, Richard, D. Garth Taylor, and Jan Dunham. 1984. *Paths of Neighborhood Change*. Chicago: University of Chicago Press.

White, Michael J., Ann Biddlecom, and Shenyang Guo. 1993. "Immigration, Naturalization, and Residential Assimilation Among Asian Americans in 1980." *Social Forces* 72(September): 93–117.

Wilson, William Julius. 1987. *The Truly Disadvantaged: The Inner City, the Underclass, and Public Policy*. Chicago: University of Chicago Press.

Yinger, John. 1978. "Racial Transition and Public Policy." Unpublished Paper. Harvard University.

19

TRANSNATIONAL COMMUNITY AND ITS ETHNIC CONSEQUENCES: THE RETURN MIGRATION AND THE TRANSFORMATION OF ETHNICITY OF JAPANESE PERUVIANS

Ayumi Takenaka

THE CONSTRUCTION of a transnational community has significant consequences for immigrants, their communities, and their assimilation processes in the host countries. This chapter examines this largely neglected aspect of the studies of transnational communities. Past studies (for example, Basch, Glick Schiller, and Szanton Blanc 1994; Smith 1995) have primarily focused on the processes in which migrants create and maintain "simultaneous multi-stranded social relations that link together their societies of origin and settlement" (Glick Schiller, Basch, and Szanton Blanc 1995). Perhaps overemphasizing the centrality of transnational ties, however, these studies have largely neglected to examine their nature as well as their differential impact on migrants and on their sending nations and communities (Foner 1997). They have assumed that maintaining transnational ties would lead to the creation of a transnational community and that such ties affect both migrants and nonmigrants. Yet transnational ties do not always transform entire immigrant sending nations into "transnational nation-states" (Glick Schiller and Fouron 1997). Maintaining transnational ties can indeed accentuate immigrants' group boundaries within both the receiving and sending countries. The process of constructing a transnational community can reinforce migrants' own ethnicity distinct from others. Exploiting international resources and connections, Japanese Peruvians have created an identity and space unique to their own. Called "Nikkei" (foreign nationals of Japanese descent), this ethnic identity denotes neither a completely Peruvian nor a completely Japanese or American identity but rather a combination of cultures. Opting to live as Nikkei, on the other hand, implies the negation of becoming "completely" Peruvian in Peru or Japanese in Japan or American in the United States. The process of transnational community formation can, therefore, hinder migrants' assimilation processes in the host societies and instead accentuate their distinct ethnic consciousness.

Migrants accentuate their group boundaries when they perceive advantages to doing so. In this sense, transnational community construction is a tool for "ethnic mobilization" (Nagel and Olzak 1982). Migrants use their transnational ties as a strategy to maximize their collective benefits (Patterson 1975). Thus, transnational community formation is a selective and strategic process of maintaining simultaneous membership in multiple countries. It is a process that reshapes the social relations of transmigrants (Glick Schiller, Basch, and Szanton Blanc 1995) and has significant consequences for migrants' ethnicity and ethnic assimilation in both sending and receiving nations. I examine these consequences here by analyzing the transformation of Japanese Peruvian communities and ethnic identity as a result of their migrations.

Like Mexicans, Dominicans, or Haitians, who have frequently been studied in the literature of transnational communities, Japanese Peruvians are geographically dispersed as a result of their repeated migrations. Unlike these groups, however, Japanese Peruvians are "twice migrants" (Bhachu 1985), cut off, until recently, from direct ties with their country of origin (Japan). Moreover, unlike other immigrant groups, Japanese Peruvians are ethnic minorities in all three countries. In Peru, they feel and are treated as Japanese or Chinese, and in the United States, as Asians or Asian Hispanics. Even in their ancestral homeland of Japan, they are treated as Peruvians or simply as foreigners.

More than twenty thousand Japanese migrated from Japan to Peru from 1899 through the 1930s. They were, for the most part, contract migrants sponsored by the Japanese government. Most were from Okinawa, the southernmost island group that was a sovereign nation until Japan annexed it in 1879. Almost a century later, the descendants of these migrants began to migrate to Japan, again, as contract factory workers. This return migration was directly triggered by Japan's ethnicity-based immigration policy specifically targeted at Nikkei. Furthermore, some of these return migrants have since migrated from Japan to the United States partly because of personal networks stemming from prior migrations. (Some Japanese Peruvians had migrated from Peru to the United States during the 1970s and 1980s as laborers, and many had emigrated from Okinawa to the United States before World War II.) Many return migrants aspire to migrate further to the United States because of their perception that it is more open than Japan to immigrants. Currently, one-third of the eighty thousand to ninety thousand Japanese

Peruvians live in Japan as contract workers, and the rest reside in Peru and the United States.

The Japanese Peruvian community has thrived for a century with a strong sense of ethnic consciousness grounded in their international movements. My analysis of this community is based on the ethnographic data I collected during a year and a half of fieldwork in Japanese Peruvian communities in Peru (Lima), Japan (Greater Tokyo), and the United States (New Jersey and New York). In these three countries, I interviewed a total of 130 Japanese Peruvians. They were mostly third-generation youths between the ages of nineteen and thirty-six who had different past migration experience as well as migratory aspirations for the future. To better assess their community in the context of larger society, I interviewed both core members who actively participated in community activities and others who were distant from the community. The data are also derived from my participant observation in the homes, workplaces, and community activities of Japanese Peruvians in my attempt to live fully among them, although as a Japanese native I was an outsider to the community.

The word "community" is used here mostly in an institutional sense. The Japanese Peruvian community in Peru is made up of more than sixty associations organized around the Japanese-Peruvian Association in Lima. Although not all later-generation Japanese Peruvians have ties with the community, this analysis focuses on central community institutions that play an important role in shaping Japanese Peruvians' ethnic identity in a broader sense.

Migration and the Transformation of the Japanese Peruvian Community

After their century-long presence in Peru, Japanese Peruvians are largely acculturated; they are overwhelmingly Spanish monolinguals and Catholics (Morimoto 1991). Yet they remain unassimilated, maintaining an ethnic community and identity distinct from that of other Peruvians. They acknowledge that they are, after all, Peruvian but that nonetheless, as Nikkei, they remain a "special type of Peruvian" (Fukumoto 1997; Nakamoto 1988). Japanese Peruvians continue to maintain endogamy as high as 65 to 75 percent (Morimoto 1991; marriage records in Lima, 1985 to 1995). They also maintain numerous associations whose membership is exclusively for "Nihonjin" (Japanese, in the Japanese language). "Perujin" (Peruvians, referring to Peruvians of non-Japanese descent) are often automatically excluded from membership in the Nihonjin community.

A century after the first Japanese immigrants arrived in Peru, the Japanese Peruvian community is undergoing a major transition as a result of its increasing distance from Japan. Replacing first-generation immigrants, second- and third-generation Japanese Peruvians, who largely have no knowledge about Japan, are increasingly taking over community leadership. The return migration, the mass-scale emigration of Japanese Peruvians back to Japan as labor migrants, has further increased this distance. Ironically, direct interactions with the Japanese have accentuated their differences from, rather than similarities with, the Japanese. Traditionally, the community has been defined as Japanese, which was considered a blood-based ethnicity. Presently, they are faced with the need to redefine what has long held the community together: Japan and "Japaneseness." This transition, spurred by generational change and return migration, has nevertheless helped to maintain, and even strengthen, the distinct community and identity.

The return migration has affected the Japanese Peruvian community in Peru in many ways. Among the negative consequences, from the prespective of community leaders, is a population loss. During the peak migration period from 1990 to 1992, as many as thirty thousand of the eighty thousand Japanese Peruvians left Peru for Japan. They were mostly third-generation youths from relatively modest economic backgrounds. Enrollment at the major Japanese Peruvian school declined from sixteen hundred to twelve hundred. The community's major athletic club was "empty," according to its director. The Japanese-style athletic meet, Undokai, held every April to celebrate the former Japanese emperor's birthday, was canceled for a lack of participants. Many Japanese Peruvian small businesses suffered as their coethnic workers left for Japan. The migration boom also changed the professional aspirations of many Japanese Peruvian youths. The director of a Japanese Peruvian school lamented, "During these [peak] years, 95 percent of our graduates did not wish to go on to a university. They all wanted to go to Japan to work, and so they left." By 1996, community activities had returned to normal. Yet the impact of the migration remains, even today.

Despite the mass exodus, however, the community has significantly benefited from the return migration. Above all, the migration has brought in revenues to the community. For instance, the return migration boom in Peru has increased the demand for instruction in the Japanese language. This has strengthened the community, which plays the primary role as intermediary between Peru and Japan and holds a virtual monopoly in Peru over all things Japanese. The number of students taking Japanese language classes at the community-run language school increased, as did the number of people who used the community's language service to translate documents required to obtain Japanese entry visas. Revenues also came from Japanese companies trying, with the assistance of the community, to recruit laborers. Another major source of revenue was the community's newly created remittance company, M, which operated in both Peru and Japan. Officially a nonprofit cooperative owned by the Japanese-Peruvian Association, the company gained economically, beyond remittances, from the sale of local products and air tickets as well as the provision of courier and translation services. In addition, M offers correspondence courses for Peruvian children residing in Japan in cooperation with a Japanese Peruvian community school in Peru. As a company administrator explained, it also engages in the real estate and housing construction businesses in Lima to "help return migrants to buy a house or land in Peru upon returning home." Their expanded businesses have brought in direct communal revenues as well as indirect benefits to the Japanese Peruvian community by utilizing community resources, such as Japanese Peruvian teachers, architects, and carpenters, for their businesses.

The return migration has also benefited the community in other ways. Some travel agencies owned by Japanese Peruvians gained from the return migration because they played a central role in recruiting workers and making their travel arrangements on behalf of Japanese companies. Newly created Japanese Peruvian–owned job recruitment firms flourished, as did remittance companies. At the individual level as well, remittances helped raise the economic status of Japanese Peruvian families. Some were now able to buy houses and cars or to move to more upscale neighborhoods, such as Miraflores.

In addition to economic benefits, the return migration has also helped raise the status of the Japanese Peruvian community. The migration boom caused a sudden interest in Japan and Japanese throughout Peru. Although the return migration was specifically targeted at Japanese descendants, many non-Japanese Peruvians went to Japan to work as factory laborers. Some entered as visa-exempt tourists before the visa exemption agreement between Japan and Peru was practically abolished in 1994. Others entered with forged passports and "koseki," Japanese family registers, purchased from Japanese Peruvian families. Before the return migration, Japan remained a remote country to many Peruvians. Over time, Japan has become better known, partly because of President Alberto Fujimori, the son of Japanese immigrants, but also because many Peruvians have family members working in Japan. This has resulted in the increase of the status of Japan as well as that of the Japanese Peruvian community. Indeed, as a recent survey shows, Japan became the second-most-admired country, after the United States, and the second-most-desired destination, also after the United States, among Peruvian emigrants (Apoyo 1997). The survey also shows that by 1992, at the peak of the return migration, Japan emerged as "the number one friend of Peru" and "the most economically important country to Peru" as perceived by Peruvians surveyed (Apoyo 1997). Because of this renewed interest in Japan, Peruvians who want to visit the country often approach Japanese Peruvians with the intention of buying koseki from them. A third-generation Japanese Peruvian told me that "Cholitos (those little mestizo Peruvians) suddenly want to become friends with us." Similarly, racially mixed Japanese Peruvians in Peru's rural areas who had no prior consciousness of their Japanese background have suddenly become aware of their heritage and intend to "maintain" Japanese customs.

To respond to the growing demand to "become Japanese," Lima's Japanese-Peruvian Association, together with the community's remittance company, M, has tried to cultivate ties with those rural, mostly racially mixed and poor Japanese Peruvians by offering them Japanese cultural seminars. In one of their recent "cultural encounters" tours in the provinces, the association organized an event to the rural Japanese Peruvian "community"—including a brief Japanese language course, a flower arrangement presentation, a medical consultant service provided by doctors from Lima's Japanese Peruvian health clinic, and a "coethnic seminar" in which Lima's community leaders taught rural "coethnics" about the importance of organizing themselves to cultivate ties with Lima and Japan. The response of rural Japanese Peruvians was simple: they wanted to know how to obtain their koseki, to restore their Japanese family name long lost through intermarriage, and to cultivate a Japanese identity, even though, as one rural informant commented, they "didn't know how to act Japanese." Their main concern was simply to claim their Japanese heritage, to work in Japan and simultaneously discover what it means to be a Japanese descendant.

These activities in Peru's provinces have played an important role in bolstering the Japanese Peruvian community. First, they serve to publicize the community and, in particular, its remittance company and to increase its future business clientele. Second, these activities help raise the status of the Japanese Peruvian community by cultivating a Japanese identity where it did not previously exist. An organization leader who visited one of Peru's poor villages told me, "Among many cultural activities we organize in the province, we provide rural Nikkei people with medical equipment and training because there are no doctors or hospitals in the village. Imagine, if the first [person to become a] doctor . . . in the village is Nikkei, our prestige and status will go up." In this way, community leaders actively cultivate Nikkei consciousness. Such an identity is beneficial and essential for the Japanese Peruvian community: without a sense of ethnic ties, the community would cease to exist. In short, although the renewed interest in Japan (owing to the return migration) helps bolster the Japanese Peruvian community; community leaders, too, actively cultivate the resurgent interest to bolster itself.

Transforming Ethnicity: Becoming Nikkei

Despite its increasing distance from Japan and the Japanese, the Japanese Peruvian community has been strengthened. A key to explaining this paradox is the transformation of the meaning of ethnicity and the development of those factors that hold the community together. In the midst of transition, the community has had to redefine itself. In this process, the Japanese Peruvian people have gradually replaced "Japanese" with the term "Nikkei" to refer to themselves. Stories of their past have come to emphasize their successful resettlement in Peru over the vague, stereotypical views of distant Japan. Their difference from the native Japanese has also been accentuated; unlike contemporary Japanese, Nikkei still maintain "good old Japanese traditional values," as they discovered in the process of return migration to Japan. These traditional values—"Nikkei values," as they are now called—are being reinterpreted to include not only the common stereotypical qualities of the Japanese prevalent in Peru—honesty, responsibility, punctuality—but also what they perceive as positive attributes that are no longer identified with contemporary Japanese—the spirit of mutual help, respect for the elderly, and care for the family. These positive values, which they claim as their own, are what almost every Japanese Peruvian I spoke with identified as the essence of being Nikkei.

Transforming their ethnic identity from Japanese to Nikkei has been the key to maintaining, and even strengthening, this later-generation immigrant community in the face of its growing distance from Japan. The transformation entails a process of reinterpreting their past or attributing positive values to their perceived tradition. In fact, ethnicity always appeals to the idealized past: the past is preserved and transformed in order to better the future (Roosens 1989). Positive meanings are attached to the past in such a way as both to accentuate differences from others (Barth 1969; Cohen 1982) and to enhance the material and social lives of the group (Patterson 1975; Roosens 1989). The transformation from a Japanese identity to a Nikkei identity, therefore, is both a social and political process: in the course of the return migration to Japan, Japanese Peruvians have become aware of their own culture, distinct from that of "the Japanese from Japan." It is also a selective and strategic process in which the Japanese Peruvian community, in its growing distance from the Japanese, has tried to maximize the socioeconomic benefits of the group. The Nikkei identity is what the community—institutionally and individually—actively creates in its particular social context, shaped by both the internal community dynamics and external factors that are outcomes of the return migration.

Ethnicity Construction as a Social Process: Encountering the "Other"

The transformation of the ethnic identity of Japanese Peruvians begins with the return migration to Japan. Japanese Peruvians in Japan are largely incorporated as "dekasegui" (temporary labor) migrants or manual contract workers in an employment system distinct from native workers. They largely remain isolated from the Japanese, partly because of language barriers and also because their social lives there are circumscribed by their work lives, as they try to save as much money as possible before returning home. The status loss and the gap between expectation and reality further increase the social distance. Many who were self-employed in Lima as owners of small businesses (restaurants and grocery stores, for example) work as contract employees in Japan. Even Japanese Peruvians with university educations engage in manual labor in Japan, with little chance of promotion. Moreover, despite having a "Japanese" face and name, Japanese Peruvians are treated "just as gaijin" (foreigners). Contrary to what their grandparents have told them about Japan, the Japan they discover is "cold," "rigid," and "too Westernized." The few Japanese words they know do not make sense to the Japanese, because they are outdated or of the Okinawan dialect. The customs they believe to be Japanese, such as the old Buddhist funeral customs, are no longer prevalent in modern Japan. Consequently, many expressed disappointment with Japan. A third-generation former migrant remarked, "Although I expected that I would feel just at home in Japan, I found people and their culture different. And to be accepted in Japan, you must be real Japanese." In this manner, many later-generation Japanese Peruvians who once dreamed about returning to the homeland experience ethnic disillusionment upon discovering that they are, after all, not quite Japanese.

The ethnic denial they experience in Japan is soon transmitted to Lima through personal communications and the ethnic media. As a result, Japanese Peruvians in Lima, regardless of their migratory experience, have come to perceive a greater distance from the Japanese. They have learned that the Japan of their imagination, an image that has served as the principal identity of their community, no longer exists: the Japanese, and Japan, have simply ceased to be the reference group for the community. Japanese Peruvians subsequently face the need to redefine themselves on some foundation beyond blood-based ethnicity. What has emerged to replace the bond of blood is a set of Nikkei values that distinguish them both from the Japanese and from other Peruvians. Nikkei values belong exclusively to Japanese descendants; they are, as one informant claimed, what "we inherited from our ancestors," and they "no longer exist in Japan, where people do not care about their families but only about themselves. The young do not treat the elderly well, men treat women horribly, and children commit suicide." In this way, Japanese descendants are, by their own definition, becoming a "race" apart from the Japanese.

In fact, Nikkei values do not always arise out of a primordial sense of tradition but, in fact, reflect a specific set of community relations. Like any institution, the Japanese Peruvian community selects membership, imposes a code of behavior, and punishes the deviant by establishing written and unwritten rules. These rules work effectively, particularly in a community like this, a small kinship-based group that maintains a high rate of endogamy. These community functions serve to justify and reinforce Nikkei values.

The establishment of the Japanese Peruvian community has itself been a selective process. Institutionally, the community attracts only a specific segment of the Japanese Peruvian population. Although anyone with Japanese blood (officially defined as possessing at least a paternal or maternal Japanese family name) is welcome to join major community associations, in reality, core members who actively participate in community affairs almost always have Japanese heritage by both parents and middle-class backgrounds. Racially mixed Japanese Peruvians are often excluded. Without Japanese phenotypical features, they are automatically stopped by the security guards at the entrance to the Japanese-Peruvian Association complex. Similarly, those who are outside the circle of active members are usually unable to obtain the Japanese Peruvian sponsors required to join an association. Poorer Japanese Peruvians, who are often racially mixed, feel excluded not only for racial but also for economic reasons, owing to high membership and activity fees imposed by the community. One third-generation Japanese Peruvian, who climbed up to a high ministerial position in his thirties, said of his case, "I participate in the community only now because they invite me to events. Coming from a poor family, I never had contact with the community, but now being in this high position, they keep calling me." Upper-class, high-ranking Japanese Peruvians, on the other hand, such as the owners of major corporations and President Fujimori, as well as intellectuals, writers, and artists tend to stay aloof from the community.

Now that the return migration has resulted in the departure of many relatively poor Japanese Peruvians, membership selectivity has further increased, as has the effectiveness of rules of conduct.

Inside the Japanese Peruvian community, many members, indeed, feel the pressure to behave in certain ways. One third-generation youth leader noted that "with Peruvians, you can act in whatever ways, but with Nikkei, you'd better behave well, because everybody knows everybody." Another active participant whose family has ties with the community explained that marrying a Peruvian of non-Japanese descent carries stigma, "as other Nikkei stare at you and might not invite you to tanomoshi," a small rotating credit union. Tanomoshi itself functions as negative reinforcement of social conduct: In this trust-based activity, practiced among small circles of Japanese Peruvian friends and relatives, according to a third-generation informant, "you must behave well, showing up punctually every time and making payment without failure. Otherwise, they will punish you; they simply will not invite you again."

These community functions are the foundation of Nikkei values. When I asked Japanese Peruvians what Nikkei values really mean, many mentioned the word "trust." One third-generation community member explained that "there's an automatic affinity with [other] Nikkei because of values. I mean, you can trust Nikkei because you can expect how they would behave. They come from the middle-class background and share the same values." Another Japanese Peruvian agreed: "I can never trust perujin but can trust Nikkei. Nikkei community centers are the only places in Peru where you can leave your belongings unattended. At Union [the Japanese Peruvian sports stadium], there is no robbery. Nikkei are honest and trustworthy." Nikkei values, as they are often understood as a sense of trust, are a concept shaped out of personal relationships. "Nikkei are honest and trustworthy" precisely because they all know one another. "Nikkei are responsible and punctual" because if they are not they will be punished.

Because they are shaped by social relations, Nikkei values, moreover, are a relative concept. Japanese Peruvians may be "more honest and responsible" than other Peruvians, but they are "not necessarily so punctual as the Japanese from Japan," said a Japanese Peruvian who appeared an hour late for our interview. It may be easier for a smaller, more selected, and less diverse group to impose rules and cultivate a sense of common values than for Peruvian society as a whole. Regardless of their contents, values are interpreted to symbolize a new ethnic identity by means of which distinct groups differentiate themselves from the "other."

Ethnicity Construction
as a Political Process:
Values as a Symbolic Ideology

Values are also used strategically as a symbolic ideology to hold the community together. For instance, community leaders often interpret the return migration positively. In the midst of their community transformation, stemming from generational change and the growing distance from the Japanese, the return migration is, in the view of one community leader, "good because [migrants] bring a little knowledge about Japan, and it strengthens our community." Many first-generation Japanese immigrants are delighted that their children and grandchildren are going back to their "homeland." An eighty-five-year-old former association president described his feeling in this way:

> For us "issei" [first-generation Japanese immigrants], it's fortunate that many "sansei" [third-generation] are going to Japan to see their roots. It was always our dream. Japan is a wonderful country with a high level of education and technology. It's a good opportunity for them to learn about Japanese culture and language. Besides, they are in Japan not only to see the country but to work and save money to help their parents economically. It's filial piety. That's Japanese value.

Although, according to many third-generation Japanese Peruvians, they do not actually "learn about Japanese culture" in Japan because they are too busy working in factories and, in any case, "there are no more traditional customs in Japan to learn about" (according to a third-generation informant), leaders take a different view. Although many return to Peru with a negative image of Japan, the leaders consider it beneficial, nonetheless, that younger-generation Japanese Peruvians are turning their eyes to Japan for the first time, even if only for economic reasons. A second-generation community leader, who himself has not worked in Japan, commented that "at least, sansei are becoming more interested in Japan through dekasegui. It is good, because otherwise they keep forgetting our values that we inherited from our parents. Thanks to dekasegui, we now have more contact with Japan, and young people are going to maintain the values." In sum, it is values, or symbolic ideologies, rather than concrete knowledge about Japanese history, literature, or language that serve to bolster the community.

Values are used effectively as symbols of ethnicity because of their abstract meanings and collective representation of culture beyond individual attributes. This is precisely the virtue of symbols; without defining their contents, they can be a tool to unify members in distinction from others, simultaneously permitting internal diversity within a group

(Cohen 1986). Indeed, values are interpreted and used differently at different levels. On a gross level, people often apply more abstract and ambiguous meanings to their collective representation, whereas to distinguish themselves from others on an individual level, they use more concrete symbols (Cohen 1982). Individually, Japanese Peruvians often understand Nikkei values as symbolic representations of their daily customs, such as "sobre" (envelope), a practice of contributing an envelope containing cash at funerals and weddings, and tanomoshi, the rotating credit union. These customs, which immigrants used to practice out of dire economic need, now serve as symbols of mutual help. When Japanese Peruvians compare themselves with others on a society level, however, Nikkei values often reflect simple stereotypes prevalent within their society, such as responsibility and honesty.

Because of such positive stereotypes, Japanese Peruvians often choose to define themselves as Nikkei. For example, a third-generation Japanese Peruvian said that he preferred to be considered Nikkei to Peruvian simply because of the respective stereotypes: "Peruvians themselves think we Nikkei are honest and responsible. So, there are many ads in newspapers looking for Nikkei cashiers. On the other hand, stereotypes attached to Peruvians are all negative—'criollo,' 'vivo'—in short, that they always try to take advantage of you." Even poor and racially mixed Japanese Peruvians in urban slums try to take advantage of the benefit. One half–Japanese Peruvian teenager I met in a slum, who said she had "nothing Japanese," now wants to use her maternal Japanese name, Takayama, rather than her paternal one, Gonzales, because "if you are Nikkei, you have gained credit even if you have done nothing." Positive Nikkei values are reinforced by President Fujimori's reputation for having lifted the country out of its economic crisis and checking the rising terrorist threat as well as the relatively successful economic status of Japanese Peruvians in Peru and of Japan as an economic power.

Japanese Peruvian institutions, too, use positive stereotypes and interpret them as their own values to bolster their community. A leader of the Japanese-Peruvian Association told me about his future vision to expand their Japanese-Peruvian Cultural Center into "Peru's biggest cultural center" because "spreading our good Nikkei values of discipline and hard work will be positive for Peru." Similarly, the director of a Japanese Peruvian school boasted of its Nikkei values in explaining the recent surge in enrollment of non–Japanese Peruvian children in his school: "These days perujin parents send their kids to our school because they think highly of our Nikkei values. So, we educate and treat all our kids as if they were Nikkei. At our school, we demonstrate what Nikkei are like—honest and hard-working, with the spirit of being superior."

Nikkei values function as a symbolic ideal of what Japanese descendants should be like. A third-generation half–Japanese Peruvian once described herself to me as "a bad Nikkei" because "even though I have a Japanese name and blood, I am neither punctual nor serious." In this way, Japanese Peruvians use Nikkei values as symbolic guidance to regulate their behavior, thereby reinforcing their positive values and a sense of their unique ethnic identity as Nikkei.

In the midst of community transition, values are increasingly replacing the notion of blood as an important criterion of group membership. What holds the Japanese Peruvian community together is no longer a notion that they belong to the same race but, rather, that they share the same culture and tradition. Although Japanese Peruvians still utilize blood relation as a mechanism to distinguish themselves from and exclude other Peruvians, they use the concept of shared values to justify and strengthen their own institutions. Thus, the long absence of ties with Japan has led not to the abolition of their traditional culture but to its transformation (Bhachu 1985). Some selective aspects of their traditional culture have survived precisely because of their extrinsic advantage; these factors have been transformed, interpreted, and used strategically to increase the material and psychological benefits of its members (Patterson 1975; Roosens 1989).

The Japanese Peruvian community was originally born out of the need for mutual help among poor immigrants. Now the more prosperous community finds it difficult to define itself in concrete terms. Its primary objective of "working for the welfare of the community members," as stipulated in the bylaws of the Japanese-Peruvian Association, seems ambiguous and unclear to many Japanese Peruvians. The symbolic interpretation of their distant heritage enables the later-generation "Japanese" community to thrive. It is the mechanism by which they retain their ethnic identity and maintain their community, by maximizing the benefits.

Nikkei Beyond Borders

A Nikkei identity is being constructed not only nationally but also transnationally. Now that Japanese Peruvians are geographically dispersed as a result of the return migration, Nikkei values are spreading beyond Peruvian borders. The personal and institutional ties that are being cultivated across the Pacific further affirm this identity. They also activate the transnational Nikkei movement, in that such ties help increase the unifying structures among Nikkei and also clarify a commonality of interests (Nagel 1986). The transnational Nikkei movement constitutes the development of an increasing number of transnationally operated companies, such as the remittance company M, that have helped promote economic ties, through remittances, as well as cultural ties. Ties are also promoted through the creation of various international Nikkei institutions connecting not only geographically dispersed Japanese Peruvians but also Japanese descendants throughout the Americas. One major international organization is the Pan-American Nikkei Association, whose biannual meetings provide important opportunities for Japanese descendants throughout the Americas to gather, share, and confirm their Nikkei identity. Another is the annual Overseas Nikkei conference, held in Tokyo under the sponsorship of the Japanese government. Although Japan plays a role in this ethnic movement, it is fundamentally a movement to cultivate a Nikkei identity among Japanese descendants, as distinct from the native Japanese. As part of this movement, Japanese Peruvian sports clubs have recently established greater ties with similar organizations in other countries, with which they hold international Nikkei sports competitions to promote friendship. Japanese Peruvian youth associations have established similar ties, organizing homestay programs and international karaoke singing contests to foster international youth exchange. The creation of Pan-American Nikkei business and medical associations is also under way. "This movement is good for our community," said one Japanese Peruvian community leader in Lima, "for cultivating ties with other Nikkei will provide us with more opportunities and greater welfare for all of us Nikkei."

According to this leader, the reason for activating such an international Nikkei movement is simple: "Being Nikkei, we all have something in common. We automatically feel affinity with other Nikkei because we all share the same values. Yes, even if we cannot quite communicate with each other because of language barriers." Thus at the transnational, as well as the national, level, Nikkei values hold these later-generation Japanese descendants together across borders. The transnational Nikkei movement is progressing, indeed, precisely because of what they share with one another: from their perceived common experiences, such as ethnic denial in Japan and minority status in their respective countries, to a sense of their idealized tradition based on distant Japan. Like the Japanese Peruvians within Peru, Japanese descendants transnationally work to create a common ethnic identity to enhance their lives together by exploiting resources beyond national borders for their mutual benefit.

The extended transnational network has reinforced a Nikkei identity among Japanese Peruvians not only in Peru but also in the United States and Japan. Their transnational activities have provided them with an additional ethnic option that can be strategically manipulated as a combination of cultures, and the transnational connections further enhance the perceived benefits of becoming Nikkei.

The transnational Nikkei community, created as a result of the ties Japanese Peruvians maintain across the Pacific, fosters an identity distinct from others within each country. Consequently, rather than being "melted into" Peruvian, Japanese, or U.S. societies, the Japanese Peruvian communities, both nationally and transnationally, continue to thrive as Nikkei, although membership is no longer based exclusively on the traditional notion of common "blood" but rather on a transformed sense of values shaped by social relations.

Conclusion

In the early 1990s, organizers at a Pan-American Nikkei conference adopted the slogan, "Become the best citizens of our continent and respective countries." To accomplish this goal, said the president in his conference speech, "we should continue to work hard to maintain the values we inherited from our parents, diffuse them widely, and use them in a way to benefit our countries and future generations." To live as Nikkei, he continued, they should adopt a strategy to exploit the multiple options of Japanese descendants, namely, to become "60 percent Japanese, 60 percent other [for example, Peruvian], and 120 percent total." Thus, to become Nikkei does not negate national membership; rather, it was presented as the best strategic option for Nikkei, both within and beyond nations.

This effort has resulted, however, in accentuating Japanese Peruvians' ethnic identity distinct from others in Peru, Japan, and the United States. The Nikkei movement—nationally and transnationally—has provided Japanese Peruvians with an alternative identity beyond the dichotomous options of assimilating to the host culture and retaining home culture. The transnational ties that Japanese Peruvians have established have resulted in a strengthening of their own community organizations within nations.

The construction of this multinational identity, however, does not result automatically from their transnational connections. It reflects Japanese Peruvians' efforts to maximize their cultural benefits. To live as Nikkei is partly a strategy that community leaders adopt to maintain the community by reinterpreting its traditions. Without some unifying ethic to sustain them, transnational communities weaken in the process of generational succession and assimilation to the national majority. It is also a useful strategy for Japanese-Peruvians, in general, to increase their personal benefits and defend against discriminatory treatment by others. Later-generation immigrants are likely to maintain transnational communities and ethnic identities as long as they perceive benefits to doing so.

A previous version of this chapter appeared in *American Behavioral Scientist* 1999, vol. 42, no. 9.

References

Apoyo. 1997. *Informe de Opinión*. Lima: Apoyo.

Barth, Frederik. 1969. Introduction to *Ethnic Groups and Boundaries: The Social Organization of Cultural Difference*, edited by Frederik Barth. Boston: Little, Brown.

Basch, Linda, Nina Glick Schiller, and Cristina Szanton Blanc. 1994. *Nations Unbound: Transnational Projects, Postcolonial Predicaments, and Deterritorialized Nation-States*. Basel, Switzerland: Gordon and Breach.

Bhachu, Parminder. 1985. *Twice Migrants: East African Sikh Settlers in Britain*. London: Tavistock.

Cohen, Anthony. 1982. "Belonging: The Experience of Culture." In *Belonging: Identity and Social Organisation in British Real Cultures*, edited by Anthony Cohen. Wolfeboro, N.H.: Manchester University Press.

———. 1986. "Of Symbols and Boundaries, or Does Ertie's Greatcoat Hold the Key?" In *Symbolising Boundaries: Identity and Diversity in British Cultures*, edited by Anthony Cohen. Wolfeboro, N.H.: Manchester University Press.

Foner, Nancy. 1997. "What's New About Transnationalism? New York Immigrants Today and at the Turn of the Century." *Diaspora* 6(3): 355–76.

Fukumoto, Mary. 1997. *Hacia un nuevo sol: Japoneses y sus descendientes en el Perú*. Lima: Asociación Peruano-Japonesa del Perú.

Glick Schiller, Nina, Linda Basch, and Cristina Szanton Blanc. 1995. "From Immigrant to Transmigrant: Theorizing Transnational Migration." *Anthropological Quarterly* 68 (January): 48–63.

Glick Schiller, Nina, and George Fouron. 1997. "The Generation of Identity: Haitian Youth and the Transnational Nation-State." Paper presented at the Conference on Transnational Communities and the Political Economy of New York in the 1990s. New School University, New York(February 21–22, 1997).

Morimoto, Amelia. 1991. *Población de origen Japonés en el Perú: Perfil actual*. Lima: Comisión Conmemorativa del 90 Aniversario de la Inmigración Japonesa del Perú.

Nagel, Joane. 1986. "The Political Construction of Ethnicity." In *Competitive Ethnic Relations*, edited by Susan Olzak and Joane Nagel. Orlando, Fla.: Academic Press.

Nagel, Joane, and Susan Olzak. 1982. "Ethnic Mobilization in New and

Old States: An Extension of the Competition Model." *Social Problems* 30(2): 127–43.

Nakamoto, Jorge. 1988. "Discriminación y aislamiento: El caso de los Japoneses y sus descendientes en el Perú." In *Primer Seminario Sobre Poblaciones Inmigrantes.* Lima, Peru: Consejo Nacional de Ciencia y Tecnología.

Patterson, Orlando. 1975. "Context and Choice in Ethnic Allegiance: A Theoretical Framework and Caribbean Case Study." In *Ethnicity: Theory and Experience,* edited by Nathan Glazer and Daniel Patrick Moynihan. Cambridge, Mass.: Harvard University Press.

Roosens, Eugeen. 1989. *Creating Ethnicity: The Process of Ethnogenesis.* Newbury Park, Calif.: Sage.

Smith, Robert. 1995. "Los Ausentes Siempre Presentes: The Imagining, Making, and Politics of a Transnational Migrant Community Between Ticuani, Puebla, Mexico, and New York City." Ph.D diss., Columbia University.

20

MIGRANTS PARTICIPATE ACROSS BORDERS: TOWARD AN UNDERSTANDING OF FORMS AND CONSEQUENCES

Peggy Levitt

M ANY Americans expect migrants to loosen their ties to their countries of origin as they assimilate into life in the United States. They assume that residence eventually equals membership because migrants will gradually shift their allegiance from the countries they leave behind to those that receive them. Increasing numbers of migrants, however, continue to participate in their homelands, even as they are incorporated into host countries. Rather than cutting off their social and economic attachments and trading one political membership for another, some individuals keep feet in both worlds. Citizenship is not the primary basis upon which individuals form their identities or express their interests. Instead, migrants use a variety of political, religious, and civic arenas, which do not require full membership or residence, to forge social relations, earn their livelihoods, and exercise their rights across borders.

The proliferation of these long-term transnational ties challenges conventional notions about how migrants are assimilated into host countries and about the impact of migration on sending-country life. How do ordinary people actually stay connected to two nations? What kinds of new social groups do they form, and how do these affect where and when they participate? Is dual membership a recipe for long-term social and political marginalization, or can participation in two polities result in a case of "two for the price of one"?

In this chapter, I present findings from an ongoing, comparative historical study of transnational migration among various communities, focusing on the experiences of Dominican migrants from the village of Miraflores, Brazilian migrants from the city of Governador Valadares, and Indian migrants from the state of Gujarat who have settled in the greater Boston metropolitan area. Though the larger study examines the effect of transnational migration on the sending and receiving country, my focus here is primarily on events in the United States.[1]

Theoretical Assumptions

Migration begins in and spreads through social networks. A social network is a set of interpersonal ties connecting migrants, return migrants, and nonmigrants in the sending and receiving countries through kinship, friendship, and attachment to a shared place of origin. Once a network is in place, it becomes more likely that additional migration to that region will occur. The risks and costs of movement for subsequent migrants are lower because there is a group of "experienced experts" already in the receiving country, who greet newcomers and serve as their guides. Because these well-established migrants help new arrivals find jobs and housing, they also increase migration's economic rewards (Massey et al. 1993).

For some immigrant groups, these social networks eventually weaken as migrants become incorporated into the host society, engaging in fewer cross-border activities, or as migration slows. For other groups, they continue as loose interpersonal connections between individuals, often reinforced by the activities of states or other political and religious groups. A transnational public sphere or social field may emerge within which some members express their interests, conduct business, or raise families across borders (Basch, Glick Schiller, and Szanton Blanc 1994; Fraser 1991; Mahler 1998). In other cases, these social networks consolidate, grow, and become organized such that a transnational community spanning two or more settings emerges.

The term "transnational community" has been used to describe a number of social groups. Alejandro Portes (1996) defines transnational community as a thick network, crossing political borders, that migrants create to achieve economic advancement and social recognition. He focuses on entrepreneurs who move across borders and use resources from the sending and receiving communities to achieve economic gain. Carol Nagengast and Michael Kearney (1990) describe a transnational community, including Mixtec Indians in Mexico and the United States, who create an emancipatory space neither the sending nor receiving state can control. Ninna Sorenson (1998) and Riva Kastoryano (1994) describe transnational communities of Dominican and Turkish migrants, living in multiple sites throughout the United States and Europe, who organize to secure greater protections and rights.

I think of transnational communities as rooted in particular, bounded sending- and receiving-country locales. Because they emerge from the social networks that precipitate migration, members tend to know one another personally or have family members or acquaintances in common during the early phases of community formation. They form organizations that express their identity as a transnational group. They exhibit some level of self-consciousness about belonging to a community spanning borders. For Dominicans, it is common knowledge that families from Sabana Iglesias are strongly connected to those living in certain neighborhoods in Queens, New York. By using the term "community," I do not wish to imply that all members feel a sense of affinity or solidarity with one another: the divisiveness and hierarchical nature of all social groups also characterizes transnational communities. Neither are the costs and rewards of transnational community membership equally distributed: long-standing patterns of privilege and access do not disappear merely because they are recreated across borders.[2]

Transnational communities include both migrants and nonmigrants, though the nature of nonmigrant participation varies considerably. Migration's impact on the sending country and the flow of social remittances may be so strong, focused, and widespread that nonmigrants also adopt values and practices, participate in organizations, and make claims across borders.[3] Actual movement, then, is not a requirement for transnational community membership.

Furthermore, in some cases, the organizations that create and are created by transnational communities also become transnational. These groups form transnational structures and conduct their activities across borders, though they do not always have the same impact in both settings. Transnational organizational activities often have a greater effect in one context. Though a political party may have parallel chapters in the sending and receiving countries and raise funds and conduct campaigns in both settings, it may exert a much stronger impact on sending-country politics.

These kinds of transnational connections are not new. Earlier groups, such as the Irish, Polish, and Italians, also remained involved in the affairs of their sending countries.[4] Several factors, however, heighten the intensity and durability of transnational ties among contemporary migrants, including ease of travel and communication; sending states' heightened economic dependence on migrant remittances; purposeful efforts by sending states to create "diasporic" nations that include migrants who reside permanently abroad; the social economics and political marginalization of some migrants in their host countries;[5] and a social climate that tolerates greater ethnic diversity.

I do not wish to suggest that all migrations produce transnational communities. In fact, one of the central empirical questions this study addresses is under what conditions and with what consequences these kinds of communities arise. To shed light on these concerns, each group in this study was chosen because it included a critical mass of migrants from a particular sending-country region who clustered residentially in the Boston metropolitan area. If a transnational community emerged, it would be more likely to form in this context. The groups were also selected to represent a variety of racial, ethnic, and religious experiences. Although this methodology allows me to compare the consequences of different migrants' transnational practices, it does not allow me to assess the generalizability of these relationships.

Patterns of Transnational Contact and Their Consequences for Participation

The unique qualities of the Dominican, Brazilian, and Indian immigrant communities included in this study, and the organizations they create and are created by, distribute their members' loyalties and energy between their home and host countries in different ways. The transnational social and political practices of migrants from Miraflores have the greatest effect on their sending country, whereas migrants from Valadares seem to be reorienting their attentions toward U.S. affairs. In the Gujarati case, migrants distribute their energies more evenly, engaging in both United States– and India-oriented activities.

Migration from the small Dominican village of Miraflores to Boston began in the late 1960s. Miraflores is located outside the city of Baní, which lies about sixty-five kilometers from the Dominican capital. Over time, migrants and nonmigrants have forged such close social and economic ties to one another that a transnational village has emerged. Its social life takes place in two settings, though not simultaneously nor with equal force. Villagers constantly exchange news, resources, social remittances, and goods. More than half speak to their relatives in Boston by phone at least once a month. These constant enduring connections have fundamentally transformed village life.[6] Many families have televisions, video-cassette recorders, and compact-disk players, though their houses have no indoor plumbing or running water. Almost everyone in Miraflores can talk about "La Mozart" or "La Centre" (Mozart Street park and Centre Street), two focal points of the community in Boston. When someone is ill, cheating on his or her spouse, or finally granted a visa, the news spreads as quickly on the streets of Miraflores as on the streets of Jamaica Plain.

When asked to comment on how migration changed their village, most migrants and nonmigrants from Miraflores described a community that now extends across borders to include those living in the United States. Both Dominican opposition political parties and the Dominican government have recognized these strong connections. Migrants make large campaign contributions. Because the remittances they send are often a critical source of income for those who remain behind, migrants also influence how nonmigrants vote. To encourage migrants' continued involvement on the island, a number of political, religious, and civic groups have actively reached out to Dominicans in the United States. Some explicitly encourage migrants to fully integrate at the same time that they remain active in Dominican affairs.

Despite these diverse opportunities for long-term dual participation, most Mirafloreños in Boston continued to devote most of their efforts toward social and political life on the island. In 1994, although 73 percent were legal resident aliens, only 1 percent were naturalized citizens. The Miraflores Development Committee, with chapters in Boston and Miraflores, saw its mission as promoting village-level development and consciously chose not to address problems facing the immigrant community (Levitt 1997). When the Dominican government approved dual citizenship and expatriate voting in 1996 and 1997, respectively, it institutionalized the means to sustain dual memberships, even among the second generation.

The Valadarense community is somewhat different. Relations between Boston and Valadares began during World War II, when Boston-based companies went to Brazil to mine mica. When mining executives returned to Boston after the war, they brought Brazilian women with them to work as domestic servants. These individuals created the social networks that later stimulated the large-scale migration that began in the 1980s, following a failed stabilization program in Brazil, which hit hard at the middle and working classes. By 1994, an estimated 1.5 million Brazilians had migrated, including six hundred thousand to the United States. Of these, as of 1992, thirty thousand were from Governador Valadares (Sales 1999). An estimated twenty thousand Valadarenses settled in the greater Boston metropolitan area, creating a second, urban-to-urban social group. Valadarenses also formed other enclaves along the eastern seaboard in New York, Florida, and Connecticut (Margolis 1994).

Migrant Valadarenses exert such a strong economic effect on their sending city that the term "Valadolares" was coined to describe the almost complete dollarization of the economy. In 1994, the municipal secretary of revenue calculated that migrants injected $10 million monthly into local coffers (Levitt and de la Dehesa 1998). Not surprisingly, our findings suggest a strong culture of migration. The Boston and Framingham Buildings are visible advertisements for the riches awaiting in the United States. New cafeteria-style restaurants are one popular cultural import. Several respondents commented that they had always had "United States fever" and had thought about migrating from the time they were very young. Again, national- and regional-level activities reinforce these attachments. Since 1992, Brazilian migrants have also been entitled to dual citizenship. They were granted the right to vote in Brazil in the late 1970s, though the first direct presidential election since 1960 was not held until 1989. An extensive transnational network of Catholic and Protestant groups is also emerging.

My research suggests that these transnational participatory options produce quite different outcomes from those in the Dominican case. Whereas Mirafloreños tend to remain more active in Dominican civic and political life, Valadarenses appear to be traversing a more traditional route toward incorporation. They have created a strong and active ethnic community in Boston. Their primary goal, however, appears to be achieving economic and political advancement in the United States, rather than influencing political and social reform in Valadares. Those Valadarenses who do sustain dual memberships tend to do so through religious arenas.

Migration between Gujarat, India, and Massachusetts forms a third type of cross-border group—a normative transnational community. In 1990, more than 815,500 Indian immigrants were living in the United States. An estimated thirty thousand of these resided in Massachusetts, more than half of whom arrived in the 1980s. Many of those living around the city of Lowell are Gujaratis from the Baroda and Anand districts. Like Indians throughout the United States, they are likely to be college educated (49 percent), well represented in professional (49 percent) and technical (47 percent) occupations, and home owners (63 percent) (U.S. Bureau of the Census 1992). There are also increasing numbers of new arrivals, from the towns and villages in these districts, who find working-class jobs in the United States.[7]

At first glance, Gujaratis might be expected to form only loose connections with one another and to sustain very weak attachments to Gujarat. Though there is a critical mass of Gujaratis in Massachusetts, there are also large communities in New Jersey, California, and Texas. The Indian government and Indian political groups have played a minimal role in reinforcing these ties. Geographic dispersion and limited transnational institutional development, however, seem to be counteracted by the multiple, overlapping identities community members share with one another. Larger, more inclusive identities, such as being from Gujarat or belonging to the same caste, are reinforced by membership in smaller endogamous marriage groups of residents from particular towns or religious organizations. The requirements of membership in many of these groups, and the substantive content of their activities, isolate members from the host society and constantly remind them of their attachments to Gujarat. In the case of Gujaratis, then, the nature of their transnational community may lead to strong continuous ties to Gujarat combined with abbreviated participation in U.S. political and civic institutions.

What Explains these Differences?

A variety of factors help explain the differences in participation and orientation among transnational social groups suggested by my findings. In the interest of space, I focus on four: the transnational characteristics of each group, the role of the state and other political organizations, institutional opportunities, and the socioeconomic characteristics of each group.

Transnational Group Characteristics

Clearly, the most important factor affecting how and where migrants participate is the type of transnational group to which they belong. Transnational villages are likely to last the longest, and keep their members most focused on their sending community, because they involve small, well-defined numbers at both ends of the migration spectrum who are in touch with one another on a regular basis. Almost all community members know one another personally. Nonmigrants' level of economic dependence on migrants is generally high. Transnational village members' contacts with one another influence so many aspects of life that both migrants and nonmigrants raise their families, establish businesses, and participate in organizations across borders. Because it is cheaper, faster, and easier to travel back and forth from the United States to the Dominican Republic than to India or Brazil, the Miraflöreños can maintain closer physical ties with their sending community. The United States also has a century-long history of involvement in Dominican political and economic affairs.

In contrast, ties between migrant and nonmigrant Valadarenses and Gujaratis are weaker and less inclusive. In the Brazilian case, these links connect a small city with several small cities in the Boston metropolitan area, though one central focus of the community is the city of Framingham. Though Valadarenses also claim that most people knew one another personally in the early days of settlement, they say that now, as the community has grown, they are more likely to have only family members or acquaintances in common. Whereas Miraflöreños send remittances monthly, Valadarenses tend to send money only periodically, when a particular need arises. It is also more difficult for Valadarenses to travel back to Brazil. Fifty percent are estimated to live in Boston illegally; once they arrive, they do not normally risk a second reentry. It is also much farther and more expensive for them to travel back to Brazil. Whereas 73 percent of all Mirafloreños had been back to visit at least once, Valadarenses seem to visit and call home much less frequently.

Gujaratis' ties to one another, though even less likely to be based on actual personal acquaintance than those of the Valadarenses, are stronger because they are rooted in religious practice. The geographic dispersion of Gujaratis throughout the United States is counteracted by the fact that they share additional identities, nested within one another like concentric circles, with successively greater degrees of exclusiveness. Many Gujaratis are also Patidars, have the last name "Patel," and belong to particular religious groups from that region. The Patidar transnational community, then, arises not so much from actual interpersonal connections as from the additional, overlapping norms and values that Gujaratis share, which entail explicit expectations and obligations to one another. Several respondents, for example, described traveling to a new city, searching for the last name "Patel," in the phone book, and being warmly received when they visited a family they had never met. Despite their distance from Gujarat, lack of economic interdependence with nonmigrants, and comparatively infrequent levels of phone contact and return travel, these migrants belong to a normative transnational community that binds them to India and to one another through these religious and cultural attachments.

The Role of the State and Other Political Groups

Another factor shaping migrants' continued transnational engagement is the nature of sending-country states' efforts to incorporate migrant members. In each of the three cases in this study, state efforts influence the character of local-level transnational ties.

After nearly fifteen years of debate, the Dominican legislature granted dual citizenship to migrants in 1996. Political parties and migrants, rather than the Dominican government, were the primary sponsors of this legislation. Although Joaquin Balaguer, the Dominican president from 1966 to 1978 and again from 1986 to 1996, feared migrants as potential political opponents, opposition political groups recognized that migrants held increasing sway over Dominican economic and political affairs. The proportion of Dominicans living in the United States grew so high that the largest voting block outside the Dominican capital was located in New York. Those who live abroad, and return migrants, had become a key force in the Dominican economy. According to Carlos Dore, an adviser to the current president, Leonel Fernández, economic remittances are the "sine qua non for Dominican macroeconomic stability, including monetary exchange rates, the balance of trade, international monetary reserves, and the national balance of payments" (quoted in Guarnizo 1998, 7).

In response, several political groups articulated a dual agenda that simultaneously addressed the needs of migrants and furthered Dominican national interests. If parties encouraged those in the United States to become integrated politically, migrants would be in a better position to advocate for Dominican national concerns. In exchange, these groups would support policies that addressed the interests of migrants, such as lower taxes on imports, dual citizenship, and the expatriate vote.

In the case of Miraflores, however, migrants continued to participate more in Dominican political life despite efforts, at both the national and the local level, to encourage transnational politics.[8] There is little evidence of political integration in Boston to date, despite attempts by the Partido Revolucionario Dominicano (PRD) and the Partido de la Liberación Dominicana (PLD)[9] to promote dual participation. In 1990, only 19 percent of all Dominicans in the state of Massachusetts were U.S. citizens. There are no official relations between Dominican political groups and the Massachusetts Democratic or Republican Party organizations. Only small numbers of Dominicans work on campaigns or have relations with individual politicians. Political groups have been more successful at organizing around Dominican causes. Candidates for senator of Peravia, the province in which Miraflores and are located, or for mayor of Baní come to campaign specifically in Boston because so many Banilejos live there. Both the PRD and the PLD have well-developed party organizations in New England. In 1994, the PRD had more than a thousand members, from Providence, Rhode Island, to the North Shore of Boston, who contributed more than $150,000 to the Dominican presidential campaign.

In contrast to the party-led incorporation of Dominican migrants, the state is behind most efforts to ensure migrants' continued participation in Brazilian affairs. The foreign ministry, Itamaraty, manages these activities, which arose out of efforts to improve consular services and in response to concerns raised by the Brazilian public that their emigrants were not being treated well abroad.[10] Though the Brazilian government approved dual citizenship, and expatriates are mandated by law to vote in presidential elections, few efforts have been made to encourage migrant participation. In fact, voter turnout in the 1994 election was low, with only 10,150 voting in the United States and 39,357 Brazilians voting worldwide (Rodriguez 1997). According to Lucio Pires De Amorin, the Director General for Legal Assistance–Related Consular Affairs for Brazilians Living Abroad, only 50,000 Brazilians registered to vote in 1998 and only 25,000 actually cast their ballots.

Instead, most of the measures adopted by the Brazilian state encourage migrants to integrate into host countries while remaining economically active in Brazil. The Brazilian Business Network in Boston, established with consular support, encourages business development in the United States as well as investment in Brazil. According to consular officials, plans are under way to open a branch of SEBRAE (Serviço Brasiliero de Apoio às Micro e Pequenas Empresas), the Brazilian equivalent of the Small Business Administration, in Boston to advise Brazilian migrants about regulations and procedures for opening small businesses in Brazil. Sheer numbers explain the lack of interest in migrants as political actors. It is simply not cost effective to devote resources to a group that represents less than 5 percent of the Brazilian population and has made minimal demands. To date, only the Workers Party has organized in Boston, and they have captured a relatively small number of supporters.

The Indian government has been the least active in seeking migrants' continued support. Because India is such a large and relatively young country, comprising multiple ethnic groups, residents generally feel a greater sense of loyalty to a particular region or state than to the Indian nation as a whole. Nonresident Indians are not allowed to vote or hold dual citizenship, and there have been no strong calls from any quarter to change this. There are signs, however, that the state will soon encourage migrants' economic ties more actively by promoting foreign investment by nonresident Indians. In August 1998, for example, officials from the State Bank of India tried to raise at least $2 billion through sales of government-guaranteed bonds offered only to migrants, which yielded higher rates of return than comparable U.S. treasury bonds. Government officials say this program responds to a convergence of migrant and state interests. Indian migrants have done well in the United States, they still feel patriotic toward their "motherland," and the government-backed securities offer them a way to express their patriotism that economically benefits India (Somini Sengupta, "India Taps into Its Diaspora," *New York Times* 1998).

The Bharatiya Janata Party (BJP) and its nonelectoral, cultural branch, the Vishwa Hindu Parishard are the only Indian political groups active in Boston. The BJP is known throughout India for its Hindu-fundamentalist platform and its advocacy of Hindutwa—the movement for an all-Hindu India. It is widely believed that the BJP receives significant support from nonresident Indians throughout the world. Because migration has traditionally been seen as a "polluting" enterprise (Chandra 1997), the BJP's call to preserve Hindu traditions resonates strongly with migrants who are concerned about their own ability to do so.

In the case of Gujaratis, then, the state has just begun to reach out to migrants to encourage stronger economic ties. Migrants participate only minimally in home-country political affairs. Similarly, the Brazilian state, though more actively involved with migrants, also views them as economic rather than political actors. Because migrants represent such a small proportion of the overall population in each of these cases, political groups understandably feel it is not worth their while to dedicate significant resources toward encouraging migrants' political involvement. In contrast, multiple constituencies in the Dominican Republic support migrants' continued economic and political role, not the least of whom are the migrants themselves.

Institutional Opportunities

The third factor influencing the shape of transnational participation is the nature of the cross-border organizations within which this occurs. Transnational social groups form organizations that are themselves transnational to varying degrees. These groups forge different kinds of alliances with receiving-country institutions. The resulting organizational arrangements afford migrants different participatory opportunities and orient their attentions in distinct ways.

Here let me focus on religious life. Dominicans in Boston and on the island already belong to the same, universal Catholic Church. The church has a long history of providing services to new arrivals. Mirafloreños became part of the Hispanic Apostalate, formed in Boston in the late 1960s to serve Puerto Ricans coming to the city. As migrants and non-migrants moved in and out of related organizational chapters, and as personal relations formed between individual priests, a constant exchange of parishioners, clergy, and resources arose between Boston and the island.

That Mirafloreños were incorporated into an already-existing organizational structure affected their participation in specific ways. Their religious integration required little self-mobilization. Because the church offered a Latino-style "product," migrants encountered something easy to adapt to and fairly familiar. In most churches, however, Mirafloreños were channeled into a "separate-but-equal" Latino parish structure. They organized their own Spanish-language masses, parish councils, and youth groups but had only minimal contact with Anglo parishioners. These organizational arrangements confined their focus to Latino religious life, mitigating against their complete assimilation and reinforcing their Latino, if not Dominican, focus.

Though many Valadarenses also join the Brazilian Catholic Church, increasing numbers seek out Protestant churches when they arrive in Boston. These tend to be "reverse missionary efforts," established by movements first introduced to Brazil earlier this century by North American religious leaders. When a large number of migrants from a particular denomination settle in a particular city, a pastor is often sent to "plant a church." Many of these churches encourage migrants to live as settlers rather than sojourners, while others afford migrants the opportunity to sustain transnational religious memberships. Some Brazilian Baptist and Presbyterian clergy, for example, have broken officially with their Brazilian church conferences and joined their American conference counterparts, while others continue to remain active in their Brazilian and North American denominations.

Patidars' seemingly greater tendency toward transnational participation arises largely from their religious history. In India, Hinduism is perceived as a largely amorphous set of beliefs and practices that are an integral part of daily life. It is both a civilization and a congregation of religions, with no beginning, no single founder, and no central authority. The experience of being a religious minority in the United States forces Hindus to organize their religious practices more formally and to assert their Hinduness consciously as a way to preserve their identity (Eck 1997; Kurien 1998). Patidars in the Boston area, many of whom are Hindu, have had to codify and simplify traditions and rituals that in India were extremely diverse and complex. They transform what are largely home-based, private rituals into public, migrant-community-affirming events. Because Patidars are few in number and display a range of affinities toward different deities and teachers, no one sect or group can afford to establish a place that belongs exclusively to them. Nonsectarian religious organizations arise, bringing together on a regular basis groups that had little contact with one another in Gujarat.

Some groups are more explicitly transnational than others because they have created structures and coordinated activities or because they are oriented toward constituencies in multiple settings. At one end of this spectrum is Gurjar, a regional cultural organization that reinforces sending-country attachments by affirming and transmitting cultural practices. At the other, the Swadhyaya movement, which is administered transnationally, organizes its meetings around videotaped messages sent from India each week by the group's leader, and adapts its obligation of charitable work to make it easier to carry out within the context of immigrant life. The requirements of membership, including vegetarianism, abstention from alcohol, modest attire, and proscriptions on dating, keep followers apart from non-Indians. Though most Patidars work in multiethnic workplaces, very few said they socialize with non-Indians in their homes.

The substantive content and membership requirements of these organizations strongly reinforces a distinct, homeland-oriented identity among their members. Most immigrants expressed the view that their ethnic identity and religious and cultural practices had to be protected from the contamination of American influences, which they considered to be culturally inferior. They also saw participation in religious activities as a way to keep their children apart from the wider group.

The Socioeconomic Characteristics of the Group

The final set of factors influencing the consequences of transnational membership are the socioeconomic characteristics of the immigrant group. Each group in this study includes individuals of color. The majority of Mirafloreños have low levels of education and limited English skills. They tend to live and work among other Dominicans, either in factory jobs or cleaning office buildings at night. The economic climate they encountered when they arrived inhibited their easy integration because they brought few of the skills required by the changing labor market.[11] This social and economic isolation constrained their incorporation and reinforced their sending-community ties.

Brazilians, by comparison, do somewhat better. They are generally more educated and have slightly better language skills. They are naturalizing at approximately the same rate as Dominicans.[12] Though Mirafloreños and Valadarenses are both heavily concentrated in the service sector, Valadarenses are more likely than Mirafloreños to clean private homes, work in hotels or restaurants, or even set up their own small cleaning businesses. Their labor market insertion generally involves higher levels of contact with non-Brazilians and requires them to develop better language and social fluency. This, in turn, encourages greater integration and attachment to the United States.

Patidars represent an interesting case.[13] They are more likely to hold professional or managerial positions. They are also more likely to own their own homes, which are often located in white neighborhoods. Because of the long-standing tradition of migration from Gujarat, families are accustomed to being dispersed between East Africa, London, and, more recently, the United States. These individuals are citizens of the world, global cosmopolites who are comfortable in many places. They have portable identities they are accustomed to taking with them, which mitigate against their deep rootedness in any particular context of reception.[14]

The migration experience differs by class. Elite Patidars are residentially, economically, and politically integrating into the United States while remaining culturally and religiously attached to India. Their peasant counterparts, who come from rural villages, follow a path more similar to that of Mirafloreño transnational villagers. They are less educated and have weaker English language skills. Even if they previously held semiprofessional or technical jobs in India, they cannot find comparable jobs in the United States. If they have family still living in India, they are likely to send economic remittances to family members, pay for improvements to the family home, or invest in small businesses in India. When I visited their homes in Gujarat, I found the same kinds of Tupperware, children's dishes decorated with Disney characters, and U.S.-made posters of puppies and kittens that I found in the homes of the Mirafloreños I visited in the Dominican Republic.

Transnational Social Groups and Participation

Findings from a comparative historical study of multiple immigrant communities in the greater Boston metropolitan area bring to light three different types of cross-border groups: a transnational village whose members continued to remain oriented toward their sending community; a Brazilian urban-to-urban transnational group, which affords members comparable opportunities for participation in both the sending and receiving countries, though they appear to be shifting their orientation toward the United States; and a normative transnational community that also provides members with the opportunity to remain active in both settings but separates them socially from the host context and reinforces their home-country ties.

Some scholars insist that transnational communities are a passing phenomenon, arguing that earlier migrants also remained attached to their homelands but eventually assimilated into life in the United States. This is undoubtedly true for some groups. For others, aspects of contemporary migration encourage the maintenance of transnational ties in unprecedented ways. First, early waves of mass migration to the United States were followed by a forty-year period of restricted entry. There was a very limited supply of raw material for the "grist mill of ethnicity, ensuring that whatever ethnic identities existed would be, for the most part, a product of the events and processes operating in the United States" (Massey 1995, 642). In contrast, contemporary migration to the United States will probably continue unabated because the conditions that encourage it, such as wage differentials, labor market segmentation, and the globalization of the economy, are unlikely to disappear. Homeland elements, aided by new communication and travel technologies, are continuously infused into the receiving-country context. New arrivals will tend to exceed the rate at which new ethnic culture is created through generational success, social mobility, and intermarriage. The character of ethnicity will be determined relatively more by immigrants and relatively less by later generations, shifting the balance of ethnic identity toward the language, culture, and ways of life in the sending society (Massey 1995, 645).

Sending-country attachments also persist because the socioeconomic integration of some groups is now more difficult than it was before. An economic boom creating hundreds of low-skilled manufacturing jobs followed the first great wave of migration. Economic restructuring during the last two decades has created more jobs for highly educated, technically trained individuals but fewer good jobs for migrants with poor language and educational skills. Contemporary migrants are more likely to be nonwhites who may face discrimination.[15] Whereas earlier groups tended to move into more heterogeneous neighborhoods as they achieved social mobility, the level of geographic concentration among new immigrant groups exceeds that of earlier arrivals at comparable stages of migration (Massey 1995; Alba and Nee 1997). Finally, institutions that encouraged integration in the past, like the ward-based political party system, are on the decline; and for some groups, such as the Catholic Church for Indian immigrants, they are irrelevant.

Given that transnational connections are likely to persist, what are the consequences for social and political life? Each transnational group creates different combinations of membership options, ranging from continued sending-country citizenship and long-term partial membership in the host society to dual citizenship. The nature of the Mirafloreño transnational village suggests that many members will be slow to naturalize and experience social and economic marginalization in the United States while they continue to participate in local-level Dominican affairs. In contrast, the Valadarense experience suggests a more traditional path toward assimilation into the United States, with some periodic involvement in sending-country affairs. Although Patidars exhibit more economic and residential assimilation than the other groups, and they naturalize at a faster rate, their religious and cultural lives may keep them strongly attached to their sending region.

These findings, and the context of increasing economic and political globalization in which they take place, bring to light new participatory forms that decouple citizenship and membership. Migrants can opt for long-term partial membership in the places they live and continue to be full, if only partially active, members of the communities from which they come. The meanings and reasons behind different participatory choices need to be distinguished from one another. Naturalization no longer signals a shift in allegiance and an end to sending-country involvement. Even migrants who become U.S. citizens may still remain active in home-country polities for an indefinite period while also exercising their rights in the United States. Similarly, those who participate actively in sending-country political parties, though they are citizens or long-time residents of the United States, may do so to promote sending-country development rather than to influence American political outcomes. The proliferation and maturation of the kinds of social groups I describe enables increasing numbers to balance dual involvements, the motivation for which may be different than they first seem.

What happens to those who chose not to become citizens but continue instead as long-term, long-distance participants in their home polities? What costs and benefits does this entail, and for whom? This study makes clear that dual citizenship is just one way that individuals keep feet in two worlds. Many religious, social, and political organizations fill the transnational public sphere that migration gives rise to. The trade-offs in protection and representation that migrants gain by participating in these different kinds of arenas must be better understood. Differences in states' abilities to intervene effectively on their expatriate citizens' behalf must also be recognized.

Finally, though I would not expect migrants from countries as large as Brazil and India to have a major impact on national politics, they may have a regional or state-level effect. Just as Mirafloreños hold sway over provincial and municipal political contests, so might Gujaratis and Valadarenses exert similar, targeted influences. This is already true with respect to economic life. The mayor of Governador Valadares, for example, announced the creation of a special investment fund for migrants to foster economic growth in the state of Minas Gerais. The fund, which pays higher interest than comparable general funds, is designed to increase remittances to the state. When candidates for provincial office conduct political and fund-raising campaigns in places in the United States where they know a concentration of migrants from a particular area resides, they also lay the foundation for such localized influences.

Notes

1. The study also includes migrants from Ireland, Portugal, Lebanon, and Israel. The research team consists of myself, colleagues in each sending country, and a group of graduate and undergraduate researchers. Most of the fieldwork on the Dominican community is complete. Approximately sixty interviews were conducted among Indian migrants in Massachusetts, and preliminary fieldwork was

carried out in 1997 and 2000 in Gujarat State. Fifty interviews have been conducted with migrants from Governador Valadares in Brazil, and fieldwork was carried out in Brazil in the summer of 1999.

2. Transnational communities are not the same as diasporas. The term "diaspora" is often used to refer to all migrants worldwide originating from a particular country. Transnational communities form a specific subset of these larger groups.

3. "Social remittances" are the ideas, behavior, social capital, and identities that flow from sending- to receiving-country communities. They are the north-to-south equivalent of the social and cultural resources that migrants bring with them that ease their transition from immigrants to ethnics. For a more detailed account, see Levitt (1999).

4. See, for example, Gerstle 1997; Foner 2000; Wyman 1993; Jacobson 1995; and Morawska, forthcoming.

5. Although this is the case for many unskilled workers, it may not be true for the new cadre of professional, highly trained workers who are now coming to the United States. Indeed, these individuals enjoy more opportunities for assimilation because many of the elite schools, social clubs, and work settings that might have been closed to them in the past are now much more accessible (Gold 2000).

6. The Dominican transnational village shares many of the characteristics of the Mexican (Smith 1994; Goldring 1992; Mountz and Wright 1996), Guatemalan (Popkin 1999), and Salvadoran (Mahler 1996) communities described by other researchers.

7. There is a long history of migration from Gujarat (Chandra 1997). In the early 1900s, Patidars, a subcaste from the region, associated with farming and business, went to East Africa to become traders. They maintained high levels of contact with India. Some respondents spent long periods in Uganda or Tanzania, followed by extended periods in India, before migrating once again to Africa. Others remained in Gujarat while their fathers worked in Africa and returned each year. The Gujarati immigrant community in Africa prospered while remaining socially apart. When independence movements spread throughout Africa in the 1960s, African nationals associated Indians with the status quo. Many returned to India, after they were forcibly expelled or their property was expropriated; others migrated to the United Kingdom or the United States.

8. There is some indication that Dominicans in New York are becoming more active in U.S. politics at the same time that they remain active in politics on the island. The Partido Revolucionario Do

minicano, in particular, lent its support to Guillermo Linares, who became the first Dominican elected to the New York City Council. Adriano Espaillat was later elected to the New York State Assembly.

9. The PRD and the PLD are two of the principal Dominican political parties. The PLD candidate, Leonel Fernández, was elected president in 1996.

10. The Brazilian case takes place within the context of an overall restructuring of consular services at the Itamaraty. The office at the foreign ministry in charge of consular affairs was elevated to a general directorate. In 1998, this change was made to heighten the profile of consular services, decrease red tape, and increase access to high ministry officials. Regional offices of Itamaraty were also opened in various Brazilian states. These structures, which are still quite new, are designed to give state governments a greater voice in foreign policy formulation. They may also serve as contact points for Brazilian consulates when arranging visits by foreign officials.

11. In 1990, 42 percent of Dominicans in Massachusetts reported that they did not speak English well or at all. Forty-eight percent reported that they had received no schooling or had attended grade school only. Only 14 percent had some college education (U.S. Bureau of the Census 1992).

12. Only 25 percent of Brazilians reported that they had no schooling or that they had attended grade school only, compared with 48 percent among Dominicans (U.S. Bureau of the Census 1992). By 1990, 17 percent of Dominicans in Massachusetts were citizens. Forty-five percent of Dominicans arrived after 1984. In contrast, 14 percent of Brazilians had naturalized by 1990, and more than 75 percent of this group arrived after 1984 (U.S. Bureau of the Census 1992).

13. Indians exhibit significantly higher rates of naturalization than both Dominicans and Brazilians. In 1990, 32 percent of Indian immigrants were naturalized citizens (U.S. Bureau of the Census 1992).

14. Parminder Bhachu (1985) identifies some Indians as "twice-migrants" because of their multiple destinations.

15. Migrants today, however, enjoy certain opportunities that both foreign and native-born minorities lacked a hundred years ago. Earlier this century, even native-born minority men, including those with Ivy League degrees, were barred from certain jobs in universities, industry, and the public sector. Present day migrants also benefit from antidiscrimination initiatives like affirmative action (Gold 2000).

References

Alba, Richard, and Victor Nee. 1997. "Rethinking Assimilation Theory for a New Era of Immigration." *International Migration Review* 32(4): 826–75.

Basch, Linda, Nina Glick Schiller, and Cristina Szanton Blanc, eds. 1994. *Nations Unbound: Transnational Projects, Postcolonial Predicaments, and Deterritorialized Nation-States.* Basel: Gordon and Breach.

Bhachu, Parminder. 1985. *Twice Migrants: East African Sikh Settlers in Britain.* London: Tavistock.

Chandra, V. P. 1997. "Remigration: The Return of the Prodigals—An Analysis of the Impact of Cycles of Migration and Remigration on Caste Mobility." *International Migration Review* 31(1): 162–70.

DeBiaggi, Sylvia Dantes. 1992. "From Minas to Massachusetts: A Qualitative Study of Five Brazilian Families in Boston." Master's thesis, Boston University.

Eck, Dianne. 1997. "Creating Hinduism in Multireligious America." Paper presented to Harvard University Center for International Affairs South Asian Seminar. Cambridge, Massachusetts, February 21, 1997.

Foner, Nancy. 2000. *From Ellis Island to J.F.K: New York's Two Great Waves of Immigration.* New Haven, Conn./New York: Yale University Press/ Russell Sage Foundation.

Fraser, Nancy. 1991. "Rethinking the Public Sphere: A Contribution to the Critique of Actually Existing Democracy." In *Habermas and the Public Sphere,* edited by Craig Calhoun. Cambridge: MIT Press.

Gerstle, Gary. 1997. "Liberty, Coercion, and the Making of Americans." *Journal of American History* 84(2): 524–58.

Gold, Steven. 2000. "Transnational Communities: Examining Migration in a Globally Integrated World." In *Rethinking Globalization(s): From Corporate Transnationalism to Local Intervention,* edited by Preet S. Aulakh and Michael G. Schechter. London: Macmillan.

Goldring, Luin. 1992. "Diversity and Community in Transnational Migration: A Comparative Study of Two Mexico–United States Migrant Communities." Ph.D. diss., Cornell University.

Guarnizo, Luis. 1998. "The Rise of Transnational Social Formations: Mexican and Dominican State Responses to Transnational Migration." *Political Power and Social Theory* 12(1): 45–94.

Jacobson, Matthew. 1995. *Special Sorrows.* Cambridge: Harvard University Press.

Kastoryano, Riva. 1994. "Mobilisations des Migrants en Europe: Du National au Transnational." *Reveu Europeenne des Migrations Internationales* 10(1): 169–80.

Kurien, Prema. 1998. "Becoming American by Becoming Hindu: Indian Americans Take Their Place at the Multicultural Table." In *Gathering in Diaspora: Migration, Ethnicity, and Religion in the United States,* edited by R. Stephen Warner and Judith G. Wittner. Philadelphia: Temple University Press.

Levitt, Peggy. 1997. "Transnationalizing Community Development: The Case of Boston and the Dominican Republic." *Nonprofit and Voluntary Sector Quarterly* 26(4): 509–26.

———. 1999. "Social Remittances: A Local-Level, Migration-Driven Form of Cultural Diffusion." *International Migration Review* 32(124): 926–49.

Levitt, Peggy, and Rafael de la Dehesa. 1998. "The Role of the State in Shaping Transnational Political Participation." Paper presented to the Latin American Studies Association meeting, Chicago(September 24–27, 1998).

Mahler, Sarah. 1996. *American Dreaming: Immigrant Life on the Margins.* Princeton, N.J.: Princeton University Press.

———. 1998. "Theoretical and Empirical Contributions Toward a Research Agenda for Transnationalism." In *Comparative Urban and Community Research,* vol. 6, edited by Michael Peter Smith and Luis Eduardo Guarnizo. New Brunswick, N.J.: Transaction publishers.

Margolis, Maxine. 1994. *Little Brasil: An Ethnography of Brazilian Immigrants in New York City.* Princeton, N.J.: Princeton University Press.

Massey, Douglas. 1995. "The New Immigration and Ethnicity in the United States." *Population and Development Review* 231(3): 431–65.

Massey, Douglas, Joaquin Arango, Graeme Hugo, Ali Kouaouci, Adela Pellegrino, and J. Edward Taylor. 1993. "Theories of International Migration: A Review and Appraisal." *Population and Development Review* 19(2): 431–65.

Morawska, Eva. Forthcoming. "International Migration and Consolidation of Democracy in East Central Europe: A Problematic Relationship in Historical Perspective." In *E Pluribus Unum: Immigrants, Civic Life, and Modes of Political Incorporation,* edited by Gary Gerstle and John Mollenkopf. New York: Russell Sage Foundation.

Mountz, Alison, and Richard Wright. 1996. "Daily Life in the Transnational Migrant Community of San Agustin, Oaxaca, and Poughkeepsie, New York." *Diaspora* 5(1): 403–28.

Nagengast, Carol, and Michael Kearney. 1990. "Mixtec Ethnicity: Social Identity, Political Consciousness, and Political Activism." *Latin American Research Review* 25(3): 61–91.

Popkin, Eric. 1999. "Guatemalan Mayan Migration to Los Angeles: Constructing Transnational Linkages in the Context of the Settlement Process." *Ethnic and Racial Studies* 22(2): 267–89.

Portes, Alejandro. 1996. "Transnational Communities: Their Emergence and Significance in the Contemporary World-System." In *Latin America in the World Economy,* edited by R. P. Korzeniewicz and W. C. Smith. New York: Russell Sage Foundation.

Rodriguez, Pedro Luiz. 1997. "Caem remessas de residentes no exterior." *Net Estado* 35(1): 3–5.

Sales, Teresa. 1999. *Brasileiros Longe de Casa.* Sao Paulo, Brazil: Cortez Editora.

Smith, Robert. 1994. "Los Ausentes Siempre Presentes: The Imagining, Making, and Politics of a Transnational Community Between Ticuani, Puebla, Mexico, and New York City." Ph.D. diss., Columbia University.

Sorenson, Ninna Nyberg. 1998. "Narrating Identity Across Dominican Worlds." In *Comparative Urban and Community Research,* vol. 6, edited by Michael Peter Smith and Luis Eduardo Guarnizo. New Brunswick, N.J.: Transaction Publishers.

U.S. Bureau of the Census. 1992. *Census of the Population: General Social and Economic Characteristics.* PC(1)-C23.1. Washington: U.S. Government Printing Office.

Wyman, Mark. 1993. *Round-Trip to America.* Ithaca: Cornell University Press.

Index

Boldface numbers refer to figures and tables.

of immigrants in New York, 159–61; naturalization, case study of (*see* Castillo family)

Donato, Katherine, 252, 387*n*3

Donelly, Nancy, 405

Dore, Carlos, 467

DuBois, W. E. B., 84

Durand, Jorge, 243

Dyer, Theodore, 412

ecological succession model, 424–25

economics: interdisciplinary research, problems facing, 46–47; variation in immigration scholars across disciplines, 31–36

Ellen, Ingrid Gould, 14

Ellis Island, 96–99

embedded liberalism, 217–18, 232

employers: labor recruitment (*see* labor recruitment); migration regulation, 223–27

ENMISA. *See* International Studies Association, Ethnicity, Nationalism, and Migration Section

entrepreneurs, immigrant. *See* immigrant entrepreneurs

Espinosa, Kristin, 242, 246–47

ethnicity: changes in immigration scholars over time, 29–30; competition among immigrant entrepreneurs (*see* immigrant entrepreneurs); construction of among Japanese Peruvians, 448–51; expectations of child care providers, 360–62; indigenous migrants and pan-ethnic identity, 150; insiders and outsiders, 37–38; political participation (*see* political participation); and residential segregation (*see* residential segregation); variation in immigration scholars across disciplines, 29–30

EU. *See* European Union

eugenics, 109

European Union (EU): migration regulation, restrictive legislation, 219,

222–23; third-party states in migration regulation, 232

Evans-Pritchard, E. E. Evans, 392–93, 395–96

EVP. *See* Exchange Visitor Program, United States

exchange programs, Filipino nurses, 121–27

Exchange Visitor Program, United States (EVP), 122–23

EZLN. *See* Zapatista Army of National Liberation

Fadiman, Anne, 51

Fairlie, Robert, 340

families: changes in and immigration, 391–92; changing gender relations among the Nuer after immigration, 396–398; cultural differences and legal context, 402–5; domestic violence (*see* domestic violence); and domestic workers (*see* domestic workers); marriage and gender relations among the Nuer in Sudan, 394–96

farm labor contracting firms, 281–83, 286–90, 292–93

Federal Glass Ceiling Commission, 318

Fernández, Leonel, 161, 467

Filipino nurses: American colonialism and nurse training, 114–21; American legislation and Filipino policy, 127–29; exchange programs, 121–27; Filipino diaspora, 129–30; migration of, 113–14

Filipino Nurses Association (FNA), 118, 123–24, 127

Fitzgerald, Alice, 118

Fix, Michael, 304

FLCs. *See* farm labor contracting firms

FNA. *See* Filipino Nurses Association

Folbre, Nancy, 395

Foner, Nancy, 5, 24, 383–84, 386

foreign workers, 62–63